PEACE DIPLOMACY, GLOBAL JUSTICE AND INTERNATIONAL AGENCY

As UN Secretary-General, Dag Hammarskjöld shaped many of the fundamental principles and practices of international organisations, such as preventive diplomacy, the ethics of international civil service, impartiality and neutrality. He was also at the heart of the constitutional foundations and principles of the UN.

This tribute and critical review of Hammarskjöld's values and legacy examines his approach towards international civil service, agency and value-based leadership, investigates his vision of internationalism and explores his achievements and failures as Secretary-General. It draws on specific conflict situations and strategies such as Suez and the Congo for lessons that can benefit contemporary conflict resolution and modern concepts such as human security and R2P. It also reflects on ways in which actors such as international courts, tribunals and the EU can benefit from Hammarskjöld's principles and experiences in the fields of peace and security and international justice.

CARSTEN STAHN is Chair of International Criminal Law and Global Justice at Leiden University, the Netherlands, and Programme Director of the Grotius Centre for International Studies, The Hague.

HENNING MELBER is Senior Advisor and Director Emeritus of the Dag Hammarskjöld Foundation, Uppsala, Sweden. He is also Extraordinary Professor at both the University of Pretoria and at the Centre for Africa Studies, University of the Free State, Bloemfontein, South Africa.

PEACE DIPLOMACY, GLOBAL JUSTICE AND INTERNATIONAL AGENCY

Rethinking Human Security and Ethics in the Spirit of Dag Hammarskjöld

Edited by
CARSTEN STAHN
and
HENNING MELBER

CAMBRIDGE
UNIVERSITY PRESS

CAMBRIDGE
UNIVERSITY PRESS

University Printing House, Cambridge CB2 8BS, United Kingdom

Cambridge University Press is part of the University of Cambridge.

It furthers the University's mission by disseminating knowledge in the pursuit of education, learning and research at the highest international levels of excellence.

www.cambridge.org
Information on this title: www.cambridge.org/9781107037205

First published 2014

Printed in the United Kingdom by Clays, St Ives plc

A catalogue record for this publication is available from the British Library

Library of Congress Cataloguing in Publication data
Peace diplomacy, global justice and international agency : rethinking human security and ethics in the spirit of Dag Hammarskjöld / edited by Carsten Stahn and Henning Melber.
pages cm
Includes bibliographical references and index.
ISBN 978-1-107-03720-5 (hardback)
1. Hammarskjöld, Dag, 1905–1961. 2. United Nations – History. 3. United Nations – Biography. 4. World politics – 1955-1965. 5. Political ethics. 6. Human security. I. Stahn, Carsten, 1971– , author, editor of compilation. II. Melber, Henning, author, editor of compilation.
D839.7.H3P43 2014
341.23–dc23
2014009000

ISBN 978-1-107-03720-5 Hardback

CONTENTS

FOREWORD BY JAN ELIASSON

Fifty years ago the second Secretary-General of the United Nations, Dag Hammarskjöld, and 15 of his collaborators died in a plane crash in the night from 17 to 18 September 1961 when approaching Ndola Airport in then Northern Rhodesia. Hammarskjöld was on his way to negotiations with Moïse Tshombe, the secessionist leader of the Katanga Province, in the former Belgian Congo.

This volume acknowledges the lasting legacy of Hammarskjöld and places the values he personified in a broader context. It focuses on the leadership and vision of internationalism that he represented. It emphasises the unique role he played during the 1950s, characterised by the Cold War policies and the decolonisation of many nations, in particular on the African continent. Through a combination of different aspects and the multi-faceted approaches personified by Hammarskjöld, this volume revisits the legacy of an outstanding global leader and the relevance of his ideas for the United Nations and the practices of global cooperation.

In his last Annual Report to the General Assembly, Dag Hammarskjöld argued that lasting peace would only be achieved on the basis of four fundamental principles, namely:

(1) equal political rights, both sovereign and individual;
(2) equal economic opportunities, through higher standards and also conditions conducive to economic and social advancement;
(3) a firm framework of the rule of law, which should underpin all activities of the international community; and
(4) the prohibition of the use of force except 'in the common interest'.

This volume raises intriguing questions regarding to what extent contemporary approaches are consistent with Dag Hammarskjöld's vision of the United Nations. The book examines whether and how Dag Hammarskjöld's legacy can still be used as a framework for reviewing

Jan Eliasson is Deputy Secretary-General of the United Nations.

recent initiatives of the international community. Such a lens is justified due to his achievements as Secretary-General as well as his ethical and philosophical approach to international service.

Hammarskjöld died a day after my twenty-first birthday, while I was serving as a cadet of the Swedish Navy during an exercise in the north of the Baltic Sea. It gave this day of entering maturity a special meaning. Since then, I have been a dedicated student of Hammarskjöld's personal and professional life. I had the privilege to deliver the annual Dag Hammarskjöld Lecture in the main hall of Uppsala University on the very day fifty years after his untimely death. Another coincidence occurred, when, during a roundtable discussion on 2 March 2012, on the occasion of the fiftieth anniversary of the Dag Hammarskjöld Foundation, Secretary-General Ban Ki-moon's appointment of me as Deputy Secretary-General was announced in New York. Dag remains a role model around the world. I hope this volume, with voices from multiple disciplines and with fresh insights on the ethics, achievements and visions of Hammarskjöld, will contribute to a better understanding of his legacy as global leader.

ACKNOWLEDGEMENTS

This book is devoted to a unique civil servant, peacemaker and intellectual: Dag Hammarskjöld, the second Secretary-General of the United Nations. His ideas remain relevant to different audiences and constituencies: the world of diplomacy, global ethics and international law. His intellectual heritage crosses disciplines. We try to capture this unique spirit in this volume.

This book is a truly collective effort. It is the result of cooperation between the Grotius Centre for International Legal Studies, The Hague Academic Coalition (HAC) and the Dag Hammarskjöld Foundation, Uppsala.

Some of the contributions grew out of discussions held at the eighth Annual Conference of HAC at the Peace Palace on 9–10 November 2011, jointly organised by the Swedish Embassy, the Dag Hammarskjöld Foundation and HAC's member institutes. The interdisciplinary nature of dialogue and the quality of contributions led to the pursuit of this collective project.

We would like to thank all contributors to this volume for their care, dedication and efforts to provide fresh thinking on Dag Hammarskjöld's legacy and contemporary relevance. We owe special thanks to individual HAC members (Prof. Jouke de Vries, Dr Sam Muller, Ed Maan and Sofia Gerards) and Dr Monica Bouman who initiated this project and supported its successful implementation.

We would also like to express our gratitude to other individuals who contributed to the creation of this volume, including Joseph Powderly who was instrumental in framing the theme, and Anda Scarlat, Daniel Huck, Nivedita S and Teodora Jugrin who provided invaluable assistance in the finalisation of the book.

At Cambridge University Press we would like to thank Finola O'Sullivan, Nienke van Schaverbeke, Elizabeth Spicer and Richard Woodham for supporting this project and ensuring publication of this volume.

This book is dedicated to the late Judge Pieter Kooijmans and Knut Olaf Hjalmar Akesson Hammarskjöld who joined us for the event in November 2011, but did not witness the publication of this work.

We hope that this book will contribute to broader discourse on human security and ethics in the spirit of Dag Hammarskjöld across scholarly disciplines. It is our hope that it will provide a modest contribution to keep Hammarskjöld's principles and legacy alive in their relevance for today.

ABBREVIATIONS

9/11	Events in New York occurring on 11 September 2001
ABAKO	Alliance des Bakongo (Diplomatic Republic of the Congo)
ADFL	Alliance of Democratic Forces for the Liberation of Congo
AJIL	*American Journal of International Law*
ANC	Armée Nationale Congolaise
API	Additional Protocol I to the Geneva Conventions of 12 August 1949
ASIL	American Society of International Law
BYIL	*British Yearbook of International Law*
CAT	Committee Against Torture
CCA	Common Country Assessments
CEPS	Centre for European Policy Studies
CFSP	Common Foreign and Security Policy (European Union)
CIA	Central Intelligence Agency (United States)
CLEER	Centre for the Law of EU External Relations
CMPD	Crisis Management and Planning Directorate (European Union)
CNN	Cable News Network
CO_2	Carbon dioxide
CPCC	Civilian Planning and Conduct Capability (European Union)
CSDP	Common Security and Defence Policy
DG	Directorate-General (European Union)
DG-E	Directorate-General for Enlargement (European Union)
DG Relex	Directorate-General for External Relations (European Union)
DH	Dag Hammarskjöld
DPA	Department of Political Affairs (United Nations)
DPKO	Department of Peacekeeping Operations (United Nations)
DRC	Democratic Republic of the Congo
E3+3	A grouping of states, namely: the three most influential European Union states (France, Germany, United Kingdom) and three other influential states (China, Russia, United States)
EBRD	European Bank for Reconstruction and Development
EC	European Community
ECOSOC	United Nations Economic and Social Council
ECOWAS	Economic Community of West African States

EEAS	European External Action Service
EIB	European Investment Bank
EJIL	*European Journal of International Law*
ENP	European Neighbourhood Policy
EU	European Union
EULEX Kosovo	European Union Rule of Law Mission in Kosovo
EUMS	European Union Military Staff
EUSRs	European Union Special Representatives
FAC	Foreign Affairs Council
FARDC	Armed Forces of the Democratic Republic of Congo
FEA	Foreign Economic Administration (United States)
GAC	General Affairs Council (European Union)
GAERC	General Affairs and External Relations Council (European Union)
GFC	Gulf Cooperation Council
HIDCs	Heavily Indebted Countries
HIPC	Heavily Indebted Poor Country
HQ	Headquarters
HR	High Representative of the Union for Foreign Affairs and Security Policy (European Union)
HR/VP	High Representative of the Union for Foreign Affairs and Security Policy/Vice-President of the European Commission (European Union)
IBM	Integrated border management (between Kosovo and Serbia)
ICC	International Criminal Court
ICCPR	International Covenant on Civil and Political Rights
ICESCR	International Covenant on Economic, Social and Cultural Rights
ICISS	International Commission on Intervention and State Sovereignty
ICJ	International Court of Justice
ICLQ	*International Criminal Law Quarterly*
ICM	International Civilian Mission (in Kosovo)
ICTR	International Criminal Tribunal for Rwanda
ICTY	International Criminal Tribunal for the former Yugoslavia
IER	International executive rule
IFIs	International Financial Institutions
IHL	International Humanitarian Law
IHRL	International Human Rights Law
ILC	International Law Commission
ILM	International Legal Materials
ILO	International Labour Organization
IMF	International Monetary Fund
ISAF	International Security Assistance Force

ITA	International territorial administration
KB DHS	Kungliga Biblioteket Dag Hammarskjöld Samling
KFOR	Kosovo Force (NATO)
LDCs	Least Developed Countries
LON	League of Nations
LTTE	Liberation Tigers of Tamil Eelam
MNC	Congolese National Movement
MONUC	United Nations Organization Mission in the Democratic Republic of the Congo
MONUSCO	United Nations Organization Stabilization Mission in the Democratic Republic of the Congo
MSU	Mediation Support Unit (United Nations)
NATO	North Atlantic Treaty Organization
NGO	Non-governmental organisation
NTC	National Transitional Council (Libya)
OAS	Organization of American States
OECD	Organization for Economic Cooperation and Development
OEEC	Organization for European Economic Cooperation
OHCHR	Office of the High Commissioner for Human Rights (United Nations)
ONUC/ UNOC	United Nations Operation in the Congo
OSCE	Organization on Security and Cooperation in Europe
OSS	Office of Strategic Services (United States)
P3	United States, United Kingdom and France (in the United Nations Security Council)
PBC	United Nations Peace-building Commission
PKOs	Peacekeeping operations
PMC	Permanent Mandates Commission (League of Nations)
PRSP	United Nations Poverty Reduction Strategy Papers
R&A	Research and Assistance Branch of the Office of Strategic Services (United States)
R2P	Responsibility to Protect
RCD	Rally for Congolese Democracy
ROL	Rule of law
RUF	Revolutionary United Front
SADS	Southern African Development Community
SRSG(s)	Special Representative(s) of the Secretary General
SSR	Soviet Socialist Republic
TEU	Treaty on European Union
TFEU	Treaty on the Functioning of the European Union
TWAIL	Third World Approaches to International Law
UK	United Kingdom

UN	United Nations
UNAMIR	United Nations Assistance Mission for Rwanda
UNCA	United Nations Constitutional Assistance
UNDAF	United Nations Development Assistance Frameworks
UNDESA	United Nations Department of Social and Economic Affairs
UNDP	United Nations Development Programme
UNEF	United Nations Emergency Force
UNEP	United Nations Environment Programme
UNGA	United Nations General Assembly
UNHRC	United Nations Human Rights Council
UNITAF	United Task Force
UNMIK	United Nations Mission in Kosovo
UNMIN	United Nations Mission in Nepal
UNOC/ONUC	United Nations Operation in the Congo
UNOCI	United Nations Operations in Côte d'Ivoire
UNOSOM II	United Nations Operation in Somalia II
UNPF/UNPROFOR	United Nations Protection Force
UNPS	United Nations Parliamentary Support
UNSC	United Nations Security Council
UNSG	United Nations Secretary-General
UNSMIL	United Nations Support Mission in Libya
UNTAC	United Nations Transitional Authority in Cambodia
UNTAET	United Nations Transitional Administration in East Timor
UNTEA	United Nations Temporary Executive Authority
UNTSO	United Nations Truce Supervision Organization
UPR	Universal Periodic Review (in the context of human rights monitoring)
USAID	United States Agency for International Development
USSR	Union of Soviet Socialist Republics
VP	Vice-President of the European Commission
WEU	Western European Union

1

Human security and ethics in the spirit of Dag Hammarskjöld

An introduction

CARSTEN STAHN AND HENNING MELBER

1.1 Introduction

The international order is undergoing transformation. Conflicts arise increasingly from aspirations for greater 'social justice' and respect of fundamental rights and freedoms inside states and societies. The Arab uprisings mark a vibrant illustration of this struggle. They have posed challenges for the capacity of the United Nations (UN) and regional organisations to respond, support and engage with a civilian revolt against repressive governance undertaken ostensibly in pursuit of the ideals of the International Bill of Rights. Concepts such as 'human security'[1] or the 'rule of law'[2] have become an integral part of the vocabulary of international peace and security. But the UN system is only gradually adjusting to these types of violence and emerging global problems. Many international responses are driven by pragmatism and/or the need to respond on short notice to events or situations of crisis. This leaves little room to engage with the normative foundations of institutional transformation and international executive rule. The ideas and ideologies underlying

Carsten Stahn is Professor of International Criminal Law and Global Justice at Leiden University and Programme Director of the Grotius Centre for International Legal Studies.
Henning Melber is Senior Advisor and Director Emeritus of the Dag Hammarskjöld Foundation and Extraordinary Professor at the Department of Political Sciences/University of Pretoria and the Centre for Africa Studies, University of the Free State.

1 See General Assembly, Follow-up to paragraph 143 on human security of the 2005 World Summit Outcome, UN Doc. A/66/L.55/rev. 1, 6 September 2012; Report of the Secretary-General, Human Security, UN Doc. A/64/701, 8 March 2010.

2 See Declaration of the High-level Meeting of the General Assembly on the Rule of Law at the National and International Levels, UN Doc. A/67/L.1, 19 September 2012.

the move towards internationalism and conflict management are rarely discussed. States are reluctant to engage openly with this dimension of institutional change. These factors are typically revealed through institutional practice, symbols, persons or values associated with these institutions. One of the traditional ideals seen in global institutions is their communitarian ethos, i.e. the commitment to interests transcending the nation-state, and their perceived autonomy and independence. This ideal is inherent in the UN Charter. This ethos is reflected in concepts, such as the notion of the 'the international community', the virtues of 'international civil service' or human rights ambitions (e.g. the fight against impunity).

Dag Hammarskjöld personified this vision like hardly any other UN Secretary-General. He defended a cosmopolitan vision of the UN and internationalism that placed the interests of Member States in the broader context of the service of the organisation.[3] He viewed the UN as an organisation in the service of 'international society'.[4] He considered it as an 'experimental operation' directed towards the development of 'higher forms of an international society'[5] and attributed 'constitutional' features to the principles and purposes of the Charter.[6] He conceived himself as an 'international' rather than a mere 'civil servant'[7] and stood up for the idea of an autonomous and effective Secretariat. His ethics, principles and credo are deeply shaped by his commitment to virtues, such as integrity and impartiality, which he used in the cause of both 'peace' and 'justice'. He shared the conviction that the organisation represents more than the

[3] In his seminal Introduction to the Annual Report of the Secretary-General on the Work of the Organization (15 June 1960–15 June 1961), he argued that 'the Charter takes a first step in the direction of an organized international community'. See GAOR, 16th Sess. Supp. No. 1 A (A/4800/Add.1), New York 1961, below as Annex 1.

[4] See J. Troy, 'Dag Hammarskjöld: An International Civil Servant Uniting Mystics and Realistic Diplomatic Engagement' (2010) 21 *Diplomacy & Statecraft* 434, at 440.

[5] See 'The Development of a Constitutional Framework for International Cooperation', Address at the University of Chicago, 1 May 1960, UN Press Release SG/910, 29 April 1960, www.un.org/Depts/dhl/dag/docs/chicagospeech.pdf, in A.W. Cordier and W. Foote (eds.), *Public Papers of the Secretaries-General of the United Nations, Vol. IV: Dag Hammarskjold, 1958–1960* (1974), at 587.

[6] *Ibid.*, at 588. See on this idea, A. Ross, *The Constitution of the United Nations – Analysis of Structure and Function* (1950).

[7] See 'The International Civil Servant in Law and Fact', Lecture delivered to Congregation at Oxford University, 30 May 1961, at www.unic.ru/news_oon/Dag_Oxford_1961.pdf, in A.W. Cordier and W. Foote (eds.), *Public Papers of the Secretaries-General of the United Nations, Vol. V: Dag Hammarskjöld, 1960–1961* (1975), 471–489.

sum of its Members. Many of his Introductions to the Annual Reports of the Secretary-General to the General Assembly and his speeches are masterfully crafted reflections which capture and re-think fundamental principles of international organisation. They address inter alia the distinction between 'impartiality' and 'neutrality' (1954), 'mediation' and 'reconciliation' (1955), 'good offices' (1959), the contours of the Charter as a 'constitutional framework for world-wide cooperation' (1960) or 'international civil service' (1961). He traced the contours of a 'United Nations ideology', based on Christian and universal notions of 'faith', 'hope' and 'charity',[8] which illustrate his ambition to embed executive action in a 'political philosophy of the UN'.[9] He viewed the UN itself as a means to an end towards the greater good, rather than an end itself. This vision is clearly expressed in his public statement that '[t]he principles of the Charter are, by far, greater than the Organization in which they are embodied, and the aims which they are to safeguard are holier than the policies of any single nation or people'.[10] Since the start of his first term of office, he stressed the need for the UN to engage with the dilemmas of decolonisation and greater social justice inside nations.

Hammarskjöld shared at the same time a strong sense of realism. Cosmopolitan and ethical principles (e.g. integrity, universality) were no abstract constructs to him. He translated these principles into a code of ethics for public service. He was committed to giving practical relevance to concepts or notions such as 'international community', 'peaceful resolution of disputes' or 'justice', through reliance on Charter norms and principles, 'active' but 'quiet' diplomacy and the creation of facts or precedents. He is thus a representative of an applied political ethic, which is founded in his spirituality and 'sacred' perception of public service. His vision departed significantly from an intergovernmental or technocratic understanding of the UN. It conflicted more than once with the power configurations at the time. The conflict of interest with the major powers in the Congo crisis culminated in the Soviet Union's request for his

[8] See 'The United Nations – Its Ideology and Activities', Address before the Indian Council of World Affairs, New Dehli, 3 February 1956, at www.un.org/Depts/dhl/dag/docs/unideologiesactivities.pdf, in A.W. Cordier and W. Foote (eds.), *Public Papers of the Secretaries-General of the United Nations, Vol. II: Dag Hammarskjold, 1953–1956* (1972), 659.

[9] Troy, *supra* note 4, at 441.

[10] See the statement of the Secretary-General, SCOR, 11th year, 751st Mtg, 31 October 1956, www.un.org/Depts/dhl/dag/docs/spv751ef.pdf, at 1.

resignation in October 1960 which he refuted as a matter of principle in the interest of the organisation as a whole.[11]

Hammarskjöld was instrumental in identifying or setting agendas for reform. But he was also acutely aware of the inherent limits of the UN and need for pragmatism in the exercise of international civil authority. This is reflected in an address to the University of California's convocation on 13 May 1954. Hammarskjöld, after a year in office, concluded, by paraphrasing Henry Cabot Lodge Jr.:

> It has been said that the United Nations was not created in order to bring us to heaven, but in order to save us from hell. That sums up as well as anything I have heard both the essential role of the United Nations and the attitude of mind that we should bring to its support.[12]

Half a century after the end of his office, there is still a considerable degree of scepticism about the role and function of the UN.[13] The UN is barely appreciated for its achievements, but often criticised for its failures. There is a striking discrepancy between norms and aspirations on the one hand, and social and political realities on the other. Some of the most ambitious ideas (e.g. the Millennium Development Goals), frameworks and institutional projects (e.g. Security Council reform) remain on the agenda, due to a lack of commitment by states or shortcomings in implementation. For some there seems little reason to celebrate. But would the world today be a better place in the absence of such frameworks, as selectively and arbitrarily as they have far too often been applied? Would we be better off without the UN?

Hammarskjöld would point to the value of the UN as a 'symbol of faith'[14] and question whether it is 'less promising than experiments …

[11] In 1960, Hammarskjöld declined to step down from office following a request from Khrushchev. He stated: 'I have no right to [resign] because I have a responsibility to all those Member States for which the Organization is of decisive importance – a responsibility which overrides all other considerations. It is not the Soviet Union or indeed any other Big Powers which need the United Nations for their protection. It is all the others.' See GAOR, 15th Sess. 883rd Mtg, 3 October 1960, A/PV.883, p. 332, para. 11. Also in Cordier and Foote, Vol. V, *supra* note 7, at 200.

[12] D. Hammarskjöld, Address at University of California Convocation. Berkeley, California, 13 May 1954 (UN Press Release SG/382, 13 May 1954), in A.W. Cordier and W. Foote (eds.), *Public Papers of the Secretaries-General of the United Nations, Vol. II: Dag Hammarskjöld 1953–1956* (1972), 301.

[13] For a critique in the area of use of force and security, see M. Glennon, *The Fog of Law: Pragmatism, Security and International Law* (2010), 21–23, 109–128 and 145–169.

[14] See Address 3 February 1956, *supra* note 8, at 659.

pursued on other lines'.[15] Some of the reflections that he offered in 1959 in his address on whether 'We need the United Nations' might still stand today:

> We need it for the constructive additions it offers in international attempts to resolve conflicts of interests. And we need it as a foundation of and a framework for arduous and time-consuming attempts to find norms in which an extranational – or perhaps even supranational – influence may be brought to bear in the prevention of future conflicts.[16]

Many goals remain unaccomplished.[17] But some achievements of UN practice are addressed in the United Nations Intellectual History Project.[18] At times, voices in the so-called global South are openly critical of UN governance or organisational policies since they are perceived as an instrument for the pursuit of 'hegemonic' interests. This critique may be compelling in some areas, such as the use of force. But it should not necessarily discredit the value of the UN as a whole. After all, the UN played a pioneering role among others not only in the decolonisation processes generally,[19] but also in declaring apartheid a 'crime against humanity' and imposing an arms embargo on the South African minority regime.[20] The organisation was decisive in bringing about the decolonisation of Namibia as a 'trust betrayed'.[21] It has played a similar role in mediating the end of conflicts elsewhere. In many instances, struggles for emancipation might have been even more burdensome or longer in the absence of the UN system. The same can be said of the many peacekeeping missions, which were established in their current form by none other than Hammarskjöld when dealing with the challenges of the so-called

[15] See Address 1 May 1960, *supra* note 5, at 587.

[16] See Address, 'Do We Need the United Nations?', Address Before the Student's Association, Copenhagen, 2 May 1959, www.un.org/Depts/dhl/dag/docs/needun.pdf, in A.W. Cordier and W. Foote (eds.), *Public Papers of the Secretaries-General of the United Nations, Vol. IV: Dag Hammarskjold, 1958–1960*, at 374.

[17] T.G. Weiss and R. Thakur, *Global Governance and the UN: An Unfinished Journey* (2010).

[18] See the initial volume by L. Emmerij, R. Jolly and T. Weiss, *Ahead of the Curve? UN Ideas and Global Challenges* (2001) and the concluding volume by R. Jolly, L. Emmerij and T. Weiss, *UN Ideas That Changed the World* (2009). For more information, see www.unhistory.org/briefing.

[19] See R. Burke, *Decolonization and the Evolution of International Human Rights* (2010).

[20] See for a summary on these specific interventions: United Nations Department of Public Information, *The United Nations and Apartheid, 1948–1994* (1994); and United Nations Special Committee Against Apartheid, *Twenty-Five Years of Commitment to the Elimination of 'Apartheid' in South Africa* (1988).

[21] United Nations, Office of Public Information, *A Trust Betrayed, Namibia* (1974).

Suez crisis in 1956. The idea of peacekeeping has stood the test of time. Some of the challenges that Hammarskjöld encountered during the mission in the Congo in the 1960s have led to reforms of UN peace operations after the end of the Cold War.[22]

More than half a century after Hammarskjöld's death during the UN mission in the Congo, the country has remained torn by violence bordering on chronic civil strife, at the cost of millions of lives and the ruin of the physical and mental health of so many more. As is so often the case, women and children have suffered most and have been the victims of a war that has not shied away from systematic rape and other forms of atrocities to the individual. UN Security Council Resolution 1325 of October 2000 paved the way for a new approach to dealing with gender issues,[23] while Security Council Resolution 1960 of December 2010 consolidated new standards and norms in the effort to protect both women and men from systematic sexual violence as a means of war-making.[24] The implementation of the latter might serve as a point of reference for the effectiveness and legal and moral weight of the UN. The situation in today's Democratic Republic of the Congo is only the tip of the iceberg. People are exposed to similar and other forms of destruction and violence in many parts of the world.[25]

Despite all setbacks and continuing mass violence, the UN entered a different phase of institutional development after Hammarskjöld.[26] Some of his approaches and ideas came to fruition only after the end of the Cold War. The spectrum of international responses to conflict has significantly

[22] See United Nations, *Review of the United Nations Peacebuilding Architecture*, UN Doc. A/64/868-S/2010/393, 21 July 2010; *Progress Report of the Secretary-General on Peacebuilding in the Immediate Aftermath of Conflict*, UN Doc. A/64/866-S/2010/386, 16 July 2010; *Civilian Capacity in the Aftermath of Conflict*, UN Doc. A/65/747-S/2011/85, 22 February 2011. It is sometimes argued that UN action has enjoyed a 'higher success rate than U.S.-led efforts'. See J. Dobbins, S.G Jones, K. Crane, A. Rathmell, B. Steele, R. Teltschik and A. Timilsina, *The UN's Role in Nation-Building: From the Congo to Iraq* (2005), at xxx, summary at www.rand.org/pubs/monographs/2005/RAND_MG304.sum.pdf.

[23] See SC Resolution 1325 of 31 October 2000.

[24] See SC Resolution 1960 of 16 December 2010. See also generally Human Security Report 2012, *Sexual Violence, Education and War: Beyond the Mainstream Narrative* (2012), at www.hsrgroup.org/human-security-reports/2012/text.aspx.

[25] See inter alia the contributions in H. Melber (ed.), *Dealing with Crimes against Humanity* (2011) 55 *Development Dialogue.*

[26] See, for example, the articles by L.L. Falkman, P. Wallensteen and T.G. Weiss in the special issue of *New Routes – A Journal of Peace Research and Action*, Vol. 16 (2011), at www.life-peace.org/resources/publications/new-routes/2011/. See also generally, S. Chesterman (ed.), *Secretary or General? The UN Secretary-General in World Politics* (2007).

shifted over time. The Human Security Report 2009/2010 has found that there is 'a decline in conflict numbers in the 1990s', including a '77 percent decline in the number of high-intensity civil conflicts since the end of the Cold War',[27] based on factors that 'reduce both the risks and the costs of international and civil wars'.[28] It relates the global decline in civil wars to a number of factors, including the demise of colonisation and the rise of democratic statehood, growing membership in international organisations, global economic interdependence, and peacemaking and peacebuilding policies. The report notes that conflict-reducing activities include:

- A fivefold increase in the number of international mediation efforts from the 1980s to the 1990s.
- A tenfold increase from 1991 to 2007 in the number of Friends of the Secretary-General, Contact Groups, and other political arrangements that support peacemaking and post-conflict peacebuilding initiatives.
- A threefold increase in UN and non-UN peace operations from 1988 to 2008 …
- An increase in the number of countries contributing troops to peace operations from 51 in 1988 to some 200 in 2008.
- A thirteenfold increase in the number of multilateral sanctions regimes between 1991 and 2008.
- A ninefold increase in the number of ongoing disarmament, demobilization, and reintegration operations from 1989 to 2008.[29]

It further links mitigation of conflict to structural factors and 'shifts in global norms', such as the impact of 'inclusive democracy' to the prevention of interstate and warfare, the contribution of 'national and international prosecutions of human rights crimes' to the 'decline in human rights abuses worldwide' and the 'substantial decline in governmental political discrimination against minority groups worldwide'.[30] Many of these developments can be related to the vision and principles of an international organisation as set out by Hammarskjöld in his Introduction to the 1961 Report to the General Assembly.[31]

But this type of internationalism also creates ambiguities and discontents. There is growing debate about the scope of 'international agency' and its relationship to regional organisations and Member State

[27] Human Security Report 2009/2010, *The Causes of Peace and the Shrinking Costs of War* (2010), www.hsrgroup.org/human-security-reports/20092010/overview.aspx, at 7.
[28] *Ibid.*, at 13. [29] *Ibid.*, at 6. [30] *Ibid.*, at 6. [31] See *supra* note 3.

responsibility. UN Security Council Resolutions 1970 and 1973 on Libya, and their reference to the concept of the Responsibility to Protect,[32] marked a controversial test case for the exercise of 'shared responsibility' under the collective security system and the UN's interaction with other international actors (e.g. the International Criminal Court, NATO, the Arab League, the African Union). The international response highlighted risks inherent in the selectivity of mandates and the decentralisation of authority that have troubled UN collective security over the past decades. Yet, despite its deficiencies, the UN system remains as important as ever. Threats to human survival, the environment and all forms of life know no territorial borders or boundaries. One can only speculate what initiatives the late Hammarskjöld would have proposed to deal with the challenges of climate change, international terrorism and organised crime as well as many other phenomena unknown at the time of his terms of office. Being a person with a deep-rooted respect for nature, culture, religion and the arts, who sought dialogue instead of polarisation, he would have approached challenges based on his commitment to mutual cooperation in a 'common interest' and shared 'solidarity'.[33] As he put it in 1956:

> Through various developments which are familiar to all, world solidarity has, so to say, been forced upon us ... In such a world, it is impossible to maintain the status of 'haves' and 'have nots', just as impossible as it has grown to be inside the national state.[34]

It is evident that many of the challenges that Hammarskjöld and his staff faced have not been solved. Nor has the UN managed to avoid mistakes associated with its involvement in the former Belgian Congo which culminated in the murder of the Congo's first Prime Minister, Patrice

[32] See the preamble of SC Resolution 1970 of 26 February 2011 ('*Recalling* the Libyan authorities' responsibility to protect its population') and SC Resolution 1973 of 17 March 2011 ('*Reiterating* the responsibility of the Libyan authorities to protect the Libyan population'). For an analysis, see C. Stahn, 'Libya, the ICC and Complementarity: A Test for "Shared Responsibility"' (2012) 10 *Journal of International Criminal Justice* 325; A. Orford, 'From Promise to Practice? The Legal Significance of the Responsibility to Protect Concept' (2011) 3 *Global Responsibility to Protect* 400–424. Orford argues that 't[h]e significance of the concept lies *not* in its capacity to transform promise into practice, but rather in its capacity to do the reverse – that is, to transform practice into promise, or deeds into words'. *Ibid.*, at 403.

[33] See Address 3 February 1956, *supra* note 8, at 659. In his world of ideas, he understood charity as a disinterested exercise, namely as 'something a brother does for a brother, not as a handing-out operation with the benevolence of the "haves" in relation to the "have-nots"'.

[34] *Ibid.*, at 661.

Lumumba and the death of Dag Hammarskjöld. But the ideal of the UN as an 'instrument of action', committed to 'mediation, negotiation and reconciliation', remains.[35] In an address on 'Asia, Africa, and the West' delivered to the academic association of the University of Lund on 4 May 1959, Hammarskjöld expressed the normative foundation of the UN as follows: 'the Organization I represent … is based on a philosophy of solidarity'.[36] Solidarity, empathy, integrity are the values for which he stood and by which he lived. He thereby created a 'moral compass' for international civil service which has often been lost in the internal politics, bureaucracy and formalism of multilateral organisations.

For Hammarskjöld, the work of the UN was to build on the commonality of humankind, its conduct and experience. During a visit to India in early February 1956, he addressed the Indian Council of World Affairs. Prompted by a moving encounter with a local cultural event performed in his honour earlier, his mainly extemporaneous speech explored the dimensions of human universalism. A commonality beyond Western – or, indeed, any culturally, religiously or geographically limited – ideology or conviction is what he spoke to:

> It is no news to anybody, but we sense it in different degrees, that our world of today is more than ever before *one* world. The weakness of one is the weakness of all, and the strength of one – not the military strength, but the real strength, the economic and social strength, the happiness of people – is indirectly the strength of all … With respect to the United Nations as a symbol of faith, it may … be said that to every man it stands as a kind of 'yes' to the ability of man to form his own destiny, and form his own destiny so as to create a world where the dignity of man can come fully into its own.[37]

Dag Hammarskjöld, as a Swedish cosmopolitan, was convinced that firm roots in one's own society, with its peculiar history and culture, are no obstacle to universal values but are, instead, a valuable point of departure, provided that history and culture are not taken as the one and only absolute truth. He shared the view that factors, such as awareness of one's own upbringing in a specific social context and the grounding of one's identity in a framework of values, offer the moral space to develop curiosity

[35] *Ibid.*, at 660.

[36] D. Hammarskjöld, Asia, Africa and the West. Address Before the Academic Association of the University of Lund. Lund, Sweden, 4 May 1959 (UN Press Release SG/813, 4 May 1959) in Cordier and Foote, *Public Papers of the Secretaries-General of the United Nations, Vol. IV: Dag Hammarskjöld 1958–1960* (1974), 384.

[37] See Address 3 February 1956, *supra* note 8, at 661 and 660.

and openness towards 'others' and to explore the 'unknown' for one's own benefits and gain. Hammarskjöld's exchanges with Martin Buber testify to this conviction, as do his practical dialogues in search of solutions to conflicts and differences deeply entrenched in sets of values, norms and specific cultural socialisations. Hammarskjöld argued that there are no risks in entering a dialogue with 'strangers' if one knows where one comes from. Five days after his re-election as the UN Secretary-General, Dag Hammarskjöld expressed his admiration for Buber's philosophy 'of unity created "out of the manifold"' in a letter to Buber (dated 16 April 1958).[38] In his role as Secretary-General, he advocated the duty of the UN to obtain complete and objective information and the need of the Secretary-General to personally form an opinion and act, based on rules and principles of the UN Charter.

On 8 September 1961, Dag Hammarskjöld addressed the staff at the Secretariat of the UN for the last time. His words then are as relevant today:

> What is at stake is a basic question of principle: Is the Secretariat to develop as an international secretariat, with the full independence contemplated in Article 100 of the Charter, or is it to be looked upon as an intergovernmental – not international – secretariat providing merely the necessary administrative services for a conference machinery? This is a basic question, and the answer to it affects not only the working of the Secretariat but the whole of the future of international relations.[39]

Hammarskjöld's legacy remains alive – not only through his Annual Reports and speeches, but also through his commitment to norms and ideas that balance the *realpolitik* of states against human interests and ideals. His ideas foreshadow the merits, as well as some of the problems, inherent in modern developments, such as the aspirations of the global human rights movement relating and shifting attitudes about accountability (i.e. 'justice cascade').[40]

1.2 Focus and perspectives in this volume

This book is both a tribute and a critical review of Hammarskjöld's thought. Qualitities such as his value-based approach to leadership, his integrity

[38] Quoted in L. Marin, *Can We Save True Dialogue in an Age of Mistrust? The Encounter of Dag Hammarskjöld and Martin Buber* (2010), 11.

[39] D. Hammarskjöld, Last Words to the Staff – from Remarks on Staff Day. New York, 8 September 1961, in Cordier and Foote, Vol. V, *supra* note 7, at 563.

[40] See K. Sikkink, *The Justice Cascade: How Human Rights Prosecutions Are Changing World Politics* (2011).

and his personalised style of diplomacy form the basis of Hammarskjöld's action and conception of duty. They were honoured with the posthumously awarded Nobel Peace Prize in 1961. But Hammarskjöld was neither flawless nor a saint. Hence, some of the contributions to this volume keep a critical distance and invite reflections on the tasks and dilemmas that a Secretary-General is facing – now and in the past.

This volume seeks to set Hammarskjöld's achievements and failures into multiple contexts, by investigating his role from different disciplines and perspectives. It examines Hammarskjöld's approach towards international civil service, agency and value-based leadership. It investigates his conception of the role of the Secretary-General and the space of peace diplomacy, including its relevance and limitations. It is further meant to serve as a platform for current inquiry. It seeks to identify lessons from specific conflict situations and peace strategies (Suez, Congo), including their impact on contemporary conflict resolution efforts and modern concepts, such as 'human security' and 'R2P'. It also reflects on ways in which other actors and institutions (e.g. international courts and tribunals, the EU) can benefit from Hammarskjöld's principles and experiences in the broader fields of peacemaking and international justice.

While special emphasis is placed on the pioneering initiatives of Hammarskjöld, contributions also include analysis of his limits and failures, especially with regard to the UN intervention in the Congo. As Secretary-General, Hammarskjöld relied extensively on ethics and a personal approach to diplomacy in order to interpret and exercise his office. He justified key choices and approaches (e.g. autonomy of the UN and its agents, international cooperation, the role of privacy in peacemaking), by reference to moral concepts and human rights and duties.[41] This 'personal' dimension is inseparable from his 'public' function,[42]

[41] This is exemplified by his public addresses and speeches, published in A.W. Cordier and W. Foote (eds.), *Public Papers of the Secretaries-General of the United Nations,* Volumes II to V (1972 to 1975).

[42] See also the statement by Rolf Edberg, Swedish Ambassador to Norway, on the occasion of the award of the Nobel Peace Prize in Oslo, 10 December 1961, at www.nobelprize.org/nobel_prizes/peace/laureates/1961/hammarskjold-acceptance.html ('It was impossible to witness that scene at the stormy session of last year's General Assembly without recalling some words that he once wrote about his own father. "A man of firm convictions does not ask, and does not receive, understanding from those with whom he comes into conflict", he wrote about Hjalmar Hammarskjöld. "A mature man is his own judge. In the end, his only firm support is being faithful to his own convictions." How aptly these words applied to himself when he rose unhesitatingly to defend the idea of a truly international body of civil servants or to uphold the principles of the Charter in the Congo operation!').

and is thus considered as equally important in this volume. After all, much of the fascination concerning Hammarskjöld's results stems from interest in his exceptional visions, practices and sometimes unexpected successes.

His legacy raises ongoing questions for contemporary law and politics: what role do his conceptions of office play for modern international organisation? To what extent are his views on international relations, international service, leadership and the role of the United Nations shaped by his own idelogical background and faith? How relevant are his ideas on international law, preventive diplomacy, international service or technical assistance today? How do his conceptions of agency, impartiality and neutrality interrrelate with modern notions of the 'responsibility to protect', 'global justice' and governance, and what are its merits and risks?

1.3 Reflections on Dag Hammarskjöld

The volume starts with personal reflections. It includes statements by former UN officials and policy-makers who have witnessed or applied Hammarskjöld's legacy in practice. These contributions engage with Hammarskjöld's institutional and intellectual heritage. They add a personal component to the volume. While some of these reflections bear traces of admiration and recognition of Hammarskjöld, they also have a documentary character and provide some evidence and testimony in UN circles.

Kofi Annan, Sir Brian Urquhart, the late Pieter Kooijmans and Hans Corell have all served as international civil servants. They were either directly or indirectly presented with the application of the ethics and principles that Hammarskjöld represented.

Kofi Annan's own footsteps as Secretary-General were shaped by Hammarskjöld's ideas. There are some interesting parallels. His report 'In Larger Freedom'[43] proposed new initiatives (e.g. Responsibility to Protect, Peacebuilding Commission) that are in line with Hammarskjöld's visions. His dynamic understanding of the architecture of the UN coincides with Hammarskjöld's view, who argued that the Charter provides sufficient flexibility to permit growth and 'continous adaptation' going beyond what seems to have been anticipated in San Francisco, even 'without formal

[43] See Report of the Secretary-General, 'In Larger Freedom: Towards Development, Security and Human Rights for All', UN Doc. A/59/2005, 21 March 2005.

revisions'.[44] In his Dag Hammarskjöld Lecture in 2001, Annan states that there is a 'rule of thumb' for a Secretary-General facing a crisis: 'How would Hammarskjöld have handled this?'. Building on Hammarskjöld's principles, he claims that the UN can only successfully meet its challenges in the twenty-first century if it is understood as 'a framework of shared values and understandings' within which 'free and voluntary efforts can interact, and reinforce each other'.

Brian Urquhart joined the UN Secretariat at its inception in 1945. He served in the Office of the Under-Secretary-General for Political Affairs during almost the entire time of Hammarskjöld's tenure.[45] He examines how Hammarskjöld developed the political mandate and powers of the office of the Secretary-General (i.e. through multilateral diplomacy). His contribution demonstrates to what extent Hammarskjöld's action and defence of 'common interest' challenged prevailing conceptions of state sovereignty and Great Power interests. He concludes that Hammarskjöld gave both the Secretariat and the UN as organisation a new self-understanding and meaning in the Cold War.[46]

Pieter Kooijmans, former Judge at the International Court of Justice, explores a different aspect of Hammarskjöld's influence. He discusses why there is still interest in Hammarskjöld. He justifies Hammarskjöld's relevance partly by his spirituality. He claims that the continuing interest in Hammarskjöld results not only from the force of specific views and ideas that he advocated, but rather from his authenticity and his way of approaching global problems. He argues that Hammarskjöld's urge for continuous reflection and self-reflection enabled him to integrate long-term policy objectives in his decisions and actions and to withstand pressures of *ad hocism* based on Charter principles.

Hans Corell, who served as UN Legal Counsel, analyses how the core principles that Hammarskjöld identified as foundation of the UN in his final Annual Report ('equal political rights', 'equal economic opportunities', 'justice' and the 'prohibition of the use of force'),[47] have developed since Hammarskjöld's death. He identifies some institutional progress as well as remaining shortcomings (e.g. lack of loyalty of UN members to aims, principles and purposes of the Charter) that need to be

[44] See Introduction to the Annual Report of the Secretary-General on the Work of the Organization, 16 June 1958–15 June 1959, GAOR, 14th Sess. Supp. No 1A (A/4132/Add.1), at 2.

[45] See also B. Urquhart, *Hammarskjöld* (1972) reprinted in 1994.

[46] For a full account, see *ibid.*, Epilogue, 596–597.

[47] See *supra* note 3.

addressed. He places particular emphasis on the development of the concept of the 'rule of law' and its potential to re-think both the obligations of 'members of the United Nations and the organization itself', including decisions and decision-making processes in the Security Council. He concurs with Hammarskjöld's vision that occasional conflicts of the Secretary-General with Member States may be an inevitable expression of loyalty to the Charter, which demonstrate the 'neutrality' of the Secretary-General, rather than his or her 'failure to observe neutrality'.[48]

1.4 Hammarskjöld's intellectual legacy and leadership

Part II of the volume examines an aspect of Hammarskjöld that is often sidelined in political science and legal scholarship: namely the influence of his spiritual and professional background on his approach towards law and politics. Particular emphasis is placed on Hammarskjöld's intellectual legacy and leadership,[49] including impulses from his posthumously published spiritual diary.[50] The entries offer manifold insights into the foundations of Hammarskjöld's ethics (integrity, authenticity, dialogue and respect for otherness), and its interrelation with diplomacy and leadership. *Markings* itself contains no express references to specific political events or people. But it becomes evident that there is a history to Hammarskjöld before taking over the office of Secretary-General and that this history and his spirituality play a key role in understanding his later approaches to UN-related challenges. His spiritual dimensions went largely unnoticed during his lifetime. They are retrieved here, based on analysis of his posthumously published notebook as well as personal correspondence. His academic training as an economist as well as his role in the establishment of the Swedish welfare state and the reconstruction of post-war Europe are also treated.[51] This section demonstrates that these

48 See 'The International Civil Servant in Law and in Fact', *supra* note 7, at 348.

49 See on this particular aspect also the PhD thesis by L.L. Andersson, *Ledarskapande Retorik. Dag Hammarskjöld och FN:s övriga generalsekreterare som scen för karisma, dygder och ledarideal* (2009).

50 D. Hammarskjöld, *Markings* (1964), Swedish original 1963; re-published since then in many different editions and languages. See also B. Erling, *A Reader's Guide to Dag Hammarskjöld's Waymarks*, at www.dhf.uu.se/publications/other-publications/a-reader%E2%80%99s-guide-to-dag-hammarskjold%E2%80%99s-waymarks/.

51 See on Hammarskjöld's formative years in the Swedish public service also H. Landberg, *På väg ... Dag Hammarskjöld som svensk ämbetsman* (2012); M. Svegfors, *Dag Hammarskjöld. Den förste moderne svensken* (2005).

dimensions shaped his political and analytical thinking, including typical 'Dag' approaches (e.g. 'personalised' and silent diplomacy as means of conflict prevention or reduction, development policy and approaches to neutrality).

The three opening chapters take a closer look at the link between spirituality and politics. Usually, these two dimensions are considered in isolation. In the case of Hammarskjöld, this separation of personal, including religious, conviction and public service is open to challenge. Hammarskjöld shared the view that both are intrinsically related.[52] He stands as an example of a statesman whose ethical views and inner convictions deeply influenced his political actions and decisions.[53] Throughout his tenure, he stressed the difference between beliefs as a private man and public service. But his moral and religious beliefs provided the basis of his political ethics. He theorised the foundations of the Charter through the lens of moral and philosophical principles. Moreover, he derived his ethic of responsibility as civil servant (e.g. self-sacrifice, service in the 'common good') from synergies to faith.[54]

His commitment to public service is partly grounded in the Swedish Lutheran tradition of duty and selfless service to God and service to men[55] and the writings of medieval mystics who called for service in the imitation of Christ.[56] These influences may also explain his sense of righteousness in the exercise of duty (Luther) and his ethics of equality.[57] The synergies between spiritual life and professional ethics are reflected in his use of religious metaphors and quotes (e.g. St Paul) to describe his mandate and his dual commitment to spiritual faith (as a private person) and the application of 'faith' in the secular world (as a civic mandate).[58] The

[52] He agreed with Martin Buber on this point and had started to translate his 'I and Thou' shortly before his death.

[53] See M. Fröhlich, *Political Ethics and The United Nations: Dag Hammarskjöld as Secretary-General* (2010), at 121.

[54] See A.J. Lyon, 'Moral Motives and Policy Actions: The Case of Dag Hammarskjöld at the United Nations' (2006–7) 9 *Public Integrity* 79–95, at 85–87.

[55] This influence may be traced back to his father, Hjalmar Hammarskjöld, a member of Swedish nobility and public servant under King Gustav V of Sweden.

[56] See St John of the Cross, Thomas à Kempis, St Teresa of Avila. See Lyon, *supra* note 54, at 83.

[57] Some of the evangelistic influences go back to contacts of his mother (Agnes Almquist Hammarskjöld) and the Lutheran community in Sweden. See Lyon, *supra* note 54, at 82.

[58] He clarified his vision of office in a prepared press statement in 1953. He said: 'In my new official capacity the private man should disappear and the international public servant take his place. The public servant is there in order to assist, so to say from the inside, those

most well-known and prominent example of this dualism is his comparison of the Secretary-General to a 'secular pope'.[59]

His reliance on Christian thought was not meant in a missionary sense.[60] He defended the secular character of the Charter and the principle of neutral integrity as part of his public function. He explained this at the World Council of Churches in 1954, where he stated:

> The United Nations stands outside – necessarily outside – all confessions, but it is nevertheless an instrument of faith. As such it is inspired by what unites and not what divides the great religions of the world.[61]

This 'faith'-based approach towards civil duty and peaceful internationalism had different implications: his spiritual worldview and Christian background might explain some of the opposition to him from the Soviet Union and the socialist bloc. But it serves at the same time as an example of how spirituality may enrich certain features of diplomatic practice and principles of international organisation, such as conflict resolution skills (e.g. confidence, diligence and long-term thinking), loyalty to norms and principles and institutional ethics.[62]

Monica Bouman analyses the foundations of Hammarskjöld's ethics of international service. She locates the origins of a duty-based approach to international service in *Markings* and his first diplomatic experiences. She shows that Hammarskjöld regarded the UN as a quasi-secular 'church' of ideals and principles.[63] She argues that his vision of international service is influenced by Christian ideas and secular traditions of thought, including Dauenhauer's philosophy of the 'politics of hope', Arendt's approach

who make the decisions which frame history. He should – as I see it – listen, analyze and learn to understand fully the forces at work and the interests at stake, so that he will be able to give the right advice when the situation calls for it. Don't think that he – in following this line of personal policy – takes but a passive part in the development. It is a most active one. But he is active as an instrument, a catalyst, perhaps an inspirer – he serves.' See Statement to the Press on Arrival at International Airport, New York, 9 April 1953, UN Press Release, SG/287, 9 April 1953.

59 See Troy, *supra* note 4, at 441, 446.

60 See Urquhart, *supra* note 45, at 23–25 ('His identification with Christian thought was not messianic, but rather in the old tradition of the imitation of Christ in sacrifice and service to others').

61 See Address World Council of Churches, 20 August 1954, in Cordier and Foote, Vol. II, *supra* note 8, at 352.

62 See also Lyon, *supra* note 54, at 92.

63 See Address by Secretary-General Dag Hammarskjöld at Dinner in his Honor Given by the American Association for the United Nations, New York, 14 September 1953, UN Press Release SG/336, at 7, at https://docs.google.com/folder/d/0BwQhqizmWFekZlhFSW1mUXZ5SFk/edit?pli=1.

to morality ('standard of the moral self') and Jasper's views on the 'unity of mankind'.[64] She claims that the interplay between spirituality and public service explains some of the success of his diplomatic initiatives (e.g. the resolution of the 1954 US–China dispute and the Taiwan Strait crisis). She sees strengths in his perception as 'practitioner of the politics of hope'.

Paul Nelson examines the link between Hammarskjöld's spirituality and negotiation, based on archival sources.[65] In 1953, Hammarskjöld identified the quest for peace as a basis of the political foundations of the UN.[66] Nelson shows how Hammarskjöld's spirituality influenced his approach towards negotiated peace and reconciliation in the Suez and the Congo crises. He argues that his diplomacy of reconciliation was deeply shaped by his faith.

Roger Lipsey analyses the spiritual and secular foundations of Hammarskjöld's political wisdom. He argues that there is continuity between 'his private reflections' in *Markings* and his 'public life'. He shows how elements of Hammarskjöld's moral code influenced specific aspects of his exercise diplomacy, namely his approach to 'dialogue' (as a professional skill and form of 'empathy') and to 'negotiation' (e.g. fair play, trust and timing, balancing of short-term and long-term objectives, use of ambiguity). He concludes that Hammarskjöld's approach to diplomacy differs from classical realism, by encouraging 'a politics of willing global interdependence that begins in the private world and issues out into the shared world'.

Ove Bring examines the link between Hammarskjöld's intellectual background and his approach towards international law. He argues that Hammarskjöld adopted a 'flexible' approach which reconciled the recognition of global norms and principles with the application of ethical principles.[67] This is reflected in his contextual vision of norms and principles. Bring shows that Hammarskjöld was one of the early defenders of the link

[64] See also M. Bouman, *Dag Hammarskjöld, Citizen of the World* (2005).

[65] See also P. Nelson, *Courage of Faith. Dag Hammarskjöld's Way in Quest of Negotiated Peace, Reconciliation and Meaning* (2007).

[66] He noted: 'We are of different creeds and convictions. Events and ideas which to some of us remain the very basis of our faith are elements of the spiritual heritage of man which are foreign to others. But common to us all, and above all other convictions stands the truth, once expressed by a Swedish poet when he said that the greatest prayer of man does not ask for victory but for peace.' Statement in the General Assembly After Taking the Oath of Office, 10 April 1953, in Cordier and Foote, Vol. II, *supra* note 8, at 31 et seq.

[67] See also O. Schachter, 'Dag Hammarskjöld and the Relation of Law to Politics' (1962) 56 *AJIL* 1.

between peace, security and human rights. He argues that Hammarskjöld interpreted fundamental concepts, such as collective security or non-intervention, through the lens of human rights and human security, namely a focus on 'men' in addition to states, and on 'dignity' in addition to security – a nexus that is recognised in UN peace maintenance today. He shows that Hammarskjöld's personal ethics explain his openness towards UN intervention and protection, when the UN crossed the boundaries between peacekeeping and peace enforcement in the Congo. He argues that Hammarskjöld's approach towards law is based on the 'natural law' understanding that written law needs to be reconciled 'with a law of a higher order' – a position in line with his Christian values.

Anne Orford investigates yet another dimension of Hammarskjöld's legacy. She addresses the influence of his economic thinking on his vision of the role of the state and of international organisations in managing reconstruction and development. Orford argues that his focus on 'executive action' and his commitment to neutrality in decolonisation are shaped by his involvement in post-war European reconstruction. She explains how Hammarskjöld's vision of the relation of state and market (e.g. his insistence on neutrality and the role of the state as arbiter) conflicted with other economists of the so-called Stockholm school (e.g. Gunnar Myrdal), who defended greater state planning and the architecture of the Swedish welfare state. She shows to what extent his approaches towards decolonisation in the Congo were shaped by the tension between his commitment to 'independence', on the one hand, and his faith in 'liberal economics', on the other.

1.5 Hammarskjöld, the UN and the Congo

Part III investigates one of the most controversial aspects of Hammarskjöld's tenure, namely the background of the Congo crisis, its consequences for UN involvement and Hammarskjöld's death. Much has been written about the UN operation in the Congo and the dubious circumstances of the airplane crash in which he and all others on board died.[68] This part revisits the history and consequences of Hammarskjöld's handling of the Congo crisis, including its impact on contemporary practice. It includes critical assessments of Hammarskjöld's efforts to

[68] See S. Williams, *Who Killed Hammarskjöld? The UN, the Cold War, and White Supremacy in Africa* (2011); R. Rembe and A. Hellberg, *Midnatt i Kongo. Dag Hammarskjölds förlorade seger* (2011).

find a peaceful solution to the conflict, which question the impartiality and the agenda of the intervention. Contributions address in particular the relationship between Hammarskjöld, Patrice Lumumba as the first elected Prime Minister of independent Congo, and the UN officials on the ground. They show that precarious personal interactions were an important dimension to the conflict, which resulted in the death of the two most prominent protagonists.

Maria Rognoni analyses Hammarskjöld's approach to the Congolese crisis, based on newly researched archival sources. Using Hammarskjöld's personal correspondence as evidence, she argues that Hammarskjöld was aware of the Cold War implications of his personal stand and of his place within the Congo confrontation, and that the confrontation with the Soviet Union helped him gain support for some of his approaches. She claims that the UN played a 'crucial role during the first Congo crisis' and that the solution Hammarskjöld sought had to take into account aspects that 'transcended the local framework and called for a difficult balance between different points of view'.

Helen Hintjens and Serena Cruz examine the vision of internationalism that surrounded the UN presence in the Congo. They argue that the 1960–1 period remains crucial for understanding the role and limits of what the UN can do to promote peace. They show that the quest for freedom was not only a question of sovereignty, but also a struggle for dignity and freedom from economic coercion and enslavement.

Jean Omasombo Tshonda contrasts Hammarskjöld's vision of neutrality with Lumumba's approach towards freedom and independence. He argues that Lumumba's historical rejection of colonial heritage reflects a conflict between political authority and national conscience that remains relevant to the perception of international forces by Congolese society until today. He claims that Lumumba's vision presents an 'alternative reading of the Congolese experience' than the one presented by Western history.

Henning Melber examines how the relationship between Hammarskjöld's ethics and his awareness of the socio-economic dimensions of inequality influenced his thinking on decolonisation. His approach and conclusions contrast with the earlier, more critical assessments of Hammarskjöld's involvement in the Congo. He revisits the circumstances of Hammarskjöld's untimely death. He concedes that 'the role of the UN under Hammarskjöld in the Congo [might be] seen as an indication of his failure to advocate the principles he claimed to stand for'.

But he claims that Hammarskjöld nonetheless set standards that have lost none of their value and relevance.

Alanna O'Malley analyses how 'quiet diplomacy' enabled the UN to position itself as an arbiter among major powers in the conflict. She argues that the combination of 'the Afri-Asian bloc' and Hammarskjöld's commitment to decolonisation made the 'General Assembly more influential during the Congo crisis than it had ever previously been'. The chapter provides a transition to the following part, which gives prominence to the diverse aspects related to the role played by the UN and its Secretary-General through Hammarskjöld.

1.6 The role of the UN Secretary-General

Part IV examines some of the innovations that Hammarskjöld introduced, as well as the development of some of his approaches in international practice. The contributions focus on the lessons learned from Hammarskjöld's conception of the role and powers of the Secretary-General, described by Tryvge Lie as 'the most impossible job in the world'.[69] It entails a tension between the function as 'Secretary' and the role as 'General'.[70] Hammarskjöld paid attention to the political dimension of the role of the Secretary-General. He gave a new space to executive action under the Charter. He devised the functions of Under-Secretary-Generals in the structure of the UN and entrusted them with roles as special advisors. He developed new means and techniques to strengthen the capacity of the Secretariat to respond swiftly and effectively to disputes. He relied on 'preventive diplomacy' and mediation in order to mitigate conflict.[71] He defended the independence of the Secretary-General vis-à-vis other organs. He derived his approach to negotiation either explicitly from the Charter or from its philosophy.[72]

[69] Quoted in Urquhart, *supra* note 45, at 15.

[70] For an excellent analysis see Fröhlich, *supra* note 53.

[71] See Report of the UN Secretary-General, 'Preventive Diplomacy: Delivering Results', UN Doc. S/ 2011/552, 26 August 2011, dedicated to the legacy of Dag Hammarskjöld. The report recalls Hammarskjöld's dictum that 'we have only begun to explore the full potentialities of the United Nations as an instrument for multilateral diplomacy'. See for the full document http://reliefweb.int/sites/reliefweb.int/files/resources/SG%20Report%20on%20Preventive%20Diplomacy.pdf.

[72] For an illustration, see Address 2 May 1959, *supra* note 16, at 373: 'The statement of objectives in the Charter is binding, and so are the rules concerning the various organs and their competence, but it is not necessary to regard the procedures indicated in the Charter as limitative in purpose. They may be supplemented by others under the pressure

In his diplomatic efforts, he claimed authority to act in his capacity as Secretary-General, rather than as a representative or spokesperson of the General Assembly.[73]

Hammarskjöld was at the same time fully aware of the implications of technology and communication on conflict management and diplomacy. Some of his statements retain relevance in relation to 'early warning' or the use of private networks in conflict prevention (e.g. Facebook):

> We are all very conscious of the fact that it is now but a question of hours for military forces to reach distant parts of the globe and that the old considerations of strategy based on geographic separation may no longer count for much.
>
> News also reaches us from all corners of the globe almost as quickly as if we had been eye-witnesses. We are parties to an action practically at the very moment it is undertaken. The nerve signals from a wound are felt at once through the body of mankind.[74]

He acknowledged that 'media of mass communications, when supplemented by education in world affairs in schools and universities, provide powerful tools for developing a better informed public opinion'.[75] But he also recognised that 'they can be misused'.[76]

When Hammarskjöld took office in 1953, he compared the qualities required by a Secretary-General to 'mountaineering'. He stressed the need for:

> perseverance and patience, a firm grip on realities, careful but imaginative planning, a clear awareness of the dangers but also of the fact that fate

of circumstances and in the light of experience. This freer interpretation permits an evolution departing from what has been expressly stated, to the extent that new procedures, perhaps combined with a modified balance in the use of various organs, prove productive in practice for the efforts to attain the objectives of the Charter ... What we are seeing is an evolution on the basis of a fundamental charter of sufficient flexibility to permit a continuous adaptation of constitutional life to the needs.'

73 In 1954, Hammarskjöld pushed for the inclusion of operative paragraph 4 into Resolution 906 (IX), which requested the Secretary-General to seek the release of US hostages 'by the means most appropriate in his judgment'. This enabled him to engage in direct talks with the Chinese side, despite the condemnation of the detention by the General Assembly in paragraph 2 of the resolution. See GA Res. 906 (IX) of 10 December 1954, adopted at its 509th Plenary Meeting, and Interim Report of the Secretary-General on the implementation of Resolution 906 (IX), 30 December 1954, UN Doc. A/2891.

74 Speech to the Foreign Policy Association at a Dinner Given in His Honor, New York, 21 October 1953, in Cordier and Foote, *supra* note 8, at 102.

75 See Address Ohio, 'The Element of Privacy in Peacemaking', 5 February 1958, UN Press Release, SG/656, 3 February 1958, at www.un.org/Depts/dhl/dag/docs/privacy.pdf., at 30.

76 *Ibid.*, at 30.

> is what we make it and that the safest climber is he who never questions his ability to overcome all difficulties.[77]

Manuel Fröhlich demonstrates how Hammarskjöld's 'principled stand' in the resolution of the Suez crisis led to the creation of the first UN peacekeeping operation (United Nations Emergency Force (UNEF)). He argues that the basic principles identified by Hammarskjöld in relation to UNEF set a constitutional precedent for the future of UN peacekeeping. He shows that UNEF presented some of the problems of Chapter VII operations, without enjoying its powers.

Aiofe O'Donoghue examines the role of Hammarskjöld in the development of 'good offices'. Hammarskjöld addressed this practice explicitly in the introduction to his 1959 Annual Report to the General Assembly. At the time, he justified it as follows:

> [I]n some recent cases of international conflict or other difficulties involving member states the Secretary-General has dispatched personal representatives with the task of assisting the governments in their efforts. This may be regarded as a further development of actions of a 'good-offices' nature, with which the Secretary-General is now frequently charged. The steps to which I refer here have been taken with the consent or at the invitation of the government concerned, but without formal decisions of other organs of the United Nations. Such actions by the Secretary-General fall within the competence of his office and are, in my view, in other respects also in strict accordance with the Charter, when they serve its purpose. As a matter of course, the members of the appropriate organ of the United Nations have been informed about the action planned by the Secretary-General and were given an opportunity to express views on it.[78]

O'Donoghue analyses Hammarskjöld's use of 'good offices' in two instances, the Congo crisis and the US–China hostage crisis, leading to the development of the 'Peking formula'. She concludes that Hammarskjöld transformed the role of 'good offices' from state-based mediation into an instrument of prevention and conflict resolution under the UN umbrella. She shows that his approach encountered initial criticism, but also paved the way for modern practices, such as the use of Special Envoys or Special Representatives of the Secretary-General.

Following Hammarskjöld's tenure, the phrase 'Leave it to Dag' has become a popular slogan in mediation and conflict resolution. Peter

[77] Statement to the Press on Arrival at International Airport, New York, 9 April 1953, UN Press Release, SG/287, 9 April 1953, in Cordier and Foote, *supra* note 8, at 30.

[78] Introduction to the Fourteenth Annual Report, New York, 20 August 1959, in Cordier and Foote, Vol. IV, *supra* note 5, at 451 et seq.

Wallensteen unpacks this notion, by analysing his record in diplomacy in twenty situations of crisis during his term of office. He assesses Hammarskjöld's action through the lens of three types of diplomacy: 'agenda diplomacy' (i.e. action to find an agreed entry point for conflict resolution between conflicting parties), 'agreement diplomacy' (i.e. arrangements to foster formal agreement) and 'implementation diplomacy' (i.e. initiatives to translate an existing agreement into practice). He argues that Hammarskjöld was most successful in 'implementation negotiations', relatively successful in 'agreement diplomacy' (with a split record of successes and failures), and least successful in 'agenda setting'. He concludes that Hammarskjöld's approach and success was characterised by four features: 'travel diplomacy', 'building trust', 'early action' and 'coalition-building'. He shows how these features were developed in crisis diplomacy by some of his successors (e.g. Annan).

Jan Anne Vos argues that the transformations and structural changes in UN practice over the past decades cannot be explained in isolation of personality and visions of international life. He takes a more systematic look at structural and thematic synergies in the mandates of Hammarskjöld and Annan. He indicates how Hammarskjöld framed major issues of international organisation through his Annual Reports and statements. He argues that Hammarskjöld's vision of the architecture of the UN marked a deep shift from a functional or intergovernmental conception of international authority. He claims that Annan's approach in his report 'In Larger Freedom' coincides largely with the 'magic triangle' developed by Hammarskjöld in the Introduction to his 1953 Annual Report to the General Assembly. He concludes that both share a 'duty-based' vision of the state in relation to human rights and the well-being of the population. He points at the same time to some of the risks that arise from a supranational conception of the UN, such as the dislocation of 'authority' and 'responsibility' and divisions caused by neo-imperialist perceptions.

In his 1960 address on the 'Development of a Constitutional Framework for International Organization', Hammarskjöld developed the foundations of his institutional understanding based on parallels to European integration. He noted:

> The institutional evolution in Europe has brought us a step in the direction of a true constitutional framework for cooperation which through experimental stages of a confederal nature, may finally lead to some kind of federal systems or even stronger forms of association … If we accept the interpretation given here to the European community … The United Nations could, in a similar sense, be called a 'community', although of

> a universal character. 'It represents in itself, with the methods of operation and the rules established, an elaboration of an institutional pattern of co-existence'.[79]

Today, some of the foundations of Hammarskjöld's community-based vision of the UN are expressly enshrined in the legal order of the EU and its Common Foreign and Security Policy. The EU is acting as a 'global peace broker' in some areas (e.g. Kosovo). Some of its structures (e.g. the role of the High Representative of the Union for Foreign Affairs and Security Policy, the use of EU Special Representatives) resemble features of UN peace diplomacy. Steven Blockmans examines this development. He argues that some of Hammarskjöld's principles of international organisation are represented in:

(1) the constitutional objectives of the EU;
(2) its instruments and methods of peace diplomacy; and
(3) the structures of the emerging European External Action Service.

1.7 Re-thinking internationalism: intervention, responsibility and the politics of R2P

Part V examines whether and how some of the foundations of Hammarskjöld's thought and ideology have developed in international practice. From a formal point of view, there is a considerable degree of continuity. There have been only a few attempts to change the normative framework or re-write basic features of UN organisation. While some areas have been developed through codification (e.g. protection of human rights, environmental protection, international justice), the organisation evolved mainly incrementally, namely through practice, including facts and circumstances created through action.[80] Many of the priorities and inherent features that Hammarskjöld found in Charter norms and principles have become more explicit.

The functions of the Secretary-General and the use of executive authority have expanded in the field of international peace and security. There is an ongoing discussion about the 'constitutional' elements of the Charter and its special functions as a multilateral instrument (e.g. a Constitution),[81] including its effect on regional organisations, states and

[79] See *supra* note 5, at 586.

[80] See also A. Orford, *International Authority and the Responsibility to Protect* (2011), at 6.

[81] See B. Fassbender, *UN Security Council Reform: A Constitutional Perspective* (1998). See also more generally J. Klabbers, A. Peters and G. Ulfstein, *The Constitutionalization of*

individuals. The 'socio-economic' and 'justice'-related dimensions of the Charter have been developed more systematically. 'Rule of law' principles have become part of peacebuilding and development assistance strategies.[82] The proposal that sovereignty should not serve as a shield for human rights atrocities has been strengthened by Chapter VII practice and the conception of 'sovereignty as responsibility' under R2P.[83] The protection of community interests is reflected in the assumption of *erga omnes* obligations,[84] the recognition of resources that form part of the 'common heritage of mankind'[85] or are of 'common concern',[86] and the administration[87] or regulation of global common goods.[88] The very concept of R2P provides a 'humanitarian' ideology for the exercise of international authority.[89]

But there are also new problems and discontents. The expansion of international executive rule has posed novel challenges to the legitimacy

International Law (2009); N. Krisch, *Beyond Constutionalism: The Pluralist Structure of Postnational Law* (2010).

[82] See S. Pahuja, *Decolonising International Law: Development, Economic Growth and the Politics of Universality* (2011).

[83] For a discussion, see C. Stahn, 'Responsibility to Protect: Political Rhethoric or Emerging Legal Norm' (2007) 101 *AJIL* 99.

[84] See ICJ, Barcelona Traction, Light and Power Company Ltd (*Belgium* v. *Spain*, ICJ Reports 1970, 3, 32, para. 33). On the 'international community' idea, see C. Paulus, *Die internationale Gemeinschaft im Völkerrecht* (2001).

[85] See Declaration of Principles Governing the Seabed and the Ocean Floor and the Subsoil Thereof, Beyond the Limits of National Jurisdiction, GA Res. 2749 (XXV), 17 December 1970, (1971) 10 ILM 220; Art. 11 (1) of the Agreement Governing the Activities on the Moon and other Celestial Bodies, 5 December 1979.

[86] See para. 1 of GA Res. 45/53, Protection of Global Climate for Present and Future Generations of Mankind. See generally J. Brunnée, 'Common Areas, Common Heritage, and Common Concern', in D. Bodansky, J. Brunnée and E. Hay (eds.), *The Oxford Handbook of International Environmental Law* (2007), 550.

[87] On 'global administration law', see D. Esty, 'Good Governance at the Supranational Scale: Globalizing Administrative Law' (2006) 115 *Yale Law Journal* 1490; B. Kingsbury, N. Krisch and R. Stewart, 'The Emergence of Global Administrative Law' (2005) 68 *Law and Contemporary Problems* 15; B. Kingsbury, 'The Concept of "Law" in Global Administrative Law' (2009) 20 EJIL 23; B. Kingsbury and L. Casini, 'Global Administrative Law Dimensions of International Organizations Law' (2009) 6 *International Organizations Law Review* 319.

[88] On the concept of 'global public goods', see M. Desai, 'Public Goods: A Historical Perspective', in I. Kaul, P. Conceicao, K. Le Goulven and R.U. Mendoza (eds.), *Providing Global Public Goods: Managing Globalization* (2003), 60–77; D. Bodanky, 'What's in a Concept? Global Public Goods, International Law, and Legitimacy' (2012) 23 *EJIL* 651; G. Shaffer, 'International Law and Global Public Goods in a Legal Pluralist World' (2012) 23 *EJIL* 669.

[89] See Orford, *supra* note 32, at 424.

of international authority, the accountability of international actors and the application of due standards in decision-making processes (e.g. individual sanctions). The decentralisation or delegation of authority to subsidiary bodies, regional organisations or states has blurred lines of communication, command and responsibility. The defence of a 'positive' conception of peace, founded on the link between security, democracy and human rights, conflicts with the traditional assumption of the UN's 'impartiality'. UN action remains dominated by selectivity and *ad hocism*.

The implementation of R2P is one of the areas in which the very foundations of the ideas of 'international community' and 'neutrality' are put to a test most severely. R2P is one of the most prominent, but also one of the most contested, new concepts. It has been associated with hopes for a new 'duty of care' in international relations.[90] But it puts the dilemma of 'agency' and 'good faith' at the forefront.[91] From Hammarskjöld onwards, proponents of international executive action have justified international action on the basis of human rights and maintaining order, and in contrast to unilateral action. There is often a thin line between 'protection' and 'tutelage' in the implementation of international mandates. In Rwanda or Srebrenica, impartiality and neutrality were criticised and associated with complicity in 'evil'. In the context of Libya, the mandate was framed in terms of a neutral '*jus in bello*' concept, the 'protection of civilians'. This vocabulary clouded many antinomies of the operation. Both the interpretation of the scope of the mandate and the idea of 'agency' became controversial in the implementation of the mandate.[92] The nexus between collective security and international justice was meant to reinforce prevention. But it also complicated the exercise of independent international justice. This last part explores these dichotomies. It treats the promises, as well as the limitations, of Hammarskjöld's heritage of international humanitarianism.

Carsten Stahn revisits Hammarskjöld's vision of international executive authority. He explores to what extent there is continuity or a shift in relation to the exercise of public authority between the colonial

[90] See L. Arbour, 'The Responsibility to Protect as a Duty of Care in International Law and Practice' (2008) 34 *Review of International Studies* 445.

[91] See also Orford, *supra* note 80, at 192 et seq. The UN placed a focus on consolidating norms through 'action'. See Report of the Secretary-General, 'Implementing the Responsibility to Protect', A/63/677, 12 January 2009.

[92] Brazil suggested to complement the R2P concept by a new dimension: the 'responsibility while protecting'.

experience of the nineteenth century and contemporary UN missions today.

Vijayashri Sripati examines 'international executive rule' – a key doctrine developed by Hammarskjöld – from a Third World Approaches to International Law (TWAIL) perspective. She suggests that criticisms of international authority have fostered a turn to UN Constitutional Assistance – an approach which may be more in line with TWAIL.

Craig Barker analyses the origins and implications of Hammarskjöld's conception of 'duty' and 'obligation' for the development of international law. He shows that basic tenets of the R2P concept can be traced back to Hammarskjöld's ideas, including his early articulation of 'the right of everyone to security and to freedom from fear'.[93] In his defence of multilateralism, Hammarskjöld advocated, in particular, a new vision of 'shared responsibility'. Drawing on Christian ethics, he placed the idea of 'solidarity' at the core of international cooperation. He stated:

> I think that it is not in keeping with the very spirit of sharing if the country which gives wants to put it on its flag that it is the donor, or if the country which receives has to be constantly reminded of the fact that it receives. It is not a gift from one to the other; it is a sharing, a sharing in the name of solidarity which is a 'must' in our world and not something of our free choice.[94]

Barker develops this line of thought. He argues that the moral theory of 'ethics of care' should be considered as a possible basis for the development of international law, in addition to the traditional ethics of justice. Drawing on arguments based on family law and feminist scholarship, he proposes to develop the role of responsibility as a 'relational concept' in order to encourage the effective implementation of international law.

Francis Kofi Abiew and Noemi Gal-Or highlight some of the antinomies arising in the application of R2P in contemporary practice. They argue that the application of R2P in the Libyan context falls short of meeting the criteria and elements set out in foundational policy documents, such as the Report of the International Commission on State Sovereignty and Intervention[95] and the 2005 Word Summit Outcome

[93] See D. Hammarskjöld, Address on Human Rights and the Work for Peace at the Fiftieth Anniversary Dinner of the American Jewish Committee, New York, 10 April 1957 (UN Press Release SG/585, 10 April 1957) in Cordier and Foote, *Public Papers of the Secretaries-General of the United Nations, Vol. III: Dag Hammarskjöld 1956–1957* (1973), 555.

[94] 'Ideology', *supra* note 8, at 662.

[95] See *The Responsibility to Protect*, Report of the International Commission on Intervention and State Sovereignty (2001).

Document.[96] They conclude that like other peace operations, the Libya intervention has failed to provide a 'skeletal model' for a more 'comprehensively articulated' doctrine of R2P.

Louise Arbour examines international responses in the context of the Arab Uprisings. She takes a closer look at the interplay of law and politics in the architecture of peace and security. She argues that 'the responsibility to protect and international criminal justice cannot be sheltered from political considerations'. She claims that the 'increasing entanglement of justice and politics is unlikely to be good for justice in the long run'.

1.8 Hammarskjöld's credo

The volume concludes with two of the last (and lasting) key texts and deliberations by Dag Hammarskjöld, testifying to the legacy he left behind for an understanding of the United Nations and the role of its Secretariat as well as the Secretary-General: his Annual Report to the General Assembly of the United Nations of 17 August 1961[97] and his Address to Secretariat Staff, 8 September 1961[98] – two documents that are frequently visible throughout the volume.

In 1961, only days after Hammarskjöld's death, Kennedy delivered his famous speech at the United Nations, at which he said:

> The problem is not the death of one man – the problem is the life of this organization. It will either grow to meet the challenges of our age, or it will be gone with the wind, without influence, without force, without respect.[99]

Dag Hammarskjöld's ethics, his concept of solidarity, his sense of fundamental values and human rights in combination with his respect for the multitude of identities within the human family, as well as his responsibility as the world's highest international civil servant to assume global leadership, set ideals that have to this day lost none of their value and relevance.[100] The way he defined and executed his duties can confidently

[96] See GA Resolution 63/308, The Responsibility to Protect, 14 September 2009, UN Doc. A/RES/63/308.

[97] See Annex 1. [98] See Annex 2.

[99] See J.F. Kennedy, Address to the United Nations General Assembly, 25 September 1961, at http://en.wikisource.org/wiki/Address_to_the_United_Nations_General_Assembly_(Kennedy, 1961-09-25).

[100] See for recent appraisals also R. Lipsey, *Hammarskjöld: A Life* (2013); M. Fröhlich, H. Klumpjan and H. Melber, *Dag Hammarskjöld (1905–1961). Für eine friedliche Welt – Ideen und Impulse des zweiten UN-Generalsekretärs* (2011); B. Thelin, *Dag Hammarskjöld.*

be qualified as an act of international solidarity of a nature we are often missing today so painfully.

Rolf Edberg, then ambassador of Sweden to Norway, received the Nobel Peace Prize posthumously awarded to Dag Hammarskjöld. In his acceptance speech on 10 December 1961, he reminded the audience that Hammarskjöld himself had no doubt about the convincing force of his ideals. As he quoted from Hammarskjöld's last article: 'Setbacks in trying to realize the ideal do not prove that the ideal is at fault.'[101]

During his time in office, Hammarskjöld left a lasting imprint on the role of a Secretary-General to the UN. He maintained that serving the family of nations required autonomy from any influence of major powers. He defined his task as a duty not to compromise to please the major powers. Hammarskjöld thereby shaped the ethics of an international civil servant, whose loyalty rests with the UN and not with a state seeking to exert influence over global governance and politics. His service was for the principles laid down in the UN Charter, and his duty to promote the values enshrined in the body's normative frameworks. In his last and most elaborate presentation of this understanding of the international civil service, which was partly a reaction to the criticisms of the Congo crisis, he maintained that:

> the international civil servant cannot be accused of lack of neutrality simply for taking a stand on a controversial issue when this is his duty and cannot be avoided ... [I]f integrity in the sense of respect for law and respect for truth were to drive [the international civil servant] into positions of conflict with this or that interest, then that conflict is a sign of his neutrality and not of his failure to observe neutrality – then it is in line, not in conflict with his duties as international civil servant.[102]

Hammarskjöld believed as firmly in the need to ensure representation of the voices often unheard in the world's choir. He advocated dialogue with others to establish common ground in search for solutions. This understanding reiterated his conviction that the members should respect the autonomy of the UN Secretariat. The UN for him had the choice between being a 'conference machinery' with the Secretariat as a mere service

FN-chefen och människan (2010); Fröhlich, *supra* note 53, and the much longer original version *Dag Hammarskjöld und die Vereinten Nationen. Die politische Ethik des UNO-Generalsekretärs* (2002).

101 Dag Hammarskjöld – Acceptance Speech, at www.nobelprize.org/nobel_prizes/peace/laureates/1961.

102 Hammarskjöld, *supra* note 7, at 488 and 489.

provider, and a Secretariat which, in the spirit of the Charter, proactively alerted the members to take initiatives and measures for active conflict prevention. As importantly, the Secretary-General never believed in the superiority of a given country. For him, the dividing line, as he elaborated, had no territorial dimensions but was in the mind and consciousness of people wherever they lived:

> The conflict [over] different approaches to the liberty of man and mind or between different views of human dignity and the right of the individual is continuous. The dividing line goes within ourselves, within our own peoples, and also within other nations. It does not coincide with any political or geographical boundaries. The ultimate fight is one between the human and the subhuman. We are on dangerous ground if we believe that any individual, any nation, or any ideology has a monopoly on rightness, liberty, and human dignity.[103]

Hammarskjöld was much respected for his integrity and honesty. He insisted that while diplomacy was also about compromises, these compromises could never be at the expense of the fundamental values. As he reiterated in his Introduction to the Annual Report presented in 1960:

> It is my firm conviction that any result bought at the price of a compromise with the principles and ideals of the Organization, either by yielding to force, by disregard of justice, by neglect of common interests, or by contempt for human rights, is bought at too high a price. That is so because a compromise with its principles and purposes weakens the Organization in a way representing a definite loss for the future that cannot be balanced by any immediate advantage achieved.[104]

To execute this mandate, the international civil servant should always be as independent as not to give up the principles codified in the UN Charter and the conventions adopted. While not seeking to romanticise or glorify the role and character of the second Secretary-General, this volume nonetheless pays tribute to a truly international civil servant. As Urquhart, one of the UN officials from the first hour, recalls:

103 D. Hammarskjöld, 'The Walls of Distrust'. Address at Cambridge University, Cambridge, England, 5 June 1958 (UN Press Release SG/684, 5 June 1958) in Cordier and Foote, Vol. IV, *supra* note 5, at 91f.

104 D. Hammarskjöld, Introduction to the Fifteenth Annual Report, New York, 31 August 1960 (General Assembly Official Records, Fifteenth Session, Supplement No. 1A (A/4390/ Add. 1)), in Cordier and Foote, Vol. V, *supra* note 7, at 139.

> Hammarskjöld effected an extraordinary transformation both in the attitude of the Secretariat and in the renewed interest and respect with which governments and outside observers began to treat the UN. It was a triumph both of personality and of intellect. In the sometimes most unbearable frustrations of later years, I have often recalled that time and that slight, indomitable, strangely innocent figure as a reminder of what can be done through leadership and commitment to an idea.[105]

While specific aspects of UN practice are subject to valid criticism and fears, the hopes associated with Hammarskjöld's vision of the UN, articulated in his Address to Staff in 1961, still stand today. His words and visions remain as powerful in 2013 as in 1961:

> It is true that we are passing through a period of unusual threats to human society and to peace. The dangers are too well known for me to add any comments here. If anything, you hear and see too much about them in the headlines of every paper. It is also true that the role of the Organization is necessarily a modest one, subordinated as it must be to governments, and through governments to the will of the peoples.
>
> But, although the dangers may be great and although our role may be modest, we can feel that the work of the Organization is the means through which we all, jointly, can work so as to reduce the dangers. It would be too dramatic to talk about our task as one of waging a war for peace, but it is quite realistic to look at it as an essential and – within its limits – effective work for building dams against the floods of disintegration and violence.[106]

It is an unplanned but welcome coincidence that the finalisation of this volume coincides with the publication of a report by a privately initiated Commission of Inquiry ('The Hammarskjöld Commission') into the death of Dag Hammarskjöld [107] The report adds further evidence to the assumption that foul play might have been involved in the plane crash, which caused the death of Dag Hammarskjöld and 15 others in his company. It suggests that '[t]here is persuasive evidence that the aircraft was subjected to some form of attack or threat'.[108] It concludes on an optimistic note. It notes that 'the last half-century, far from obscuring the facts,

[105] B. Urquhart, *A Life in Peace and War* (1987), 127.

[106] Last Words to the Staff, *supra* note 39, at 566.

[107] See Report of the Commission of Inquiry on whether the evidence now available would justify the United Nations in reopening its inquiry into the death of Secretary-General Dag Hammarskjöld, pursuant to General Assembly Resolution 1759 (XVII) of 26 October 1962, The Hague, 9 September 2013. For more information, see www.hammarskjoldcommission.org/ and Chapter 14, this volume.

[108] See Report, *supra* note 107, at 15.4.

may have brought us somewhat closer to the truth about an event of global significance which deserves the attention both of history and of justice'.[109] Keeping the legacy of the second Secretary-General alive is, therefore, an even more adequate and timely form of commemoration. It pays tribute to the continuing relevance of his approaches to modern practice.

[109] *Ibid.*, at 15.17.

PART I

Reflections on Dag Hammarskjöld

2

Dag Hammarskjöld and the twenty-first century

KOFI ANNAN

As Secretary-General of the United Nations, I have to give many speeches, and even quite a few lectures. But I can think of no invitation to speak that is a greater honour, or a greater challenge, than this one.

It will not surprise you to hear that Dag Hammarskjöld is a figure of great importance for me – as he must be for any Secretary-General. His life and his death, his words and his action, have done more to shape public expectations of the office, and indeed of the organisation, than those of any other man or woman in its history. His wisdom and his modesty, his unimpeachable integrity and single-minded devotion to duty, have set a standard for all servants of the international community – and especially, of course, for his successors – which is simply impossible to live up to. There can be no better rule of thumb for a Secretary-General, as he approaches each new challenge or crisis, than to ask himself, 'How would Hammarskjöld have handled this?' If that is true for any Secretary-General, how much more so for one of my generation, who came of age during the years when Hammarskjöld personified the United Nations, and began my own career in the UN system within a year of his death. And how much more true, also, for one who has the special relationship that I do with this, his home country!

So you see, it is quite a solemn thing for me to give this lecture, especially so close to the fortieth anniversary of Hammarskjöld's death. And I feel all the more solemn about it coming here, as I do, directly from the part of Africa where he met that death – and where, forty years later,

Seventh Secretary-General of the United Nations (1997–2007). The text is based on the Fourth Dag Hammarskjöld Lecture, organised by the Dag Hammarskjöld Foundation and Uppsala University. It was delivered in Uppsala on 6 September 2001 and subsequently published by the Dag Hammarskjöld Foundation. For its original publication see: www.dhf.uu.se/pdffiler/Kofi%20Annan.pdf. Reproduced in a slightly edited version with kind permission of the Dag Hammarskjöld Foundation. The editors of this volume have added the references to the sources quoted.

the United Nations is again struggling to help restore unity and peace to the Democratic Republic of Congo. I can tell you that the Congolese have never forgotten Dag Hammarskjöld. Four days ago, during my visit to the Congo, I met with the parties involved in the Inter-Congolese Dialogue. Their spokesman began the meeting by telling me how much they appreciated the late Secretary-General's dedication, and the fact that he gave his life for peace in their country. And he asked us to pay tribute to Hammarskjöld's memory by observing a minute of silence. I found it very moving that people could feel like that about him after forty years.

In Zambia, too – which, as you know, was where he actually died – Hammarskjöld's death is commemorated annually. The Zambian government, together with your own and with the United Nations system, has launched a 'living memorial', which includes a programme to educate young Africans as 'messengers of peace', as well as a Centre for Peace, Good Governance and Human Rights. There could be no better way to commemorate him than by promoting these ideals, which he held so dear.

If Dag Hammarskjöld were to walk through that door now, and ask me what are the main problems the United Nations is dealing with today, I could easily answer in a way that would make him think nothing much had changed. I could talk to him not only about the Congo, but about the Middle East, or Cyprus, or the relations between India and Pakistan, and it would all seem very familiar. But I could also tell him things that he would find very unfamiliar – though some would surprise him less than others, and some would gratify him more than others. He would probably be relieved, but not surprised, to hear that China is now represented at the United Nations by the government that actually governs the vast majority of Chinese people. It would surprise him much more to learn that the Soviet Union no longer exists. But he could only be pleased to find that there is no longer an unbridgeable ideological difference between the permanent members of the Security Council. He might be struck by the number of conflicts the United Nations is dealing with today that are within, rather than between, states – though the experience of the Congo would have prepared him for this – and also by the number of regional organisations that have developed as partners for the UN in different parts of the world.

I feel sure, in any case, that he would be pleased to see the way United Nations peacekeeping has developed, from the model that he and Lester Pearson so brilliantly improvised in 1956 to something much more diverse and complex, which is often more accurately described as 'peacebuilding'.

And I imagine he would be equally impressed by the wide range of issues that the United Nations is now called upon to face outside the traditional security arena – from climate change to HIV/AIDS. He would be gratified, and perhaps not all that surprised, to hear that human rights and democracy are now generally accepted as world norms – though he might well be distressed to see how far, in many countries, the practice still falls short of the rhetoric.

He would definitely be distressed to learn that, within the last decade, genocide had again disfigured the face of humanity – and that well over a billion people today are living in extreme poverty. I think he would see preventing the recurrence of the former, and putting an end to the latter, as the most urgent tasks confronting us in this new century. He would no doubt be impressed by the speed and intensity of modern communications, and momentarily confused by talk of faxes and sat-phones – let alone emails and the Internet. But I'm sure he would be quick to grasp the advantages and disadvantages of all these innovations, both for civilisation as a whole and for the conduct of diplomacy in particular. What is clear is that his core ideas remain highly relevant in this new international context. The challenge for us is to see how they can be adapted to take account of it.

One idea which inspired all his words and actions as Secretary-General was his belief that the United Nations had to be a 'dynamic instrument', through which its members would collectively 'develop forms of executive action'. During his time in office he became increasingly sensitive to the fact that some Member States did not share this vision, but regarded the United Nations as only 'a static conference machinery for resolving conflicts of interests and ideologies with a view to peaceful coexistence'.[1]

In the Introduction to his last Annual Report – a magisterial work, which reads almost as if he was consciously writing his political testament – Hammarskjöld argued that those who regarded the organisation in this way were not paying adequate attention to certain essential principles of the Charter. He showed that the Charter clearly implies the existence of an international community, for which the organisation is an instrument and an expression. The overriding purpose of this commu-

[1] D. Hammarskjöld, Introduction to the Sixteenth Annual Report, New York, 17 August 1961, General Assembly Official Records, Sixteenth Session, Supplement No. 1A (A/4800/Add.1), in A.W. Cordier and W. Foote, *Public Papers of the Secretaries-General of the United Nations, Vol. V: Dag Hammarskjöld 1960–1961* (1975), 542.

nity was to save succeeding generations from the scourge of war, and to do this it had to follow certain key principles. These were:

- First, 'equal political rights' – which encompassed both the 'sovereign equality' of all Member States, in Article 2 of the Charter, and 'respect for human rights and fundamental freedoms', in Article 1.
- Second, 'equal economic opportunities' – spelt out in Article 55 as the promotion of 'higher standards of living, full employment, and conditions of economic and social progress and development', as well as 'solutions of international economic, social, health, and related problems'.
- Third, 'justice' – by which he meant that the international community must be 'based on law ... with a judicial procedure through which law and justice could be made to apply'.
- And finally, the prohibition of the use of armed force, 'save in the common interest'.

These principles, Hammarskjöld argued, are incompatible with the idea of the United Nations as merely a conference or debating chamber – as indeed is the authority the Charter gives to its principal organs, and particularly to the Security Council, which clearly has both legislative and executive powers. The context in which he put forward these arguments was, of course, the Cold War, and particularly the Soviet campaign against him during the Congo crisis of 1960–1. That campaign is happily long past. But we still face, from time to time, attempts by Member States to reduce the United Nations to a 'conference mechanism'. Those attempts no longer come systematically from one particular ideological camp. Instead, they tend to vary according to the subject under discussion.

Broadly speaking, industrialised countries remain reluctant to see the United Nations act on Hammarskjöld's second principle – the promotion of 'equal economic opportunities'. And the governments of some other countries are equally loath to see it actively promote 'respect for, and observance of, human rights and fundamental freedoms for all'. In both cases, I believe the Secretary-General has no choice. He has to follow in the footsteps of Hammarskjöld, upholding the right and duty of the United Nations to pursue the aims laid down for it by the Charter.

Of course there is always a need for negotiation and discussion on the appropriate forms of action. But the United Nations will fail in its duty to the world's peoples, who are the ultimate source of its authority, if it allows itself to be reduced to a mere 'static conference', whether on economic and social rights or on civil and political ones.

The same applies to Hammarskjöld's exalted view of the 'international civil servant', which he also pursued in that last Annual Report, and in a lecture given that same summer at Oxford University.[2] His argument here was that the people charged with carrying out the executive functions of the United Nations could not be neutral in relation to the principles of the Charter. Nor could they be regarded, or allowed to regard themselves, as nominees or representatives of their own nations. They had to represent the international community as a whole. Here too, Hammarskjöld based his argument on a very careful reading of the Charter itself – in this case Articles 100 and 101. Article 100 forbids the Secretary-General or any of his staff either to seek or to receive instructions from states. And Article 101 prescribes 'the highest standards of efficiency, competence, and integrity' as 'the paramount consideration in the employment of the staff'. Once again, Hammarskjöld was arguing in the context of the Cold War, in which first one side and then the other had tried to insist on the right to be represented, within the Secretariat, by people who were loyal to its political or ideological point of view.

Again, the context has changed, and I am glad to say that states today, while extremely keen to see their nationals appointed to senior positions, no longer seek – or at least, not in the same way – to exercise political control over them, once appointed. But the principle of an independent international civil service, to which Hammarskjold was so attached, remains as important as ever. Each successive Secretary-General must be vigilant in defending it, even if, on occasion, changing times require us to depart from the letter of his views, in order to preserve the spirit. To give just one example: Hammarskjöld insisted that the bulk of United Nations staff should have permanent appointments and expect to spend their whole career with the organisation. That may have been appropriate in his time. It is less so now that the role of the United Nations has expanded, and more than half of our employees are serving in missions in the field. This is a development which Hammarskjöld would surely have welcomed, since it reflects a transition from the 'static conference' model to the 'dynamic instrument' model which he so strongly believed in. But what is clear is that his ideal of the United Nations as an expression of the international community, whose staff carry out decisions taken by states

[2] D. Hammarskjöld, 'The International Civil Servant in Law and in Fact', Lecture Delivered in Congregation at Oxford University, Oxford, England, 30 May 1961, UN Press Release SG/1035, in Cordier and Foote, *supra* note 1, 471–489.

collectively rather than bending to the will of any one of them, is just as relevant in our times as in his.

And that, of course, has very important implications for the role of the Secretary-General himself. Hammarskjöld pointed out that Article 99 of the Charter – which allows the Secretary-General, on his own initiative, to bring matters to the Security Council's attention when in his view they may threaten the maintenance of international peace and security – makes him clearly a political rather than a purely administrative official.[3] In practice, successive Secretaries-General, including Hammarskjöld, have invoked this article very sparingly. I myself have never yet found it necessary to do so. But the fact that the Secretary-General has this power crucially affects the way he is treated by the Security Council, and by the Member States in general. Few people now question the responsibility of the Secretary-General to act politically, or to make public pronouncements on political issues.

In fact, the boot today is if anything on the other foot: I find myself called on to make official statements on almost everything that happens in the world, from royal marriages to the possibility of human cloning! I do my best to satisfy this demand with due respect for the decisions of the Security Council and General Assembly. But those bodies would find it very strange if on each occasion I sought their approval before opening my mouth! Their members can, and do, take exception to some of my statements – and thank goodness they do. There must be freedom of speech for governments, as well as for international officials! But they do not question my right to make such statements, according to my own understanding of the purposes and principles of the United Nations as set out in the Charter. No doubt Dag Hammarskjöld would also disagree with some of the specific positions I have taken. But I suspect he would envy me the discretion I enjoy in deciding what to say. And I have no doubt he would strongly endorse the principle that the Secretary-General must strive to make himself an authentic and independent voice of the international community.

What he might not have foreseen is the way our concept of that community has developed in recent years. In his time it was essentially a community of separate nations or peoples, who for all practical purposes were represented by states. So if we go back to the things about today's world that we would have to explain to him, if he unexpectedly joined us now, probably the most difficult for him to adjust to would be the sheer

[3] *Ibid.*, at 477.

complexity of a world in which individuals and groups of all kinds are constantly interacting – across frontiers and across oceans, economically, socially and culturally – without expecting or receiving any permission, let alone assistance, from their national governments. He might well find it difficult to identify the precise role, in such a world, of a body like the United Nations, whose Charter presupposes the division of the world into sovereign and equal states, and in which the peoples of the world are represented essentially by their governments. He might find that difficult – and if so, he would not be alone! But I am convinced he would relish the challenge. And I am sure he would not stray from his fundamental conviction that the essential task of the United Nations is to protect the weak against the strong. In the long term, the vitality and viability of the organisation depend on its ability to perform that task, by adapting itself to changing realities. That, I believe, is the biggest test it faces in the new century.

How would Hammarskjöld approach that task? First of all he would insist, quite correctly, that states are still the main holders of political authority in the world, and are likely to remain so. Indeed, the more democratic they become – the more genuinely representative of, and accountable to, their peoples – the greater also will be their political legitimacy. And therefore it is entirely proper, as well as inevitable, that they will remain the political masters of the United Nations. He would also insist, I am sure, on the continuing responsibility of states to maintain international order – and, indeed, on their collective responsibility, which their leaders solemnly recognised in last year's Millennium Declaration, 'to uphold the principles of human dignity, equality and equity at the global level'.[4] And he might well say that, with a few honourable exceptions, the more fortunate countries in this world are not living up to that responsibility, so long as they do not fulfil their long-standing commitments to much higher levels of development assistance, to much more generous debt relief, and to duty- and quota-free access for exports from the least developed countries. But then he would also see that his own lifetime coincided, in most countries, with the high-water mark of state control over the lives of citizens. And he would see that states today generally tax and spend a smaller proportion of their citizens' wealth than they did forty years ago. From this he might well conclude that we should not rely exclusively on state action to achieve our objectives on the international

[4] Resolution adopted by the General Assembly, A/55/L.2 as United Nations Millennium Declaration at the Millennium Summit on 8 September 2000, at I.2.

level, either. A great deal, he would think, is likely to depend on non-state actors in the system – private companies, voluntary agencies or pressure groups, philanthropic foundations, universities and think tanks, and, of course, creative individuals. And that thought would surely feed into his reflection on the role of the United Nations.

Can it confine itself, in the twenty-first century, to the role of coordinating action by states? Or should it reach out further? Is it not obliged, in order to fulfil the purposes of the Charter, to form partnerships with all these different actors? To listen to them, to guide them, and to urge them on? Above all, to provide a framework of shared values and understanding, within which their free and voluntary efforts can interact, and reinforce each other, instead of getting in each other's way?

Perhaps it is presumptuous of me to suggest that this would be part of Hammarskjöld's vision of the role of the United Nations in the twenty-first century – because it is, of course, my own vision. No doubt if he were alive today he would offer us something nobler and more profound. But I like to think that what I have just described would find some place in it.

3

A beacon of hope

Dag Hammarskjöld and the United Nations

BRIAN URQUHART

Far more important was the status and standing of Hammarskjöld's UN. It is hard to remember what a beacon of hope it was in the 1950's: indeed, it was every young man's dream to serve.[1]

3.1 Introduction

It is now fifty years since Dag Hammarskjöld died in an air-crash near Ndola in what was then Northern Rhodesia, on his way to put a stop to a battle between UN peacekeeping troops and the mercenary-led forces of Moïse Tshombe, the secessionist leader of the Congolese province of Katanga.

In 1953 the United Nations had long outlived the enthusiasm and apparent common purpose of its early, post-war days. The nations, and especially the Great Powers, were anything but united. The Cold War had frozen many of the hopes and possibilities of the UN. Trygve Lie, the first Secretary-General, had had a particularly difficult time. His support of the UN's forceful intervention against North Korea's invasion of South Korea, which the Security Council had authorised in the

Sir Brian Urquhart was the second person to be recruited to the UN Secretariat in 1945 as personal assistant to Trygve Lie, the first Secretary-General. In 1954–71 he worked with Ralph Bunche, whom he succeeded in 1972 as UN Under-Secretary-General for Special Political Affairs. This text was originally published in a special issue of *New Routes: A Journal of Peace Research and Action*, Vol. 16, No. 2/2011 on 'Dag Hammarskjöld and the United Nations: Vision and Legacy – 50 Years Later', published by the Life & Peace Institute in Uppsala in collaboration with the Dag Hammarskjöld Foundation (www.life-peace.org/resources/publications/new-routes/2011/).

[1] Sir Raymond Appleyard, recalling his time at the UN in the 1950s setting up the UN Scientific Committee on the Effects of Atomic Radiation (1953–61), 'The Birth of UNSCEAR – the Midwife's Tale' (2010) 30 *Journal of Radiological Protection*, at 622.

absence of the Soviet representative (in protest at the exclusion from UN membership of the recently victorious People's Republic of China), had caused the Soviet Union to sever all relations with him. At the same time the US congressional, anti-communist witch-hunt, led by Senator Joseph McCarthy, had found a happy hunting ground among the American members of the Secretariat. Lie had struggled with this intricate problem and in the process lost the respect of the Secretariat, where morale had plummeted. Lie put his resignation before the General Assembly in November 1952. On 9 April 1953 at New York's Idlewild Airport, he welcomed his successor, Dag Hammarskjöld, to 'the most impossible job on this earth'.

Hammarskjöld had been chosen as Lie's successor on 31 March 1953 after a long stalemate in the Security Council. He was not well known except to a few European negotiators and, of course, in his own country. There was a general feeling that he would be a good but relatively colourless civil servant who would not rock the international political boat. He inherited a dismal situation at the UN, and to many observers it seemed unlikely that this youthful-looking and ostensibly diffident Swede would be able to deal with it. However, as was his habit, Hammarskjöld had arrived with firm principles already formulated, as well as imaginative ideas on the nature and execution of his new responsibilities. Recent developments were also in his favour. The advent of a new US administration, the death of Stalin in March 1953, and the prospect of an armistice in Korea all gave hope of improvement in East–West relations and of a more constructive role for the Secretary-General.

Hammarskjöld devoted his first eighteen months at the UN to discreetly winning the confidence of member governments and to reorganising the Secretariat and reinforcing its discipline and morale. He showed himself to be a master administrator who could combine principle and practical common sense in the resolution of controversial problems. He also dealt firmly but quietly with the anti-communist US witch-hunt, emphasising the Secretary-General's overall responsibility for the Secretariat. He strongly defended the independent position of the fledgling international civil service and reinforced both its discipline and its efficiency.

3.2 The first political intervention

Hammarskjöld had said that the Secretary-General should not 'jump up on the stage' on political matters unless there was a critical situation which he was best suited to deal with. Such a situation arose at the end of

1954. Seventeen American air force members had come down in China during the Korean War and were convicted as spies by Chinese courts. They were still being held, and the United States, having refused to recognise the People's Republic of China, was in no position to get them freed. Enormous internal pressure on the Eisenhower administration had built up in Washington. Nuclear strikes on the Chinese mainland had even been suggested, and the administration was desperate.

The UN Security Council and the General Assembly, in neither of which the Peking government was represented, had been able to do no more than censure the Chinese government and ask the Secretary-General to seek the release of the airmen and all other captured UN personnel. Immediately after the Assembly had adopted its resolution, Hammarskjöld announced his intention to go to Peking. He knew, however, that a government, which was excluded from the UN and had just been severely criticised by the UN General Assembly, was unlikely to cooperate with him as the Assembly's representative. He therefore had to find a rationale for his mission which Zhou Enlai, the Chinese Foreign Minister, might be able to accept. This rationale, which is a good example of Hammarskjöld's genius for improvisation and which added a new dimension to the work of the Secretary-General, became known as the 'Peking formula'. Its essence was that under the terms of the UN Charter the Secretary-General has an obligation to reduce international tensions anywhere in the world. He was coming to Peking as a result of this legal obligation, not on the basis of the General Assembly resolution, which had censured China. Zhou Enlai accepted this formula. The negotiations proceeded on the high intellectual level that both participants preferred, and the release of the last of the US airmen on 1 August 1955 was announced in a message from Zhou Enlai, who also congratulated Hammarskjöld on his fiftieth birthday. The date of the airmen's release was not a coincidence.

The successful solution of a highly explosive international problem showed governments that in the person of the new UN Secretary-General they had a major resource for resolving dangerous problems at a time when the Cold War had severely limited the effectiveness of the Security Council. Hammarskjöld's achievement was based on the elements which also made possible his future successes – determined independence and objectivity, absolute honesty with all concerned, rigorous intellectual and practical preparation, ingenuity in creating innovative alternatives in order to break deadlocks, intuition and understanding of the positions and difficulties of those he was dealing with, and the integrity and moral courage which gave him a unique and respected position in the world.

3.3 Major international crises

During the Cold War, regional crises had an extra and terrifying dimension. This was the possibility that what had started as a regional conflict could develop into the cause of nuclear confrontation between the two superpowers. This threat strengthened Hammarskjöld's effort to develop conflict resolution mechanisms involving the Secretary-General and his representatives. Among these mechanisms was the new concept of peacekeeping forces.

Hammarskjöld continued to develop the UN's capacity for conflict resolution in a series of major crises. During the Suez crisis of 1956 he displayed not only his ability as a mediator, but also his flair for emergency political/administrative action, improvising the first UN peacekeeping force and deploying it within ten days of the decision to establish it. In 1958 he played a central role in defusing the Lebanese crisis, during which the United States landed troops in Lebanon and the British in Jordan. Hammarskjöld conducted a score or more of 'quiet diplomacy missions' in different parts of the world during his eight years as Secretary-General. 'Leave it to Dag' became a familiar slogan in the world press.

At mid-summer 1960 the mounting chaos in the newly independent Congo demanded a UN operation that included a large civilian administrative element as well as a large peacekeeping force. The Congo situation presented the UN with highly complex demands in a vast and often violent tribal country in which both superpowers had a strong interest. It later involved Hammarskjöld in disagreements with Nikita Khrushchev and to a lesser extent with Charles de Gaulle, the latter embittered by Hammarskjöld's efforts to protect Tunisia from an armed French incursion in the summer of 1961. His relations with the United States, the United Kingdom and several African countries were also severely strained by disagreements over the Congo. Hammarskjöld died during an effort to resolve the Katanga problem which, for the previous two years, had poisoned the UN's work in the Congo as well as the mood of the General Assembly and the Security Council.

3.4 The legacy

Hammarskjöld became Secretary-General of a world organisation that was divided and paralysed by the mutual ideological and political hostility of the nuclear superpowers and was thoroughly demoralised by both governmental and public disillusionment. By his leadership, skill and creativity he not only gave the Secretary-General and the international secretariat a new position in world affairs. He also renewed and strengthened the standing and performance of the world organisation itself. His achievement has remained an inspiration to his successors.

In May 2010, at a symposium in Delphi, Greece, a group of former foreign ministers, UN permanent representatives, and members of the Secretariat discussed the role and the process of selection of the UN Secretary-General.[2] Of the desirable qualities for a UN Secretary-General, their report included:

- integrity, independence, moral courage, and impartiality;
- moral and intellectual as well as political leadership;
- diplomatic skills essential for a mediator and crisis manager;
- capacity to manage the organisation effectively and to provide leadership to the wider UN system;
- problem-solving capacity and sure political instincts;
- charisma and contemporary media skills.

Not altogether coincidentally, Dag Hammarskjöld displayed most, if not all, of these qualities. In doing so he set an admittedly high standard for his successors. That is perhaps the most basic part of his legacy. Hammarskjöld championed and personified the principles of the Charter, and especially those that applied to the Secretary-General. He was a dedicated intellectual, actively participating at the highest and most demanding level of international politics – an international civil servant of unique integrity and passion.

In a world of power politics haunted by the Cold War, Hammarskjöld generated a strong and welcome feeling of hope. He had proved his ability to act effectively in dangerous situations where the UN Security Council was frustrated by the conflicting interests of the major powers. He became widely trusted to solve life-endangering problems that no one else could tackle. He seemed undaunted by powerful governments. In times of crisis he showed that one man, if sufficiently spirited and courageous, could stand up for principle against even the greatest powers and have an influence on important events. Thus Hammarskjöld greatly expanded the scope of the political functions of the Secretary-General, as well as the respect of both governments and the public for the office. He left to his

[2] Athens Development and Governance Institute, *The UN in the 21st Century: The Role and Selection of the Secretary General of the United Nations*. The Delphi Symposium in honour of Javier Perez de Cuellar, Athens and Delphi, 27–30 May 2010 (2010).

successors a position and a range of responsibilities far greater than the limited role outlined in the Charter.

Charisma is an important quality for any public figure, and of all human qualities it is the most elusive and unaccountable. Hammarskjöld was not a sociable or gregarious man. He was naturally shy and had little interest in social life. He was not a particularly good public speaker. He was a very private person who valued and protected his privacy. He spurned supposedly crowd-pleasing gestures. Nonetheless, ordinary people all over the world knew who he was, why what he did was important, and why the Secretary-General was relevant to their lives. This kind of charisma is a quality that cannot be handed on, but it is particularly important in an office which has none of the normal attributes of power.

3.5 Enhancing UN presence

Hammarskjöld not only expanded the role of the Secretary-General; he also created new methods of conflict control and bridged at least part of the very large gap that the Cold War had made in the UN's principal function of maintaining international peace and security. Peacekeeping forces, quiet diplomacy, UN 'presences', and representatives of the Secretary-General were just four of such creations.

Hammarskjöld realised that the permanent representatives of the Member States at UN headquarters could be immensely valuable to the work of the Secretary-General. He established close cooperation with them to such effect that some of them said that they sometimes found it hard to remember whether they were national representatives or members of the Secretariat. This new alliance was passed on to his successors, most of whom greatly benefitted from it.

The basic element of Hammarskjöld's famous confrontation with Khrushchev in the 1960 General Assembly was the degree of independence and authority of the Secretary-General and the Secretariat. The operation in the Congo became so controversial that neither the Security Council nor the General Assembly could agree on the necessary directives. Hammarskjöld was therefore forced either to make the important decisions himself, or to close the operation down. He rightly chose the first and more difficult alternative. Thus the Congo operation came to represent everything that Khrushchev found intolerable about the independent action of the Secretary-General. Khrushchev therefore proposed replacing the Secretary-General with a *troika* of three senior officials – from the capitalist West, the socialist countries, and the third world.

Hammarskjöld knew that such an arrangement would in effect extend the veto power that had paralysed the Security Council into the Secretariat, and he fought it with all his strength. The UN, he argued, would be reduced by the *troika* to a mere conference machinery with no capacity to resolve critical problems or to take action in controversial emergencies, a development that in the current circumstances could well prove to be the 'Munich of international cooperation'.

Khrushchev's *troika* was soundly defeated in the General Assembly, but Hammarskjöld still felt that the essential and vital nature of a truly international civil service owing no allegiance to any national government was not sufficiently understood. In his last major speech, at Oxford University on 30 May 1961, he addressed the subject with a text, 'The International Civil Servant in Law and in Fact', which remains the classic pronouncement on the nature and reality of the international civil service, a central principle of the UN Charter.[3] It is a text that should be studied and discussed again at the present time when both the concept and the practice of international civil service are subject to neglect and serious erosion.

3.6 Long-term development of the UN

Finally there is Hammarskjöld's vision of, and contribution to, the long-term development of the United Nations. He was acutely aware that the world organisation was still in a very early stage of development and needed a constant effort to establish new precedents and ideas in order to keep up with contemporary problems and grow with the times. He took great care to lay a strong foundation for new ideas and techniques. He personally engaged, for example, in the laborious negotiation of a Status of Forces Agreement with Egypt to define the relationship of the first peacekeeping force with its host country. When criticised for spending so much time and energy on this, he replied that if the agreement was sound enough it would benefit future peacekeeping operations by establishing an accepted legal basis for them. He has proved to be right.

Hammarskjöld believed that a reliable and just world order could eventually be built only by a process of precedents and case law. He hoped that by this process the world organisation would be gradually transformed from an institutional mechanism into a constitutional instrument creating obligations that were recognised and respected by all nations. In a

[3] Text in A.W. Cordier and W. Foote (eds.), *Public Papers of the Secretaries-General of the United Nations, Vol. V: Dag Hammarskjöld 1960–1961* (1975), at 471–489.

speech given at the University of Chicago Law School on 1 May 1960, he stated:

> Working at the edge of the development of human society is to work on the brink of the unknown. Much of what is done will one day prove to be of little avail. That is no excuse for the failure to act in accordance with our best understanding, in recognition of its limits, but with faith in the ultimate result of the creative evolution in which it is our privilege to cooperate.[4]

The view of the United Nations as a work in progress, a 'creative evolution' which, especially at the most critical times, must be believed in, supported, and sustained by innovative practical work and ideas, is a vision of profound importance for those who believe that a just and peaceful world is the greatest of humanity's objectives. Hammarskjöld's ideas and his unsurpassed record of international service have left a generous legacy for the fulfilment of this vision.

[4] Text in A.W. Cordier and W. Foote (eds.), *Public Papers of the Secretaries-General of the United Nations, Vol. IV: Dag Hammarskjöld 1958–1960* (1974), at 592.

4

Dag Hammarskjöld 1905–1961

A remarkable man, a remarkable Secretary-General

PIETER KOOIJMANS

If Dag Hammarskjöld had lived up to the expectations the Member States of the UN – and in particular the major powers – had when they elected him to the office of Secretary-General, we would not be here today to commemorate him. He was expected to be a competent administrator without political ambitions, but willing to serve the interests of the Member States and not to antagonise the leading nations as his predecessor had done. A competent administrator he was, but he decided to serve the interests of the world organisation as such, as the embodiment of the world community, and steadfastly refused to allow it to become a tool in the hands of the major powers. He certainly was no starry-eyed idealist but was well aware – to use his own words – that 'the role of the organization is necessarily a modest one, subordinated as it must be to governments, and through governments to the will of the peoples'.[1] But that did not restrain him from adding immediately that 'it is quite realistic to look at the work of the organization as an essential and – within its limits – effective work for building dams against the floods of disintegration and violence'.[2] And he strongly appealed to the members of the Secretariat to meet this challenge jointly. He ardently believed in the values and principles contained in the Charter and in the possibilities the UN, as an organisation, had in being instrumental in restructuring world conditions. And he was able to pass on this belief to a group of people he had gathered around him and

The late Pieter Kooijmans (6 July 1933–13 February 2013) was Minister of State, State Secretary and Minister of Foreign Affairs of the Netherlands and Judge at the International Court for Justice.

[1] D. Hammarskjöld, 'Last Words to the Staff – from Remarks on Staff Day', New York, 8 September 1961, in A.W. Cordier and W. Foote (eds.), *Public Papers of the Secretaries-General of The United Nations, Vol. V: Dag Hamarskjöld 1960–1961* (1975), 566. See also Annex 2 of this volume.

[2] *Ibid.*

who were willing to explore with him new horizons and set off on new daring adventures, like, for example, the instrumentation of peacekeeping, preventive diplomacy and early warning.

The international climate in which Hammarskjöld carried out his office was as ominous and volatile as the present one, even if the differences are evident. But the similarities are evident as well. Although the international system in his time was bipolar, whereas the present one is multipolar if not diffuse, the problems of a great number of newly independent states at that time are not unlike those of failed or fragile states today; the Palestine question has remained a powder keg and social-humanitarian emergencies are as urgent today as they were in his time. It is therefore no matter of surprise that from time to time one wonders – as, for example, Kofi Annan did during his time in office when presenting the fourth annual Dag Hammarskjöld Lecture in September 2001:[3] how would Hammarskjöld have handled this matter? What would his approach have been?

To give only one highly topical example: Hammarskjöld certainly would have welcomed the decision of the Security Council in Resolution 1973 to authorise 'Member States … acting in cooperation with the Secretary-General, to take all necessary measures … to protect civilians and civilian populated areas under threat of attack in the Libyan Arab Jamahiriya'[4] as a clear recognition of the principle of the Responsibility to Protect (R2P), a principle wich was not yet known in his time but clearly reflects a number of his ideas. But would he have agreed with the interpretation given to that authorisation by a number of the states, which carried out that mandate as including regime change, or would he have been of the view that that is beyond the range of the R2P principle and at any rate might make future references to it by the Security Council more difficult, as seems to be borne out in the case of Syria? And – a not irrelevant question – would he, in light of the condition (contained in the resolution) that action must take place in cooperation with the Secretary-General, have seen it as part of his responsibility as highest official of the organisation to give expression to his views? If he had decided to do so, he would with certainty have antagonised some permanent members of the Security Council, whatever position he would have taken. Hammarskjöld was not afraid to do so,

[3] See Chapter 2, this volume.

[4] United Nations Security Council, S/RES/1973(2011), 17 March 2011, para. 4, at www.un.org/ga/search/view_doc.asp?symbol=S/RES/1973%282011%29.

although he certainly did not seek it. He categorically stated in response to the demand by a permanent member for his resignation:

> It is very easy to bow to the wish of a big power. It is another matter to resist. ... If it is the wish of those nations who see the Organization as their best protection in the present world, I shall now do so again.[5]

Why is it that we are so eager to know what Hammarskjöld's views and position on our present world problems would have been? Is it because we intuitively realise that what moved him in last instance was a deeply felt sense of justice combined with a sense of urgency; is it because we recognise that he was a man who was in balance with himself and thus exuded composure but at the same time was driven by an unremitting commitment since so much could and should be done?

But if that is the case, it is not so much his political views that fascinate us but the approach he took to the problems that confronted him and still confront us? What enabled him to tackle newly arisen or long-dormant problems in an innovative way; what gave him the stamina to pursue tenaciously the new or not so new courses he had embarked upon? And what was it that made him a source of inspiration for so many who were proud to call themselves his fellow workers?

Since the publication of *Markings* – that remarkable book of personal annotations – some years after Hammarskjöld's untimely death, we know even better than during his life what was at the source of his mind and methods, what 'made him tick': his deep spirituality and his need for continuous reflection and self-reflection. That was already clear when, on his initiative, the meditation room in the General Assembly building was remodelled and enlarged. During the opening ceremony in 1957 he said: 'This house, dedicated to work and debate in the service of peace, should have one room dedicated to silence in the outward sense and stillness in the inner sense.'[6] And he concluded: 'It is for those who come here to fill the void (of this room) with what they find in their center of stillness.'[7] For Hammarskjöld this was no free-floating vagary but a strong conviction that important decisions should not be taken without a preceding deep

[5] D. Hammarskjöld, 'I Shall Remain in My Post ...', Second Statement of Reply, New York, 3 October 1960 (General Assembly Official Records, Fifteenth Session, 883rd plenary meeting), in Cordier and Foote, *supra* note 1, at 201.

[6] D. Hammarskjöld, 'A Room of Quiet' (The United Nations Mediation Room), December 1957, in Cordier and Foote, *Public Papers of the Secretaries-General of The United Nations, Vol. III: 1956–1957* (1973), 710.

[7] *Ibid.*, at 711.

reflection on the issue at hand and the mindframe with which it should be approached, taking into consideration the consequences of the various alternatives.

Roger Lipsey, who completed a book on Hammarskjöld's mind and methods and in particular his spirituality,[8] says that the best way to honour a chosen model – and Hammarskjöld is beyond any doubt a chosen model for many people even in our time – is to study every big and little thing about him and then to release and step back into one's own life and time, to meet the challenges which confront us there, nourished but not constricted by the admired model.

Maybe the best tribute to this remarkable man is a continuing awareness that his state of mind is direly needed also today to plot the course which may lead to a more stable and just world society. I am quite sure that such a course will include those items which were dear to Hammarskjöld's heart: early warning and preventive steps which are both concepts which ask for a long-term policy. Maybe if these long-term policy goals are taken more seriously, it will not be necessary to resort to short-term action like the use of force, as happened in the case of Libya. Such short-term action may at a given moment be *necessary*, but the real question should be: was such action *inevitable* or could it have been prevented by taking other measures earlier?

In an interview given on 1 August 2011, Edward Luck, Special Advisor to the UN Secretary-General on the Responsibility to Protect, argued that in the case of Libya most of the negative response has focused on the use of force, which – he stresses – is not R2P's main goal and therefore should not be the litmus test of its success.[9] And he added: 'For us the job is not response, the job is prevention. Many people think that the R2P is all about the use of military force after the bodies start piling up. For us, that is not morally acceptable.'[10]

I feel that that is the correct state of mind: the short-term action is not morally acceptable if the long-term approach has not seriously been given a chance.

But that does not alter the fact that Libya and Syria – both failures in their own way – determine to a large extent the present state of the world and that success stories seem to be scarce. It was not different in

[8] See R. Lipsey, *Hammarskjöld: A Life* (2013). See also Chapter 8, this volume.

[9] Interview with Edward Luck, Special Advisor to the Secretary-General, UN News Centre, 1 August 2011, www.un.org/apps/news/newsmakers.asp?NewsID=38.

[10] *Ibid.*

Hammarskjöld's time and he had to admit that it was often nearly impossible to indicate whether and where progress was made. Yet, he told the press in 1958:

> I cannot belong to or join those who believe in our movement toward catastrophe. I believe in growth, a growth to which we have a responsibility to add our few fractions of an inch ... It is not the facile faith of generations before us ... it is in a sense a much harder belief ... the belief and the faith that the future will be all right because there will always be enough people to fight for a decent future.[11]

These are not the words of a bold adventurer who dreamed of changing the world overnight, but the words of a man who knew, as he admonished his staff:

> that if we feel that what we do we is purposeful, not to say essential for the progress of men and human society in a broader sense ... we are willing to accept hardships and serve gladly for the value of serving.[12]

That is exactly what he did – he served for the value of serving and that made him a most remarkable Secretary-General and a most remarkable man.

[11] D. Hammarskjöld, Transcripts of Extemporaneous Remarks, Correspondents Association Luncheon in His Honor at the Beginning of His Second Term, New York, 9 April 1958, in Cordier and Foote, *Public Papers of the Secretaries-General of The United Nations, Vol. IV: 1958–1960* (1974), 63–64.

[12] See Hammarskjöld, *supra* note 1, at 565.

5

Dag Hammarskjöld, the United Nations and the rule of law in today's world

HANS CORELL

This chapter will focus, first, on Dag Hammarskjöld as a person and, second, the relevance of the principles outlined in his final Annual Report to the General Assembly for the United Nations and the rule of law in today's world. It will then discuss briefly the ethics of an international civil servant in light of Hammarskjöld's thinking, ending with some brief conclusions.

5.1 Dag Hammarskjöld

Dag Hammarskjöld was born in 1905. His father was a judge and later governor. Between 1914 and 1917 his father was Prime Minister of Sweden. Dag took degrees in humanities, economics and law. In 1934, he took a doctoral degree in economics. He had a distinguished career in the Swedish civil service and government office, culminating in 1951, when he became the Deputy Foreign Minister. He took up his position as the Secretary-General of the United Nations in April 1953 and served in this position until his death in a plane crash outside Ndola in Northern Rhodesia (today's Zambia) on 18 September 1961.

There are many books written about Dag Hammarskjöld, including in particular by persons who served with him during his tenure at the UN. One of his most renowned biographers is Brian Urquhart, who served in the United Nations Secretariat from 1945 until his retirement in 1986,

Hans Corell served in the Swedish judiciary from 1962 to 1972 and in the Ministry of Justice from 1972 to 1984. He was Ambassador and Head of the Legal Department of the Swedish Ministry for Foreign Affairs from 1984 to 1994 and Under-Secretary-General for Legal Affairs and the Legal Counsel of the United Nations from 1994 to 2004. This chapter is based in part on an address delivered at Dag Hammarskjöld University College of International Relations and Diplomacy in Zagreb in November 2011.

the last fourteen years as Under-Secretary-General for Special Political Affairs.[1]

Personally, I never met Dag Hammarskjöld in spite of the fact that I was a student at his hometown Uppsala in the late 1950s and early 1960s. However, I was present as a steward in Uppsala Cathedral at his funeral in September 1961. Since then, I have often reflected on Dag Hammarskjöld and his life. As so many others, I read his book *Markings* when it was published shortly after his death.[2]

Of particular interest in this context is the following quote from Oscar Schachter, one of the senior lawyers in the United Nations Office of Legal Affairs with whom Dag Hammarskjöld worked very closely:

> In the tributes paid him there was universal recognition of his extraordinary personal qualities: the depth and brilliance of his intellect, his strength of spirit, dedication, courage, and incredible stamina. He was that rare, indeed almost incomparable, combination of a man who could act with energy, boldness and consummate skill in meeting the harsh conflicts of our time, and at the same time could lead a life of inner contemplation and aesthetic experience. For those privileged to work closely with him, he had a contagious vitality and zest which, even in the most discouraging moments, inspired renewed effort. He brought to these personal qualities a tough-minded awareness of political realities and a talent for creative political innovation. The result was an era of international action in which the United Nations moved from the plane of words to that of deeds in facing some of the most perilous crises of this generation. It may well be that, with the death of Mr. Hammarskjöld, this era has come to a close, but it is not likely that its example will be forgotten.[3]

Schachter then goes on to discuss Dag Hammarskjöld and the relation of law to politics.[4]

The Preamble of the Charter of the United Nations states that the responsibility of the organisation is 'to save succeeding generations from the scourge of war'. In his final Annual Report to the General Assembly in 1961, Dag Hammarskjöld argued that this objective was to be progressively achieved via the international community's realisation of four fundamental principles, namely:

[1] B. Urquhart, *Hammarskjold* (1972, reprint 1994). See also Chapter 3, this volume.

[2] Dag Hammarskjöld, *Markings*. Translated by L. Sjöberg and W.H. Auden (1964); 1983 edition.

[3] O. Schachter, 'Dag Hammarskjold and the Relation of Law to Politics' (1962) 56 *AJIL* 1–8.

[4] *Ibid*. On Hammarskjöld's approach to international law, see Chapter 9, this volume.

(1) equal political rights, both in terms of sovereign equality and individual respect for human rights and fundamental freedoms;
(2) equal economic opportunities, thereby promoting higher standards of living through the creation of conditions conducive to development and economic and social advancement;
(3) a firm rule of law framework underlying the actions and activities of the international community; and
(4) the prohibition of the use of force contrary to the common interest of the international community.[5]

5.2 Reflections on Dag Hammarskjöld's principles

In the following, I touch briefly on the first, second and fourth principles while the main focus will be on the third element – the rule of law, in which I include also peaceful settlement of disputes[6] – without which in my view the other three will not be attainable.

But let me start by setting the scene, as it has changed dramatically since the UN was established in 1945 and since Dag Hammarskjöld passed away more than fifty years ago. Originally, the UN had fifty-one members. In 1953, when Dag Hammarskjöld took up his position, there were sixty members. When he died in 1961, there were 104 members. Today, the organisation has 193 members.[7] This increase in membership has been accompanied by a tremendous development in many fields, not least in the fields of science and technology. In addition, there has been a dramatic rise in the world population. In 1945, we were about two billion. We are now seven billion. By mid-century the world population is expected to be 9.3 billion.[8] Undoubtedly, today's world is literally a world of difference when it comes to administering the United Nations and its members. However, Dag Hammarskjöld's four fundamental principles are just as relevant today as they were when he framed them. Let us now reflect on them.

[5] Introduction to the Annual Report of the Secretary-General on the Work of the Organization 16 June 1960–15 June 1961, New York, 17 August 1961, UN Doc. A/4800/Add. 1, see Annex 1, this volume.
[6] See Article 33 of the UN Charter.
[7] See www.un.org/en/members/growth.shtml.
[8] See www.un.org/esa/population/unpop.htm.

5.2.1 Equal political rights

With respect to the first principle – equal political rights, both in terms of sovereign equality and individual respect for human rights and fundamental freedoms – there has been a tremendous development over the last fifty years. Dag Hammarskjöld could make reference to the 1948 Universal Declaration of Human Rights, and he was certainly fully aware of the European Convention on Human Rights, adopted by the Council of Europe in 1950.

However, today there are numerous human rights treaties, most prominently the two Covenants from 1966: the International Covenant on Economic, Social and Cultural Rights and the International Covenant on Civil and Political Rights. In the wake of the two Covenants, a great number of treaties for the protection of human rights have been adopted, the latest being the International Convention for the Protection of All Persons from Enforced Disappearance from 2006.[9] In addition, there are regional conventions and, most importantly, regional courts, that can adjudicate disputes with respect to how states honour their obligations under some of these treaties. In Europe there is the European Court of Human Rights with its seat in Strasbourg. Certainly, much remains to be done for the protection of human rights, and, sadly, violations are committed also by states from which we have reason to expect a better performance. However, all in all, there has been a remarkable development in this field and if states respected the commitments they have already made, the world would certainly be a different place.

5.2.2 Equal economic opportunities

With respect to the second principle – equal economic opportunities, thereby promoting higher standards of living through the creation of conditions conducive to development and economic and social advancement – much remains to be done. Addressing poverty is one of the Millennium Development Goals.[10] In spite of positive trends, too many people in the world still live under very poor conditions. There is still famine in many places, and the access to water is increasingly becoming a major issue. It is true that many states do make efforts to assist people

[9] See the United Nations Treaty Collection at https://treaties.un.org/pages/Treaties.aspx?id=4&subid=A&lang=en.

[10] See www.un.org/millenniumgoals/reports.shtml.

who live under less fortunate circumstances, and Official Development Assistance is taken very seriously in many capitals.

In this context it should also be emphasised that the business community can contribute. If business observes the standards that are now expected from this community in accordance with the Global Compact,[11] and the standards of corporate social responsibility that are now gradually being implemented by serious actors in this field, business could make a great contribution to a positive development.[12] An important factor here is foreign direct investment, which by far surpasses the Official Development Assistance.

In this field there is also a connection with the idea of transferring financial resources in order to assist developing countries in addressing issues connected to climate change. In the Bali Action Plan[13] it was foreseen that major transfers of financial resources would be made to these countries. However, very little has happened after the meetings in Copenhagen in 2009, in Cancún in 2010, and in Durban in 2011. This whole issue also has an ethical component, related to the way in which we lead our lives around the globe. One indicator is the release of CO_2 per capita in the world.[14]

5.2.3 The prohibition of the use of force

With respect to the fourth principle – the prohibition of the use of force contrary to the common interest of the international community – we have seen a positive development, but much remains to be done here. In the news, the reports of use of force in violation of this principle are constant companions. The difference in relation to the time when Dag Hammarskjöld was Secretary-General of the United Nations may be that conflicts between states are less common, while intrastate use of force is a tragic fact.

Since 2011 we have all followed intensely the development in northern Africa and the Middle East. The so-called 'Arab Spring' has brought about

[11] See www.unglobalcompact.org/.

[12] See in particular 'Guiding Principles on Business and Human Rights: Implementing the United Nations "Protect, Respect and Remedy" Framework', Human Rights Council, Doc. A/HRC/17/31 of 21 March 2011, adopted by the UN Human Rights Council, at www.ohchr.org/Documents/Issues/Business/A-HRC-17-31_AEV.pdf. See also www.unglobalcompact.org/news/130–06–17–2011.

[13] See UN Framework Convention on Climate Change, FCCC/CP/2007/L.7/Rev.1, under 1/CP.13, at http://unfccc.int/meetings/bali_dec_2007/meeting/6319.php.

[14] See, for example, http://data.worldbank.org/indicator/EN.ATM.CO2E.PC.

dramatic changes, and we are all hoping that peoples in these regions will gain their freedom and will be allowed to live in dignity in their respective countries.

The two main elements under this heading that need attention at the highest political level are disarmament, in particular in the field of nuclear arms, and responsibility to protect. A determined action is needed, in particular by the UN Security Council, when people are subjected to genocide, war crimes, ethnic cleansing and crimes against humanity.[15]

5.2.4 *The rule of law*

In the past, I have focused extensively on the need for a firm rule of law framework both at the national and international levels. A case in point is my farewell lecture to the United Nations on 24 February 2004, entitled 'Prospects for the Rule of Law among Nations'.[16]

An important point of departure in discussing the rule of law is the Preamble to the 1948 United Nations Universal Declaration of Human Rights. A famous paragraph in this Preamble reads: 'Whereas it is essential, if man is not to be compelled to have recourse, as a last resort, to rebellion against tyranny and oppression, that human rights should be protected by the rule of law.'

The meaning of the English expression 'rule of law' can always be discussed. There are several ways in which one can define the concept and there is ample literature available.[17] The World Justice Project applies the following definition:

1. The government and its officials and agents are accountable under the law;
2. The laws are clear, publicized, stable and fair, and protect fundamental rights, including the security of persons and property;
3. The process by which the laws are enacted, administered and enforced is accessible, fair and efficient;

[15] See paragraphs 138 and 139 in the 2005 World Summit Outcome, General Assembly Resolution A/RES/60/1.

[16] Available at http://legal.un.org/ola/media/info_from_lc/Vienna_24_2_04final.doc. For a discussion, see also H. Corell, 'A Challenge to the United Nations and the World: Developing the Rule of Law' (2004) 18 *Temple International & Comparative Law Journal* 391–402, at www.havc.se/res/SelectedMaterial/20040331achallengetotheuntemple1.pdf.

[17] See, for example, The Hague Institute for the Internationalisation of Law, Rule of Law Publications at www.hiil.org/publications.

4. Access to justice is provided by competent, independent, and ethical adjudicators, attorneys or representatives, and judicial officers who are of sufficient number, have adequate resources, and reflect the makeup of the communities they serve.[18]

For my part, I always maintain that four elements are needed to establish the rule of law, namely:

(1) democracy;
(2) proper legislation meeting relevant international standards;
(3) institutions – administrative as well as judicial – to administer the law; and, most importantly,
(4) individual civil servants and other officials, including judges, with the necessary knowledge and integrity to handle this administration.

The mission of the World Justice Project, just mentioned, is to lead a global, multidisciplinary effort to strengthen the rule of law for the development of communities of opportunity and equity. It is based on two complementary premises:

(1) the rule of law is the foundation for communities of opportunity and equity; and
(2) multidisciplinary collaboration is the most effective way to advance the rule of law.[19]

It is important to be aware of the fact that developing the rule of law is not a one-time exercise. In reality, it is a major effort that will never be completed. It cannot be completed, and it must not be said to be completed for the simple reason that it has to reflect the current needs and circumstances at any time. And most importantly: the rule of law must be applied both at the national level and the international level.

Having said this, there is a very serious aspect that I must highlight. It is a sad fact that the protection of human rights and thus the rule of law has backtracked in several respects in later years. If we analyse the situation, it is clear that what happened on 9 September 2001 – commonly referred

[18] See www.worldjusticeproject.org/about/.

[19] Within the World Justice Project, a Rule of Law Index has been developed. It is a new quantitative assessment tool designed by the Project to offer a detailed and comprehensive picture of the extent to which countries adhere to the rule of law in practice. It can be accessed at www.worldjusticeproject.org/rule-of-law-index/. Reference should in this context also be made to 'Innovations in Rule of Law', published by the Project and others on 26 June 2012 and accessible at www.hiil.org/data/sitemanagement/media/WJP&HiiL%20UN%20Report-UNGA%20Event(1).pdf.

to as '9/11' – is a turning point. In the wake of this horrible crime, which I witnessed from my office on the thirty-fourth floor of the UN building, actions were taken, both legislative and administrative, that are not in conformity with international human rights standards. The misnomer 'war on terror' has caused great damage by confusing the distinction between human rights law and humanitarian law. To quote the Madrid Agenda Against Terrorism, adopted on 11 March 2005 by the Club de Madrid, an organisation of former heads of state and government:

> Any successful strategy for dealing with terrorism requires terrorists to be isolated. Consequently, the preference must be to treat terrorism as criminal acts to be handled through existing systems of law enforcement and with full respect for human rights and the rule of law.[20]

The fight against terrorism has entailed serious violations of human rights standards that flow from the international agreements referred to in the foregoing and the case law of the institutions established to monitor and implement the human rights standards. Unfortunately, my own country is among those that have failed to stand their ground with determination here.

A most regrettable occurrence is a case of so-called 'rendition', where Swedish officials handed over two Egyptian asylum seekers, Ahmed Agiza and Mohammed al-Zari, to representatives of the United States (the CIA) at a Swedish airport from where they were flown to Cairo, where both of them were tortured. In May 2005, the Committee against Torture (CAT) concluded that Sweden was in breach of both substantive and procedural provisions of Article 3 of the Convention against Torture and Other Cruel, Inhuman or Degrading Treatment or Punishment in respect of the summary expulsion of Ahmed Agiza. Article 3 deals with the prohibition on expelling, returning or extraditing a person to another state where there are substantial grounds for believing that the person would be in danger of being tortured or otherwise ill-treated (*refoulement*).[21] In a decision of 10 November 2006, the UN Human Rights Committee found that Sweden's involvement in the transfer by the CIA of Mohammed al-Zari to Egypt breached the absolute ban on torture, despite assurances of humane treatment provided by Egyptian authorities prior to the rendition.[22]

[20] See http://summit.clubmadrid.org/agenda/the-madrid-agenda.html.

[21] Decision of the Committee against Torture (CAT/C/34/D/233/2003), Thirty-fourth session, 24 May 2005, at www.unhchr.ch/tbs/doc.nsf/MasterFrameView/4dec90a558d3057 3c1257020005225b9?Opendocument.

[22] Communication No. 1416/2005: Sweden. 2006-11-10. CCPR/C/88/1416/2005, at www.unhchr.ch/tbs/doc.nsf/0/13fac9ce4f35d66dc12572220049e394?Opendocument.

In exemplifying violations of human rights standards, I felt obliged to mention these cases, which should be thoroughly investigated, since I often criticise other states for violating human rights standards and have to be objective. The same objectivity should be applied by states. As I said in my farewell address to the UN, in order for a state to criticise others with legitimacy, that state must pay attention to its own observance of human rights. I suspect that no state is above criticism in this field.

Looking to the future, there is an obvious need to reform both the members of the United Nations and the organisation itself. In the past, I have argued that it is the members who need reforming the most.[23] This is still the situation. A more active and systematic approach is needed at the national level. The following should be clear to anyone who gives thought to world governance:

- Rule of law is necessary to create a society in which human beings can live in dignity with their human rights protected.
- Rule of law as it is (or must be) understood today can only exist in a democracy.
- There is a direct correlation between the rule of law and a state's ability to attract foreign and domestic investments, to address poverty, and to protect the environment.
- There is a need for a coordinated, coherent and integrated approach to post-conflict peacebuilding and reconciliation in order to achieve a sustainable peace.
- To enhance the rule of law in post-conflict societies, it is necessary to assist countries emerging from conflict.

An examination of the present situation demonstrates that much is being done in this field today. The question is, however, if there should not be a more active and systematic engagement to enhance the rule of law. This applies, in particular, to countries that need assistance before a conflict erupts; every country falling short in this respect is a potential source of conflict that eventually could threaten international peace and security. When UN peacekeepers have to be sent to a country or region it is in a sense addressing the symptoms of what is wrong. Conflicts invariably are caused by the absence of the rule of law and lack of protection of human rights.

[23] See H. Corell, 'Who Needs Reforming the Most – the UN or its Members?' (2007) 76 *Nordic Journal of International Law* 265–279, also available at www.havc.se/res/SelectedMaterial/20071108corellwhoneedsreforming.pdf.

Obviously, the responsibility to make advances in the field of the rule of law rests with the states themselves and their governments. Member States of the United Nations should make a determined effort to systematically address the rule of law deficiency in today's world. But everybody should be encouraged to participate in this work, in particular, civil society and non-governmental organisations. These efforts should also be supported by intergovernmental organisations.

This brings me to the United Nations and the need to reform the organisation from a rule of law perspective. This can be done only with the full support of its members and in particular of its most powerful member. In addressing this dilemma in the past, I made reference to Dag Hammarskjöld's famous quote from a statement before the Security Council on 31 October 1956:

> The principles of the Charter are, by far, greater than the Organization in which they are embodied, and the aims which they are to safeguard are holier than the policies of any single nation or people.[24]

It should, however, be recognised that the rule of law has gradually become part of the day-to-day activities of the United Nations. The Brahimi Report focused on it.[25] In 2003, at the initiative of the United Kingdom, the rule of law was introduced as a distinct item on the agenda of the Security Council. In September 2004, the Secretary-General devoted his address to the General Assembly to the rule of law.[26] The Secretariat has also focused on these issues. The annual treaty event initiated by the Treaty Section of the UN Office of Legal Affairs is now a traditional ingredient in the high-level meetings of the General Assembly in September every year, now also with the support of the 2005 Summit.[27] In this context should also be mentioned the 'Strategy for an Era of Application of International Law', which was adopted by the UN Senior Management Group and approved by the Secretary-General in June 2000.[28] Among

[24] See H. Corell, 'Reforming the United Nations' (2005) 2 *International Organizations Law Review* 373–390, also available at www.havc.se/res/SelectedMaterial/2005iolrreformingtheun.pdf.

[25] See Report of the Panel on United Nations Peace Operations, UN Doc. A/55/305 – S/2000/809, 21 August 2000, at www.un.org/ga/search/view_doc.asp?symbol=A/55/305&referer=/english/&Lang=E.

[26] Note in particular Doc. S/2004/616, 23 August 2004, at www.un.org/ga/search/view_doc.asp?symbol=S/2004/616&referer=http://search.un.org/search?ie=utf8&Lang=E.

[27] See 2005 World Summit Outcome Resolution, A/RES/60/1, 16 September 2005, para. 134(b). See also http://treaties.un.org/Pages/Publications.aspx?pathpub=Publication/TE/Page1_en.xml.

[28] See 'Strategy for an Era of Application of International Law: Action Plan', at http://legal.un.org/ola/action_planA.aspx.

other things, the programme recommended an increase in the assistance provided by the United Nations system to needy countries to enable them to participate in the international treaty framework.

Recognising the difficulties involved in domestic jurisdictions in realising this goal, the Secretary-General observed that, all too often, individuals and corporations find that they are denied the rights and benefits that international law and treaties provide. Sometimes national authorities refuse to recognise and respect their obligations under international law, even where the state has voluntarily subscribed to the relevant treaties. More often though, such authorities simply lack the necessary expertise or resources to ensure that their obligations are properly implemented and applied.[29]

Against this background, every office, department, programme, fund and agency of the United Nations was requested to review its current activities and to consider what else it might do, within its existing mandate and given existing resources, to promote the application of international law. The focus should be on building national capacities to implement treaties more effectively by providing technical assistance to help governments implement their commitments under the treaties to which they are or might wish to become parties. A special effort was made to map all legal technical assistance provided by the United Nations system. A designated website was established for this purpose.[30]

An important development within the United Nations was the adoption by the General Assembly of the 2005 Summit Resolution.[31] In this resolution Member States recommitted themselves to actively protect and promote all human rights, the rule of law and democracy.[32]

The 2005 Summit Resolution also contained a decision to establish a Peacebuilding Commission, and expressed support for the idea of establishing a rule of law assistance unit within the Secretariat.[33] Both of these entities are now established, the latter working under the Rule of Law Coordination and Resource Group.[34]

[29] See Report of the Secretary-General on the work of the Organization, Supplement No. 1 (A/55/1) (2000), para. 278.

[30] See United Nations' Legal Technical Assistance Website, at www.un.org/law/technical/technical.htm.

[31] See GA/RES/60/1, *supra* note 27.

[32] Reference is made to paragraphs 11, 16, 21, 24 (b), 25 (a), 119 and 134 of the resolution.

[33] See GA/RES/60/1, paras. 97 and 134 (e).

[34] See www.un.org/en/peacebuilding/ and www.unrol.org/article.aspx?article_id=2.

Furthermore, a practice has now been established, according to which the Secretary-General submits Annual Reports on the UN rule of law activities. According to the Third Annual Report of the Secretary-General, the UN is providing rule of law assistance in over 150 Member States spanning every region of the world.[35] These activities take place in all contexts, including development, fragility, conflict and peacebuilding.[36] Reference should in this context also be made to the work performed by the United Nations Development Programme (UNDP).[37] In the wake of the Brahimi Report, it is now also being recognised that rule of law assistance is an essential tool to help maintain peace and security around the world.[38] As it appears from the Secretary-General's rule of law report just referred to, this activity has become a prominent feature in all peace operations.

The General Assembly has decided to convene a high-level meeting on the topic 'The rule of law at the national and international levels'[39] during the high-level segment of its 67th Session, i.e. in September 2012.[40] On this occasion, representatives of non-governmental organisations active in the field of the rule of law were invited to speak at the plenary. The high-level meeting resulted in a Declaration on the 'Rule of Law at the National and International Levels' which recognises that 'the rule of law applies to all States equally, and to international organizations, including the United Nations and its principal organs', and 'all persons, institutions and entities, public and private, including the State itself, are accountable to just, fair and equitable laws and are entitled without any discrimination to equal protection of the law'.[41]

[35] See 'Third Annual Report on Strengthening and Coordinating United Nations Rule of Law Activities', Report of the Secretary-General (A/66/133), 8 August 2011, para. 2, at www.unrol.org/files/Third%20Annual%20Report%20of%20the%20Secretary-General.pdf.

[36] *Ibid.*, para. 2.

[37] See the UNDP Rule of Law Global Programme Annual Report 2011, entitled 'Strengthening the Rule of Law in Crisis-affected and Fragile Situations', at www.undp.org/content/dam/undp/library/crisis%20prevention/UNDP%20Rule%20of%20Law,%20Annual%20Report_web%202011.pdf.

[38] See United Nations Peacekeeping, 'Rule of Law', at www.un.org/en/peacekeeping/issues/ruleoflaw.shtml.

[39] See also 'Delivering Justice: Programme of Action to Strengthen the Rule of Law at the National and International Levels', Report of the Secretary-General, UN Doc. A/66/749, 16 March 2012, at www.unrol.org/files/SGreport%20eng%20A_66_749.pdf.

[40] See GA Res. 66/102, 'The Rule of Law at the National and International Levels', UN Doc. A/RES/66/102, 9 December 2011, at www.un.org/en/ga/search/view_doc.asp?symbol=A/RES/66/102.

[41] See GA Res. 67/1, 'Declaration of the High-level Meeting of the General Assembly on the Rule of Law at the National and International Levels', 24 September 2012, para. 2, at http://unrol.org/files/Declaration%20HLM_A%20RES%2067%201.pdf.

The Declaration emphasises 'the importance of the rule of law as one of the key elements of conflict prevention, peacekeeping, conflict resolution and peacebuilding'. It stresses 'that justice, including transitional justice, is a fundamental building block of sustainable peace in countries in conflict and post-conflict situations'.[42] Of particular interest is the commitment to ensure:

> that impunity is not tolerated for genocide, war crimes and crimes against humanity or for violations of international humanitarian law and gross violations of human rights law, and that such violations are properly investigated and appropriately sanctioned, including by bringing the perpetrators of any crimes to justice.[43]

A closely related problem is corruption. It is like a poison that destroys many efforts to establish the rule of law and to assist developing countries in enhancing government and achieving better living conditions for their populations.[44] This is an area which requires attention in all countries. In this context, the Corruption Perceptions Index provided by Transparency International may be of use.[45]

With respect to the international level, much remains to be done. In the past, I have in this context focused in particular on the members of the Security Council, in particular the five permanent members. It is imperative that they bow to the UN Charter for the simple reason that they are entrusted with the primary responsibility for the maintenance of international peace and security. When permanent members of the Security Council violate the Charter, the observance of which they are mandated to supervise, it sends a terrible message to the rest of the world. The situations that I have highlighted in the past are the armed attacks on Iraq in 2003 and Georgia in 2008. I refer in this context to a letter that I sent to the members of the United Nations on 10 December 2008, entitled 'Security Council Reform: Rule of Law More Important Than Additional Members'.[46] In this letter, I suggested that the permanent five members, who, because of their veto power, can block any amendment to the UN Charter, rather than considering at the present stage additional members of the Council, should adopt a binding declaration containing the following four elements:

[42] *Ibid.*, para. 18. [43] *Ibid.*, para. 22. [44] See also para. 25 of GA Res. 67/1.

[45] Available at www.transparency.org/policy_research/surveys_indices/cpi/2010/results.

[46] The text of this letter is available at www.havc.se/res/SelectedMaterial/20081210corelllettertounmembers.pdf.

- To scrupulously adhere to the obligations under international law that they have undertaken and in particular those laid down in the Charter of the United Nations.
- To make use of their veto power in the Security Council only if their most serious and direct national interests are affected and to explain, in case they do use this power, the reasons for doing so.
- To refrain in their international relations from the threat or use of force against the territorial integrity or political independence of any state unless in self-defence in accordance with Article 51 of the Charter of the United Nations or in accordance with a clear and unambiguous mandate by the Security Council under Chapter VII.
- To take forceful action to intervene in situations when international peace and security are threatened by governments that seriously violate human rights or fail to protect their populations from genocide, war crimes, ethnic cleansing and crimes against humanity or when otherwise the responsibility to protect is engaged.

Is this realistic? Does anyone believe that the permanent five members of the Security Council are prepared to take such a step? My response today would be: look at the pledges suggested in the letter and repeated here and compare them to the declaration on the rule of law adopted by the General Assembly on 24 September 2012.[47] Do the first three pledges not fall squarely within the framework of an international society under the rule of law? Is it too much to ask that the body entrusted with the primary responsibility for the maintenance of international peace and security bow to the very law they are set to supervise and apply? The fourth pledge may be a little more complex.

Let us take the situation in Syria as an example. At present, the absence of a unanimous, clear and firm condemnation by the Security Council of the violence applied by the Syrian regime against its own citizens is deplorable. One of the points made in the letter just quoted is that the Council is actually in a formidable position to make a difference in the world if its members, and notably the permanent members, joined hands and agreed to adhere strictly to international law and in particular the UN Charter.

The inability of the Council to unite in the case of Syria is a painful illustration of its shortcomings. The fact that, on 16 February 2012, the General Assembly with overwhelming majority (137 votes in favour to 12 against,

[47] See *supra* note 41.

with 17 abstentions) adopted a resolution strongly condemning widespread and systematic human rights violations by the Syrian authorities,[48] demonstrates that there is a disconnect between the vast majority of the UN membership and the permanent members of the Security Council, in this particular case, China and the Russian Federation. A united stand by the Security Council would have sent a very powerful signal to the regime in Damascus – and to the allied forces and armed groups.

What is lacking is a determined effort by the Council to send, already at the outset, a strong unanimous message to the parties that what is happening in Syria is unacceptable in modern day society. The message should also have included an indication that further measures would be considered in case the violence did not stop. And why did the Council hesitate in sending the signal that those responsible for the international crimes committed in Syria will be brought to justice?[49] Compare this with the very clear contents of the 24 September 2012 Declaration on the Rule of Law.[50]

To a long-time observer of the Council it is incomprehensible that the permanent five members seem to be unable to unite when people are being abused by their own governments. To maintain, in today's world, that such situations are internal matters is simply not acceptable. Irrespective of the reasons underlying the position by the two vetoing states, they could never excuse the fact that innocent people suffer. To be fair, the double standards applied by certain Western states, e.g. in relation to the ongoing conflict between Israel and Palestine, should be mentioned here too.

This short-sighted and shameful attitude actually breeds conflict instead of promoting an atmosphere where more and more people around the world will be allowed to participate in their governance in a meaningful way. The Security Council, and in particular the permanent five members, not only have the primary responsibility for the maintenance of international peace and security – they actually hold the key to international peace and security.

An interesting question is what Dag Hammarskjöld would have said, had he observed this situation while at the same time reading the 24 September Declaration of the General Assembly or the following

48 See para. 2 of GA Res. 66/253 'The Situation in the Syrian Arab Republic', 16 February 2012. See also GA Res. 66/253 B, 'The Situation in the Syrian Arab Republic', 3 August 2012.

49 In the 6849th Meeting of the Security Council Security Council on 17 October 2012, many speakers urged the Council to act on the crisis in Syria. See Press Release available at www.un.org/News/Press/docs/2012/sc10793.doc.htm.

50 See paras. 22 and 23 of Res. 67/1.

paragraphs from the Preamble to GA Resolution 66/102 on 'The rule of law at the national and international levels':

> *Reaffirming its commitment* to the purposes and principles of the Charter of the United Nations and international law, which are indispensable foundations of a more peaceful, prosperous and just world, and reiterating its determination to foster strict respect for them and to establish a just and lasting peace all over the world,
>
> *Reaffirming* that human rights, the rule of law and democracy are interlinked and mutually reinforcing and that they belong to the universal and indivisible core values and principles of the United Nations,
>
> *Reaffirming also* the need for universal adherence to and implementation of the rule of law at both the national and international levels and its solemn commitment to an international order based on the rule of law and international law, which, together with the principles of justice, is essential for peaceful coexistence and cooperation among States,
>
> ...
>
> *Convinced* that the promotion of and respect for the rule of law at the national and international levels, as well as justice and good governance, should guide the activities of the United Nations, and of its Member States.[51]

5.3 The ethics of an international civil servant in light of Dag Hammarskjöld's thinking

Let us now focus on the question of what Dag Hammarskjöld would have said and done if he had been confronted with the issues that the UN is facing today. It would of course be presumptuous to suggest any particular manner in which he would have approached the situation. However, I am convinced that with the integrity and determination that he demonstrated during his tenure as UN Secretary-General, he would not have hesitated to take action.

On the occasion of a commemorative event, I reflected on his famous address at Oxford University on 30 May 1961, entitled 'The International Civil Service in Law and in Fact'.[52] I attempted to highlight the most salient elements in Dag Hammarskjöld's reasoning.[53] Among the most important conclusions in his address is that the responsibilities of the

[51] See preamble, GA Res. 66/102, *supra* note 40.

[52] Dag Hammarskjöld's 30 May 1961 address is available at www.un.org/Depts/dhl/dag/docs/internationalcivilservant.pdf. See also www.un.org/Depts/dhl/events/lectures/civil_servant.htm.

[53] Lecture delivered at Uppsala on 18 September 2009 at a Commemorative Event organised by the Dag Hammarskjöld Foundation on the 48th Anniversary of Dag Hammarskjöld's

Secretary-General under the Charter cannot be laid aside merely because the execution of decisions by him is likely to be politically controversial. The Secretary-General remains under the obligation to check out the policies as adopted by the organs. The essential requirement according to Dag Hammarskjöld is that the Secretary-General does this on the basis of his exclusively international responsibility and not in the interest of any particular state or group of states.

He then draws attention to the ambiguity of the word 'neutrality' in such a context:

> It is obvious from what I have said that the international civil servant cannot be accused of lack of neutrality simply for taking a stand on a controversial issue when this is his duty and cannot be avoided. But there remains a serious intellectual and moral problem as we move within an area inside which personal judgement must come into play. Finally, we have to deal with the question of integrity or with, if you please, a question of conscience.[54]

Against this background, Dag Hammarskjöld maintains that the international civil servant must keep himself under the strictest observation. He is not requested to be neutral in the sense that he has to have no sympathies or antipathies, that there are to be no interests which are close to him in his personal capacity or that he is to have no ideas or ideals that matter for him. However, says Dag Hammarskjöld, he is requested to be fully aware of those human reactions and meticulously check himself so that they are not permitted to influence his actions. This is nothing unique, he says, and ends with the rhetorical question: is not every judge professionally under the same obligation?

The very essence of Dag Hammarskjöld's thinking in this matter appears in the penultimate paragraph of his address:

> If the international civil servant knows himself to be free from such personal influences in his actions and guided solely by the common aims and rules laid down for, and by the Organization he serves and by recognized legal principles, then he has done his duty, and then he can face the criticism which, even so, will be unavoidable. As I said, at the final last, this is

Death, available at www.havc.se/res/SelectedMaterial/20090918hammarskjold.pdf, also published as H. Corell, 'The Need for the Rule of Law in International Affairs – Reflections on Dag Hammarskjöld's Address at Oxford University on 30 May 1961, The International Civil Service in Law and in Fact', in H. Corell, Inge Lønning and H. Melber, 'The Ethics of Dag Hammarskjöld', Dag Hammarskjöld Foundation 2010, at www.dhf.uu.se/publications/other-publications/the-ethics-of-dag-hammarskjold/.

[54] See Dag Hammarskjöld, 30 May 1961 address, *supra* note 52.

> a question of integrity, and if integrity in the sense of respect for law and respect for truth were to drive him into positions of conflict with this or that interest, then that conflict is a sign of his neutrality and not of his failure to observe neutrality – then it is in line, not in conflict with, his duties as an international civil servant.[55]

In my reflections, I ventured to suggest that what the United Nations needs are persons who can make assessments and decisions in accordance with the clear guidelines that follow from Dag Hammarskjöld's address. Based on my experiences during my ten years as the Legal Counsel of the UN, I also believe that it is inevitable that the Secretary-General, from time to time, is likely to have an argument with one or more Member States and notably the major powers.[56]

I am not suggesting that this is something that the Secretary-General should be looking for. But it is the unavoidable result of the Secretary-General performing the duty that follows with the position. In conclusion I maintained:

> If this situation should occur, the Member States should not simply jump into conclusions that produce confrontation but rather step back for a moment and reflect. Is this situation not rather a sign of health – that the Secretary-General is doing his or her job? On second thought, maybe the firm stand of the Secretary-General is in both the short and long term interest of the Member States, including those that may have been displeased in the particular situation.[57]

5.4 Conclusions

The obvious conclusion to be drawn from Dag Hammarskjöld's thinking is that international civil servants, with the Secretary-General of the United Nations in the lead, could make a difference by applying the standards that Dag Hammarskjöld promoted. This is something that should be borne in mind by all within the international civil service. The question is, however, if the fundamental ethical principles that he applied in his reasoning could not be a lodestar also to other actors and in particular when it comes to respecting the law.

All too often, international civil servants observe that UN Member States are lacking in loyalty to the aims, principles and purposes of the

[55] *Ibid.*

[56] See H. Corell, 'The Ethics of an International Civil Servant' (2011) 16 *New Routes* 12–16, at www.dhf.uu.se/wordpress/wp-content/uploads/2011/06/NR112.pdf.

[57] *Ibid.*

United Nations. It is sometimes said that the questions that the UN organs deal with are more political than legal. This is certainly true in many instances. But this argument is not acceptable when it comes to applying clear and unambiguous rules, such as the core provisions of the UN Charter and fundamental human rights standards. Here the law is clear and there should be no room for political manoeuvring based on reasons that in many cases probably would not bear the light of day. In a state under the rule of law, political bodies must also bow to the law. The same must apply at the international level.

In the present discussions relating to the Middle East, there is talk of the use of force against Iran as if the UN Charter did not even exist. It is therefore important to remind the most aggressive participants in the discussion, that the UN Charter is legally binding and that the obligations flowing from it actually trump national law, including national constitutions. If a state has concluded an international agreement, the state in question is bound by that agreement in relation to other parties to the treaty. This is the concept upon which the whole international system is based. It is a matter of law, but equally a matter of ethics. Another way of describing the concept is to do it in a way that Dag Hammarskjöld might have done if he had observed today's world: it is a matter of civilisation.

PART II

Hammarskjöld's intellectual legacy and leadership

6

Dag Hammarskjöld and the politics of hope

MONICA BOUMAN

6.1 Introduction

This chapter introduces Hammarskjöld's philosophical model of international service, which he developed based on Western philosophy. It relates Hammarskjöld's world of ideas to three philosophical schools of thought: the 'politics of hope' (Bernhard Dauenhauer), the 'standard of the self' (Hannah Arendt) and the 'unity of humanity' (Karl Jaspers). It argues that his conception of international service was shaped by his personal and diplomatic experiences in the 1950s, the Peking mission and the Bandung Conference. It then discusses the contemporary scope and relevance of the model.

6.2 Context

US President Eisenhower was not a Romeo, and Chinese Premier Zhou Enlai was certainly not his Juliet. Both men were at opposite sides of the political spectrum at the height of Cold War hostility, marked by antagonistic disputes and political bloc formation. But they played a crucial role in peace negotiations. In June 1953, they agreed on a truce in the Korean War, with Zhou Enlai negotiating on the communist side, and Eisenhower on the South Korean side. In 1955, their diplomacy was again needed in light of the threat of a nuclear world war caused by the Taiwan Strait crisis. This time, tension was avoided with the help of the United Nations and its Secretary-General, i.e. Dag Hammarskjöld's Peking mission and the Bandung Conference, which gave Zhou Enlai a platform for international diplomacy.

Dr Monica Bouman studied psychology and theology at the Catholic University of Nijmegen and humanities at the University of Amsterdam, where she defended her PhD thesis ('Internationale dienstbaarheid als vrijheid en plicht: De levensweg van Dag Hammarskjöld' [International Service as Freedom and Duty: The Life of Dag Hammarskjöld]) in 2001. She is author of *Dag Hammarskjöld: Citizen of the World* (2005).

On 30 December 1954, Hammarskjöld set off on a diplomatic visit to Peking. The purpose of his mission was to ask Zhou Enlai to release eleven American flyers who had been captured by China and accused of espionage. Hammarskjöld considered it his duty to remind the Chinese Premier of the vital importance of the treatment of flyers to international peace. Commenting on his mission, Hammarskjöld said to Zhou Enlai:

> [this incident] has brought me around the world in order to put before you, in great frankness and trusting that we see eye to eye on the desperate need to avoid adding to existing frictions, my deep concern both as Secretary-General and as a man.[1]

Seven months later, when Hammarskjöld was in Sweden to celebrate his fiftieth birthday, he heard that Peking had released the American flyers. His visit to Peking had established a channel of communication between communist China and the United States and averted a potential world war in Southeast Asia. The mission was a great success for Hammarskjöld's diplomacy.

Hammarskjöld perceived this mission as an experiment in world organisation, the process of which was as interesting to him as its diplomatic result. He reflected on these experiences, searched for their meaning and integrated them into his model of international service. He elaborated contours of this model in two public speeches given in June 1955: 'International Service' and 'The World and the Nation'. Further reflections can be found in his spiritual diary *Markings*, in particular his entries for 1 August 1955 and 19–20 October 1955, which describe his attitude towards diplomacy ('Concerning men and their way to peace and concord').[2]

This chapter examines Hammarskjöld's model of international service and the cases that gave rise to the model. The title of the chapter builds on the argument by political philosopher Bernhard Dauenhauer, who described Hammarskjöld as a 'practitioner of the politics of hope'.[3] A politics of hope stands radically opposed to all forms of tyranny and totalitarianism. It is guided by the effort to nurture as effectively the full range of human activity and to foster the idea of unity of humankind. It

[1] B. Urquhart, *Hammarskjöld* (1972), 106. The quote from the Hammarskjöld/Zhou Enlai talks is taken by Urquhart from Hammarskjöld's own records.

[2] D. Hammarskjöld, *Markings* (1965), 114.

[3] B. Dauenhauer, *The Politics of Hope* (1986), 123. Drawing upon Western political philosophy, Dauenhauer acknowledges in his book that man, in his aims as well as in his deeds, is always and essentially en route and finds in this acknowledgement a stimulus

cherishes the differences among men while seeking further harmonisation of human relations. The philosophy of the United Nations has synergies with the politics of hope. This is reflected in the commitment of the UN Charter to mediation, negotiation and reconciliation in the settlement of disputes.

6.3 Hammarskjöld's model of international service

Hammarskjöld's conception of international service is rooted in his ethics. In June 1955, on the occasion of the tenth anniversary of the United Nations, Hammarskjöld delivered two speeches which illustrate his thinking: one on 'International Service'[4], given at Johns Hopkins University, Baltimore, Maryland, and another one on 'The World and the Nation'[5], delivered at Stanford University, Palo Alto, California. Both speeches addressed Hammarskjöld's ethics of international service. I will first introduce the general content of each speech and then relate them to models of the 'politics of hope', the 'standard of the self' and the 'unity of humanity'.

6.3.1 'International service'

On 14 June 1955, Hammarskjöld opened his 'International Service' address at Johns Hopkins University with a general sketch of the global political landscape. He then turned to the theme of ethics:

> At this time of great ideological conflicts and violent clashes of interests, technological and economic developments have, as never before, brought us together as members of one human family, unified beyond race or creed on a shrinking globe, in face of dangers of our own making.
>
> In such a situation, many ethical problems take on a new significance and our need to give sense to our lives exceeds the inherited standards. True, our duties to our families, our neighbours, our countries, our creeds have not changed. Yet something has been added. This is a duty to what I shall call international service, with a claim on our lives equal to

to unremitting cooperative effort. A responsible politics, then, both respects the human condition and takes optimal advantage of the opportunities available to men.

4 D. Hammarskjöld, 'International Service', in W. Foote (ed.), *The Servant of Peace: A Selection of the Speeches and Statements of Dag Hammarskjöld, Secretary-General of the United Nations 1953–1961* (1962), 80–85.

5 D. Hammarskjöld, 'The World and the Nation', in W. Foote (ed.), *The Servant of Peace: A Selection of the Speeches and Statements of Dag Hammarskjöld, Secretary-General of the United Nations 1953–1961* (1962), 86–91.

> that of the duty to serve within those smaller units whose walls are now breaking down.[6]

Hammarskjöld regarded international service as an obligation and as a privilege:

> International service requires of all of us first and foremost the courage to be ourselves. In other words, it requires that we should be true to none other than our ideals and interests – but these should be such as we can fully endorse after having opened our minds, with great honesty, to the many voices of the world. The greatest contribution to international life that anyone can render – be it as a private citizen or as one professionally engaged in international work – is to represent frankly and consistently what survives or emerges as one's own after such a test. Far from demanding that we abandon or desert ideals and interests basic to our personality, international service thus puts us under the obligation to let those ideals and interests reach maturity and fruition in a universal climate.[7]

Hammarskjöld expressly acknowledged that international service implies the resolution of conflicts. He argued that this capacity requires a certain maturity of mind. He said:

> The international civil servant who works for an Organization with members of different ideologies and interests, remains under the obligation that applies to all of us – to be faithful to truth as he understands it. In doing so, he is loyal – both in relation to the Organization and to his country. In doing so, he must, of course, subordinate himself to rules of good order, as all of us should do.[8]

He regarded subordination to the 'rules of good order' as the essence of service to all fellow men. He framed this ideal as follows:

> The attitude basic to international service places the pursuit of happiness under the laws of conscience which alone can justify freedom. In accepting such a way of life we recognize the moral sovereignty of the responsible individual.[9]

Hammarskjöld further stressed the role of dignity. He shared the view that human dignity forms part of the inherited values of all Western civilisation, i.e. that each man is an end in himself and of infinite value as an individual. He noted that this ideal may become a reality

> when we, ourselves, follow a way of life, individually and as members of a group, which entitles us personally to the freedom of a mature individual,

[6] *Ibid.*, at 80. [7] *Ibid.*, at 80. [8] *Ibid.*, at 82.
[9] See Hammarskjöld, *supra* note 4, at 83.

> living under the rules of his conscience. And it becomes the key to our dealings with others only when inspired by a faith which in truth and spirit gives to them the value which is theirs according to what we profess to be our creed.[10]

Hammarskjöld referred to 'The Dignity of Man', an unfinished book by the essayist Russell W. Davenport, published after his death. He recommended the subject and its writer as follows:

> It is apparent what he wanted to say: that the dignity of man, as a justification for our faith in freedom, can be part of our living creed only if we revert to a view of life where maturity of mind counts for more than outward success and where happiness is no longer to be measured in quantitative terms.[11]

Hammarskjöld was convinced that 'the final reply is not one that can be given in writing, but only in terms of life'.[12] He notes:

> There is no formula to teach us how to arrive at maturity and there is no grammar for the language of inner life. [Davenport's] study, like the effort of every single individual, finally led him to the doorstep where the rest is silence because the rest is something that has to be resolved between a man and himself. The rest is silence – but the results of the inner dialogue are evident to all, evident as independence, courage and fairness in dealing with others, evident in true international service.[13]

At the end of his speech, Hammarskjöld stated that the thoughts expressed mark conclusions from 'a most practical experience'.[14] He argued that achievements in politics and diplomacy are not merely the result of will and skill, but determined by the consistency of the actors and the validity of their ideals. He noted:

> Contrary to what seems to be popular belief there is no intellectual activity which more ruthlessly tests the solidity of a man than politics. Apparently, easy successes with the public are possible for a juggler, but lasting results are achieved only by the patient builder. Those who are to be called teachers or leaders may profit from intelligence but can only justify their positions by integrity.[15]

6.3.2 'The World and the Nation'

In 'The World and the Nation', his commencement address at Stanford University on 19 June 1955, Hammarskjöld examined the balance between

[10] *Ibid.*, at 83, 84. [11] *Ibid.*, at 84. [12] *Ibid.*
[13] *Ibid.* [14] *Ibid.* [15] *Ibid.*, at 85.

national and international politics in international relations, and the role of the United Nations. He argued that:

> nationalism and internationalism represent essential parts of the mental and spiritual equipment of all responsible men in our time ... when understood as meaning recognition of the value and the rights of the nation and dependence of the nation on the world.[16]

He made these remarks at a time when decolonisation was advancing and when interstate relations were shaped by conflicts of interest between 'old' nations and 'new' states. Hammarskjöld welcomed decolonisation and the emergence of 'new' states. He encouraged his audience 'to meet this new enthusiasm with understanding, in full appreciation of the rich gifts it may bring to a world of many nations and peoples in friendly competition'. He also pointed to leadership qualities necessary for true statesmanship:

> History places a burden on our shoulders. The creative urges of the emergent nations are tinged with strong emotions from the past. It is for all of us, denying neither the goods nor the ills from the past, to look ahead and not to permit old conflicts to envenom the spirit of the creative work before us.[17]

Hammarskjöld noted that some of the existing states were reluctant to accept such change. He cautioned against such reservations. He argued that 'older' nations should not isolate themselves in this process of transformation.[18] He took the view that this challenge should be approached with an independent and open attitude towards dialogue and mutual relations.[19] In the context, he used the metaphor of 'the way', i.e. the idea of a path to maturity, in order to support his view. He advocated 'a vigorous and self-confident development, in free contact with the world, of the special qualities and assets of their nation and their people – a development which should give them their just weight in the international balance'.[20]

Hammarskjöld acknowledged at the same time that nations were far from ready for the responsibility of world government. In this context, he addressed the function and tasks of the United Nations:

[16] Hammarskjöld, *supra* note 5, at 86.

[17] *Ibid.*, at 87, 88. [18] *Ibid.*, at 88.

[19] 'Giving thus to the world what is specifically ours, we could manifest and protect our national character, while accepting change and opening our minds to the influences of the world.' *Ibid.*, at 89.

[20] *Ibid.*, at 90, 91. See on this, also Chapter 14, this volume.

> The United Nations is an expression of our will to find a synthesis between the nation and the world, overcoming being one-sided … It is an attempt to provide us with a framework inside which it is possible to serve the world by serving our nation, and to serve our nation by serving the world. Whatever the past shortcomings of this experiment in world organization might be, it has given meaning and direction to the efforts of all men who are striving towards a better world.[21]

In the second, more ideological part of his argument, Hammarskjöld explained the historical context and foundation of his argument. He addressed the idea of world community by reference to the 'brotherhood of men'. He argued that both internationalism and nationalism remain effective forces in history. He made reference to the idea of a hero/saint of the international community:

> Every nation has its heroes, its martyrs and its saints. The world also has its heroes and saints. One who long ago spoke among a small, oppressed people for the brotherhood of men was sacrificed as a danger to the safety of his own nation. Western civilization has aspired for nearly two thousand years to follow the life and teachings of this apostle of peace. Nevertheless, all through those two thousand years, nationalism in the narrow and dangerous sense of the word has remained a major force. In the light of history, one might well ascribe to mankind the words of Milton's Lucifer: 'For only in destroying I find ease for my relentless thoughts.'[22]

Hammarskjöld argued that scepticism towards progress in history could be overcome through spirituality and inspiration by faith. He stated:

> Whatever doubts history may cast, I believe that the hope for a world of peace and order, inspired by respect for man, has never ceased to agitate the minds of men. I believe that it accounts for the great and noble human spirit behind the ravaged exterior of a history whose self-inflicted wounds have become more and more atrocious. I believe that at the point we have now reached in our technical development, our creed may gain new possibilities to shape history.[23]

Hammarskjöld closed his speech with confidence in the role of the United Nations. He argued that the United Nations gave sense and direction to the efforts of people striving for a better world.

[21] See Hammarskjöld, *supra* note 5, at 90, 91.
[22] *Ibid.*, at 89, 90. [23] *Ibid.*, at 90.

6.3.3 Substantiating Hammarskjöld's model of international service

In his 'International Service' speech, Hammarskjöld relied on Kant's enlarged mentality ('erweiterte Denkungsart'). This was also the point of departure of Hannah Arendt's concept of the moral self. Arendt considered the 'standard of the self' as the core of morality.[24] She derived this conclusion from the experiences of the collapse of all established moral standards in public and private life during the 1930s and 1940s, including Hitler's Germany and Stalin's Russia. Based on these experiences, Arendt insisted that a truly thinking person should not look for rules or laws in a crisis, but rather remain true to oneself: 'I must be true to myself. I must not do anything that I cannot live with, that I cannot bear to remember.'[25]

Arendt related morality to the individual in his or her singularity. According to her model, moral conduct implies being faithful to – not forgetting – what was and is true in oneself and for oneself. It involves internal dialogues, through which humans are prepared to consult others who also think in this way and are thus prepared to judge reflectively. Individuals should be prepared to submit their thinking to a community of spectators with enlarged mentality.[26] According to Arendt, this process involves thinking, judging and will.

This position is also inherent in Hammarskjöld's approach. He considered the maturity of mind as the basis of international service. He refers to the 'undivided self', which Arendt associated with lovingly related will (an enduring 'I') and reflective judging,[27] i.e. the ability to include multiple positions in thought-processes and judgement. Characters trained by love recommit to the world and act in the public realm. They try to preserve the common world or the public realm in which *who* a person is can make an appearance.

Hammarskjöld went further than Arendt on one point. He stressed the central position of silence in ethics. He refers to inner dialogue until the point 'where the rest is silence'.[28] He does not elaborate on its meaning. But he gives dialogue at the edge of silence a central position. He noted:

[24] E. Young-Bruehl, *Why Arendt Matters* (2006), 200.

[25] H. Arendt, *The Life of the Mind* (1978), 97, 102.

[26] Those who do not have this ability do wrong in action. Arendt seems to imply that 'to do wrong is to spoil this ability'. *Ibid*., at 94.

[27] Young-Bruehl, *supra* note 24, at 203.

[28] Hammarskjöld, *supra* note 5, at 84.

> The rest is silence – but the results of the inner dialogue are evident to all, evident as independence, courage and fairness in dealing with others, evident in true international service.[29]

If one applies the 'standard of the moral self' to Hammarskjöld's 'Peking formula', one may note that he interprets international service as a commitment to Charter principles and to faithfulness and consistency with the moral self. Hammarskjöld engaged in open dialogue with Zhou Enlai, in an attempt to learn to understand 'the other side'. The inner strength of these dialogues made a deep impression on him. Hammarskjöld's reflections on these dialogues, his enlarged mentality and his judgements strongly influenced his diplomatic style. This becomes evident in Hammarskjöld's reflections in *Markings* after the June speeches, which added further refinements to the international service model (see Section 6.5).

In his speech 'The World and the Nation', Hammarskjöld expanded the model to include leadership and world citizenship in the international world of the 1950s. As noted in the introduction, the goals and principles of the United Nations correspond to the politics-of-hope model. According to Dauenhauer:

> A responsible politics is one which both respects the human condition and at the same time takes optimal advantage of the opportunities available to men. A politics of hope acknowledges that man, in his aims as well as in his deeds, is always and essentially *en route* and finds in this acknowledgement the stimulus to unremitting cooperative effort. Actualized hope in man ascribes positive worth both to the future possibilities arising from this routedness and to the concrete relations which constitute it.[30]

Hammarskjöld's speech focused on differences in attitude concerning nationalism or internationalism. This is reflected in his above-mentioned statement:

> nationalism and internationalism represent essential parts of the mental and spiritual equipment of all responsible men in our time … when understood as meaning recognition of the value and the rights of the nation and dependence of the nation on the world.[31]

To him, this recognition is an act of mature judgement. Hammarskjöld took the view that international service is incumbent on everyone, by being a citizen of a nation and of the world. But he recognised, at the same

[29] *Ibid.* [30] See Dauenhauer, *supra* note 3, at 119.
[31] See *supra* note 16.

time, that world order requires mature leadership, i.e. the ability to deal constructively, peacefully and justly with the conflicts that arise under changing national circumstances. He argued that the United Nations has a central role in establishing an adequate balance.

Hammarskjöld was, in particular, convinced that the organisation should play a key part in the politics of hope of nations. This is reflected in his introduction to the Eleventh Annual Report to the General Assembly. He notes that 'we have to foster understanding, cooperation and a mutual accommodation of interests', in an effort to 'nurture as effectively as possible the full range of human activity and achievement and to bring about brotherhood'.[32] He also points to cherishing 'the differences among men while harmonizing them'.[33]

By introducing the concept of the 'apostle of peace', Hammarskjöld linked his ethics of international service to the spiritual traditions of mankind and the idea of the unity of mankind. He explained his ideas on faith and spirituality related to the UN in public on several occasions. His conception combined moral aspirations with professional discipline and realism. In his speech 'The New Santa Maria' he described the United Nations as an adventure (i.e. a new 'Santa Maria'). He compared its journey to the mission of Christopher Columbus' famous battleship. He further recalled the ancient Asian saying, 'We cannot mould the world as masters of a material thing ... But we can influence the development of the world from within as a spiritual thing'.[34] He applied these ideas to the UN. He conceived the organisation as the expression of 'a secular "church" of ideals and principles in international affairs', and the Secretariat and the Secretary-General as its representatives to the governments.[35] He acknowledged that the organisation necessarily stands outside all confessions. But he viewed it as an instrument of faith, i.e. an entity inspired by the common heritage of the great religions of the world. He encouraged his audience 'to show the strength that follows from the courage to meet others with trust' – a feature that characterises people of faith.[36]

[32] *Ibid.*, at 118. [33] *Ibid.*

[34] See Address by Secretary-General Dag Hammarskjöld at Dinner in his Honor Given by the American Association for the United Nations, New York, 14 September 1953, UN Press Release SG/336, at 2, reprinted in W. Foote (ed.), *The Servant of Peace: A Selection of the Speeches and Statements of Dag Hammarskjöld, Secretary-General of the United Nations 1953–1961* (1962).

[35] *Ibid.*, at 7.

[36] D. Hammarskjöld, 'An Instrument of Faith', in W. Foote (ed.), *The Servant of Peace: A Selection of the Speeches and Statements of Dag Hammarskjöld, Secretary-General of the United Nations 1953–1961* (1962), 56, 57, 60.

In this context, it is useful to explore synergies between Hammarskjöld's thought and Karl Jaspers' view on the unity of humanity. To Jaspers, Jesus was one of the great philosophers connected to the Axial period,[37] along with the Buddha, Socrates and Confucius. In his conception,[38] the Axial period was a unifying phase in history that provided a common frame of historical self-comprehension for all peoples – for the West, for Asia, and for all men on earth, without regard to particular articles of faith. He found this axis of history in the period around 500 BC, in the spiritual process that occurred between 800 and 200 BC. In this period, mankind, as we know it today, came into being. Man became conscious of being, and its limitations. This was a new phenomenon in all three areas of the world. Jaspers noted:

> He [i.e. man] experiences the terror of the world and his own powerlessness: he asks radical questions and, face to face with the void, he strives for liberation and redemption. By consciously recognising his limits he sets himself the highest goals. In the depths of selfhood and in the lucidity of transcendence he experiences absoluteness. The many spiritual conflicts that arose were accompanied by attempts to convince others through the communication of thoughts, reasons and experiences. As a result of this process, hitherto unconsciously accepted ideas, customs and conditions were subjected to examination, questioned and liquidated. In so far as the traditional substance still possessed vitality and reality, its manifestations were clarified and thereby transmuted.[39]

Jaspers considered the present age as one of technological and political remoulding, rather than spiritual creation. He argued that there is a need to reconstruct humanity from its origin. He asked

> the fateful question as to how we can, in faith, become specifically human beings? In this process of self-understanding through the knowledge of whence we come the mirror of the great Axial period of humanity will perhaps, once more, prove one of the essential assurances.[40]

In this respect, Jaspers' hope lies in preserving the stream of philosophy. He stated: 'In view of the possibility of a totalitarian world empire and a totalitarian doctrinal truth corresponding to it, the only hope left for the individual, is to preserve the stream of philosophy.'[41]

Jaspers argued that the last refuge is 'the independence from both Church and State of the deepest inner being of the man related to

[37] K. Jaspers, *Die Massgebenden Menschen, Sokrates, Buddha, Konfuzius, Jesus* (1975), 165–193.

[38] K. Jaspers, *The Origin and Goal of History* (1953/2010), 1–21.

[39] *Ibid.* [40] *Ibid.*, at 139–140. [41] *Ibid.*, at 227.

transcendence, his liberty of soul, that draws courage from discourse with the great cultural heritage'.[42] In the end,

> philosophy leads us along the road to the point at which love acquires its depth in real communication. Then in this love, through the success of communication, the truth that links us together will be disclosed to those who are most remote in the diversity of their historical origin.[43]

Hammarskjöld's conception of the UN as 'a secular "church" of ideals and principles', and his understanding of 'international service' were shaped by this thinking. Hammarskjöld's ideas embrace a distinction between 'Christian hope' which 'refers to God' and 'political hope' which has no superhuman reference, but relies on the bonds that people share with others and unite 'genuine human life'.[44] Both 'political hope' and 'Christian hope' differ from Stoic resignation, or even despair, on the one hand, and presumptuous optimism, on the other.[45]

At the end of his speech, Hammarskjöld formulated his belief in hope in strong terms, with relevance to the past, the present and the future:

> Whatever doubts history may cast, I believe that the hope for a world of peace and order, inspired by respect for man, has never ceased to agitate the minds of men. I believe that it accounts for the great and noble human spirit behind the ravaged exterior of a history whose self-inflicted wounds have become more and more atrocious. I believe that at the point we have now reached in our technical development, our creed may gain new possibilities to shape history.[46]

These lines echo the words of Albert Schweitzer's Nobel Peace Prize Lecture, delivered on 4 November 1954 at Oslo University. Hammarskjöld admired Schweitzer's work and corresponded with the Alsatian theologian, doctor and surgeon of the Lambarene hospital in Equatorial France (now Gabon). The subject of Schweitzer's lecture was 'The Problem of Peace', and it focused on the spirit of humanitarianism.[47] In his view, the

[42] *Ibid.* [43] *Ibid.*, at 228.

[44] B. Dauenhauer, 'Ricoeur's Model of Translation and Responsible Political Practice', in F.J. Mootz III and G.H. Taylor (eds.), *Gadamer and Ricoeur* (2011), 195.

[45] What has been said about Christian hope may also be said about political hope, namely: 'Just as patience helps hope to continue and endure, so, in return, hope helps one to be patient, to resist, to struggle. There is a reciprocal influence. Courageous in its desire, serene in its courage, hope is a principle of action.' *Ibid.*, quote from S. Harent, 'Espérance', in *Dictionnaire de Theologie Catholique*, edited by A. Vacant and E. Mangenot (1939), Vol. V, part 1, at 611.

[46] See Hammarskjöld, *supra* note 5, at 90.

[47] A. Schweitzer, 'The Problem of Peace', see www.nobelprize.org, from F.W. Haberman (ed.), *Nobel Lectures, Peace 1951–1970* (1972).

United Nations had been unable to bring about peace, since its efforts were undertaken in a world where there was no prevailing spirit directed towards peace. He noted: 'Only when an ideal of peace is born in the minds of the peoples will the institutions set up to maintain this peace effectively fulfil the function expected of them.'[48]

Schweitzer argued for 'a spirit of humanitarianism', i.e. an ethical spirit. He claimed that one is true to oneself and capable of creating, when one is inspired by humanitarianism. He warned against the 'spurious nationalism, which is rampant especially among those peoples who formerly lived under white domination and who have recently gained their independence'.[49] He was convinced that such nationalism could be overcome through a humanitarian ideal. He stated:

> All men, even the semi civilized and the primitive, are as beings able of compassion, able to develop a humanitarian spirit. It abides within them like tinder ready to be lit, waiting only for a spark.[50]

Like Jaspers, Schweitzer assumed a common spiritual legacy of all people:

> The idea that the reign of peace must come one day has been given expression by a number of peoples who have attained a certain level of civilization. In Palestine it appeared for the first time in the words of the prophet Amos in the eighth century B.C. (Amos 9: 11–15) and it continues to live in the Jewish and Christian religions as the belief in the Kingdom of God. It figures in the doctrine taught by the great Chinese thinkers: Confucius and Lao-tse in the sixth century B.C., Mi-tse in the fifth and Meng-tse in the fourth. The situation today is such that it must become reality in one way or another; otherwise mankind will perish.[51]

For Schweitzer this truth went hand in hand with the certainty that 'the human spirit is capable of creating in our time a new mentality, an ethical mentality, inspired by this certainty'.[52] He postulated this truth in the hope that the testimony 'may help to prevent its rejection as an admirable sentiment but a practical impossibility'.[53] He added: 'Many a truth has lain unnoticed for a long time, ignored simply because no one perceived its potential for becoming reality.'[54]

6.4 Two cases

The cases of the Peking mission and the Bandung Conference illustrate the interplay between political leadership and humanitarian spirit. They

[48] *Ibid.* [49] *Ibid.* [50] *Ibid.* [51] *Ibid.*
[52] *Ibid.* [53] *Ibid.* [54] *Ibid.*

marked a decisive point in Hammarskjöld's approach towards ethics and 'international service'.

6.4.1 *Hammarskjöld's Peking mission*

Hammarskjöld's approach was marked by practical experience and reflective thinking. His diplomatic experiences were important sources for reflection. This was also the case in the context of his diplomatic visit to Peking. In the course of this mission, Hammarskjöld pleaded not only for the release of the American flyers; he also promoted the goals and methods of the United Nations and practised the 'politics of hope'. His talks with Zhou Enlai in January 1955 marked the start of a mutual relationship, based on responsible leadership for the common cause of peace. In April 1955 at Bandung, Zhou Enlai contributed to the success of the Bandung Conference. Later, on 1 August 1955, this initiative was followed by the release of the American flyers, which supported the United Nations' policy and aims. Through this common endeavour by Hammarskjöld and Zhou Enlai, the United Nations developed new working methods. The encounter also refined Hammarskjöld's model of ethical leadership, through increased understanding, successful action and cooperation.

Hammarskjöld's intervention was triggered by a dispute between the United States and communist China. In November 1954, the Chinese sentenced eleven American pilots to long prison terms for crimes of espionage. The pilots had been shot down during the Korean War. They were imprisoned in China, together with other American flyers. The pilots had been working under UN mandate at the time of their capture. This turned the action into a matter of international peace and security. Secretary of State Dulles' strategy of 'brinkmanship' put the Far East on the verge of serious war. Relations between the United States and communist China were extremely hostile.

On 10 December 1954, the United Nations General Assembly passed Resolution 906 (IX). The resolution condemned the detention and imprisonment of the eleven American airmen as a violation of the Korean Armistice Agreement. The Assembly requested the Secretary-General to work for their release and make 'continuing and unremitting efforts to this end by the means most appropriate to his judgment'.[55] Hammarskjöld was

[55] See GA Res. 906 (IX) of 10 December 1954, adopted at its 509th Plenary Meeting, and Interim Report of the Secretary-General on the implementation of resolution 906 (IX), 30 December 1954, UN Doc. A/2891.

concerned about the US approach, which favoured condemnation over negotiation.[56] He fought for the inclusion of a passage in the second part of the resolution which gave him flexibility and a legal base for negotiation. The UN had been involved in the conflict against China during the Korean War and had directed sanctions. Moreover, the People's Republic was not represented in the UN, while the Chiang Kai-Shek regime at Formosa held China's seat in the Security Council.

Hammarskjöld expected that China would not welcome a UN delegation. But on the day on which the resolution was passed, he decided to ask Zhou Enlai, Prime Minister of the State Council and Minister of Foreign Affairs of the People's Republic of China, whether he could come to visit him in Peking. Hammarskjöld felt that his personal diplomatic activity was required in order to bridge the gap in communications between the United States and China.[57]

Hammarskjöld undertook this visit for several reasons. One of his purposes was to serve as mediator, i.e. to try to get the Chinese side to accept certain positions advocated in the General Assembly resolution. A second purpose was to serve as a neutral channel of communication, i.e. as a soundboard through which the conflicting parties could exchange and understand their mutual views and motives. A third consideration was Hammarskjöld's fear that the situation in the Far East might escalate into a greater threat to international peace. Hammarskjöld wanted to know and understand the leaders of one of the major parties in the area, in order to enable the United Nations to play an active settlement role in any future conflict in the region.[58] Hammarskjöld decided to visit China in his independent authority as Secretary-General of the United Nations, based on the General Assembly resolution and the principles of the UN Charter.

Hammarskjöld viewed the Charter as a procedural and normative framework within which the members and Secretary-General could create new 'working methods' for promoting the goals of the organisation. Each means of action had to be fitted to the particular circumstances of the situation that it was trying to influence.[59] Hammarskjöld defended the position that the Secretary-General does not represent the specific interests of any one nation or a coalition of states (e.g. a majority in decision-making by a UN body), but the interests of the organisation as a whole. In

[56] Urquhart, *supra* note 1, at 98.

[57] M.W. Zacher, *Dag Hammarskjöld's United Nations* (1970), 58–62.

[58] *Ibid.*, at 60. [59] *Ibid.*, at 39.

his view, he derived his responsibilities from the general purposes set out in the Charter, which are applicable to members and non-members of the United Nations alike. This understanding, i.e. the assertion of the independent position and right of intervention by the Secretary-General, later became known as the 'Peking formula'.[60]

It has its origin in the talks with Zhou Enlai. On 30 December 1954, soon after he received the invitation to visit Peking, Hammarskjöld set off on his trip to Asia. From 5 to 11 January 1955, he conducted intensive negotiations with Zhou Enlai. Their mutual respect and understanding were important factors in their interaction. Both Zhou Enlai and Hammarskjöld were intellectuals as well as highly professional diplomats.[61] Together with their advisors, they held four talks.

Hammarskjöld started the conversation with a detailed presentation of his position, i.e. the claim that the airmen acted under United Nations command in Korea and should therefore be released. Zhou Enlai replied in a detailed statement why he thought the airmen were spies. A second round of discussions focused on complaints by Zhou Enlai against the United States and its allies in Asia, including their motives and aggressive conduct against the People's Republic of China. Hammarskjöld noted that he had encountered similar claims from the West in relation to the motives of the People's Republic. He expressed the hope that this mission might be able to break the mutual distrust and hostility between China and the United States and improve relations.[62] A quote from Hammarskjöld's own records illustrates how he dealt with the differences in opinion and how he managed to find common ground and purpose:

> When the Secretary-General of the United Nations has engaged himself and his office, with all the weight it carries in world opinion, for the fate of the prisoners – and although I refer primarily to the eleven plus four, I have also the others in mind – it does not mean that I appeal to you or that I ask you for their release. It means that – inspired also by my faith in your wisdom and in your wish to promote peace – I have considered it my duty as forcefully as I can, and with deep conviction, to draw your attention to the vital importance of their fate to the cause of peace … [T] heir fate may well decide the direction in which we all will be moving in the near future – towards peace or away from peace … This case is one of those which history sudden lifts up to key significance – as is evidenced by the sheer fact that, against all odds, it has brought me around the world in order to put before you, in great frankness and trusting that we see eye

[60] See Urquhart, *supra* note 1, at 105. [61] *Ibid.*
[62] See Zacher, *supra* note 57, at 58–62.

> to eye on the desperate need to avoid adding to existing frictions, my deep concern both as Secretary-General and as a man.[63]

On 8 January, during the longest of their meetings, Hammarskjöld responded to the fears and resentments that Zhou Enlai had expressed the day before, in particular resentments concerning American 'imperialism'. Chinese positions, in turn, were regarded with suspicion by other countries, who feared that communist ideology might be a driving force for revolution or world domination by China. At this breaking point, Hammarskjöld said:

> we have run into what I would call a tragedy of errors, in a most serious form reflecting the situation in that little Peking opera which we saw yesterday night, where two men were fighting each other in the dark, each of them believing that he had been threatened by the other man.[64]

Hammarskjöld was convinced that someone had to take the first step, in order to improve relations and prepare the ground for a solution to some of the major problems. For him, the main question was what could be done to improve international relations beyond ideological divides.[65]

Hammarskjöld responded with sympathy to two claims made by Zhou Enlai, namely (1) the argument that communist China had wrongly been denied admission to the United Nations, and (2) criticism by China that the United States had unduly refused to allow Chinese students to return to the People's Republic of China. Hammarskjöld agreed to take up the topic of student visas in talks with US government officials.[66] Zhou Enlai remained reluctant to accept Hammarskjöld's position regarding the detention of the prisoners. But at the end of the talks, he agreed to comply with two of the Secretary-General's requests. He agreed that the People's Republic of China would comply with the policy terms regarding treatment of foreign prisoners, announced at Geneva, which implied lenient sentences. He also proposed to supply information to the prisoner's families regarding their health. By conceding that the families of the prisoners could come to visit them in China, he went even beyond Hammarskjöld's request.[67]

A joint communiqué concluded:

> In these talks reference was made at the same time to questions pertinent to the relaxation of world tension. We feel that these talks have been

[63] See Urquhart, *supra* note 1, at 106. All quotes from the Hammarskjöld/Zhou Enlai talks are taken by Urquhart from Hammarskjöld's own records.

[64] *Ibid.*, at 109, 110. [65] *Ibid.*, at 110.

[66] See Zacher, *supra* note 57, at 58–62. [67] *Ibid.*

> useful and we hope to be able to continue the contact established in these meetings.[68]

Hammarskjöld issued a brief explanatory statement designed, as he later told Lester Pearson, Canadian Minister of Foreign Affairs, 'to ward off desperate reaction when unrealistic expectations are not fulfilled'.[69] At the airport he said:

> My visit to Peking was a first stage in my efforts to achieve the release of the eleven fliers and other UN Command personnel still detained. I feel that my talks with Mr. Chou En-Lai were definitely useful for this purpose. We hope to be able to continue this contact. The door that has been opened can be kept open, given restraints on all sides.[70]

After his return, a brief communiqué confirmed that the talks had proceeded smoothly, that contact had been established, and that Hammarskjöld perceived the talks in Peking as the beginning of a new era.

On 1 August 1955, the Associated Press in Tokyo announced that Peking had released the American flyers. Hammarskjöld was in Sweden, where he was privately celebrating his fiftieth birthday, when he received the news by post. On the next day, 8 August, he was in Geneva for the opening of the First International Conference on the Peaceful Uses of Atomic Energy. He read out a cable from the Swedish Ambassador informing him that the Chinese government had decided

> to release the imprisoned flyers; with regard to maintaining friendship with Hammarskjöld and no connection with the UN resolution; with the express hope of the Chinese government to continue the contact established with Hammarskjöld; and with Chou En-Lai's congratulations to Hammarskjöld on his 50th birthday.[71]

Urquhart notes that the successful Peking experience stimulated in Hammarskjöld 'a new taste and new ideas for using his office and his position to tackle difficult problems'.[72] The release of the American flyers was a triumph for his diplomatic style. From this time on, the Secretary-General was seen as a major resource of the international community for dealing with difficult problems. The Peking mission opened the door for new forms of diplomacy and conflict resolution in line with the Charter. The Secretary-General was seen as organ competent to handle some of the great issues of the time.[73]

[68] See Urquhart, *supra* note 1, at 112. [69] *Ibid.*, 113.
[70] *Ibid.* [71] *Ibid.*, at 125–126. [72] *Ibid.*, at 131. [73] *Ibid.*, at 127.

6.4.2 *The Bandung Conference, 1955*

Hammarskjöld was not the only one impressed by Zhou Enlai's personality and diplomatic skills. In April 1955, Zhou Enlai attended the Bandung Conference of Asian and African nations, a historically unique meeting of leaders of formerly colonised peoples. Ali Sastroamidjojo, Prime Minister of Indonesia, had conceived the idea of a conference of leaders of the newly independent Asian and African nations while he was Indonesian ambassador at the UN and in Washington from 1950 to 1953. The conference became a key element of his government's foreign policy.[74] The conference took place from 18–25 April 1955, at Bandung in Indonesia. It was sponsored by Indonesia, Burma, Ceylon, India and Pakistan. It was driven by the incentive to reduce the threats of the Cold War era and to end colonial rule. It was further meant to improve relations between China and the West, i.e. (1) to put an end to the isolation, demonisation and non-recognition of the government of the People's Republic of China by the United States and its allies, and (2) to restore its place as representative of China in the Security Council.

The Conference was overshadowed by the traces of the Taiwan Strait crisis and the presence of the American Seventh Fleet in the Strait of Taiwan. The fleet was deployed as a result of the struggle between the People's Republic of China and the Republic of China (Taiwan) over the strategic islands Quemoy and Matsu. It was regarded as a provocation. In the United States, a strong lobby favoured confrontation with communist China. Admiral Radford, Chairman of the Joint Chiefs of Staff, supported an attack against the mainland and fight for the Tachen islands. Republican Senator Knowland preferred a blockade of the coast. Secretary of State Dulles threatened to use nuclear weapons if Peking were to attack Quemoy.[75] He rejected the idea of the Bandung Conference, arguing that no country should be non-aligned. Eisenhower defended a more moderate position. On 18 April, he issued a statement in which he recalled the 'grave implications of the Chinese Communist build-up against Taiwan'. But he expressed 'the President's hope that the Bandung Conference would seek agreement to a general renunciation of force with respect to the realization of national claims and objectives'.[76]

[74] J. Mackie, *Bandung 1955, Non-Alignment and Afro-Asian Solidarity* (2005), 58.

[75] T. Hoopes, *The Devil and John Foster Dulles* (1973), 283.

[76] *Ibid.*, at 282.

The Asian-African delegates of the conference were keen to avoid a war off the China coast. They sought to convince the People's Republic of China to renounce on the use of force in relation to Taiwan. There was considerable support for a proposal by the Prime Minister of Ceylon, Sir John Kotelawala,[77] which called for an immediate ceasefire in the Straits and a five-year international trusteeship for Taiwan, to be followed by a plebiscite. But offering self-determination to Taiwan was a non-issue for both Chiang Kai-Shek and Mao Tse Tung. Zhou Enlai responded quietly, but forcefully. He supported a 'relaxation of tensions' in line with Asian-African views, while rejecting multilateral negotiation over Taiwan or a formal ceasefire. He stressed that the People's Republic of China did not want to go to war with the United States and that the government was willing to settle international disputes by peaceful means. He rejected a ceasefire on the ground that there was no war between China and the United States. He also expressed the willingness of the Chinese government to enter into negotiations with the United States to discuss the question of relaxing tensions in the Far East, especially in the Taiwan area. The US government first rejected this offer, but then sent a more considered and positive response on 26 April.[78]

At Bandung, Zhou Enlai declared that China had come to the conference to 'seek unity and not to quarrel, to seek common ground and not to create divergences'.[79] He argued that this should be the goal of the conference. He noted:

> The conference should seek common ground among us, while keeping our differences. None of us is asked to give up his own views, because differences in viewpoints are an objective reality.[80]

The Conference brought further progress, also in another regard. It led to the signing of an agreement on Dual Nationality between China and Indonesia. The agreement marked the first occasion on which the Chinese government allowed Chinese living in Southeast Asian countries to opt for the nationality of that country, if they wished.[81]

The Conference ended with a final communiqué, with included a ten-point statement. In that statement, participating nations declared their intention to settle their conflicts with peaceful means in adherence to the principles of the UN Charter, to respect human rights and the principles of the United Nations, and to abstain from the use of arrangements

[77] *Ibid.*, at 282–283. [78] *Ibid.* [79] Mackie, *supra* note 74, at 83.
[80] *Ibid.*, at 85. [81] *Ibid.*

of collective defence to serve the particular interests of any of the major powers.

The Bandung Conference thereby helped avert threats of a potential nuclear war in the mid 1950s. Zhou Enlai received wide recognition for his skilful diplomacy and pragmatic negotiations. Until the Geneva and Bandung Conferences, he had not been well known outside China. Through his personal approach and diplomacy, the image of the People's Republic of China changed in the eyes of other Asian and African leaders, enabling China to develop new diplomatic initiatives later in the 1950s.[82] The Bandung Conference also mitigated the differences between the aligned and non-aligned camps in the UN.

6.4.3 *Hammarskjöld comments*

Hammarskjöld took additional steps to mitigate risks of a nuclear crisis in the Cold War. Inspired by President Eisenhower's 'Atoms for Peace' speech, given in the autumn of 1953, he gave full UN support to two initiatives: the establishment of an International Agency for Atomic Energy, and the organisation of the International Conference on the Peaceful Use of Atomic Energy. In his view, these two initiatives were extremely important, not only scientifically, but also politically. He took an active role in leading the preparations. Urquhart reports:

> The Advisory Committee started off extremely badly in full Cold War gear. Hammarskjöld, by being the chairman of this, by a really masterly display of good chairmanship of this group and intellectual grasp of the subject, completely derailed the Cold War part of it and we had after that, forever after, as long as those people remained in that committee, one of the most constructive, most collegial and hard working and efficient committees I have ever attended.[83]

The fortnight-long International Conference on the Peaceful Use of Atomic Energy took place in August 1955 in Geneva. It was the largest international conference since the Second World War. It received much publicity. According to Urquhart, the event marked a breakthrough on the nuclear front. It showed that the UN was capable of running conferences that were not strictly political or diplomatic. This was the start of a tradition of UN conferences bringing together great and small nations.

82 *Ibid.*, at 48.

83 United Nations Archives (UNA), United Nations Oral History, (02)/U79, Interview with Brian Urquhart conducted by Leon Gordenker, 15 October 1984.

Hammarskjöld communicated his reflections on the Bandung Conference during a visit to India in February 1956:

> A year ago there was a significant conference in Bandung. Some people looked upon it as a warning – or even as a threat – from the United Nations angle. I confess that I saw it never in that way, and I must say that the results of the conference, as expressed in its decisions and resolutions, with their strong emphasis on adherence to the principles of the United Nations Charter, confirmed those who felt that this was a sound and natural development which, in its final results, should strengthen the processes of international cooperation embodied in the United Nations. But the conference did indicate one thing: it indicated the need for a broadened field of international cooperation, a broadened platform for the Asian people speaking to the world.[84]

In March 1956, on his return from a business trip through a number of Asian countries, he gave a speech at the Metropolitan Museum of Art in New York, on the occasion of the opening of an Asian art exhibit. He expressed his increased appreciation for mutual cooperation and understanding between Eastern and Western countries. He also recognised that there were still barriers in the mutual understanding. He noted:

> We talk these days much about the Renaissance of Asia and the Asian peoples. We talk about a new nationalism, about the urge for independence and wider political influence for the peoples of Asia. I am afraid that in doing so we are sometimes so preoccupied with the specific problems and interests of what history calls 'the West' that we view these developments less in the light of what they contribute to the growth of all humanity than in the light of what they might detract from the predominance of Western peoples. We see what we may lose. We do not realize what we are gaining.[85]

In Hammarskjöld's view, a true interchange of ideas required far more. He added:

> It is my conviction that when Asia can speak – as Asia – to the West, and when the West learns to listen and to respond in the spirit of a new and equal relationship, mankind all over the world will profit by it. A true interchange of ideas and a fruitful collaboration requires that we accept

[84] D. Hammarskjöld, 'The United Nations its Ideology and Activities', in A. Cordier and W. Foote (eds.), *Public Papers of the Secretaries-General of the United Nations, Vol. III: Dag Hammarskjöld 1956–1957* (1973), at 672.

[85] D. Hammarskjöld, 'Remarks at the Metropolitan Museum of Art on the Occasion of the Opening of a Special Loan Exhibition, "Asian Artists in Chrystal"', in A. Cordier and W. Foote (eds.), *Public Papers of the Secretaries-General of the United Nations, Vol. III: Dag Hammarskjöld 1956–1957* (1973), at 59–61.

> what *is* – is, in its own right – without narrowing our ability to comprehend and appreciate by rigid ideas about what *should be*.[86]

Hammarskjöld did not regard this attitude as weak acquiescence or unprincipled tolerance. On the contrary, he saw it as reflecting constructive acceptance that there are many equally valid standards to measure human achievement.[87]

Taking into account the experiences of the Peking mission and the Bandung Conference, it is easier to understand Hammarskjöld's reaction to Soviet premier Khrushchev, who had requested him to resign from office. Hammarskjöld famously replied on 3 October 1960:

> It is not the Soviet Union or indeed any other Big Power which need the United Nations for their protection. It is all the others. In this sense, the Organization is first of all their Organization and I deeply believe in the wisdom with which they will be able to use it and guide it. I shall remain in my post during the term of office as a servant of the Organization in the interest of all those other nations as long as they wish me to do so.[88]

6.5 Refining the international service model

Hammarskjöld's interaction with Zhou Enlai marked the opening of a new 'politics of hope' in East–West relations. He undertook these travels at a time when the People's Republic of China was excluded from membership of the UN. Hammarskjöld established a new way of communication and reciprocal understanding. In Zhou Enlai, he met an equally minded interlocutor with diplomatic courtesy and intellect. They acknowledged their differences of opinion, as well as their responsibilities. Both of them were willing to overcome these differences. The meeting with Zhou Enlai made a deep impression on Hammarskjöld. This is apparent from his letter to Uno Willers, Swedish National Librarian and Secretary of the Swedish Academy:

> The mission was not only unique in diplomatic history but also unique as a human experience. What is so appalling is the basic lack of realism as to the assumptions on which very much of Western policy is built. And now I am thinking not only of the situation in China, but of China's role in Asia and of the position of the present regime in Peking. It is a little bit humiliating when I have to say that Chou En-Lai appears to me as the most superior brain I have met so far in the field of foreign policy. Of course,

[86] *Ibid.* [87] *Ibid.*

[88] A. Cordier and W. Foote (eds.), *Public Papers of the Secretaries-General of the United Nations, Vol. V: Dag Hammarskjöld, 1960–1961* (1975), at 200–201.

> that does in no way mean that I have found a wider area of agreement than I anticipated, but it does mean that policy making without taking into account his personal qualities is likely to lead to disaster. As I said to one of the Americans: Chou is so much more dangerous than you imagine because he is so much better a man than you have ever admitted.[89]

Hammarskjöld's vision of international service was not only influenced by diplomatic experiences, but also by other creative and cultural aspects of his personality. The negotiations with Zhou Enlai over the release of US flyers coincided with important other events in his life. In 1953, his father, Hjalmar Hammarskjöld, who had served as Prime Minister of Sweden from 1914 to 1917, died. In December 1954, Hammarskjöld was elected to the Swedish Academy[90] to fill the seat left vacant by his father. This was the first case in which a son succeeded his father in the Academy. One of the traditions of the Academy is that a new member gives an address on the life and work of his predecessor, in the presence of the royal family and government. On this occasion, Hammarskjöld's made a point which captures not only his father's worldview, but also his own standpoint. He said:

> In the classical spirit, he [Hjalmar Hammarskjöld] felt that the scholar, the orator and the legislator stood shoulder to shoulder with the poet and the narrator in their responsibility for the language as the voice of the spirit.[91]

Dag Hammarskjöld took this responsibility for 'the language as the voice of the spirit' very seriously. He regularly organised cultural meetings with well-known modern writers and artists in his apartment in New York. His spiritual diary contains references to works of world literature. The inner dialogues and haikus in his diary represent Hammarskjöld as a poet and philosopher.[92]

During his tenure as Secretary-General, Hammarskjöld managed to find spare time for studying. He translated works of literature into Swedish. Among the writers he translated are Djuna Barnes, Eugene O'Neill and Alexis Leger (Saint-John Perse). During what appeared to be his final mission to Africa, he began translating the work *Ich und Du* from

89 Urquhart, *supra* note 1, at 117.

90 The Swedish Academy, founded in 1786 by King Gustav III, aims to preserve and enrich the Swedish language and literature. With eighteen members elected for life, its most widely known responsibility is awarding the annual Nobel Prize for Literature.

91 D. Hammarskjöld, 'Hjalmar Hammarkjöld', in W. Foote (ed.), *The Servant of Peace: A Selection of the Speeches and Statements of Dag Hammarskjöld, Secretary-General of the United Nations 1953–1961* (1962), at 77.

92 Originally written in Swedish, after Hammarskjöld's death, the British poet W.H. Auden, working together with Leif Sjöberg, produced an English translation of *Markings*.

Jewish philosopher Martin Buber. He had long admired Buber's work. They met each other, once in New York in 1958 and twice in Jerusalem in 1959.

In 1959, Hammarskjöld nominated Buber as a candidate for the Nobel Prize for Literature. In his presentation, Hammarskjöld called him a spokesman for 'humanistic internationalism' with a 'unique position in modern Jewish thought based fundamentally on Jewish religious thinking'.[93] In his view, Buber represented neither a 'rational materialism' typical of Ben Gurion, nor a 'formalistic orthodoxy and religious intolerance'.[94] He had developed a 'personal mystique' under the influence of Chassidism and the medieval mystics. Hammarskjöld argued that Buber had 'revitalized essential features of Israel's prophetic legacy ... while Ben Gurion and his predecessor continued the legacy of a strident nationalism as a feature of historical Israel'.[95] Buber's humanistic internationalism promoted Israeli–Arab friendship on the grounds of their common historical legacy and as an expression of an essential feature in Jewish and Muslim thinking.[96]

Hammarskjöld applied this creativity and 'humanistic internationalism' in the context of the Peking mission. His meeting with Zhou Enlai gave him the chance to study the Chinese perspective on life. Because of their direct contact, he could experience the 'other side', i.e. approach the encounter 'from the side of the person one meets as well as from one's own side' and perceive 'the other person in the actuality of his being, while being oneself (Buber)'.[97] This approach guided Hammarskjöld's way of interaction and international service. In meeting the other, he opened not only diplomatic doors, but also inner doors.

Hammarskjöld's inner dialogues, i.e. the thinking, judgement and will that shaped his moral character, can be found in *Markings*. He explains this in a letter which was found together with the manuscript of his notes in his New York apartment after his death.[98] These entries provide, as he put it, 'a sort of white book concerning my negotiations with myself – and with God'. The entry written in early January 1955 resembles what he said about his mother's teachings in 'This I believe', a 1954 Canadian radio interview:[99]

[93] D. Hammarskjöld, 'Dag Hammarskjöld om Martin Buber' (1966) 39 *Judisk Tidskrift* 2, 18–21, at 18 (translated from the Swedish by Monica Bouman).

[94] *Ibid.* [95] *Ibid.* [96] *Ibid.*

[97] M. Friedman, *The Life of Dialogue* (1960), 81.

[98] Hammarskjöld, *supra* note 2, at V.

[99] D. Hammarskjöld, 'Old Creeds in a New World', in W. Foote (ed.), *The Servant of Peace: A Selection of the Speeches and Statements of Dag Hammarskjöld, Secretary-General of the United Nations 1953–1961* (1962), at 23, 24.

> From scholars and clergymen on my mother's side I inherited a belief that, in the very radical sense of the Gospels, all men were equals as children of God, and should be met and treated by us as our masters in God.

In the same interview, he also explained what he had learned from his father, Hjalmar Hammarskjöld:

> From generations of soldiers and government officials on my father's side I inherited a belief that no life was more satisfactory than one of selfless service to your country – or humanity. This service required a sacrifice of all personal interests, but likewise the courage to stand up unflinchingly for your convictions.[100]

It is clear that Hammarskjöld made these beliefs his own and that he approached Zhou Enlai with complementary visions, both as UN Secretary-General and as a human being. One entry refers most certainly to his negotiations with Zhou Enlai.

> What! *He* is now going to teach me! Why not? There is nobody from whom you cannot learn. Before God, who speaks through all men, you are always in the bottom class of nursery school.[101]

Cordier, US Chief of Staff at the time, reports that Hammarskjöld was deeply moved after a meeting with a distinguished world scientist. Hammarskjöld and the scientist discussed the intellectual and spiritual qualities required in diplomatic negotiations to achieve mediation and conciliation. The scientist said that the matter finally comes down to a short, simple word: 'love'. Hammarskjöld's thinking is reflected in an entry in *Markings*, which states: 'You can only hope to find a lasting solution to a conflict if you have learned to see the other objectively, but at the same time, to experience his difficulties subjectively.'[102] It reflects Hammarskjöld's admiration for the work of Buber.[103]

One can find this insight among a series of entries which Hammarskjöld wrote on the night of 19–20 November 1955, under the heading, 'Concerning Men and Their Way to Peace and Concord'.[104] In these reflections, Hammarskjöld goes to the core of personal ethics in diplomacy, formulating principles for dialogue and silent diplomacy. He derived

[100] *Ibid.*, at 23. [101] Hammarskjöld, *supra* note 2, at 104. [102] *Ibid.*, at 114.

[103] A. Cordier, 'Motivations and Methods of Dag Hammarskjöld', in A. Cordier and K. Maxwell (eds.), *Paths to World Order* (1967), at 3.

[104] W.H. Auden, who with Leif Sjöberg translated *Markings* into English, translated the Swedish 'vág till enighet' as 'way to peace and concord'. A translation in the same line of meaning would be 'mankind's way to unity'.

these rules of thumb from the Peking experience and his reflective thinking. They refined his model of international service:

> The truth is so simple that it is considered a pretentious banality. Yet it is continually being denied by our behaviour. Every day furnishes new examples.
>
> It is more important to be aware of the grounds for your own behaviour than to understand the motives of another.
>
> The other's 'face' is more important than your own.
>
> If while pleading another's cause, you are at the same time seeking something for yourself, you cannot hope to succeed.
>
> You can only hope to find a lasting solution to a conflict if you have learned to see the other objectively, but, at the same time, to experience his difficulties subjectively.
>
> The man who 'likes people' disposes once and for all of the man who despises them.
>
> All first-hand experience is valuable, and he who has given up looking for it will one day find that he lacks what he needs: a closed mind is a weakness, and he who approaches persons or painting or poetry without the youthful ambition to learn a new language and so gain access to someone else's perspective on life, let him beware.
>
> A successful lie is doubly a lie, an error which has to be corrected is a heavier burden than truth: only an uncompromising 'honesty' can reach the bedrock of decency which you should always expect to find, even under deep layers of evil.
>
> Diplomatic 'finesse' must never be another word for fear of being unpopular: that is to seek the appearance of influence at the cost of its reality.[105]

This attitude enabled Hammarskjöld to entertain relations with both Zhou Enlai and Eisenhower at the same time. US Senator Joseph McCarthy perceived this approach as a weakness. But it was, in fact, Hammarskjöld's strength.

A second refinement of Hammarskjöld's thinking on international service is reflected in a text 'Respect for the Word', which is based on an inner dialogue written on 1 August 1955. It was written when Hammarskjöld received word of the release of the flyers. In order to understand Hammarskjöld's entry, it is important to return to the standard of the self, articulated by Arendt. Arendt argued that:

> [a] person whose character has been trained by love will want to preserve the world as a place where acts that ultimately flow from love – acts of solidarity, acts of mutual pledging – can exist.[106]

[105] D. Hammarskjöld, *Markings* (1964), 114.

[106] H. Arendt, *The Human Condition* (1958, 1998), 243.

She related this effort of preservation to respect. She noted that '[r]espect is a kind of "friendship" without intimacy and without closeness; it is a regard for the person from the distance which the space of the world puts between us'.[107] According to Arendt, this space allows us to appreciate another person's point of view as different from our own. It allows us to be spectators – judges – and to enjoy in respectful friendship the differences among our judgments and opinions, and to reconcile differences for the sake of political life.[108]

Arendt's vision is well illustrated by Hammarskjöld's thoughts and actions. His insights are reflected in a key passage from *Markings* which addresses the role of 'respect'. It reads:

> *Respect for the word* is the first commandment in the discipline by which a man can be educated to maturity – intellectual, emotional, and moral.
>
> Respect for the word – to employ it with scrupulous care and an incorruptible heartfelt love of truth – is essential if there is to be any growth in a society or in the human race.
>
> To misuse the word is to show contempt for man. It undermines the bridges and poisons the wells. It causes man to regress down the long path of his evolution.
>
> 'But I say unto you, that every idle word that men speak ...' (Mt 12.36)[109]

These words also reiterate Hammarskjöld's commitment to the 'politics of hope' (Dauenhauer),[110] and his belief in the idea of the unity of humanity (Jaspers).[111]

6.6 Conclusion

In the 1950s, the United Nations and global leaders were in need of peaceful, just and constructive solutions to overcome the tensions of the Cold War. The principles of the Charter, as well as the diplomacy and mediation of Hammarskjöld and other responsible leaders, were of vital importance

[107] *Ibid.* [108] See Young-Bruehl, *supra* note 24, at 200–206.

[109] Hammarskjöld, *supra* note 2, at 112.

[110] Dauenhauer, *supra* note 3, at 119 ('man, in his aims as well as in his deeds, is always and essentially *en route* and finds in this acknowledgement the stimulus to unremitting cooperative effort. Actualized hope in man ascribes positive worth both to the future possibilities arising from this routedness and to the concrete relations which constitute it').

[111] Jaspers, *supra* note 38, at 228 ('Philosophy leads us along the road to the point at which love acquires its depth in real communication. Then in this love, through the success of communication, the truth that links us together will be disclosed to those who are most remote in the diversity of their historical origin').

in this process. Hammarskjöld's quiet diplomacy and application of (what would later be called) the 'Peking formula' created a breakthrough in a major international political conflict. Later, Hammarskjöld developed his concept of the spirituality, ethics and pragmatics of international service, through reflective and philosophical thinking. This approach helped him to exercise and improve his own role in ethical leadership.

Hammarskjöld's public papers and spiritual diary *Markings* provide us, his readers, with access to his thoughts. This is a basis upon which we can reconstruct his approach towards 'international service'. It continues to remain relevant until today for conflict prevention, mediation and resolution, as well as intercultural and interreligious dialogue.

His general vision of hope is expressed in this final quote, taken from his last words to his United Nations staff:

> We are not what we should be. We have not reached the full strength of our possible contribution until we have managed to develop within ourselves, and in our relations with others, the sense of belonging. We are no Vatican, we are no republic, we are not outside the world, we are very much in the world. But even within the world, there can be this kind of sense of belonging, this deeper sense of unity. I hope that we are on our road to that sense. I feel that we have moved in that direction and, to the extent that it depends upon me, I can give you one assurance: Whatever I can do for that purpose I will do.[112]

[112] D. Hammarskjöld, 'Remarks at Special Meeting, United Nations Staff, New York, New York, April 10, 1958', in A. Cordier and W. Foote (eds.), *Public Papers of the Secretaries-General of the United Nations, Vol. IV: Dag Hammarskjöld 1956–1957* (1973), at 68.

7

Dag Hammarskjöld's spirituality and the quest for negotiated peace, reconciliation and meaning

PAUL R. NELSON

7.1 Introduction

This chapter[1] deals with Dag Hammarskjöld's 'visionary realism', i.e. his faith in human solidarity and reconciliation in times of 'planetary crisis'.[2] Hammarskjöld's own understanding was inspired by an 'ecumenical' worldview. His commitment to authentic universality and human solidarity beyond national and racial barriers is inter alia reflected in his correspondence with English sculptor Henry Moore. Hammarskjöld viewed Moore's creative art as a breakthrough which represents humanity beyond lines of colour or cultural prejudice. He regarded Henry Moore's creations as symbols of the spirit that characterises the idea of the United Nations (UN). Hammarskjöld reflected on this idea in *Vägmärken* (*Markings*):

> It is an *idea* you are serving – an idea which must be victorious if a mankind worth the name is to survive.
>
> It is this idea which you must help towards victory with all your strength – not the work of human hands which just now gives you responsibility and the responsibility-creating chance to further it.[3]

Hammarskjöld commissioned Henry Moore's 'Reclining Figure: Hand' which was placed on the north side of the garden of the UN Secretariat in New York. He wrote to the artist:

Paul R. Nelson is a researcher at Uppsala University.

[1] This chapter is based in part on a PhD thesis, published as 'Courage of Faith: Dag Hammarskjöld's Way in Quest of Negotiated Peace, Reconciliation and Meaning' in 2007 (Peter Lang, Frankfurt/Main). It is reproduced here with kind permission of the publisher. All English translations of Hammarskjöld's Swedish correspondence cited are by the author. The Swedish original versions are fully reproduced in the book volume, so are the original Swedish entries in *Vägmärken* (1963).

[2] Dag Hammarskjöld's dialogue with Martin Buber uses this term in their correspondence, cf. Dag Hammarskjöld Papers, Royal Library, Stockholm (cited as *DH Papers*).

[3] D. Hammarskjöld, *Markings* (1964), 119 (cited as *Markings*).

> I have long felt that your work has stripped man of so many of the superficial covers and faces, the colours, and has revealed instead essential elements and qualities that belong to us all. The posture, the gaze, the harmonious formation are all elements of a human drama revealed in spiritual terms. That is so much at the heart of what we should be trying to do in the United Nations.[4]

The idea of '[a] human dream revealed in spiritual terms' applies also to Hammarskjöld's appreciation of the creative approach and language of reconciliation used by Jewish philosopher Martin Buber. Barely seven years after Auschwitz, Buber gave an address at Carnegie Hall in New York (1952), entitled 'Hope for this Hour' in which he addressed the dilemmas of dialogue and understanding at a time when both sides of the so-called Iron Curtain questioned their loyalty. Buber questioned whether communication and reconciliation was possible in a climate of ideological mistrust in which one side regards 'the other' as the embodiment of falsehood and itself as the embodiment of truth.[5] He was sceptical as to whether East or West could claim a monopoly regarding an authentic interpretation of reality. Having read Buber, Dag Hammarskjöld quoted him extensively in his address, entitled 'The Walls of Distrust' delivered at Cambridge University.[6] Buber rejected a 'vague idealism' and pleaded in favour of a 'more comprehending more penetrating realism, a greater realism, the realism of a greater reality!'[7] Hammarskjöld shared this commitment to faithful realism and authentic 'dialogical immediacy'.

The Dag Hammarskjöld papers in the Royal Library Stockholm contain a dialogue between Hammarskjöld and Swedish author Eyvind Johnson which reveals the significance of this normative-ethical problem:

> You may well guess that the events of the last three months have given me ample reasons to reflect on how responsibilities are carried – or not carried – by those who are called by their fellow men to lead. At least in politics I know what may justly be called the sin against the Holy Ghost: to invert the words of the High Priest and to say about oneself that it is better that the people suffer for one man than that the one man perishes. You would not believe me, but it is true of more than one of the political leaders, hailed by their peoples, that they basically act and speak guided by this perverted concept.

4 Letter to Henry Moore, 7 April 1961, *DH Papers*.
5 M. Buber, 'Hope for this Hour', in *Pointing the Way: Collected Essays* (1957), 220–229.
6 D. Hammarskjöld, 'The Walls of Distrust', address at Cambridge University, 5 June 1958. In A.W. Cordier and W. Foote (eds.), *Public Papers of the Secretaries-General of the United Nations* (Volumes II to VI; cited as *PPSG*), *PPSG* IV.
7 Buber, *supra* note 5, at 227.

> However, I am sure that digging into the time of Charles the Great you have them before you, those Over-Lords who believe that history is made for their sake. Thus, what I can tell you is only what you know already: we have not changed since the Middle Ages, in spite of the somewhat more fanciful political suits we wear and the somewhat more high-sounding phrases we use.[8]

7.2 Beyond the walls of distrust

In Hammarskjöld's personal correspondence with Eyvind Johnson in 1958, he referred to Martin Buber's advice to deal with threats resulting from mistrust and lying. Buber's insight would later become Hammarskjöld's own path through the ideological cleavages of the time:

> Buber: 'The only reply to distrust is candor … We must create the simple trust which alone makes human speech possible in a world where we have forgotten how to talk to each other … In our meeting we must affirm their being.'[9]

Based on this vision, Hammarskjöld maintained a sense of optimism, despite the threats to the future. He shared

> an irrational conviction that we shall overcome to break through the chain of causality of fear, clumsiness, self-assertion and ordinary simple folly … As a practitioner in the risky field of international politics I can only confirm how right you are: behind the development lies a sickness which infects some of the simplest but also the most vital of elements in ordinary human life in common. If it is not possible to do anything else in this post, at least in Buber's meaning, one can try to remain 'healthy'. That can mean something in the present situation – just as always – and it provides a direction in which what I try to do in my job and what you have taken as your task in a significant area seems to me to run in parallel ways.[10]

Hammarskjöld was aware of 'the threat to the future'. But he saw at the same time a way out of the impasse, based on authentic universality, integrity and negotiated peace. He noted in a candid letter to Bo Beskow:

> One of the lasting experiences from the last months and weeks is that, with our so-called rising civilization, we do in no way see a decline in the art of lying. The modern media of communication, the modern entanglement of interests all over the world, have opened a door to a paradise for

[8] Letter to Eyvind Johnson, 4 October 1958, *DH Papers*.
[9] Letter to Eyvind Johnson, 29 April 1958, *DH Papers*. [10] *Ibid*.

> those who fight with words representing mala fide assumptions, false presentations, invidious comments, outright slander – and so on. If I were Hieronymus Bosch, I could paint a beautiful triptych in the colors of Hell and in celebration of this new great Harlot.[11]

Hammarskjöld sought to overcome mistrust, suspicion and animosity through action. In this way, he attempted to break what he termed 'the chain of causality',[12] i.e. the spiral of violence and injustice.[13]

7.3 The diplomacy of reconciliation

The foundations of Hammarskjöld's diplomacy of reconciliation may be traced back to the Suez crisis. The formation of the United Nations Emergency Force (UNEF) by the UN marked a decisive turning point for negotiated peace.[14] Hammarskjöld held the view that peacekeeping forces were ultimately geared towards a diplomacy of reconciliation. This point is made clear by correspondence between Hammarskjöld and UN Press Officer George Ivan Smith.[15] In the aftermath of Suez and the emerging crisis in Lebanon, the agenda of the United Nations was shaped by the 'walls of distrust' in the Middle East. There was deep resentment in Great Britain over Hammarskjöld's action during the Suez crisis. When George Ivan Smith spoke at Oxford University in November 1957, he expected sharp criticism of the United Nations' management of the Suez matter and direct personal criticism of the Secretary-General. He decided to focus his remarks on the necessity of a diplomacy of reconciliation. The reaction by the Oxford audience was encouraging. Smith wrote to Hammarskjöld: 'The response was incredible. Controversial questions died on the questioners' lips.'[16] It thus became obvious that Hammarskjöld's diplomacy of reconciliation embraced the aims of the United Nations Charter.

In the aftermath of crises in Suez and Hungary, Hammarskjöld stood by his conviction that a diplomacy of reconciliation marked the way

[11] Letter to Bo Beskow, 16 March 1957, in Bo Beskow, Krokodilans Middag (1969), 137, Bo Beskow archive (copy on file with the author).

[12] *Vägmärken*, *supra* note 1, at 160.

[13] Letter to Bo Beskow, *supra* note 11.

[14] See for details B. Urquhart, *Hammarskjold* (1972), 176 et seq.

[15] On the relationship between Hammarskjöld and Smith, see also Dag Hammarskjöld Foundation, Occasional Paper Series, 'Beyond Diplomacy: Perspectives on Dag Hammarskjöld from the Papers of George Ivan Smith and the Ezra Pound Case' (2008) 2 *Critical Currents*.

[16] Letter to Dag Hammarskjöld, 13 November 1957, *DH Papers*.

through 'the awful labyrinth of supposedly irreconcilable conflicts and insolvable problems':[17]

> If properly used the United Nations can serve a diplomacy of reconciliation better than other instruments available to the Member States. All the varied interests and the world meet in its precincts upon the common ground of the Charter.[18]

Hammarskjöld was convinced that a diplomacy of reconciliation would bring hope and introduce a new logic that breaks the 'causality' of the spiral of violence and injustice in the region. In his view, the possibilities of peace required dialogical immediacy by faithful representatives of the people, faithful to their mission, i.e. 'a genuine dialogue, a genuine dealing with one another out of which would emerge in all clarity the fact that the common interests of the peoples were stronger still than those which kept them in opposition to one another'.[19]

Hammarskjöld gained insights and support for his diplomacy of reconciliation from Martin Buber's *Pointing the Way* (1957). Buber's essays treat 'signs, about the Single One and his responsibility, with references also to the political sphere'.[20] Hammarskjöld shared Buber's plea for the imperative of human dignity. He expressed openly how essential faithful realism is for political responsibility and ethical action:

> It is easy to turn the responsibility over to others, or perhaps, to seek explanations in some kind of laws and history. It is less easy to look for the reasons within ourselves or ... where, we all of us, carry a major responsibility. However, such a search is necessary, because finally it is only within ourselves ... that we can hope, by our own actions to make a valid contribution to a turn of the trend of events.[21]

Hammarskjöld knew that a diplomacy of reconciliation is a patience-straining process. He regarded it as 'the greatest need today'.[22] His approach had profound and decisive significance for national security. It met with scepticism by members of both Houses of Parliament in London in April 1958. His approach to negotiation, leading to UNEF, marked

[17] *PPSG II*, 285.
[18] Introduction to the Annual Report, 22 August 1957, *PPSG III*.
[19] Conversations between Dag Hammarskjöld and Martin Buber at the United Nations, October 1958, in M. Buber, *A Believing Humanism: My Testament 1902–1965*. Translated by M. Friedman (1967), 57, 58.
[20] Letter to Martin Buber, 17 August 1961, *DH Papers*.
[21] D. Hammarskjöld, 'The Walls of Distrust', *PPSG IV*, 92.
[22] D. Hammarskjöld, 'Introduction to the Twelfth Annual Report', *PPSG III*, 636.

a counter-model to the use of military intervention by powers, such as Great Britain, France and Israel. It alleviated the threat of a nuclear stalemate by the major powers and the existential mistrust that Martin Buber had predicted. Hammarskjöld sought to go beyond the walls of distrust:

> A diplomacy of reconciliation – I use the term of the Charter – practiced under the Charter, must be guided toward the goal of justice, and it is not a pious phrase. On the contrary, whatever success that can be achieved in this direction would be the greatest contribution that could be made to the reality of national security for the member states.[23]

Hammarskjöld was a pathfinder who pursued an ecumenical worldview of existence on 'the great human way'.[24] He stressed the virtues of human rights and righteousness, rather than force, and combined ethical mysticism with faithful realism in his diplomacy of reconciliation. Together with Martin Buber, Hammarskjöld knew that 'the end never sanctifies the means, but the means can certainly thwart the end'.[25]

7.4 A practice of global ethics of human rights and reconciliation

Hammarskjöld's practice faced criticism. Critics have questioned whether dilemmas of power involved the UN as an organisation in the application of double standards, and whether Hammarskjöld was a priest of moral relativity.[26]

The Congo crisis became the moment of truth for the UN and Hammarskjöld's approach. Urquhart has described the flow of events from the decision of the United Nations Security Council (July 1960) to the fatal plane crash in Ndola, Northern Rhodesia (today Zambia), on 17/18 September 1961. Hammarskjöld, who 'was in no doubt of the potential dangers of the situation', told the Security Council:

> There should not be any hesitation, because we are at a turn of the road where our attitude will be of decisive significance. I believe, not only for the future of this Organization but also for the future of Africa. And Africa may well in present circumstances mean the world.

[23] D. Hammarskjöld, 'Before both Houses of Parliament', London, April 1958, *PPSG IV*, 47–48.

[24] Buber, *supra* note 5.

[25] Dag Hammarskjöld, quoting Martin Buber's 'Pointing the Way' in a letter to Eyvind Johnson, *DH Papers*.

[26] Cf. P. Johnson, *A History of the Modern World 1917 to the 1980s* (1983), 514 et seq. and 537.

> I know these are very strong words, but I hope that this Council and the Members of the Organization know that I do not use strong words unless they are supported by strong convictions.[27]

During August and September 1960, the Congo crisis developed with hurricane velocity. Hammarskjöld evaluated the turn of events as part of the big picture of human history. This is reflected in this graphic account of events to Swedish Academy Chairman Eyvind Johnson, written from the 'eye of the hurricane' at the UN headquarters:

> Time has flown away and the endless two months are, at the same time, really as if they had never existed. They have made 'big news', but I wonder how many feel how big the story really is back of the headlines; the story of how a whole continent breaks into history and of the fight for its soul, staged by the Powers that be, through men as petty, as dishonest, as unintelligent – and as human – as any of those who were the protagonists in the French Revolution of the Soviet Revolution or the Nazi revolution. It is a fourth great turn in modern history, which has, however, got its specific, nearly apocalyptic character.[28]

He revealed the depth of the turn of events and the role of the UN and his own destiny in a dramatic rendering:

> It is a curious but perhaps logical play of destiny that the UN should be placed in the key position in this revolution. And it is an even more curious play of destiny for me to be the one forced into all those daily and hourly decisions which will determine the *sense* of the outcome – whatever the outcome.[29]

This corresponds to a 'waymark' in which Hammarskjöld indicated that he was not indifferent, but deeply engaged with the 'outcome' of the turn of events:

> *Yes* to God: yes to Destiny: yes to yourself. This reality can wound the soul, but has the power to heal her.[30]

In both instances, Hammarskjöld clarified that the Swedish *ödet* refers to 'logical play of destiny' implying invincible aim and direction, rather than blind fate defined as power of necessity predetermining events.[31]

Hammarskjöld was painfully aware of the thinly veiled attacks on his integrity and impartiality as UN Secretary-General during those

[27] Urquhart, *supra* note 14, at 406.
[28] Letter to Eyvind Johnson, 18 September 1960, *DH Papers*. [29] *Ibid.*
[30] *Markings*, *supra* note 3, at 135.
[31] *Vägmärken*, *supra* note 1, at 126; translated into 'fate' in *Markings*, *supra* note 3, at 135.

'endless two months'. Prime Minister Lumumba alleged that the Secretary-General had sided with Belgium. In Brussels, the Secretary-General was believed to be strongly biased in favour of the Congolese position. Being blamed by both sides in a conflict situation was the usual destiny which Hammarskjöld patiently endured. For him, strict reliance on the principles of the UN Charter implied that the United Nations was obliged to resolve the issue in Katanga by negotiation, rather than through force.[32]

Destiny meant for Hammarskjöld a choice of good and evil, i.e. *to create* rather than *to destroy*. This may explain his decision to remain in office. It meant that he could continue to pursue his political ethics and diplomacy of reconciliation. Hammarskjöld's inner dialectics shed some light on his motives. In a letter to author and poet Lagerkvist, he referred to

> a moral compulsion on me. No matter how tired I am, honestly, so often of this perpetual responsibility, these never ending demands for initiative, these endless conflicts – and how terrifying the perspective of five more years might seem – I had no right in these circumstances to provoke difficulties which all the governments were united to try to avoid. Even less could I respond from pure 'homesickness', no matter how strong that is in this foreign and humanly rootless environment.[33]

As the weeks and months went by, he continued to reflect on his destiny, goal and meaning:

> The other day a persistent journalist got me to formulate the primary requirement which would facilitate the process toward peace and reason. I found no better formulation than the following: he must push his awareness to the utmost limit without losing his inner quiet. He must be able to see with the eyes of others from within their personality without losing his own.[34]

Archive correspondence shows in some detail how Hammarskjöld approached power ambition (*härsklysten*) and his personal spiritual life. 'The process toward peace and reason' prevailed in his efforts, despite unrelenting moral critiques of his capacity, integrity and action. Hammarskjöld was deeply committed to the vision of the United Nations Charter as a 'universal synthesis'. For him, the realisation of this vision required patient, consistent and imaginative exploration of the possibilities for human rights, justice, righteousness and reconciliation, through negotiation, rather than unilateral use of force.

[32] Urquhart, *supra* note 14, at 407.
[33] Letter to Pär Lagerkvist, 11 October 1957, *DH Papers*.
[34] Letter to Eyvind Johnson, 31 January 1958, *DH Papers*.

7.5 Hammarskjöld's retrospection of his destiny and meaning of life

In his diary, Hammarskjöld asserts that each human being is 'a cosmos of whose riches we can only catch glimpses'.[35] He applied this to his own life and his negotiations with himself and with God. The Dag Hammarskjöld Papers in Stockholm and the Secretary-General Papers in New York illustrate Hammarskjöld's reflections, including his 'enumeration of moves and countermoves and threats and intrigues'[36] – a chess analogy which he had also used in the correspondence with his mentor, Swedish Foreign Minister Östen Undén. Hammarskjöld communicated with Undén in the spring of 1961, when the events in Congo took a tragic turn. Undén had a wealth of experience in international relations and was familiar with the challenges of *realpolitik*, due to Sweden's involvement in the League of Nations and his experience relating to the United Nations. Hammarskjöld shared his analysis and evaluation of the situation in the Congo in March 1961 with Undén, after the announcement of the tragic murder of Prime Minister Lumumba had become public. The question as to how the major powers would react to the situation occupied a central place in Hammarskjöld's mind:

> This has now developed in a problem of qualified chess, as there are clear indications that the Soviets have not managed to convince themselves of their arguments in favour of the theory that there has been here any lack of objectivity on my side. It is funny when time in this way, even among those responsible, eliminates even the last vestige of an emotional involvement in the coldly calculated tactical moves in so-called politics. I am afraid I am so much of an intellectual as to take a certain pleasure in the game when it is scaled down to these terms of an abstract problem concerning the right way to get or avoid checkmate in three moves.[37]

In late May 1961, when Hammarskjöld was on a retreat over Whitsunday/Pentecost, Soviet and American cultural representatives discussed the fate of the Secretary-General in the Crimea. The meeting preceded the Kennedy–Khrushchev talks in Vienna.[38] The discussions focused on

[35] *Markings, supra* note 3, at 148; *Vägmärken, supra* note 1, at 141.

[36] Letter to his brother Sten Hammarskjöld, 3 June 1961, *DH Papers*.

[37] Letter to Östen Undén, 18 March 1961, *DH Papers*.

[38] These consultations were revealed by the participating Alexis Johnson in a letter to Andrew Cordier in August 1961; cf. Andrew Cordier Papers on microfilm. UN Headquarters Archive, New York.

several themes. One topic was the prospect for change in the administrative organisation of the UN. Participants discussed the role and the impartiality of the Secretary-General in addition to the composition of Secretariat staff. Criticisms were expressed in relation to Hammarskjöld's stance and action, but received robust rebuttal. The meeting also addressed the role of peacekeeping. There was disagreement as to whether peacekeepers could be considered as 'police forces'. Participants further debated understandings of peace, human dignity and the rule of law, including the question to what extent these concepts are objective or subject to manipulation. The meeting revealed the tensions relating to the role of the Secretary-General and the UN among the major powers.

The seriousness of the situation is reflected in Hammarskjöld's reaction to Willy Brandt's planned visit to the UN in spring 1961. Hammarskjöld felt that it would be unwise to pursue a dialogue with Brandt in light of the situation. At that time, there were protests at the UN headquarters relating to the events in the Congo which were partly guided by efforts to make Hammarskjöld resign from office. Hammarskjöld wrote to Mayor Willy Brandt: 'I do not believe that there is any possibility to arrange a meeting without the publicity that seems unavoidable in this country around persons who have the bad luck to be in the public eye.'[39] He felt that he had become a 'symbolic target'[40] for intense verbal attack following the assassination of Patrice Lumumba.

Hammarskjöld viewed Khrushchev's 'troika' proposal as an indication that his approach and his reliance on Charter principles had gained some respect. It contained a de facto admission of the impartiality of the UN measures. It implied that Charter principles and international civil service stand above the individual interests of the East or the West. Hammarskjöld communicated to Undén that the Secretary-General's standpoint was 'an expression of a straight civil service philosophy, geared solely to the best interest of the Organization'.[41]

Undén confirmed Hammarskjöld's analysis of the situation. He acknowledged that the opposition to Hammarskjöld resulted from the fact that he had become 'a power factor in international politics' that could not be controlled by a superpower.[42] Hammarskjöld's approach to UN practice implied that action by the Secretary-General was not subject

[39] Letter to Willy Brandt, 15 March 1961, *DH Papers*. [40] *Ibid.*

[41] Letter to Östen Undén, 18 March 1961, *DH Papers*.

[42] Letter to Dag Hammarskjöld, March 1961, *DH Papers*; published in Y. Möller, *Östen Undén* (1986), 459.

to the right of veto. 'It meant that … under the leadership of an effective Secretary-General', the UN [could] 'function even in essential questions without hindrance of the lack of unity in the Security Council' and that it could act in cases where 'the Assembly was not able to procure a required majority'.[43] Hammarskjöld responded as follows:

> I guess that in the general effort, between Moscow and Washington, to 'scale down the agenda' that is to say to eliminate points which create difficulties for their relations, the Soviets have tried a bargain to the effect that they, on their side, promise to shelve for the time being the 'troika' on the understanding that the United States, on their side, agree with the Russians on an Afro-Asian Secretary-General now, so as to 'render the Organization effective again' and to get rid of 'a cause of differing opinions and continued friction' prior to substantive discussions ahead.
>
> As I said, I take for granted that the Soviets should have tried this, although I have not heard anything so far. What the Washington reaction has or will be, of course, is anybody's guess. I do not at all exclude that at least Kennedy would consider the bargain a possible one. He is not likely to give too much weight to its implications by way of an implicit endorsement of the attempt at character assassination, although it is made for obvious partisan reasons. Nor do I think he will be too afraid of the consequences of what – on its limited scale – would be a Munich-type compromise with blackmail. Were the politician in Kennedy to make him accept the bargain, the whole question would of course be resolved in substance, as it is most unlikely that the Afro-Asians would stand up, especially if flattered by the appointment.
>
> If this development were to come about, I believe that the future interest of the United Nations require that in some form, the elements of the bargain are on the General Assembly record, so that there is no misunderstanding about what the deal involves in more general terms.[44]

The correspondence between Hammarskjöld, Eyvind Johnson, Östen Undén and Bo Beskow shows that Hammarskjöld was deeply aware of the vested interests and methods of *realpolitik*.

In his response to Hammarskjöld, Undén expressed concern that Khrushchev had become so deeply engaged with the matter, that the Soviet Union would continue to push for a turnover of the Secretary-General, even if Hammarskjöld managed to obtain enough votes in the first round of voting. He noted: 'I have difficulty in conceiving that a "compromise" between the most powerful member states … should be a surprise. You will certainly be put on notice and get the chance to consider your tactics in the circumstances.'[45]

43 *Ibid.* 44 Letter to Östen Undén, 19 March 1961, *DH Papers*.

45 Letter to Dag Hammarskjöld, *supra* note 42.

Hammarskjöld chose his tactics with resolve. In the week in which cultural representatives from the Soviet Union and the United States deliberated over his destiny in the Crimea, he formulated his political ethics for his famous address at Oxford University on 30 May 1961.[46] Oscar Schachter, who was involved in the preparation of the address, indicated how carefully Hammarskjöld prepared for this occasion.[47] He presented his principles and ethics under the title 'The International Civil Servant in Law and Fact'. The document stands as a testimony of his commitment to public service, moral judgement and international law. Following the presentation, he answered questions at a press conference with direct reference to his lecture. He explained and defended his integrity and impartiality in personal terms:

> It may be true that in a very deep, human sense there is no neutral individual, because, as I said in Oxford, everyone, if he is worth anything, has to have his ideas and ideals – things which are dear to him, and so on. But what I do claim is that even a man who is in that sense not neutral can very well undertake and carry through neutral actions, because that is an act of integrity. That is to say, I would say there is no neutral man, but there is, if you have integrity, neutral action by the right kind of man. And 'neutrality' may develop, after all into a *jeu de mots*. I am not a neutral as regards the Charter, I am not neutral as regards facts. But that is not what I mean. What is meant by 'neutrality' in this kind of debate, is of course, neutrality in relations to interests; and there I do claim that there is no insurmountable difficulty for anybody with the proper kind of guiding principles in carrying through such neutrality one hundred percent.[48]

An entry in *Vägmärken* (*Markings*), dated 8 June 1961 reveals his reflections about the consequences of his approach:

Sleepless questions

In the small hours:
Have I done right?
Why did I act
Just as I did?
Over and over again

[46] See 'The International Civil Servant in Law and Fact', Lecture delivered to Congregation at Oxford University, 30 May 1961, at www.unic.ru/news_oon/Dag_Oxford_1961.pdf, published in A.W. Cordier and W. Foote (eds.), *Public Papers of the Secretaries-General of the United Nations, Vol. V: Dag Hammarskjöld, 1960–1961* (1975), 471–489.

[47] Interview by the author with Oscar Schachter, former Legal Advisor to the Secretary-General. Columbia University, New York, May 1983.

[48] Press Conference Comments arising from lecture at Oxford. From Transcript, 12 June 1961, *PPSG V*, 492.

The same steps,
The same words:
Never the answer.[49]

His final entry in *Vägmärken* (*Markings*) shows courage of faith and self-knowledge about his destiny and meaning of life:

The seasons have changed
And the light
And the weather
And the hour.
But it is the same land.
And I begin to know the map
And to get my bearings.[50]

Despite intense pressures, Dag Hammarskjöld maintained integrity and impartiality as UN Secretary-General. The negotiations with himself and with God were basic elements of his personal ethics and his action for negotiated peace and reconciliation. He applied the courage of faith in order to overcome ideology and destructive chaos in his era.

49 *Markings*, *supra* note 3, at 171.

50 *Ibid.*, at 181.

8

From the unwritten manual

Dag Hammarskjöld's political wisdom

ROGER LIPSEY

8.1 Introduction

He would have written, had he lived. While serving as Secretary-General of the United Nations, Dag Hammarskjöld occasionally let friends know how much that would matter. But what would he have written? From a man so various – a uniquely resourceful international leader, a spiritual seeker of depth and learning, an essayist, poet, translator, and naturalist – much and various could be expected. 'I dream of private writing down at Hagestad after the five years of fighting here. *Then*, if ever …',[1] he wrote to his friend, the artist Bo Beskow, in the course of his first term in office. Hagestad was the site of a farmhouse in southern Sweden acquired for him by Beskow, just a few miles inland from Backåkra, the larger seaside house purchased for him by Beskow a few years later. Sometime after that first letter, he again wrote to the artist:

> I often think of your stained glass windows and your preoccupation with the eternal problems of the space of the canvas. I hope I will still have enough of patience, humility and stillness left when one day I shall be allowed to return to a life along the same lines. Then, maybe, I should be able to say in the right way something of what should be said.[2]

But what should be said? The liveliest clue is in a letter quoted by the poet Erik Lindegren in his address of December 1962 to the Swedish Academy. The Academy had invited him to occupy the seat left vacant

Roger Lipsey, PhD, is the author of *Hammarskjöld: A Life* (2013) and 'Dag Hammarskjöld and *Markings*: A Reconsideration' (2011) 11 *Spiritus*.
In the notes, Dag Hammarskjöld is referenced as DH and the English-language edition of his private journal (see *infra* note 22) is referenced as *Markings*.

[1] B. Beskow, *Dag Hammarskjöld: Strictly Personal – a Portrait* (1969), 17.
[2] *Ibid.*, 60.

by Hammarskjöld's untimely death and, following custom, his inaugural address concerned the life and achievements of his predecessor. The letter must have forcibly struck Lindegren; it was the substance of his opening paragraph. 'The mission and formula for our generation', Hammarskjöld had written in December 1960, 'I think I know it, perhaps I even live it. But I could not formulate it in a way that would help others. Perhaps I shall be able to do so one day when I can see what I experience every day in a freer perspective'.[3] No matter where else his creative energies took him, something of this kind could be expected. He would stay close to experience; he would reach for understandings both inspiring and practical – such is the implication of his provocative phrase 'mission and formula' (Swedish: *uppgift och formel*); and his wish to write from an attitude of 'patience, humility, and stillness' implies that his strong spirituality would not be absent.

During the UN years, he gave importance to what he called white papers that captured the broad narrative and 'inside story' of major crises.[4] They were not for immediate publication, although their time might come. He wrote his own confidential account of the Beijing negotiation of 1954–5 and passed along to staff members for similar treatment his personal notes on the Suez crisis. In late correspondence he still had in mind the need to document while memories are fresh and intricacies easily recalled: '[t]he Congo crisis continues its wild course of events', he wrote to a trusted Swedish friend,

> with frightening elements of irresponsibility, intrigues, untruthfulness, and cruelty. This really is a history that soon must be written, written by a cold head and a sharp pen, as a frightening picture of our world and of our present-day humanity.[5]

It is unlikely that he saw himself in that role. He was a man of meticulous discretion, and the Congo crisis called for revelations – of irresponsibility and intrigues, of grave misconduct on the part of powerful nations, of both courage and awkwardness within the UN. He might have enriched the record on some matters but left the grand narrative to others. We

[3] E. Lindegren, *Dag Hammarskjöld*. Translated by T. Palmlund (1962), 1.

[4] With Per Lind, his personal aide in the first three years, DH discussed the need for interpretive documents of this kind. See B. Thelin, *Dag Hammarskjöld: FN-chefen och människan* (2010), 130ff.

[5] DH letter to Uno Willers, 10 February 1961, Hammarskjöld Collection, Swedish National Library.

must look elsewhere for insight into what he might have written in later years.

Hammarskjöld knew the literature of diplomacy and its wide range of voices; his exploration of mission and formula would have contributed to it. There are systematic textbooks – *Satow's Diplomatic Practice* comes to mind, now nearly a century old and fresh in its sixth edition.[6] There are personal books of advice to the young diplomat or courtier – for example, the works of Baltasar Gracián and Baldassare Castiglione.[7] There are fascinating diaries and memoirs, such as the diplomat and parliamentarian Harold Nicolson's account of Churchill and his government in the Second World War – unsystematic, observed on the fly, but enormously instructive.[8] There are case studies of all kinds, from Kissinger to analyses of specific diplomatic crises. And there is Machiavelli, in a class by himself owing to the pitiless rigor of his thought and precision of language: *The Prince* was and is a work of extraordinary intellect. Hammarskjöld once acknowledged it in a toast to the President of Italy: '[e]ven the much decried principles of Machiavelli', he said, 'can from time to time give us useful lessons because they teach us to recognise and measure our illusions, and that is a discipline we can hardly neglect in the midst of the dangers of the atomic age'.[9] *The Prince* is the kind of book Hammarskjöld might well have written, individual in voice and perspective, closely reasoned, plain-spoken but eloquent, with a wealth of attitudes and strategies tied to a definite worldview. But Hammarskjöld's thought bore little relation to Machiavelli's school for tyrants.

If the author of *The Prince* and *The Discourses* taught something of how to write, but not what to write, two masterworks had earned Hammarskjöld's unreserved respect and would almost certainly have influenced his approach. Their poetic, gnomic style suited him to perfection; their theme was his theme – human relations and our place and obligations in the scheme of things; and they were warm, not chilly. The

[6] Sir I. Roberts (ed.), *Satow's Diplomatic Practice* (2009).

[7] B. Gracián, *L'Art de la prudence*. Translated by A. de la Houssaie with a preface by J.-C. Masson (1994); B. Castiglione, *The Book of the Courtier*. Translated by Sir T. Hoby (1975).

[8] H. Nicolson, *Diaries and Letters 1939–1945*, edited by N. Nicolson (1967).

[9] A.W. Cordier and W. Foote (eds.), *Public Papers of the Secretaries-General of the United Nations, Vol. III: Dag Hammarskjöld 1956–1957* (1974), From Toast Proposed at Dinner in Honor of President Giovanni Gronchi of the Republic of Italy, New York, 12 March 1956, 64.

first is ancient: writings from the circle around Confucius on good governance, the design of life, and the character of leaders, in Ezra Pound's translation.[10] The second is contemporary: Martin Buber's *I and Thou* and his essays on dialogue.[11] Both texts, closely read and enormously valued, nourished Hammarskjöld's search for political wisdom as UN Secretary-General and breadth of being as a private individual. In 1957, when the Suez crisis was winding down, he wrote to Pound:

> [i]t may amuse you to hear that your Confucius, especially *The Unwobbling Pivot*, is one of the books to which I have most often returned during the past years when most policy-making has been of a kind somewhat different ... from the one our Chinese friends recommended.[12]

By 'our Chinese friends' he meant Confucius and his circle. Where Buber was concerned, he described *I and Thou* as 'one of the few great poems of this age', and, setting out at the end of his life to translate it into Swedish, told his publisher that 'this is really something I am very happy to do – also for the publicly unavowable reason that this translation in a certain sense is a personal declaration'.[13]

Such was the universe of ideas and sensibilities in which Hammarskjöld would have situated his future literary efforts. There were, of course, other voices, other minds for which he cared enormously: among early moderns, Blaise Pascal; among twentieth-century authors, the novelists Joseph Conrad, Hermann Hesse and Julien Gracq, the philosopher Henri Bergson, the poet Saint-John Perse; in South Asia, the battlefield conversation between Krishna and Arjuna, known as the *Bhagavad Gita*; in Swedish cultural history, many but none more admired than Carl Linnaeus, the eighteenth-century naturalist of genius whose 'freshness and precision, enthusiasm without lyricism, [and] instinctive eye for meaning and causality', as Hammarskjöld said of him, set an unforgotten standard for observation and report.[14] And behind all this lay Hammarskjöld's deep knowledge and love of the Gospels, Psalms, and

[10] E. Pound, trans. and commentary, *Confucius: The Unwobbling Pivot, The Great Digest, The Analects* (1951).

[11] M. Buber, *Ich und Du* (1958); *I and Thou*. Translated by R.G. Smith (1958). These are the editions used by DH, the former a revision of the 1923 original.

[12] M.-N. Little, *The Knight and the Troubadour: Dag Hammarskjöld and Ezra Pound* (2011), 111; text available online at www.dhf.uu.se, accessed 21 November 2012.

[13] DH letter to Georg Svensson, 12 September 1961, Hammarskjöld Collection, Swedish National Library.

[14] Cordier and Foote, *supra* note 9, The Linnaeus Tradition and Our Time (Presidential Address at the Annual Meeting of the Swedish Academy), 702.

the writings of the medieval Christian mystics. He had long since assimilated these sources. They were his culture, internal and available. They were lines of kinship assuring him of what he once called, in another connection, 'a sort of fellowship under the same stars'.[15]

The notion of political wisdom was congenial to Hammarskjöld – not as a high-flown, flattering concept but as a necessity in the life he led. He would use the phrase on occasion, and others used it about him. 'Impatience is a useful goad', he once said, 'but a very poor guide. There are times when it is political wisdom, in the best sense, to mark time'.[16] Ralph Bunche, one of his two closest Secretariat colleagues, said of him that he 'left a great legacy of high idealism wedded to great political and practical wisdom and imagination'.[17] The literary work he all but promised in the letter cited by Lindegren would have been a book of political wisdom founded on his experience and infused with his values. We shall never know what form it might have taken, but we can know a very great deal about his political wisdom. In the quite vast legacy of his public papers and correspondence, as in the compact text of his private journal, *Markings*, there is a structure.

8.2 Begin in the private world

'Our work for peace must begin within the private world of each one of us', he said in his year-end radio message in 1953:

> [t]o build for man a world without fear, *we* must be without fear. To build a world of justice, *we* must be just. And how can we fight for liberty if we are not free in our own minds? How can we ask others to sacrifice if *we* are not ready to do so? Some might consider this to be just another expression of noble principles, too far from the harsh realities of political life … I disagree.[18]

While year-end 1953 was still early days in his tenure as Secretary-General, throughout the UN years he reverted often, and powerfully, to this point

[15] Beskow, *supra* note 1, at 37.

[16] A.W. Cordier and W. Foote (eds.), *Public Papers of the Secretaries-General of the United Nations, Vol. II: Dag Hammarskjöld 1953–1956* (1972), Address at a Public Meeting Organized by the United Nations Association at the Royal Albert Hall, London, 17 December 1953, 205.

[17] R. Bunche, 'The UN Operation in the Congo' (1964), in C.P. Henry (ed.), *Ralph J. Bunche: Selected Speeches and Writings* (1995), 204.

[18] Cordier and Foote, *supra* note 16, From New Year's Message as Broadcast over United Nations Radio, New York, 31 December 1953, 209.

of view. He was acutely aware, of course, of systems for international cooperation, of national sovereignties, non-governmental organisations, and customary patterns of diplomacy, many of them enshrined in the UN Charter and related policy. He worked within systems constantly, and he and his colleagues built complex systems such as peacekeeping operations. But the primal fact remained for him what he called 'the moral sovereignty of the responsible individual'[19] – primal in the sense that in his experience all else, for good or ill, proceeds from the awareness and choices of individuals. He had little interest in ideologies that describe individuals in leading roles as puppets of larger economic or social forces, although as an economist in earlier years he had managed macro realities and could not be described as naïve in that regard. 'It is easy to turn the responsibility over to others', he said in 1958,

> or, perhaps, to seek explanations [for difficulties] in some kind of laws of history. It is less easy to look for the reasons within ourselves or in a field where we ... carry a major responsibility. However, such a search is necessary, because finally it is only within ourselves and in such fields that we can hope, by our own actions, to make a valid contribution.[20]

There is a corollary to his insistence on the primal role of the 'mature individual, living under the rules of his conscience':[21] fate is what we make it. This perspective is perhaps surprising in a man of religious faith who sometimes intuited, and sometimes prayed for, the participation of providential guidance in harsh circumstances. But he was not a man of lazy faith. 'Why do you seek rest? You were only created to labour.'[22] These are words transcribed into his private journal from the pages of a revered medieval Christian source, Thomas à Kempis. If there is indeed something like divine providence, in Hammarskjöld's view it has an affinity for people who don't count on it but work exhaustively to build and set things right. He didn't hesitate to express

> the conviction that perseverance and patience, joined with the calm trust in the possibility to overcome all difficulties which is proper to men who

[19] Cordier and Foote, *supra* note 16, 'International Service' – Address at Johns Hopkins University Commencement Exercises, Baltimore, Maryland, 14 June 1955, 506.

[20] A.W. Cordier and W. Foote (eds.), *Public Papers of the Secretaries-General of the United Nations, Vol. IV: Dag Hammarskjöld 1958–1960* (1974), 'The Walls of Distrust' – Address at Cambridge University, Cambridge, England, 5 June 1958, 92.

[21] Cordier and Foote, *supra* note 16, at 506.

[22] DH, *Markings*. Translated by Leif Sjöberg and W.H. Auden (1964), dated entry for 29 July 1955, 107.

> know that fate is what they make it, are the qualities most needed at the present difficult juncture in history.[23]

Perseverance, patience, calm trust – these are individual traits and, from Hammarskjöld's point of view, earned traits. The human being is a workshop, and the first and recurrent focus of work is oneself.

Those who are familiar with Hammarskjöld will recognise that we have moved into terrain midway between the public life of UN service and the private life recorded in *Markings*. The distance is not as great as many have thought: an essay could be written solely on the politics of *Markings*. For example, in his last major address he adjured that 'the international civil servant must keep himself under the strictest observation'.[24] He went on to say that:

> [one] is not requested to be a neuter in the sense that he has to have no sympathies or antipathies, that there are to be no interests which are close to him in his personal capacity or that he is to have no ideas or ideals that matter for him. However, he is requested to be fully aware of those human reactions and meticulously check himself so that they are not permitted to influence his actions.[25]

In Hammarskjöld's view, the basis for probity and good judgement in diplomatic life is strict self-observation – which he understood not as if there were some packet of sensible notions about oneself that could be acquired once and for all, but as something more like 'self-knowing' in the course of events. It is a demanding ideal; it must need practice. It is also a foundational element of the spiritual path reflected in *Markings*. Before the UN years, Hammarskjöld described it in *Markings* as 'conscious self-scrutiny': '[a] grace to pray for', he wrote, 'that our self-interest, which is inescapable, shall never cripple the capacity for conscious self-scrutiny with a sense of humor, which alone can save us'.[26] During the UN years, the pages of *Markings* record sometimes astonishing examples of self-observation, among which the most notable may be the following:

23 Cordier and Foote, *supra* note 16, Remarks at the United Nations Press Club, New York, 9 April 1954, 279.

24 A.W. Cordier and W. Foote (eds.), *Public Papers of the Secretaries-General of the United Nations, Vol. V: Dag Hammarskjöld 1960–1961* (1975), 'The International Civil Servant in Law and in Fact' – Lecture Delivered in Congregation at Oxford University, Oxford, England, 30 May 1961, 488.

25 *Ibid.*

26 *Markings*, 1950, 43 (translation slightly revised by the author); 'conscious self-scrutiny' translates Sw. *igenkännande självsyn*.

> When you are irritated by his 'pretentiousness', you betray the character of your own: it is *just as it should be* that he increases while you decrease. Choose your opponents. To the wrong ones, you cannot afford to give a thought, but you must help the right ones, help them and yourself in a contest without tension.[27]

Conscious self-scrutiny in Hammarskjöld's practice was transformative: perception led to resolve and, in light of his rich internal culture, resolve could have a large dimension – as here, where the observed correlation between his own and his adversary's pretentiousness ends in a call to himself, rooted in Christian teaching (Matthew 5:44) but refreshed and new.

Management of one's self – of the fluid, changing, thoughtful thing one is – was central to Hammarskjöld's political wisdom. To the students of Amherst College at a commencement exercise in spring 1954, he expressed this need once again. He appreciated their enthusiastic wish to enter into and master one of the great systems of society – business, finance, the professions, public life – but in his view that was half of the challenge. 'We learn in order to know', he said,

> and we wish to know in order to master, not other men, but the tools put in our hands for establishing a satisfactory life for ourselves and for all men. Too often our learning, our knowledge, and our mastery are … concentrated on techniques and we forget about man himself… When I speak of knowledge in this context I do not mean the kind of knowledge which you can gain from textbooks, but the knowledge which you can derive only from a study of yourself and your fellow men, a study inspired by genuine interest and pursued with humility. The door to an understanding of the other party, with whom you may have to deal in business, in politics, or in the international sphere, is a fuller understanding of yourself, since the other party, of course, is made fundamentally of the same stuff as you yourself.
>
> Thus, no education is complete, in a world basically united, which does not include man himself, and is not inspired by a recognition of the fact that you will not understand your enemy without understanding yourself, and that an understanding of your enemy will throw considerable light also on yourself and on your own motives.[28]

[27] *Ibid.*, 1955, 119. Is the unnamed subject here Indian Ambassador V.K. Krishna Menon? He had a history of competing with Hammarskjöld, with results ranging from harmless upstaging to actual interference. See Lipsey, *Hammarskjöld: A Life* (2013), Chapter 10.

[28] Cordier and Foote, *supra* note 16, Address at Commencement Exercises of Amherst College, Amherst, Massachusetts, 13 June 1954, 303–304.

8.2.1 *A political primer*

In his magisterial biography of Hammarskjöld, Brian Urquhart calls attention to a page from late 1955 in *Markings* that amounts to a political primer.[29] It is by no means the only passage of that character, but it is the most direct and unmistakable. '"Of human beings and their way to unity –?"', Hammarskjöld began questioningly, quoting a source still unknown to us. He continued in the compact style of an enchiridion, a handbook of good counsel of a kind familiar in the West since the teachings of Pythagoras and the biblical Proverbs were first recorded.

> The truth is so simple that it's considered a pretentious banality. Yet it is continually being denied by our behaviour. Every day furnishes examples.
>
> It is more important to be aware of the grounds for your own behaviour than to understand the motives of another.
>
> The other's 'face' is more important than your own.
>
> If, while pleading another's cause, you are at the same time seeking something for yourself, you cannot hope to succeed.
>
> You can only hope to find a lasting solution to a conflict if you have learned to see the other objectively, but, at the same time, to experience his difficulties subjectively.
>
> One who has 'a liking' for people has the upper hand over one who despises them.
>
> All first-hand experience is valuable, and he who has stopped searching will one day find – that he lacks what he needs: rigidity is a weakness, and he who approaches persons or painting or poetry without the youthful ambition to learn a new language and so gain access to someone else's perspective on life, let him beware.
>
> A successful lie is doubly a lie, an error set right is weightier than truth.
>
> Only a compromise-free 'honourableness' can reach the bedrock of decency which you should always expect to find, even under deep layers of evil.
>
> Flexibility must not mean fear of going on the offensive.
>
> The semblance of influence is sought at the cost of its reality.[30]

We could explore every element of this primer; threads reach out in many directions into Hammarskjöld's political philosophy and practice. But to respect the boundaries of an essay, we might take up just one theme, which he restated several years later with unforgettable clarity and

[29] B. Urquhart, *Hammarskjold* (1972), 32, referring to *Markings*, 1955, 114.

[30] *Markings*, 1955, 114 (translation revised by the author).

persuasiveness. See the other objectively, experience his difficulties subjectively, he writes. In 1958, a reporter from the internal Secretariat newsletter rather diffidently approached Hammarskjöld for an interview. One question so compelled Hammarskjöld's interest that he returned to it a few days later in a letter to a trusted Swedish friend.

> *Reporter:* One last question, Mr. Hammarskjöld: What, in your opinion, are the main qualities that an international official should possess?
>
> *DH:* Well, that is a difficult question to answer straight away. You should give me a little while to think about it. First off, however, I would say that a heightened awareness combined with an inner quiet are among these qualities. Also, a certain humility, which helps you to see things through the other person's eye, to reconstruct his case, without losing yourself, without being a chameleon, if you see what I mean.[31]

A few days later, Hammarskjöld revisited the question by letter with a fellow member of the Swedish Academy:

> The other day I was forced by a journalist to try to formulate my views on the main requirements of somebody who wishes to contribute to the development of peace and reason. I found no better formulation than this: 'He must push his awareness to the utmost limit without losing his inner quiet, he must be able to see with the eyes of the others from within their personality without losing his own.'[32]

The continuity is evident between Hammarskjöld's private reflections in *Markings* and his public life. Diplomacy, in his practice, is a discipline of awareness and reserved empathy – empathy that experiences the other's point of view and circumstances without losing objectivity. Following this discipline without calling attention to it, Hammarskjöld developed a remarkable understanding of political processes and shared his understanding serially, so to speak, as matters came up and new thought was needed. He never had time to set it all in order. The manual, if it was to be that, remained unwritten, but the balance of this chapter assembles a sample of the key points he cared for. It is the political wisdom of a 'patient builder'. This quietly provocative term occurred in a talk of mid 1955. 'Politics and diplomacy are no play of will and skill', he said,

> where results are independent of the character of those engaging in the game. Results are determined not by superficial ability but by the consistency of the actors in their efforts and by the validity of their ideals.

[31] *Secretariat News*, 14 February 1958, 3–4.

[32] DH letter to Eyvind Johnson, 31 January 1958, Hammarskjöld Collection, Swedish National Library.

> Contrary to what seems to be popular belief there is no intellectual activity which more ruthlessly tests the solidity of a man than politics. Apparently easy successes with the public are possible for a juggler, but lasting results are achieved only by the patient builder.[33]

8.3 Every day counts, every action

In a circle of ideas, all points tie to one another without losing distinctiveness. Hammarskjöld's political wisdom forms such a circle: one can start nearly anywhere on the circumference and advance, encountering observations and insights that imply and need the next and next – until one finds oneself again and quite naturally at the point of departure. For example, the topic of dialogue leads to discussion of negotiation, which raises the question of timing and – a Hammarskjöld favourite – the healing power of time. Those issues tie to the search for common ground, the need for patience, perseverance and realism – and the strategic uses of ambiguity. And those in turn tie to certain values often mentioned by Hammarskjöld – integrity, maturity of mind, faith, duty, courage – all of which support sustained dialogue. As we explore of necessity just a few arcs in the circle of ideas, it is worth remembering that we are not speaking of a political wisdom elaborated in sheltered circumstances.

Hammarskjöld's thought was for the most part situational and often enough fired in exceedingly difficult circumstances. 'I don't think it will surprise you', he wrote to a fellow diplomat during the Congo crisis, 'to hear that we all manage to remain in good health and in good heart, catching as they pass those bricks which can be built into the structure and dodging, if we can, those that we fail to catch'.[34] While he obviously had strong ideals, among them the values of the UN Charter, he was thoroughly practical. Rajeshwar Dayal, his trusted Indian colleague in two crises, has written that 'he frequently told me that the perfect recipe for a diplomat was great shrewdness combined with great integrity'.[35] In a freely conversational moment with a Foreign Minister who in fact caused him serious difficulty, Hammarskjöld once revealed something of his shrewdness. The report is from Christian Pineau, French Foreign Minister during the Suez crisis:

[33] Cordier and Foote, *supra* note 16, 'International Service' – Address at Johns Hopkins University Commencement Exercises, Baltimore, Maryland, 14 June 1955, 506–507.

[34] DH letter to Sir Pierson Dixon, 10 March 1961, Hammarskjöld Collection, Swedish National Library.

[35] R. Dayal, *Mission for Hammarskjöld: The Congo Crisis* (1976), 306.

> He had no illusions about the possibilities for settling the great conflicts that divide the planet, nor even the difficulties among neighbours in Asia, Africa, or Latin America. His sole objective was to avert or limit bloodshed.
>
> 'To that end,' he explained to me one day, 'I start by seizing on the problem in the name of the United Nations. Then I guard against proposing a solution too quickly. Coming from me, it would immediately be suspect and rejected. But I complicate matters as much as possible; I multiply exploratory conversations. I act like a spider tying up an insect to immobilize it before eating it. I weave my threads around the problem to the point of making it invisible or, if you prefer, incomprehensible. In the end people no longer have a clear notion of what made them adversaries and renounce fighting.'
>
> 'Alas,' he added, 'it's not always a success!'[36]

This charming account is impressionistic, but it reflects the wisdom, verve and frequent good humour with which Hammarskjöld approached challenges – and, no less, his well-developed sense of irony. He thoroughly disliked shrewdness in the absence of integrity, but Dayal's recollection need not be doubted.

8.3.1 Dialogue

'I do believe … that … dialogue is badly needed', he said in 1960, 'but dialogue requires quite a few things: objectivity, a willingness to listen, and considerable restraint. Those are all human qualities. No one of them is very remarkable, but they are all called for'.[37]

The slightly wistful tone here is not misleading: the seemingly endless Cold War, the war of words at the UN between the Western democracies and the Soviet bloc, the hypocrisy and deceptiveness even of the democracies when key interests were at stake, the threat and reality of violence in many parts of the world had convinced Hammarskjöld that dialogue had become as rare as it was urgently needed. He was not a pessimist, far from it; but on this particular point he shared his doubts – for example in a press conference of early 1960 – perhaps because by expressing doubt he could prod the worldwide audience that listened to him to think again about the need for peaceful dialogue:

[36] C. Pineau, *1956 Suez* (1976), 117 (translation by the author).

[37] Cordier and Foote, *supra* note 20, From Transcript of Press Conference, New York, 19 May 1960, 606.

> We are sadly lacking in the art of dialogue generally, within the political field and outside it. We make all sorts of attempts, and whether they will prove successful or not depends very much on the spirit. So far, I have not on that point revised my opinions in a more optimistic direction.[38]

However grave the topic, however highly placed the individual, he preferred private informal conversation to all other forms of dialogue. He said as much to David Ben-Gurion, Prime Minister of Israel, with whom he had both ferocious disagreements and an underlying sense of kinship. 'One of the most positive elements in my previous efforts to help towards bettering the situation in the Middle East', Hammarskjöld wrote to him in spring 1956,

> was the strong feeling I got that back of all problems and difficulties and – sometimes – even marked differences of views, there was between us, on a much deeper level, a meeting of minds where you understood what I was trying to do and where I could see eye to eye with you concerning your basic aims and fears. It is unavoidable that this common denominator be overshadowed by current events and worn thin by time if it is not maintained. That can be done only by personal contact. Whatever the excellence of the intermediaries, neither they nor any exchange of messages can maintain fully vital the basis on which I hope to continue my co-operation with you for peace.[39]

Readers of Hammarskjöld know his high regard for Martin Buber, whom he had gone out of his way to meet personally, first at his UN office and later in Jerusalem. Writing to the Swedish poet Erik Lindegren, he converted some elements of his first long meeting with Buber into a charge to 'poets', by which he surely meant all who care for the word. 'Things are not going so well', he wrote,

> and I think the time has come for the so-called intellectuals to make their voice heard with greater urgency. I saw the other day old Martin Buber – he really is a great man … He talked about our dehumanized existence in which language has ceased to have its normal function of communication in order to establish a living contact between human beings. I think he is basically right, and I think that is one reason why poets should add a new dimension to their task as guardians of straight human communication where respect for the word still is maintained.[40]

[38] *Ibid.*, From Transcript of Press Conference, New York, 24 March 1960, 558.

[39] DH letter to David Ben-Gurion, 26 June 1956, Hammarskjöld Collection, Swedish National Library.

[40] DH letter to Erik Lindegren, 3 May 1958, Hammarskjöld Collection, Swedish National Library.

It may sound as if we are encountering a strident, moralistic attitude in Hammarskjöld. It is true that at times he was utterly fed up. A letter to Beskow catches that mood:

> With our so-called rising civilisation, we do in no way see a decline in the art of lying. The modern media of communication, the modern entanglement of interests all over the world, have opened the door to a paradise for those who fight with words representing *mala fide* assumptions, false presentations, invidious comments, outright slander – and so on … But why be bitter?[41]

Over against this, we should recognise that he had a strikingly positive attitude towards the wars of words that not infrequently broke out in the Security Council or General Assembly. 'I feel that what very many people call negative sides', he once commented in a press conference, 'the talking, the conflicts, the flux of events, the uncertainties about outcomes and so on and so forth – are not negative sides but positive sides'.[42] For the most part he remained poised, interested and interesting as he engaged in dialogue at every level in many settings. In a letter of 1959 referring to 'the odd ways in which we men run our business',[43] he added a charming and quite poignant observation bearing on our topic. He had just returned from the Middle East. 'My last trip', he wrote,

> repeated the experience of the importance of friendly but critical common sense in keeping some of our friends away from mischief; the pathetic thing is that it should be so easy to nip some conflicts in the bud provided you manage to say the simplest things in a way that registers.[44]

Reflected here is his preference whenever possible for a light touch. As we read him on the value of a light touch in political processes, we edge towards the topic of negotiation. 'In many matters', he wrote in *Markings*,

> profound seriousness can only be expressed in words which are light-hearted, amusing, and detached; such a conversation as you may expect to hear from someone who, while deeply concerned for all things human, has nothing he is trying to gain or defend.[45]

[41] DH letter to Bo Beskow, 16 March 1957, Hammarskjöld Collection, Swedish National Library.

[42] Cordier and Foote, *supra* note 16, From Transcript of Press Conference, New York, 22 December 1955, 631.

[43] DH letter to Sir Dennis Robertson, 19 January 1959, Hammarskjöld Collection, Swedish National Library.

[44] *Ibid.* [45] *Markings*, 1955, 121.

Perhaps a year earlier, he made a closely related point in a press conference:

> A good driver makes only slight movements of the wheel in order to give direction at the critical moment … It is a question of remaining wide awake and … saying our word in the way which seems to us to be appropriate to give that touch to the wheel which helps to keep the car on the road. In any case, there is no one else to say that word, to give that touch to the wheel.[46]

Committed to clarity of awareness and moved by empathy, Hammarskjöld had mastered what he called 'the art of dialogue'.[47] He recognised it as the central skill in international life – and as more than a skill. It reflects one's sense of kinship with others and for that reason is a modest form of love. 'One who has "a liking" for people has the upper hand over one who despises them.'[48]

8.3.2 Negotiation

'How do you go about building bridges?'[49] he once asked when the topic was South Africa, still shackled by apartheid in 1960.

> The building of a firm bridge … over which you can pass without any difficulties may be a long story, but you can at least put the first stones down into the water or get a first piece of wood across the water, a little bit out into it.[50]

The remark is in character, both warm and quietly entertaining. He made a similar remark about Middle East negotiations:

> This particular job is a little bit like building an arch. I feel that I have now added a second stone to the first one, and that it is just as good as the first one. However, you know that in building an arch the construction is not stable until all the stones have been fitted in.[51]

He viewed negotiation as a stepwise process. He was not really a list maker, but we do have a list of the traits of character he regarded as essential to sound negotiation, with the implications he drew from the list.

46 Cordier and Foote, *supra* note 16, From Transcript of Background Press Conference, New York, 10 February 1954, 225.

47 See *supra* note 38. 48 See *supra* note 30.

49 Transcript of Press Conference, New York, 8 April 1960, Hammarskjöld Collection, Swedish National Library.

50 *Ibid.* 51 Urquhart, *supra* note 29, 145.

> The other day I read some observations on the perennial laws of peacemaking made by an outstanding observer of foreign affairs. He enumerated what he called the fundamentals of good negotiation – careful preparation, truthfulness, precision, patience, impassivity, and modesty. These are good qualities on all roads of life. They are essential in dealings between nations or inside nations where we have to carry responsibility for the fate of others. There is a widespread view that diplomacy is a game where it pays to be shrewd, where moral laws are somehow suspended, and where it is laudable to fool your adversary. Need I tell you that such a view is wrong? Diplomacy of this kind may yield temporary and limited successes, but it will never lay the foundation for lasting agreements or understanding. Frankly, how can anyone believe that the road to a world of justice and peace is one of deceit and the destructive use of force? In international politics the right road is to defend to the best of your ability the interests which you are called upon to represent, but always in ways that uphold the principles which you want to see realised in the world of tomorrow. The laws applicable to constructive politics are not different from the laws applying to a game based on fair play: fight for your team, but remember that your adversaries of today were your friends of yesterday and will have to be your friends of tomorrow.[52]

Hammarskjöld did not need to have the best of feelings for the person or persons across the table. In a conversation with his first (and very able) biographer, the journalist Joseph Lash, he said that he viewed negotiation

> as a process of working out a mutually satisfactory arrangement with someone I had to live with. To negotiate with someone never meant to me I had to like him or approve of him, much less that I was willing to sell out my principles.[53]

He thought it best to be forthright early in the process: 'In a negotiation, is not the very first step to make your own attitude, and the basis for your own attitude, perfectly clear?'[54] He preferred, as noted earlier, private meetings at which there was no reason to posture, no reason to seem brilliant; it was often necessary to grope awkwardly towards solutions. 'There has always been this practice of private – or quiet – diplomacy in the United Nations', he once wrote,

> and there has been a marked increase in its use … But the need for it is not sufficiently understood. The best results of negotiation between two parties cannot be achieved in international life, any more than in our

52 Cordier and Foote, *supra* note 16, From Statement Before New York Herald Tribune Youth Forum, New York, 26 March 1955, 464–465.

53 J.P. Lash, *Dag Hammarskjold: Custodian of the Brushfire Peace* (1961), 148.

54 Cordier and Foote, *supra* note 16, Transcript of Press Conference, New York, 14 January 1955, 443–444.

> private worlds, in the full glare of publicity with current public debate of all moves, unavoidable misunderstandings, inescapable freezing of position due to considerations of prestige, and the temptation to utilise public opinion as an element integrated in the negotiation itself.[55]

This may well have been a lesson learned, or at least thoroughly relearned, in the course of the Beijing negotiation of 1954–5. Hammarskjöld was quite passionate about ensuring calm and quiet around that delicate enterprise.

> The contact [with China] … does reflect an attitude of … playing fair on the basis of objective study of facts. It is obvious that it's a rather tender plant when you open talks of this type, and under a blast of strong emotional reactions which, so to say, wreck the basis laid in one respect or another – that is to say, to introduce an element of propaganda on either side – the other one would of course find it rather difficult to continue.[56]

As you will recall, that nearly came to pass. Hammarskjöld and his negotiating partner, Zhou Enlai, needed to be notably steady despite ill-timed blasts from other parties to reach what they both regarded as the proper outcome.

In Hammarskjöld's experience, negotiation is a search for common ground in which timing is immensely important. He remarked to Zhou Enlai that it is hopeless to begin negotiations with large questions; better 'to find solutions for the lesser problems first, and thus prepare the ground for solution of major issues'.[57] Later, in the context of Middle East negotiations, he aired the same thought. 'It may be quite possible', he said in a press conference,

> that there are points in this whole setup where an Israeli interest and an Arab interest, because of some development, happen to coincide because it happens to fit in with the plans on both sides. If that is so … it obviously would be nonsensical not to try to get it down and, at least, to get somewhere.[58]

The closing words reflect his realism.

At the beginning of his second term as Secretary-General, Hammarskjöld shared with a reporter some of his thinking about the search for common

[55] Cordier and Foote, *supra* note 20, 'The Element of Privacy in Peacemaking' – Address at Ohio University, Athens, Ohio, 5 February 1958, 27.

[56] Cordier and Foote, *supra* note 16, Transcript of Press Conference, New York, 14 January 1955, 448.

[57] *Ibid.*, Editors' Introduction, 439.

[58] *Ibid.*, From Transcript of Press Conference, New York, 20 April 1954, 290.

ground. 'He follows three rules for the negotiation of intractable issues', wrote the reporter:

(1) Don't let a situation get frozen.
(2) Keep trying in the areas in which there is a possibility that agreement can be reached.
(3) Don't let yourself be sidetracked by fears that the other fellow has cards up his sleeve.[59]

About this last he was vehement in a letter to Ben-Gurion:

> I cannot work on the general assumption of people trying to double-cross me even when this runs counter to their own interest. Being afraid of being fooled to that extent, I would fool myself. I could then just as well stop all efforts, thus sacrificing the chance of getting the right thing – however small – because I was always fearing to get what is of no value.[60]

The right thing, however small, was the beginning of common ground.

On timing, Hammarskjöld was richly thoughtful – and for some reason had recourse to metaphors and proverbs when talking the issue through. For example, he once said that:

> when one prepares a soup, it is sometimes part of that preparation to take the soup off the fire. That may also be the case in this special field. There are times when one furthers the purpose of negotiation by not sitting at the table all the time. If there is an interval of silence, even such an interval may result in a wider perspective, greater calm, and lesser heat, and in that way may serve the purposes of negotiation.[61]

In one of his most colourful remarks, he responded as follows to a reporter who cast doubt on the ability of the UN to achieve its goals: 'If the elephant walks and walks in the right direction, we should not be impatient. It does not move too quickly, but we shall certainly arrive at a goal.'[62]

Deeply impressed as a young man by the philosopher Henri Bergson's concept of creative evolution, Hammarskjöld had underlying confidence – more than that, he had faith – in the healing power of time and the tendency, fragile yet real, of human beings to work things out with

[59] T.J. Hamilton, 'Hammarskjold's View of His U.N. Role Today', *New York Times*, 13 April 1958.

[60] DH letter to David Ben-Gurion, 31 July 1956, Hammarskjöld Collection, Swedish National Library.

[61] Cordier and Foote, *supra* note 16, From Transcript of Press Conference, New York, 19 April 1955, 479.

[62] S. Ask and A. Mark-Jungkvist (eds.), *The Adventure of Peace: Dag Hammarskjöld and the Future of the UN* (2005), 198.

each other. Speaking as a largely undeclared Bergsonian, he once wrote that 'nothing is of greater importance for … peaceful and constructive development … than to respect the laws of natural growth, guiding and helping the necessary change without impatience for overnight results'.[63] The results of a negotiation may not satisfy all parties to it, but there too the healing power of time comes into play. 'We have to maneuver … in such a way as to give free swing to those forces which are constructive and conciliatory',[64] he once said.

> And if we can do that, we shall do well enough. Nature has a certain healing quality and ability which is likely to bring us to a state of affairs where people may still be grudging and unhappy but where they see what is irreversible.[65]

He was quite insistent on this point.

> Time, when it is used wisely by men endowed with a sense of history and imbued by a humane and tolerant faith, can be a great healer of hate, a solvent of conflict and a bridge from fear to understanding in a measure that seems today to be beyond our reach. The United Nations was created and must be sustained by such men as we move painfully, slowly, but surely toward that world community which is the destiny of civilisation.[66]

Elephants, stone arches, uncertain bridges, the long view – it can sound as if Hammarskjöld's sense of timing favoured length. In point of fact, he was pragmatic. If his own and the Secretariat's activities were necessarily, as he once put it, 'to a large extent … a slow, patient, undramatic operation based on continuing negotiations with all parties concerned',[67] he also recognised the need for rapidity. 'Basically, the Secretary-General's responsibility … is to use whatever right he may be given, and may be acknowledged to have, with the utmost flexibility and a very quick reaction, because time means so very, very much in these matters.'[68] On another occasion, he addressed the issue somewhat differently:

[63] Cordier and Foote, *supra* note 16, From Address at Commencement Exercises of University of Pennsylvania, Philadelphia, Pennsylvania, 13 February 1954, 258.
[64] Cordier and Foote, *supra* note 9, From Transcript of Remarks at UN Correspondents Luncheon, New York, 8 March 1956, 56.
[65] *Ibid.*
[66] Cordier and Foote, *supra* note 16, Address at Pilgrims Dinner, London, 18 March 1954, 272.
[67] *Ibid.*, From Address at Luncheon at the Empire Club, Toronto, Canada, 25 February 1954, 263.
[68] *Ibid.*, From Transcript of Background Press Conference, New York, 20 April 1954, 289.

> I feel that when a danger does exist, we should act on the basis of that very fact that there is a danger and not give ourselves any leeway as to false speculations that the danger is far off in time; that is to say, whatever your guesses are concerning the time of certain possible threatening developments, you should act as if things might happen tomorrow.[69]

Whether rapid or lengthy, his timing was careful; he was clear about the danger to the UN of missteps:

> The United Nations' responsibility is not only to act, but to act at the right moment and in the right way, and I hope that nobody will consider it wise for the United Nations to act irrespective of the value of action merely in order to show up with an action.[70]

While Hammarskjöld highly valued clarity – and in that spirit hoped for the development of international law far beyond its scope in his era – he recognised the need on occasion for ambiguity. The clarity of law is by far best ("The truest safeguard of sovereignty in an interdependent world is … effective international law'[71]), but meanwhile ambiguity can help. Some unknown wit in the Secretariat suggested that Hammarskjöld's motto should be '*Per ambigua ad astra*' – through ambiguity to the stars.[72] Ambiguity was a tactic. Just peace was the goal. The great example was Suez. 'In order to gain the necessary time', he told his advisory committee in that crisis, 'I accepted a certain lack of clarity'.[73] Either he or his trusted Canadian colleague Lester Pearson, with Hammarskjöld's approval, noted about Suez that '[the arrangements] are becoming almost metaphysical in their subtlety. I have no complaint about that because if, from the beginning of this operation, we had attempted to be specific, we would not have had an operation at all'.[74] He could be satisfyingly witty about this feature of negotiation. 'Much as I will try to slip around all corners', he once said,

> and avoid saying whether the cat is white or black, because it is so dark all around, I am very much afraid that someone may have a torch and discover the sad secret the very moment the cat tries to catch a rat – that is to say, to do something.[75]

[69] *Ibid.*, From Transcript of Press Conference, New York, 5 April 1955, 474.

[70] *Ibid.*, From Transcript of Press Conference, New York, 19 April 1955, 477.

[71] *Ibid.*, 'Liberty and Law in International Life' – Address at Annual Convention of the American Bar Association, Philadelphia, Pennsylvania, 22 August 1955, 592.

[72] E. Kelen, *Hammarskjöld* (1966), 83.

[73] B. Urquhart, *Ralph Bunche: An American Life* (1993), 270.

[74] Urquhart, *supra* note 29, 192. [75] *Ibid.*, 212.

It was with a sense of tragedy averted by a thin margin that he wrote retrospectively to a trusted journalist about his approach to Suez:

> In the vacuum which suddenly developed in the Suez crisis, I had, for what it was worth, to throw in everything I had to try to tide over; it was one of those irrational and extremely dangerous situations in which only something as irrational on a different level could break the spell.[76]

8.3.3 *Half-hearted measures lead nowhere*

At a gathering in 1960, Hammarskjöld said: 'In the development of an experiment of international co-operation like this one, every day counts, every action, yes, even every word counts in establishing the record on which the final outcome will be judged.'[77] One has the impression of his tautness, and the tautness of thought and act he expected of his immediate colleagues and of member-nation delegates whom he knew to have in mind the best interests of the organisation. The day-to-day situation was, of course, far from tidy; tautness could sag. He often spoke of trial and error and once at least sounded like the leader of any enterprise that relies on generosity. A reporter asked him what steps he envisaged 'to increase and improve technical assistance activities'.[78] Hammarskjöld responded, 'Well, I have to go on very much in the same way. I and all my colleagues pleading, pleading, pleading.'[79] It was funny; it was also accurate.

We have only touched on the riches of Hammarskjöld's political wisdom, but we must touch on one further point: the aphoristic power of his mind. Aphorisms – compact statements that flash a light of understanding – came to him quite naturally. *Markings* has many; they are often memorable. 'On the field where Ormuzd has challenged Ahriman to battle, he who chases away the dogs is wasting his time.'[80] Who can forget these words, once heard? They are part of the politics of *Markings*. But in his political discourse the same is true, although less obviously so because he necessarily pursued whole topics in all of their complexity. Remarkable aphorisms pass quickly by. It is so also in

[76] DH letter to Max Ascoli, 29 November 1956, Hammarskjöld Collection, Swedish National Library.

[77] Cordier and Foote, *supra* note 24, Remarks at Unveiling of Portrait of Trygvie Lie, New York, 21 November 1960, 294.

[78] Transcript of Secretary-General's Press Conference, Palais des Nations, Geneva, 9 July 1954, Hammarskjöld Collection, Swedish National Library.

[79] *Ibid.*

[80] *Markings*, 1956, 128.

his correspondence – for example to his colleague and friend Per Lind during later months of the Suez crisis: 'It is difficult ... to hear the low voice of reason or see the clear little light of decency, but, of course, both endure and both remain perfectly safe guides.'[81] Or to his Chief of Staff Andrew Cordier during negotiations in the Middle East: 'We happen to be those on the spot, and we have to play ball with both guts and prudence.'[82] In the same note he also wrote: 'Once you go head first into it, even the most impossible task may show unexpected opportunities.'[83] This vernacular eloquence was in character. To the friend of his youth, Rutger Moll, recently returned from a Parisian holiday, he confessed that 'you cannot both fight at the front line and see the battle in perspective. But a week in Paris could correct that.'[84]

In political discourse he was certainly more careful but no less capable of aphoristic brilliance. For example, speaking at an early stage of his tenure at the UN, he observed that 'no institution can become effective unless it is forced to wrestle with the problems, the conflicts, and the tribulations of real life'.[85] Obvious, one may say – but can the thought be more compactly or effectively expressed? In the same vein, with a satisfactory echo of Churchill, he once remarked that 'even with the best of men, half-hearted and timid measures will lead nowhere. The dynamic forces of history will overtake us unless we are willing to think in categories on a level with the problem'.[86] To do so requires what he often called 'maturity of mind', a theme of private importance to Hammarskjöld in *Markings* and of public importance to him, particularly where the decolonisation of Africa and Asia was concerned. 'There is a maturity of mind required of those who give up rights', he said in 1959, and continued: 'There is a maturity of mind required of those who acquire new rights. Let us hope that, to an increasing extent, the necessary spiritual qualities will be shown on all sides.'[87] Hammarskjöld's aphoristic turn of mind appeared even in press

[81] DH letter to Per Lind, 16 March 1957, Hammarskjöld Collection, Swedish National Library.

[82] DH memorandum to Andrew W. Cordier from Beirut, 21 April 1956, Hammarskjöld Collection, Swedish National Library.

[83] *Ibid.*

[84] DH letter to Rutger Moll, 10 June 1956, Hammarskjöld Collection, Swedish National Library.

[85] Cordier and Foote, *supra* note 16, Address at a Public Meeting Organized by the United Nations Association at the Royal Albert Hall, 17 December 1953, 203.

[86] Cordier and Foote, *supra* note 9, Address before the International Law Association at McGill University, Montreal, 30 May 1956, 157.

[87] Cordier and Foote, *supra* note 20, 'The Walls of Distrust' – Address at Cambridge University, Cambridge, England, 5 June 1958, 91.

conferences. On 30 June 1960, as the Belgian Congo attained independence, he didn't spare the press his foreboding. 'We must accept the risks',[88] he said. 'We can accept them as an act of faith or an act of conviction, but we should do so.'[89]

We must conclude, perhaps best on two quite different notes, the first of good-hearted irony about what we have heard Hammarskjöld call 'the odd ways in which we men run our business';[90] the second, a classic statement of perseverance. 'You will certainly hear me preach very many more sermons', he said in late 1955, 'before I have converted those I want to convert, if I ever do it. I am quite sure that if I do not convert them, events will'.[91] The dry truth of his words remains compelling. About efforts in his era towards nuclear disarmament, he summoned a timeless and still inspiring attitude: 'There have been no precedents or experiences which entitle us not to try again.'[92]

We cannot know what Hammarskjöld's witness to the 'mission and formula' of his generation would have been. Who can doubt that he set the limit too narrowly: his thought would remain evergreen, important for subsequent generations. But we can know his political wisdom over eight years and more of UN service, and we can be certain that this treasury of insight would have guided some portion of the unwritten manual. With clarity and conviction fully equal to Machiavelli's, it would have taught a different lesson: a politics of willing global interdependence that begins in the private world and issues out into the shared world is just what is needed.

[88] *Ibid.*, From Transcript of Press Conference, New York, 30 June 1960, 638.
[89] *Ibid.*
[90] Cordier and Foote, *supra* note 16, From Transcript of Press Conference, New York, 22 December 1955, 637.
[91] *Ibid.*
[92] *Ibid.*, From Transcript of Press Conference, New York, 19 May 1955, 488.

9

Hammarskjöld's dynamic approach to the UN Charter and international law

OVE BRING

9.1 Introduction

Dag Hammarskjöld had a flexible approach to international law. On the one hand, he strongly relied on the principles of the UN Charter and general international law; on the other, he used a flexible and balanced ad hoc technique, taking into account values and policy factors whenever possible, to resolve concrete problems. Hammarskjöld was inclined to express basic principles in terms of opposing tendencies, to apply a discourse of polarity or dualism, stressing for example that the observance of human rights was balanced by the concept of non-intervention or the concept of intervention by national sovereignty, and recognising that principles and precepts could not provide automatic answers in concrete cases. Rather, such norms would serve 'as criteria which had to be weighed and balanced in order to achieve a rational solution of the particular problem'.[1] Very often it worked.

Dag Hammarskjöld has gone down in history as an inspiring international personality, injecting a dose of moral leadership and personal integrity into a world of power politics. He succeeded Trygve Lie as Secretary-General in April 1953, in the midst of the Cold War; in addition to East–West rivalry, he was confronted with Third World problems and the agonising birth of the new Republic of Congo, a tumultuous crisis, during which he lost his life in the Ndola air crash of 17/18 September 1961.

Ove Bring is Professor Emeritus at Stockholm University and the Swedish National Defense College.

[1] O. Schachter, 'Dag Hammarskjöld and the Relation of Law to Politics' (1962) 65 *AJIL* 2–5. Hammarskjöld recognised that there was a tension between principles and concrete needs; by taking account of both, he sought to achieve (in his own words) 'that combination of steadfastness of purpose and flexibility of approach which alone can guarantee that the possibilities which we are exploring will have been tested to the full'. *Ibid.*

9.2 Legal 'roots', intellectual background and personal philosophy

Dag Hammarskjöld was born in 1905 in Jönköping, Sweden, the fourth son of Hjalmar Hammarskjöld, President of the Göta Court of Appeal and a member of the Swedish government. At the time of Dag's birth, his father was part of a Swedish delegation that negotiated the dissolution of the union between Sweden and Norway.

Hjalmar Hammarskjöld had studied trade law and legal history under Professor Paul Laband in Strasbourg and he later fulfilled his doctorate at Uppsala University with a thesis on contracts of affreightment (1886). He was appointed Professor of Law at Uppsala in 1891, served as a non-political Minister of Justice in 1901–2, and was appointed member of the Hague Permanent Court of Arbitration in 1904. During most of the First World War he served as Prime Minister (1914–17) and pursued a 'strict' policy of neutrality which was widely criticised for being legalistic and, at the same time, biased to the advantage of Germany through the application of the principle of 'normal trade' ('*courant normal*'). In the Prime Minister's own words, he wanted Sweden and the other Nordic countries to stand up for the law of neutrality for the benefit of European civilisation. Hammarskjöld authored a joint Nordic diplomatic note to the belligerent states to this effect (in November 1914). In 1924 he published the legal treatise *La Neutralité en general*.

Dag's elder brother Åke became in 1920 a member of the League of Nations Secretariat. From 1922 until 1936 Åke was Registrar of the Permanent Court of International Justice in The Hague. In that function he assisted the President of the Court, Judge Max Huber. When Huber was appointed arbiter in the dispute between the United Kingdom and Spain in the *Spanish Zone of Morocco Claims* in 1923, he asked Åke Hammarskjöld to function as Secretary of the arbitration commission. They cooperated smoothly and Hammarskjöld was probably involved in the different decisions that were delivered during 1924 and 1925. He published a number of articles on international law issues.[2] He was appointed judge of the Permanent Court in 1936, but died prematurely the following year. Dag always held his brother Åke in high esteem.

Dag's eldest brother, Bo Hammarskjöld (1891–1974), was appointed member of the Supreme Administrative Court of Sweden in 1934 and a

[2] Åke Hammarskjöld's writings were after his death collected in the book *Juridiction Internationale* (1938), with a foreword ('In Memoriam') by Max Huber.

District Governor in 1935. The father and his sons were groomed in a typical Swedish civil service tradition (‘*ämbetsmannatradition*’) in which the concepts of ‘duty’ and ‘responsibility’ reflected time-honoured values.

Oscar Schachter, who was a member of the UN Secretariat between 1953 and 1956, has said of Dag Hammarskjöld that ‘he had a manifest pride in his family’s legal background’ and that he ‘regarded himself as a man of law’.[3] Hammarskjöld had an academic training in both law and economics, and he would later become a professional economist. After studying Romanic languages, social philosophy and political economy at Uppsala University, he spent the autumn of 1927 at the University of Cambridge and attended the seminars of John Maynard Keynes. He majored in economics at Uppsala in 1928 and obtained a Bachelor of Law degree there in 1930. He produced a doctoral thesis in Stockholm in political economy in 1933. The thesis was entitled *Konjunkturspridningen* (*The Spread of the Business Cycle*) and led to an assistant professorship in political economy.

Two years later Hammarskjöld became an influential civil servant, first with the National Bank of Sweden, then with the Ministry of Finance, and in 1947 he was appointed to a leading function in the Ministry for Foreign Affairs. During this time, as Monica Bouman has pointed out, he founded his belief that it was just not desirable but also possible to have an impartial civil service, and he later worked hard to realise the goal of an independent international civil service as Secretary-General of the United Nations.[4] In 1947 and 1948 Hammarskjöld participated in the conferences in Paris on the Marshall Plan and on the structure of European Economic Cooperation. During these negotiations fellow diplomats discovered his technical and analytical gifts and his talent for finding compromises to complicated problems. In 1951 he joined the Swedish cabinet as (a non-political) Minister without Portfolio. He became, in effect, Deputy Foreign Minister, dealing with economic cooperation. This was his position when he, in the spring of 1953, was approached for the function of Secretary-General of the United Nations.

Hammarskjöld’s personal philosophy would play an important role during his time as Secretary-General. He had a very close relationship to

[3] See Schachter, *supra* note 1, at 1.

[4] M. Bouman, *Dag Hammarskjöld, Citizen of the World* (2005), 26. Bouman also points out that at the same time as Hammarskjöld was Under-Secretary of the Ministry of Finance his brother Bo was Secretary of State for Social Affairs. ‘It is said that together the two brothers were responsible for working out all the financial and technical details of the Swedish Welfare State.’ *Ibid.*

his mother Agnes, a religious and pious woman, and from her he inherited a simple wish to 'do good' in concrete cases. Already as a young man he was interested in medieval religious thinking. His early correspondence includes references to mystics like Meister Echart (d. 1327) and Thomas à Kempis (d. 1471). He had received Thomas à Kempis' *De imitatione Christi* from his mother in 1921 and kept the book for the rest of his life. Later he also referred to Thomas Aquinas (d. 1274), the more empiric and realist philosopher who tried to combine Christian doctrine with Aristotelian thinking, and St John of the Cross (d. 1591), who combined Christian mysticism with religious reformism and poetry. What these thinkers had in common was a focus on meditation and seclusion, a stress on the importance of a man's inner life in relation to God, in preparation for individual choices and individual action. Hammarskjöld was throughout his life attracted to this personal approach to moral decision-making. It also connected to the societal values of 'duty' and 'responsibility' conveyed by his father and the pious-moral influence exerted by his mother.[5] Thus, while the wish to 'do good' seems to be inherited from his mother, it has been said that the ideals 'duty, righteousness and self-less service' were inherited from the Swedish paternal tradition.[6]

After Hammarskjöld's death, the manuscript of a diary was found in his New York apartment. Together with it was a letter addressed to a Swedish friend and diplomat, where Hammarskjöld described the text 'as a sort of white book concerning my negotiations with myself – and with God'.[7] The diary was published in Sweden in 1963 as *Vägmärken* (*Markings*). An English translation was published in 1964 under the title of *Markings*.[8] The entries do not tell us anything about Hammarskjöld 'on the job' as Secretary-General (other than obliquely), but they tell us something about his thinking on values and personal guidelines. His religious and moral reliance on Meister Eckhart and Thomas Aquinas (in that order) was confirmed. In addition, it became clear (or was confirmed) that he had an intense relationship to world literature. He used the works of Joseph Conrad, Herman Hesse, Henrik Ibsen, Fyodor Dostoyevsky and others for personal reflection in situations where decisions needed to be taken. It was manifest from his correspondence and

[5] G. Aulén, *Dag Hammarskjöld's White Book: An Analysis of Markings* (1969), 14.

[6] *Ibid.*

[7] The letter is rendered on the introductory page in Dag Hammarskjöld, *Markings*, translated from the Swedish by L. Sjöberg and W.H. Auden (1964).

[8] *Ibid.*

diary that these and other authors played a significant role in his world of ideas since student years.[9]

Dostoyevsky's *The Brothers Karamazov* includes references to each individual's universal responsibility for other individuals, to the ideas of 'service to mankind' and 'brotherhood and inclusiveness of men', and to individual action 'for the sake of future'. The novel foreshadowed the ethics of Albert Schweitzer, and Hammarskjöld always kept a copy of it in his apartment. Hammarskjöld was much attracted to the idea of moral individual action. He also felt that Joseph Conrad's novels *Lord Jim* and *Heart of Darkness* conveyed strong moral messages; and that Herman Melville's *Moby Dick* and Henrik Ibsen's *Brand* caught the dilemmas of strong-willed individuals who frantically pursue their chosen path of life in constant uphill battles.

Hammarskjöld was not afraid of uphill battles. He saw the appointment as Secretary-General as a challenge and a chance to be of real service to the international community. At last he was in a position to put into action the ethics of Albert Schweitzer embraced by himself, the ideal of service to man. His diary entries following 7 April 1953 (the day of his election by the General Assembly upon the recommendation of the Security Council) seemed to express a certain self-confidence: 'To say Yes to life is at one and the same time to say Yes to oneself.'[10] He was ready to take on a role of leadership vis-à-vis the international community.

9.3 In the United Nations

Not long after Hammarskjöld's appointment as Secretary-General in 1953, it was already becoming clear that he had an innovative approach to the possibilities of the United Nations. He was not a formalist, he wanted to go forward and act in line with the purposes of the UN Charter. The purposes of the Charter were fixed and binding, but the working methods of the organisation must be flexible and innovative. He did not want to feel fettered by concrete provisions of the Charter that did not explicitly provide for things he wanted to do, options he wanted to test in his capacity as Secretary-General. If he felt that the purposes of the UN made it possible, he would envision a mandate

[9] See Karl E. Birnbaum (ed.), *Dag Hammarskjöld: Ungdomsårens vittnesbörd: Brev och uppteckningar 1925–1931* (2001).

[10] See Hammarskjöld, *supra* note 7, at 92. On Hammarskjöld's use of the phrase 'to say Yes', see H.P. van Dusen, *Dag Hammarskjöld: The Statesman and His Faith* (1967), 99–102.

flowing from the Charter to act in accordance with his conscience as an international civil servant.

Hammarskjöld set out his views on the role of the UN organisation and his approach to the UN Charter in the Annual Reports to the General Assembly. In this context he developed a doctrine on the independence of the international civil servant, including an active role for the Secretary-General under an expansive interpretation of Articles 97–100 of the Charter. He introduced new mechanisms for a UN presence in conflict areas, for example the appointment of Special Representatives of the Secretary General (SRSGs).

He did not make a very sharp distinction between law and politics. Nor did he look upon international law as mainly 'written law', but emphasised, in the vein of Myres McDougal, 'the whole international pattern of rules and behavior'.[11] Already before Wolfgang Friedman had published his famous book *The Changing Structure of International Law* (1964), Hammarskjöld used the distinction between the traditional 'law of coexistence' and the more dynamic 'law of cooperation'. The world, in his view, was slowly moving into the latter more advanced area, which included supranational decision-making.

During his time as Secretary-General (1953–61), Hammarskjöld set forth a number of general themes regarding the role of the UN, but he did not articulate specific doctrines on human rights, intervention or security. Nevertheless, as we shall see, he developed new methods for the functioning of the system of collective security, and he was a forerunner in the field of what today is called human security.

One of Hammarskjöld's first tasks as Secretary-General was to negotiate, in the aftermath of the Korean War, the release of American pilots taken prisoners by China. In this context, he felt the support of the wisdom of the Jewish philosopher Martin Buber as expressed in the book *Ich und Du* (1923). Buber stressed the importance of human dialogue and Hammarskjöld's visit to Beijing in January 1955 was marked by fruitful intellectual dialogue with Chinese Premier Zhou Enlai. The chemistry between the two men made the conversation sparkle. Later the same year, the US airmen were released. The release coincided with Zhou Enlai's

[11] See W. Foote (ed.), *The Servant of Peace: A Selection of Speeches and Statements of Dag Hammarskjöld* (1962), 242. The quoted words may indicate an intellectual link to the New Haven school, but at the same time as Hammarskjöld was guided by universal 'policies and goals' (including the concept of human dignity), he nevertheless gave priority to the legal elements over the political ones in the decision-making process. Cf. Schachter, *supra* note 1, at 2.

personal congratulations to the Secretary-General on his fiftieth birthday. Hammarskjöld is famous for having coined the concepts of preventive and quiet diplomacy, but in this case it was more a matter of personal diplomacy.

9.4 The introduction of peacekeeping

Hammarskjöld is best known for his innovative approach to the UN Charter. The first example here is the matter of peacekeeping, which was not, and still is not, mentioned in the Charter. Hammarskjöld elaborated the new concept during the Suez crisis of 1956. As the Security Council was blocked by a joint British and French veto, the Secretary-General had to rely on the General Assembly. As a procedural matter, he used the Uniting for Peace resolution of 1950 to summon an extra Emergency Session of the Assembly. Together with the Canadian External Affairs Minister, Lester Pearson, he thereafter introduced the option of a UN mandated military peace operation in the conflict area, with the consent of the parties to the conflict. On 7 November 1956, the General Assembly adopted a resolution which launched the first peacekeeping operation in UN history, the UN Emergency Force in the Middle East (UNEF).

Although UN observer missions had been fielded in 1948 and 1949, the deployment of armed troops to assist in the implementation of agreements reached between the UN and parties to a conflict added a new dimension to international relations. To govern these operations, Hammarskjöld laid down three principles:

(1) consent from the territorial state and other parties involved;
(2) impartiality on the UN side to secure credibility in the operation; and
(3) non-use of force by the UN side, unless in individual self-defence or collective mission defence.

Over the years it became clear that the Security Council should be the UN body to decide on all forms of UN peace operations, not only with regard to peace enforcement under Chapter VII of the Charter, but also with regard to cooperative peacekeeping. When UNEF was established, Hammarskjöld considered it a new departure. 'It is', he said, 'certainly not contrary to the Charter, but is in a certain sense outside the explicit terms of the Charter'.[12] Thus peacekeeping operations, PKOs, were not

[12] For a comprehensive survey, see www.un.org/en/peacekeeping/missions/past/unef1backgr2.html.

foreseen under either Chapter VI or VII of the Charter, but fell somewhere in between, and not surprisingly the unwritten Chapter VI½ has been suggested as their legal basis. It is submitted that this 'VI½ perception' is appropriate and useful; appropriate because PKOs are a more ambitious involvement than anything provided for in Chapter VI; and politically useful because it shows that innovations, even without textual support, can be legitimised under the system of the Charter if they fulfil the purposes of the UN organisation.

9.5 Hammarskjöld on idealism and realism

Dag Hammarskjöld was appointed Secretary-General five years after Hans Morgenthau had published his influential realist opus *Politics among Nations*. In a speech in 1956, Hammarskjöld had reason to comment on the divide between idealism and realism. Assertions that the UN had failed were often misleading, he said:

> Do we refer to the purposes of the Charter? They are expressions of universally shared ideals which cannot fail us, though we, alas, often fail them. Or do we think of the institutions of the United Nations? They are our tools. We fashioned them. We use them. It is our responsibility to remedy any flaws there may be in them.[13]

And he continued:

> This is a difficult lesson for both idealists and realists, though for different reasons. I suppose that, just as the first temptation of the realist is the illusion of cynicism, so the first temptation of the idealist is the illusion of Utopia.[14]

Hammarskjöld was an idealist in the sense that he believed in the purposes and principles of the UN Charter and in the possibilities of the UN organisation. At the same time, he was a realist in the sense that he did not want to stretch the potential capacities of the organisation too much if Member States were not ready for it. For example, he opposed the idea of a standing UN military force, because he felt it was politically premature in view of the strong feelings related to national sovereignty, and also because he felt it was impractical to have a ready-made military

[13] 'An International Administrative Service', from an address to the International Law Association at McGill University, Montreal, 30 May 1956. See Foote, *supra* note 11, at 116.

[14] *Ibid.*

unit standing by, when it was much better to tailor a unit to the specific demands of an impending situation.[15]

It goes without saying that he wanted the UN to respond to the demands of the international community, and in reflecting how that should be done he again fell back on a distinction between existing legal norms and innovative procedures. On the one hand, he could refer to the UN normative framework in a natural law oriented manner that included an implicit static element. Thus, in 1956 he stated that 'the principles of the Charter are, by far, greater than the Organisation in which they are embodied, and the aims which they are to safeguard are holier than the policies of any single nation or people'.[16]

On the other hand, he often used a dynamic and evolutionary approach to the system of the UN Charter, repeatedly arguing that although the objectives and rules of the Charter were binding, the working methods of the system could be supplemented by new procedures. As he put it in 1959:

> As is well known, such an evolution has in fact taken place, and it has ... been recognized that ... new procedures may be developed when they prove productive in practice for ... the objectives of the Charter. In this respect, the United Nations, as a living organism, has the necessary scope for a continuous adaptation of its ... [system] to the needs [of the international community].[17]

This organic approach was in line with his views on the Uniting for Peace Resolution and the establishment of UNEF. But Hammarskjöld developed it further into a dynamic conception of the UN organisation. His successor, U Thant, once remarked that Hammarskjöld was prone to use his great gift for innovation and improvisation. He 'discovered new ways to help keep the peace' – an emergency force in one situation, an observer group in another, and a UN presence in a third context.[18]

The dynamic approach of Hammarskjöld was also stressed by Ralph Bunche, who was among his close collaborators in the UN Secretariat. Bunche indicated in a speech in 1964 that Hammarskjöld consciously

[15] B. Urquhart, *Hammarskjöld* (1973), 230.

[16] Statement during the Suez Crisis, 31 October 1956. *Official Records of the Security Council*, 751st meeting. Quoted in Urquhart, *supra* note 15, at 174.

[17] See Introduction to the Annual Report of the Secretary-General on the Activities of the Organization 1958–59, 22 August 1959, in Foote, *supra* note 11, at 223.

[18] U Thant, 'Looking Ahead', Address given at Columbia University, 7 January 1964. See A.N. Cordier and W. Foote (eds.), *The Quest for Peace: The Dag Hammarskjöld Memorial Lectures* (1965), 40.

strove to make the UN a progressive force for human advancement. Wherever there was a conflict situation, actual or threatening, he believed the UN should actively seek to contain or avert it: '[B]y quiet diplomacy when the circumstances permitted, in the form of good offices if the parties themselves demonstrated an inability to deal with the situation; and, if necessary by overt United Nations action.'[19] He added that Hammarskjöld saw clearly that the UN 'must do more than hold meetings and talk and adopt resolutions'.[20] Hammarskjöld himself said at a press conference in early 1959 that the UN simply must respond to those demands which might be placed upon it. If those demands would go beyond the 'present capacity', that must not in itself be a reason to exclude action. The capacity of the UN could prove to be greater than expected. He referred to the organisation as a machine, thrusting its way through the terrain of international politics. He said: 'I do not know the exact capacity of this machine. It did take the very steep hill of Suez; it may take other and even steeper hills.'[21]

Hammarskjöld was not confronted with the issues of human security and UN intervention until the summer of 1960, but he had reason before that to comment upon some of the elements of that discourse. With regard to the protection of national sovereignty, he referred in a speech in 1953 to the classical Chinese philosopher and poet Tao-Tse-Tung, who is reported as stating that 'whoever wants to grip the world and shape it will fail, because the world is a spiritual thing that cannot be shaped'.[22] Hammarskjöld later in his speech made clear that the

> United Nations has no power to encroach upon the national sovereignty of any state against the will of its government and people. It would indeed not only be against the letter and the spirit of the Charter ... to attempt to impose its will in domestic matters. It would also be against the elementary wisdom expressed ... [by] Tao-Tse Tung.[23]

With regard to the protection of human rights, Hammarskjöld said at one point that behind the Universal Declaration of Human Rights 'we find literally thousands of people who directly or indirectly participated

[19] R.J. Bunche, 'The United Nations Operation in the Congo', in Cordier and Foote, *supra* note 18, at 121f.
[20] *Ibid.*
[21] Quotation by Lester B. Pearson, in Cordier and Foote, *supra* note 18, at 100.
[22] See Address by Secretary-General Dag Hammarskjöld at Dinner in his Honor Given by the American Association for the United Nations, New York, 14 September 1953, UN Press Release SG/336, at 2, reprinted in Foote, *supra* note 11.
[23] *Ibid.*, at 4, in Foote, *supra* note 11, at 43.

actively in its drafting'.[24] He thereby implied that the Declaration was not mainly a contribution of the West. He further stated that the Declaration could be called a 'universal expression' on the subject in a world where the memory was still fresh of some of the worst infringements of human rights ever experienced in history.

With regard to the principle of collective security, Hammarskjöld sometimes referred to the Chapter VII procedure as a necessary requirement for armed action. At the same time he was prone to relate the matter of collective peacemaking to the other objectives of the Charter. Not surprisingly, he then used a contextual approach. In his view, peace was not solid without human rights, and human rights could not be fully realised unless peace was at hand.[25]

In a similar vein, he also saw the creation of the UN as something going beyond the exclusive interests of states and governments. In 1958 he made the point that a global cooperative project – a universal body – was not a new idea. The UN organisation was a body for collective efforts established after centuries of human struggle. He said: 'It is the logical and natural development from lines of thought and aspiration going far back into all corners of the earth since a few men first began to think about the decency and dignity of other men.'[26]

The choice of emphasis on 'men' instead of 'states', and on 'dignity' instead of 'security', is perhaps telling about how Hammarskjöld regarded the objectives of the UN Charter. Collective security included human dignity. Or, as we would express it today, collective security is not only state security but also human security. The interests of the international society of states could and should not differ from the interests of mankind.

9.6 The issue of UN humanitarian intervention in peace operations, a 'responsibility to protect'

When the political situation in the Republic of Congo deteriorated in the summer of 1960, a UN peace operation was launched, ONUC. In August there were tribal massacres in the province of Kasai. Hundreds of Balubas were killed by government soldiers. Villages had been pillaged and burned

[24] 'The International Significance of the Bill of Rights', Address at Celebration of the 180th Anniversary of the Virginia Declaration of Rights 1776–1956, Williamsburg, Virginia, 14 May 1956. See Foote, *supra* note 11, at 106.

[25] Address in New York, 10 April 1957, in Foote, *supra* note 11, at 127.

[26] 'The Uses of Private Diplomacy', Address in the Houses of Parliament, London, 2 April 1958, in Foote, *supra* note 11, at 174.

and their inhabitants, including children, killed simply for the reason of their ethnicity. Hammarskjöld felt – and made clear to his associates – that the UN could not stand aside and remain passive in what he called 'a case of incipient genocide'. He indicated that the central government had to accept this responsibility of the UN.

True, the Kasai situation was a delicate one for the UN to interfere in, against the background of an unclear mandate and the non-intervention principle of Article 2(7) of the Charter. But, on the other hand, Hammarskjöld concluded in a cable to his emissary in Leopoldville: 'Prohibition against intervention in internal conflicts cannot be considered to apply to senseless slaughter of civilians or fighting arising from tribal hostilities.'[27]

After a meeting with his advisors in New York, he authorised the interposing of UN troops, using force if necessary, to stop the massacres.[28] As it happened, in the beginning of September 1960, the situation calmed down and there was no need to act upon these instructions. In reporting to the Security Council on 9 September, Hammarskjöld referred to the atrocities as international crimes. He stated:

> They involve a most flagrant violation of elementary human rights and have the characteristics of the crime of genocide since they appear to be directed towards the extermination of a specific ethnic group, the Balubas.[29]

Hammarskjöld did not at this point ask for an extended ONUC mandate to deal with the humanitarian threats. His moral gut reaction was – as is shown by the cable to Leopoldville – that it was not necessary. But diplomatic prudence would of course have it that any humanitarian crossing of the borderline between peacekeeping and peace enforcement should be mandated by the Security Council, and if there is no time for that, that Council approval should at least be registered *ex post facto*.

Hammarskjöld's position, in principle, was clear. We can assume that it was not exclusively a legal position. His moral 'do good' inclination was probably influenced by his Christian values and he was not prepared to compromise with his personal conviction. In his report to the General Assembly he made clear: 'You try to save a drowning man without prior authorization.'[30]

[27] Unpublished statement quoted by Urquhart, *supra* note 15, at 438.
[28] *Ibid.*, at 438.
[29] *Security Council Official Records*, 896th Meeting, 9 September 1960, para. 101.
[30] Statement on UN Operations in Congo before the General Assembly, 17 October 1960.

There was probably also a policy element of human rights involved. Hammarskjöld was normally not a driving force in the field of human rights. The issue was tainted with Cold War controversy and he regularly approached it with caution. In this case, however, he was prepared to use the Secretary-General's power of interpretation to protect human rights and play the card of 'incipient genocide' to increase his power of persuasion. To him, obviously, it was a matter of values and a mix of law and morality. He was not alien to the incorporation of extra-legal elements in the process of international law. Although he laid heavy emphasis on the non-intervention principle of Article 2(7) of the Charter, he nevertheless thought that the Kasai massacres were outside the scope of that provision. His personal ethics coincided with the natural law proposition that *lex scripta* had to be reconciled with a law of higher order.

Hammarskjöld's policy-related instincts, focused on a kind of 'UN responsibility to protect' perception, did not leave a significant imprint in the peacekeeping discourse during the Cold War. It is noteworthy, though, that the principle of protecting civilians during peace operations has been brought into the present millennium by the Brahimi Report (2000)[31] and through the broader concept of Responsibility to Protect (2005).[32] Hammarskjöld's instinctive approach to the matter has come to stay and is now codified in the peacekeeping doctrine of the United Nations.[33]

9.7 Concluding remarks: leadership and legal development

The future of the UN organisation lies, as always in the case of intergovernmental organisations, in the hands of Member States. Political will is essential, as is international leadership. Unfortunately, the world today suffers from a lack of both. As to political will, Hammarskjöld did not expect it to surface in multilaterally negotiated documents; he saw it develop through precedents created by a responsible international leadership. Thus, the Hammarskjöld approach to the UN and international law

[31] Report of the Panel on United Nations Peace Operations, chaired by Ambassador Lakhdar Brahimi (Algeria), transmitted to the Secretary-General on 17 August 2000. UN Doc. A/55/305-S/2000/809.

[32] General Assembly Resolution 60/1, World Summit Outcome Document (2005), paras. 138–139.

[33] Report of the Secretary-General, Implementation of the Recommendations of the Special Committee on Peacekeeping Operations, UN Doc. A/60/640 (2005). Cf. my earlier article 'Dag Hammarskjöld and the Issue of Humanitarian Intervention', in J. Petman and J. Klabbers (eds.), *Nordic Cosmopolitanism: Essays in International Law for Martti Koskenniemi* (2003), 485–518.

was not to rely on drawn out political compromise, but on ad hoc arrangements responding to urgent and concrete needs in line with the purposes of the UN. As Hammarskjöld's biographer Brian Urquhart has pointed out, the then Secretary-General believed that a just and reliable world order had to rely on precedents (state practice) made possible through political acquiescence.

Hammarskjöld's contribution to international law, beyond his value-based decision-making and his innovative and flexible use of the UN Charter, lies in this development feature. He realised that a progressive development of international law could not be achieved exclusively through multilateral treaty-making, but that, in addition, an element of development through practice would be needed. However, development through precedents presumes that those international actors which are prepared to take the lead – statesmen of governments and organisations – can inspire confidence in their initiatives vis-à-vis the rest of the international community. To find and promote such actors of global leadership, sensitive to political feelings and aware of political opportunities, with distinct transcultural outlooks, will be a challenge for nation-states and international organisations alike.

10

Hammarskjöld, economic thinking and the United Nations

ANNE ORFORD

10.1 Introduction

Outside Sweden, Dag Hammarskjöld is usually remembered for his role as the second Secretary-General of the United Nations (UN) from 1953 until his death in 1961. The legacy of his time in that office includes his expansion of the authority of the Secretary-General, and his transformation of the UN from an organisation devoted to 'static conference diplomacy' to one that functioned as an instrument of 'dynamic executive action'.[1] Hammarskjöld's development of international tools such as fact-finding, preventive diplomacy, technical assistance, peacekeeping and civilian administration ensured that the UN would play a major role in the management and policing of the decolonised world for decades to come.[2]

Yet the entry on Hammarskjöld that appeared in the 1952 edition of Sweden's principal encyclopaedia, *Svensk Uppslagsbok*, listed him as an 'economist'.[3] Hammarskjöld's approach to the role of the international civil servant, and the model of the state and of administration that he applied in the decolonised world, were influenced by the milieu in which his economic expertise had developed during the 1930s and 1940s. Hammarksjöld's vision of the proper role of the state in relation to society and the market was informed by his early involvement with two dynamic generations of Swedish economists, his experience as a senior Swedish civil servant involved in fiscal and monetary policy, and his role as an

Anne Orford is the holder of the Michael D. Kirby Chair of International Law and an Australian Research Council Future Fellow at Melbourne Law School.

[1] UN Secretary-General, *Introduction to the Annual Report of the Secretary-General on the Work of the Organization*, UN Doc. A/4800/Add.1 (1961), at 1.

[2] See generally, A. Orford, *International Authority and the Responsibility to Protect* (2011).

[3] B. Kragh, 'Dag Hammarskjöld: The Economist' (2005) 3 *Economic Review* 82.

international negotiator involved in planning for the reconstruction of Europe after the Second World War. His biographer, Brian Urquhart, suggests that 'political economy' remained Hammarskjöld's lasting interest even after he became Secretary-General.[4] Economics was for Hammarskjöld a pragmatic science, which he understood as 'one aspect of a wider picture of society, an instrument for the achievement of political, social, and ethical objectives'.[5]

This chapter explores Hammarskjöld's approach to economic questions, and the ways in which economic thinking shaped, and in some ways limited, the strategies he adopted as Secretary-General. It focuses in particular upon two key ideas that underpinned Hammarskjöld's vision of the role of the state and of international organisations in the context of decolonisation – the desirability of international executive action and the commitment to the principle of neutrality. As this chapter will show, these ideas were shaped by Hammarskjöld's immersion in the task of planning for post-war European reconstruction – a site of intense ideological struggle in 1940s Europe.[6] While the commitment to executive rule and to administrative neutrality were controversial positions to take in relation to the restructuring of European war economies, they would prove even more radical when applied to the development of Europe's former colonies.

10.2 Dag Hammarskjöld, economist

Hammarskjöld was one member of the group of dynamic young economists that emerged in Sweden during the 1920s and 1930s. Remembered today as the Stockholm School, the group was known for the 'leftist leaning in its political outlook' and for 'proposing Keynesian policies before Keynes'.[7] Having come of age during a period of rising unemployment in Sweden and depression globally, the Stockholm School economists on the whole took a different approach to that of the earlier (and more classically liberal) generation of economists that had established the discipline in Sweden, such as Gösta Bagge, Gustav Cassell, David Davidson, Eli

[4] B. Urquhart, *Hammarskjöld* (1992), 369. [5] *Ibid.*

[6] See generally, A. Orford, 'Europe Reconstructed' (2012) 75 *Modern Law Review* 275.

[7] L. Jonung, 'Introduction and Summary', in L. Jonung (ed.), *The Stockholm School of Economics Revisited* (1991), 1, at 6. Economists associated with the Stockholm School include Dag Hammarskjöld, Olf Johansson, Karin Kock, Erik Lindahl, Erik Lundberg, Gunnar Myrdal, Bertil Ohlin and Ingvar Svennilson.

Heckscher and Knut Wicksell.[8] Where that earlier generation had focused on price stabilisation as the principal goal of monetary policy and were critical of central planning and government intervention, the Stockholm School economists were more concerned with the stabilisation of employment levels and favoured state planning and government intervention as tools to achieve social objectives. The new generation of economists was also far more involved in public life than their predecessors, with many of them serving on government committees, providing expert advice to the Riksbank or the Finance Ministry, or holding office as civil servants.[9] Yet while Hammarskjöld was associated with the Stockholm School, in some ways his approach to economic questions was more aligned with that of the older generation.

Hammarskjöld graduated with a licentiate in political economy from Uppsala University in 1928,[10] and continued his studies in economics at Cambridge with John Maynard Keynes.[11] In 1930 he began work for the *Arbetslöshetsutredningen*, the Swedish governmental Committee on Unemployment, which had been established in 1927 to analyse why there was still permanent unemployment in Sweden despite the boom of the 1920s.[12] Today, the Committee on Unemployment is seen as one of the key institutional settings in which the ideas of the Stockholm School developed.[13] Hammarksjöld used the expert report he wrote for the Committee as the basis for his doctoral dissertation, which he completed in less than two years and defended in 1933 at the University of Stockholm.[14] That dissertation, entitled *Konjunkturspridningen: en Teoretisk och Empirisk Studie* (translated, *The Spread of Business Cycles: A Theoretical and Empirical Study*), offered a highly schematic and abstract account of

[8] *Ibid.*

[9] Gunnar Myrdal notes, however, that although the earlier generation of economists 'abstained as a matter of principle from entering politics or even from formally belonging to a political party', they were nonetheless 'definitely active politicians in another sense, *viz* as political economists' who had an enormous influence over public opinion in Sweden and presented their liberal views 'as clear and almost self-evident truths'. G. Myrdal, 'Postscript', in P. Streeten (ed.), *Value in Social Theory: A Selection of Essays on Methodology by Gunnar Myrdal* (1958), 237, at 246.

[10] H. Landberg, 'Time for Choosing: Dag Hammarksjöld and the Riksbank in the Thirties' (2005) 3 *Economic Review* 13.

[11] Urquhart, *supra* note 4, at 368. Keynes reportedly thought Hammarskjöld 'highly intelligent but not original or creative as an economist' and told Hammarskjöld's colleague Bertil Ohlin 'I don't think we can expect much from *him*'. *Ibid.*

[12] E. Wadensjö, 'The Committee on Unemployment and the Stockholm School', in L. Jonung (ed.), *The Stockholm School of Economics Revisited* (1991), 103.

[13] *Ibid.* [14] Landberg, *supra* note 10, at 19.

the spread of business cycles and price movements internationally and was fiercely critiqued by Hammarskjöld's doctoral opponent, the great Stockholm School economist Gunnar Myrdal.[15] In 1934, Hammarskjöld took up a position at the Finance Ministry and began working in close relationship with the Social Democratic Minister of Finance, Ernst Wigforss, while also continuing his work at the Committee on Unemployment.[16] In 1941 Hammarskjöld was appointed as State Secretary (the most senior official position) in the Department of Finance,[17] and served as Chair of the Board of Governors of the *Riksbank*, the Swedish National Bank, from 1941 to 1948.[18]

During this period, Hammarskjöld played a major role in shaping the economic policy of the social democratic government. In his varied roles as an economic advisor and Swedish civil servant, Hammarskjöld became 'one of the most important, but unacknowledged architects of the practical economic policy of Swedish Social Democracy'.[19] In particular, Hammarskjöld influenced the subtle shift that took place between the formulation and implementation of Swedish economic policy during the 1930s. While advisors to the social democratic government such as Myrdal had developed government policy prioritising the goals of full employment and public works as a means of responding to the economic crises of the period,[20] it was Hammarskjöld who was responsible for translating the general policy into practical measures at the Finance Ministry and the *Riksbank*.[21] In that process of translation, Hammarskjöld sought to prioritise price stability over full employment and state neutrality over state intervention.

Hammarskjöld also played a significant role in determining Sweden's post-war economic policy. By as early as 1935, Hammarskjöld had begun to establish himself as 'an independent voice in economic policy' in relation to questions of international monetary cooperation and stabilisation.[22] In 1945 he was appointed as an advisor to the Swedish Cabinet on economic and financial issues, and was involved in the development

[15] Ö. Appelqvist, 'A Hidden Duel: Gunnar Myrdal and Dag Hammarskjöld in Economics and International Politics 1935–1955', *Stockholm Papers in Economic History No. 2* (2008), at 3–4, at http://swopec.hhs.se/suekhi/abs/suekhi0002.htm.

[16] *Ibid.*, at 5. [17] *Ibid.*, at 7.

[18] Ö. Appelqvist, 'Civil Servant or Politician? Dag Hammarskjöld's Role in Swedish Government Policy in the Forties' (2005) 3 *Economic Review* 33.

[19] Appelqvist, *supra* note 15, at 6.

[20] Appelqvist, *supra* note 18, at 34–35; Urquhart, *supra* note 4, at 369.

[21] Appelqvist, *supra* note 18. [22] Landberg, *supra* note 10, at 23.

of international economic policy as Under-Secretary in the Ministry of Foreign Affairs from 1949 and as Minister without Portfolio (effectively Deputy Foreign Minister) from 1951.[23] In these roles he shaped Sweden's post-war economic and financial planning, led trade and financial negotiations with countries including the United States and the UK, was the Swedish delegate to the Paris Conference at which the administration of the Marshall Plan was negotiated, and was a key player in shaping the terms of Sweden's accession to the Bretton Woods institutions.[24] In short, 'Hammarskjöld was the principal actor behind Sweden's position in the postwar world of trade and money'.[25]

The positions that Hammarskjöld took on questions relating to the goals of post-war monetary policy suggest his distance from the emerging social democratic orthodoxy with its commitment to full employment and active government intervention in the market. This is particularly well illustrated by the debate over the question of what sectors of society should bear the burden of repaying Sweden's public debt after the war.[26] Hammarskjöld brought his liberal economic orientation to bear on Sweden's plans for post-war Europe, pushing to prioritise price stability and the protection of government bondholders as policy goals. The group of experts he established to develop post-war monetary policy for Sweden advocated deflationary government policy so that the value of government bonds could increase and bondholders could be repaid.[27] In order to achieve this, they recommended that salaries should be kept frozen and any increase in real wages should come from decreases in prices.

That approach to post-war planning was challenged by Gunnar Myrdal. Myrdal played his own role in European reconstruction. Within Sweden, he acted as a consultant to the *Arbetarrörelsens Fredsråd* (the Peace Council of the Labour Movement) and as Chair of the Royal Commission for Economic Post-War Planning. Later, he served as Executive Secretary of the UN Economic Commission for Europe on a pan-European scale.[28] The Peace Council was hostile to prolonged austerity after the war on the basis that workers had already sacrificed by accepting price increases without salary increases during the war. In discussions within the Council, Myrdal argued that the perceived contradiction between repaying the war debt and meeting social needs could be transcended, provided the

[23] G. Ahlström and B. Carlson, 'Hammarskjöld, Sweden and Bretton Woods' (2005) 3 *Economic Review* 50, at 52; Urquhart, *supra* note 4, at 369.

[24] *Ibid.* [25] Ahlström and Carlson, *supra* note 23, at 52.

[26] Appelqvist, *supra* note 18, at 8. [27] *Ibid.*, at 9.

[28] W.J. Barber, *Gunnar Myrdal: An Intellectual Biography* (2008), 97–120.

economy grew fast enough so that sufficiently increased tax revenues were generated to enable both goals to be achieved.[29]

Örjan Appelqvist describes an informal meeting on financial policy held in June 1944, at which Hammarskjöld responded to Myrdal's proposal for a growth-oriented Swedish budgetary policy.[30] Hammarskjöld put forward the principle of neutrality as an argument against expansionary economic policy. If Sweden were to rely upon growth as a means of fuelling the repayment of its public debt, this would mean that taxpayers would effectively be repaying government bondholders. As it was not certain that these groups were identical, Hammarskjöld argued that Myrdal's policy proposal thus represented 'a complicated intrusion in the process of income distribution' – a critique that could of course be levelled against any government policy.[31] Central to Hammarskjöld's argument was his view of the proper role of the state in relation to the market:

> Dominating Hammarskjöld's perception was the general view of the Civil Service aristocracy of the state as an arbiter between conflicting interests and as the highest expression of the general interest in society. This could be seen in his insistence on 'neutrality' as the leitmotif in the moments of decision in the after-war years in Sweden. Neutrality between debtors and creditors, between the Swedish Treasury and the government bond holders, were invoked as a central argument underlying the goal of the post-war monetary policy: to reflate the price levels to the 1940 level. Neutrality was also invoked by Hammarskjöld as the main argument against a growth oriented financial policy: it was by no means certain that the advantages of such a policy would accrue to those who would bear its costs in terms of higher taxation levels.[32]

The gap between Hammarskjöld's views and those of economists and policy-makers who were more committed to state planning can also be seen in his approach to issues concerning the role of governments in regulating the market, such as the role of central banks versus parliamentary bodies in economic planning, and the desirability of forms of international monetary cooperation that would require constraints on government policy-making. For example, in his presentation to a meeting of Nordic economists in 1935, Hammarskjöld discussed the possibility of establishing a new international monetary standard and the common policies that would be needed in order for monetary cooperation to be possible.[33]

[29] Appelqvist, *supra* note 18, at 9. [30] *Ibid.*, at 9–10.
[31] *Ibid.*, at 10. [32] Appelqvist, *supra* note 15, at 22.
[33] Landberg, *supra* note 10, at 24, citing *Førhandlinger ved det tiende nordiske nasjonaløkonomiske møte I Oslo den 17–18 juli 1935* (1935).

Hammarskjöld's description of the ways in which economic integration would require constraints on state planning bears a strong resemblance to the arguments developed by Friedrich Hayek only a few years later.[34] According to Hammarskjöld:

> It would ... be necessary to consider some constraint on the individual country's fiscal policy and on the whole on the government's economic operations. I am well aware that in considering such consequences it is a far cry from what looks feasible in practice today. But I am inclined to believe that in time we shall be forced to realise that the sacrifice of national independence that may lie in such agreements can be worth more than it costs.[35]

Similarly, Hammarskjöld referred to the desirability of constraining the economic operations of governments in a paper presented to the 1935 Swedish Bankers' Association Annual Meeting on 'Central Banks in Contemporary Economic Life'.[36] The question of the role to be played by central banks had become increasingly significant in 1930s Europe, given the effective abandonment of the gold standard during the interwar period and the consequent loss of the principal mechanism for stabilising commodity prices.[37] Hammarskjöld argued that in the absence of the gold standard, central banks had a major role to play in actively intervening to ensure price stability, not only through setting interest rates but also through liaising with commercial banks and other lenders to withdraw credit from overheated sectors of the economy.[38] Governments were increasingly confronted with strong groups able to wield power 'on a scale that was inconceivable earlier'.[39] As a result, new forms of state intervention were needed to ensure that 'regular open market operations' could take place.[40] Hammarskjöld made clear that the forms of market intervention he envisaged were liberal in intention and effect, designed to create the necessary conditions for a competitive economic order:

[34] F. Hayek, 'The Economic Conditions of Interstate Federalism', in *Individualism and Economic Order* (1948), 255. See further the discussion in Section 10.3.

[35] Landberg, *supra* note 10, at 24.

[36] *Ibid.*, at 25, referring to D. Hammarskjöld, 'Centralbankerna i nutidens ekonomiska liv', föredrag vid Svenska Bankföreningens årsmöte 1935' (1935) 61 *Skrifter utgivna av Svenska bankföreningen*.

[37] B. Eichengreen and M. Flandreau, 'Editors' Introduction', in B. Eichengreen and M. Flandreau (eds.), *The Gold Standard in Theory and History* (1997), 1.

[38] Landberg, *supra* note 10, at 25, citing Hammarskjöld, *supra* note 36.

[39] *Ibid.*, at 28.

[40] *Ibid.*, at 29.

> If, in the altered situation, the central institutions of the state feel obliged to try new paths, to focus their objectives more clearly than before, and, if necessary, to try to achieve these objectives even against the wishes of the interest groups, this as such does not mean that they switch to the implementation of a policy that is the opposite in principle of the policy up to now of liberal reform – however justified the dangerous epithet national economic planning may seem to be to the critics. For the fact that economic policy has, to put it bluntly, increasingly become an experimental workshop rather than a traditional routine and that, accordingly, the objectives of economic policy are up for debate, does not necessarily mean – and as far as Sweden is concerned has neither, as far as I can judge, yet meant – that there has been a departure from the earlier set of motives for this policy.[41]

Hammarskjöld considered that the new experiments in economic planning should not, however, be carried out by parliamentary bodies subject to capture by special interest groups. He argued that while new functions were required of governments due to developments in the market, it was preferable that those functions be entrusted to 'institutions that, like central banks, are essentially removed from the direct influence of party politics'.[42] The responsibility to work for the public good was best left to institutions that were apolitical and free from influence by any organised groups, including political parties.

As the following part of this chapter will show, Hammarskjöld's position on these questions echoed the arguments developed by the Ordoliberal School of economics that emerged in Germany during this period. The support for state intervention designed to create a space for 'a social embedded and well-functioning competitive order', the concern with the capture of the state by economic special interests, and the consequent scepticism about entrusting economic decision-making to parliamentary bodies were all strong features of Ordoliberal thought.[43] While the commitment to administrative neutrality rather than state planning, and the preference for executive and expert rule over democratic interest-based politics, would prove controversial even in Europe, the application of this model of economic thinking in the context of decolonisation would have tragic consequences.

[41] *Ibid.*, at 28–29, citing Hammarskjöld, *supra* note 36. [42] *Ibid.*

[43] R. Ptak, 'Neoliberalism in Germany: Revisiting the Ordoliberal Foundations of the Social Market Economy', in P. Mirowski and D. Plehwe (eds.), *The Road from Mount Pèlerin: The Making of the Neoliberal Thought Collective* (2009), 98, at 109–111.

10.3 Liberal economics and the reconstruction of Europe

While Hammarskjöld's liberal economic vision of the role of the state in European reconstruction was influential, its dominance was neither inevitable nor uncontested. The idea that the state had a limited role to play in planning, redistribution, or the provision of social welfare did not, at least *initially*, achieve the same centrality to the project of European reconstruction as it did to the project of development.[44] Long before the Second World War had come to an end, many of Europe's most innovative thinkers had gone to work on the task of envisaging what the post-war project of reconstruction and integration should entail. The idea that the state and international organisations had a limited role to play in post-war reconstruction was challenged both within Europe and among US officials working on questions of post-war planning. In particular, Hammarskjöld's ideas about executive action and about neutrality can be usefully compared with ideas being developed in four other sites of economic thinking about reconstruction: the proposals being developed by the Office of Strategic Services in the United States; the forms of economic administration and integration being proposed by Jean Monnet in France; the attacks on state planning drafted in response by Friedrich Hayek, then based at the London School of Economics; and, the comprehensive proposals for rebuilding a market economy being developed by the Ordoliberal School in Germany.

10.3.1 Social revolution and the Frankfurt School at war

Within the United States, post-war planning was undertaken by a range of US agencies – the War Department, the Department of State, the Foreign Economic Administration (FEA), and the newly created Office of Strategic Services (OSS).[45] The positions those agencies took reflected fundamental differences in thinking about the role of the state in economic planning – differences that would come to have enormous significance both for European reconstruction and for decolonisation. Disputes about the proper role of government in managing the economy were at

[44] For the argument that the European economic integration project has led to the implementation of a controversial Hayekian answer to the question of what role the state should play in contemporary Europe, see generally Orford, *supra* note 6.

[45] P. Marquardt-Bigman, 'Behemoth Revisited: The Research and Analysis Branch of the Office of Strategic Services in the Debate of US Policies Towards Germany, 1943–46', (1997) 12 *Intelligence and National Security* 91.

the heart of debates about US post-war policy towards Germany, and about the reconstruction of Europe more generally. For example, the War Department considered that the role of post-war occupation should be limited to establishing law and order and that the occupying administration should not have long-term planning ambitions. Both the State Department and the FEA 'intended US military government in Germany to be part of a lengthy and comprehensive democratisation process', while in addition the FEA also wanted to see the military government working to mould Germany 'into a fair replica of the New Deal'.[46]

Of particular relevance to this chapter, however, are the proposals for German reconstruction developed by Franz Neumann, Herbert Marcuse, Otto Kirchheimer, and their band of émigré intellectuals from their posts at the Research and Analysis Branch of the OSS (R&A) in Washington.[47] The OSS was a new agency, and while it was viewed with some suspicion (in part because it was staffed with leftist Ivy Leaguers and émigré scholars from institutions such as Max Horkheimer's Institute for Social Research, now collectively known as the Frankfurt School), its well-developed position on US post-war policy towards Germany appears to have had a great deal of support within the US administration.[48] The R&A studies were initially produced as intelligence for American officials dealing with the German question, and then after July 1943 the R&A was asked 'to support the War Department's Civil Affairs Division in planning and preparing for the occupation and military administration of Germany'.[49] In cooperation with agencies such as the State Department and the FEA, the R&A prepared 'a series of guides and handbooks intended for the use of military government officers'.[50] The resulting reports offer a remarkable insight into the ways in which these members of the Frankfurt School managed 'to enter into the historical struggle against fascism on the basis of their intellectual calling, not in spite of it'.[51]

The OSS took quite a similar line to the War Department on the question of long-term planning, while also being committed to the goals of democratisation and economic reconstruction. However, where the OSS differed from the other agencies was in its vision of how these goals could be accomplished. The OSS position was strongly shaped by Franz Neumann,

[46] *Ibid.*, at 94.

[47] B.M. Katz, *Foreign Intelligence: Research and Analysis in the Office of Strategic Services, 1942–1945* (1989).

[48] Marquardt-Bigman, *supra* note 45, at 91. [49] *Ibid.*, at 94. [50] *Ibid.*

[51] B.M. Katz, 'The Criticism of Arms: The Frankfurt School Goes to War' (1987) 59 *The Journal of Modern History* 439, at 443.

a former student activist and labour lawyer who had fled Germany in 1933 after being warned of his imminent arrest. Neumann was the author of the hugely influential *Behemoth: The Structure and Practice of National Socialism 1933–1944*, an analysis of National Socialism published in 1942 that had an immediate influence on American ideas about Germany both within and beyond the academy.[52] His view, as expressed in his book and in reports he wrote while at the OSS, was that National Socialism was 'a consequence of structural problems with roots in Germany's social and economic system', particularly the struggle for power that had developed between the landed nobility and the industrialists on the one hand and the remainder of the German people on the other.[53] Similarly, a study authored by Marcuse had argued that the root cause of the German problem was 'a fundamental antagonism between "ruling" and "ruled groups", which could be solved only by a profound and comprehensive democratization of social, economic and political structures'.[54] From these analyses the R&A developed its recommendations for post-war Germany, including eliminating the influence of industrialists on the German state through the development of a liberalised economy, the re-establishment of the freedom to organise, land reform, and the democratisation of political and economic organisations.

Of particular interest however was the emphasis in R&A studies on 'social revolution' as the 'indispensable precondition for a democratization and pacification of Germany'.[55] In debates over what should go into the guides and handbooks for military officers, the R&A 'consistently warned against the notion that the Allies could solve the problems in Germany by imposing a democratization "from above"'.[56] Given the fundamental antagonism that they perceived between ruling and ruled groups in Germany, the R&A considered

> that the end of the war will release political forces in Germany which, given time to develop and assume adequate organization forms, will be capable of accomplishing all or at any rate a large part of our basic objectives in Germany.[57]

Their reports made clear that they considered that these forces were 'the potential followers of the underground remnants of organized labor and the parties of the left'.[58] It was for that reason that the R&A wanted a more

[52] F. Neumann, *Behemoth: The Structure and Practice of National Socialism 1933–1944* (1966).

[53] Marquardt-Bigman, *supra* note 45, at 92–93.

[54] *Ibid.* [55] *Ibid.*, at 93. [56] *Ibid.*, at 95. [57] *Ibid.* [58] *Ibid.*

restricted role for the military government than even the War Department was advocating. They urged that:

> military government should recognize that a strict enforcement of 'law and order' in the initial stages of the occupation might be detrimental for the momentum of the 'social revolution' which the branch considered to be an absolutely indispensable precondition for a genuine democratization of Germany.[59]

In other words the solution proposed by the R&A was to avoid authoritarian international administration as far as possible so as to enable a social revolution.

These reports appear to have been well received and part of mainstream American policy thinking. But as differences between the Allies over the future of Europe became more apparent, the possibility of achieving the vision proposed by the R&A faded away. It became clear that 'military government was not willing, perhaps not able, to compromise on "law and order"', that the German people had only a lukewarm reaction towards the democratisation project urged upon them by the Americans, and that the policies that had been envisaged for a united Germany and a united Europe would not be implemented in a divided Germany by a divided Europe.[60]

10.3.2 Planning and the administrative vision of Jean Monnet

The focus on social revolution in the policies developed by the Frankfurt School can be compared to the plans for executive-led reconstruction developed by Jean Monnet, the international financier, former deputy director of economic affairs for the League of Nations, and soon to be architect of European integration. Throughout the war, Monnet had developed and refined his vision for the rationalisation of production and the management of allied resources. This is encapsulated well in his report for the French government on 'The Organization of Franco-British War Supplies', in which he argued that the Allies had to adopt new forms of administrative authority if they were to avoid the supply shortages that had threatened their populations during the First World War at the height of the submarine offensive. Monnet wrote:

> France, Britain and Italy all faced a supply shortage. The problem was to share it out; then, to devote to the most urgent needs those resources

[59] *Ibid.* [60] *Ibid.*, at 98.

> that could be procured – and finally to procure such resources on the best possible terms ... It is no exaggeration to say that supplies for the armies and the civil population in 1917 and 1918 could be ensured only by a system with almost dictatorial powers, whose strength lay in France's and Britain's agreement to pool their resources and act together in carrying out decisions.[61]

The result was the decision to set up joint Executive Committees to oversee purchases of food, armaments, raw material, petroleum, aircraft and shipping.[62] The mandate of the Committees was:

> to draw up a programme of what was needed and an inventory of what was available, to ensure the best use, in the common interest, of the two countries' resources of raw materials, means of production, etc., and to share fairly between the two countries any cuts that may be imposed by the need to reduce the programmes.[63]

Monnet was appointed as the Chair of the Anglo-French Coordinating Committee that oversaw the work of these Executive Committees, and in consequence was called by a British paper 'the first federal official of the New World'.[64] For Monnet, 'the only way to win this war, like the first war, was to pool the two countries' material resources and productive potential'.[65]

Monnet, like many others, could not see why the achievement of peace should bring these new techniques of rational management to an end. By the end of the war, he had already begun his work on the French post-war, five-year *Plan de Modernisation et d'Équippement* (Plan for Modernisation and Equipment), the most significant theme of which was the importance of guaranteed access to German resources and markets for French national reconstruction.[66] For exponents of state planning like Monnet, there was no sense that the expansion of planned economies should come to an end with the return to peace – rather, they envisaged 'a gradual shift from warfare state to welfare state'.[67]

10.3.3 Friedrich Hayek, the rule of law, and the end of planning

It was in the face of such proposals that Friedrich Hayek began to draft his attacks on state planning, aimed at the perceived threats posed to liberty

[61] J. Monnet, *Memoirs* (1978), 125.
[62] *Ibid.* [63] *Ibid.* [64] *Ibid.* [65] *Ibid.*, at 18.
[66] J. Gillingham, *European Integration, 1950–2003: Superstate or New Market Economy?* (2003), 20.
[67] *Ibid.*, at 4.

not only by communism and fascism, but also by the proposed post-war planned economies of the UK, the United States and France.[68] Hayek opposed planning to the rule of law. For Hayek, state planning involved the authorities usurping the role of the individual and was the precursor to totalitarian rule. He argued that a clear distinction could be drawn between 'the creation of a permanent framework of laws within which the productive activity is guided by individual decisions, and the direction of economic activity by a central authority'.[69] This distinction between individual decision-making and state planning could be understood as 'a particular case of the more general distinction between the Rule of Law and arbitrary government'.[70] If a government was to act in accordance with the rule of law, it should leave it to individuals to decide the ends for which available resources were to be used. Any rules that the government introduced must 'be made in advance, in the shape of *formal rules* which do not aim at the wants and needs of particular people'.[71] Such rules 'are, or ought to be, intended for such long periods that it is impossible to know whether they will assist particular people more than others'.[72] Planning, in contrast, 'necessarily involves deliberate discrimination between particular needs of different people' and thus 'the decline of the Rule of Law'.[73]

The state and the law must therefore remain impartial as between individuals. The state must remain impartial for moral reasons, because to fail to do so would be to take the first step on the road to serfdom and discriminatory rule. The state must also remain impartial for reasons of efficiency, because central authorities are not capable of gaining the knowledge or making the calculations necessary to govern a complex market economy. The state should not intervene to change the economic status quo and will only fail as an agent of planning, control or redistribution. Thus the state did not have a legitimate role to play in post-war reconstruction except to the extent that it enabled markets and protected economic freedom.

For Hayek, one means of dismantling planned economies was through a systematic process of interstate economic integration. Hayek argued that the removal of tariff walls and other barriers to the movement of goods and capital had 'certain important consequences which are frequently overlooked'.[74] In particular, the absence of such 'economic frontiers' made

68 See particularly, F. Hayek, *The Road to Serfdom* (2001/1944).

69 *Ibid.*, at 76. 70 *Ibid.* 71 *Ibid.*, at 76–77.

72 *Ibid.*, at 77. 73 *Ibid.*, at 82.

74 F. Hayek, 'The Economic Conditions of Interstate Federalism', in *Individualism and Economic Order* (2009/1948), 255 at 258.

it much more difficult to 'create communities of interest on a regional basis' and of an 'intimate character'.[75] For Hayek, the destruction of any 'solidarity of interests' was the most important overlooked consequence of economic integration.[76] In a 1948 article on the subject, Hayek states:

> That there will always be communities of interest which will be similarly affected by a particular event or a particular measure is unavoidable. But it is clearly in the interest of unity of the larger whole that these groupings should not be permanent and, more particularly, that the various communities of interest should overlap territorially and never become lastingly identified with the inhabitants of a particular region.[77]

The absence of economic frontiers would make it more difficult for states to identify national economic and political interests. That in turn would limit the capacity of states to develop monetary policy, regulate methods of production, set minimum wages, limit working hours, prohibit child labour, tax commodities, and so on.[78] Hayek also considered it unlikely that 'restrictive or protective' forms of government regulation would be taken over by the newly created interstate government.[79] People would be much less willing to make sacrifices or pay more for goods in order to help producers in other states – as a result, there would be no support for restrictive or protective measures aimed at helping other groups of producers within an internationalised market:

> It seems clear that, in a federation, the problem of agreeing on a common tariff will raise problems different in kind from those that arise in a national state. It would lack the support of the strong nationalist ideologies, the sympathies with the neighbor; and even the argument of defense would lose much of its power of conviction if the Union were really strong enough to have little to fear. It is difficult to visualize how, in a federation, agreement could be reached on the use of tariffs for the protection of particular industries. The same applies to all other forms of protection.[80]

Thus removing 'economic frontiers' and dissolving the sense of community and sympathy created by the nation-state was conceived of by Hayek as an instrument to attack planning:

> Planning, or central direction of economic activity, presupposes the existence of common ideals and common values; and the degree to which planning can be carried out is limited to the extent to which agreement on such a common scale of values can be obtained or enforced.[81]

[75] *Ibid.*, at 257. [76] *Ibid.*, at 258. [77] *Ibid.* [78] *Ibid.*, at 258–259.
[79] *Ibid.*, at 261. [80] *Ibid.*, at 263. [81] *Ibid.*, at 264.

Economic integration was not envisaged by Hayek as a means of attacking the capacity of the state to discriminate between national producers and foreign producers, as it is often argued today, but rather it was envisaged from the beginning as a means of attacking the capacity of the state to discriminate – that is, to plan – at all. Inherent in Hayek's argument for economic federation was the goal of limiting legislation in many fields and making it more difficult for groups to reach agreement on what forms of economic regulation were appropriate. Hayek argued:

> The main point is that, in many cases in which it will prove impossible to reach such agreement, we shall have to resign ourselves rather to have no legislation in a particular field than the state legislation which would break up the economic unity of the federation. Indeed, this readiness to have no legislation at all on some subjects rather than state legislation will be the acid test of whether we are intellectually mature enough for the achievement of suprastate organization.[82]

Hayek concluded that 'the abrogation of national sovereignties and the creation of an effective international order of law is a necessary complement and the logical consummation of the liberal program'.[83]

Hayek's view of the consequences of interstate economic integration was strikingly prescient. As the next part of this chapter will suggest, the commitment to international economic integration and the resulting constraints on the capacity of governments to exercise economic powers would have serious implications for newly independent states. Yet Hayek's account of the relation between planning and the market was already anachronistic. The growth in the size and complexity of business enterprises in the United States and Europe by the 1930s meant that there was 'an inherent degree of planful activity inherent in market-based economies'.[84] Critics had already begun to point to the emergence of a new elite group of corporate managers whose power and privileges appeared increasingly unconstrained.[85] Thus, already by the time Hayek was writing, it no longer, if it ever had, made sense to suggest an opposition between plan and market. In order to understand the economic theory that proved best placed to address the challenges then facing liberal officials involved in European reconstruction and later colonial development, we need to turn to that developed by the Ordoliberal School based in Freiburg.

[82] *Ibid.*, at 266. [83] *Ibid.*, at 269.

[84] K. Tribe, *Strategies of Economic Order: German Economic Discourse 1750–1950* (1995), 150.

[85] Neumann, *supra* note 52, at 284–285. See also, A. Berle Jr. and G. Means, *The Modern Corporation and Private Property* (1933).

10.3.4 *Ordoliberalism and the constitution of economic order*

The Ordoliberal or Freiburg School is the name given to another loosely affiliated group of economists and lawyers, generally taken to include Walter Eucken, who was Professor of Economics in the Faculty of Law and State Sciences at Freiburg University from 1927 until his death in 1950, the legal scholars Franz Böhm and Hams Großmann-Doerth, and the liberal economists Alexander Rüstow, Wilhelm Röpke and Alfred Müller-Armack.[86] The group's name comes from its yearbook *ORDO*, itself derived from the term *Ordnungspolitik* (policy of order) coined to describe their collective project.[87] Ordoliberalism rejected the strong opposition between market and plan, and instead saw the market economy 'as a complex order in which, at many levels, planning and regulation are required for it to function'.[88]

In the aftermath of the Great Depression, Eucken, Rüstow, Röpke and Müller-Armack had analysed what they saw as a crisis of the capitalist economy and had sought to develop the foundations of a new liberalism.[89] They criticised the Weimer Republic as an 'economic state' that had too easily become the prey of organised special interests and was unable to act for the collective good. Drawing particularly on the critique of parliamentary democracy by Carl Schmitt,[90] Rüstow and Müller-Armack argued that liberalism required a strong state that could stand above all other powers or interests.[91] Limiting parliamentary democracy would make it possible to free the market from special interests, enable competition, and realise the social potential of the economy.[92] For the Ordoliberals, the problem with democracy was its dependence upon interests as expressed through political parties and popular voting – the result was that the government lacked authority, the ability to assert leadership, and the capacity to act.[93] The solution was to allow for temporary dictatorship, which would make it possible to implement the measures necessary for the maintenance of social order and the market economy in a timely fashion, while providing for such measures later to be subjected to democratic debate.[94]

After the Second World War, the problem of how to build a market in Germany could not be addressed with such authoritarian solutions. Instead, the focus of liberal economic thinking during this period turned to the social conditions necessary to recreate a competitive economic

[86] Ptak, *supra* note 43, at 98–99. [87] *Ibid*., at 101; Tribe, *supra* note 84, at 207.
[88] Tribe, *supra* note 84, at 215. [89] Ptak, *supra* note 43, at 110.
[90] C. Schmitt, *The Crisis of Parliamentary Democracy* (1988/1932).
[91] Ptak, *supra* note 43, at 111. [92] *Ibid.* [93] *Ibid.* [94] *Ibid.*

order in Germany – one that would guarantee that a coalition of statist, militarist and monopolistic economic interests could not again emerge. After the Second World War, the Ordoliberals were specifically concerned with 'the problems of economic reconstruction in the remnants of the broken and occupied German nation'.[95] The challenge they faced was not that of the economists of the eighteenth century – that is, 'given the existence of a legitimate state, which is already functioning in the fully and completely administrative form of a police state, how can we limit this existing state and, above all, allow for the necessary economic freedom within it'.[96] Rather, the challenge facing liberal German economists after the Second World War was, 'given a state that does not exist, how can we get it to exist on the basis of this non-state space of economic freedom'.[97] The contribution of the Ordoliberal School, with its close collaboration between economists and legal scholars, was to approach this as a question of constitutional order.[98] The diagnosis of the problem facing Germany was that the capture of the state by special interests had led to forms of regulation that obstructed the effective functioning of the market, and more specifically, of the price mechanism.[99] The role of the state in reconstruction (and more generally) was to put in place the conditions that would allow competition to take place. Competition (not exchange) was seen as the key ordering 'principle of the market'.[100] It was competition that would ensure the proper formation of prices, and prices would in turn provide the means of regulating the choices made by individuals.[101] Stated differently, perfecting the process of competition would produce a fair price, and the price mechanism was itself the appropriate form of economic regulation.

Ordoliberalism was not a closed or fully elaborated theory, but it was marked by its commitment to the need for governmental action both to enable competition and to preserve the social balance in order to suppress conflict (or revolution).[102] In addition, the Ordoliberals had a distinctively anti-modernist dislike of bureaucratisation, urbanisation and

[95] Gillingham, *supra* note 66, at 10.

[96] M. Foucault, *The Birth of Biopolitics: Lectures at the Collège de France 1978–1979* (2008), 86.

[97] *Ibid.*, at 86–87.

[98] V. Vanberg, 'The Freiburg School: Walter Eucken and Ordoliberalism', *Freiburg Discussion Papers on Constitutional Economics, No. 04/11* (2004), at www.econstor.eu/handle/10419/4343.

[99] Tribe, *supra* note 84, at 212–213.

[100] Foucault, *supra* note 96, at 118.

[101] *Ibid.*, at 119.

[102] Ptak, *supra* note 43, at 124–125.

redistributive social policies.[103] Thus their agenda differed fundamentally from contemporary social democratic and other left-wing programmes directed to achieving egalitarian redistribution, higher wages, better working conditions, and other 'classical labor movement demands'.[104]

10.3.5 *Hammarskjöld and varieties of economic thinking*

Hammarskjöld's views on the role of the state in post-war planning echo these trends in European economic thought. As we have seen, Hammarskjöld did not prioritise the goals of social democrats or the labour movement, such as full employment, higher wages, better working conditions, land reform, the democratisation of political and economic organisations, or the redistribution of wealth. Rather, he demonstrated his sympathy for liberal economic thinking about the proper role of the state through his commitment to neutrality and price stability as goals of Swedish economic policy. His presentations to economists and bankers throughout the 1930s and 1940s demonstrated that, unlike Hayek, he was willing to support state planning, provided however that it was directed towards the liberal goals of enabling open markets and securing prices. Hammarskjöld did not place much value on parliamentary processes, sharing with the Ordoliberals a concern with the capture of the state by special interests. His starting premise – like that of many liberal economists of his age, but *unlike* many of his social democratic colleagues – was that the state is grounded upon and legitimised by economic freedom, and that executive rule may be necessary to create the conditions needed to secure that freedom.

Hammarskjöld's approach to economic and social policy may have been one reason he was an attractive candidate for UN Secretary-General from the American perspective.[105] Throughout his time as Secretary-General, he remained closely allied with a US administration that was shaped by an increasingly strident anti-communism and by an emergent liberal (if not yet neoliberal) economics. Hammarskjöld's liberal economic worldview was the foundation for his principled commitment to decolonisation and to the equality of the new states,[106] but it was also the foundation for his faith in the free market and in a particular model of international

103 *Ibid.*, at 104–105. 104 *Ibid.*, at 105.

105 Appelqvist, *supra* note 15, at 2 (arguing that Hammarskjöld's performance as a Swedish civil servant goes some way to explaining 'why he was nominated and accepted by the representatives of the United States as UN Secretary-General').

106 See further, H. Melber, 'Dag Hammarskjöld, the United Nations and Africa' (2012) 39 *Review of African Political Economy* 151.

economic integration. As the next part of this chapter will show, the effect was that while Hammarskjöld considered that the UN had a significant role to play as a neutral administrator of the decolonisation process, he insisted that the scope of governmental action, whether undertaken by the UN or by decolonised states themselves, should be limited.

10.4 Decolonisation and the role of the state

Hammarskjöld's vision of the role of the UN in the context of decolonisation was premised upon two ideas that can be traced to the forms of economic thinking discussed so far – the need for executive intervention to maintain order, and the commitment to governmental neutrality. Hammarskjöld's responses to the serial crises of decolonisation that marked his tenure – including those involving the Suez Canal in 1956, Lebanon in 1958 and the Congo in 1960 – transformed both the UN and the new states of the Middle East and Africa. Hammarskjöld's solution to those crises saw the introduction and development of forms of executive action such as fact-finding, preventive diplomacy, technical assistance, peacekeeping, and international administration aimed at maintaining order and protecting life until what he called the 'political vacuums' caused by decolonisation could be filled.[107] Hammarskjöld considered that the UN could not fulfil its function of protecting self-determination and the independence of all peoples if it were limited to relying upon decisions of the General Assembly or the Security Council taken 'within the framework of a conference pattern'.[108] The challenges of decolonisation in the context of the Cold War meant that new forms of executive action were necessary to protect the independence of newly decolonised states and to create an international order that ensured 'equal economic opportunities for all individuals and nations'.[109]

10.4.1 Executive rule, neutrality and the administration of decolonisation

Hammarskjöld was particularly concerned with 'the problem of Africa and its importance for the international community'.[110] There had been

[107] UN Secretary-General, Introduction to the Annual Report of the Secretary-General on the Work of the Organization, UN Doc. A/4800/Add.1 (1961), at 1.
[108] *Ibid.*, at 7. [109] *Ibid.*, at 2.
[110] UN Secretary-General, Introduction to the Annual Report of the Secretary-General on the Work of the Organization, UN Doc. A/4390/Add.1 (1960), at 1.

'mixed' reactions to independence from outside Africa, with some trying 'to maintain what history has already judged' and others trying 'to put in place of the past new and more subtle forms of predominance and influence'.[111] In that situation, the UN had a particular 'responsibility' to put in place a 'framework' within which independent African states could determine their own 'political personality' within 'the setting of universality as represented by the United Nations'.[112] Hammarskjöld believed that the UN was the proper actor to play this role because it was neutral – a 'universal organization neutral in the big Power struggles over ideology and influence in the world' and 'free from any aspirations of its own to power and influence over any group or nation'.[113] According to Hammarskjöld, the UN represented an advance beyond older forms of internationalism premised upon 'conference diplomacy' because it introduced 'joint permanent organs, employing a neutral civil service, and the use of such organs for executive purposes on behalf of all the members of the organizations'.[114] That 'radical innovation in international life' depended upon the belief that the Secretary-General in particular, and the international civil service more broadly, were capable of acting 'on a truly international basis' and carrying out their tasks 'without subservience to a particular national or ideological attitude'.[115] From his reorganisation of the Secretariat through to the conduct of the UN operation in the Congo, Hammarskjöld treated the commitment to neutrality as a core requirement both of the office of the Secretary-General and of the Secretariat. While neutrality is often interpreted as a political concept, it is useful to remember that economics was the mode of politics in which Hammarskjöld's thinking about neutrality, as well as his belief in the necessity of executive rule, had been shaped.

As we have already seen, the liberal economic idea that the state had a limited role to play in relation to the market was a radical one within post-war Europe. It was an even more radical idea in the context of decolonisation. The decolonised state was confronted with an economic system designed to enable the profitability of colonial enterprises. After the Second World War, the newly dominant United States was opposed to the continuation of colonialism as a coercive order premised upon the concentration of ownership and control in the hands of a particular colonial

111 *Ibid.* 112 *Ibid.* 113 *Ibid.*

114 D. Hammarskjöld, 'The International Civil Servant in Law and in Fact', in W. Foote (ed.), *The Servant of Peace: A Selection of the Speeches and Statements of Dag Hammarskjöld* (1962), 329.

115 *Ibid.*, at 346.

power. It sought to replace this with a regime of open access, free trade, non-discrimination, and the international management of resources in the decolonised world.[116] Yet at the same time, in the name of resisting communism, the United States prevented attempts to restructure the colonial state and its relation to the broader international economy. Without such restructuring, decolonisation would merely shift the comparative advantage in accessing and controlling resources and labour located in the former colonies from the former colonial powers to the emergent United States. In other words, a new power would simply occupy the colonial position in the name of free access and non-discrimination.

And this shift in occupation was indeed the effect. It was achieved through the American political project of reconstruction in Europe and development in the decolonised world. The UN played a key role in this process of transforming an empire of land appropriation to an empire of economic administration. Central to this process was the meaning that Hammarskjöld gave to the principle of 'neutrality' in the project of managing decolonisation. Hammarskjöld had already indicated his sympathy for this economic way of thinking about the proper role of the state in his role as a civil servant in Sweden. In particular he did this through advocating neutrality as a policy goal. Hammarskjöld again realised his vision of the state through the meaning he gave to the concept of neutrality in the context of the UN interventions. The tension between Hammarskjöld's commitment to independence on the one hand, and his faith in liberal economics as the means for development on the other, informed the practices he introduced for managing decolonisation. The idea that the government should remain neutral in relation to the market as it existed had significant implications for the project of decolonisation.

10.4.2 The limits of the liberal project: UN intervention in the Congo

The conduct of the UN intervention in the Congo provides a particularly good illustration of the ways in which ideas about the role of government in relation to the market and the commitment to economic order at the expense of parliamentary democracy informed Hammarskjöld's decision-making. In order to grasp the implications of Hammarskjöld's economic thinking for the project of decolonisation, it is necessary first to consider the political economy of the Belgian Congo and of its newly independent successor.

[116] See generally, Orford, *supra* note 2.

The Belgian Congo inherited 'the economic and social rationality' of the Congo Free State, which had been established by King Leopold II as a personal fiefdom and source of income.[117] The Congo Free State saw the 'expansion of production for export dependent on the use of force and even of terror', and effectively guaranteed the investments of foreign capital in railways and mines.[118] Once the Belgian state took over the Congo from Leopold, it softened but still continued to use existing forms of political and economic constraint 'to create a labour market and to facilitate the accumulation of capital'.[119] During the colonial period from 1910 until 1960, the foreign minority continued to exercise significant control over the means of production directed towards facilitating commodities for export.[120] The agricultural and mining surplus of the Belgian Congo contributed to the development of an industrial sector in Brussels.[121]

In order for entrepreneurs to be able to access new markets, cheap labour, and raw materials, they depended upon the intervention of the colonial administration.[122] By the 1920s, 'the density of administration in the Congo was unequalled in Africa'.[123] 'No Congolese, rural or urban, could have failed to perceive that he was being administered'.[124] This was true both of those living in the urban centres and those living in rural areas – 'what differentiated the Belgian system from others in Africa was the extent of its occupation and organization of the countryside'.[125] Colonial policies were directed towards the recruitment of labour for the mines, plantation and army, as well as halting the rural exodus and preserving the health of the workforce through public immunisation and other health programmes. The Belgian administration was striking in its lack of commitment to education and in the limitations it placed on union activity, political organisation and free speech. As a result, the situation confronting the Congolese at independence was that 'the foreign minority in 1958, though it represented only 1 percent of the population, controlled 95 percent of the assets, 88 percent of private savings and 82 percent of all the firms'.[126] Until independence, the Congo remained a major source of profit for Belgian firms. While Belgian firms in general

[117] J. Peemans, 'Capital Accumulation in the Congo under Colonialism: The Role of the State', in P. Duignan and L. Gann (eds.), *Colonialism in Africa 1870–1960: The Economics of Colonialism* (1975), Vol. IV, 165, at 168.

[118] *Ibid.*, at 171–179. [119] *Ibid.*, at 180. [120] *Ibid.*

[121] *Ibid.*, at 165–166. [122] *Ibid.*, at 167.

[123] C. Young, *Politics in the Congo: Decolonization and Independence* (1965), 10.

[124] *Ibid.*, at 11. [125] *Ibid.*

[126] Peemans, *supra* note 117, at 181.

averaged returns of 8 to 9 per cent during the 1950s, those operating in the Congo averaged 20 per cent.[127] Belgium's economic stake in its former colony 'motivated Brussels' post-independence efforts to retain its economic lock on the Congo's economy'.[128] In order for decolonisation in the Congo to be meaningful, it therefore required the redistribution of property and power both locally and internationally.

The UN intervention in the Congo was necessitated by the Belgian response to the initiation of just such a process of redistribution by the post-independence Congolese government. The crisis in the Congo began when soldiers of the *Armée Nationale Congolaise* (formerly the *Force Publique*) revolted against their Belgian officers soon after the Congo's accession to independence, demanding immediate appointment of Congolese officers and, along with other public servants, seeking higher wages and promotions.[129] The new government responded to the soldiers' demands by agreeing to Africanise the officer corps and raise army wages by 30 per cent. This was interpreted by outside observers as an invitation to 'public employees and the black proletariat in mines and factories to follow the soldiers' lead and consolidate independence with social demands'.[130] Ralph Bunche, the Secretary-General's special advisor in the Congo, wrote to Hammarskjöld: 'Strikes continue and spread, encouraged and triggered originally by successful tactics of army.'[131]

On 10 July Belgium intervened, justifying its military action as a 'humanitarian intervention in the Congo' undertaken 'with the sole purpose of ensuring the safety of European and other members of the population and of protecting human lives in general'.[132] The Belgian intervention started in the resource-rich province of Katanga, which declared its independence on 11 July, and extended to the occupation of the Port of Matadi, which was also of commercial significance to the Belgians.[133]

127 C. Collins, 'The Cold War Comes to Africa: Cordier and the 1960 Congo Crisis' (1993) 47 *Journal of International Affairs* 243, at 251.

128 *Ibid.*

129 G. Nzongola-Ntalaja, *The Congo from Leopold to Kabila: A People's History* (2002), 89.

130 See L. de Witte, *The Assassination of Lumumba*. Translated by A. Wright and R. Fenby (2001), at 8.

131 *Ibid.*

132 Security Council Official Records: Fifteenth Year, UN Doc. S/PV.873 (13/14 July 1960), at 34–37.

133 The cable from Kasavubu and Lumumba claimed that the Belgian government had 'carefully prepared the secession of the Katanga with a view to maintaining a hold on our country' and declared that the Congolese government, 'supported by the Congolese people, refuses to accept a "fait accompli" resulting from a conspiracy between Belgian imperialists and a small group of Katanga leaders'. See Cable dated 12 July 1960, 13 July

The subsequent recognition of the State of Katanga by the Belgians had enormous strategic implications for political developments in the Congo more generally. In part this was due to the economic and fiscal implications of the attempted secession. Direct taxes on companies operating both in the Congo and in Belgium were collected in Brussels, and those taxes accounted for more than one-third of the revenues of the Congo.[134] After the Katangese secession, Belgian mining companies recognised the authority of Katanga to levy taxes and export duties, so that all revenues formerly paid by Belgian companies to the Congo were subsequently paid to the State of Katanga.[135] Those revenues, which would otherwise have formed the basis of the Congolese economy, were then used to form, train and equip the armed forces of Katanga.[136] In addition, secessionist forces seized local branches of para-statal institutions such as the central bank, and in so doing seriously limited the capacity of the central government to exercise 'the chief economic control instruments of the state'.[137] The Belgian intervention also shifted the military balance of power in favour of Katanga. While Belgian forces in other parts of the Congo were instructed to 'intervene when Belgian lives are threatened', in Katanga they were instructed to occupy 'all centres of importance'.[138] Belgian troops in Katanga rounded up and neutralised the *Force Publique*, attacked troops loyal to the central government in their barracks, and trained the Katangese *gendarmerie*.[139]

On 12 July, Lumumba and the President of the Republic of the Congo, Joseph Kasavubu, jointly wrote to the UN Secretary-General condemning 'the dispatch to the Congo of metropolitan Belgian troops' and requesting UN military assistance 'to protect the national territory of the Congo from the present external aggression which is a threat to international peace'.[140] In his report to the Security Council placing the Congo on the agenda and successfully requesting UN intervention, the Secretary-General recharacterised UN involvement as necessary to achieve 'the maintenance of order

1960. For analyses of the relation between the Congolese secessionists and Belgian military forces, see Collins, *supra* note 127, at 250, and G. Abi-Saab, *The United Nations Operation in the Congo 1960–1964* (1978), 21–53.

134 R. West, 'The United Nations and the Congo Financial Crisis: Lessons of the First Year' (1961) 15 *International Organization* 603.

135 C. O'Brien, *To Katanga and Back: A UN Case History* (1962), 87.

136 See West, *supra* note 134, at 612.

137 *Ibid.*, at 612.

138 Abi-Saab, *supra* note 133, at 41.

139 *Ibid.*

140 Telegram from the President and Prime Minister of the Republic of the Congo to the Secretary-General of the United Nations, UN Doc. S/4382, (1960), at 11.

in the country and the protection of life'.[141] Hammarskjöld made clear his understanding that 'were the United Nations to act as proposed' and as a result 'the national security forces are able to fully meet their tasks', the Belgian government would then 'see its way to a withdrawal'.[142]

While Hammarskjöld made clear that the UN required Belgian forces to withdraw from Katanga, he also declared that the UN Force could not 'be a party to any internal conflict', nor could it 'intervene in a domestic conflict'.[143] Hammarskjöld characterised the Katangese succession as an internal matter that was outside the jurisdiction of the UN.[144] Ralph Bunche met with the Katangese leader, Moïse Tshombe, in early August to negotiate the conditions on which UN troops would be stationed in Katanga. On 9 August 1960, the Security Council passed a resolution calling upon the Belgian government 'to withdraw immediately its troops from the province of Katanga', yet stating 'that the United Nations Force in the Congo will not be a party to or in any way intervene in or be used to influence the outcome of an internal conflict, constitutional or otherwise'.[145] The latter paragraph had been proposed by Hammarskjöld as a means of giving Belgium and Katanga an 'assurance that the deployment of the UN Force in Katanga would not affect the outcome of the political controversy between Katanga and the Central Government'.[146]

On 12 August, Hammarskjöld himself made a controversial visit to Elizabethville, the capital of Katanga, to meet with Tshombe and his government. On the way, he drafted a memorandum setting out his interpretation of the UN's position on the situation in Katanga for use in his talks with Tshombe.[147] That memorandum dealt in detail with the question of how the UN would relate to the competing claimants for authority within the Congo. According to Hammarskjöld, guidance for the interpretation of paragraph 4 could be gained from looking to earlier UN practice – in particular, the case of Lebanon that came before the Security Council in

[141] See UN Doc. S/PV.873, *supra* note 132, at 3. [142] *Ibid*., para. 26.

[143] D. Hammarskjöld, 'Statement in the Security Council Introducing Report: New York, July 20, 1960', in A.W. Cordier and W. Foote, *Public Papers of the Secretaries-General of the United Nations, Vol. V: Dag Hammarskjöld 1960–1961* (1975), 43.

[144] See also Second Report of the Secretary-General on the Implementation of Security Council Resolutions S/4387 of 14 July 1960 and S/4405 of 22 July 1960, S/4417, 6 August 1960, para. 10.

[145] See SC Res. 146, S/4426, 9 August 1960, adopted by nine votes with two abstentions (France and Italy).

[146] Abi-Saab, *supra* note 133, at 33.

[147] D. Hammarskjöld, 'Exchange of Messages with Tshombé on Entry of the United Nations Force in Katanga, August 10', in A.W. Cordier and W. Foote, *Public Papers of the*

1958 involving a conflict between the Lebanese President and a group of insurgents. The President had sought assistance from the UN on the basis that the insurgency was being led from outside Lebanon. In granting that assistance and sending an observer group to monitor the border, the Security Council had concerned itself solely with preventing intervention from outside Lebanon in assistance to rebels and had not otherwise intervened in support of either 'the government side' or the rebels.[148]

Based on his interpretation of the resulting non-intervention principle governing the Katanga question, and his characterisation of the dispute between Katanga and the central government as a purely internal matter, Hammarskjöld drew the following broad conclusions about the limits of UN action:

> Applying the line pursued by the Security Council in the Lebanese case to the interpretation of operative paragraph 4, it follows that the United Nations Force cannot be used on behalf of the central government to subdue or to force the provincial government to a specific line of action.[149]

In a heated exchange of letters with Hammarskjöld, Lumumba rejected Hammarskjöld's interpretation of the Katangese secession as an internal matter, accused Bunche of behaving improperly in meeting with the Belgian government's 'homme de paille', Tshombe, and argued that it was clear from the initial Security Council resolution that the UN was charged, in consultation with the government of the Republic of the Congo, with providing the government with the military assistance it considered necessary.[150]

Hammarskjöld's determination that the UN could not assist the central government in regaining control over Katanga marked a turning point in the relation between the UN and the central government. In response to that determination, Lumumba decided that if the secession were an internal security matter, the central government would have to respond to it through military action.[151] The Congo government accepted

Secretaries-General of the United Nations, Vol. V: Dag Hammarskjöld 1960–1961 (1975), 82, at 84.

148 D. Hammarskjöld, 'Interpretation of Paragraph 4 of the Security Council's Third Resolution on the Congo, Leopoldville, The Congo, August 12', in A.W. Cordier and W. Foote, *Public Papers of the Secretaries-General of the United Nations, Vol. V: Dag Hammarskjöld 1960–1961* (1975), 85, at 86.

149 *Ibid.*

150 See particularly, Incoming Code Cable from Bunche to Hammarskjöld, 5 August 1960, National Library of Sweden, MS L179:132.

151 See De Witte, *supra* note 130, at 14.

Russian military assistance of 100 trucks and sixteen planes to transport troops to the secessionist provinces in order to stage a military campaign against the insurgents.[152] The situation deteriorated when inadequately resourced troops seeking to requisition food and vehicles began fighting local groups and massacred more than seventy civilians seeking shelter in a local school.[153] The receipt of Russian aid and the attack on civilians firmed up Hammarskjöld's view that the UN should not support the central government. According to Hammarskjöld, any external support to the central government was an illegal interference in the internal affairs of the Congo. In making that argument, Hammarskjöld equated the authority of the central government with that of the insurgents in Katanga:

> I have already referred to Belgian assistance in Katanga. But the Belgians are not alone. There are others who follow a similar line, though they justify their policy by a reference to the fact that assistance is given to the constitutional government of the country. Admittedly, there is a difference … I think, however, it should be recognized that this is no longer a question of form and legal justification, but a question of very hard realities, where the use to which the assistance is put is more important than the heading in an export list under which it is registered, or the status of the one to whom it is addressed.[154]

For the USSR, in contrast, the status of the one to whom assistance was addressed was the key question. The UN had no authority to 'control the relation between the Republic of the Congo and other states', and neither the UN Charter nor the Security Council gave 'any United Nations administrative officer, whoever he may be, the right to intervene in relations between sovereign States unless they request his intervention'.[155]

It was in that context of deteriorating relations between the government of Lumumba and the UN that the constitutional crisis in the Congo erupted in early September, when, in a brief speech broadcast from the Leopoldville radio station, Kasavubu announced that he was dismissing Lumumba.[156] According to General von Horn, commander of the UN force, the atmosphere at UN headquarters after the announcement was of

[152] Abi-Saab, *supra* note 133, at 54. [153] *Ibid.*, at 55.

[154] D. Hammarskjöld, 'Opening Statement in the Security Council September 9', in A.W. Cordier and W. Foote, *Public Papers of the Secretaries-General of the United Nations, Vol. V: Dag Hammarskjöld 1960–1961* (1975), 162, at 169.

[155] UN Doc. S/4503/II (10 September 1960), as cited in Abi-Saab, *supra* note 133, at 56.

[156] M.G. Kalb, *The Congo Cables: The Cold War in Africa – From Eisenhower to Kennedy* (1982), 71.

'relief, almost of satisfaction'.[157] Less than an hour later, Lumumba delivered a speech that was broadcast three times over the radio that evening, both in French and in Lingala.[158] Lumumba stated that, 'Kasavubu had no power to dismiss a Prime Minister who enjoyed the confidence of the Parliament and that by doing so he had defied the Parliament and the people'.[159] On 7 and 8 September, Lumumba won the overwhelming support of both the lower house of parliament, the Assembly, and the upper house, the Senate. Nonetheless, for Hammarskjöld, given the conflict between 'the chief of state whom the United Nations must recognize' and 'a cabinet which continued in being, but the chief of which put himself in sharp opposition to the chief of state', the only response available to UN representatives in the Congo was 'to avoid any action by which, directly or indirectly, openly or by implication they would pass judgement on the stand taken by either one of the parties in the conflict'.[160] For that reason, as Hammarskjöld stated, in making decisions about emergency action the UN representatives were effectively unable to consult any Congolese:

> With whom could the United Nations representatives consult in this situation without taking sides? In the light of what I have said, the answer is obvious: they had to act on their own responsibility, within their general mandate, in order to meet the emergency which they were facing. Let me repeat it, there was nobody, really nobody, with whom they could consult without prejudging the constitutional issue.[161]

In response to Hammarskjöld's statement, Kasavubu expressed his 'gratitude', while Lumumba considered it a 'confirmation' of 'the flagrant interference of the United Nations in the internal affairs of the Congo'.[162] According to Lumumba, Hammarskjöld's interpretation 'runs counter to the sovereign decisions taken by the Congolese Parliament, which has annulled by two separate votes, each by a large majority, Mr Kasavubu's illegal decree'.[163] He concluded that '[i]t is not for the Secretary-General of the United Nations to interpret the Fundamental Law; that is the responsibility of the Congolese Parliament'.[164]

[157] *Ibid.*, at 74. [158] Urquhart, *supra* note 4, at 442.
[159] Abi-Saab, *supra* note 133, at 59–60.
[160] Hammarskjöld, *supra* note 154, at 164. [161] *Ibid.*, at 165.
[162] See Communication dated 10 September 1960 from the Prime Minister of the Republic of the Congo Addressed to the Secretary-General of the United Nations, UN SCOR, 15th Sess., UN Doc. S/4498, 10 September 1960.
[163] *Ibid.*
[164] S/4498, 10 September 1960, as cited in Abi-Saab, *supra* note 133, at 67.

On 14 September, Colonel Mobutu took to the airwaves and announced that 'he was neutralizing the Chief of State, the two rival governments, and the Parliament until the end of the year and would meanwhile call in "technicians" to run the country'.[165] According to the Financial Advisor of ONUC during that period, power was exercised during the constitutional crisis 'by a group of non-political technicians, composing a council of commissioners which undertook to reactivate the administrative machinery of the state'.[166] From September onwards, ONUC officials 'decided to collaborate, as far as civilian operations were concerned, with the *de facto* authorities'.[167] Once Mobutu had come to power, Lumumba remained under virtual house arrest until his escape and subsequent murder by Belgian officers and Katanga leaders in January 1961.

For Hammarskjöld and many other Western UN officials, the fact that Lumumba 'was the democratically elected and legitimate leader of the Congo government, who had received significantly more votes than Kasavubu in the May elections and commanded predominant support in the Congo parliament' was not decisive.[168] In the words of Hammarksjöld's executive assistant and interim Special Representative to the Congo, Andrew Cordier:

> There is really no such thing as a Congolese Government. Several weeks ago I sent a cable to Dag suggesting that he see someone in the Government about a certain matter. He replied, 'But who can I see?' There is a cabinet, but Lumumba uses it as his tool. Some members of the Cabinet share his vision and lust for power, while the few moderates ... are understandably fearful to take any positive line.[169]

Hammarskjöld clearly indicated that he found the question of whom to recognise as the legitimate authority in the Congo a difficult one. In a lecture presented at Oxford University in May 1961, he commented:

> [T]he unanimous resolution authorizing assistance to the Central Government of the Congo offered little guidance to the Secretary-General when that Government split into competing centres of authority, each claiming to be the Central Government and each supported by different groups of Member States within and outside the Security Council.[170]

Hammarskjöld nonetheless did make decisions about which actors to recognise as having lawful authority in the Congo. In making those decisions, he preferred the capacity of the executive to guarantee order over

[165] Urquhart, *supra* note 4, at 451. [166] West, *supra* note 134, at 608.
[167] *Ibid.* [168] Collins, *supra* note 127, at 258. [169] *Ibid.*
[170] Hammarskjöld, *supra* note 114, at 344.

support for parliamentary democracy, and he preferred actors whom he thought would act responsibly in relation to economic matters. He was for neutrality in the economic sphere and against revolution, and he was committed to 'bringing the underdeveloped countries into the world market in the proper way'.[171] Lumumba's project of 'national unity, economic independence and pan-African solidarity' was a threat to that vision of decolonisation.[172] Hammarskjöld made clear his contempt for Lumumba's government in the following statement to the Security Council, presented at the height of the constitutional crisis and just a little over two months after the Congo had gained its independence:

> Members will have gathered from the report that, in spite of the great natural resources of the country, the financial situation is one of bankruptcy. True, there are financial assets, but they are hopelessly insufficient. And with a complete disruption of civilian and economic life, where are the new revenues, where the foreign exchange, where the taxes, where the customs duties? We face a nation with a budget with all the necessary outlays and nothing to cover them ...
>
> In this situation spokesmen of the central government speak about the assistance rendered by the international community through the United Nations as if it were an imposition and treat the Organization as if they had all rights and no obligations. They seem to believe that the independence of the Republic of the Congo, in the sense of the international sovereignty of the state which everybody respects, means independence also in a substantive sense of the word which, in our interdependent world of today, is unreal even for a country living by its own means and able to provide for its own security and administration.
>
> A government without financial means is dependent on those who help it to meet its needs. It may depend financially on another state, or group of states, and thereby tie its fate to that of the donors. Or it may depend on the international community in its entirety, represented by the United Nations, and so remain free. There is no third alternative this side of a complete breakdown of the state through inflation or a speedy disintegration of all social and economic services.
>
> ... There are the hard facts which should be remembered when the relations of the United Nations with the central government are discussed.[173]

This indictment of the Congolese government was premised upon economic thinking. Hammarskjöld did not suggest that the Congo was no longer sovereign in a formal sense, or that its rulers were political opponents or even evil tyrants who should be punished. Instead, Hammarskjöld

[171] Urquhart, *supra* note 4, at 376. [172] Nzongola-Ntalaja, *supra* note 129, at 84.
[173] Hammarskjöld, *supra* note 154, at 163.

simply dismissed the Lumumba government as 'a clumsy, inadequate government that does not do the proper thing'.[174]

10.5 Conclusion: 'economic thinking at its best'

Hammarskjöld enshrined a particular form of economic thinking at the heart of the UN. In this chapter, I have suggested that this may prove to be one of his most important legacies. In reflecting upon the choices Hammarskjöld made in the Congo and elsewhere, it is important to stress that he was not a dogmatic economic thinker. Throughout his career, Hammarskjöld was 'interested in major matters of principle in the borderland between theory and practical policy'.[175] He did not take up the position of Secretary-General with a doctrinaire agenda for economic liberalisation. When asked at a press conference in 1957 whether the retirement of Gunnar Myrdal from the Economic Commission for Europe would mean a shift in the nature of economic thinking at the UN Secretariat, Hammarskjöld commented:

> I think that our duty is collectively to reflect as well as we can not this or that trend in political thinking in economics, but certainly the development of economic thinking at its best. It is eclectic; it is pragmatic, if you want. From that point of view, the scientist may sometimes feel a little unhappy because everyone who has this kind of academic background, whether it is Mr Myrdal or Mr Hammarskjöld, of course likes to think in his own way. But I think we are all solidly and well coordinated and subordinated to the major responsibility.[176]

Nonetheless, the combined effect of Hammarskjöld's working alliance with the Republican administration of Dwight D. Eisenhower, his desire to limit communist influence in the Middle East and Africa, the pragmatic milieu in which he and other civil servants operated at the UN, and his version of liberal economic thinking meant that the model of the state that emerged in the decolonised world under his leadership was much closer to that proposed by the emerging Ordoliberal School than might have been expected from someone with his background and links to social democratic governments in Sweden. Hammarskjöld considered that it was necessary to support the expansion of international cooperation in order to allow economic and political institutions to develop in the proper

[174] For this characterisation of economic approaches to governmentality, see Foucault, *supra* note 96, at 10.

[175] Landberg, *supra* note 10, at 23.

[176] Urquhart, *supra* note 4, at 370–371.

way, both in a Europe ruined by war and in the former European colonies. In addition, he considered that government (whether by states or by international administrators) should be premised upon principles of neutrality and impartiality. Finally, he had little time for legal formalities or issues of representation when they stood in the way of establishing rational government. As this chapter has shown, these ideas about the proper relation of state and market, the desirability of executive action, and the significance of neutrality were informed by Hammarskjöld's background both as a Swedish civil servant working in the financial sector and as an economist.

In some ways, the model of the state that took hold in the decolonised world during the following decades was the worst of all worlds. It was enabled by the vision of executive rule introduced by Hammarskjöld rather than the vision of social revolution championed by Neumann and his fellow OSS émigré analysts, yet it lacked Hammarksjöld's commitment to equal economic opportunities for all nations. It was initially justified by reference to the neutrality of international civil servants and the need for dynamic executive action to guarantee the freedom of nations and individuals, but it resulted in the intensification of uneven development and the growth of the monopolistic power of multinational corporations. By the 1980s, international intervention in the name of achieving development and security would be combined in over ninety states with the imposition of a model of structural adjustment that incorporated elements of Malthusian thinking about population control with neoliberal resistance to state planning and redistribution.

While a version of liberal economic thinking about the state shaped the internationalist management of decolonisation, that approach initially proved far more contested in the context of European reconstruction. State-building took quite a different direction in Europe. It is true that the light-touch approach to post-war reconstruction and the enabling of social revolution envisaged by the R&A did not eventuate. Nonetheless, the idea that the state had a limited role to play in planning, redistribution, or the provision of social welfare did not receive the same support in the practice of European reconstruction as it did in the practice of postcolonial development. Yet, over recent decades we have increasingly come to see an expansion of executive rule and a very contested economic argument for limiting state planning and redistribution begin to transform the European state in the name of achieving austerity and enabling economic growth.

The two projects of reconstruction and development are thus beginning to converge again in the twenty-first century. Central to that convergence is the role increasingly being played by the neoliberal vision of the rule of law in reconstructing the state – for a long time in Europe's former colonies, and now increasingly throughout Europe. As nation-states throughout Europe are subjected to another round of public sector funding cuts to protect the financial health of the Eurozone, however, the occupation of streets and squares across Europe by protestors and rioters signals the crisis of an international project of state reconstruction to which much of Africa, Asia and Eastern Europe has been subjected. Rather than demand that European states be reconstructed along the same lines that states of Asia, Africa and Latin America have been, this may be an opportune moment to re-examine the alternatives to liberal economic thinking that might yet be available.

PART III

Hammarskjöld, the UN and the Congo

11

Dag Hammarskjöld and the Congo crisis, 1960–1961

MARIA STELLA ROGNONI

11.1 Introduction

Fifty years after Dag Hammarskjöld's death, the approach adopted by the Secretary-General of the United Nations to confront the Congo crisis in 1960–1 is still of great significance. The same issues that were debated then – the form and extent of UN interventions and their broader political considerations – are relevant and questioned in today's UN interventions to secure peace and justice. Therefore it is useful to examine in detail Hammarskjöld's approach to the Congolese crisis in a highly complex political process, which has been perceived as a turning point in relations between newly independent countries, former colonial powers, and the superpowers.

Looking back at the time when the Congolese crisis transformed itself into one of Hammarskjöld's biggest diplomatic challenges, suffice it to recall that from the beginning of July 1960, a few days after the proclamation of the independence of the Congo on 30 June 1960, the Secretary-General had to find the best way to respond to an appeal from the new Congolese government for immediate military assistance. This call came against the backdrop of what, from the start, looked to be a major crisis that went beyond the troubled African context and had dangerous implications for the Cold War.

Although the scope and limits of the United Nations mission to the Congo, and its instruments, had been agreed upon in a number of Security Council resolutions, starting with Resolution 143 of 14 July 1960, the questions posed by the UN intervention in the huge African country continued to be debated. How far should the intervention go in helping

Maria Stella Rognoni is Senior Lecturer of History and Institutions of Africa at the Department of Political and Social Sciences, University of Florence.

the Congo to solve its internal problems, thus ceasing to be a menace to international peace and security? In the Cold War circumstances prevailing at that time, how could the independence of UN involvement be guaranteed given, for instance, that one of the two superpowers, the United States, provided the bulk of the funding? How would the broader context of the impressive changes taking place in the rest of Africa affect the viewpoints of the decision-makers within the UN and of the various governments, African and non-African, that were seeking to find a solution to the crisis?

If we separate these questions from the historical context of the Congo crisis, we realise how some of them – the extent and freedom of intervention in an internal crisis by an external force, funding of multilateral military and civilian operations, broader political considerations, and promotion of 'democratic rules of the game' – still matter in present UN actions and, more generally, in current international interventions in internal crises and conflicts.

If these premises are indeed true, then it is interesting and useful, even fifty years on, to analyse in detail Hammarskjöld's approach to the Congolese crisis to determine how he managed the constraints that faced him in discharging a duty whose risks and difficulties he understood very clearly and which ultimately brought him to his death. This is the aim of this chapter, the origins of which lie in broad research conducted into primary sources available in Belgian, American, French and British archives,[1] research that has been enriched and sharpened by consulting the Dag Hammarskjöld Collection held at the National Library of Sweden in Stockholm.

Hammarskjöld's role in the crisis forms the core of this analysis, and the chapter is divided into four sections: the origins of UN involvement in the crisis, the Katanga issue and the confrontation with Lumumba, the ousting of Lumumba, and new counterparts, old problems. These sections basically follow the chronological development of the crisis from its start in June 1960 to Hammarskjöld's death in September 1961.

Interestingly, the Hammarskjöld Collection, which is crucial in illuminating the decision-making process in the higher ranks of the UN, does not often appear among the sources used by researchers who have given their attention to the Congolese crisis, specifically the UN role in it. Significantly, even the most recent works on the topic are based

[1] See M. Rognoni, *Scacchiera Congolese: Materie Prime, Decolonizzazione e Guerra Fredda Nell'Africa dei Primi Anni Sessanta* (2003).

on American and European sources,[2] which are essential for grasping important aspects of the issue, but which can be usefully complemented by UN documents as well. The perspective of the world body is indeed different from that of a government – as different as their respective aims and instruments – and, by taking it into account, the overall picture is enriched. One can better grasp the issues at stake and the complexity of a political process that, far from dealing with just the Congo and Belgium, was perceived by the actors involved – and certainly by Dag Hammarskjöld – as a turning point in relations between the newly independent countries, the former colonial powers, and the superpowers.

11.2 The opening of the crisis and UN involvement

In the words of the Secretary-General as early as 19 July 1960:

> Congo operation is likely to go far beyond Suez story in all directions. If we succeed and if Seco [Security Council] accepts lines and philosophy developed in my report of yesterday, it will probably mean the opening of new and decisive chapter in history of under-developed countries and UN. For first time we come to grips with realities of post-colonial era, and I hope that we will not fail.[3]

From the start, Hammarskjöld realised that the dimensions of the crisis, triggered by the mutiny of part of the Congolese army, the secession of the richest province Katanga, and Belgium's military intervention, went far beyond the regional context. Cold War issues were certainly at stake, both in the field and in New York, where the decisions regarding the UN mission were made. Nevertheless, the bipolar confrontation of the Cold War, despite its many implications, was but one of the possible constraints that Hammarskjöld had to take into account in trying to define a policy for the Congo.

The United States and the Soviet Union, as superpowers, were certainly interested in mastering the African game and in not losing ground to one another, but they were by no means the only players on the scene. There was the Congolese political arena, as frail and fragmented as could be after a rushed decolonisation process. Far from sharing a common vision, the Prime Minister, Patrice Lumumba, the President of the republic,

[2] See, for instance, J. Kent, *America, the UN and Decolonisation: Cold War Conflict in the Congo* (2010).

[3] Outgoing Code Cable from Hammarskjöld to de Seynes. 19 July 1960. National Library of Sweden, MS L179:155.

Joseph Kasavubu, and the President of Katanga province, Moïse Tshombe (to cite only the most significant figures), were clearly not ready to compromise. There was the former colonial power, Belgium, which was trying to build through its Congolese bet – '*le pari congolais*' – the credibility it had failed to establish for itself during the decolonisation process. The goal in Brussels was to retain political and economic influence in the rich African country while accepting the surrender of formal power. Exerting maximum power and influence where possible was a goal fully shared by the big corporations (Belgian, but also British, French, American, Scandinavian, etc.) with interests in the Congo, especially in Katanga. For them, as for the majority of Belgian and Western settlers, preservation of the status quo was soon perceived as a matter of survival.

Meanwhile, as soon as the crisis erupted, the geographic position of the Congo, its economic relevance and its political frailty called out for the involvement of several significant African governments, which perceived the situation in Leopoldville, and in New York, as both a risk and an opportunity. During 1960, the UN's 'Year of Africa', international attention was being partly diverted from the usual hot spots, such as the Middle East and the Far East, to the heart of the African continent, opening up unexpected room for initiative and possibly for asserting new leadership. Finally, there was the Congolese population, fourteen million people unevenly distributed across a country as big as Western Europe, who had managed to survive one of the harshest of colonial administrations. Very few of them belonged to the privileged class of so-called '*evolués*', who, thanks to a certain level of education, filled the lower ranks of the colonial administration or enjoyed the status of small entrepreneurs and, with independence, could aspire to improve their social position. However, the great majority of the Congolese people, despite the high expectations linked to independence, did not have much to rely on and were far removed from the richness of their own country.

Against this complex backdrop, the Secretary-General of the United Nations, who was in the third year of his second mandate by the summer of 1960, recognised the stakes involved in the Congo, including the possibility of turning the crisis into an opportunity, thus opening the way for either a fundamental and seminal success, or a failure that might have serious consequences for the organisation. On 30 September 1960, in a stressful phase of the crisis, answering a cable sent by Dayal and comparing the situation in New York with that in Leopoldville, Hammarskjöld wrote: 'We also sit on volcano with the pleasant quality that, if it erupts, even the Organisation is likely to disappear underground. This may be meager consolation but it creates the proper kind of philosophical approach.'[4]

In any event, the risk was perceived to be so high that every decision had to be pondered cautiously, but under great pressure and often without adequate time. That is why analysis of the decision-making process at the apex of the Secretariat still provides, fifty years on, invaluable evidence of the Secretary-General's diplomatic skills. Apart from evaluating the role he played, one can appreciate his ability to place each choice within a broader picture in a constant attempt to mediate between constraints and opportunities, using all his capabilities for the ultimate accomplishment of the organisation's mission, thoughts about which he shared throughout his mandate. The Secretary-General made constant efforts to share his thoughts and worries with his closest team members as part of his decision-making. For instance, in a communication to A.M. Dayal, his special representative during the crisis, Hammarskjöld wrote:

> have strongest understanding for the enormous scope of the problem you are facing. We would be happy to be of any assistance but we cannot add anything of value to your own thinking, planning and action. And we are happy to know that the team we have on the spot is one in which we have the fullest confidence. We know that you are doing what is humanly possible with the means at your disposal in the mad situation.[5]

On the eve of Congolese independence there was a general fear, shared by major Western diplomatic missions, that neither the new Congolese political leaders nor the Belgian government were fully aware of the challenges and risks in the transfer of power. Even before the sensational speech delivered by Lumumba at the independence ceremony,[6] which showed that not everything was following the course the Belgians were trying to set for their former colony, there were rumours about the weaknesses of the newly independent country and the risk of a possible vacuum created by the transfer of power.[7]

[4] Outgoing Code Cable from Hammarskjöld to Dayal. 30 September 1960. National Library of Sweden, MS L179:155.

[5] Outgoing Cable Code from Hammarskjöld to Dayal. 28 September 1960 National Library of Sweden, MS L179: 155.

[6] J. Willame, *Patrice Lumumba: La Crise Congolaise Rivisitée* (1990), 112; T. Kanza, *The Rise and Fall of Patrice Lumumba: Conflict in the Congo* (1972), 181.

[7] See, for instance, Ministère des Affaires Etrangères, Archive Diplomatique, Paris (MAEF), Série Amérique- Lévant (AL) 1960–65, Sous-série Congo ex Belge (SSCeB), Congo Belge (CB) 7, tel.-lett. 135, P. Charpentier a Ministère des Affaires Etrangères, Léopoldville, 7 July 1960.

The idea of UN intervention in the Congo through a technical assistance programme was already being discussed before 30 June 1960. As early as 17 June 1960, Philip de Seynes, UN Under-Secretary for Economic and Social Affairs, wrote from Geneva to Hammarskjöld about talks among Belgian officials: 'Opinion unanimously and emphatically favourable to United Nations intervention and technical assistance in Congo as soon as possible.'[8] In the same cable, de Seynes also recounted some impressions of the Congolese Prime Minister: 'Lumumba is considered somewhere between Sekou Touré and Nkrumah, but more along Sekou Touré lines, yet more pragmatic and less doctrinaire. Considered unpredictable and given to quick decisions.'[9] When Ralph Bunche reached Leopoldville as Special Representative of the Secretary-General to attend the independence ceremonies, Lumumba himself explicitly asked for economic and financial experts – 'preference for expert from a small neutral country'[10] – to assist the new government in the negotiations with the Belgians on infrastructural projects, such as the Inga hydroelectric scheme.[11] The UN representative, in underlining the importance of a quick and positive response to the request ('it is a striking example of difficulty confronting this government, so uniquely lacking in technicians of every kind')[12] added a further consideration in his report to the Secretary-General: 'We also think it would be tactically advantageous to respond helpfully to this first request.'[13] It is not surprising, therefore, that as soon as the mutiny by part of the Congolese army broke out on 5 July 1960, quickly followed by Belgian military intervention and, a few days later, by Katanga's declaration of secession, both Kasavubu and Lumumba appealed to the UN

[8] Incoming Code Cable from De Seynes to Hammarskjöld and Bunche. 17 June 1960. National Library of Sweden, MS L179:155.

[9] *Ibid.*

[10] Incoming Code Cable from Bunche to Hammarskjöld and Léo. 6 July 1960. National Library of Sweden, MS L179:155.

[11] The reference is to a study presented at that time to the new Congolese government by a Belgian and other European firms on the development of a project of exploitation of hydroelectric power at Inga on the Congo River, 250 km west of Kinshasa in the Lower Congo Region. Later on, during Mobutu's years, two dams have been built: Inga I, in 1972, and Inga II, in 1982. In recent years, a new 'Grand Inga Project', that would represent the world's largest hydropower scheme, is under consideration. For basic information see for instance www.internationalrivers.org/resources/grand-inga-hydroelectric-project-an-overview-3356. See also http://postconflict.unep.ch/congo/en/content/inga-hydroelectric-projects.

[12] Incoming Code Cable from Bunche to Hammarskjöld and Léopoldville. 6 July 1960. National Library of Sweden, MS L179:155.

[13] *Ibid.*

as the first source of support.[14] Within a few days, similar appeals were made to the United States[15] and Ghana,[16] whereas Moscow received a sort of pre-alarm on 14 July 1960, stating that the Soviet Union might be called on for assistance in case the Western powers refused to stop the act of aggression against the Congo.[17]

Less than a week after independence, the situation in the field was becoming more and more worrying. Acts of disobedience among the ranks of the Force Publique, now called Armée Nationale Congolaise (ANC), were spreading.[18] On 8 July 1960, in trying to meet the requests of the army, Lumumba and Kasavubu announced a process of Africanisation aimed at drastically reducing the Belgian presence among the higher ranks of the ANC. However, the riots did not stop, and panic started to spread among the white population.[19]

The cables sent by Ralph Bunche to the Secretary-General from 7 July 1960 until the final breaking off of diplomatic relations between the Congo and Belgium on 14 July 1960, with the subsequent Security Council resolution of the same day, give a vivid picture of a tension that nobody seemed to be able to calm.[20] 'Powder keg here', wrote Bunche on 9 July 1960, 'but full explosion may be averted. Terrific tension among Europeans owing to shock of disillusionment about reliability of corps publique'.[21] The answer Hammarskjöld gave on the same day expresses his initial view of the crisis but already includes several critical points that would last

[14] Incoming Code Cable from Bunche to Hammarskjöld. 10 July 1960. National Library of Sweden, MS L179:155.

[15] In the face of the Belgian military intervention in Katanga, Luluabourg and Matadi on 12 July 1960, while Lumumba and Kasavubu were out of the capital, Foreign Minister Justin Bomboko, with the consent of the Vice-Prime Minister Antoine Gizenga, appealed to Washington. See Rognoni, *supra* note 1, at 68.

[16] This request was made by Antoine Gizenga on 13 July 1960. See J. Gérard-Libois and B. Verhaegen, *Congo 1960* (1961), 546.

[17] The text of the cable sent to Khrushchev and signed by Kasavubu and Lumumba is in Gérard-Libois and Verhaegen, *supra* note 16, at 555.

[18] *Ibid.*, 333–370.

[19] On the Africanisation of the ANC see *ibid.*, 406–407; see also Willame, *supra* note 6, 131–151; Rognoni, *supra* note 1, 57–58. On the reactions of the white population see C. Young, *Politics in the Congo: Decolonization and Independence* (1965), 316–317.

[20] See, for instance, Incoming Code Cable from Bunche to Hammarskjöld and Léo. 7 July 1960. National Library of Sweden, MS L179:155. In that cable, Bunche reported on the intervention of the Belgian ambassador, Van den Bosch, who avoided a disaster by refusing to follow General Janssens's request for the general intervention of Belgian troops without the necessary prior consent of the Congolese minister of defence (Lumumba).

[21] Incoming Code Cable from Bunche to Hammarskjöld and Léo. 9 July 1960. National Library of Sweden, MS L179:155.

much longer and affect his approach to the whole Congolese operation: 'Deeply worried by your evaluation of the situation which indicates that we all deal now not with authorities but with an excitable and demoralized mob.'[22] The lack of reliable counterparts among the Congolese politicians would remain a constant concern throughout the crisis.[23] Moreover, Hammarskjöld added:

> What worries me most, apart from considerable risks that may be run by many, is possibility that situation will develop where European military intervention becomes a psychological necessity with a breakdown for African-Western relations and very serious repercussions for the whole independence development.[24]

The Secretary-General's words show his anxiety about the broader and longer term implications of possible mistakes in the Congo beyond only the Congolese or Belgian perspectives.

Suddenly, after almost eighty years of a close and exclusive relationship between the Congo and Belgium, the newly independent African country was being projected on to the international stage in the most dramatic and least manageable way. As the Secretary-General quickly realised, the forces involved and the challenges to be faced called for an extraordinary effort by the international community and the United Nations in particular.[25] From the field, in the face of the developments prompted by the secession of Katanga and the continuation of Belgian military intervention despite the protests of the Congolese government, the moderate initial position taken by Bunche turned into an open request for intervention.

> In a situation such as this where fear is profound throughout European community and is manifest also among Africans, where excitement holds at fever pitch and tension is unrelaxing, one who is in the midst of it as I am unavoidably questions both his power of observation and analysis

[22] Outgoing Code Cable from Hammarskjöld to Bunche. 9 July 1960. National Library of Sweden, MS L179:155. It's worth noting that Hammarskjöld's considerations came before the declaration of secession of Katanga, which further exacerbated the situation and confirmed his worst fears.

[23] *Ibid.* Commenting from Léopoldville, Hammarskjöld wrote: 'I feel there is nobody, repeat nobody, on Congolese side combining reason and authority in way which enables me to explore matter before phrasing bid. I must therefore probably again work very much on instinct.' Incoming Code Cable from Hammarskjöld to Cordier. 4 August 1960. National Library of Sweden, MS L179:155.

[24] *Ibid.*

[25] US Department of State, *Foreign Relations of the United States, 1958–1960*, Vol. XIV, *Africa* (1992), Doc. 262.

wrote Bunche to Hammarskjöld on 13 July 1960. He continued:

> there has been considerable deterioration ... this leads now to lean heavily to view that only some manifestation of 'third presence' which definitely should be international, military but not indispensably fighting men, can save the situation ... But there must be a quick and impressive manifestation of 'moving in' by the UNATIONS on the situation here if our effort is to be effective.[26]

Despite this belief and the fact that he followed all the moves made by the Congolese leadership in those dramatic days from close up, Bunche admitted he had been taken by surprise when Kasavubu and Lumumba had formalised the request for UN military intervention.[27]

The following steps are well known. The Secretary-General, under Article 99 of the UN Charter, brought the issue before the Security Council.[28] After intense negotiations, a Tunisian resolution asking Belgium to withdraw its troops and authorising the Secretary-General to provide the needed military assistance, passed with eight votes and the abstentions of France, the United Kingdom and China.[29] The miracle of the success at the Security Council could not hide the weaknesses of the text that was agreed upon, despite the Cold War constraints of the time, precisely because it left room for at least two different interpretations. According to Western countries and, to a certain extent, to the Secretary-General, the UN operation should assist the Congolese government to maintain internal order, whereas the Soviet Union, Poland and Tunisia thought of it as an instrument to help the Congolese government to face Belgian aggression.[30]

26 Incoming Code Cable from Bunche to Hammarskjöld. 13 July 1960. National Library of Sweden, MS L179:155.

27 *Ibid.* Bunche continues: 'Congo request for UN troops was complete surprise. No prior discussion or indication. Most if anything anticipated as result of activities Belgian troops was protest to UN about violation of treaty. Apparent reason for the extreme request was reports of serious engagements between Congolese and Belgian troops at Matadi on 11th. 2. Certain alternative to quick UN action is extension of Belgian troops intervention and probable involvement before long of French forces across river.'

28 'Summary Diary' by Hammarskjöld. 10–19 July 1960. National Library of Sweden, MS L179:141.

29 See A.W. Cordier and F. Wilder (eds.), *Public Papers of the Secretaries-General of the United Nations*, Vol. V, *Dag Hammarskjöld, 1960–1961* (1975), 16–27. On the Belgian position see Ministère des Affaires Etrangères, du Commerce Extérieur et de la Coopération au Développement, Bruxelles (MAECC), Direction des Archives (DA), Archives Diplomatiques (AD) Afrique, Congo, général (AF I-1), Juillet, note, W. Loridan, New York, 28.7.60.

30 See Rognoni, *supra* note 1, 72–77.

The compromise secured in New York was essential for the establishment of UNOC (as the operation of the United Nations in the Congo was called). At the same time, through it, the long Cold War shadows reached the African country and started to count, not as the only important factor, but certainly as a crucial one. To what extent was the Secretary-General able to cope with the constraints arising from the difficult situation in the field and the fragile bases of his mandate? This question opened up a political debate that was bound to characterise much of the UN intervention in the Congo and to continue for a long time. The end of the Cold War has partly helped us to look back on that period with a different perspective, giving weight to factors other than those exclusively inspired by the bipolar confrontation.[31]

Simply put, the fact that the Congo continued to be the scene of violence and instability after the end of the Cold War and the collapse of Mobutu's regime calls for deeper analysis that takes into account long-term trends together with contingent factors. The same approach could be applied to analysis of UNOC and Hammarskjöld's role in it. Besides the Cold War dimension, he had to consider a series of other factors, the first of which was the impact of the crisis on the newly independent countries which would form the bulk of the UN's members in the near future. The decision to implement the mandate conferred by United Nations Security Council Resolution 143 through a regional approach is a good illustration of this double concern: by asking only African or neutral countries to contribute troops to the UN forces in the Congo, Hammarskjöld managed to keep the major powers[32] out of Congolese territory while offering to countries looking for international recognition and visibility an opportunity to assume wider responsibility.

[31] See, for instance, the interesting contribution by D. Gibbs, *The Political Economy of Third World Intervention: Mines, Money, and U.S. Policy in the Congo Crisis* (1991).

[32] For the Secretary-General's attitude towards France in this respect, see in particular the note he wrote on 14 July 1960 after meeting with the French ambassador to the UN, Armand Bérard: 'Paris had a feeling that I was in principle excluding French from all possible functions in the UN operation. I said this was complete misunderstanding … He should know that the French were excluded in a UN paramilitary unit in line with principles which were clearly established in UN common law. That meant that there would be no Frenchmen in any function in the UN Force in the Congo, nor would be any US, UK and USSR.' Continuing in the same vein but with a bit of irony, he says: 'Paris further was eager to see true universality in the international Force. I said that true universality would give me an army as the minimum national unit (and in a sense also the maximum) was roughly a battalion. We did not need initially more than some 2000–3000 men and with the Congo approach to Ghana and the Tunis and Morocco approaches to me, in turn leading on to Mali and Guinea I had safely in hand that number already in one integrated corner of Africa.' 'Summary Diary' by Hammarskjöld. 14 July 1960. National Library of Sweden, MS L179:141.

11.3 The Katanga issue and the confrontation with Lumumba

When UNOC was launched as a regional approach, it soon became clear that there were many obstacles to its implementation. Some could be tackled by intensifying UN assistance, but others appeared riskier. The secession of Katanga and the role played by the Belgian government (by certain ministers, in particular)[33] and by Belgian and other Western economic interests became the issue. As early as 14 July 1960, in a top secret cable to Hammarskjöld, Bunche wrote: 'If Government cannot forestall secession of Katanga strongly rumoured here night 11th, it could be start of rapid disintegration of this State.'[34] Meanwhile, evaluation of the leading Congolese counterpart, whose collaboration was crucial to the implementation of the resolution, was beginning to take place both in Leopoldville and New York.[35] 'Talked Lumumba two hours and half morning 16th', wrote Bunche the same day. 'He is fluent but utterly maniacal child. With Leo and entire country on verge of disaster UN troops pouring in etc. his main and excited concern was a UN aircraft fly him to Stanleyville for obvious political reasons.'[36] In a subsequent message, the Special Representative talked in different terms about Thomas Kanza (governmental delegate for relations with the UN) and Justin Bomboko (Minister of External Affairs), whom he described as the only ones to have 'education, comprehension but little authority'.[37] Just a few days after 14 July 1960, Lumumba became the target of criticism in Western diplomatic circles – as one would expect – but also among UN staff. Certainly, his firm and outspoken refusal to countenance

[33] Harold d'Aspremont Lynden was one of these ministers. Rognoni, *supra* note 1, at 93, and at 202–203.

[34] Incoming Code Cable from Bunche to Hammarskjöld. 14 July 1960. National Library of Sweden, MS L179:155. See also, Incoming Code Cable from Bunche to Hammarskjöld and Léo. 21 July 1960. National Library of Sweden, MS L179:155, in which Bunche gave his first impression of Tshombe: 'Tshombe is a puppet and nothing more. He represents relatively few people, in fact.'

[35] United Nations Security Council Resolution 143 was explicit on this point: 'The Security Council … decides to authorize the Secretary-General to take the necessary steps, in consultation with the Government of the Republic of the Congo, to provide the Government with such military assistance as may be necessary until, through the efforts of the Congolese Government with the technical assistance of the United Nations, the national security forces may be able, in the opinion of the Government, to meet fully their tasks', UN Doc. S/RES/143 (1960).

[36] The cable continued by stating: 'Have disabused him in clearest language that UN not here to assist any political purposes. UN troops will not repeat not fight Belgians or anyone else here, and that they will remain completely and exclusively under UN orders.' Incoming Code Cable from Bunche to Hammarskjöld. 16 July 1960. National Library of Sweden, MS L179:155.

[37] *Ibid.*

hesitation in accomplishing what he thought should be the UN mission did not help to forge a good relationship between him and UN personnel, or the Secretary-General himself.[38]

It was not Lumumba's supposed communism or radicalism that affected his relationship with the Secretary-General, nor Hammarskjöld's alleged tendency to lean towards Western positions or to be soft on the Belgians. In other words, it was not only or mainly a Cold War issue that stood in the way of their relationship, but their differing and contradictory visions of the role of the UN in the Congo. In Lumumba's view, the UN had been called by the Congolese government to help it regain full control of the internal situation. Thus, for instance, it was essential to put an immediate end to Katanga's secession. In no way could he conceive of a role for his government subordinate to that of the UN.[39] Hammarskjöld believed ONUC should assist the Congolese government in re-establishing law and order in the country, but this mandate should be accomplished by taking into account and safeguarding the impartiality and universal mission of the organisation.[40] Whereas Lumumba, since the beginning of the UN operation, criticised the lack of action and slowness on the part of UN officials as an 'imperialist trick',[41] Hammarskjöld made time-consuming efforts to find a

[38] An example was Lumumba's declaration – received by the Secretary-General on 18 July 1960 – to appeal to the Soviet Union if UN troops did not replace within 24–48 hours all Belgian troops throughout the country. Incoming Code Cable from Bunche to Hammarskjöld. 18 July 1960. National Library of Sweden, MS L179:155; see, Hammarskjöld's answer, Outgoing Code Cable from Hammarskjöld to Bunche. 18 July 1960. National Library of Sweden, MS L179:155; see also, Hammarskjöld's reflections in 'Summary Diary of Congo Operation' by Hammarskjöld. 19 July 1960. National Library of Sweden, MS L179:141.

[39] A good example of the divide between the two sides can be found in a minute of conversation between Ralph Bunche and Patrice Lumumba. Notes on Conversation with Mr. Lumumba. 12 August 1960. National Library of Sweden, MS L179:141. See also Cordier and Wilder, *supra* note 29, at 97–121.

[40] In order to strengthen his position, the Secretary-General insisted on the importance of understanding the UN force as a 'major manifestation of Africa solidarity'. Against any attempt to introduce the big powers into the picture (as threatened by Lumumba in his controversial ultimatum), he was very straightforward: 'This is a question of an either-or: either assistance from African nations within the framework of African solidarity, or assistance from big powers from outside the region.' In the second case, he continued, 'this would undoubtedly mean a major blow to the peaceful evolution of African independence and might well lay open to a major conflict with possible disastrous consequences for Congo and Africa as a whole'. Outgoing Code Cable from Hammarskjöld to Bunche. 18 July 1960. National Library of Sweden, MS L179:155.

[41] *Ibid.*

formula of intervention capable of preserving unanimity, or at least broad consensus, among UN members. 'We cannot permit ourselves to bring havoc in another nation situation', wrote the Secretary-General to Cordier from Leopoldville on 1 August 1960.[42] Hammarskjöld continued: 'This does not mean playing soft, but it does mean playing reasonably. My main responsibility to the Security Council is for peace, justice and quiet in general, not to any one specific point at a cost which may be immeasurable in case of rash action.'[43]

On 22 July 1960, a second Security Council resolution called on Belgium to 'implement speedily' the withdrawal of its troops from the Congo and requested all states to 'refrain' from direct or indirect intervention that might worsen the domestic situation and compromise Congolese territorial integrity and political independence.[44] The message should have been clear both to Belgium[45] and to all those within or outside the country who might want to conspire against Congo's 'territorial integrity' and 'political independence'. As for the Secretary-General, the resolution gave him further credit by strengthening his mandate. Despite the difficulties encountered in dealing with his counterparts in the field and in New York so far, it was evident that he wanted to master the timing of, and approach to, the implementation of his mission. His main concern during the summer of 1960 was finding an equilibrium among various and contradictory pressures,[46] the juridical framework of his mandate, the Congolese

[42] Incoming Code Cable from Hammarskjöld to Cordier and Léo. 1 August 1960. National Library of Sweden, MS L179:155.

[43] 'What must be impressed on people', wrote Hammarskjöld, 'is a. that in this as in other cases, military action is follow up on diplomatic action, and that it is more important here than anywhere else, as we want to preserve the frail basic unity of the Congolese people and their very frail constitution. My view on this point is shared by all Congolese with any political experience and any nation feeling. b. there is a certain rhythm in the deployment of military force over this vast territory. This rhythm is determined by the strength of the force in relation to needs, by the development of logistics support and by transport and similar technicalities ... Such a potential is not yet reached ... this is hard fact but it has to be faced also by eager braves'. *Ibid.*

[44] UN Doc. S/RES/145 (1960).

[45] Some of those in the UN's higher ranks were very critical of the Belgian attitude towards the Congo. See, for instance, Incoming Code Cable from Bunche to Hammarskjöld and Léo. 24 July 1960. National Library of Sweden, MS L179:155.

[46] The difficulty of the effort is well conveyed in Hammarskjöld's words: 'I thought I had experienced the maximum of diplomatic and political complications, committed with risks, in UN activities, – but this -!'. Incoming Code Cable from Hammarskjöld to Cordier and Léo. 31 July 1960. National Library of Sweden, MS L179:155.

government's frailty and fragmentation,[47] the requests from the countries that contributed most to UNOC (the United States in terms of money; some African and Asian countries in terms of troops), and the concerns of colonial or former colonial powers.[48] On Katanga – the issue that did the most to exacerbate his divergences with Prime Minister Lumumba – Hammarskjöld's position was straightforward: Katanga was a decisive test and the UN should take action there in order not to lose the support of African and anti-colonial powers.[49] Once again, the disagreements with Lumumba were not about the aims – since both of them favoured an end to the secession – but the methods and timing in achieving it.

Of course, delay in ending the secession in Katanga (and the various influences at play in the field) could imply – this was Lumumba's main point – a weakening of the central government in a crucial phase. Hammarskjöld's detractors saw in his attitude an attempt to indirectly influence the internal debate among Congolese political forces, which was particularly heated in those weeks of late July and August.[50] On the contrary, during his trip to the Congo, Hammarskjöld made up his mind to foster quick action to avoid an extremist drift. He wrote to Cordier on 3 August:

> If we are scared of risks, the outcome seems too certain: a dictatorial regime with clear orientation seemingly requested by Congolese people itself in frustration with conditions and in reaction against difficulties encountered in first international contacts with one side.[51]

[47] For instance, Hammarskjöld wrote, 'I have found Katanga problem deeply intertwined with domestic politics and members of Central Government keen on keeping its political lead in the matter', after talks with various Congolese leaders. Incoming Code Cable from Hammarskjöld to Cordier and Léo. 29 July 1960. National Library of Sweden, MS L179:155.

[48] Outgoing Code Cable from Hammarskjöld to Bunche. 26 July 1960. National Library of Sweden, MS L179:155.

[49] Ministère des Affaires Etrangères, du Commerce Extérieur et de la Coopération au Développement, Bruxelles, Direction des Archives, Archives Diplomatiques Afrique, Congo, général (AF I-1), Juillet, memorandum of conversation (P. Wigny, D. Hammarskjöld, W. Loridan, A. Holvoet, C. Schuurmans *et al.*), Brussels, 27 July 1960.

[50] See, for instance, D. Gibbs, 'The United Nations, International Peacekeeping and the Question of "Impartiality": Revisiting the Congo Operation of 1960' (2000) 38 *Journal of Modern African Studies* 3, 359, at 359–377. The contrary was also true. At the beginning of August, when Hammarskjöld was visiting the Congo, he became convinced of the need for the UN forces to enter the secessionist province as soon as possible for 'lifting Katanga question out of fight between extremists and others'. Incoming Code Cable from Hammarskjöld to Cordier. 3 August 1960. National Library of Sweden, MS L179:155.

[51] *Ibid.* At the end of the same cable the Secretary-General noted: 'Afraid I cannot impress on you how things are in this never-never land. For the second time in this crisis we were today on the eve of Korea, and I do not know if countermove led to postponement for

Additional support for the Secretary-General's approach was given by Security Council Resolution 146 of 9 August 1960 (approved by nine votes and one abstention), which reiterated the prohibition on the UN to 'be a party' in or 'in no sense to exert influence' on the issue between the provincial government and central government.[52] The point was further reaffirmed by the Secretary-General's memorandum to the Security Council of 12 August 1960, which, not surprisingly, provoked a negative reaction from Lumumba, who criticised the UN's ineffectiveness in ending Katanga's secession, Hammarskjöld's interpretation of his mandate and his decision to start direct negotiations with Tshombe.[53]

A harsh confrontation between the Congolese Prime Minister and the UN Secretary-General lasted until late August[54], when the majority of the Security Council members endorsed Hammarskjöld's interpretation, thus weakening Lumumba's international standing.[55] The deterioration of the relationship with Western countries and the UN increased the political isolation of the Prime Minister, whose domestic position was also under pressure. Rivals from the outset, like Jean Bolikango or Albert Kalonji, were gaining support, colleagues such as Cyrille Adoula and Joseph Ileo[56] were dissociating themselves from what they judged to be excessive centralisation and misuse of power, and criticism of the approach and content of Lumumba's leadership was spreading even within his cabinet.[57] Thomas Kanza, one of Lumumba's closest friends,

more than couple of day. Long-term we are facing a China problem. It is now that action must be taken, inspired in no way by choice of side in cold war, but simply in the interest of peace for people whose innocence no party should be permitted to abuse for its own purposes and with disastrous consequences.'

52 UN Doc. S/RES/146 (1960).

53 UN Doc. S/4417/Add.6 (12 August 1960). For some of the UN senior officials' comments on Lumumba's reaction to Secretary-General's memorandum see Incoming Code Cable from Bunche to Cordier and Léo. 12 August 1960. National Library of Sweden, MS L179:155.

54 See, for instance, Notes on conversation with Mr. Lumumba. 12 August 1960. National Library of Sweden, MS L179:141.

55 See www.un.org/en/sc/repertoire/59–63/Chapter%208/59–63_08–8-Situation%20in%20the%20Republic%20of%20Congo.pdf, at 166.

56 In a cable sent to the Secretary-General, Bunche reported: 'Morning 25 Ileo told me in confidence that at least 13 ministers were opposed to Lumumba but dared not to speak out ... His view is that Lumumba called for UN only when he thought it politically advantageous to do so. Now, finding that UN will not permit him to use it as an instrument on behalf of his political ends, he is against it.' Incoming Code Cable from Bunche to Hammarskjöld. 25 August 1960. National Library of Sweden, MS L179:155.

57 For instance, Minister of External Affairs Joseph Bomboko, for instance, did not approve of the total break with Belgium and kept informal contacts with Ambassador Van den

was particularly worried by the possible outcome of the confrontation with the upper echelons of the UN: 'Certainly we were all too aware of the harm done when Lumumba effectively broke off all personal relations with Hammarskjöld – in one of the worst diplomatic errors he committed during that August 1960.'[58] But it was among the grassroots of the *Alliance des Bakongo* (ABAKO) movement that strong opposition grew to Lumumba's premiership, thus laying the basis for his ousting in the first days of September 1960.[59]

Certainly, the pressures to get rid of the Prime Minister were spreading among Western governments as well, and the CIA was working out a plan for his 'removal'.[60] Against this general backdrop, Lumumba's decision to fight an open battle with UNOC and the Secretary-General himself proved to be a decided mistake. Probably for want of alternatives, the Prime Minister called an All African Independent States Conference in Leopoldville, for 25–31 August 1960, in the hopes of building an African consensus on his struggle. The delegates, from various African countries,[61] were struck by the general climate of tension and, following a position put forward by Tunisia[62] and contrary to Lumumba's expectations, advocated a more moderate line towards the UN and its Secretary-General in

Bosch. Willame, *supra* note 6, at 373. See also, on Bomboko's attitude, Incoming Code Cable from Bunche to Hammarskjöld. 21 August 1960. National Library of Sweden, MS L179:155.

[58] Kanza, *supra* note 6, at 262.

[59] See, for example, D. Bacquelaine, F. Willems and M.T. Coenen (eds.), *Rapport fait au nom de la Commission d'Enquête Parlamentaire Visant à Déterminer les Circonstances Exactes de l'Assassinat de Patrice Lumumba et l'Implication éventuelle des Responsables Politiques Belges dans Celui-ci* (Chambre des représentants de Belgique) (2001), at 105–106; Willame, *supra* note 6, at 379–381; A. Maurel, *Le Congo de la Colonisation Belge à l'Indépendence* (1962), at 322. See also Rognoni, *supra* note 1, at 131–139.

[60] US Department of State, *Foreign Relations of the United States, 1958–1960*, Vol. XIV, *Africa* (1992), Doc. 189; see also, United States Senate, *Alleged Assassination Plots Involving Foreign Leaders: An Interim Report of the Select Committee to Study Governmental Operations with Respect to Intelligence Activities* (1975), 15. For the French position, see US Department of State, *Foreign Relations of the United States, 1958–1960*, Vol. XIV, *Africa* (1992), Doc. 177.

[61] The conference was attended by the ministers of external affairs of Tunisia, Sudan, Liberia, Togo, Ethiopia, Morocco, Guinea, Ghana, the United Arab Republic, Mali, the Provisional Government of Algeria, Congo Brazzaville, and other representatives of non-independent countries. Rognoni, *supra* note 1, at 135.

[62] See, Incoming Code Cable from Bunche to Hammarskjöld. 27 August 1960. National Library of Sweden, MS L179:155; see also, Incoming Code Cable from Bunche to Hammarskjöld and Léo. 30 August 1960. National Library of Sweden, MS L179:155.

particular, thus clearly manifesting Lumumba's isolation.[63] Lumumba's showdown with the Secretary-General (probably stemming from his frustration at what he saw as misuse of the UN force in the Congo) represented a new defeat for the Prime Minister. His subsequent decision to appeal directly to the Soviet Union for help was the last step in his political fall. From the Secretary-General's perspective, this attempt to gain support outside the UN framework by involving a superpower contradicted all the efforts made until then and confirmed the image of Lumumba as the essential obstacle to a positive outcome for UNOC.[64]

Reassessing the UN position in the context of developments in the field after the African conference had ended, Hammarskjöld wrote rather bluntly: 'There is one page that has to be turned and that is Lumumba's and Gizenga's and, for example, Gbenye's with their complete misconception of rights in relation to the UN and their role in the world.' Concluding in an ironic tone and with a good measure of self-confidence, he added:

> For the rest: visitors galore, repainted planes, formal protests written in Leo and possibly also civil war trucks speak their eloquent language. But in spite of that and other worries I believe that the risk of another Korean situation is now back of us.[65]

11.4 The ousting of Lumumba: new counterparts, old problems

When, on 5 September 1960, using a debatable (and much discussed) article of the *Loi Fondamentale*, President Kasavubu dismissed Lumumba from office, the UN's immediate response was mainly left to officials in the field. Cordier felt it necessary to take prompt action to avoid the spread of violence, so he ordered UN forces to keep control of all ports, airports and the national radio.[66] The decision was eventually endorsed by

[63] Ghana in particular had been very close to Lumumba's position since the beginning of the crisis, but followed the Tunisian line. Nkrumah tried hard to induce the Prime Minister to adopt a more moderate course. See, National Archives and Records Administration (NARA), Record Group 59, General Records of the Department of State (GRDS), Central Decimal File (CDF) 1960–63, box 1956, 770G.00, tel. 321, W. C. Flake a Sec. of State, Accra, 6.9.60.

[64] See, in particular, a top secret draft note on the evolution of the situation on the field by the UN Secretary-General dated 4 September 1960, National Library of Sweden, MS L179:141. See also US Department of State, *Foreign Relations of the United States, 1958–1960*, Vol. XIV, *Africa* (1992), Doc. 180 and 190.

[65] Outgoing Code Cable from Hammarskjöld to Cordier. 1 September 1960. National Library of Sweden, MS L179:155.

[66] On 5 September the correspondence from and to Léopoldville is particularly intense. For the instructions given by Cordier to local UN commanders see, for instance, Incoming

the Secretary-General, who became the target of strong criticism by the Eastern bloc and many African states.[67] They considered Cordier's action as new and heavy-handed interference and the final proof of UNOC's biased role.[68] Although the sources give no clear evidence of direct involvement by Hammarskjöld or his closest staff in Lumumba's ousting, the general climate of tension and mistrust prevailing at the time between the Prime Minister and the high echelons of the UN Secretariat allows us to think that Kasavubu, with or without a precise *placet* from Cordier,[69] acted in the knowledge that his decision might please many, even in the UN. For present purposes, it is interesting to note how Hammarskjöld tried to counter the attacks and criticism by keeping the issue in the realm of principle, justifying the UN's taking control of the most important communication lines only as a measure to avoid a general uprising, thus accomplishing its mandate.[70]

On the other hand, and with perfect timing, the replacement of Cordier by the Indian officer Rajeshwar Dayal as the Secretary-General's Special Representative in the Congo on 8 September 1960 did mark a significant change in UNOC's general approach to the crisis. Dayal did not hide his view of the need for the UN to get back on 'the path of legality and even-handed justice',[71] thus indirectly admitting a diversion from that path in the recent past.[72] This new attitude was a response (fully endorsed by Hammarskjöld) to the need for the UN to regain the essential support of Asian and African states at a moment when it was losing credibility and

Code Cable from Cordier to Hammarskjöld. 5 September 1960. n. B-797, National Library of Sweden, MS L179:155. In a subsequent cable to the UN Secretary-General Cordier writes: 'Blocking of runways regarded as necessary in grave national emergency involving threat to international peace and security. It represented not a deviation but an extension of the measures taken in implementation of Security Council resolutions to maintain peace and security ... Our action was not taken in compliance with the presidential order nor even with the order as a necessary basis, but rather on our own appreciation.' See text of cable to UN Secretary General from Mr Cordier. 7 September 1960. National Library of Sweden, MS L179:155.

67 See, for instance, Outgoing Code Cable, from Hammarskjöld to Cordier. 5 September 1960. n. 1553. National Library of Sweden, MS L179:155. See also A. James, *Britain and the Congo Crisis, 1960–63* (1996), 42.

68 The sources show no evidence of a direct involvement of the UN in the ousting of the Prime Minister.

69 See Willame, *supra* note 6, at 394–395.

70 See Rognoni, *supra* note 1, 148–152.

71 R. Dayal, *Mission for Hammarskjöld: The Congo Crisis* (1976), 47.

72 Dayal also showed great concern over the desperate conditions of the country, stating in one cable, 'With complete and utter recklessness, the political struggle – if it can be so called – is going on without logic or sense. Meanwhile the country is hurtling head

the very office of the Secretary-General was under attack by the Soviet Union.[73] Consistently, UN forces prevented the arrest of Lumumba ordered by Mobutu on 12 September 1960 (and again in October 1960),[74] ensured his protection in the following weeks, and adopted a strong stand in favour of the definite withdrawal of Belgian personnel ('military, para-military and civilians') from the Congo, including Katanga.[75]

In the face of the political turmoil produced by the confrontation between the President and the Prime Minister that resulted in Mobutu's takeover on 19 September and the ensuing formation of the *College des Commissaires*,[76] later recognised by President Kasavubu, Hammarskjöld and his closest entourage in the Congo managed to retain a neutral position.[77] Significantly, he continued to be criticised by both camps. Nevertheless, he succeeded in securing basic consensus among Asian and African countries.[78] Resisting the pressures coming at him from both

long on the road to disintegration and chaos'. Incoming Code Cable from Dayal to Hammarskjöld. 15 September 1960. National Library of Sweden, MS L179:155.

[73] Commenting on those attacks, Hammarskjöld wrote to Dayal: 'Round up in a day of cold war ... My basic feeling however is that the very venom of certain statements is a recognition of defeat, which again is of interest for it means that it is our duty to continue in the interest of those who wish only the best for the people of the Congo.' Outgoing Code Cable from Hammarskjöld to Dayal. 23 September 1960. National Library of Sweden, MS L179:151.

[74] See, for instance, Incoming Code Cable from Dayal to Hammarskjöld and Léo. 29 September 1960. National Library of Sweden, MS L179:155.

[75] Ministère des Affaires Etrangères, du Commerce Extérieur et de la Coopération au Développement, Bruxelles, Direction des Archives, Archives Diplomatiques, Afrique, Congo, général (AF I-1), Octobre, ONUC, copie de note, Dag Hammarskjöld à W. Loridan, Léopoldville, 8.10.60.

[76] For an assessment of Mobutu's attitude, see Incoming Code Cable from Dayal to Hammarskjöld and Léo. 19 September 1960. National Library of Sweden, MS L179:155. Rumours of a possible takeover by Mobutu had been circulating since 14 September. See, Incoming Code Cable from Dayal to Hammarskjöld. 14 September 1960. National Library of Sweden, MS L179:155.

[77] 'It is charmingly ironical counterpoint daily to be told here how we have disorganised the central government, paralysed administration, put up Mobutu, support Tshombe and act for the Belgians at the same time as your reports and even newspapers in their biased way tell about the attacks on UN from those same quarters. The role of strict impartiality is not one for somebody who "wants to be loved". Aesthetically the balance would be perfect if both sides in the cold war used the same degree of publicity in voicing their dissatisfaction.' Outgoing Code Cable from Hammarskjöld to Dayal. 23 October 1960. National Library of Sweden, MS L179:156.

[78] 'If the Afro-Asian stick together, or even if only the Africans stick together, they represent new big power to which certain others have to bow', wrote Hammarskjöld in a cable to Dayal after the meeting of the General Assembly that had confirmed its support for the Secretary-General against the expectations of the Soviet Union. 'You know', he continued, 'this is a theory on which I have worked now for two months. Today it was fully

sides, he tried to work for the implementation of his mandate, with priority being given to preserving the legitimacy and credibility of the UN and of his office. In his own words, the UN must 'keep clean on the record, wherever it may lead'.[79]

The attempt to find a solution to the crisis brought Hammarskjöld to a now well-known endpoint. In the months following the dismissal of Lumumba, many were the moments of tension and the difficult choices he had to face. Certainly the most dangerous one was the arrest[80] and the subsequent murder of Lumumba[81] with the consent of President Kasavubu and General Mobutu and the active participation of Katanga's government officers. Again, from the UN's perspective – in the face of a human tragedy that could have been predicted, leaving room for all kinds of speculations – the death of Patrice Lumumba represented both a failure and a risk. A failure because, despite the direct responsibilities that should be searched for elsewhere,[82] the UN was in the Congo to secure law and order, and the death of Lumumba and two of his companions, Joseph Okito and Maurice Mpolo, showed the world how far UNOC had still to

vindicated and I regard the fact that the Afro-Asian group in this way stood up to the test, found its own strength and a new cohesion, is more important than any other result'. Outgoing Code Cable from Hammarskjöld to Dayal. 20 September 1960. National Library of Sweden, MS L179:155.

79 This comment was made by the Secretary-General during a discussion with the United States representative at the UN. Hammarskjöld noted in particular the complexity of the legal aspects involved in the confrontation between the President and the Prime Minister and the ensuing role of Ileo's Cabinet. Significant also is the comment reported in the memorandum of conversation that described the US reaction to Hammarskjöld's stand: 'Our strongest impression is that he sees no clear course of action in Léopoldville to deal with the present situation and has fallen back on a completely do nothing "impartiality", although he realizes that this may be working in Lumumba's favour.' US Department of State, *Foreign Relations of the United States, 1958–1960*, Vol. XIV, *Africa* (1992), Doc. 249. See also, Rognoni, *supra* note 1, at 147.

80 Immediately after Lumumba's arrest, Hammarskjöld wrote to Dayal: 'We are in the middle of an extraordinarily complicated and indeed politically dangerous situation. I believe all we can do is to fall back on our right and duty to stand firmly on Charter principles, as overriding all other considerations, even if this would lay us open to allegations of partisanship – perhaps even from both sides.' Outgoing Code Cable from Hammarskjöld to Dayal. 12 December 1960. National Library of Sweden, MS L179:156.

81 On Lumumba's murder see, in particular, Daniel Bacquelaine, Ferdy Willems, Marie-Thérèse Coenen, Bruxelles, Chambre des Représentants de Belgique, *Rapport fait au Nom de la Commission d'Enquête Parlementaire visant à determiner les circonstances exactes de l'assassinat de Patrice Lumumba* (Doc. 50 0312/006, 16 November 2001), in particular 336–430. See also C. Braeckman, *Lumumba, un Crime d'Etat (2009)*; L. De Witte, *L'Assassinat de Lumumba* (2000), 190–206.

82 After 13 January 1960, the correspondence between the Secretary-General and his team in the Congo shows strong concern over the fate of Lumumba and his companions and over the consequences of their probable mistreatment. See, for instance, Incoming Code

go in accomplishing its mission. A risk, because Lumumba's murder was a terrible blow to UN credibility, and its detractors could now shout to the world the organisation's shortcomings and ask for its definite withdrawal, with all the political consequences that might entail.

Against this difficult backdrop, Hammarskjöld kept to the line he had followed since the beginning of the crisis. In New York, he looked and worked for constant and clear support by the Security Council, which was his ultimate point of reference, while trying to maintain a broad consensus among Asian and African states over his approach to the crisis.[83] In the Congo, with the help of a staff that he managed to keep very close despite enormous pressures,[84] he pursued a dialogue with all political parties in order to overcome the stalemate of the summer of 1960 and to help to create the conditions for the formation of a government of national unity.[85]

When the Adoula cabinet received the approval of the Congolese parliament on 2 August 1961, and the quick recognition of the majority of the international community, including the Soviet Union, the Secretary-General could look upon this development as a personal success.[86] The Katanga secession was not yet over, but the participation of the Lumumbists in the new political framework left open the possibility of building the hoped-for united domestic front needed to tackle Tshombe's resistance. It was precisely during a new attempt to negotiate with Katanga that the Secretary-General and 15 other people died in a plane crash, the exact circumstances of which have never been fully explained.[87]

Cable from Dayal to Hammarskjöld and Léo. 14 February 1961. National Library of Sweden, MS L179:157.

[83] For a personal interpretation of his role in the Congo and the constraints and challenges he had to face, see the very interesting letter Hammarskjöld sent to the Swedish minister for foreign affairs. 'Letter from Dag Hammarskjöld to H.E. Mr. Östen Undén' by Hammarskjöld. 26 February 1961. National Library of Sweden, MS L179:141.

[84] Among others, this was especially the case with Dayal. See, Rognoni, *supra* note 1, at 231–232; Kent, *supra* note 2, at 47. 'In this "Battle of Britain"', wrote Hammarskjöld to Dayal, 'those who try to be in the deeper sense the friends of all are bound to be treated as the enemies of all. This you know as well as we do, and therefore things I believe somehow will work out right'. Outgoing Code Cable from Hammarskjöld to Dayal. 28 February 1961. National Library of Sweden, MS L179:157.

[85] See, for instance, Incoming Code Cable from Linner to Hammarskjöld and Léo. 25 May 1961. National Library of Sweden, MS L179:162.

[86] 'My congratulation and gratitude to the UN Congo team', wrote the Secretary-General immediately after the vote of confidence in Adoula's Cabinet, 'and especially to you and your close collaborators, on this encouraging forward step. The way may now be opened to a much more constructive effort on our part'. Outgoing Code Cable from Hammarskjöld to Linner. 2 August 1961. National Library of Sweden, MS L179:160.

[87] The commission of inquiry instituted to investigate the crash worked on three hypotheses, a direct attack, sabotage, or an accident, without reaching straightforward

The climate in the Congo in mid-September 1961, after the enthusiasm generated by the formation of the government of national unity in August, was becoming tense again. The UN – through its new representative in Elizabethville, the Irish official Conor Cruise O'Brien – was now convinced of the urgent need to end the secession of Katanga in order to ensure the unity of the country and implement the reforms it badly needed.[88] At the end of August 1961, eighty-one foreign officials had been peacefully expelled from the province,[89] the Katangese Minister of the Interior Godefroid Munongo had been arrested, and the radio station temporarily seized by UN forces to secure the final expulsion of all mercenaries. This move by UN forces, fully endorsed by the central government in Leopoldville, the Soviets and the majority of Afro-Asian states, met with scepticism (if not open opposition) among many Western countries,[90] while Tshombe continued to adopt delaying tactics.

In this situation of impasse, the Secretary-General hoped to facilitate a solution by becoming involved in direct negotiations with Tshombe. The correspondence he exchanged with his closest staff and with Bunche, in particular, until the last hour, shows a confidence in his mission and the absolute belief in the need to make all possible efforts to achieve a positive outcome in the interests of the UN and of the Congo as a whole. In one of his last cables from Leopoldville, the Secretary-General, upset at the Western lack of comprehension of the difficulties encountered in Katanga, stated in very clear terms:

> It is better for the UN to lose support of the US because it is faithful to law and principles than it survive as an agent whose activities are geared to political purposes never avowed or laid down by the major organs of the UN.[91]

conclusions. The issue gave rise to a lively debate. In a letter to the editor published in the *Guardian* on 9 September 1992, Conor Cruise O'Brien – UN representative in Katanga at the time of the crash – and his aide George Ivan Smith argued that the crash was the result of a direct attack by Katanga's mercenaries paid by Union Minière. This thesis has been challenged. B. Rösiö, 'The Ndola Crash and the Death of Dag Hammarskjöld' (1993) 31 *Journal of Modern African Studies* 4, at 661–671. On this issue, see also D. Gibbs, 'Dag Hammarskjöld, the United Nations, and the Congo Crises of 1960–61: A Reinterpretation' (1993) 31 *Journal of Modern African Studies* 1, at 173–174.

[88] See C. O'Brien, *To Katanga and Back: A UN Case History* (1966).

[89] At the beginning of August 1961, there were 500 mercenaries left in the province, and by mid-September 1961 more than 100 had still to be expelled. See O' Brien, *supra* note 88, at 123; and Rognoni, *supra* note 1, at 409.

[90] See, for instance, Outgoing Code Cable from Bunche to Hammarskjöld. 14 September 1961. National Library of Sweden, MS L179:162.

[91] Outgoing Code Cable from Hammarskjöld to Bunche. 15 September 1961. National Library of Sweden, MS L179:162.

11.5 Conclusion

The UN played a crucial role during the first Congo crisis. The Secretary-General was convinced from the time the Security Council had first endorsed the relevant mandate on 14 July 1960 that the crisis was an immense challenge for the future of the organisation. In the framework of the great transformations taking place in the international system as a result of decolonisation, a success in the Congo would have enormously increased the prestige and the very role of the UN, while a defeat would have been a severe blow to its future development.

Thus the Secretary-General, despite the many constraints and challenges he had to face – the high economic dependence on the United States, by far the largest economic supporter of UNOC, the resistance of Belgium in giving up its influence, and the discordant views of Congolese political leaders, to mention but a few – tried constantly to work out a balanced approach. The post he occupied and his personal experience allowed him to place the Congo crisis in broader perspective – not always to the advantage of the Congo, one must say. The solution being sought had, in fact, to take into account aspects that transcended the local framework and called for a difficult balance between different points of view. Certainly Hammarskjöld – as clearly shown by the sources – was aware of the Cold War implications of his personal stand and of his place within that confrontation.

The peak of the Congo crisis coincided – and not accidentally, of course – with a tough Soviet campaign over the functions and powers of the Secretary-General. Paradoxically, that campaign, far from producing positive results for the Soviet Union, helped Hammarskjöld to preserve a strong consensus not only in personal terms, but also in terms of his conduct in regard to the Congo, even in the face of the most controversial of events, such as Lumumba's murder. The analysis of the UN's internal papers allows some insight, cable by cable, into how this effort at mediation was pursued, and to appreciate aspects of the Secretary-General's personality that do not emerge from other sources. Those sources demonstrate his irony and his ability to play down difficulties and obstacles in a spirit of understatement that probably helped him to perform his duties and to deeply enjoy his work, despite the frustrations and disenchantments that were part of it.

12

Continuities of violence in the Congo

Legacies of Hammarskjöld and Lumumba

HELEN M. HINTJENS AND SERENA CRUZ

> They have corrupted some of our countrymen; they have bought others; they have done their part to distort the truth and defile our independence ... What is important is the Congo, our poor people whose independence has been turned into a cage, with people looking at us from outside the bars.[1]

> The members of the Mapping Team were able to observe the constant fear on the part of affected populations that history would repeat itself, especially when yesterday's attackers are returning in positions that enable them to commit new crimes with complete impunity.[2]

> The death of Hammarskjöld took place in the context of intense competition among Western mining companies for access to Katanga, and had very little to do with the rivalry between East and West.[3]

12.1 Introduction

In 1964, President Mobutu renamed Congo. It became Zaire. After the fall of Mobutu's regime, the country was renamed Democratic Republic of Congo (DRC). It is distinguished from the former French Congo (Congo-Brazzaville), by its name Congo-Kinshasa (with Kinshasa as capital city). Despite the

Helen M. Hintjens is Senior Lecturer, International Institute of Social Studies, Erasmus University, The Hague. Serena Cruz is a PhD candidate, Florida International University; Research Associate, International Institute of Social Studies, The Hague.

1 Extract from the text of Patrice Lumumba's last letter to his wife, cited in L. de Witte, *The Assassination of Lumumba* (2001), 185.

2 Report of the United Nations High Commissioner for Human Rights on the situation of human rights and the activities of her Office in the Democratic Republic of the Congo, UN OHCHR Mapping document DRC, unofficial English translation, 2003, at: www2.ohchr.org/english/bodies/hrcouncil/docs/13session/A-HRC-13-64.pdf.

3 D. Gibbs, 'Dag Hammarskjöld, the United Nations, and the Congo Crisis of 1960–1: A Reinterpretation' (1993) 3 *The Journal of Modern African Studies* 163–174, at 174.

changes in name, peace in the Congo today seems as elusive as ever, and prospects of socio-economic justice are as unlikely as they were in 1960 when UN forces intervened under Secretary-General Dag Hammarskjöld. Forty years after the first UN peacekeeping mission was sent to Congo, UN troops returned. Their mission is to 'keep the peace'. But even with 20,000 UN troops in the country, it remains a challenge to address the underlying injustices of a violent economic and political order for ordinary Congolese. This time, the UN presence is better armed, with 'heavy fire-power, and robust mandates and rules of engagement', under Chapter VII of the UN Charter, instead of the more pacific Chapter VI powers.[4] But there are striking parallels. Today, as then: '(s)eizing and retaining power is associated with direct violence in Congo, and elites have ... deliberately fuelled and exploited insecurity to impose and maintain a particular political order'.[5] This chapter explores continuities of violence between the past and the present. It argues that both internal and international efforts to promote justice and peace in the Congo are compromised by systems of entrenched physical violence that underpin the economy and politics of the DRC. Today, as much as in 1960–1, continuities of violence remain a key problem that requires resolution before peace and justice can be practically addressed.

This contribution addresses this dilemma through the lens of the contrasting, yet interconnected, legacies of UN Secretary-General Dag Hammarskjöld[6] and Congo's first elected Prime Minister, Patrice Lumumba.[7] These two great historical figures share a common legacy, which has been obscured by their sharp inter-personal and political differences in life. Yet their life trajectories show how fate can inextricably entwine different individuals, despite their contrasting understandings of the roots of the 'Congolese problem' at the time of independence.

4 The quotation is from William Swing, 'War, Peace and Beyond', *The UN-DRC Newsletter*, 3 December 2007, at www.un.int/drcongo/un-news.htm. The author was Chief of MONUC at the time.

5 See Z. Marriage, 'Flip-flop Rebel, Dollar Soldier: Demobilisation in the Democratic Republic of Congo' (2007) 7 *Conflict, Security and Development* 281–309, at 285.

6 For recent accounts of Hammarskjöld, see Gibbs, *supra* note 3, at 163–174 (discussing the US investigations, and Swedish interest in the Congo).

7 For biographical treatment, see J. Omasombo and B. Verhaegen, 'Patrice Lumumba: jeunesse et apprentissage politique 1925–1956' (1998) 33–34 *Cahiers Africains* 1–265, and J. Omasombo and B. Verhaegen, 'Acteur politique: de la prison aux portes du pouvoir: Juillet 1956–février 1960' (2005) 68–70 *Cahiers Africains* 1–406. As Zeilig comments, these studies are the best around and Lumumba's legacy is recounted 'often through the words of his contemporaries – and much which has never before been published'. L. Zeilig, 'From "Whiteman in Rags" to Revolutionary Nationalist: Patrice Lumumba 1925–1960' (2008) 34 *Social Dynamics: A Journal of African Studies* 227–258, at 229.

Lumumba 'intended to jettison the deadweight of colonial heritage and combat any neo-colonial designs on the country'.[8] The UN Secretary-General, by contrast, was preoccupied with the idea of a 'liberal peace' and the maintenance of public order.[9] Both agendas were closely related to Belgian efforts to retain control over the Congo after formal political independence in 1960. There are some remarkable similarities in the deaths of Hammarskjöld[10] and Lumumba.[11] Both were victims of the vested interests that sought to protect post-independence Congo as a *chasse gardée*, including Belgian mining interests. But the approaches of both personalities differed. Hammarskjöld defended a more or less liberal conception of justice in the confrontations of the 1960–1 Congo crisis. This is illustrated by his insistence on UN 'neutrality' and his emphasis on the protection of political and civil rights and 'law and order'. Lumumba, and other anti-colonial nationalists, placed greater focus on the defence of 'social' interests and included economic and social rights as part of decolonisation. They regarded the protection of territorial integrity as a means to ensure reforms for the benefit of all Congolese.[12]

These differences shaped the course of events.[13] Since 1884, the army in the Congo has used violence against Congolese people, rather than protecting them. King Leopold's conquests were based on violence on such a massive scale that the death rate was unprecedented. These experiences had repercussions on the Congo crisis. The conflict at independence between Lumumba and the Belgian authorities affected the relationship between Lumumba and Hammarskjöld. Their encounter became partially a conflict about the meaning of history.[14] Lumumba and Hammarskjöld came into direct confrontation in relation to the role of the UN in the context of African decolonisation. Hammarskjöld may not have appreciated

[8] De Witte, *supra* note 1, at 6. [9] *Ibid.*

[10] S. Williams, *Who Killed Hammarskjöld? The UN, the Cold War and White Supremacy in Africa* (2011).

[11] On the death of Lumumba, see Parliamentary Committee of enquiry in charge of determining the exact circumstances of the assassination of Patrice Lumumba and the possible involvement of Belgian politicians to be found at: www.lachambre.be/kvvcr/pdf_sections/comm/lmb/312_6_volume1.pdf.

[12] For a description of different views in the *Mouvement National Congolais*, led by Lumumba, see Zeilig, *supra* note 7, at 249.

[13] The best and most accessible being the work of G. Nzongola-Ntalaja, *The Congo: From Leopold to Kabila: A People's History* (2002).

[14] While the 'official' history of events in 1960–1 has largely been rewritten by Congolese historians since independence, colonial mythologies remain a powerful lens through which the dominant account of events was constructed at the time. See *supra* note 7.

the depths of Belgian self-deception over the bloody history of the Congo. East–West obsessions added another layer to the disputes over the legacy of the colonial past.

In subsequent years, the Congo crisis was critical in forming the state which collapsed thirty-five years later, after the genocide in Rwanda spilled over into Zaire.[15] The state structures inherited at independence in 1961 were further weakened under Mobutu and collapsed following the Rwanda genocide of 1994. Congo's rich natural and mineral resources have been pillaged and exploited throughout all historical periods since Leopold.[16]

MONUC – now known as MONUSCO (with the addition of the word 'stabilisation') – entered this context after forty years of independence. Its presence remained controversial. As in 1960–1, UN peacekeepers have been unable to 'contain' the violent situations they find themselves caught up in. UN forces have been criticised for complicity, or even active participation, in the looting of the Congo's mineral resources and inaction in case of violence against civilians, including action by the Armed Forces of the DRC (FARDC). MONUC troops have themselves been accused of sexual abuse, and illegal resource extraction and trading.

Based on the history of Lumumba and Hammarksjöld and contemporary operations, one may question the role of outside actors in the DRC today.[17] Systemic violence has remained a constant factor throughout 'modern' Congolese history. As Zoe Marriage put it: '(t)he colonial regime,

[15] See G. Nzongola-Ntalaja, *The Congo: From Leopold to Kabila* (2002), 214–252.

[16] The Annex to the 2003 Report of the UN Panel of Experts includes a number of companies importing minerals from the Democratic Republic of the Congo via Rwanda, among which just a few can be listed. There were many more companies, especially from Belgium, plus others from India, Malaysia and Kenya, for example: Cogem/Muka-Enterprise/Soge, Belgium – cassiterites, coltan; Issa/Chpistopa/Geologistics Hannover, Germany – cassiterites, coltan; Redemi/Extano-Office/Coopimar, Rwanda – cassiterites and coltan; Banro-Resources Corp, Malaysia – cassiterites, coltan; Bharat, United Republic of Tanzania – cassiterites; Rwasibo-Butera, Switzerland – coltan; Eagleswings/ Veen Netherlands/Warehouse, Netherlands – coltan Afrimex, United Kingdom of Great Britain and Northern Ireland – coltan. See *Report of the Panel of Experts on the Illegal Extraction of Natural Resources and Other Forms of Wealth of the Democratic Republic of Congo*, UN Doc. S/2002/1146, submitted on 16 October. Full UN Panel's report available at: www.irinnews.org/drc%20panel_english.pdf, accessed 12 April 2006. The report was followed up with Security Council Resolution 1457 (2003) of 24 January: www.securitycouncilreport.org/atf/cf/%7B65BFCF9B-6D27–4E9C-8CD3-CF6E4FF96FF9%7D/DRC_SRES%201457.pdf.

[17] For analysis, see B. Pouligny, *Peace Operations Seen from Below: UN Missions and Local People* (2006).

the regime of Mobutu and the rebellions of the Alliance of Democratic Forces for the Liberation of Congo (ADFL, led by Laurent Kabila) and the Rally for Congolese Democracy (RCD) have each demonstrated that force is the means to power'; yet none has proven capable of bringing peace or justice to the Congo.[18] Before peace and justice become possible it is necessary to address the root causes of the violence that underpins the social and economic order in the DRC today.

12.2 The legacy of violence and injustice

If one takes a closer look at the status quo, one may note that physical violence remains structurally entrenched in the DRC, just as it was in 1960–1, when private companies and militias in the newly independent Congo used military force and forced labour to organise political practices based on coercion throughout the country. In 2010, a UN report found that: 'government security forces and irregular armed forces continue to commit acts of sexual violence and to subject artisanal miners and other civilians living in the area to forced labour, illegal taxation and extortion.'[19] According to the definition of the International Labour Organization, slavery takes different forms, including 'physical abduction, followed by forced labor'.[20] Slavery as a form of economic ownership is complemented by systems of violent exploitation and economic abuse that involve 'total domination over another through physical and/or psychological violence for purposes of extracting unpaid labour'.[21] There are, in particular, few dividing lines between different forms of violence in a system where threats of physical force and actual physical violence, including sexual violence, serve multiple purposes, including that of gaining material, symbolic and economic control over fractured families and communities. This is as true today as it was for King Leopold in the 1890s.[22]

[18] See Marriage, *supra* note 5, at 286.

[19] See Report of the United Nations High Commissioner for Human Rights on the situation of human rights and the activities of her Office in the Democratic Republic of the Congo, p. 11, available at: www2.ohchr.org/english/bodies/hrcouncil/docs/13session/A-HRC-13–64.pdf.

[20] ILO reports confirm that such practices remain widespread in the Congo today. See ILO, HREA: Slavery and Forced Labour, at www.hrea.org/index.php?base_id=160.

[21] See A.Y. Rassam, 'International Law and Contemporary Forms of Slavery: An Economic and Social Rights-Based Approach' (2005) 23 *Penn State International Law Review* 809, at 809.

[22] See A. Hochschild, *King Leopold's Ghost: A Story of Greed, Terror, and Heroism in Colonial Africa* (1998).

Parts of the economic system of the country have been based on forced labour and protected by armed violence. In 2010, for example, it was estimated that almost half the working population involved in mining had been in a situation of slavery at some time over the past two years in Eastern Congo.[23] In this context, sexual violence has become part of wider violent methods to force local communities into forced labour.[24] Conditions in many artisanal mines are similar to chattel slavery or debt bondage, with many mining families heavily indebted to their 'recruiters'.[25] Specific war political economies in Eastern DRC show remarkable continuity with colonial forms of coerced labour, including Leopold's 'rubber terror' which required villages to meet quotas on rubber collection.[26]

Through networks in the wider Great Lakes region and beyond, an economy of violent plunder and human enslavement linked to distant corporate interests and profits has remained a constant factor throughout colonial and post-independence history in the Congo.[27] UN interventions may have had a share in this, by contributing to the protection of global commercial and mining interests, i.e. Belgian companies in 1960–1,

[23] In June 2011, an organisation called Free the Slaves produced a report, entitled *The Congo Report: Slavery in Conflict Minerals*, which exposed the connection between global mineral trade and various forms of slavery, including sexual slavery, peonage slavery, slavery by armed groups, debt slavery and child slavery. See Open Square Foundation, *Free The Slaves: The Congo Report – Slavery in Conflict Minerals* (2011), 12, at www.freetheslaves.net/Document.Doc?id=243.

[24] S. Meger, *Minerals and Masculinity: A New Understanding of Sexual Violence in War: The Case of the Democratic Republic of Congo* (2012), PhD, University of Melbourne (copy on file with the authors).

[25] See *supra* note 23.

[26] For a criticism of Leopold's rule, see A. Conan Doyle, *The Crime of the Congo* (1908).

[27] See generally S. Pavan, *Beyond Men and Guns: Making DDR Work for Men and Women alike in the Democratic Republic of the Congo* (2010), at http://en.justitiaetpax.nl/userfiles/file/Beyond%20men%20and%20guns.pdf. One report on the slavery of indigenous people in Congo, reports that: local Mayi Mayi groups were exporting 'as much as $80 million worth of tin ore per year, mostly through the exploitation of an informal and desperately poor local labor force working under the direct threat of violence', and the stories in that report are horrendous. See World Peazant Organization & The Advocacy Project, *The Mineral Trade and Badja Slaves in Eastern Congo: Testimonies of Former Badja on their Forced Participation in the Eastern Congo Mineral Trade and the Lingering Effects of Slavery after their Liberations* (2009), at www.ecaair.org/wp-content/uploads/2010/07/BANJA-PROFILES. The following quotation from p. 4 of this document is just one of many examples: 'M. Nyamigangu was enslaved in a mine in North Kivu, probably on a coltan deposit located in Nyamukubi. She worked in the mine from 1996 to 2000, and despite being found working in 1997 by WPIO field workers, discussions concerning her freedom took until 2000 to succeed.' Curiously, no Human Rights Watch report on the DRC deals with forced labour or slavery.

and interests of other Western companies to invest and trade 'freely' in modern times.[28]

Today, Congo remains, as Lumumba's opening quotation suggested, to some extent an 'open prison'. Few Congolese have benefited from the vision that Lumumba associated with independence, despite an estimated cost of US$8.73 billion spent on UN troops stationed in the DRC by 2010.

It is well known that Hammarskjöld and Lumumba shared contrasting positions on the causes and meanings of the civil war that emerged in the Congo immediately after independence. For Lumumba, the outbreak of armed violence marked a deliberate sabotage of independence, provoked by the economic and political interests of Congolese collaborators, Belgian companies and white Belgian settlers. Hammarskjöld, in turn, did not understand the situation in quite the same way. He had been advised that ethnic diversity in the Congo was such that conflict would almost inevitably arise. Initially, none of the two believed that the Katanga separatism required 'Cold War' confrontation. But both then became unavoidably entangled in a Cold War logic that divided the stance of the UN from the cause of Congolese politicians, such as Lumumba and his allies. Although Hammarskjöld insisted on UN neutrality, certain Belgian interest groups saw UN troops as 'interfering' in Congolese internal affairs and resented their involvement. It is reported that '[m]uch of the Belgians' animus was directed against Hammarskjöld personally', which made it an unpleasant job for the Secretary-General, who was fairly sympathetic, at least initially, to Belgian points of view.[29] At first, Hammarskjöld asked 'the Belgians to leave peacefully', since he was not willing to confront the Belgians directly. When asked by Lumumba to intervene to end the secession in Katanga, Hammarksjöld refused. As observed later, it almost seemed that '[t]he UN was acting as though it was the governing authority in the Congo'.[30]

Hammarskjöld was of the view that the UN was in the Congo to protect democratic interests in general, and not a specific Congolese government. His preoccupations were driven by what we would associate today with the 'liberal peace' idea.[31] But Hammarskjöld's social-democratic vision of an

[28] On the competition between Belgian and Swedish-American mining interests during the 1960–1 crisis, see Gibbs, *supra* note 3, at 170–172.

[29] See Gibbs, *supra* note 3, at 169.

[30] Georges Nzongola-Ntalaja quoted in a report on a conference: *Centenary of Ralph Bunche Celebrated by Conference at UCLA*, report available at: www.international.ucla.edu/article.asp?parentid=11977.

[31] See generally, R. Paris, 'International Peacebuilding and the "Mission Civilisatrice"' (2002) 28 *Review of International Studies* 637–656; R. Paris, *At War's End: Building Peace*

ideal political order for the Congo did not necessarily include protection of the elected government.[32] His hostility to Lumumba was well known. It may have been grounded in his belief that Lumumba was challenging UN authority to decide on its mandate. In reality, however, the greatest threat to peace came not from Lumumba, but from the Belgians, as he would later find out. In 1961, Hammarskjöld focused on rapidly ending the 'separatist war' in Katanga. At that point, Western interests had become sharply divided. Belgian interests competed with other, more globalised corporate interests, including those of the United States.[33] Hammarskjöld put the UN's legitimacy to the test when deciding that it was time to address the separatist war. The success of his mission may have been compromised by a perception that he would end the Katanga war and then favour US and Swedish mining interests over Belgian interests.[34]

In response, priority was given to control of immediate military threats to peace. But some of the deeper root causes of violence, resulting from social injustice and economic exploitation, remained unaddressed. Due to the prevalent role of mining interests and use of militarised and forced labour systems, no decolonisation of social structures could take place in the Congo.[35]

The 'ethnic conflict' argument was used in 1960 to claim that Lumumba was engaging the army in 'genocide'. But the conflict in 1960–1 was rooted in delimmas of colonial rule, including exploitation of natural resources. These experiences raise continuing problems. From the nineteenth century to the present day, military interventions have partly served global financial and commercial interests.[36] Among ordinary Congolese,

After Civil Conflict (2004); R. Newman, R. Paris and O. Richmond, *New Perspectives on Liberal Peacebuilding* (2009).

[32] M. Salih, 'Poverty and Human Security in Africa: The Liberal Peace Debate', in D. Francis (ed.), *Peace and Conflict in Africa* (2008), 171–184.

[33] See Gibbs, *supra* note 3, at 170–171. [34] *Ibid.*

[35] The economic foundations of war and injustices against civilians are gradually coming to be recognised, including by the UN, and by NGOs that have tried to work in the DRC to directly address issues of slavery, forced labour, and connected practices of militarisation and sexual violence. Amnesty and smaller organisations like the Anti-Slavery Society and Free the Slaves are among those working on and researching these issues. See Amnesty International's report: 'Democratic Republic of Congo: "Our brothers who help kill us": Economic Exploitation and Human Rights Abuses in the East', 2003, No. AFR 62/010/2003, can be seen at: http://amnesty.org/en/library/info/AFR62/010/2003/en. This report showed evidence of looting of harvests, stealing of medical supplies and food aid, extortion and 'taxation' of civilians, forced labour and displacement combined with sexual exploitation.

[36] See Meeger, *supra* note 24, at 254 ('(i)n the hegemonic political and economic global order, core states do not require stable regimes in peripheral states in order to access the natural resources therein').

international presence is still associated with this heritage, i.e. the defence of hegemonic political and ecomomic interests that keep African people 'on their knees'.[37]

12.3 Continuity and change in the Congo

Henry Morton Stanley predicted that the Congo river[38] would one day become the commercial artery of Central Africa, uniting transport routes and promoting a combination of 'free' trade and prosperity for commercial interests in the region.[39] But this vision was hampered by colonial rule which took advantage of profitable opportunities in the shortest and crudest way possible, with minimal investment in social or physical infrastructure. King Leopold's regime was marked by forced taxation and forced labour for the purpose of rubber production. Villagers were forced to produce for the king. Land was declared the property of the king. Community needs were subordinated to rubber export. Raising revenue for the king, without investing in wages or the infrastructure of the colony, became the priority.[40] Locals were obliged to collect and deliver rubber and to work and pay taxes, without adequate returns. Leopold's agents used violence and the threat of violence, in order to increase productivity and profit. Colonial violence had devastating consequences for agricultural communities. This is evidenced by the drastic decline in population, from between 20 and 30 million in 1884 to just 8.5 million by 1911. Even by 1924, the population of Congo barely reached 10 million.[41] Yet Leopold's Free State was recognised by the United States, Great Britain, France and Germany.

Many of these atrocities have been recorded and publicised. But before handing Congo over to the Belgian state in 1908, Leopold ordered the destruction of all state archives on the Congo, in Brussels and in Congo.

[37] For a full exploration of the implications of US policy, see D. Gibbs, *The Political Economy of Third World Intervention: Mines, Money and U.S. Policy in the Congo Crisis* (1991).

[38] The African Great Lakes region is hugely diverse. Today, the lakes continue to act as barriers, protecting the relatively strong public authority structures in Rwanda from the less stable Eastern DRC. While Uganda and Burundi have been termed 'hybrid-democracies', the DRC is more often described as a 'failed state'. See A. Mari Tripp, *Museveni's Uganda: Paradoxes of Power in a Hybrid Regime* (2010), Chapter 1.

[39] See Hochschild, *supra* note 22, Chapter 2.

[40] *Ibid.*, at 129–135.

[41] See Nzongola-Ntalaja, *supra* note 13, at 22. This is portrayed in the documentary film entitled *Congo: White King, Red Rubber, Black Death* (2003) which presents the same estimate of around ten million deaths under the rule of King Leopold.

Through historical reconstruction, some testimonies of the 'rubber-terror' have re-emerged.[42] The trauma imposed on Congolese people was largely transmitted through oral testimony and documentation by visitors and activists, such as Morel and Roger Casement.[43] It was less known to Hammarskjöld in the context of 1960, when little research had revealed the 'true' history of the Congo.

'Leopold's ghost' continued to haunt the Congolese people. It resulted in a legacy of fear, including the fear 'that history would repeat itself'.[44] Violence against women was part of the 'battleground of an economic war'. Congolese women experienced rape alongside economic coercion.[45] The connection of sexual and non-sexual forms of violence may be traced back to Leopold, who put in place a system of state violence that was carried out mainly by Congolese armed forces, the *Force Publique*, recruited by force and overseen by agents working for various companies and the king.[46] Persons who were 'unwilling or unable to meet the assigned daily quotas of production were subject to rape, arson, bodily mutilation and murder'.[47] Compulsory work practices included the legalised kidnapping of women. Women were held until village men returned with a specified quantity of rubber. Those who refused or did not bring enough rubber could be punished through the systematic raping and killing of their wives, children or elders.[48] At the time of the UN intervention in 1960, 'corporate greed, fueled by capitalist consumption, and the rape of women' had 'merged into a single nightmare'.[49] The UN Secretary-General may not have been fully aware of this at the time of the Congo crisis.

42 See Hochschild, *supra* note 22, at 294, 297.

43 In *Leopold's Ghost*, Hochschild argues that the rubber terror 'branded people with memories that remained raw', *ibid.*, at 165.

44 On the relationship between conflict, land and migration see C. Huggins and J. Pottier, 'Land Tenure, Land Reform and Conflict in Sub-Saharan Africa: Towards a Research Agenda', in C. Huggins and J. Clover (eds.), *From the Ground Up: Land Rights, Conflicts and Peace in Sub-Saharan Africa* (2005), 383–392.

45 Labour coercion in mining and forest-extraction areas include practices around public sexual violence and public forms of rape, as well as forced labour for all ages. See Hochschild, *supra* note 22, at 160–163.

46 *Ibid.*, at 123 ('The framework of control that Leopold extended across his enormous realm was military').

47 See Nzongola-Ntalaja, *supra* note 13, at 22.

48 See Hochschild, *supra* note 22, at 162.

49 Eve Ensler speaking at US Senate hearings on 13 May 2009, cited in Dominique Soguel, 'Rape Crisis in East Congo Tied to Mining Activity', Women's e-news, 1 June, at http://womensenews.org/story/090601/rape-crisis-in-east-congo-tied-mining-activity.

The experiences of colonial rule set a dangerous example.[50] As Shantz reminds us: 'Congo has remained subject to imperialist interests pursuing private gain; such external actors (and their internal allies) have always played a significant and sinister part in the ongoing Congo tragedy.'[51] Leopold took over all lands, through royal decree. Congolese 'brutality' was used as a pretext to justify the neglect of the well-being of the Congolese people until independence in 1960. Later, Mobutu ruled Congo as if it was his personal possession.[52] The use of slave labour by Belgian rulers to exploit rubber, ivory and timber set a precedent for local militias, and the army, who continue to work through violence to protect interests of international mining, banking and trading corporations.[53] The 'rubber terror' has become the 'coltan terror'. This exploitation relies on a 'system that rewards illicit trade and discourages legal and stable commerce'.[54]

Lumumba and his nationalist supporters hoped that this legacy of colonialism could be overcome with the help of the United Nations. They sought greater peace and justice for all Congolese. This vision might have been shared by the UN, and by its Secretary-General, had they been more fully aware of the violent (neo-)colonial context into which they were about to intervene.

12.4 Congolese independence unravels: 1960–1961

It is well known that neither Hammarskjöld nor UN Envoy Ralph Bunche met Lumumba eye to eye. Their relationship was allegedly marked by 'clashes in the personal chemistry, suspicion on both sides and miscommunication'. This resulted in a 'toxic personal relationship characterized by animosity and mutual contempt'.[55] Hammarskjöld was 'never able to

[50] See generally M. Nest, F. Grignon and E.F. Kinsangani, *The Democratic Republic of Congo: Economic Dimensions of War and Peace* (2006). Ongoing systemic violence and continuous disregard by the state for even the most basic well-being of the Congolese population leads donors to claims that there is not much they can do to help the population, besides sending in MONUSCO. See Z. Marriage, 'Defining Morality: DFID and the Great Lakes' (2006) 27 *Third World Quarterly* 477–490.

[51] See J. Shantz, Review of *The Democratic Republic of Congo: Economic Dimensions of War and Peace* (2007) 50 *African Studies Review*, at 187.

[52] See Nzongola-Ntalaja, *supra* note 13, Chapter 4.

[53] See Report Amnesty International, *supra* note 35, at 12; Hochschild, *supra* note 22, at 278–279.

[54] See Report *Free the Slaves*, *supra* note 23, at 6.

[55] See H. Melber, 'Review of R. A. Hill and E. J. Keller (eds.), *Trustee for the Human Community: Ralph J. Bunche, the United Nations, and the Decolonization of Africa* (2010)', (2011) 1 *Africa Spectrum*, 111–114, at 112–113.

relate to the African realities on the ground'. This may explain the serious misunderstandings that resulted in the tragic end of both Lumumba and Hammarskjöld himself, who did not heed Lumumba's warnings about the greatest threat to peace in the Congo in 1960.[56]

Hammarskjöld was well known for wanting to steer a middle course between Soviet and US interests at the UN. He had a clear idea that UN 'neutrality' should not be compromised. The actively supportive UN that Lumumba had hoped for was not part of Hammarskjöld's vision. He did not want to be seen as 'serving' the interests of any one side in the conflict. The UN's failure to act decisively to retain the territorial integrity of the Congo compromised the process of independence. Neo-colonial dismemberment began and Lumumba's primary goal, i.e. to promote national unity, failed. When Hammarksjöld decided that the war in Katanga needed to be ended to secure law and order, it was almost too late.[57]

Under Hammarskjöld, the UN defended a 'liberal' conception of peace.[58] The maintenance of 'law and order' was the first priority, but it was embedded in the idea of protecting liberal democracy. Hammarksjöld expected the Belgians to behave 'reasonably' towards the UN, with him as a fellow European in charge. Peace and justice were his sole priorities, and this arguably implied a peace that would allow for 'business as usual' without disruption to the economy and to trade. Until the UN failed to act, Lumumba still believed the UN would support the territorial integrity of a Member State. He did not expect his own agenda, including restoration of land rights to Congolese, to meet such fierce resistance by the Secretary-General. In the end, Lumumba was abandoned and killed by his enemies. It is reported that he 'was captured on 1 December at Lodi, on the left bank of the Sankuru River, and denied UN protection by the Ghanaian contingent at Mweka the following morning'.[59] Vital questions remain, including how Hammarskjöld – and his Special Aide Bunche – came to the conclusion that the elected Prime Minister of the country posed a greater threat to peace than a violent war of secession. It also remains questionable why the UN allowed Lumumba's illegal arrest.

The sheer violence unleashed following Congo's independence may have posed an unparalleled challenge to the logistical and political capacities of the UN and its top officials. Yet Hammarskjöld responded to the

[56] *Ibid.*, at 113.
[57] De Witte, *supra* note 1, at 6.
[58] On the 'liberal peace' idea, see *supra* notes 31 and 32.
[59] Nzongola-Ntalaja, *supra* note 13, at 110.

Kasai uprisings in 1960 in a very different way from his response to the Katanga secessionist war, by characterising the killings in Kasai as genocide. This allegedly implied that Lumumba instigated deliberate and targeted violence against civilians – an allegation that was later disproven. By undermining Lumumba's legitimacy, Hammarskjöld reinforced his vulnerability. Lumumba was soon placed under house arrest. He was tortured, including by Mobutu, and then killed in January 1961.[60]

It might have been only later that Hammarskjöld realised to what extent Belgian mining interests posed a threat to peace and justice in Congo's independence transition. Forces supporting Katanga separatism included private Belgian mining companies, who sought to dismember the Congo so as to protect their own investments. The MNC, associated with Lumumba, prioritised national unity and opposed territorial dismemberment. The UN was narrowly 'neutral' in 1960. It was less committed to the territorial integrity of the Congo than to its law and order. The Secretary-General failed to lend support to the elected government of the Congo. Had he done so, events might have taken a different turn. Belgian goodwill was taken for granted. The threat posed by Belgian interests to ordinary Congolese people was acknowledged too late.

The Katanga war caused tensions that threatened to extend civil war among the Congolese. But Lumumba was not in a strong position to make his views known to Hammarskjöld. Ludo de Witte notes that Hammarksjöld had referred to Tshombe's separatist aims for Katanga as 'legitimate'.[61] In view of this, it is puzzling that UN troops were not used to protect Patrice Lumumba, the popularly elected Prime Minister who led his country into independence.[62]

Belgian and other whites received vital UN protection in 1960 and shored up their vested interests in mining and in the region. This was significant since 'Belgian investments in the Congo produced profit rates that were two or three times higher than those in the metropole, with the largest financial group, the *Societe Generale de Belgique*, gaining some 40 per cent of its total profits from holdings in the Congo'.[63] Belgians clearly wanted to retain this privilege after 1960. Lumumba accused Moïse Tshombe, the leader in Katanga, of being a European puppet. He argued that Moïse Tshombe sought to help Belgians retain control of the country's resources after independence. Hammarskjöld, however, trusted

[60] *Ibid.*, at 102–110. [61] See De Witte, *supra* note 1, at 14.
[62] *Ibid.*, at 58. [63] See Gibbs, *supra* note 3, at 165.

claims that Katangan demands for separation were tribal, rather than based on mining interests.

The UN stood by when Lumumba's government was dissolved and when he was illegally arrested, detained, mistreated and eventually murdered. The argument that the UN could not interfere in domestic affairs was used to defend inaction in favour of the the former Prime Minister. Hammarskjöld's role was ambiguous. Perhaps '(t)he most charitable explanation of his position is that he was convinced that the Belgians would leave without confrontation once UN troops had restored law and order and brought the situation under control'.[64] He seems to have been mistaken.

It was clear from some historical writing and novels, such as Joseph Conrad's *Heart of Darkness*,[65] that Belgian Congo was a place of horror, and that Europeans, perhaps more than Africans themselves, were behind the crimes committed for the sake of profit, often crimes committed by Africans against fellow Africans. This record might have provided an incentive to Hammarksjöld to distrust Belgian claims. Lumumba's worst crime was his 'rudeness', i.e. his firm denial of the 'glorious' achievements of Belgian colonialism by King Baudouin at the independence ceremonies.[66] King Baudouin's speech was a provocation to those aware of Congolese history, given the scale of historical violence. Lumumba spoke out against this vision and challenged attempts by Belgium to rescue its reputation. Afterwards, 'Washington, New York and Brussels ... succeeded in eliminating Lumumba and his radical followers from the political scene and in replacing them with moderate leaders'.[67]

As long as Lumumba was alive, Hammarskjöld seemed unaware of the dangerous mix of economic and military interests in the Katangan war. He failed to appreciate to what extent corporate economic interests continued to influence almost all aspects of the violence in the Congo. His decision in 1961 to end the Katanga war may have led to his untimely death. His vision of law and order was peculiarly Western, and had nothing to do with the priorities of Lumumba, who wanted to decolonise the country, or the narrow profit-motives of Belgian mining corporations. Hammarskjöld's intentions were guided by other aspirations, including

[64] Nzongola-Ntalaja, *supra* note 13, at 113.

[65] See J. Conrad, *Heart of Darkness* (1902).

[66] On Lumumba's reaction to Baudouin's patronising speech, see also Chapter 13, this volume.

[67] Nzongola-Ntalaja, *supra* note 13, at 95.

his 'vision of turning the United Nations into a world government' and his wish to increase the legitimacy of the UN in the eyes of the international community.[68]

Once Hammarskjöld started to identify the interests behind violence after independence, he tried to change tack. Secret cables between the UN headquarters in New York and the UN mission in Congo conveyed 'the growing frustration of Hammarskjöld and his officials over the tactics used by the powerful mining company Union Minière ... to obstruct and undermine the UN mission in Congo'.[69] Lumumba could no longer be blamed for the continuing violence, since he was dead. Hammarskjöld may have realised belatedly that Belgian Katanga interests, as opposed to the MNC, were funding and fuelling civil violence among the Congolese. Hammarskjöld decided to enter into earnest efforts to use UN troops to end the Katanga war.

Evidence of CIA involvement in the killing of Lumumba became apparent earlier than evidence of foul play in Hammarskjöld's death.[70] Yet the manner of Lumumba's death might also reveal something about the way in which the Secretary-General died some months later. Violence was obviously regarded as a legitimate means in Belgian resentment against both the nationalists and the UN. A US Senate investigation from 1975 revealed that CIA personnel plotted Patrice Lumumba's assassination and that Mobutu, who had been Lumumba's chief of the army (and later became Lumumba's 'Judas'), had ties to the CIA.[71]

Taking into account these factors, one might argue that Lumumba's and Hammarskjöld's deaths are closely related. Both were fatalities of a war fought over mineral resources and Belgian control over the Congolese

[68] *Ibid.*, at 114.

[69] Quotation is from Göran Björkdah, "I have no Doubt ...", see also J. Borger, 'Dag Hammarskjöld Unable to Overcome Congo's Troubled History', *Guardian*, 17 August 2011, at www.guardian.co.uk/world/2011/aug/17/dag-hammarskjold-congo-troubled-history. See also J. Borger and G. Smith, 'Dag Hammarskjöld: Evidence Suggests UN Chief's Plane was Shot Down', *Guardian*, 17 August 2011, at www.guardian.co.uk/world/2011/aug/17/dag-hammarskjold-un-secretary-general-crash.

[70] The official Belgian report on Lumumba's assassination is available in French; Chambre des Représentants de Belgique, 'Enquête parlementaire visant à déterminer les circonstances exactes de l'assassinat de Patrice Lumumba et l'implication éventuelle des responsables politiques belges dans celui-ci', Vol. I, 16 November 2001. For a full discussion see Chapter 13, this volume.

[71] See US Congress, Senate, Interim Report: Alleged Assassination Plots Involving Foreign Leaders, Select Committee to Study Government Operations with Respect to Intelligence Activities, 94th Congress, 1st Sess. 20 November 1975. See Nzongola-Ntalaja, *supra* note 13, at 107–108.

state. Mining companies sought to continue their violent business 'in peace'. The course of events was dramatically altered by this ambition, and many innocent people, including Hammarksjöld and Lumumba, were killed in the process. Genuine independence, as Lumumba had envisaged it, was geared at making the Congo safe for the Congolese. This aim conflicted with business interests in the extraction of the country's wealth.[72] The hopes of Congolese nationalists to gain genuine independence were dashed. Unfortunately the UN did not assist early enough in securing genuine peace and justice. Ultimately, this failure reflected on Hammarskjöld himself.

12.5 The sequel: continuing violence in the DRC

Since the critical 1960–1 period, the fall of Mobutu with the coming to power of Laurent Kabila in 1998, the Rwandan invasion and war from 1996 onwards have resulted in new forms of violent predation. In response to ongoing violence, UN peacekeeping troops returned once more to the Congo. For older Congolese, this return of UN troops produced an uncomfortable déjà vu, as peacekeeping, law and order, and disarmament in the Congo were once again on the international agenda, as in 1960. This time, some atrocity crimes, including child recruitment and sexual violence, were prosecuted by the International Criminal Court following a referral by the Congolese government.[73] Unlike in 1960, when Katanga and Kasai were the main focus, UN troops were mainly deployed in Eastern DRC, close to mineral-rich regions producing cassiterite and coltan, in particular, and diamonds.

In the thirty-five years during which Mobutu remained in power, he retained some of the questionable practices of the former colonial power. Slave-based economic activity continued under his regime. It is reported that Mobutu robbed the country of its riches while neglecting the government's most basic functions for more than three decades. The jungle

[72] The 2002 report of the UN Panel on the Illegal Exploitation of the Congo asked for all mining and related contracts granted in the DRC since 1997 to be reviewed. This recommendation was made since the evidence collected showed that direct violence and crime were involved in mineral extraction in the Congo. Lengthy debates, denials and indecision followed. In 2010 a mining suspension order was imposed by President Joseph Kabila in parts of Eastern DRC. This measure seemed to have encouraged Congolese army personnel to take over direct control of more mines, and to organise mining away from the proscribed areas. See Meger, *supra* note 24, at 116.

[73] For a record of ICC cases, see www.icc-cpi.int/EN_Menus/ICC/Situations%20and%20Cases/Situations/Situation%20ICC%200104/Pages/situation%20index.aspx.

literally grew up over the country's network of roads; unpaid soldiers turned to living off the people; and the people did whatever they could to survive. A corrupt informal economy flourished, fertile ground for modern forms of slavery.[74]

Independence did therefore not entail tangible improvements in the lives of ordinary Congolese people as Lumumba had hoped.[75] The fragile state system collapsed with the Rwanda genocide, which brought venomous nineteenth-century theories of 'Hamitic' and 'Bantu' races back to life, inserting them into the political lexicon of Zaire.[76] Both Rwandan and Ugandan armies entered Eastern DRC in 1998 and initiated 'a war of partition and plunder' that continues until the present.[77] The Congolese media became xenophobic, tending to identify the 'racially' different populations as responsible for all the country's ills. This was reinforced by Congolese nationality law, which is rooted in the colonial tradition. A Belgian colonial law dating from 1885 specified that a Congolese national should be 'a member of a tribe settled in Congo', within Congolese boundaries as established at the Berlin Conference on 1 August 1885. This law was later modified but not revoked.[78] In 1981, Mobutu redefined Zairean nationality law to exclude those of Rwandan origin. In this setting, the Rwanda genocide resulted in growing statelessness, displacement and refugee flight across the Great Lakes region. An often highly racialised political ideology extended the damaging and divisive consequences of the Rwandan genocide beyond Rwanda.[79]

According to a major study, the DRC counts as the country with the largest population affected by slavery in the world.[80] In 2010, a survey was conducted in Eastern Congo based on a sample of over 700 people. The report found that the majority of these people had direct personal experience with forced labour, in areas such as military recruitment, public

[74] See *Free the Slaves*, *supra* note 23, at 4.

[75] See Nzongola-Ntalaja, *supra* note 13, at 121 et seq.

[76] See H. Hintjens, 'When Identity Becomes a Knife: Reflecting on the Genocide in Rwanda' (2001) 1 *Ethnicities* 25–55.

[77] See G. Nzongola-Ntalaja, 'Citizenship, Political Violence and Democratization in Africa' (2004) 10 *Global Governance* 403–409.

[78] See C. Malangana Nguya-Ndilo, 'The Motivations behind Kinshasa's Nationality Legislation', in R. Doom and J. Gorus (eds.), *Politics of Identity and Economics of Conflict in the Great Lakes Region* (2000), 289–309, at 305.

[79] See generally, Nest *et al.*, *supra* note 50, at 20–24; Nzongola-Ntalaja, *supra* note 77.

[80] See K. Bales, *Disposable People: New Slavery in the Global Economy* (1999). See also *Free the Slaves*, *supra* note 23.

sexual violence, and debt bondage in mining areas.[81] Economic, military and sexual slavery remains thus a reality, in addition to forced labour, in particular in mining and areas controlled by the Congolese army.

Refugees and indigenous people, women and young children have been particularly vulnerable to practices of forced labour, including in mines, since they usually possess no land of their own. During the post-genocide period in the Eastern DRC, there was a boom in coltan mining. According to some sources, farmers shifted

> into mining communities, exploiting their own lands, selling it in concessions to speculators or dispersing as itinerant miners. An estimated 95 per cent of those involved were drawn from the region's rural poor, and civilian miners may have numbered up to 50,000 during the boom [in 2002].[82]

The entire Great Lakes region has been affected by mass movement of population, in particular since the 1994 Rwanda genocide.[83] This has coincided with a 'seemingly unstoppable flow of small arms and light weapons into the region'. These factors have supported armed conflict and militia operations.[84] Weapons are stockpiled in silos. Small arms are a common currency throughout the region. Many young men are unable to earn a 'decent' living or to marry. A gun is often the sole means through which they imagine a better living. They seize the land of others or coerce others to work in the mines, through threat or use of violence.[85] In this context, individuals 'can become slaves, and … an entire group can lose its corporate integrity', be it in a civilian or a military capacity.

[81] The forms of slavery identified in Eastern Congo included the following: 'forced labor enforced by armed groups, debt bondage, peonage, sexual slavery, forced marriage, the use of children by armed groups, and other forms of child slavery'. See *Free the Slaves*, *supra* note 23, at 11. According to the report: 'Statistics presented on the artisanal mining population are based on data gathered from a non-random sample of 354 men, women and children in the Bisie mine, 177 children in Omate, and 211 children in Bibatama. Data collection was conducted over a three-month period, from July to September 2010 … Both organizations followed their surveys with community consultations in directly affected communities. The purpose of these consultations was to corroborate the findings in the survey, as well as to understand the communities' priorities and how they might address the problems identified'. *Ibid.*, at 10.

[82] See Amnesty International, *supra* note 35, at 29.

[83] See H. Hintjens, 'Conflict and Resources in Post-genocide Rwanda and the Great Lakes Region' (2006) 63 *The International Journal of Environmental Studies* 599–615.

[84] See K. Austin, 'Light Weapons and Conflict in the Great Lakes Region of Africa', in J. Boutwell and M.T. Klare (eds.), *Light Weapons and Civil Conflict* (1999), 29–47, at 29.

[85] See Meger, *supra* note 24, at 102–105.

This creates a climate in which violent conflicts tend to re-emerge in the long term.[86]

Agents and middlemen who control communication with outside traders and markets are in a privileged position. They set the terms and conditions of the commodity chain. Military forces have an interest in controlling the mines wherever possible, since the wages of soldiers are low or not paid at all. In many cases, there is a system in which '[t]he buyer pays the leader of the armed group for the transport, and the commander then sends out troops to abduct and force individuals to carry the bags, without pay or choice'.[87] This system bears some resemblance to the structures that prevailed more than a century ago.

Global networks involved in mineral trading are linked to networks of armed groups and humanitarian organisations. It is reported that 'some of the cargo companies based in Europe, South Africa and China that have been involved in the shipments of military equipment to governments or sub-state actors in the Great Lakes area have also been contracted to carry humanitarian relief supplies for some of the international aid agencies'.[88] Senior army and government officials in Uganda, Rwanda and Zimbabwe have been involved in trading minerals mined illegally in DRC. They typically deny involvement. But the minerals from Congo 'end up for sale in jewelers across the globe, and [in] ... our mobile phones'.[89] Legitimate global businesses are the main buyers of resources mined in DRC. Mining remains at the heart of the Congolese economy. It provides three-quarters of the DRC's export revenue and employment to an estimated one million workers. Yet, only 35,000 of them are formally registered.[90] It is thus still a long way towards a culture of accountability where 'international measures' would ensure that 'global companies' refrain from 'undermining poverty reduction goals' through 'profit sharing arrangements' or taking short-cuts on 'property rights, human rights, environmental and labour standards'.[91]

[86] See generally S. Miers and I. Kopytoff (eds.), *Slavery in Africa: Historical and Anthropological Perspectives* (1977).

[87] See *Free the Slaves, supra* note 23, at 12.

[88] See Austin, *supra* note 84, at 39.

[89] See Hintjens, *supra* note 83, at 611.

[90] See C. Braeckman, 'Congo's Abandoned Miners', *Le Monde Diplomatique* 2006, at http://mondediplo.com/2006/07/06congo, accessed 26 January 2012.

[91] House of Commons International Development Committee, Working Effectively in Fragile and Conflict-Affected States: DRC and Rwanda, Twelfth Report of Session 2010–12, House of Commons, 12 December 2011, p. 8, at www.publications.parliament.uk/pa/cm201012/cmselect/cmintdev/1133/1133vw.pdf, accessed 12 March 2012.

Following inter-community violence, civilians flee from their homes and typically leave their farms behind. Sites of abandoned farmland in war-torn areas (like Kisangani and Ituri) are then taken over by senior military or civilian leaders or armed militia groups allied with local business intermediaries.[92] This seizure and reallocation of land is partially 'used as one of the elements in the "reconstruction" of identity' along ethnic and race lines.[93]

Violence has thus remained a key instrument of economic and political governance in the Congo. The country has witnessed an unbroken succession of abusive political administrations, military authorities and armed political groups that have looted the region and committed human rights abuses with impunity. In 1960–1, the competing mining interests involved mainly Belgian, European or North American actors. Today the companies involved in the Congo's mineral trade and extraction are truly global.[94] These global economic interests receive at times greater concern than the well-being of Congolese people. Some of the few public institutions that used to function during the Mobutu era (universities, some hospitals, trading and farming groups) are in disarray.[95] Outside interventions, including foreign donor support and UN presence, produce some ambiguous effects. They sometimes protect the rights of international private investors and their local business partners, instead of reducing entrenched violence and forced labour practices.[96]

12.6 A future for peace and justice in the DRC?

The future is even harder to envisage today than in 1960, when Lumumba voiced his plea for genuine independence. Lumumba associated freedom not only with sovereignty, but also with freedom from economic coercion and enslavement.

[92] K. Vlassenroot and C. Huggins, 'Land, Migration and Conflict in Eastern DRC', in Huggins and Clover, *supra* note 44, 116–194.

[93] Huggins and Pottier, *supra* note 44, at 384.

[94] Examples from Annex I of the UN Panel of Experts Report (2003) include cassiterites trading via companies in Belgium, Germany, Malaysia, Tanzania, Switzerland, Netherlands, United Kingdom, Kenya, India, Pakistan and the Russian Federation (source: www.un.org/news/dh/latest/drcongo.htm).

[95] See M. Giovanni, T. Trefon, J. Kasongo Banga and C. Mwema, 'Acting on Behalf (and in Spite) of the State: NGOs and Civil Society Associations in Kinshasa', in T. Trefon (ed.) *Reinventing Order in the Congo* (2004), 99–115.

[96] This is not unique to the Congo. Elsewhere too UN forces are viewed as an interest group, which is unable to remain a neutral military arbiter, but becomes instead a party in the violent conflicts they are sent to prevent. See Pouligny, *supra* note 17.

Would it have been possible to envisage a Marshall Plan for the Congo that would not become neo-colonial? Western powers did have the time to make up for the consequences of the past. But thus far, no outside or inside forces have produced a solution capable of reducing, or putting an end to, the violence that makes peace and justice impossible, in daily life, in economic processes and in politics.

The 'Democratic Republic of the Congo Relief Security and Democracy Promotion Act',[97] adopted in September 2006, proposed tight controls over 'Conflict Minerals'. This was done as a follow-up to the recommendations of the UN Panel of Experts on the Illegal Exploitation of the Congo (2003) and the UN Group of Experts on the Democratic Republic of the Congo (2010). These recommendations identified factors for the reduction of resource-related violence against Congolese civilians, including: 'strengthening company management systems, identifying and assessing supply chain risks, designing and implementing strategies to respond to identified risks, conducting independent audits, and publicly disclosing supply chain due diligence and findings.'[98] These proposals were implemented by the Congolese government by way of a ban on mineral trade in 2010. But further international action is needed to support the government's efforts, since the global economic demand surrounding trade in minerals continues to fuel illegal and violence-based labour practices and sexual violence against ordinary Congolese.

Meeting this challenge requires a combined effort, with:

> active and courageous international diplomacy, pressure from all quarters on Congolese and neighboring governments including Rwanda, Uganda and Burundi; regulatory, consumer and investor pressure on companies to clean slavery out of their supply chains; and the strengthening of mining communities at the local level.[99]

Trading of 'conflict minerals' is a problem for the Congo. President Kabila's mineral trading suspension in 2010 was a first effort to acknowledge the source of the problem. However, armed groups responded by moving their operations to more remote areas, or forcing villagers to work

[97] See Bill S.2125 (109th Congress), 14 December 2006, at www.govtrack.us/congress/bills/109/s2125/text.

[98] See United Nations, 'Due Diligence Guidelines for the Responsible Supply Chain of Minerals from Red Flag Locations to Mitigate the Risk of Providing Direct or Indirect Support for Conflict in the Eastern Part of the Democratic Republic of the Congo' (2011), at www.un.org/News/dh/infocus/drc/Consolidated_guidelines.pdf. See also www.sec.gov/comments/s7-40-10/s74010-346.pdf.

[99] See *Free the Slaves*, *supra* note 23, at 5.

in illicit mineral extraction and trading, and imposing 'taxation' through force of arms on local populations. Local people interviewed about the presidential mining suspension in one part of Eastern DRC, i.e. the mineral-rich Walikale, doubted that it would improve security. They accepted the President's characterisation of networks that dominated production in the mineral sector. But they remained uncertain as to whether any disciplinary measures would be taken against the most prominent beneficiaries of violent methods of production, including international business partners outside the DRC.[100]

Civilians and local businesses, and perhaps even international investors, need to consider more carefully whether and how they can make a contribution to active peacebuilding and reconstruction efforts, rather than feeding a 'coercive pillage economy'. Foreign investors are unable to make longer-term investments as long as armed violence and short-term exploitation continues.

'Stabilisation' under MONUSCO requires the UN to gain the goodwill of the ordinary Congolese population, especially in Eastern DRC. Ensuring public safety remains, in principle, the sole justification of armed UN intervention. But in many situations, UN forces are unable to offer civilians realistic promises of protection.

Finally, donors and scholars from outside the Congo especially, need to be more self-critical and aware of the limits of their understanding. They are often unable to critically assess 'the impact of their assistance'. It is important to recognise that aid and even research can involve 'alliances with ... elements that benefit directly from that insecurity'.[101]

12.7 Conclusion

In his final letter before he was killed, Lumumba stated:

> History will one day have its say; it will not be the history taught in the United Nations, Washington, Paris or Brussels ... but the history taught in the countries that have rid themselves of colonialism and its puppets.[102]

[100] United Nations Security Council, Final report of the Group of Experts on the DRC, submitted in accordance with paragraph 6 of Security Council Resolution 1896 (2009), S/2010/596, 29 November, http://daccess-dds-ny.un.org/doc/UNDOC/GEN/N10/615/06/PDF/N1061506.pdf, at 49.

[101] See Marriage, *supra* note 5, at 306.

[102] See Letter to Pauline Lumumba, reprinted in J. Van Lierde (ed.), *Lumumba Speaks: The Speeches and Writings of Patrice Lumumba, 1958–1961* (1972), 422–423.

The history of the Congo indeed needed to be rewritten since independence. Two or more generations of Congolese historians and Africanist historians have been able to gain access to previously classified information and sources, including at the UN, in Belgium and in the Congo itself. The 'new Congolese history', written by Jean Omasombo, Georges Nzongola-Ntalaja and many others, has sought to correct many errors of the past, and some serious distortions that have arisen from the rewritings of colonial historiography and hagiography.[103] Stories invented by Leopold, by the Belgian colonisers and later by the UN and Western powers took on a life of their own and still compromise public perceptions of the Congolese past. For many Congolese, who have trusted in the stories told to them, Lumumba was a communist and a ghost whose legacy should be relegated to the past. In the collective memory, Hammarskjöld is presented as another man who failed to understand the Congo.

Many would agree that the deaths of both Lumumba and Hammarskjöld changed the course of events in Congo in 1961 quite radically, undermining more nationalist alternatives. Had both men made more effort to understand each other's positions, then perhaps both might have lived, and the continuity of violence in Congo's economy might have been interrupted, or even transformed. Yet it is doubtful as to whether these two individuals could have really changed the broad direction of historical events. In the context of the Cold War, even the best-intended efforts of Congolese and outsiders to promote genuine independence, greater justice, meaningful peace and democratic transformation were undermined by neo-colonial and imperialist politics, and dominant economic interests which left the social and economic structures of violence in place.

One should also not exaggerate the importance of individuals, despite their legacies. Each man may have misunderstood the position of the other. They were working through lenses of the Cold War. Lumumba and his supporters were let down by the UN's failure to protect the elected Prime Minister from arrest, torture and death. One might argue that there were perhaps not enough 'honest brokers' who were willing to bring the UN Secretary-General and Lumumba together, despite their mutual antagonism.[104] With the help of such brokers, it might have been possible to create a better understanding between the two. But this was prevented

103 See *supra* note 7.

104 See C. Young, 'Ralph Bunche and Patrice Lumumba: The Fatal Encounter', in R.A. Hill and E.J. Keller (eds.), *Trustee for the Human Community: Ralph J. Bunche, the United Nations, and the Decolonization of Africa* (2010), 128.

by prejudices and mistrust in the relations between Hammarskjöld and Lumumba, and vested intests in existing economic and political structures.

Lumumba's view challenged not only Belgian interests, but a broader vision of Congo's colonial history, i.e. the perception that the Congolese population had benefited from Belgian-led 'development'. Hammarskjöld was almost as unpopular as Lumumba among Belgian settlers and miners. He was unable to see that Lumumba represented a type of leader who could have assisted the UN to fulfil its ambitious mandate in the Congo. Had Lumumba not been detained, tortured and killed, a better future might have been possible, perhaps with UN assistance.

13

Lumumba vs. Hammarskjöld

A story of confrontation

JEAN OMASOMBO TSHONDA

13.1 Introduction

In contemporary readings on the Congo crisis, Congolese leader Patrice Lumumba is frequently presented as an object of devotion or someone to be feared.[1] Although his death was followed by much commentary, there is still limited critical engagement.[2] The involvement of a range of actors, including the 'Great Powers', has made it difficult to understand the circumstances surrounding his fate. It is important to re-think parts of the existing historiography. Unfortunately, some facts have been distorted by mishandled evidence and colonial mythologies. This makes it difficult to understand the complex factors relating to his legacy.[3]

Lumumba lived for only thirty-five years (1925–61). He spent twenty years of his youth in a poor rural environment. He was in prison for twenty months and spent two years in active politics. He rose to fame as a political leader (i.e. Congolese Prime Minister) before his atrocious end. Both the United Nations and the international community bear some

Jean Omasombo Tshonda is Researcher at the Musée Royal de l'Afrique Centrale, Tervuren, Belgium.

[1] See P. Halen and J. Riesz (eds.), *Patrice Lumumba entre Dieu et Diable. Un héros africain dans ses images* (1997); B. Jewsiewicki, 'Corps interdits. La représentation christique de Lumumba comme rédempteur du peuple zaïrois' (1996) 36 *Cahiers d'Études Africaines* 113–142; B. Jewsiewicki (ed.), *A Congo Chronicle: Patrice Lumumba in Urban Art* (1999); L. De Witte, 'Lumumba et le péché originel du roi Baudouin?', (2011) Centre D'Études Wallonnes.

[2] Belgian Chamber of Deputies (*Chambre des Représentants de Belgique*), Enquiry to Determine the Exact Circumstances of the Assassination of Patrice Lumumba and the Ultimate Implications of the Responsibility of Belgian Political Leaders in this Event (*Enquête parlementaire visant à déterminer les circonstances exactes de l'assassinat de Patrice Lumumba et l'implication éventuelle des responsables politiques belges dans celui-ci*) (16 November 2001) Vol. I, at 587.

[3] *Ibid.*

responsibility for his fate. In his last statement, he identified the Secretary-General of the UN as one of his primary political adversaries.

Rather than providing a biography of Lumumba,[4] this chapter seeks to analyse the differences that arose between Lumumba and Hammarskjöld. It is meant to shed some further light on the dramatic events in the Congo, without claiming to present a full analysis.

13.2 Lumumba: a prototype, and the itinerary of broken dreams

Patrice Lumumba has a very specific role in the history of the Congo. He was born to a farmer family in the Kasaï province of Congo. His family was Catholic. But he was not significantly influenced by this background. He shared a deep sense of perceptiveness, becoming a self-taught scholar, regional head of the Cercles of Stanleyville and member of the Belgium Liberal Party. His rise came as a surprise to the Belgian colonial power.[5]

Until 1956, i.e. four years before Congo's independence, Lumumba still believed that it was possible to envisage a future '*Belgo-Congolese Community*', based on mutual respect and reciprocal freindships between blacks and whites. He held this belief even though he had experienced and witnessed racial abuse and mistreatment in his country. The idea of improving inter-racial relations was the main inspiration behind his earliest political choices. During his working visit to Belgium (in April–May 1956), he drew up a list of the most urgently-felt priorities of the Congolese.[6] These included: a better salary policy; recruitment of capable and worthy Congolese to positions of responsibility; the progressive integration of the Congolese into the colony's administration; greater efforts to promote the education of Congolese girls; and the extension of the social policies in place for whites to the Congolese 'évolués' who would be gradually integrated into the white population. The central line in his struggles was expressed in the poem he published in late September

[4] See J.-C. Willame, *Patrice Lumumba. La crise congolaise revisitée* (1990); J. Omasombo and B. Verhaegen, *Patrice Lumumba: jeunesse et apprentissage politique (1925–1956)* (1998); J. Omasombo and B. Verhaegen, *Patrice Lumumba, acteur politique: de la prison aux portes du pouvoir. Juillet 1956-février 1960* (2005) at 47–51.

[5] See J. Omasombo Tshonda, *Lumumba, drame sans fin et deuil inachevé de la colonisation*, (2004) 44 *Cahiers d'Études africaines* 221.

[6] Z. Aziza Etambala, 'Lumumba en Belgique, du 25 avril au 23 mai 1956: son récit de voyage et ses impressions: document inédit', in M. Quaghebeur (ed.), *Figures et paradoxes de l'histoire au Burundi, au Congo et au Rwanda* (2002), 191.

1959: 'Cry, O My Beloved Black Brother'. [7] He aimed to be the voice of all Congolese, if not the voice of all black people.

Lumumba was disappointed by the delays, hesitations and contradictions of Belgian decolonisation. He felt that many of the self-justificatory promises of colonialism were based on false promises or lies. He declared his dissatisfaction with colonial oversight and his own demands and hopes in a study written in prison in 1956. It is entitled 'Is the Future of Congo in Danger?' (*Le Congo terre d'avenir est-il menacé?*).[8] This title captured future reality. Lumumba started to engage in social struggle, and later in political struggle for the advancement of the cause of all Congolese.

Following his release from prison, he was instrumental in setting up the *Mouvement National Congolais* (MNC) in 1958. The MNC was victorious in the general elections organised by the Belgian colonial power in May 1960. Lumumba became the Prime Minister of independent Congo. At the official Independence Ceremony on 30 June 1960, Lumumba took the floor to counter the official speeches given by Belgian King Baudouin I, and the new Congolese President, Joseph Kasavubu. In his address (also known as the 'tears, fire and blood' speech), Lumumba described the painful colonial past of the Congo, which he felt was coming to an end with independence. He emphasised the changes required to make the Congo a 'rich, free, and prosperous country'. He made it clear that independence was the fruit of a struggle provoked by the 'humiliating slavery' of colonialism. He argued that this struggle should form the basis of meaningful independence in the future, i.e. 'liberation of the entire African continent' and the birth of a new kind of 'man'. He said:

> For this independence of the Congo, even as it is celebrated today with Belgium, a friendly country with whom we deal as equal to equal, no Congolese worthy of the name will ever be able to forget that it was by fighting that it has been won, a day-to-day fight, an ardent and idealistic fight, a fight in which we were spared neither privation nor suffering, and for which we gave our strength and our blood.

[7] The title of Lumumba's poem is inspired by the well-known work of South African author Alan Paton, *Cry, Beloved Country* (French translation: *Pleure, ô pays bien aimé*, 1950), which denounced the policy of racial segregation and described the miserable existence of the black man in his own country. Lumumba's poem was republished in *La pensée politique de Patrice Lumumba, textes et documents recueillis et présentés par Jean Van Lierde* (1963), 69.

[8] P. Lumumba, *Le Congo terre d'avenir est-il menacé?* (1961).

> We are proud of this struggle, of tears, of fire, and of blood, to the depths of our being, for it was a noble and just struggle, and indispensable to put an end to the humiliating slavery which was imposed upon us by force ...
> We are going to show the world what the black man can do when he works in freedom ...
> We are going to keep watch over the lands of our country so that they truly profit her children. We are going to restore ancient laws and make new ones which will be just and noble. We are going to put an end to suppression of free thought and see to it that all our citizens enjoy to the full the fundamental liberties foreseen in the Declaration of the Rights of Man.[9]

This speech caused anger and generated a sense of panic. Lumumba was accused of being a communist sympathiser. This strategy was used to unite opposition against him and to prevent him from governing. Lumumba called on the United Nations to intervene in his favour. But he failed to get the necessary support. The Western powers, led by the United States, France and Belgium, remained opposed to him. Under pressure from the Western powers, President Kasavubu signed a document authorising Lumumba's dismissal on 5 September 1960. This decision was contested by Lumumba and the two parliamentary chambers, i.e. the Parliament and the Senate, which reaffirmed his power to remain in office. Lumumba learned that real power and authority lay elsewhere, outside the Congo. He lacked the support of the National Army of the Congo (ANC), led by Colonel Mobutu. He was first placed under house arrest under the surveillance of UN and Congolese soldiers. In October 1960, he was arrested and tortured, with the support of various Western and Congolese networks. On 17 January 1961 he was killed in a brutal manner on the outskirts of Elizabethville in Katanga. His body was hacked into pieces and burned in acid in order to prevent memorialisation.[10]

Lumumba was neither intimidated nor surprised by the prospect of violent death. He knew since 1959 that he might be condemned to death. He stated this in some of his public speeches. He was conscious that he fought for a cause bigger than his own person. He stated:

> Neither brutal assaults, nor cruel mistreatment, nor torture have ever led me to beg for mercy, for I prefer to die with my head held high, unshakable

[9] See P. Lumumba, Independence Day Speech, 30 June 1960, in P. Lumumba *The Truth about a Monstrous Crime of the Colonialists*. Translated by T. Schmidt (1961), 44–47.

[10] G. Soete, *Het verhaal van de Lumumba* (1978); J. Bazinnen and J. Kestergat, *Qui a tué Patrice Lumumba?* (1991); L. De Witte, *L'assassinat de Lumumba* (2000).

> faith, and the greatest confidence in the destiny of my country rather than live in slavery and contempt for sacred principles.[11]

These words, and his decision to make the ultimate sacrifice, are reflected in his last letter addressed to his wife.[12] He concluded:

> whether dead or alive, free or in prison by order of the colonialists, it is not my person that is important. What is important is the Congo, our poor people whose independence has been turned into a cage, with people looking at us from outside the bars, sometimes with charitable compassion, sometimes with glee and delight. But my faith will remain unshakable. I know and feel in my very heart of hearts that sooner or later my people will rid themselves of all their enemies, foreign and domestic, that they will rise up as one to say no to the shame and degradation of colonialism and regain their dignity in the pure light of day …
>
> Do not weep for me, my companion; I know that my country, now suffering so much, will be able to defend its independence and its freedom. Long live the Congo! Long live Africa![13]

Lumumba maintained his principled commitment to unconditional freedom and independence. His fate, and the confrontation with Hammarskjöld, reveal a contest between different priorities, i.e. the quest for 'truth' (i.e. true independence for Congolese) and the promotion of 'order' (favoured by the UN and Western powers). Lumumba experienced that successs is not driven by determination alone, but dependent on the force and power of actors involved. In light of his ideals, he refused to acknowledge the power configurations that existed at the time, although such knowledge might have secured his own survival. He is sometimes criticised for his lack of understanding of the influences of power. Some extracts from the Belgian Parliamentary Commission of Enquiry report, which is based on Belgian documentary sources, illustrate this point:

> Lumumba never accepted his deposition. He disputed the legality of Kasavubu's intervention (and Lumumba was supported in this by most Afro-Asian countries). He maintained the support of both Parliament and the army.[14]

Lumumba came into friction with the major powers. This included the Belgian leadership which coordinated operations:

[11] See Letter to Pauline Lumumba, reprinted in J. Van Lierde (ed.), *Lumumba Speaks: The Speeches and Writings of Patrice Lumumba, 1958–1961* (1972), 422–423.

[12] *Ibid.* [13] *Ibid.*

[14] See Belgian Chamber of Deputies, *supra* note 2, at 132.

> Available sources … make it possible to infer that the Belgians (individually and through the governmental authorities) played an active role in the preparation of Lumumba's deposition … First of all, the Belgian government funded certain opposition activities through the means of 'secret' funds, and with the help of some Belgians *in situ*. Secondly, Belgian diplomats provided President Kasa-Vubu with the legal arguments he needed to depose Lumumba. Indirectly, but no less decisively, the Belgian government significantly weakened the position of the Lumumba government by supporting the secessions in Katanga and in South Kasai … in their telex of 3 September 1960, Davignon and Westhof referred to 'the overthrow of the government according to our wishes'. To say that the Belgian government was implicated amounts to confirming the responsibility of the Prime Minister (Eyskens) first and foremost, and of the Minister of Foreign Affairs (Wigny) and the Minister of African Affairs (Scheyven). Wigny was the one to develop the legal arguments, and Scheyven provided the funds for the operations. Eyskens, the Prime Minister, gave the green light for this funding and was generally speaking, kept informed of all the most important issues through the permanent office of the cabinet. At the end of August 1960 Harold d'Aspremont Lynden, who had returned from Elizabethville to Brussels, was permanently in place. On 2 September 1960 he took over the post of Scheyven as Minister of African Affairs. This reshuffle of the Cabinet represented a shift towards a more active Belgian policy in the Congo, which went beyond being purely symbolic.[15]

The anti-Lumumba strategy of Belgian authorities was intended to extend the circle of his enemies, right up to and including the UN. Wigny insisted on the Belgian position, 'especially in the meeting of the Security Council to take place that very evening [10 September 1960]'.[16]

Lumumba based his struggle on words, i.e. speech echoing conviction. He was ready to face any consequences, even death, if this was required to safeguard the interests of the Congo. His principled stance had a sacrificial element, which gave him some sense of immortality. Lumumba's goals were dignity, freedom, in the ideal sense, at whatever price. He refused to negotiate over independence of the Congo. For him, 'independence' and 'sovereignty' were an inherent right of the Congolese, and a 'sacred task'.[17] His 'sublime' struggle and his tragedy reflected those of the entire country. Lumumba became a figure who symbolised the destiny of the Congo.[18] This adds weight to the burden of those who share responsibility for his death.

[15] *Ibid.*, at 125–126. [16] *Ibid.*, at 133.

[17] He spoke of the 'sacred task of rebuilding our independence, our sovereignty', see Letter, *supra* note 11.

[18] J.P. Sartre, 'Préface', in J. Van Lierde, *supra* note 11.

13.3 Hammarskjöld or Lumumba

To understand the background of events, it is important to reflect on some of the factors that contributed to the opposition to Lumumba. The tension between Lumumba and Hammarskjöld is explored in the Belgian Parliamentary Report entitled 'Parliamentary Enquiry into the Exact Circumstances of the Assassination of Patrice Lumumba and the Ultimate Responsibility therein of the Belgian Political Authorities' (*Enquête parlementaire visant à déterminer les circonstances exactes de l'assassinat de Patrice Lumumba et l'implication éventuelle des responsables politiques belges dans celui-ci*).[19] The report addresses the controversy between Hammarskjöld and Lumumba on different occasions, i.e. in a section entitled 'Pressure from the United States and the United Nations' (*Pressions exercées par les États-Unis et les Nations unies*), and in Chapter 2, devoted to the 'decline and fall of the Lumumba government' (*Le sape et le renversement du gouvernement Lumumba*).[20] The report suggests that it was partly the role of Secretary-General Hammarskjöld, rather than that of the UN as a whole,[21] that led to the 'political elimination' of Patrice Lumumba. It states:

> Straight away – that is to say from the time of the UN Resolution of 14 July [1960] – Lumumba and Hammarkskjöld had different conceptions of the role of UN intervention. In the eyes of the Congolese Prime Minister, the UN troops should be placed at the disposal of the Republic of Congo and of its government in order to help maintain the territorial integrity of the country, and to expel the Belgian aggressors [Belgian troops] out of the Congo. Several times, Lumumba expressed his dissatisfaction with the delay in the withdrawal of Belgian troops, and in relation to UN actions in Katanga. For Hammarskjöld, the UN operation was intended to restore law and order in the Congo, and also in Katanga. The troops were not to be used to resolve internal political differences through force of arms. These differences had to be resolved under the auspices of the United Nations, through negotiations between Congolese leaders. Belgian troops were not seen as aggressors [from this perspective] … Their withdrawal had to be achieved in agreement with the United Nations, and depending on the capacity of the UN to maintain overall security. Such differences of opinion progressively grew, leading to the breaking off of negotiations on 15 August [1960].[22]

In the conclusions, the report becomes even more specific. It notes:

> Crucial to the final fall of Lumumba was the split between the Congolese Prime Minister and the UN Secretary General Hammarskjöld, because

[19] See Belgian Chamber of Deputies, *supra* note 2.

[20] *Ibid.*, at 120–121. [21] *Ibid.*, Conclusions, under I.A.

[22] *Ibid.*, at 120–121.

> it forced Lumumba on the one hand to (openly) ask for the support of the Soviet Union and on the other hand encouraged the United States (behind the scenes) to organise active opposition against Lumumba (with the first plans of physical elimination).[23]

These findings imply that Hammarskjöld became a handicap for the Congolese government, and especially for Lumumba. The different key actors (i.e. Belgium, Hammarskjöld and Lumumba) shared a different understanding of the proclamation of Congolese independence on 30 June 1960. Belgian authoritities failed to perceive their former colony as a fully 'Free State'. Hammarskjöld appeared to sympathise with this point of view, and effectively turned his back on Lumumba, together with others, as of July 1960.

The dispute between Belgium and Lumumba was rooted in a fundamental difference over the history and legacy of the colonial past. Belgium considered Congolese independence essentially as a Belgian success story. This is reflected in King Baudouin's address in Leopoldville on 30 June 1960, which glorified Belgian colonialism and the achievements of his ancestor King Leopold II.[24] King Baudouin, then thirty years old, said:

> The independence of the Congo is the crowning of the work conceived by the genius of King Leopold II, undertaken by him with courage and continued by Belgium with perseverance ...
>
> For 80 years, Belgium has sent to your land the best of her sons – first to deliver the Congo basin from the odious slave trade which was decimating her population, later to bring together the different tribes which, though former enemies, are now preparing to form the greatest of the independent states of Africa. [These] pioneers deserve admiration from us and acknowledgment from you.
>
> They built communications, founded medical service, modernized agriculture and built cities, industries and schools ... It is now up to you, Gentlemen, to show that you are worthy of their confidence.[25]

Lumumba replied to the king's speech, in his 'tears, fire and blood' speech, directed to the 'men and women of the Congo'. He addressed the injustices of colonial rule:

> [F]or eighty years ... [w]e have known harassing work, exacted in exchange for salaries which did not permit us to eat enough to drive away

[23] *Ibid.*, Conclusions, under I.A.

[24] See generally A. Hochschild, *King Leopold's Ghost: A Story of Greed, Terror, and Heroism in Colonial Africa* (1999).

[25] Text in D. Renton, D. Seddon and L. Zeilig, *The Congo: Plunder and Resistance* (2007), at 81.

hunger, or to clothe ourselves, or to house ourselves decently, or to raise our children as creatures dear to us.

We have known ironies, blows that we endured morning, noon, and evening, because we are are Negroes. Who will forget that to a black one said 'tu,' certainly not as to a friend, but because the more honorable 'vous' was reserved for white alone?

We have seen our hands seized in the name of allegedly legal laws which in fact recognized only that might is right.

We have seen that the law was not the same for a white and for a black, accommodating for the first, cruel and inhuman for the other.

We have witnessed atrocious sufferings of those condemned for their political opinions of religious beliefs; exiled in their own country, their fate truly worse than death itself.

We have seen that in the towns there were magnificent houses for the whites and crumbling shanties for the blacks, that a black was not admitted in the motion-picture houses, in the restaurants, in the stores of the Europeans; that a black traveled in the holds, at the feet of the whites in their luxury cabins.

Who will ever forget the massacres where so many of our brothers perished, the cells into which those who refused to submit to a regime of oppression and exploitation were thrown?

All that, my brothers, we have endured.[26]

This speech 'confirmed the mutual distrust between Lumumba and the Belgian government' and 'influenced ... reactions to the subsequent events'.[27] Lumumba's reaction to the king was perceived as a sign of ingratitude and 'treason' by Belgium. His account of the colonial presence turned him into a persona non grata in the eyes of the Belgian government. These events led to a 'fundamental split' between Lumumba, the Belgian government, and others, which contributed to Lumumba's political downfall.[28]

As of July 1960, the Belgian government took measures to influence a change of government, i.e. through military intervention and disruption of diplomatic ties with the Lumumba government. Belgium supported Katanga and the rising Tshombe government. Belgian leaders did not directly intend to further secession, but sought to 'remov[e] the economic base of power from Lumumba and his Unitarian MNC movement'.[29] Belgium provided de facto assistance to Katanga, through a Belgian Technical Mission in Elisabethstad, led by Harold d'Aspremont

[26] See Patrice Lumumba, Speech at the ceremony of the proclamation of Congo's independence', 30 June 1960, *supra* note 9.

[27] See Belgian Chamber of Deputies, *supra* note 2, Conclusions, under I.A.

[28] *Ibid.* [29] *Ibid.*

Lynden. This mission 'played an important role in the development of the legal and military structures of Katanga as well as for the information and intelligence services'.[30] Actions against the Lumumba government were complemented by Belgian support for 'opposition press and politicians', radio campaigns and 'undercover operations',[31] and the role of the Union Minière, which facilitated secession by deciding to pay taxes to the Tshombe government. [32]

13.4 Lumumba face to face with Hammarskjöld

Hammarskjöld was not willing to consider the intervention by Belgium in the Congo as an act of aggression. Taking this position was a fundamental choice. Whether this was an error of judgement, or Hammarskjöld's misunderstanding of history, is not clear. Was it a case of '*realpolitik*' and of choosing the side that had the advantage of both force and the ability to guarantee economic interests? J. Gérard-Libois and B. Verhaegen note:

> After the Katangan declaration of independence of 11 July, the political evolution of the Congo as a whole, and of behaviour of the main players: Belgium, the Lumumba government, the United Nations, the Ileo September government, the Collège des Commissaires, was conditioned by the reality of Katangan secession. No political authority was able to impose itself in Leopoldville, and receive the support of international opinion, given their failure to exercise their control over Katanga.[33]

Hammarskjöld became entrenched in the quarrels of the Congo crisis as a key actor. This shaped the subsequent course of events, including the dramatic events concerning Lumumba. Lumumba could no longer come to an agreement with Hammarskjöld. He felt that he could no longer rely on the UN. From this moment on, he started to envisage an alternative solution to the Congo crisis. As head of the Congolese government, Lumumba's first priority was to restore national unity and, to achieve this, he embarked on the use of armed force. His hostility to Hammarskjöld was no longer a case of differences of opinion. It turned into a direct confrontation on the ground. As the Belgian commission's report notes:

[30] *Ibid.* In a message addressed to Belgian officials at the end of July, Harold d'Aspremont-Lynden noted: 'Henceforth, you must act in the name of the Councillors, with the aim of loyally supporting the Katangan authorities.' *Essor du Congo*, 26 Juillet (July) 1960.
[31] *Ibid.* [32] *Ibid.*
[33] J. Gérard-Libois and B. Verhaegen, *Congo 1960* (1962), Vol. II, 1083.

> The United Nations operation became an obstacle for Lumumba. He [Lumumba] wanted to militarily recover the secessionist provinces of South-Kasaï et Katanga, with the help of the ANC [*Armée nationale congolaise* – Congolese National Army] and with the support of friendly African countries which already had troops in the Congo and support from the Soviet Union. Hammarskjöld understood this as a threat to the general operations of the UN, which risked becoming dislocated. He predicts a conflict with an international dimension, and fears that the whole reputation of the organisation could be damaged. By the time of the Security Council of 20 August [1960], the situation was clearly one of: either Hammarskjöld or Lumumba.[34]

Hammarskjöld's declared that the pro-Lumumba troops were 'perpetrating the start of a génocide' in Bakwanga. This argument discredited Lumumba and brought comfort to his enemies. The stakes were high. Events turned into a political duel. As the Belgian commission's report states:

> The Belgian government [was] more and more aware that a conflict more and more openly [pitted] Lumumba against Hammarskjöld, and this no doubt reinforced the [Belgian government's] decision to intervene even more actively from the second half of August [1960]. Did the United Nations perhaps even assist in the planning and preparation on the ground of the removal from power of Lumumba? We did not look into the intervention of the United Nations, and the documents related to this as such, but the Belgian documentation also contains some indications of this. On 28 August [1960] an indication was received in Brussels from the Belgian representative at the United Nations that the United Nations ONUC force in the Congo would no longer abstain from taking a position, and would henceforth intervene against Lumumba. In the coming crisis, General Van Hom, the commander of the ONUC forces, would – we insist 'would' – be authorised to use force. At the end of August [1960], Cordier arrived in Léopoldville as a temporary UN Emissary, in the interim of the arrival of Dayal, who would come to replace Bunche. As suggested elsewhere, it is not unreasonable to see in the temporary arrival of the American Cordier, a conscious decision of Hammarskjöld, as seems clear from the exchange of messages between [Hammarksjold] and Cordier. In any event, the UN attitude on 5th-6th September [1960] would be critical to the collapse of the Lumumba government.[35]

After the break of diplomatic ties with Belgium, the policies of Lumumba's government were criticised in the Congolese Senate. The ANC campaign against the secession of South Kasaï reinforced internal tensions

[34] See Belgian Chamber of Deputies, *supra* note 2, at 121.

[35] *Ibid.*, at 121.

and 'eventually led to a split between Lumumba and Kasavubu'.[36] But Lumumba did not accept defeat easily. On 7–8 September 1960, the two Congolese Chambers renewed their trust in Lumumba, by way of a vote of confidence. This led to a situation of confusion. Lumumba refused to step down from office, while his rival Ileo 'was unsuccessful in consolidating his position'.[37]

When Lumumba tried to reassert his authority, he was blocked by the UN. On 11 September 1960, Ghanaian UN troops prevented Lumumba from speaking on Radio Leopoldville. On 12 September, he was again prevented from speaking. On 13 September, Jean Bolikango announced via radio that Lumumba would soon be judged for his regime of terror. Lumumba sent a telegram to the Secretary-General to ask for immediate military assistance. He threatened to seek help elsewhere if his request was refused.[38]

President Joseph Kasavubu hastened to dismiss Lumumba. Colonel Mobutu came into the picture on 14 September 1960. Following Lumumba's refusal to step down from office, he 'neutralised' the central executive and legislative authorities. Mobutu justified this action in a speech on radio. He stated:

> In order to help get this country out of an impasse, the Congolese National Army has decided to neutralise the Head of State, the two rival governments, and the two Legislative Chambers of Deputies, until the 31 December 1960.[39]

Mobutu's decision led to the establishment of the Council of Commissioners-General (also known as the 'Collège des commissaires' or 'College of Commissioners'). The Council was officially installed on 29 September 1960 by a constitutional decree of Head of State Kasavubu. The two Chambers were suspended. All legislative and executive powers previously devolved to ministers were transferred to this new body.

This was a decisive turning point in the course of events. Lumumba was silenced in Leopoldville at a time when Moïse Tshombe set up the Katangan authority structures in Elizabethville. Lumumba's supporters hoped to restore the rightful government. But Leopoldville was the centrepoint of shifting alliances:

[36] See Belgian Chamber of Deputies, *supra* note 2, Conclusions, under I.A.

[37] *Ibid.*

[38] See UN, Questions Relating to the Situation in the Republic of the Congo, 52, at www.un.org/Depts/dhl/dag/docs/congo60.pdf.

[39] See Belgian Chamber of Deputies, *supra* note 2, at 869.

> The administrative infrastructure of the country was at Léopoldville's disposal. The Embassies and the UN base were also located in Leo, which made contact with the outside world much easier. Despite the precarity of the situation in September 1960, the College of Commissioners and the Ileo government, had some solid foundations for their authority, thanks to Mobutu who controlled the army and Nendaka who reorganised the security police.[40]

Leopoldville received most of the technical assistance provided by the UN. Belgium was keen on preventing Lumumba's return to power and pushed for his arrest.[41] Mobutu's troops arrested Lumumba on 10 October 'in exchange for a Belgian promise to provide technical and military support to the [National Army of the Congo]'.[42] President Kasavubu's delegation was recognised by the UN General Assembly in November 1960. As of then, Lumumba was convinced that UN troops would not intervene in his favour. He fled from captivity on 27 November, but was captured on 1 December by Mobutu's troops, not far from areas in which ONUC troops were stationed. ONUC did not make any move to support him. On 4 January 1961, Lumumba sent a secret message to the new UN mission chief, M. Dayal. This message turned out to be his second to last written communication. In this, he wrote: 'I remain calm and hope that the United Nations will help us out of this situation.'[43] At that time, the Secretary-General was visiting Congo, first Leopoldville and then Katanga. He showed no apparent concern for the fate of Lumumba. Lumumba was assassinated on 17 January 1961.

13.5 Lumumba names Hammarskjöld as an enemy of the Congo

In his last letter, which became his final testatment, written to his wife, Lumumba named opponents of genuine independence in the Congo. He made reference to certain 'high officials' of the UN, which included Hammarskjöld. He noted:

> I write these words without knowing if they will ever reach you, when they will reach you, or whether I will be alive when you read them. Throughout my struggle for the independence of my country, I never doubted for a

[40] C. Young, *Introduction à la politique congolaise (trad. de Politics in the Congo – 1965)* (1968), at 180.

[41] See Belgian Chamber of Deputies, *supra* note 2, Conclusions, under I.A.

[42] *Ibid.*

[43] See Letter to A.M. Dayal, Special Representative of the UN Secretary-General, Thysville, 4 January 1961, at www.marxists.org/subject/africa/lumumba/1961/01/letter.htm.

> moment that the sacred cause to which I and my companions have dedicated our whole lives, would be achieved eventually. But the things that we wished for our country, namely its right to an honourable living, to dignity without blemish, and to an independence without restrictions, was not what was wanted by the Belgian colonisers and their Western allies, who obtained direct and indirect support, deliberate and not deliberate, from certain high officials of the United Nations, that organisation in which we placed all our trust when we called for its help.[44]

As if to continue accusing the West or to challenge the UN Secretary-General's interpretation of events, Lumumba suggested an alternative reading of Congolese experience. He wrote:

> History will one day have its say, not the history taught at the United Nations, in Washington, Paris or Brussels, but the history taught in countries liberated from colonialism and from its accomplices. Africa will write its own history, and from the North as well as the South of the Sahara, this history will be one of glory and dignity.[45]

After Hammarskjöld's death, U Thant was appointed interim Secretary-General and tasked with the mandate to complete Hammarskjöld's mission. U Thant was appointed as head of the UN peace mission to Congo. He dedicated himself to his task. In July 1962 he raised the prospect of 'the threat of economic sanctions against Katanga'.[46] On 10 August 1962, he presented a 'National Reconciliation Plan' ("Thant Plan') by which he requested the Congolese government to elaborate a Federal Constitutional proposal.

The Katangan secession was the most difficult issue to resolve. After the elimination of Lumumba, a key issue was whether Katanga should rejoin the Congo. As Gérard-Libois notes:

> For Adoula [the new Prime Minister], 'Katanga province, which at a certain moment withdrew from the national community, has to become reintegrated in that community. There had never been and would never be a Katangan State'. For Tshombe, Katanga was a 'State' which would be willing to 'give up its absolute sovereignty' in order to achieve 'internal sovereignty'.[47]

The Katangan secession finally ended on 14 January 1963, following several UN Security Council Resolutions, deliberations behind closed doors,

[44] See Letter, *supra* note 11. [45] *Ibid.*

[46] J. Gérard-Libois, 'Les structures du Congo et le Plan U Thant' (1962) 8 *Études Congolaises*, 1, at 14.

[47] *Ibid.*, at 4.

different negotiations and agreements and military actions by the ANC and ONUC. It resulted in the publication of the Thant Plan.

The colonial blunders at the time of independence, and the continuous crisis of the Congo are the extended embodiment of the vision of Lumumba. Today, Lumumba is celebrated as a hero in the Congo. At his time, he might have been right, but he did not win the fight. He continues to be part of the 'ever-present past'.[48] In his case, 'the myth went beyond history, which has implications for the very notion of responsibility'.[49] Even while dead, Lumumba will never cease to torment his executioners.

Lumumba's sacrifice was not sufficient, and the unity of the Congo remains fragile more than fifty years after his assassination. From the moment of the proclamation of independence in 1960 until the present day, UN troops have been in Congo, first called ONUC, then MONUC and now MONUSCO. Whether one is for or against their presence there, even to refer to the case of Lumumba is still an accusation against this institution.

[48] Belgian Chamber of Deputies, *supra* note 2, at 844.
[49] *Ibid.*, at 589.

14

Dag Hammarskjöld and Africa's decolonisation

HENNING MELBER

14.1 Introduction

Dag Hammarskjöld was serving as the highest international civil servant when the United Nations (UN) entered its transformation from a predominantly Western, post-Second World War body into one assembling a variety of cultures and regions from all parts of the world. In the Cold War era, the organisation was increasingly affected by polarisation under the growing influence of the Soviet-led Eastern bloc. In this context, the UN moved towards being a more global governance institution, in the true sense of the word. This was the result of a growing number of newly independent countries, not least from the African continent. As the 'Third World', they became since the 1950s a major arena for East–West confrontation, and were of geopolitical interest to maintain, or secure and expand, spheres of influence. Emancipated from their former colonial status, the sovereignty and representation of the emerging new states and their governments in the world body impacted on international policy and geostrategic interests during the bipolar times of the so-called superpower rivalry.

As the second Secretary-General, Hammarskjöld had to position the UN within the new processes and global shifts accompanying the times of the 'winds of change'; and he did so proactively. According to one of his close companions during the years in the UN, he had 'hoped that the UN, having no past in many African countries, could play a special role in their future'.[1] This chapter focuses on his approach to, and role in, the decolonisation of societies on the African continent, with special reference to the Congo as his most prominent and final engagement.

Henning Melber is Senior Advisor (Director Emeritus) of the Dag Hammarskjöld Foundation and Extraordinary Professor at the Department of Political Sciences/University of Pretoria and the Centre for Africa Studies, University of the Free State.

[1] B. Urquhart, *Hammarskjöld* (1972), 383.

Hammarskjöld's policy principles and ethics applied within this transition phase – adding a growing number of independent countries to the UN as Member States – were to some extent also indicative of his general understanding of the role and function of the UN and its Secretariat as a global governance body.

Hammarskjöld was aware of the need to address the structural imbalances existing in the global power hierarchies, both politically and economically. Furthermore, he saw the need to establish the necessary fundament for democracy and human rights as ingredients towards more peaceful societies, which in turn are constituent parts of a peaceful global order. The era of decolonisation was an obvious reference point for the organisation of world affairs and the interaction between independent countries. Even under the difficult circumstances of the Cold War polarisation, he was trying to keep the organisation, as far as possible, outside of the realm of influence of the dominant states; at the same time, he tried to defend the autonomy of the Secretariat and its authority over operations vis-à-vis the efforts of the major powers to assert their dominance also through the UN.

Dag Hammarskjöld occupied the commando bridge of the UN Secretariat at a time during which, under his navigation and as his legal advisor Oscar Schachter stated in his homage, 'the United Nations moved from the plane of words to that of deeds in facing some of the most perilous crises of this generation'.[2] He did so in a way which for Schachter resembled 'more art than engineering'.[3] This chapter will make deliberate use of many direct quotes from the rich source of the speeches Dag Hammarskjöld delivered over the years. They testify to the principles and values he represented and their continued relevance in meeting the challenges of today.

14.2 Economic justice

Already at the beginning of his term in office, Hammarskjöld used his 'Introduction to the Eighth Annual Report' (which was his first one) to identify two fundamental trends in human society as his credo: one directed 'towards wider social justice and equality for individuals', the other 'towards equality and justice between nations, politically but also

[2] O. Schachter, 'Dag Hammarskjöld and the Relation of Law to Politics' (1962) 56 *American Journal of International Law* 1.

[3] *Ibid.*, at 4.

in the economic and social sense'.[4] As he continued: 'International equality and justice were prerequisites of the domestic social development of all the peoples of the world and, together, they are the decisive factors if we are able to build a world of peace and freedom.'[5] And he reiterated, 'The search for peaceful settlements, for collective security and for ultimate disarmament ... has to be based upon an orderly and steady advance towards higher living standards for all peoples'.[6]

A year later, during the opening debate on the world economic situation for the 18th Session of the UN's Economic and Social Council (ECOSOC), he identified the problem of internal economic stability in both economically advanced and underdeveloped areas, and the linkage and interdependence between domestic policies and international developments. Economic stability had, for him, national and international significance. He therefore pleaded for more awareness about this interconnectivity and the need for the greatest possible cooperation by all.[7] During all of his subsequent years, he returned to these pleas and advocated a greater responsibility of the developed economies to assist the less advanced. But he also was of the view that this assistance should happen through an international institution such as the UN and not through a club of the wealthy executing power and control on their own terms. As Urquhart explains:

> Hammarskjold's deep sense of the inequality of nations, in terms both of opportunity and of actual position, led him to believe that some form of international social consciousness should be fostered through a well-equipped and powerful system of international organizations, and he was determined to preserve and develop the possibilities of the UN system in this role.[8]

Hammarskjöld was determined to strengthen the role of the UN in international assistance. At the end of 1960, the Organization for European Economic Cooperation (OEEC), which was established subsequent to the Marshall Plan in 1947–8 (with the direct involvement of Hammarskjöld, then representing the Swedish government), joined with Canada and the

[4] D. Hammarskjöld, 'Introduction to the Eighth Annual Report', 15 July 1953, in A.W. Cordier and W. Foote (eds.), *Public Papers of the Secretaries-General of the United Nations, Vol. II: Dag Hammarskjöld, 1953–1956* (1972), at 68.

[5] *Ibid.*, at 70. [6] *Ibid.*, at 74.

[7] D. Hammarskjöld, 'Statement in the Economic and Social Council Opening Debate on the "World Economic Situation"', Geneva, 7 July 1954, in Cordier and Foote, *supra* note 4, at 318–320.

[8] Urquhart, *supra* note 1, at 370.

United States to form the OECD (Organization for Economic Cooperation and Development). From 1961 onward, the OECD claimed a responsibility by the most advanced (in the sense of industrialised) economies for international development and assistance; Hammarskjöld 'regarded this change as the intrusion of a rich man's club into problems that were within the rightful jurisdiction of the more democratic and broadly based United Nations'.[9] He had a strong sense of the need for economic justice. In his last address to ECOSOC, he linked the principles of national sovereignty to the belief that international solidarity and social consciousness must go hand in hand by:

> accepting as a basic postulate the existence of a world community for which all nations share a common responsibility ... to reduce the disparities in levels of living between nations, a responsibility parallel to that accepted earlier for greater economic and social equality within nations.[10]

Being aware of the need to give weight to the social and economic tasks of the UN, he stressed in one of his few mainly extemporaneous speeches during a visit to India:

> that the main trouble with the Economic and Social Council at present is that, in public opinion and in practice, the Council has not been given the place it should have in the hierarchy of the main organs of the United Nations. I guess that we are all agreed that economic and social problems should rank equal with political problems. In fact, sometimes I feel that they should, if anything, have priority. While the Security Council exists primarily for settling conflicts which have arisen, the Economic and Social Council exists primarily to eliminate the causes of conflicts by working to change these conditions in which the emotional, economic, and social background for conflicts develop.[11]

He testified further to this awareness of the needs for global economic justice only a few months later in his opening statement during a debate on the world economic situation in ECOSOC. In his remarks, he bemoaned

> the absence of a framework of international policy that compels the underdeveloped countries each to seek its own salvation in its own way

[9] *Ibid.*

[10] Quoted in S. Fukuda-Parr, 'Poverty and Inequality – Challenges in the Era of Globalisation', in S. Ask and A. Mark-Jungkvist (eds.), *The Adventure of Peace: Dag Hammarskjöld and the Future of the UN* (2005), 222.

[11] D. Hammarskjöld, 'The UN – its Ideology and Activities', Address before the Indian Council of World Affairs. New Delhi, India, 3 February 1956 (UN Department of Public Information Pamphlet, April, 1956), in Cordier and Foote, *supra* note 4, at 668.

> without reference to wider horizons. How often have we not heard the voices of those who bewail the fact that this underdeveloped country is moving along the slippery path to autarky, that that country is neglecting its exports, whether agricultural or mineral, or that yet a third country is manipulating its exchange rates in a manner contrary to the letter and spirit of the Bretton Woods agreements? And yet how many of those who belabor the underdeveloped countries in this fashion have given adequate thought to the structure of world economic relationships which has forced these countries into unorthodox patterns of behavior?[12]

The introduction to the Sixteenth Annual Report of the UN became Hammarskjöld's last programmatic statement. Submitted a month before his untimely death, it underlined his firm belief in the equality of peoples and societies, as different from each other as these might be perceived to be:

> In the Preamble to the Charter, Member nations have reaffirmed their faith 'in the equal rights of men and women and of nations large and small,' a principle which also has found many other expressions in the Charter. Thus, it restates the basic democratic principle of equal political rights, independently of the position of the individual or of the Member country in respect of its strength, as determined by territory, population or wealth. The words just quoted must, however, be considered as going further and imply an endorsement as well of a right to equal economic opportunities.[13]

Importantly, Hammarskjöld once again does not content himself with proclaiming noble postulates by making lofty reference to an abstract equality. As a trained economist, who was also involved in the reconstruction of post-Second World War Western Europe through the Marshall Plan,[14] he never lost sight of the socio-economic dimensions of inequality. It is therefore no coincidence that he returns to stress the right to equal economic opportunities:

> So as to avoid any misunderstanding, the Charter directly states that the basic democratic principles are applicable to nations 'large and small' and to individuals without distinction 'as to race, sex, language and religion,'

[12] D. Hammarskjöld, '1. Statement in the Economic and Social Council Introducing Debate on the World Economic Situation', Geneva, 16 July 1956 (UN Press Release SG/493, 16 July 1956), in A.W. Cordier and W. Foote (eds.), *Public Papers of the Secretaries-General of the United Nations, Vol. III: Dag Hammarskjöld 1956–1957* (1973), 190f.

[13] D. Hammarskjöld, 'Introduction to the Sixteenth Annual Report', New York, 17 August 1961, in A.W. Cordier and W. Foote (eds.), *Public Papers of the Secretaries-General of the United Nations, Vol. V* (1975), 544.

[14] See Chapter 10, this volume.

> qualifications that obviously could be extended to cover other criteria such as, for example, those of an ideological character which have been used or may be used as a basis for political or economic discrimination ... The demand for equal economic opportunities has, likewise, been – and remains – of specific significance in relation to those very countries which have more recently entered the international arena as new states. This is natural in view of the fact that, mostly, they have been in an unfavourable economic position, which is reflected in a much lower per capita income, rate of capital supply, and degree of technical development, while their political independence and sovereignty require a fair measure of economic stability and economic possibilities in order to gain substance and full viability.[15]

As the statements quoted above document, Hammarskjöld had a clear understanding of the importance of the socio-economic dimensions involved in societies obtaining meaningful self-determination. The support for their aspirations to play a relevant role in the world organisation therefore, in his view, required that fair exchange relations and economic structures in support of their legitimate interests allow them to develop in a way which secures also the establishment of peaceful relations, both domestically and internationally.

14.3 Decolonisation

Hammarskjöld considered the Bandung Conference, at which the global South was in a way constituting its agency based on shared common grounds, as a legitimate expression of aspirations to enter the global policy sphere with own interests and identities.[16] He believed in the need to support the initiatives in Asia and Africa to seek independence from the dominance of the Western colonial world and argued for assistance to these countries in finding their own ways for sovereign rule and development.

Hammarskjöld had no closed mindset. When once asked over dinner by his friend John Steinbeck what would matter most during a world tour, Hammarskjöld reportedly answered: 'Sit on the ground and talk to people. That's the most important thing.'[17] He followed a similar approach (though not necessarily sitting on the ground) during a five-week trip

[15] See Hammarskjöld, *supra* note 13, at 545 (original italics).

[16] See Chapter 6, this volume.

[17] Quoted in P. Lind and B. Thelin, 'Nature and Culture: Two Necessities of Life', in Ask and Mark-Jungkvist, *supra* note 10, at 99.

through large parts of Africa between 22 December 1959 and the end of January 1960. It took him to more than 20 countries on the continent, over which the 'winds of change' had begun to blow. Upon his return on 31 January, he declared at the airport in New York:

> I would say that this experience over this long journey makes me less inclined than ever to generalize, less than ever willing to say this or that about Africa or this or that about the Africans, because just as there is very much in common, especially the aspirations, there is also an enormous diversity of problems, of attitudes, and of traditions. In such a way, the journey makes me both a little bit wiser and a lot more humble.[18]

In a subsequent press conference, Hammarskjöld elaborated further on the approach he had outlined to his friend Steinbeck:

> You can say that to stay in a country one night or two nights cannot give much of an experience. Well, first of all, it can. It can because, if you break through the walls and if you have the necessary background knowledge, even a talk of one hour can tell you more than volumes ... It is not in particular what you can learn in this or that city or from this or that man that gives you valuable understanding of the situation. It is what he says and what you see in one city seen in the light of what you have heard others say and what you have seen in other cities.[19]

The trip attested to his general mindset and practice of seeking dialogue with others to explore the common ground of humanity. For Hammarskjöld, the UN was, as already stated in an address at Stanford University in June 1955, 'an expression of our will to find a synthesis between the nation and the world'.[20] When, upon his return from his visit to the African countries, a journalist inquired at the press conference whether the ideological trends in Africa 'stem from the inner realities facing African life today or whether they reflect the often repeated clichés of foreign ideology', Hammarskjöld's clarification left no doubt:

> I do not think that the rights of man is a foreign ideology to any people and that, I think, is the key to the whole ideological structure in Africa

[18] D. Hammarskjöld, 'Airport Statement on Return from African Trip', New York, 31 January 1960 (UN Press Release SG/895, 31 January 1960), in Cordier and Foote, *supra* note 13, at 522.

[19] 'From Transcript of Press Conference', New York, 4 February 1960 (UN Note to Correspondents No. 2108, 4 February 1960), in Cordier and Foote, *supra* note 18, at 525.

[20] D. Hammarskjöld, 'The World and the Nation'. Commencement Address at Stanford University, Palo Alto, California, 19 June 1955 (UN Press Release SG/426, 18 June 1955), in Cordier and Foote, *supra* note 4, at 512.

> at present. It may be that the most eloquent and the most revolutionary expressions of the rights of man are to be found in Western philosophers and Western thinking, but that certainly does not make the idea a Western idea imposed on anybody.[21]

His role as the highest international civil servant was based on values that were permeated by a notion of solidarity. On 26 January 1960, towards the end of his African journey, he declared at the second session of the Economic Commission of Africa in Tangier:

> Partnership and solidarity are the foundations of the United Nations and it is in order to translate these principles into practical measures of economic cooperation that we are gathered today in this hall ... The emergence of Africa on the world scene, more than any other single phenomenon, has forced us to reappraise and rethink the nature of relationships among peoples at different stages of development, and the conditions of a new synthesis making room for an accelerated growth and development of Africa.[22]

Hammarskjöld then reverted to a speech he had given a few months earlier at the University of Lund in Sweden, on 'Asia, Africa, and the West'. On that occasion, he had reminded his audience that

> nobody should forget that colonization reflected a basic approach which may have been well founded in certain limited respects, but which often mirrored false claims, particularly when it touched on spiritual development. Applied generally, it was untenable.[23]

Commenting on the Western perspectives of the early twentieth century, Hammarskjöld found it striking 'how much they did *not* see and did *not* hear, and how even their most positive attempts at entering into a world of different thoughts and emotions were colored by an unthinking, self-assured superiority'.[24] For Hammarskjöld, the 'richest satisfaction' lay in 'meeting different spiritual traditions and their representatives', provided one 'approaches them on an equal footing and with a common future goal in mind'. He was confident that this approach would ensure

[21] 'From Transcript of Press Conference', *supra* note 19, at 533–534.

[22] D. Hammarskjöld, 'Statement at the Second Session of the Economic Commission for Africa', Tangier, Morocco, 26 January 1960 (UN Press Release SG/890, 25 January 1960), in Cordier and Foote, *supra* note 13, at 517.

[23] D. Hammarskjöld, 'Asia, Africa, and the West', Address Before the Academic Association of the University of Lund, Lund, Sweden, 4 May 1959 (UN Press Release SG/813, 4 May 1959), in A.W. Cordier and W. Foote (eds.), *Public Papers of the Secretaries-General of the United Nations, Vol. IV: Dag Hammarskjöld 1958–1960* (1974), 381.

[24] *Ibid.*, at 382 (original emphasis).

progress 'in the direction of a human community which, while retaining the special character of individuals and groups, has made use of what the various branches of the family of man have attained along different paths over thousands of years'.[25]

He clearly dismissed any claims to superiority over others based on any kind of naturalist concept of dominance rooted in supposed biological advancement and also questioned the legitimacy sought by dominant classes to justify their privileges:

> The health and strength of a community depend on every citizen's feeling of solidarity with the other citizens, and on his willingness, in the name of this solidarity, to shoulder his part of the burdens and responsibilities of the community. The same is of course true of humanity as a whole. And just [as] it cannot be argued that within a community an economic upper class holds its favored position by virtue of greater ability, as a quality which is, as it were, vested in the group by nature, so it is, of course, impossible to maintain this in regard to nations in their mutual relationships.[26]

He therefore concluded:

> We thus live in a world where, no more internationally than nationally, any distinct group can claim superiority in mental gifts and potentialities of development ... Those democratic ideals which demand equal opportunities for all should be applied also to peoples and races ... no nation or group of nations can base its future on a claim of supremacy.[27]

At a time when many of the colonial societies were engaged in often violent anti-colonial resistance, at times resorting to full-scale wars of liberation, Hammarskjöld held a clear view on the equality of people. It is noteworthy, however, that at the same time the international power relations impacted on the possibilities – and limits – his office faced. There is no comment by the UN, as a moral authority, on the British policy in Kenya, where the brutal response to the so-called Mau Mau rebellion could have justified some critical observations. Also, any critical engagement with the French war waged against the Algerian liberation movement was missing. The efforts to address the South African Apartheid policy were overshadowed by the emerging crisis over the situation in the Congo. A visit to South Africa – against the initial resistance of the government there and negotiated as a compromise, which limited the access to the opposition under the African National Congress – was originally

[25] *Ibid.* [26] *Ibid.*, at 383. [27] *Ibid.*, at 384.

planned after the Sharpeville massacre. It had to be postponed and only materialised in early 1961, but remained inconclusive.[28] Hence, the strong moral positions taken by the Secretary-General clearly faced their limits in the *realpolitik* the UN was forced to practise, in the light of the power and influence held by its dominant members.[29]

14.4 Intervention in the Congo

The crisis unfolding after the independence of the Congo as a former Belgian colony during 1960–1 was the biggest and ultimate test for Hammarskjöld's role on the commanding height of a world organisation which he strongly felt had to be autonomous from any individual state interests. Already on 31 October 1956, during the Suez crisis, Hammarskjöld had stated before the Security Council in no uncertain terms that, in his view, 'the discretion and impartiality … imposed on the Secretary-General … may not degenerate into a policy of expediency'.[30] As he reiterated in his introduction to the Annual Report to the UN for 1959–60:

> It is my firm conviction that any result bought at the price of a compromise with the principles and ideals of the Organization, either by yielding to force, by disregard of justice, by neglect of common interests or by contempt for human rights, is bought at too high a price. That is so because a compromise with its principles and purposes weakens the Organization in a way representing a definite loss for the future that cannot be balanced by any immediate advantage achieved.[31]

There is also anecdotal evidence of such steadfastness. In this case, the last personal assistant to Dag Hammarskjöld recalled:

> During an intermission in a debate in the Security Council, Dag was talking with the British Ambassador Sir Pierson Dixon in the corridor

[28] See C. Saunders, 'Hammarskjöld's visit to South Africa' (2011) 11(1) *African Journal of Conflict Resolution*; T. Sellström, 'Hammarskjöld and Apartheid South Africa: Mission Unaccomplished', C. Saunders, 'Dag Hammarskjöld and Apartheid South Africa', in H. Melber and M. Schoeman (eds.), *The United Nations and Regional Challenges in Africa – 50 Years After Dag Hammarskjöld* (2011) 57 *Development Dialogue*.

[29] This was also illustrated by the inability of the UN and its Secretary-General to make any difference when it came to the US imperialism in Central America and the Soviet invasion of Hungary, to mention only two of the more visible geopolitical issues illustrating the big power influence over global policy matters.

[30] Quoted from K. Falkman (ed.), *To Speak for the World: Speeches and Statements by Dag Hammarskjöld* (2005), 120f.

[31] *Ibid*., at 71.

> behind the podium. Sir Pierson suggested that the Secretary-General should make a statement in support of the British position. Dag refused. The ambassador insisted that, 'After all, there is something called political sense.' I stood there together with Dixon's assistant, Douglas Hurd (later to become Mrs. Thatcher's foreign secretary), when Dag, stressing each syllable, declared, 'And there is something called integrity,' turned around and closed the door behind him.[32]

Hammarskjöld's efforts to steer the UN in the Congo crisis, however, were in the midst of escalating Cold War antagonisms, similar to the challenges faced by navigating through Scylla and Charybdis. What made it worse was an authorisation of the UN presence in the country by a Security Council resolution, which lacked any clear and concrete guidance. While this provided space for navigation – at times deliberately used by Hammarskjöld at his discretion – it also risked that, in the absence of clarity, parties with their own interests involved were critical of whatever the Secretariat under the Secretary-General did (or did not) do:

> in directing the Secretary-General to eliminate any justification for foreign intervention by restoring law and order, as far as possible with the help of the Congo government but without using force or interfering in internal affairs, the Council from the start injected an inherent contradiction into the Congo operation.[33]

The Western interests vested in the Congo, and seeking to influence Hammarskjöld's policies, put enormous pressure on his office. After an initial (short) period of mutual support, he faced suspicions and criticism for almost every decision from the hegemonic states either in the East or in the West, who were all eager to influence him enough to give in to what they considered their interest. Hammarskjöld tried to escape these efforts of big states to hijack the UN's role and derail its policies, by seeking the cooperation of as many states as possible from the non-aligned movement. India (Nehru), Egypt (Nasser), Guinea (Touré), Ghana (Nkrumah) and Tunisia (Bourguiba) became important counterparts and at times even allies to bring a visible involvement of the South in international affairs and peacekeeping efforts. He stressed time and again – as late as a day before the fatal flight to Ndola – that 'the solution of the problem of the Congo lies in the hands of the Congolese people themselves

[32] W. Wachtmeister, 'Leader – Statesman – Friend', in M.L. Hanley and H. Melber (eds.), *Dag Hammarskjöld Remembered: A Collection of Personal Memories* (2011), 82.

[33] Urquhart, *supra* note 1, at 403f.

without any interference from outside'.[34] This is of course a contradictory position, given that the United Nations had already been tasked to intervene, though explicitly also reminded that this intervention should not be interference in internal affairs. Talk about a mission impossible!

When Lumumba was ousted from the office he held as Prime Minister of the Congo's first government, Hammarskjöld and his staff were at pains to decide how the UN should position itself. The Congo mission was tasked by the Security Council resolution to act in consultation with the constitutional government. But when President Kasavubu and Prime Minister Lumumba clashed in early September 1960, the question was who, by virtue of the position held, can claim to represent the government. Hammarskjöld concluded that the provisional constitution for the Congo, the *Loi Fondamentale*, allowed the Chief of State (which was the President), under Article 22, to dismiss the Prime Minister and appoint a new one, if his action was endorsed by at least one minister, which had been the case.

> On the other hand, there could be no doubt that the Prime Minister's attempt to dismiss the President was unconstitutional and had put Lumumba in a very doubtful position. For all practical purposes, it seemed that in the present circumstances the UN must inevitably regard the Chief of State as the only unquestioned constitutional authority.[35]

After the rapidly escalating conflicts between the internal factions culminating in the ousting of Lumumba, the Soviet leader Nikita Khrushchev accused Hammarskjöld of being a lackey of Western interests. When demanding his resignation at the UN General Assembly in early October 1960, the Secretary-General responded with the following historical words:

> It is not the Soviet Union or indeed any other Big Power who needs the United Nations for their protection, but all the others. In this sense, the Organisation is first of all their Organisation, and I deeply believe in the wisdom with which they will be able to use it and guide it. I shall remain in my post during the term of my Office as a servant of the Organisation in the interest of all those other nations, as long as they wish me to do so.[36]

[34] D. Hammarskjöld, First Message to Mr. Tshombé, 16 September 1961. Security Council Official Records, Sixteenth Year, Supplement for July, August and September 1961, document S/4940/Add.4, in Cordier and Foote, *supra* note 13, at 570.

[35] Urquhart, *supra* note 1, at 443f. He refers to C. Hoskyns, *The Congo since Independence–January 1960 to December 1961* (1965), at 208–210, for a discussion of this constitutional question.

[36] Quoted from Falkman, *supra* note 30, at 86.

Hammarskjöld continued to stay on course also in the subsequent debates in the Security Council. He refuted allegations that the UN acted in compliance with Western interests and that it could be held responsible for the brutal murder of Patrice Lumumba. He stated on 13 February 1961, in another response in the Security Council to the continued demands for his resignation (which now were also increasingly made by the Belgian, French and British, who saw their vested economic interests at stake):

> For seven or eight months, through efforts far beyond the imagination of those who founded this Organization, it has tried to counter tendencies to introduce the Big-Power conflict into Africa and put the young African countries under the shadow of the cold war. It has done so with great risks and against heavy odds. It has done so at the cost of very great personal sacrifices for a great number of people. In the beginning the effort was successful, and I do not now hesitate to say that on more than one occasion the drift into a war with foreign-power intervention of the Korean or Spanish type was avoided only thanks to the work done by the Organization, basing itself on African solidarity. We effectively countered efforts from all sides to make the Congo a happy hunting ground for national interests. To be a roadblock to such efforts is to make yourself the target of attacks from all those who find their plans thwarted ... From both sides the main accusation was a lack of objectivity. The historian will undoubtedly find in this balance of accusations the very evidence of that objectivity we were accused of lacking, but also of the fact that very many Member nations have not yet accepted the limits put on their national ambitions by the very existence of the United Nations and by the membership of that Organisation.[37]

His even-handedness towards the major powers is documented by another incident, shared by Sture Linnér (1917–2010) with an audience attending his presentation at the annual Dag Hammarskjöld Lecture in October 2007 in Uppsala. Linnér was, at the time of Hammarskjöld's death, Under-Secretary-General in charge of the UN mission in the Congo. In July 1961 President J.F. Kennedy tried to intervene directly. Afraid of Antoine Gizenga coming into political power, then campaigning for election as Prime Minister and suspected of representing Soviet interests, Kennedy demanded that the UN should prevent Gizenga from seizing office. If not in compliance, the United States and other Western powers

[37] D. Hammarskjöld, Second Statement After Soviet Demand for His Dismissal. New York, 13 February 1961. Security Council Official Records, Sixteenth Year, 933rd meeting, in Cordier and Foote, *supra* note 13, at 349f.

might withdraw their support to the UN.[38] Reportedly, Hammarskjöld in a phone conversation with Linnér dismissed this unveiled threat with the following words: 'I do not intend to give way to any pressure, be it from the East or the West; we shall sink or swim. Continue to follow the line you find to be in accordance with the UN Charter.'[39]

Sture Linnér ended his Dag Hammarskjöld Lecture with the conclusion:

> The Congo crisis could easily have provoked armed conflicts in other parts of Africa, even led to a world war. It was Dag Hammarskjöld and no one else who prevented that. And it is certain that for a suffering people he came to be seen as a model; he brought light into the heart of darkness.[40]

While many have, like Linnér, praised Hammarskjöld for his foresight and diplomatic skills to avoid worse through the specific way he handled the Congo crisis, others have been less positive in their assessment.[41] There were indeed disturbing contradictions and inconsistencies, which suggested that the UN intervention in the Congo was at times more so dependent upon individuals than being an organised and concerted, well planned action based on a clear strategy. There were initiatives by locally deployed high-ranking UN officials (both civilian and military staff) on an ad hoc basis, which were not always properly discussed in advance, nor always endorsed by Hammarskjöld, who explicitly disapproved afterwards of some of the decisions taken. The situation on the ground was at times confusing and contradictory, while often requiring quick action, which risked being wrong – and at times was. Furthermore, the communication with varying competing Congolese partners was – to put it mildly – not always reliable and often confusing. Exasperation was at times a crucial factor; it made even the highest-ranking officials (including Hammarskjöld), during the events from mid 1960 to fall 1961 in their interactions with the local counterparts, 'more impatient and less diplomatic than they might have been in a more normal situation'.[42]

[38] See for this period and the unusual blunt intervention the comprehensive documentation in M.G. Kalb, *The Congo Cables: The Cold War in Africa – From Eisenhower to Kennedy* (1982), 274–276.

[39] S. Linnér, 'Dag Hammarskjöld and the Congo Crisis, 1960–61', in S. Linnér and S. Åström, *UN Secretary-General Hammarskjöld: Reflections and Personal Experiences. The 2007 Dag Hammarskjöld Lecture* (2008), 26.

[40] *Ibid.*, at 29. [41] See Chapters 12 and 13, this volume.

[42] Kalb, *supra* note 38, at 290.

One might also explain these flaws by the extreme pressure exerted through the direct interests of the many different parties involved. This included the variety of Western – anything but identical – interests as represented most prominently by Belgium; but it also included the United Kingdom and the United States, the British settler colonial minority regimes of the Central African Federation (Northern and Southern Rhodesia and Nyasaland) and Apartheid South Africa, as well as the opposite interests of the Soviet camp in securing a stake in the resource-rich territory – or at least preventing the West from establishing another satellite regime.[43]

For Hammarskjöld this required a constant navigation through rough waters, with winds blowing from different directions. Failure was almost programmed; both the assassination of Patrice Lumumba and the loss of his own life, the loss of fifteen others on board the plane that crashed on approach to Ndola, as well as the loss of so many more lives of civilians and soldiers on all sides of the conflict – including the killing of many blue helmets – testified to the mission being impossible. The 'Congo Club', those UN higher staff members who were directly involved in the operations both in the Secretariat and on the ground, most notably on the civilian side the Americans Ralph Bunche and Andy Cordier, the Irish Conor Cruise O'Brien and the Indian Rajeshwar Dayal, but also the Swedish commander of the UN forces von Horn (who reportedly had absolutely no grasp of the local realities), created a special mixture, where the personal chemistry played an important but rather negative role.

The personal account of Conor Cruise O'Brien[44] is a detailed narrative illustrating 'how an international civil service can be forged from men whose national cultures and working experience necessarily have a heavy hold on their minds'.[45] As claimed by one of the critical assessments of the UN's Congo mission of the early 1960s, the UN officials having the most

[43] Matters became even more complicated through a policy change in the US administration under President J.F. Kennedy, who since 1961 in office deviated from the earlier US foreign policy under Dwight D. Eisenhower by seeking to enter closer relations with the newly independent African countries at the expense of uncritically backing the interests of the European colonial powers in maintaining control over their 'backyards'. See P.E. Muehlenbeck, *Betting on the Africans: John F. Kennedy's Courting of African Nationalist Leaders* (2012).

[44] C. Cruise O'Brien, *To Katanga and Back: A UN Case History* (1962). See for other important perspectives R. Dayal, *Mission for Hammarskjold: The Congo Crisis* (1976), B. Urquhart, *A Life in Peace and War* (1987), 145–188.

[45] L. Gordenker, 'Conor Cruise O'Brien and the Truth About the United Nations' (1969) 23 *International Organization* 908.

influential decision-making impact 'shared a common Cold War outlook with Western policy makers, and saw their mission in the Congo as that of preserving the then existing balance of forces in the world'.[46] However, given the evidence available, it seems to be somewhat unfair, if not wrong, to include in this rather sweeping statement someone of Hammarskjöld's calibre.

14.5 The murder of Lumumba

The complicated personal dimensions within the Congo conflict should not be ignored or downplayed. Ralph Bunche's interaction with Patrice Lumumba highlights a mismatch due mainly to a personality clash, suspicion on both sides and miscommunication. Altogether, this escalated into a relationship characterised by animosity and mutual contempt. As ridiculous as it sounds, the interaction between the Afro-American Bunche and the Congolese Pan-African nationalist Lumumba displayed strong racist undertones on both sides. The unfortunate role played by the Swedish commander von Horn in charge of the UN military operations, who was never able to relate to the African realities on the ground, was an addition to the recipe for disaster. But neither was Lumumba's behaviour a reliable criterion for policy decisions. The complicated mixture of domestic political rivalries, external influences by other states, an unclear framework for UN intervention and personality clashes, ended in deadly consequences for Lumumba and one of the biggest failures of a mission in the history of the UN, even though it averted another conflict of even bigger magnitude. Diagnosed as a 'fatal encounter', the mismatch between Bunche and Lumumba resulted in a tragic constellation in as much as 'the flow of information that shaped their understandings was so completely at odds that one might imagine that they were engaged in wholly separate settings'.[47]

Hammarskjöld was personally blamed for not restoring Lumumba's role in the government of the Congo after he was ousted as Prime Minister by the State President. While Hammarskjöld held the view that this would have been an undue intervention into the domestic affairs of the country (and that the dismissal was within the discretion of the constitutional

[46] G. Nzongola-Ntalala, *The Congo from Leopold to Kabila: A People's History* (2002), 114.

[47] C. Young, 'Ralph Bunche and Patrice Lumumba. The Fatal Encounter', in R.A. Hill and E. J. Keller (eds.), *Trustee for the Human Community: Ralph J. Bunche, the United Nations, and the Decolonization of Africa* (2010), at 129.

powers of the State President), others even in the UN administration reached opposing conclusions. It therefore remains a contested matter: to what extent the passivity of the UN was at least an indirect support to the Western interests in removing Lumumba from office and finally taking initiatives to eliminate him physically. Along similar lines, it remains a matter of controversy to what extent the UN should have protected Lumumba even after he had decided to leave at his own risk the house in which he stayed under UN observation. As Hammarskjöld and others argued, by removing himself from the direct protection offered, in order to mobilise for the restoration of his political influence, Lumumba was returning by his own decision into Congolese politics. Protecting him in this role would therefore have been tantamount to an undue interference into the political affairs of the country.

The most pronounced critique of the passive role of both the UN and its Secretary-General Hammarskjöld with regard to the domestic policy matters in the Congo and the subsequent assassination of Patrice Lumumba has hitherto been presented by Ludo de Witte. In the preface of the English edition of his study, he maintains that without the involvement not only of the Western powers but also the UN, 'the assassination could never have been carried out'.[48] The critical review of the English edition of his book by Brian Urquhart,[49] who was also a member of the closer circle of high-ranking UN officials surrounding Hammarskjöld, sparked off an illuminating exchange. De Witte repeated his accusation that 'UN Secretary-General Hammarskjöld played a decisive role in the overthrow of the Congolese government of Patrice Lumumba', thereby willingly accepting his assassination. For him the 'UN was the most important vehicle of destroying the Congolese government and laying the groundworks for the dictatorship of Mobutu'. He considered Western criticism of aspects of the UN operation as being merely 'for public consumption, or a counterweight to the Afro-Asian pressure on the UN leadership to help Lumumba'.[50]

[48] L. De Witte, *The Assassination of Lumumba* (2001), xv; this interpretation is shared at least in tendency in the chapters by Hintjens and Cruz (Chapter 12) and to a lesser extent by Omasombo Tshonda (Chapter 13) in this volume. For a less romanticising appreciation of Lumumba's role and his personality see L. Zeilig, *Patrice Lumumba: Africa's Lost Leader* (2008). The author also resists the temptation to blame Hammarskjöld for Lumumba's death.

[49] B. Urquhart, 'The Tragedy of Lumumba', *The New York Review of Books*, 4 October 2001.

[50] L. De Witte in 'The Tragedy of Lumumba: An Exchange', *The New York Review of Books*, 20 December 2001 (www.nybooks.com/articles/archives/2001/dec/20/the-tragedy-of-lumumba-an-exchange/?pagination=false). During an informal exchange on the occasion of a seminar on 'Dag Hammarskjöld, the United Nations and the End of Empire' at

Interestingly, a highly credible observer participated in this controversy as a witness. As he claimed, he spoke to a stressed and intoxicated Lumumba, who acted rather irrationally hours before his clandestine escape from UN protection. In his view this 'discounts the many erroneous versions of what happened given by critics who have sought to show UN collaboration in Lumumba's ghastly fate'.[51] Urquhart, in his response, qualifies De Witte's 'elaborate fantasy of Hammarskjöld's conspiracy with the Belgians' as 'absurd to anyone who worked with Hammarskjöld at the time and experienced his frustration and his frequent rages at, and denunciations of, both the Belgians and their protégé, the Katangese leader, Moïse Tshombe'.[52]

At the same time, however, it seems difficult to object to a critical conclusion when glancing through the evidence available with regard to the unfortunate, if at times not disastrous, impact of some members of the 'Congo Club' mentioned above. In their role within the Congolese UN mission, they 'wittingly or unwittingly' might have 'provided to those seeking Lumumba's demise the justification and the opportunities they needed to remove a democratically elected leader from office by illegal means'[53] – with deadly consequences. While an ultimate verdict on the role of the Secretary-General in this affair seems impossible, it is at least noteworthy that the death of Lumumba did not remain without a personal comment indicating some degree of empathy from Hammarskjöld's side. In a letter to John Steinbeck he wrote:

> Your approach to the Lumumba tragedy – his murder was in Tallyrand's words: 'more than a crime, it was a major stupidity' is unique, no one in these parts, at least, has suggested it, and it invited thought ... I incline to the conclusion that *no* one, in the long pull, will really profit from

the University of London Senate House on 2 September 2011, De Witte rebuked the reference to the statements of Hammarskjöld in the UN Security Council as purely cosmetic smokescreen, drafted by the American diplomats to create the impression of a UN neutrality, which according to De Witte never existed. The assumption that Hammarskjöld would read out statements, which diplomats from permanent missions at the UN drafted for him, is for those familiar with Hammarskjöld's character and thinking so far-fetched that it borders on nonsense and reveals the degree of a mind anchored in conspiracy theory.

51 Colin Legum (1919–2003), author of *Congo Disaster* (1960), was a widely recognised and respected South African senior journalist, who because of his anti-Apartheid convictions was living in exile until 1991.

52 See Urquhart, *supra* note 49.

53 G. Nzongola-Ntalala, 'Ralph Bunche, Patrice Lumumba, and the First Congo Crisis', in Hill and Keller, *supra* note 47, at 156.

Lumumba's death, least of all those outside the Congo who now strain to do so but should one day confront a reckoning with truth and decency.[54]

14.6 Operation Morthor and Hammarskjöld's death

Dag Hammarskjöld, and with him fifteen other persons (entourage and crew), died in the wreckage of the DC6 airplane 'Albertina', which crashed a few miles away from the airport when approaching the Northern Rhodesian mining town of Ndola in the night from 17 to 18 September 1961. Hammarskjöld was to meet close to the border of the Congo the leader of the Katangese secessionist movement, Moïse Tshombe, in an effort to negotiate a peaceful solution to the civil war; previous military efforts of the UN to bring an end to the Katangese secession had dismally backfired in late August and early September 1961, when UN troops failed to solve the impasse by force of arms.[55]

The circumstances of the plane crash remain – despite the findings of several official commissions of enquiry concluding that it was most probably a pilot's error (while, importantly, the UN enquiry did not rule out foul play) – a matter of speculation. Too many questions have not been answered in a satisfactory manner, and it is not surprising that half a century later these simmering doubts and unanswered questions resurface with new vigour.[56]

In one of the many review articles welcoming the latest investigative study, Michaela Wrong found herself

> chafing at the detail, hungry instead to know more about the ideological convictions and strategic calculations that set Hammarskjöld, his Irish deputy Conor Cruise O'Brien and others at the UN on their high-risk

[54] Letter to John Steinbeck, 28 February 1961. Dag Hammarskjöld Papers. Royal Library, Stockholm. Quoted in P. Nelson, *Courage of Faith: Dag Hammarskjöld's Way in Quest of Negotiated Peace, Reconciliation and Meaning* (2007), 218 (fn. 734).

[55] Operations 'Rumpunch' on 28 August 1961 and 'Morthor' on 13 September 1961 were disastrous attempts to bring an end to the Katangese secession and clearly executed beyond the original mandate for UN peacekeeping intervention in the Congo through the deliberate application of military means in a domestic conflict. For details see the personal account of C. Cruise O'Brien, *supra* note 43, 195ff.

[56] For a concise overview on the different speculations and explanations see M. Fröhlich, 'The Unknown Assignation: Dag Hammarskjöld in the Papers of George Ivan Smith', in *Beyond Diplomacy: Perspectives on Dag Hammarskjöld* (2008), 27–33. See as the latest, hitherto most comprehensive effort to explore the dubious aspects of the plane crash further, S. Williams, *Who Killed Hammarskjöld? The UN, the Cold War and White Supremacy in Africa* (2011).

> course of geopolitical confrontation. Hammarskjöld once said 'It is better for the UN to lose the support of the US because it is faithful to law and principles, than to survive as an agent whose activities are geared to political purposes never avowed or laid down by the major organs of the UN.' I would have liked to know what UN officials in New York think of such sentiments today, whether they regard Hammarskjöld as dangerously naïve or superbly high-minded, and how UN policy since then has been influenced by the sneaking, terrible suspicion that a former boss paid for such defiance with his life.[57]

Meanwhile, similar to the inconclusive discussion as to what extent the UN and Hammarskjöld could have been blamed for sharing responsibility, if not even complicity, in the murder of Lumumba, the controversy continues over the possible theories for the cause of the fatal plane crash. While this chapter cannot provide an overview on all circumstantial evidence discussed elsewhere, which motivates and fuels the ongoing debate, it is noteworthy that the political constellation of the time would not have excluded an interest of several parties in the prevention of a meeting between Hammarskjöld and Tshombe – if not the removal of the Secretary-General from his office by all means. Hammarskjöld had decided on short notice to seek a conversation with Tshombe as a follow up to the botched attempt to bring the Katanga secession through the application of (legally dubious) UN force of arms to an end.

An exchange of cables just ahead of the flight to Ndola and prior to Operation Morthor, seems to suggest that the Secretary-General was more involved in the discussions preceding the failed military interference than one might have assumed. It is a matter of interpretation how much Hammarskjöld knew in detail before Morthor and to what extent he endorsed the operation, but he was clearly informed about such plans. Published recently by the *Guardian*,[58] the material reproduced shows that he had consulted his legal advisor Oscar Schachter, who on 7 September 1961 warned strongly against such forms of engagement as undue 'violation of the ban against intervention in domestic political conflicts'.[59] But on 10 September 1961 Hammarskjöld cabled to Sture Linnér that, 'the speed of developments and the stage reached means that short of a

[57] M. Wrong, 'Who Killed Hammarskjöld? By Susan Williams', *The Spectator*, 29 October 2011, www.spectator.co.uk/books/7342003/who-killed-hammarskjld-by-susan-williams.thtml.

[58] A series of stories and reproduced cables were posted on the website of the *Guardian*: guardian.co.uk, 17 August 2011.

[59] www.guardian.co.uk/world/interactive/2011/aug/17/un-cable-hammarskjold-katanga-operation-morthor?INTCMP=SRCH.

change for the better in Katanga we are beyond the point of no return'.[60] While some take this as proof that Hammarskjöld endorsed Morthor, it still leaves open the question of to what extent Hammarskjöld explicitly authorised the operation. Often before, he had used a form of language which bordered on that of an oracle and allowed for ambiguous meanings and interpretations. There are however sufficient indications that he was involved in the discussion, regarding if and how the military presence of the UN might be instrumental in reversing the secession of Katanga. The governments in the Western states also became aware of Hammarskjöld's involvement and their strong disapproval was conveyed to him. Dismissing criticism by the United States, Hammarskjöld – as already quoted in part in the review article by Wrong above – cabled on 15 September 1961 to Bunche:

> It is better for the UN to lose the support of the US because it is faithful to law and principles than to survive as an agent whose activities are geared to political purposes never avowed or laid down by the major organs of the UN ... Generally speaking, I have one advice and that is that the major powers do not react until they know the facts and further, that they do remember that they are most likely to keep their positions if they respect principles than if they expect others to break them on their behalf or on behalf of the Welenskys.[61]

There is hitherto no conclusive evidence that the plane crash was the result of external influence upon instruction or with the encouragement of any of the parties who were interested in preventing the UN under Hammarskjöld to end the Katangese secession. But it is not far-fetched to conclude that the 1961 UN military operations 'were seen as a sacrifice of Western economic interests ... in return for Soviet support of a negotiated end to the civil war'.[62]

It therefore came as no surprise that a recent privately initiated Commission of Inquiry ('The Hammarskjöld Commission') reached the conclusion that, after a year-long investigation between August 2012 and

[60] www.guardian.co.uk/world/interactive/2011/aug/17/un-cable-hammarskjold-operation-morthor?INTCMP=SRCH.

[61] www.guardian.co.uk/world/interactive/2011/aug/17/un-cable-hammarskjold-american-criticism?INTCMP=SRCH. Sir Roy Welensky had been the CAF Prime Minister and a fierce opponent to the UN's role in the Congo, which was considered a threat to white supremacy in Southern Africa. Kalb, *supra* note 38, at 297 describes Hammarskjöld's reaction to the Western demands as 'somewhat annoyed'.

[62] T. Scarnecchia, 'The Congo Crisis, the United Nations, and Zimbabwean Nationalism, 1960–1963' (2011) 11(1) *African Journal of Conflict Resolution* 65.

August 2013 collecting and reappraising all evidence still available, the ultimate verdict on the real circumstances of the plane crash is still pending.[63] The four internationally renowned jurists – after a careful balancing of all available (often hitherto not yet considered) factual hints – concluded that the puzzle seems to suggest that:

> There is persuasive evidence that the aircraft was subjected to some form of attack or threat as it circled to land at Ndola, which was by then widely known to be its destination. Accepting, as we do, that there is – as the experts advise – no need for such an explanation to account for the crash and that it is capable of being fully explained as a controlled flight into terrain, we nevertheless consider that the possibility that the plane was in fact forced into its descent by some form of hostile action is supported by sufficient evidence to merit further inquiry.[64]

The Commission refused to speculate about the concrete motives or the actual initiators of the possible hostile aerial act, but maintained that the investigation whether such an act had likely occurred and 'whether it is considered to have caused the descent of the plane by direct damage or by harassment, or to have triggered some form of disabling harm to the plane, is in our judgment capable of proof or disproof'.[65] The Commission therefore feels that a follow-up by the United Nations resuming further investigations would be an appropriate process. Such a decision would remain, however, purely within the authority and discretion of the member states and requires a submission adopted in the General Assembly.

14.7 Hammarskjöld's legacy

The legacy of Hammarskjöld as second Secretary-General of the UN remains a lasting reference point over and above such efforts to investigate further the circumstances of his death. Suffice to conclude that it is an interesting aspect that suspicions are not completely unfounded or dismissed that some Western and settler-colonial interests, in alliance with the big mining companies in control of the mineral wealth in Katanga, could have been at play when it came to the plane crash. This in itself points to the outstanding relevance attached to Hammarskjöld's role as second UN Secretary-General. But critics remain unconvinced and see

63 See for further details the information presented at its website, including the final report, submitted in September 2013: www.hammarskjoldcommission.org/.

64 The Hammarskjöld Commission, *Report of the Commission of Inquiry*, The Hague, 9 September 2013 (amended on 15 September 2013), 48.

65 *Ibid.*

him as a willing collaborator of the Western hegemonic interests. His numerous speeches testifying to the contrary do not impress them. The similar testimonies of numerous colleagues working with him are considered biased, especially as the role of the UN under Hammarskjöld in the Congo is seen as an indication of his failure to advocate the principles he claimed to stand for.

But others maintain that Hammarskjöld's ethics, his concept of solidarity, his sense of fundamental universal values and human rights in combination with his respect for the multitude of identities within the human family, as well as his responsibility as the world's highest international civil servant to assume global leadership, set standards that have lost none of their value and relevance. The way he defined and executed his duties also with regard to the people of Africa can in their view confidently be qualified as an act of international solidarity, even though it might not have been flawless. His efforts to find solutions under difficult circumstances at the same time testify to the relevance of the words, with which he was greeted when leaving the plane upon arrival at Idlewild Airport in New York on 9 April 1953, a day after his election. His predecessor Trygve Lie then had welcomed him to 'the most impossible job on this earth'.[66]

In his last words to the staff, Hammarskjöld reiterated the autonomy of the Secretariat from the direct influence of UN Member States as one of his fundamental principles. When the Secretariat, as he stated, 'is regarded as truly international, and its individual members as owing no allegiance to any national government', then it 'may develop as an instrument for the preservation of peace and security of increasing significance and responsibilities'.[67] One should maybe give him the benefit of the doubt that he indeed meant what he said and tried to live up to these standards.

As he had stressed so often before and once again in his introduction to the Sixteenth Annual Report just a month before his death, the Charter 'has committed the Organization to the furtherance of self-determination, self-government, and independence'.[68] He also insisted that the

[66] Quoted in Urquhart, *supra* note 1, at 15.

[67] D. Hammarskjöld, 'Last Words to the Staff – from Remarks on Staff Day', New York, 8 September 1961, in Cordier and Foote, *supra* note 10, at 564.

[68] D. Hammarskjöld, Introduction to the Sixteenth Annual Report. New York, 17 August 1961. General Assembly Official Records. Sixteenth Session, Supplement No. 1A (A/4800/Add.1), in Cordier and Foote, *supra* note 10, at 544.

fundamental principles, as laid down in the Charter, were of special significance for the practical work of the organisation

> in relation to countries under colonial rule or in other ways under foreign domination. The General Assembly has translated the principles into action intended to establish through self-determination a free and independent life as sovereign states for peoples who have expressed in democratic forms their wish for such a status … The resolution on colonialism, adopted by the General Assembly at its fifteenth session, may be regarded as a comprehensive restatement in elaborated form of the principle laid down in the Charter. Results of developments so far have been reflected in the birth of a great number of new national states and a revolutionary widening of the membership of the Organization.[69]

In conclusion, and after the accounts presented above, it seems somewhat unfair to blame the Secretary-General for having ultimate responsibility in the miscarriage of the birth of the Congolese state. Not that this would be merely a moral or ethical question. Rather, documentary evidence seems unable to substantiate the claims that Hammarskjöld willingly allowed his office and the UN to promote a Western imperialist agenda. If at all, the evidence suggests that then as now, the hegemonic powers in our world seek to influence global policies above all in their interests, not in the spirit of the principles they adopted and ratified through the Charter and many subsequent conventions and other normative frameworks supposedly guiding global policies.

The following seems to be a fair assessment of Hammarskjöld's role with regard to the Congo:

> Hammarskjöld was certainly pro-Western but did not always go along with the United States, particularly when he determined (or was forced to see) that its goals were not conducive to overall international security (as he saw it). Yet Hammarskjöld was also a diplomat extraordinaire, and had he lived longer the crisis might have ended sooner or more peacefully. A major problem with his legacy is that his imprint on ONUC was so subtly managed and dependent on his personal relationships that it was impossible for others to follow. He was not supposed to die, and his untimely death threw into jeopardy all he had carefully crafted and managed in the Congo.[70]

Brian Urquhart, who joined the UN system as the second public official in the organisation's history and who served Hammarskjöld (as one of

[69] *Ibid.*, at 545.
[70] L. Namikas, *Battleground Africa: Cold War in the Congo 1960–1965* (2013), 226.

five Secretaries-General) throughout his time in office, found some of the most moving words in his effort to cope with the loss of his 'boss', as the UN staff often with respect and fondness referred to the second Secretary-General:

> I have had news of the death of many friends in my life, but none has affected me as this did, and I believe that others had the same experience. The death of Hammarskjöld was not only an appalling blow to the UN and to all who had worked with him. There was also an agonizing sense of irreparable personal loss which I still find hard to account for. None of us knew Hammarskjöld really well, but he had come to occupy a unique place in our lives, thoughts, and affections by the nature of his leadership and his character. For a long time it was hard to think of him without tears, not least because one would never see his like again. To this day I can see and hear him in my mind as if I had only just left his presence.[71]

[71] Urquhart, *supra* note 44, at 175.

15

The Dag factor

How quiet diplomacy changed the role of the Secretariat during the Congo crisis, 1960–1961

ALANNA O'MALLEY

15.1 Introduction

Asked if I have the courage
To go on to the end,
I answer Yes without
A second thought.
Dag Hammarskjöld,
April 1961[1]

When the Central African country of the Congo was gripped by conflict just days after its independence from Belgium on 30 June 1960, there was little indication that the struggle of another African nation would prove to have a fundamental impact on the United Nations, creating a quagmire for the organisation and ultimately resulting in the untimely loss of the Secretary-General in mysterious circumstances. The Swedish diplomat Dag Hammarskjöld would pioneer an independent, interventionist position for the organisation: militarily, with the launch of its groundbreaking peacekeeping mission to the Congo, but also politically, casting the organisation in the role of arbitrator between the major powers.

The focus of this chapter will be on the specific role envisaged for the organisation during the international crisis by its most interventionist Secretary-General to date. With the development of what would later be termed quiet diplomacy, Hammarskjöld helped the institution to function by sidestepping the deadlocked Security Council, and the riotous

Alanna O'Malley is Assistant Professor of International Studies at, Leiden University, formerly Research Assistant, Max Weber Postdoctoral Programme, European University Institute.

[1] D. Hammarskjold, *Markings* (1965), 206.

General Assembly through advocation of the role of soft power. This argument is based on two premises. First, it is context-specific as the rise of the Afro-Asian bloc and the addition of forty-seven new members within two years diluted the traditional power base of the West within the UN. This allowed Hammarskjöld to wrench back more control over the institution, helping it develop into more than just an arm of the United States abroad. Crucially, however, it was exactly Hammarskjöld's championing of the Afro-Asian cause which would create a new role for soft power within the organisation. Due to Cold War tensions, the Security Council was often hamstrung in negotiations, particularly during the Congo crisis which was seen as a battleground for the various interests of the superpowers. By invigorating the General Assembly and the new voices within it, Hammarskjöld helped develop a role for soft power whereby international prestige became a currency to motivate states into action. This was to be a key component in helping the organisation to stride an activist and neutral path during the crisis and carve out a hitherto unprecedented role for soft power within the organisation.

The United Nations was to become the central battleground for the complex, and often intractable problems, as the growing number of independent nations sought to have their voices heard on the world stage, eroding the traditional power base of the West and openly contesting their foreign policies. Not only did these newly independent nations see their collective fate hanging in the balance of the Congo crisis, but in the UN they 'believed that the bipolar conflict between the United States and the Soviet Union made them mere pawns in a bipolar Cold War game, especially when "hot wars" broke out between the two superpowers'.[2] Moreover the whole episode at the United Nations was to prove a microcosm for the broader events of international affairs emphasising the changing role of the institution and the struggle of powerful nations like Britain and the United States to deal effectively with the dual challenges of the Cold War and decolonisation. As Paul Kennedy outlines it: 'what was happening, in fact, was that one major trend in twentieth century power politics, the rise of superpowers, was beginning to interact with another, newer trend – the political fragmentation of the globe'.[3] The UN was set to become the central battleground, both in terms of ideology and diplomacy for both the East–West conflict and also the growing intemperance

[2] J. Hoff, 'The American Century: From Sarajevo to Sarajevo', in M.J. Hogan (ed.), *The Ambiguous Legacy: US Foreign Relations in the 'American Century'* (1999), 183 at 191.

[3] P. Kennedy, *The Rise and Fall of the Great Powers: Economic Change and Military Conflict from 1500–2000* (1987), 394.

of the true believers of the Third World, for whom the international forum of the UN provided a structure, coherency and a platform from which to denigrate the West.

15.2 Into the 'Heart of Darkness'[4]

> Dag Hammarskjöld has gone to history as an inspiring international personality injecting a dose of moral leadership and personal integrity into a world of power politics.[5]

Following Congolese Premier Patrice Lumumba's appeal to the UN to intervene in defence of Congolese sovereignty in July 1960 the stage was set for this drama to be played out between Western nations, as the crisis gained momentum. It was their intervention in the region in the name of protecting humanity which brought the UN to a crisis of its own over the issue. The UN intervention would ultimately have the effect of exacerbating hostilities between superpowers on the Security Council, making it very difficult for the UN to effectively and efficiently formulate policy.[6] Some historians claim that the UN was complicit in events in the Congo: '[f]ew events in Africa during the 1960's better illustrate the hypocrisy of western powers or their determination to control the newly independent countries of Africa by any means at their disposal';[7] however, others contend that the ONUC[8] mission was the swiftest and largest operation ever mounted and the '[UN's] stock never stood higher'.[9] ONUC was factionalised by Cold War politics. The UN operated in the context of the shifting global order with the rise of the ideals of nationalism, which saw a move towards decolonisation all over the world and the emergence of many burgeoning new nations on to the world stage, eager to discard the shackles of colonial oppression. The organisation sought to find ways to maintain its authority and integrity through a crisis which brought its Secretary-General Dag Hammarskjöld and the office of the Secretariat under fire

[4] *Heart of Darkness* is the novel by Joseph Conrad in which a fictional Englishman, Charles Marlow, uncovers the horrors of the Belgian colonisation of the Congo.

[5] O. Bring, 'Dag Hammarskjöld and the Issue of Humanitarian Intervention', in J. Petman and J. Klabbers (eds.), *Nordic Cosmopolitanism: Essays in International Law for Martti Koskenniemi* (2003), 485 at 486. See also Chapter 9, this volume.

[6] N. MacQueen, *Humanitarian Intervention and the United Nations* (2011), 27.

[7] G. Arnold, *Africa: A Modern History* (2006), 77.

[8] Operation des Nations Unies au Congo (ONUC) was the name of the UN peacekeeping mission undertaken in the Congo in 1960.

[9] C. Legum, *Congo Disaster* (1961), 130.

and called into question the very survival of the organisation. In his striving for the principles of righteousness and morality in all UN conduct in the Congo (to which he would eventually lose his life), Hammarskjöld established operational precedent for the conduct of peacekeeping missions. He also subtly reformed the way in which the UN would do business with regard to its central doctrine of keeping the international peace. This had not only have profound effects on the organisation itself, but also cast a long shadow over the foreign policies of some of the major participating nations such as Britain and the United States.

The objective for the UN was the containment of the Congo crisis and in particular the prevention of the internationalisation of it by ensuring that all aid and support came through the official channels of that organisation, thereby preventing any one power from gaining a foothold in the country and drawing it into the Cold War.[10] This seems to concur with the aim of the mission as viewed by members of the Afro-Asian bloc in the General Assembly; led by Ghana, they urged for the 'Africanisation' of the crisis, by 'forestalling all *non-African* and in particular imperialist and neo-colonial intervention'.[11] From the outset, the Secretary-General adopted a 'hands on' approach to the crisis, evoking formally for the first time Article 99 of the UN Charter in response to Lumumba's appeal on 13 July 1960.[12] By choosing to bring the Congo crisis to the immediate attention of the Security Council, Hammarskjöld thereby inscribed it on the global security agenda.

In his opening statement to the Council on 13 July 1960, Hammarskjöld recommended that the United Nations accede to the request from the government of the Congo for military assistance in defending their independence following the dispatch of Belgian troops to the Congo.[13] This was in response to the mutiny in the Force Publique against Belgian commanding officers on 8 July 1960.[14] The challenge, as described by *The Economist*,

[10] J. Mohan, 'Ghana, Congo and The United Nations' (1969) 7 *Journal of Modern African Studies* 369, at 375.

[11] *Ibid.*

[12] Article 99 of the UN Charter grants the Secretary-General the power to 'bring to the attention of the Security Council, any matter which in his opinion may threaten the maintenance of international peace and security'.

[13] 'Opening Statement in the Security Council, New York, 13 July 1960', in A. Cordier and W. Foote (eds.), *Public Papers of the Secretaries-General of the United Nations, Vol. V: Dag Hammarskjöld, 1960–1961* (1975), at 23.

[14] The inequitable system, which the Belgians had constructed in the Congo, is evident in the structure of the army and the mutiny offers a firm indication of not only the strength

constituted 'a task that has no precedent'.[15] Never before had the UN been asked to intervene in a sovereign country to protect its independence. By invoking his powers under Article 99, Hammarskjöld further defined the nature of his tenure in the Secretariat as independent and activist. It should be pointed out that the formulation of Article 99 is permissive. Indeed, as Norman Bentwich and Andrew Martin describe, 'it is for the Secretary-General to determine at his discretion which is a proper case for the use of his exceptional powers under this article'.[16] In addition, the unanimous agreement of the members of the Security Council was extraordinary as it superseded the usual division between the West and the communists.[17] However, Hammarskjöld's action to 'sweep away all before him at the outset of the crisis'[18] was met with not a little consternation, among Western powers in particular. This level of activism and direct investment of the Secretary-General was unprecedented and, as Alan James describes, 'states tend to be unenthusiastic about the prospect of an international organisation's top official building up a quasi-independent power base'.[19]

From the British perspective, as long as Hammarskjöld's interpretation of the Congo crisis remained in line with theirs, that being that Lumumba posed an immediate threat to law and order, no direct challenge to their policy was immediately envisaged by the outbreak of a crisis in the Congo. As Macmillan recorded in his diary on 10 July 1960: 'The Prime Minister called Lumumba (or some such name) is a communist and a Russian agent.'[20] He revealed his unease about the summer of 1960, recalling that 'it has a terrible similarity to 1914. Now Congo may play the role of Serbia'.[21] For his part, Eisenhower was increasingly alarmed by Lumumba's leanings towards the Soviets when the UN refused to help

of the resentment with which most Congolese regarded the colonial system, but also where this antipathy stemmed from. In 1960 the Force Publique comprised some 24,000 Congolese soldiers and non-commissioned officers, and about 1,000 Belgian officers. This inequality was maintained by blocking Congolese troops from entering the upper cadres of the army. On 6 July 1960, the Congolese soldiers mutinied and locked up their Belgian officers after it was announced by the commander, General Emile Jassens, that independence would have no bearing on the structure of the military nor the service conditions of the troops. E. Nwaubani, 'Eisenhower, Nkrumah and the Congo Crisis' (2001) 36 *Journal of Contemporary History* 599, at 607. See Legum, *supra* note 9, at 106.

15 'Congo Expressed Derailed', *The Economist*, 16 July 1960, 16.

16 N. Bentwich and A. Martin (eds.), *A Commentary on the Charter of the United Nations* (1969), 173.

17 See Legum, *supra* note 9, at 126.

18 A. James, *Britain and the Congo Crisis, 1960–63* (1996), 65.

19 *Ibid.*

20 A. Horne, *Macmillan, The Official Biography* (1988/2008), 207.

21 *Ibid.*, at 208.

him end the secession. This lack of a coherent direction manifested itself at the United Nations, especially during the first year of the crisis when the United States failed to provide firm leadership during negotiations, reflected by their passive stance at the Security Council. Ambrose outlines that Eisenhower sided with the European colonists, not because he wanted to keep Western access to resources in Katanga, but because he was fearful that the Soviets would use the Congo as a military base from which they could expand their power and influence.[22]

Regardless of the increasing discomfort of Western nations at the direct involvement of the Secretariat and the swift exercise of power by Hammarskjöld in the initial stages of the crisis, it is debatable where his exact position stood vis-à-vis the West. James maintains that, until the presidential coup of 5 September, Hammarskjöld was close to the Western view that Lumumba was a communist stooge. That he was spearheading the campaign for his removal from the Congo suited the British in particular as they viewed the volatile Congolese Premier as a threat to the stability of the region as a whole. As he puts it, 'Britain, the United States, the West as a whole, the United Nations as exemplified by its deeply respected Secretary-General – all were marching crisply in step'.[23] However, such a partisan stance is not reflected elsewhere. The wording of the first Security Council resolution on the Congo unambiguously called upon Belgium to withdraw its troops from the Congo.[24] This reflected some distance from the position of other Western nations who did not condemn Belgian activities. Even in the first meetings of the Congo Advisory Committee,[25] established by Hammarskjöld to advise him, through regular deliberations, on the best course of action in the Congo, the Secretary-General is riveted to the position of an 'open-door policy' in discussions, stating: 'Any time anybody can give us information or advice, we are happy to get it. For that reason there are no closed

[22] S. Ambrose, *Eisenhower: The President, 1952–1969* (1984), Vol. II, 587.

[23] See James, *supra* note 18, at 72.

[24] 'United Nations Resolution S/4387', in A. Cordier and W. Foote (eds.), *Public Papers of the Secretaries-General of the United Nations, Vol. V: Dag Hammarskjöld 1960–1961* (1975), at 25.

[25] The Congo Advisory Committee had been established by Hammarskjold in 1960 and was designed to help him gain leverage to steer the complex and controversial ONUC operation through the General Assembly. It was composed of representatives from the eighteen countries which had contributed troops to the operation. See also, concerning the use of advisory committees, T. Whitfield, 'Groups of Friends', in D.M. Malone (ed.), *The UN Security Council: From the Cold War to the 21st Century* (2004), 311 at 315.

doors, there is nothing that is definitive ... under these circumstances I think that you are fully safeguarded.'[26]

This was viewed by the Western nations – including France, Great Britain, the United States and Italy – as an indirect censure of Belgian actions, which in their view were justified to protect European lives in the Congo. These growing tensions in New York, between members of the Security Council and members of the delegations of the 'West', were sharpened due to behaviour of bad faith by the Belgian government. Instead of withdrawing its forces from the Congo, Belgium proceeded to relocate them in Moïse Tshombe's 'independent' state of Katanga. It was the duplicitous nature of their behaviour which caused the greatest problems however, because, although they were unequivocal in their non-recognition of Katanga as an independent state to the rest of the world, to Tshombe they promised support and recognition. The Belgian government argued that they had to maintain a presence in the region to guarantee the safety of the European community there and also the Belgian-owned profitable Union Miniere enterprise.

Katanga, a south-eastern province of the Congo, had seceded less than one month after the country gained independence. It was by far the wealthiest province in the whole of the Congo which in size is about equal to Western Europe and on which the fiscal solvency of the entire country depended, as the extraction of its rich mineral deposits – such as copper – produced about 60 per cent of total Congolese revenue. For its part, Belgium's support of Katanga and its behind-the-scenes efforts to influence Western countries to recognise the independence of the province isolated its own position in the West. Belgium retaliated to this hostility by threatening to abandon NATO which further damaged its reliability and credibility and contributed to mounting tensions in New York. Within the UN, Belgium's position was also becoming increasingly untenable as, despite assurances to the Secretary-General that it would initially withdraw all troops by 29 August 1960,[27] there was consistent evidence to the contrary. By 26 August, it was being reported by the Reuters press agency that not only were Belgian spy planes in the air over the south-eastern region of the country, but Belgian troops,

[26] Items-in-United Nations Advisory Committee on the Congo: Meetings Nos. 1–8, Aug.-Oct. 1960: Vol. 1, United Nations Web Drawer Archival Item S-0849–0001: EOSG – Advisory Committee on the Congo, UN Doc. S-0849–0001–01–00001 (1960), at 16.

[27] Assurances from Belgium made to, and repeated by, the Secretary-General and General Rhikye during the first and second meetings of the Congo Advisory Committee. *Ibid.*, at 11.

rather than being removed, were simply being relocated on the Ruanda-Urundi and Angolan borders. As Mr Caba, the Guinean representative on the Committee commented, '[t]his is extremely dangerous, and perhaps just when we thought that the fire in the Congo was extinguished, other fires on the frontiers may break out'.[28] Though these allegations were denounced as 'wild stories' by both General Rhikye, Military Commander of ONUC, and the Secretary-General, the effect on the Secretariat, and Hammarskjöld in particular, was damaging. It appeared that as he sat in New York urging the Belgians to honour the resolutions and making assurances that they would hold to the agreement to withdraw, the reality of their movements in the Congo itself was very different. This complicated the discussions no end, raising allegations of collusion and partisanship between the West and the Secretary-General, while simultaneously the Belgian actions undermined his authority. It created 'the impression of a United Nations vacillating between different aspirations, now giving its favour, now withdrawing it'.[29]

The fracas among Western nations, caused by the behaviour of Belgium, increased Hammarskjöld's determination to appear impartial; furthermore, it was highly significant not only for the independence of action that it represented for the Secretariat as a whole, but also because this was in line with the Afro-Asian position, which was united in condemnation of the Belgian action. In a telegram the following month to the President of Guinea, Hammarskjöld indicated his position even more clearly, pointing out that the United Nations would be the instrument which would safeguard the peace and independence of Africa, and that this could be achieved through the cooperation of the African Member States.

> The strongest support we have in this great test in the instrument of the independent nations of the world – the United Nations – is the confidence and solidarity of the African Member states, acting with a common purpose, that of maintaining Africa in peace and free of all interference alien to the African world.[30]

[28] Comment from Mr. Caba, representative of Guinea to the Congo Advisory Committee. *Ibid.*, at 47.

[29] *The Economist*, 5 November 1960, 20.

[30] 'S/4417/Add.1/Rev. II. Telegram dated August 7 1960, from the Secretary General to the President of the Republic of Guinea, Security Council Official Records, Fifteenth Year, Supplement for July, August, September 1960', in A. Cordier and W. Foote (eds.), *Public Papers of the Secretaries-General of the United Nations, Vol. V: Dag Hammarskjöld 1960–1961* (1975), at 68

This is a good example of what later became known as quiet diplomacy,[31] a method of negotiation, as Maurice Keens-Soper describes, which took place behind the grandiose verbose parley of the public forums of the General Assembly and the Security Council. It would be going too far perhaps to suggest, as he does, that 'the sessions of the committees, their "debates", resolutions and vetoes are a voluminous sham whose sole merit is the conduct of an ideological fraud on the publics of the world for the convenience of governments'.[32] Rather, such public statements from the Secretary-General reflected his commitment to the support of African states. Behind this rhetoric lay the real function of quiet diplomacy as negotiations between the Secretary-General and the African states revealed his efforts to foster a cooperative relationship with the newly independent nations. It was indicative of Hammarskjöld's overall vision of the UN as a forum for the fostering of newly independent states whereby the major powers would 'bring their wisdom and expertise to bear on the world scene'.[33]

Indeed, Afro-Asian cooperation on resolutions relating to the Congo was clear from the outset. This was not least because Hammarskjöld engineered the African representative on the Security Council to table all draft resolutions on the Congo, and further supported the proposed draft resolution from Mongi Slim of Tunisia of 8 August 1960, which called for the immediate withdrawal of troops from the province of Katanga and reaffirms the authority of the United Nations troops there.[34] This was a strategic move from Hammarskjöld to ensure that there would not be a Soviet veto on the resolution (as it may be contended there may have been, had the proposal been tabled by a member of the Western bloc). Imperative to this argument is the presumption that Hammarskjöld was broadly formulating policy which would be amenable to the West; but, the strong wording of successive resolutions for the first year of the crisis indicate that he was determined to hold Belgium accountable for its actions in the region which was perceived by many among the Western bloc as a condemnation of their ally. Moreover, the move in promoting the Afro-Asian

[31] T.G. Weiss, D.P. Forsythe, R. Coate and K. Pease, *The United Nations and Changing World Politics* (2007), at 11.

[32] M. Keens-Soper, 'The General Assembly Reconsidered', in G. Berridge and A. Jennings (eds.), *Diplomacy at the UN* (1986), 75 at 84–85.

[33] B. Urquhart, *Hammarskjöld* (1972), 595.

[34] 'S/4426, Security Council Official Records, Fifteenth Year, 885th Meeting', in A. Cordier and W. Foote (eds.), *Public Papers of the Secretaries-General of the United Nations, Vol. V: Dag Hammarskjöld 1960–1961* (1975), at 77–78.

representative was not only linked to Hammarskjöld's personal view that the Afro-Asian bloc be granted his full support,[35] but also more generally reflected the changing composition of the General Assembly.

In what has been termed a 'Koskenniemian' vein of analysis by Ove Bring, Hammarskjöld tended to operate in a dichotomous fashion, whereby his dynamic approach to the Charter allowed for upholding of existing norms with the simultaneous application of innovative procedures.[36] The growing prominence of the Afro-Asian bloc in the General Assembly was a direct manifestation of shifting world order and challenges posed by such to the West. For his part, Hammarskjöld's approach was to advocate the tenets of international law in all areas of multilateral action through the United Nations in order to safeguard the sovereignty of these newly independent nations in particular. Given the context of escalating danger to international peace, posed by deteriorating stability in the heart of Africa, the notion of a moral guardian for the world held particular attraction for newly independent nations who soon began to look to Hammarskjöld as the custodian of their independence, a counterweight to the world powers, many of which they viewed as former colonial oppressors. 'Hammarskjöld … had given the United Nations a focus of moral authority which could attract an international loyalty, and use it in the cause of peace and justice.'[37] The growing empathy with these ideals and the responsibility of the General Assembly to execute them led to the development of a sense of brotherhood between the Secretary-General and the small nations of the central chamber. Rather than being dictated to from an ivory tower, for the first time burgeoning countries had their voices heard on the world stage producing an alternative to the trite rhetoric of the Cold War.

The significance of the Secretary-General's bolstering of the position of the Afro-Asians lies in the fact that it reflected, and it could be argued, legitimated, the changed balance of power within the institution. As much as his efforts to ensure that the Congo did not become 'a gaping wound in the side of every independent state on the continent'[38] were

[35] Subject Files of the Secretary-General: Dag Hammarskjöld: ONUC, United Nations WebDrawer Archival Item S-0845-0001-02, UN Doc. S-0845-0001-02-00001 (1960), at 82.

[36] See Bring, *supra* note 5, at 500–501.

[37] C. Cruise-O'Brien, *To Katanga and Back* (1962), 15. Irishman Conor Cruise-O'Brien was the Special Representative of the Secretary-General in the Congo, 1960–1961.

[38] *The Economist*, 5 November 1960, 20.

a manifestation of his vision for the role of the UN in guaranteeing the sovereignty of all nations, his dynamic interpretation of the Charter and his innovative techniques would also prove politically important for the nature of the institution which he fostered and with which the 'West', and Britain and the United States in particular, would grapple.

As the largest financial contributor to the mission and the institution as a whole,[39] the United States would come to play a central part in what Cruise-O'Brien referred to as a 'sacred drama', whereby the floor of the General Assembly became the central battleground for rhetorical combat between the opposing factions, 'a stage upon which … to avert bloodshed by substituting ritual for real conflict'.[40] As part of this 'ritual', Hammarskjöld would come under fire for his actions over resolutions adopted for the Congo crisis, and his attempt to avoid catastrophe would eventually cost him his life. The United States was also forced to reposition itself in world affairs as the Cold War and decolonisation presented successive, inconceivable choices between its European allies and the rising voices of beleaguered nations around the world. More importantly, it was during Hammarskjöld's tenure that the United States discovered that the instrument it had created to serve its post-war aims in 1945 was fast developing beyond its control. This evolution of the role of the General Assembly was critical to the development of the soft power function of the organisation as it was where the true colonial heritage of many of the major powers was fully exposed. This sudden exposure was directly linked to the changing nature of the institution at the time.

It is imperative to briefly analyse at this point why the institution itself was undergoing dramatic changes in its composition and power structure. In 1960, often hailed as the 'annus mirabilis' for African independence, an explosion of independence movements across the African continent introduced sixteen new African states to the General Assembly, making up a quarter of total UN membership. To the world stage, these new members brought with them bitter memories of colonial experience and extensive economic, political and social problems; furthermore, most significantly, they brought the determination to redirect the global agenda

39 As Nicholas confirmed at the time, 'But above all it has been the broad shoulders of the United States which have carried the main burden, contributing almost half the cost of the entire operation' [Estimated to be in the region of US$120 million]. H. Nicholas, *The United Nations as a Political Institution* (1962), 169.

40 N. Dorr, 'Ireland at the UN: 40 Years On' (1996) 7 *Irish Studies in International Affairs* 41, at 43.

to address the cause of nations still under the colonial yoke. As Bernard Firestone describes, 'the newly independent states of African and Asia were determined to wrest control of the UN's agenda from its founders and to refocus global attention and resources on issues such as poverty, dependency, imperialism and post-colonialism'.[41] The advent of these new nations to the world stage brought with them a changed set of ideals which was to have a significant impact on the core ideology of Western foreign policy. As notions of self-determination for all peoples and ideals of democratic peace found a loud voice on the international stage, the old patriarchal, colonial system was gradually becoming less acceptable. The level of importance attached to this ideal in international relations is reflected not only by its eminent position in the Charter but is also evident in the attempts by the General Assembly to establish a precedent in the treatment of colonies.

In accordance with Hammarskjöld's emphasis on bolstering the position of weaker countries within the international system, the nations of the Afro-Asian bloc now found they had a voice and a position on the international stage and within an institution which would bolster nationalistic ideals, protect the sovereignty of burgeoning nations and further the cause of autonomy for those nations still under a colonial yoke. Together with the Bretton Woods institutions, such as the World Bank, developing nations were now gaining both the means and the opportunity to make themselves heard. Though the process of decolonisation was to be 'lengthy, painful and discontinuous'[42] for all sides, Article 1, Chapter 1 of the UN Charter, officially signed into law on 26 June 1945,[43] was further enshrined into international law by a resolution on 15 December 1960 entitled 'Declaration on the Granting of Independence to Colonial Countries and Peoples'.[44] This resolution had been passed in the General Assembly by an overwhelming vote of 90–0 (with nine abstentions) signifying the organisation's statement that colonialism, in any form, was no longer acceptable state behaviour. Such was the invigoration of the

41 B. Firestone, *The United Nations Under U Thant, 1961–1971* (2001), vii.

42 P. Gifford and R. Louis, *Decolonization and African Independence: The Transfers of Power, 1960–1980* (1988), xxix.

43 Paragraph 2 of Article 1, Chapter 1 of the United Nations Charter, states that one purpose of the United Nations is to 'develop friendly relations among nations based on respect for the principle of equal rights and self-determination of peoples, and to take other appropriate measures to strengthen universal peace'.

44 The General Assembly Resolution 1535 of 15 December 1960, complemented Chapter XI, Article 73.

General Assembly as 'a place in the world where the weak, the poor and the aggrieved can feel at home',[45] and the success of these ideals, that British Foreign Minister Alec Douglas-Home ruefully noted in 1961, '[The UN] was now run by the Afro-Asian bloc'.[46]

With the emergence of many newly independent nations onto the world stage, the true extent of the colonial heritage of many European states was exposed, casting, in most cases, a shadow over their foreign policy initiatives. This was particularly damaging at the General Assembly where the major powers found their influence diluted against the dissenting voices of their former colonial possessions. Indeed, as Bring has pointed out, 'under the international law of the Cold War, when the dogma of sovereignty was stronger than today, the UN Charter was often interpreted by the majority of the members of the UN General Assembly'.[47] Sovereignty had become a key word at the UN during the Congo crisis precisely because the ONUC mission was designed to protect Congolese sovereignty. Now the Afro-Asian bloc had an accepted ideal, a force with which to both safeguard their own nations and batter the major powers as it bounced around the chamber of the General Assembly with spectacular effect. This was because another part of the rhetoric which pervaded the Cold War was the idea of international 'prestige' and any violation of sovereignty or interpretation of such, on behalf of the major powers, immediately granted a battering rod to the Afro-Asian bloc.

In the case of the Congo, the behaviour of Belgium helped to polarise the response in the General Assembly and added credence to the arguments of the Afro-Asian bloc of every peoples' right to self-determination. It also impacted upon the integrity of Western alliances as any interpretation of action, which in any way promoted neo-colonialism, now dramatically affected the international standing of that nation. This was precisely where the impact of soft power was felt, as although the resolutions of the General Assembly were not binding, the climate of international opinion was now very different. As *The Economist* surmised:

> In 1960 when the last sods on the grave of colonialism are being pressed down (in the West at any rate), it would be unthinkable for anyone outside of Africa to take the Congo by the scruff of its neck and tutor it out of chaos.[48]

[45] Keens-Soper, *supra* note 32, at 88.
[46] James, *supra* note 18, at 73.
[47] See Bring, *supra* note 5, at 504.
[48] *The Economist*, 5 November 1960, 20.

The 'currency' of international prestige was becoming an even more crucial part of the United Nations policy of the major powers, as they found themselves confronted with the new coercive power of the Third bloc. However, it was also an essential anti-Soviet strategy, aimed at offsetting the very real threat of the Cold War, which was as much a reality at UN HQ in New York as anywhere else, to the extent that US Secretary of State Dean Rusk commented that: 'the Soviets seem determined to join the "Battle of Africa"'.[49]

15.3 Cold War, hot tempers

> The spectre that haunts the United Nations is not that of a world in agony wrestling with its fate but of men stalemated in the futility of their proceedings.[50]

The struggle for the 'hearts and minds'[51] of Cold Warriors at the United Nations was no less taxing in the debate chambers of the United Nations Headquarters in New York than anywhere else. It would prove to be an extremely influential process at play at the UN at this time which expanded the opportunities to make fundamental changes to the international system. It can be argued that the Cold War had multiple effects on the conduct on international relations there at this time.

First was the dichotomous impact of the conflict which saw the institution hamstrung in many instances where escalating tensions between the two superpowers often spilled over into rhetorical combat. From the outset of the crisis in 1960, the Congo was an issue which particularly exposed the rift between the superpowers as they saw it as a direct threat to their relative geopolitical positions. Not only did this serve to exacerbate the overall sense of polarity, but it also prevented the institution from functioning as efficiently as possible and, in many cases, where the conflict was directly exposed, halted proceedings altogether. In one infamous

[49] *Foreign Relations of the United States (FRUS), 1961–1963*, Volume XX, Rusk Telegram from the Department of State to the Embassy in Belgium, Washington, DC, 28.1.61, confidential.

[50] Keens-Soper, *supra* note 32, at 90.

[51] This quote has long been associated with US President Lyndon B. Johnson who used it repeatedly during the Vietnam War campaign. However it is originally thought to have been drawn from a quote from John Adams, the second President of the United States who spoke of the revolution being 'in the minds and hearts of the people'. See J. Adams, 'The Meaning of the American Revolution', *Niles' Weekly Register*, 7 March 1818, at www.britannica.com/presidents/article-9116854.

incident, the then Irish President of the General Assembly, Freddy Boland, shattered the presidential gavel while calling the rambunctious First Secretary of the Communist Part of Russia Nikita Khrushchev to order after he had earlier demonstrated his displeasure with the debate by banging his shoe on the table.[52] Incidentally, the Soviet Premier had been deliberately disrupting a speech by Harold Macmillan, who denounced the Soviet attack on the West over the Congo, stating, 'words like "colonialism" and "imperialism" have been slung about here without much regard to the facts'. The British Prime Minister replied to Khrushchev's interruption with one of his trademark, dry witticisms: 'Mr. President, perhaps we could have a translation, I could not quite follow.'[53] The significance of this incident alone displays how acts of Soviet aggression had the impact of severely disrupting the work of the UN in attempting to provide tangible solutions to the crisis.

Even within Security Council negotiations on resolutions, the Soviet predilection to disruption was evident from the outset. Following the First Report from the Secretary-General on Assistance to the Republic of the Congo, there was a 'cold war exchange' between Ambassador Henry Cabot-Lodge of the United States and Vasily V. Kuznetsov, First Deputy Foreign Minister of the USSR. Kuznetsov introduced a draft resolution which called for the withdrawal of Belgian troops in three days. 'In the course of a speech denouncing Western "colonialism" he said that if "the aggression" continued, more effective measures would be necessary, both by the United Nations and by the "peace-loving states" that sympathized with the Congo "a cause".'[54] The US Permanent Representative to the United Nations Cabot-Lodge replied immediately. He first pointed out that the United States had demonstrated its full support for the United Nations operation not only in words but by such practical assistance as providing the airlift for most of the UN troops and large quantities of equipment, supplies and food as well. He then warned: 'With the other United Nations members we will do whatever may be necessary to prevent the intrusion of any military forces not requested by the United Nations.' Not only did this rhetorical combat hold up the proceedings of

[52] J. Skelly, *Irish Diplomacy at the United Nations, 1945–1965: National Interests and the International Order* (1997), 273.

[53] Horne, *supra* note 20, at 278–279.

[54] 'First Report from the Secretary-General to the Security Council on Assistance to the Republic of the Congo, New York, July 18, 1960, Security Council Official Records, Fifteenth Year, 877th Meeting', in A. Cordier and W. Foote (eds.), *Public Papers of the Secretaries-General of the United Nations, Dag Hammarskjöld 1960–1961* (1975), at 28.

the UN's various committees, it reflected the mounting tensions between the two superpowers and generated an atmosphere of hostility. Moreover, it also unwittingly entrenched the Congo episode as one of Cold War proportions, leading, in one particularly acrimonious incidence on 17 September 1960, to the suspension of Security Council negotiations as the lack 'of unanimity among its members ... has prevented it from exercising its primary responsibility for the maintenance of international peace and security'.[55]

It was precisely the suspension of the Security Council due to Cold War hostilities which led to the reinvigoration of the General Assembly as a chamber for debate. This was not the first time the General Assembly had adopted this role. The 'Uniting for Peace' resolution in 1950[56] had previously granted the General Assembly an instrument for the discussion of security issues in cases where the Security Council was hamstrung.[57] However, the support enjoyed by Hammarskjöld from this organ at this particular moment was crucial. It allowed him to fully exercise his preferred method of quiet diplomacy as a form of preventative diplomacy or preventative negotiation. As Ramesh Thakur describes, 'preventative diplomacy was used to forestall the competitive intrusion of the rival power blocs into conflict situations'.[58] This was the greatest function of Hammarskjöld's initiative, as the Congo crisis was exactly a predicament

[55] United Nations Security Council, Resolution of 17 September 1960, UN Doc. S/4526 (1960). The full text of the resolution is as follows: 'The Security Council, Having considered the item on its agenda as contained in document S/Agenda/906, Taking into account the lack of unanimity of its permanent members at the 906th meeting of the Security Council has prevented it from exercising its primary responsibility for the maintenance of international peace and security, Decides to call an emergency special session of the General Assembly, as provided in General Assembly resolution 377 A(V) of 3 November 1950, in order to make appropriate recommendations.' *Ibid.*

[56] United Nations General Assembly, The Uniting for Peace Resolution, UN A/RES/377(V) (1950), Resolution 377 provides in part that, 'if the Security Council because of lack of unanimity of the permanent members, fails to exercise its primary responsibility for the maintenance of international peace and security in any case where there appears to be a threat to the peace, breach of the peace, or act of aggression, the General Assembly shall consider the matter with a view to making the appropriate recommendations to the Members for collective measures, including in the case of a breach of the peace or act of aggression the use of armed force when necessary to maintain or restore international peace and security'. *Ibid.*

[57] P. Wallensteen and P. Johansson, 'Security Council Decisions in Perspective', in D.M. Malone (ed.), *The UN Security Council: From the Cold War to the 21st Century* (2004), 17 at 21.

[58] R. Thakur, *The United Nations, Peace and Security: From Collective Security to the Responsibility to Protect* (2006), 34

which posed a threat to the balance of international security and could potentially have resulted in a superpower intervention in the region. By invigorating the General Assembly as an organ of debate, Hammarskjöld effectively used quiet diplomacy as a means of exercising soft power among the members in order to draft resolutions for the crisis. This was made possible by the support of the Afro-Asian bloc which essentially created a mechanism by which Cold War hostilities could be side-stepped in order to formulate productive UN policy for the Congo. Through this application of quiet diplomacy, Hammarskjöld provided leadership to the paralysed institution, with the Security Council and General Assembly responding to this initiative quickly and with promising results.

One of the ways in which the UN sought to deal with this was through reorganisation of the structure of the Secretariat, including the position of the Secretary-General. In addition, the issue of Chinese representation had raised concerns over whether or not the councils of the organisation, and the Security Council in particular, should be enlarged to accommodate the increasing number of Member States.[59] Officials in the State Department had previously noted that even the UK had recognised that the 'winds of change' were blowing and the structure and composition of the UN was undergoing some drastic changes.[60] This reorganisation of the Secretariat was also linked to dealing with what may be termed here the 'function creep' between the Security Council and the General Assembly, which was taking place at the time. The General Assembly was now invigorated as a site for action more than a mere talking shop. Hammarskjöld's preferred method of quiet diplomacy was a workable option in this tense atmosphere which pervaded proceedings there. It was here that this developed into a tangible form of soft power, where the major powers harnessed the opportunity to work in the corridors to avoid clashing and reduce opportunities for further denunciation of their policies. On the other side of the room, the Afro-Asian bloc seized the chance to table resolutions in their own right and prise compromises out of their former colonial masters.

One of the efforts of the United States in this vein was the proposed restructuring of the Secretariat as a means by which not only to blunt the

[59] Telegram, Department of State to the American Embassy in London, May 1961, 'National Security Files', Folder 1, Box 175. John F. Kennedy Library (JFKL). This telegram deals with the areas of Anglo-American cooperation agreed between the British Home Office and Secretary of State Rusk.

[60] Position Paper, State Department to President Kennedy, 21 March 1961. 'Briefing Book Macmillan Visit', Folder 3, Box 127A, JFKL.

Soviet troika proposal but also to try to reassert some influence over the rancorous Afro-Asian bloc in the General Assembly. The State Department had been working the diplomatic channels with Prime Minister Jawaharlal Nehru and Prime Minister Hayato Ikeda of Japan in order to mobilise the group to maintain support to the UN and the Secretary-General, even as the crisis deepened and accusations of collusion were levelled against the institution.[61] It was emphasised that the USSR was 'continuing to exploit every possibility to attempt to denigrate the Secretary-General and the UN operation in the Congo'.[62] In response, the Afro-Asians maintained that they were critical of Khrushchev's attacks on the Secretary-General and recognised the 'value of the UN as now constituted to their security as small and weak countries'.[63] The mobilisation of the Afro-Asians behind Hammarskjöld was almost immediately effective. On 15 April 1961 the General Assembly passed three resolutions on the Congo, voting 83–11 in favour of the Secretary-General's plan, displaying overwhelming support for Hammarskjöld.[64]

In a secret memo to Rusk, Assistant Secretary of State for International Organisation Affairs Harlan Cleveland in New York noted the Secretary-General's satisfaction with what he termed a 'major water-shed in his career'. What he was referring to was the revised Soviet position on the Congo, which indicated a defeat of its sustained battery on his office. 'The signal for the end of the round apparently', observed Cleveland,

> is the new Soviet resolution on the Congo in which the USSR backs down from its two main previous positions: that the UN operation in the Congo should be folded up forthwith, and that the Secretary-General should resign, and be replaced by a three man directorate.[65]

61 National Archives and Records Administration (NARA), Department of State, UN files, 310/1–561, Telegram to the American Embassy in New Delhi from the State Department, 26 March 1961.

62 *Ibid.*

63 National Archives and Records Administration (NARA), Department of State, UN files, 310/1–561, Telegram from the American Embassy in Tokyo to the Secretary of State, 29 March 1961.

64 United Nations General Assembly Resolutions 1599, 1600 and 1601 each called on Belgium to comply with previous General Assembly and Security Council resolutions (with particular reference to the Security Council resolution of 21 February 1961), and demanded its complete withdrawal from the Congo. In addition, General Assembly Resolution 1600 urged that 'necessary and effective measures be taken by the Secretary-General immediately to prevent the introduction of arms, military equipment and supplies into the Congo'.

65 National Archives and Records Administration (NARA), Department of State, UN files, 310/1–561, Harlan Cleveland to Dean Rusk, Memorandum of a Conversation with Hammarskjold, 10 April 1961.

Not only was this significant for the Secretary-General in terms of the fact that he considered that he had 'won' that battle with Khrushchev, in which he and his office had been pilloried by the Soviet Premier and his representatives since September 1960; but it also indicated the importance of the role of the Afro-Asians in the general battle of the wills against the USSR. Hammarskjöld remarked that one of the lessons the Soviets had learned was that it was 'difficult to deal with the situation where the Afro-Asian group and the UN executive are together on an issue'.[66] While this was obviously very significant for the Secretary-General and the Secretariat, in that the General Assembly resolutions essentially legitimised the operation in the Congo and reinforced the authority of his office, it was also important for US perceptions of the UN. The exercise in diplomatic pressure from the combined forces of both the United States and the Afro-Asians in this instance had demonstrated that the UN Charter was a flexible instrument, 'capable of development along lines not originally foreseen, and that one of the most significant of these is the expanding role of the Secretary-General'.[67] It was fast becoming apparent that 'the international political conjuncture was therefore more favourable to the particular conception of the office of the Secretary-General, which had become identified with Hammarskjöld'.[68]

The consolidation of the Afro-Asian bloc not only served to unite the voices of opposing factions within that group, it provided a means by which developing nations could bring their limited influence to bear. The sharp division of the chamber between two powerful blocs meant that there was a power vacuum into which the Afro-Asian bloc moved and from where their dissenting voices and concerns about neo-colonialism would carry most weight. The bipolarity of the international system at this point also indirectly granted even more importance to developing nations to advance their agenda as, due to the geopolitical nature of the conflict, strategic allies became even more important to both sides. Having found that their position in the UN was beginning to wane due to the advent of more nations to the General Assembly, the United States and Britain were ready to pay more attention to the demands of smaller nations. This was also tied to the broader conflict, which meant that countries were placing even more emphasis on the maintenance and strengthening of alliances.

[66] *Ibid.*

[67] National Archives and Records Administration (NARA), Department of State, UN files, 310/1-561, Letter from Harlan Cleveland to Helen Stewart, 25 April 1961.

[68] Cruise-O'Brien, *supra* note 37, at 45.

All of these factors combined created a particular dynamic which generated an unprecedented situation, changing the traditional balance of power at the UN. Now, not only were developing nations having their voices heard on the international stage, but their calls for European colonial powers to end colonisation were generating a movement behind which powerful players like the United States and the USSR threw their weight for a variety of reasons. Chief among their concerns was not only the retention of existing allies but the prevention of a civil or ethnic war in one of these nations becoming a full blown Cold War conflict and the expansion of their spheres of influence in order to bolster their overall geopolitical position.

In this instance, the United States moved to embrace the Afro-Asians, which had the effect of achieving a minor victory over the Soviets and consolidating the position of the Secretary-General. However it was also highly significant for two further reasons. First, it demonstrated the US recognition of the Afro-Asian bloc as an effective and legitimate force in the General Assembly. Second, the US move to embrace the Afro-Asians reflected their acceptance of the UN in its form under Hammarskjöld; even though, as previously stated, they were sometimes at odds with the increasingly independent stance of the organisation, they recognised that quiet diplomacy at the UN in the style of the Secretary-General was a real and effective force in international relations. In this case, the United States displayed its willingness to adopt and operationalise quiet diplomacy as a means of circumventing the Soviets, which had the effect of further bolstering the concept and enhancing the role of soft power within the UN.

15.4 Conclusion: defeating the spectre

> Anyone of integrity, notwithstanding his own views, can act in an exclusively international spirit and can be guided in his actions on behalf of the Organisation solely by its interests and principles, and by the instructions of its organs.[69]

Hammarskjöld seized upon the Congo as an opportunity to motivate the diplomatic machinery of the UN, operationalising the idea of quiet diplomacy in the shifting power balance with the General Assembly. In this context, it was critical for the UN to accept responsibility for the Congo's

[69] Dag Hammarskjold, Introduction to the Annual Report, 1960–1961, in A. Cordier and W. Foote (eds.), *Public Papers of the Secretaries-General of the United Nations, Vol. V: Dag Hammarskjöld 1960–1961* (1975), 6.

welfare. But the area became a battleground for East and West, as well as for 'Africans verses Africans'.[70] Hammarskjöld himself came under particular fire from the Soviet delegation, with Khrushchev denouncing ONUC at every opportunity and seeking to undermine the Secretariat. The personal investment of the Secretary-General had clear benefits in reinvigorating the General Assembly as a scene of debate and a forum for the exercise of soft power, to the extent that it would now be controlled by the Third World for whom it became an 'anvil upon which power and privilege are to be browbeaten into their images of right and justice'.[71] By invigorating the General Assembly in particular, Hammarskjöld was changing the nature of the institution which the major powers had to deal with. The United States in particular would find that no longer could it 'abuse the Assembly as a revivalist meeting-hall to rally the West'.[72] Indeed, as Firestone remarks:

> The history of the United Nations would therefore be a story of transition – as Third World concerns consumed more and more of the UN's attentions – balanced by continuity as the organization maintained its preoccupation with the Cold War, which tenaciously clung to the centre of the UN's agenda.[73]

It may be argued that the functioning of the United Nations as a public forum for debate, and also in its regulatory role for the behaviour of nations, was of particular significance in how it helped to change perceptions with regard to the treatment of colonies and the granting of independence. The combination of the Afro-Asian bloc and Hammarskjöld's determination that the UN act as an 'agent for the liquidation of colonialism',[74] would make the debate which took place in the General Assembly more influential during the Congo crisis than it had ever previously been. This was because, now that they had a conjoined bloc within the chamber, the Afro-Asians could table resolutions on the Congo in accordance with how they believed the crisis should evolve. The effect of this for the role of the UN in the Congo was significant; indeed, as James puts it, 'the modification of the UN's approach can largely be attributed to the rise, particularly in the Congolese context, of the Afro-Asian states'.[75]

[70] Nicholas, *supra* note 39, at 170.

[71] Keens-Soper, *supra* note 32, at 85.

[72] *Ibid.*, at 89.

[73] Firestone, *supra* note 41, at xxiv.

[74] Speech by Frank Aiken, Irish Minister for External Affairs, for general debate at the General Assembly, 15 October 1960. P104/6256. Private Papers of Conor Cruise O'Brien, University College Dublin Archives (UCDA).

[75] James, *supra* note 18, at 73.

The importance of the ability of the Afro-Asian bloc to bring its influence to bear on the more powerful players within the General Assembly is significant in that it helped to change perceptions of acceptable international behaviour with regard to colonialism, to the extent that the hegemonic tendencies of powerful nations were no longer regarded as tolerable. By asserting the right to self-determination of all peoples, there was an alteration in the way states are structured together and the ways in which they interrelate.[76] It was through the vehicle of the UN, the fact that Western nations found their traditional base of power to be significantly eroded due to the advent of newly independent nations and the innovative use of soft power, that the opportunity to radically modify the behaviour of states, especially the former colonial masters of the West, was realised by the challenges posed by the Congo crisis. Such was the extent of the empowerment of the UN to constrain the foreign policies of Western nations, that in 1961 Britain announced that, in future, information on the political and constitutional progress of its self-governing territories would be submitted to the UN.[77]

Not only was the international system truly able to operationalise the concept of self-determination for nations both within and outside it, but the institution took on a role of fostering the emergence of these states. This was directly linked to Hammarskjöld's promotion of the tenets of international law in all areas of multilateral action through the United Nations, in order to safeguard the sovereignty of independent nations. Through its reinvigoration, the General Assembly could now produce pragmatic, tangible results through absolute devotion to the principles of the Charter. By promoting the 'greater good', Hammarskjöld attempted to divert the deadlock over East and West ideological conflict, creating what would later be alluded to as 'a priesthood of a new and better ideology, a form of supra-national religion of which he is the head'.[78] At the core of this doctrine was the notion that the UN would act not only as a force for good but also as a moral authority. In this role, promotion of

[76] Finnemore and Sikkink define an institution as 'a collection of practices and rules'. M. Finnemore and K. Sikkink, 'International Norm Dynamics and Political Change', in P. Katzenstein, R. Keohane and S. Krasner (eds.), *Exploration and Contestation in the Study of World Politics* (1999), 247 at 251.

[77] This was a hugely significant compromise to have drawn from the British who up to this point were adamant that the UN had no grounds on which to 'interfere' in its agenda for decolonisation and had repeatedly refused to cooperate with such demands. General Assembly Official Records, 16th Session, 1017th Plenary Meeting, 27 September 1961.

[78] D. Fisher, 'The Future of the UN', *The Irish Press*, 12 January 1961.

principle was the first responsibility of the institution; this idea, alongside the fact that under Hammarskjöld in particular the UN delineated itself as an institution with considerable powers which were not tied to the will or whims of the United States, led to the UN for the first time asserting its own power. Crucially, this manifested as a form of soft power which had never previously been implemented in this way.

Through the Congo crisis, the United Nations would cut its teeth in terms of dealing with international crises. The UN Secretariat would become the site for the clash of new social and political ideas with the rise of newly decolonised nations to the world stage. This battleground provided a unique moment for Hammarskjöld, in which he provided strong leadership and forged a new agenda for the international community. The position of Secretary-General changed under his tenure to a political role in international relations which was no longer subject to the whim of the major powers. This chapter contends that it was the political development of the office of the Secretary-General under Hammarskjöld, with his method of quiet diplomacy, which gained the United Nations greater prestige and helped it position itself as an effective arbitrator in international relations through harnessing the prospects offered by the use of soft power. The two major indications of this can be drawn from Hammarskjöld's lecture at Oxford University in May 1961 entitled, 'The International Civil Servant in Law and in Fact', and his Introduction to the Annual Report 1960–1961.[79] In both of these instances, Hammarskjöld was adamant that a Secretary-General must play an independent political role with the guidance of the Charter and the principles of international law, rather than the political organs of the UN itself.[80]

By invigorating the General Assembly and with the support of the Afro-Asian bloc, Hammarskjöld seized upon the shifting world order to implement quiet diplomacy during the Congo crisis as a means to prevent the episode becoming a conflict of Cold War proportions and casting the UN in a role of international arbitrator, with unprecedented use of soft power to resolve the conflict. This innovative use of soft power had the effect of casting forever the Afro-Asian bloc in the role of Banquo's ghost which, from this point onwards, would haunt the efforts of the major powers to control the agenda of UN.

[79] For further reading, the texts and an insightful analysis of some of Hammarskjöld's public speeches, see M. Bouman, *Dag Hammarskjöld, Citizen of the World* (2005).

[80] A. Rovine, *The First Fifty Years: The Secretary-General in World Politics 1920–1970* (1970), 332–340.

PART IV

The role of the UN Secretary-General

16

The 'Suez story'

Dag Hammarskjöld, the United Nations and the creation of UN peacekeeping

MANUEL FRÖHLICH

16.1 Introduction

The Suez crisis in 1956 was a defining moment for the United Nations. While it started with an obvious denial of the UN Charter system of collective security, it ended with the establishment of the first UN peacekeeping operation, thus setting a precedent that until today accounts for much of the UN's work. The world organisation and especially its Secretary-General, which originally had been bypassed by the plan of 'Operation Musketeer', found themselves centre-stage in resolving one of the most serious crises after the Second World War.[1] When the crisis

Manuel Fröhlich is Professor of International Organisations and Globalisation, Friedrich-Schiller-University, Jena.

[1] The full background of the crisis goes beyond the scope of this study which tries to focus on Hammarskjöld's account; for details see: R.I. Miller, *Dag Hammarskjöld and Crisis Diplomacy* (1961), 59–125; H. Thomas, *The Suez Affair* (1967); K. Kyle, *Suez* (1991); A. Eden, *Memoirs*, Vol. II (1962), 475–657, in particular 552–629; M. Heikal, *The Cairo Documents* (1973), 158–183; B. Urquhart, *Hammarskjöld* (1972), 159–194; S. Bailey, *How Wars End: The United Nations and the Termination of Armed Conflict 1946–1964*, Vol. II (1982), 535–666; B. Urquhart, *A Life in Peace and War* (1987), 131–144; W. Roger Louis and R. Owen (eds.), *Suez 1956: The Crisis and its Consequences* (1989); E. Luard, *A History of the United Nations*. Vol. II: *The Age of Decolonialization 1955–1963* (1989), 18–57; M. Ghali, 'United Nations Emergency Force', in W.J. Durch (ed.), *The Evolution of UN Peacekeeping: Case Studies and Comparative Analysis* (1993); J. Düllfer, 'Die Suez- und Ungarn-Krise', in M. Salewski (ed.), *Das Zeitalter der Bombe. Die Geschichte der atomaren Bedrohung von Hiroshima bis heute* (1995); W. Heinemann and N. Wiggershaus (eds.), *Das internationale Krisenjahr 1956: Polen, Ungarn, Suez*, Beiträge zur Militärgeschichte, Vol. XLVIII (1999); S.C. Smith (ed.), *Reassessing Suez 1956: New Perspectives on the Crisis and its Aftermath* (2008). Valuable information as well as the principal documents can also be obtained from the edition of Hammarskjöld's speeches by A.W. Cordier and W. Foote (eds.), *Public Papers of the Secretaries-General of the United Nations, Vol. II: Dag Hammarskjöld*

was still not settled on 14 November, US President Eisenhower stated in a press conference:

> We must avoid in any way interfering with the delicate negotiations now going on under the leadership of Secretary-General Hammarskjöld. We must not do anything that could in any way delay his operations, hinder, or harm them. And I should like to use a moment to speak of what he is doing. He has not only shown his ability. The man has displayed a physical endurance that is highly remarkable, if not unique. Night after night he has made do with one or two hours sleep, and worked both day and night, and, I might say, worked with intelligence and devotion.[2]

The days of October and November 1956 were indeed filled with hectic and intensive diplomatic activities that – at least partly – found their focus on the UN premises in New York.

The Secretary-General clearly felt that the myriad of meetings, cables, telephone calls and resolutions that would eventually settle the crisis were an important step in the development of the world organisation. In 1956 and 1957 he made a number of notes and aide-memoires that should allow a detailed reconstruction of the crisis from a UN perspective. In addition to that, he had some of his staff put together a sort of annotated diary supplemented with documents that contained a day-by-day, and at times hour-by-hour, account of the events. This material, labelled 'Suez story' and kept safe in his office at the UN headquarters, most probably should have formed the basis of an assessment by Hammarskjöld once he would have been out of office.[3] After the Secretary-General's death in the plane crash at Ndola in 1961, the material was transferred from New York to Dag Hammarskjöld's private archives at the Royal Library in Stockholm. Among these papers there is a document from August 1957

1956–1957 (1973), 304–404. For references to Hammarskjöld and the Suez crisis see also M. Fröhlich, 'Keeping Track of UN Peace-keeping – Suez, Srebrenica, Rwanda and the Brahimi Report' (2001) 5 *Max Planck Yearbook of United Nations Law* 185, as well as M. Fröhlich, *Political Ethics and the United Nations: Dag Hammarskjöld as Secretary-General* (2008). The latter publication contains a comparatively brief discussion of the Suez crisis (at 148–164) which does, however, not make full use of the files and documents integrated into this more comprehensive study.

[2] Urquhart, *supra* note 1, 194.

[3] Kungliga Biblioteket Dag Hammarskjöld Samling (henceforth 'KB DHS'), *Suez Story*, as put together and marked by D.H. and kept in his safe in his office at UN HQ, New York 1956–1957. The possible plan for a later analysis can inter alia be drawn from remarks such as the beginning of an aide-memoire of 9 November 1956 where Hammarskjöld states that these are notes 'of importance for a final analysis of the chain of events' (KB DHS, *Dag Hammarskjöld*, Aide Mémoire 9 November 1956, 1).

entitled 'Notes on part of my personal participation in the developments 29 October – 20 November 1956'. This document recounts the crucial events from Hammarskjöld's perspective and, by way of cross-references, points to supplementary information from a number of other sources.[4] These and other documents offer a unique insight, from a UN perspective, into some of the events that shaped the resolution of the Suez crisis. The following text aims to reconstruct some of the aspects of diplomacy at the UN and assess Hammarskjöld's role in it. Section 16.2 gives a day-by-day account of events and negotiations from 29 October to 10 November 1956 when the first UNEF contingents actually arrived at Naples and UNEF commander General E.L.M. Burns had flown to Egypt in order to directly negotiate with the government in advance of Hammarskjöld's own trip to Cairo. This is also where Hammarskjöld's detailed notes end. The ensuing Section 16.3 then considers some of the problems and challenges that Hammarskjöld and the UN encountered even after the idea of an international force had been accepted. The discussion and resolution of these problems can be derived from the verbatim records held at UN archives which protocol the meetings of the advisory committee which was established with the creation of UNEF.[5] Section 16.4 offers some concluding observations on the role of Hammarskjöld and the UN in the Suez crisis.

16.2 The diplomacy of almost thirteen days

On 26 July 1956 Gamal Abdel Nasser nationalised the Suez Canal Company.[6] With this action at the very least, some Western countries perceived Nasser as a ruthless and unpredictable Arab leader who sought to extend his personal sphere of influence. Shortly before, with Egypt's recognition of the People's Republic of China and the agreement to buy Soviet weapons via Czechoslovakia, the United States had withdrawn the financial assistance promised for the construction of the Aswan

[4] The basic information is contained in five different sources: 1. Hammarskjöld's Notes from 2 August 1957 consisting of twenty-six numbered paragraphs (henceforth 'Notes'). 2. A collection of twenty-five verbatim documents from 8 to 14 November 1956 put together as annexes to Hammarskjöld's recollections. 3. Hammarskjöld's aide-memoire from 9 November 1956 consisting of six Special Notes (henceforth 'Special Notes'). 4. A calendar-like synopsis of some fifty pages covering events between 20 October and 20 November 1956 and 5. Hammarskjöld's aide-memoire from 5 August 1957.

[5] These 'verbatims' are kept mainly in UN Archives DAG-1 5.0.1.0. Box 1; henceforth quoted as 'AC UNEF [date]'.

[6] Cf. Fröhlich, *Political Ethics*, *supra* note 1, 149–161.

Dam. Thus, from the start, the crisis affected the relationship between the superpowers. After the nationalisation of the Suez Canal Company, though, the reactions of the United States and the Soviet Union were fairly muted. By contrast, France and Great Britain, the countries directly affected by the nationalisation and with strategic interests in the former mandate territory, began to consider the option of using military force against Egypt. In the course of August and September, a series of secret meetings and consultations took place between France and the UK on the one side, and France and Israel on the other.[7] Under the surface, the conflict over political order in the Middle East was taking on new forms. Meanwhile, the UN was also dealing with the conflict. Immediately after the nationalisation, UN Secretary-General Dag Hammarskjöld had, as an exercise in private diplomacy, initiated a series of informal meetings with Foreign Ministers Selwyn Lloyd, Christian Pineau and Mahmoud Fawzi in his office in New York. They focused on the questions of the future use of the canal and a settlement of the different claims and interests. To general surprise, these talks produced acceptable results in a relatively short time. The heart of the agreement consisted of six principles on the use of the canal, which the Security Council officially endorsed on 13 October.[8]

The following day, however, the French Prime Minister, Guy Mollet, unofficially proposed a coordinated military action with Israel, code-named 'Operation Musketeer', to his British counterpart Anthony Eden.[9] The plan was for Israel to attack Egypt from Sinai, whereupon Britain and France would give the two parties an ultimatum to cease hostilities and withdraw. The plan also assumed that the Egyptians would not accept that ultimatum, whereupon French and British units – as forces of law and order, as it were – would land in Egypt to occupy the Canal Zone, separate the combatants and secure the waterway. Moreover, re-establishing de facto Franco-British influence and inflicting a military defeat on Egypt could possibly precipitate the overthrow of Nasser, whom France, in addition, suspected of supporting the Algerian independence movement. Eden agreed to the plan and immediately withdrew his unsuspecting Foreign Minister from New York, where he was busy with the final negotiations of the Six-Point Plan.

[7] Cordier and Foote, *supra* note 1, 8–25. [8] *Ibid.*, 292–303.

[9] Urquhart, *supra* note 1, 159. See also A. Shlaim, 'The Protocol of Sèvres, 1956: Anatomy of a War Plot' (1997) 73(3) *International Affairs* 509.

16.2.1 Monday, 29 October 1956

News of the Israeli surprise attack on 29 October reached New York at around 3 p.m., when the Security Council had just begun a meeting on the concomitant Hungarian crisis.[10] After the meeting, Hammarskjöld and the representatives of the United States, UK and France met at US representative Henry Cabot Lodge's office in order to discuss a reaction to the Israeli attack. At the end of the meeting, all participants agreed that they would need more information before bringing the attack to the Security Council. Hammarskjöld recalls that at 9 p.m. he had heard from the news that the United States had taken the initiative and wanted to convene the Council. He tried to contact Lodge, but the US ambassador was attending a performance at the Metropolitan Opera. Later in the evening, Hammarskjöld was called by the French permanent representative Bernard Cornut-Gentille, who complained that the initiative of the United States should have been properly communicated to him, the current President of the Security Council. The mutual understanding of the Western powers from that afternoon had obviously shown its first cracks. Cornut-Gentille asked Hammarskjöld to see him at his apartment, where he received the Secretary-General with a 'fairly aggressive'[11] reaction on the US initiative that had slighted the President of the Security Council. During the night, Lodge, his deputy James Barco as well as the deputy of the British mission, Ponsonby Moore Crosthwaite, joined the meeting. Lodge officially confirmed his request to call a meeting. Hammarskjöld recalls the reaction of Crosthwaite: 'He seemed somewhat upset by the US initiative, but added with an initiated smile that the Sinai issue was much more serious than he had believed and we were likely to think.'[12] This reaction supported the impression Lodge had gained from UK permanent representative Pierson Dixon, whom he had met at the Metropolitan and informed about the US initiative. Hammarskjöld notes: 'Pierson Dixon's reaction had been one which Lodge "would never forget", as it did indicate that Dixon knew far too much and that the US initiative crossed the lines.'[13] The United States aimed at an invocation of the 1949 Tripartite Declaration in which the United States, UK and France had pledged assistance to any victim of aggression resulting from the Middle Eastern situation. Dixon clearly stated that Britain would not support such a

[10] See Notes, *supra* note 4, 1–2.
[11] *Ibid.*, 2. [12] *Ibid.* [13] *Ibid.*

policy.[14] On the other hand, right from the beginning the United States wanted to avoid the Soviet Union taking the lead in reacting to the Israeli offensive. Eisenhower had told the British Chargé d'affairs in Washington: 'We plan to get to the United Nations the first thing in the morning – when the doors open ... before the U.S.S.R. gets there.'[15]

16.2.2 Tuesday, 30 October 1956

The Security Council met at 11 a.m. and Lodge announced that he would introduce a resolution calling for Israeli withdrawal behind the armistice lines.[16] Hammarskjöld also spoke and reported that through the commander of the United Nations Truce Supervision Organization (UNTSO), General Burns, he had learned that the Israeli forces had expelled the UN observers from the demilitarised El Auja zone. After a brief discussion, the Soviet representative, Arkady Sobolev, read out a wire agency report stating news of the British–French ultimatum that had just been published via a speech by Eden in parliament. The Council reconvened in the afternoon and the text of the Eden speech was circulated. Against Dixon's efforts, Lodge introduced his original resolution calling for Israeli withdrawal, but expanded with a further call on all UN members to refrain from using force or assisting Israel. After the resolution, the Secretary-General would report on compliance and was given the chance to present further recommendations for peace and security in the area. The resolution, however, was vetoed by France and Great Britain. Sobolev then introduced an amended resolution, omitting the expanded paragraphs from Lodge's resolution, but this draft also was vetoed in the subsequent evening meeting of the Council. The Council was therefore blocked and this prompted the Yugoslav representative Josa Brilej, at Hammarskjöld's suggestion,[17] to introduce the idea of convening the General Assembly in accordance with the emergency procedure of the 'Uniting for Peace' resolution.[18] The

[14] Cordier and Foote, *supra* note 1, 306; Urquhart, *supra* note 1, 172, reports that Dixon in this context had said to Lodge: 'Don't be so damned high-minded.' From the transcript of a telephone conversation between Lodge and Dulles we get a similar record: 'When Lodge spoke of living up to the Tripartite Declaration Dixon said, "Don't be silly and moralistic. We have got to be practical".' See also J.P. Glennon (ed.), *Foreign Relations of the United States*. Vol. XVI: *Suez Crisis July 26-December 31, 1956* (1990), 841.

[15] Cited in Urquhart, *supra* note 1, 172; see also Glennon, *supra* note 14, 835.

[16] Cordier and Foote, *supra* note 1, 306–308. [17] Miller, *supra* note 1, 70.

[18] Cf. B. Nolte, 'Uniting for Peace', in R. Wolfrum (ed.), *United Nations: Law, Policies, Practice*, Vol. II (1995), 1341–1348; J. Delbrück, *Die Entwicklung des Verhältnisses von Sicherheitsrat und Vollversammlung der Vereinten Nationen* (1964), 87–99.

Council adjourned until the next afternoon and Hammarskjöld started working on a statement for that session. In his report of August 1957 he writes:

> The situation seemed to me to be one where the whole position of the UN was at stake and where the very least I could do was to play my position in order to get freedom of action in relation to the two permanent Members, which appeared to have put the UN aside, both in substance and in form.[19]

16.2.3 Wednesday, 31 October 1956

On the afternoon of 31 October, Hammarskjöld spoke at the meeting of the Security Council to establish the principles of his position as Secretary-General in the new circumstances. He started by saying that he himself would have called a meeting of the Council if no Member State had taken the initiative. He thus alluded to the political competences of the Secretary-General that derive from Article 99 of the UN Charter, which gives him the option of bringing to the attention of the Council 'any matter which in his opinion may threaten the maintenance of international peace and security'. He added:

> The principles of the Charter are, by far, greater than the Organization in which they are embodied, and the aims which they are to safeguard are holier than the policies of any single nation or people. As a servant of the Organization, the Secretary-General has the duty to maintain his usefulness by avoiding public stands on conflicts between Member Nations unless and until such an action might help to resolve the conflict. However, the discretion and impartiality thus imposed on the Secretary-General by the character of his immediate task, may not degenerate into a policy of expediency. He must also be a servant of the principles of the Charter, and its aims must ultimately determine what for him is right and wrong. For that he must stand. A Secretary-General cannot serve on any other assumption than that – within the necessary limits of human frailty and honest differences of opinion – all Member Nations honor their pledge to observe all articles of the Charter.[20]

Hammarskjöld went on to state that if Member States did not share the Secretary-General's conception of his office they were, of course, free to act accordingly. Behind this stood nothing less than the implicit

[19] Notes, *supra* note 4, 2.
[20] Cf. Cordier and Foote, *supra* note 1, 309.

threat of either his resignation or the challenge of a vote of confidence. Hammarskjöld was taking a risk, but he calculated correctly: the members of the Security Council vied with one another in offering messages of confidence and support. Louis de Guiringaud for France[21] and Dixon for Great Britain joined in the chorus. Like the American representative, both had already received Hammarskjöld's text in the morning. Just at the moment at which the United Nations appeared to be excluded, this move of Hammarskjöld focused attention on the significance of his office and reminded Member States of the legal and ethical commitments resulting from the UN Charter. Following up on Brilej's proposal from the day before, the Council voted with the necessary majority of seven affirmative votes to invoke the 'Uniting for Peace' procedure. The UK and France had tried to question the legality of this move, but a motion to that effect was rejected by six votes to four, with one abstention.[22] Thus, ironically, the procedure originally devised by the United States to circumvent a possible Soviet veto in the Council was now to be applied 'against' two Western allies.

Because of 'Operation Musketeer', numerous problems, including questions of economic relationships and oil supply, were suddenly out of control and various lines of conflict intersected: France and Great Britain, 'old' colonial powers, opposed a 'young', newly independent country that belonged to the group of non-aligned states. Nasser's ambitions of pan-Arabic leadership pitted him against Israel. At the superpower level, the United States and the Soviet Union were in a competition for predominance in the Middle East – including the crucial question as to who would win the support of the growing number of non-aligned states. The simultaneous crisis over Hungary lent additional drama to that line of conflict: Moscow clearly wanted to distract attention from Budapest by focusing on Suez. The United States, just days ahead of a presidential election, strongly disapproved of the unilateral action of the UK and France. At the same time, it had to take into account the danger that the British and French operation posed to the future of the Western alliance. Only a face-saving solution for all participants could evade further damage and escalation.

21 The deputy representative had taken over from Cornut-Gentille who, under the immense stress of the negotiations, was suffering from depression. Cf. Bailey, *supra* note 1, 597.

22 SC Res. S/3719, 31 October 1956. The vote was seven in favour, two against (France, UK) and two abstentions (Australia, Belgium). See also A/3648 Supplement No. 2, para. 283–310.

16.2.4 Thursday, 1 November 1956

The General Assembly convened for its first emergency session on 1 November at 5 p.m. In view of the sensitive context, Washington put on a show of public reserve – while putting intense diplomatic, and above all economic, pressure on France and Britain behind the scenes.[23] Instead, Canada intervened in the negotiations. Ottawa was also heavily affected by the crisis since it threatened central pillars of its foreign policy, as personified by its Foreign Minister Lester B. Pearson:[24]

> All that Canada had feared had come to pass – aggression against Egypt, Anglo-American relation in disarray, the unity of the Commonwealth in jeopardy, loyalties and friendships strained by anger, moral outrage, confusion, and disillusionment, the United Nations flouted and even abused, and an opportunity handed to the Soviet Union.[25]

Canada not only maintained special relations with the United States, but also with its 'mother countries', Great Britain and France. At the same time, it also held a position in the Commonwealth that could prove useful for mediation between the newly independent countries and the former colonial powers. When the session opened, Pearson exploited his country's position to guide the debate towards a proposal that he had developed soon after the Korean War and now dusted off: the UN could deploy its own international peacekeeping troops.[26] This idea also drew some support from developments in the UK where the Eden government had come under intense domestic criticism. In the House of Commons, just a few hours before the emergency session in New York started, Eden had signalled that British and French troops in Suez were there to separate Egypt and Israel with speed and determination. This did not, however, mean that they were meant to stay after fulfilling that immediate task. Eden said:

[23] D.B. Kunz, 'The Importance of Having Money: The Economic Diplomacy of the Suez Crisis', in Louis and Owen, *supra* note 1, 215–232.

[24] Cf. M.G. Fry, 'Canada, the North Atlantic Triangle, and the United Nations' in Louis and Owen, *supra* note 1, 285–316 as well as M.B. Oren, 'Faith and Fair-Mindedness: Lester B. Pearson and the Suez Crisis' (1992) 3(1) *Diplomacy & Statecraft* 48. J.-E. Schulte, 'Ein nationaler Weg: Kanada und die Schaffung der UN-Blauhelme in der Suez-Krise 1956' (2000) 68 *Militärgeschichtliche Zeitschrift* 49, portrays the domestic dynamics of Pearson's role which did not find unambiguous support in his home country.

[25] Fry, *supra* note 24, 306.

[26] L.B. Pearson, *Mike: The Memoirs of the Right Honourable Lester B. Pearson*. Vol. II: *1948–1957*, edited by J.A. Munro and A.I. Inglis (1973), 244–278; L.B. Pearson, 'Force for U.N.' (1957) 36(3) *Foreign Affairs* 395.

'If the United Nations were then willing to take over the physical task of maintaining peace in that area, no one would be better pleased than we.'[27] In recognition of Canada's special position, London had transmitted an advance copy of Eden's speech to the Canadian delegation in New York.[28] Pearson repeatedly raised this subject with Hammarskjöld, who was initially very sceptical. The emergency session dragged into the night.

16.2.5 Friday, 2 November 1956

Just after midnight and in the early hours of Friday, the General Assembly brought up two concrete texts that shaped further developments. For the United States, Secretary of State John Foster Dulles introduced a draft resolution reaffirming the substance of the resolution that had been vetoed in the Security Council. The Assembly adopted the resolution by 64 votes in favour, five against and six abstentions. Canada also abstained, with Pearson arguing that the resolution did not 'provide for any steps to be taken by the United Nations for a peace settlement, without which a ceasefire, which will be only of temporary value at best', and hinting at his larger idea for a UN force that could keep the peace while a political settlement could be negotiated.[29] Paragraph 5 of the resolution did, at least, request the Secretary-General to 'observe and report promptly on the compliance with the present resolution to the Security Council and to the General Assembly, for such action as they may deem appropriate in accordance with the Charter'.[30] Furthermore, the Assembly decided to remain in emergency session 'pending compliance with the present resolution'. Besides the ceasefire and withdrawal issues thus established, Pearson, who had wanted to include into the US resolution the need for a political settlement in Palestine and the option of an international force, spelled out the idea 'of a United Nations force large enough to keep [the] borders at peace while a political settlement is being worked out' in a statement to the Assembly.[31] That proposal had been presented to the Americans before the sitting. Under the agreement between Pearson and his colleague Dulles, the latter

[27] Cf. Cordier and Foote, *supra* note 1, 316. [28] Pearson, *supra* note 26, 246.

[29] UN General Assembly, Official Records, First Emergency Meeting, 1 November 1956, para. 296–306.

[30] GA Res. 997 (ES-I), 2 November 1956. The vote was sixty-four in favour, five against (Australia, France, Israel, New Zealand, UK) and six abstentions (Belgium, Canada, Laos, Netherlands, Portugal, Union of South Africa) and one non-voting member (Luxembourg).

[31] Cf. Cordier and Foote, *supra* note 1, 316.

rose to speak as soon as Pearson finished his speech and asked Canada to submit a concrete proposal for such a force.[32]

Over lunch with Pearson on 2 November, Hammarskjöld was still hesitant[33] on account of the enormous risk involved for the UN. He writes in his recapitulation of the events: 'Not by way of opposition, but in order to see to it that the Canadian initiative would be taken on the basis of realistic assumptions, I spelled out some of the obvious difficulties in which we would run.'[34] These questions included: could the legal problems relating to such a force be solved? Was the UN actually in a position to organise such a force? Would Franco-British influence allow it to operate as an international force rather than as a belated legitimation of intervention? Pearson's original proposal had run into problems precisely on the last point, as it had foreseen a UN force that could in effect supplement and transform a primarily British and French force, but not on their terms.[35] In a special note Hammarskjöld wrote:

> Mr. Pearson still had no clear idea at all about what kind of arrangements might be possible ... His main hope was to gain the tactical advantage of having put forward something positive which might help the British off the hook; his main concern was the split of the Western Bloc.[36]

Pearson consulted with the government in Ottawa and presented a draft to Hammarskjöld that was scrutinised over dinner with Pearson, Hammarskjöld's chief of the executive office, Andrew Cordier, and the Secretary-General's trouble-shooter for diplomatic assignments, Under-Secretary-General Ralph Bunche, in Pearson's suite in the Drake Hotel. Hammarskjöld articulated his ongoing reservations about Pearson's plan.[37] However, the idea of an international force survived the discussion.

[32] Pearson, *supra* note 26, 247. [33] Cordier and Foote, *supra* note 1, 319–322.

[34] Notes, *supra* note 4, 3. Bailey, *supra* note 1, 35 argues that there were 'widely differing views' on the functions of the force: 'To Egypt and the Arab States the purpose should be simply to secure and supervise the withdrawal of the foreign forces which had invaded Egyptian territory, after which it should be disbanded. To Britain and France it was to be merely a replacement of their own forces, to be stationed along the Canal itself until such time as Egypt had agreed satisfactory international arrangements for the Canal's operation. To Lester Pearson and others it was to keep the peace between Israel and the Arabs for a considerable time.'

[35] A.W. Rovine, *The First Fifty Years: The Secretary-General in World Politics 1920–1970* (1970), 288; Eden, *supra* note 1, 611; Kyle, *supra* note 1, 436.

[36] Special Note 6, *supra* note 4.

[37] A.W. Cordier, *Recollections of Dag Hammarskjöld and the United Nations* (1964), 424.

Hammarskjöld also had to concentrate on fulfilling the task of furthering a ceasefire as spelled out in Resolution 997. He sent a number of cables to the respective capitals. Britain and France replied in a joint statement that listed conditions in order for their military actions to be stopped.[38] They would only cease their activities when Egypt and Israel would accept a UN force and an Arab-Israeli peace settlement would be reached. In the meantime, they considered their own military operations justified. Egypt, for its part, accepted Resolution 997 (that did not include any reference to a UN force) 'on the condition of course that it could not implement the resolution in case attacking armies continue their aggression'.[39] Later that night, Hammarskjöld was visited in his home apartment by the Iranian permanent representative Djalal Abdoh, who, on behalf of the Afro-Asian states, asked him to intervene personally and negotiate for a ceasefire, thus expanding the mandate of the US-sponsored ceasefire resolution. Abdoh announced that he would present a draft resolution to that effect on the next day. Two resolutions, one on ceasefire and one on an international force, were expected for Saturday.

16.2.6 Saturday, 3 November 1956

Under the pressure of events and after receiving clarification about some of his concerns, Hammarskjöld finally declared himself convinced of the Pearson idea at lunch in his office on the 38th floor.[40] After making this decision in principle, he got to work exceptionally quickly, meeting with several heads of delegations in the course of the day.[41] The possible creation of a peacekeeping force in accordance with the 'Uniting for Peace' procedure needed to find broad support among Member States in the General Assembly. Hammarskjöld and Pearson coordinated this with a small circle of UN delegations that took a positive view of the plan and represented their respective regional groups in the General Assembly. Initial members of the group were Hans Engen (Norway), Arthur Lall (India) and Francisco Urrutia (Colombia).[42] It was Lall who passed on to John Holmes, one of Pearson's staff, the crucial information that after being informed by Egyptian UN representative Omar Loutfi, Nasser agreed to

[38] Cf. Cordier and Foote, *supra* note 1, 318.

[39] Cf. *ibid.*, 319. [40] E. Kelen, *Hammarskjöld* (1966), 75.

[41] Special Note 6, *supra* note 4. The delegations comprised Canada, Colombia, India, Norway and later on Denmark, Finland, Sweden, Brazil, Mexico, New Zealand and Iran. See also J.P. Lash, *Dag Hammarskjöld: Custodian of the Brush-fire Peace* (1961), 97–111.

[42] Cordier and Foote, *supra* note 1, 319.

the Canadian plan in principle.[43] Building on the efforts to coordinate and convince various Member States, that same evening Canada proposed a draft resolution that included, in addition to the efforts to reach a cease-fire, the following passage:

> The General Assembly ... Requests as a matter of priority, the Secretary-General to submit to it within forty-eight hours a plan for the setting up, with the consent of the nations concerned, of an emergency international United Nations force to secure and supervise the cessation of hostilities in accordance with all the terms of the aforementioned resolution.[44]

Canada's text was, of course, intensively coordinated with Hammarskjöld.

The prior efforts to sound out and take account of the voting positions in the different groups paid off: Canada's resolution was passed by fifty-seven votes in favour, none against and nineteen abstentions.[45] A major factor in this success was tying and limiting the functions of the Emergency Force directly to the goal and monitoring of the ceasefire. Once the resolution was passed, the ball was in Hammarskjöld's court. His only concrete instruction was to present a plan within forty-eight hours, an almost impossible deadline. Yet, before it expired, Hammarskjöld proposed to the General Assembly that a UN command be established for the future Emergency Force. As its head he recommended the chief of staff of UNTSO, General Burns, who was familiar with the problems of the region. In a telegram to Burns, Hammarskjöld expressed doubts about the idea – but also the necessity of testing the only concrete option for a solution: 'My personal lack of optimism is of course no excuse for not exploring the field.'[46]

At the same time, India and eighteen other Afro-Asian countries presented a stronger version of the US ceasefire resolution. This resolution, adopted by fifty-nine votes in favour, five against and twelve abstentions, also placed a personal role (and a time limit) on the Secretary-General since it

> [a]uthorizes the Secretary-General immediately to arrange with the parties concerned for the implementation of the cease-fire and the halting of

[43] Pearson, *supra* note 26, 251. [44] GA Res. 998 (ES-I), 3 November 1956.

[45] The abstentions came from Albania, Australia, Austria, Bulgaria, Byelorussian SSR, Czechoslovakia, Egypt, France, Hungary, Israel, Laos, New Zealand, Portugal, Romania, Ukranian SSR, Union of South Africa, UK, USSR. See also Cordier and Foote, *supra* note 1, 322.

[46] Cf. Urquhart, *supra* note 1, 178.

> movement of military forces and arms into the area and requests him to report compliance forthwith and, in any case, not later than twelve hours from the time of adoption of the present resolution.[47]

Hammarskjöld had already given a first report on compliance following the US ceasefire resolution (Resolution 997) based on the initial reactions from Britain, France and Egypt. Only after that report, Israel also issued its reply to the Secretary-General in which it accepted a ceasefire (provided that Egypt did the same), but at the same time stressed that the armistice agreement could no longer be seen as defining the relevant lines of withdrawal – a move that did of course substantially alter the terms of negotiation. After the General Assembly meeting, the Security Council also held a session which lasted until 3 a.m. Hammarskjöld directly followed up on the resolutions and, together with Bunche, wrote cables to the parties concerned regarding the ceasefire. These cables were finished at 7 a.m. In the cable to Jerusalem, Hammarskjöld maintained the position of the General Assembly resolution, thus rejecting the Israeli condition on a ceasefire. There could be, however, no doubt that the problem of a ceasefire had become more complicated and pressing with Egypt simultaneously complaining about the continuing attack. The double task of working on an international force (Resolution 998) and a ceasefire (Resolutions 997 and 999) had landed Hammarskjöld in a rather typical diplomatic dilemma since the parties made their acceptance of one item dependent upon the realisation of another and vice versa.

16.2.7 Sunday, 4 November 1956

Sunday saw an 11:30 a.m. meeting of the delegations engaged in the peacekeeping proposal. Hammarskjöld consulted with them in his efforts for an interim report which he presented the same day. In that report, the Secretary-General made a first crucial decision as far as the composition of the force is concerned. He stated that 'as a matter of principle, troops should not be drawn from countries which are permanent members of the Security Council'.[48] Besides keeping out the rival superpowers, which were competing for influence in the region, the principle reflected

[47] GA Res. 999 (ES-I), 4 November 1956. The no-votes came from Australia, France, Israel, New Zealand and the UK. The abstentions came from Belgium, Denmark, Dominican Republic, Finland, Iceland, Laos, Luxembourg, Netherlands, Norway, Portugal, Sweden, Union of South Africa.

[48] Cf. Cordier and Foote, *supra* note 1, 335.

the desire to exclude the participation of Britain and France, who could have used the UN cover to legitimise their intervention after the event. Hammarskjöld closely coordinated the report with Washington which offered its support for the airlift of troops to Egypt.[49] Hammarskjöld's principles were transformed into a draft resolution introduced by Canada, Colombia and Norway, adopted just after midnight by fifty-seven votes in favour, none against and nineteen abstentions. The resolution also established a UN Command under General Burns. Again it included a personal – and wide-ranging – mandate for Hammarskjöld. Paragraph 4 '[i]nvites the Secretary-General to take such administrative measures as may be necessary for the prompt execution of the actions envisaged in the present resolution'.[50]

Regarding the ceasefire, Hammarskjöld presented a second report in the General Assembly session that had begun at 9:45 p.m. The Israeli position had hardened even more since its denial of the armistice agreement had resulted in asking UNTSO to also withdraw its personnel from Gaza and Beersheba. At the same time, the bombing of Egypt continued and the Anglo-French fleet was approaching Port Said.

16.2.8 *Monday, 5 November 1956*

On 5 November Hammarskjöld dictated his second report on UNEF during breaks in the General Assembly sitting and between further meetings with Pearson, Holmes, Cordier, Bunche and the Chief of the Secretariat's legal office, Constantin Stravopoulos.[51] The report was finally ready at 2 a.m. the following day – Pearson had sat polishing it with the Secretary-General until the very end.[52] Hammarskjöld and Bunche brought it to Dixon in order to have it cabled to Foreign Minister Lloyd.

[49] Glennon, *supra* note 14, 977–980; Telegram from the Mission at the United Nations to the Department of State.

[50] GA Res. 1000 (ES-I), 5 November 1956. The abstentions came from Albania, Australia, Bulgaria, Byelorussian SSR, Czechoslovakia, Egypt, France, Hungary, Israel, Laos, New Zealand, Poland, Portugal, Romania, Turkey, Ukranian SSR, Union of South Africa, UK, USSR.

[51] Notes, *supra* note 4, 3–4.

[52] See KB DHS, *Dag Hammarskjöld*, Notes, *supra* note 3, 5: 'The procedure was that first Bunche and Cordier read the draft and made their corrections, later I, thereafter Pearson and Holmes, thereafter Stravopoulus, and thereafter I, myself, again, after which the text was directly retyped for reproduction.'

As far as the ceasefire was concerned, Hammarskjöld was still frustrated about the first, and defiant, reply from Israel.[53] On Monday morning he had sent a reply to Israel expressing his concerns and asking for clarifications.[54] The time limit of the resolution was expiring. In the afternoon, Hammarskjöld received a new reply with a general acceptance of the ceasefire (although tied to a number of questions regarding Egypt's position).[55] With the general acceptance by Israel and Egypt concerning the ceasefire and Cairo's acceptance in principle of the international force, Hammarskjöld again contacted London and Paris,[56] where the conditions for a ceasefire were officially still upheld. Against this new background, Hammarskjöld received a message from Dixon stating that a ceasefire at Port Said had been ordered.[57] Partial and yet not communicated progress on the ceasefire issue was, however, threatened by a new initiative from Moscow. In a letter to President Eisenhower, Soviet Prime Minister Nikolai Bulganin had proposed that the two superpowers join forces in countering the aggression in the Middle East.[58] The Soviet Union also requested a meeting of the Security Council in order to act on the obvious non-compliance regarding the ceasefire. The Soviets referred to Article 42 of the UN Charter and thus wanted to open the door for military action under Chapter VII of the Charter.[59] Hammarskjöld consciously decided to speak before Sobolev when the Council met at 8 p.m. 'and to present an oral progress report [regarding the ceasefire] which might give the debate a positive accent'.[60] This tactic proved successful since it decreased the thrust of the Soviet initiative that the United States, for its part, answered in the negative and with a clear reference to similarities with the situation in Hungary.[61] The Soviet draft resolution was not put to vote. Pressure did not, however, go down; fears of a possible intervention of Soviet or other 'volunteers' into the conflict, as well as hostile actions from Jordan and

[53] Kyle, *supra* note 1, 452. [54] Special Note 1, *supra* note 4.

[55] Hammarskjöld, therefore, had to be careful in choosing his words before the Security Council speaking of 'a statement to the effect that in the light of Egypt's declaration of willingness to cease fire, Israel wishes to confirm its readiness to agree to a cease-fire' – see Cordier and Foote, *supra* note 1, 339.

[56] GA Res. 3310 (XXIX), 14 December 1974

[57] Cf. Cordier and Foote, *supra* note 1, 333.

[58] Glennon, *supra* note 14, 993–994.

[59] Cordier and Foote, *supra* note 1, 338. [60] Notes, *supra* note 4, 5.

[61] Lodge had answered in the Security Council stating that the letter marked a 'new record of cynicism'. Although a bit milder in tone, Eisenhower's formal reply to Bulganin followed the same line of argumentation (Glennon, *supra* note 14, 1111–1112).

Syria (that just days before the crisis had taken first steps towards a joint military command with Egypt), were still reasonably grounded.[62]

16.2.9 Tuesday, 6 November 1956

Time was as much of the essence as ever. Notwithstanding the Anglo-French stop of bombings, British and French paratroopers had already landed in Port Said. The number of angry voices was growing, not only in Moscow but also among the Commonwealth countries. During 5 November, Hammarskjöld had used the recesses of the Assembly to write drafts of his second report on UNEF. In this process he again included Pearson, Cordier, Stravopolous and Bunche. In the early morning hours of 6 November, the report was finished.[63] In this report Hammarskjöld laid down further principles for the first UN peacekeeping mission.[64] Partly for pragmatic reasons and with the command given to General Burns, the constitutional structure of UNTSO became the model for the independent command and composition of UNEF. In Hammarskjöld's view, this settled two other points:

> On the one hand, the independence of the Chief of Command in recruiting officers is recognized. On the other hand, the principle is established that the force should be recruited from Member States other than the permanent members of the Security Council.[65]

On the basis of this view Hammarskjöld rejected British, French and also Egyptian proposals that the parties involved should have a voice in the selection of the different national contingents. Hammarskjöld also underlined the 'emergency' character of the force and thus from the start the temporary nature of its mandate. Its function was 'to secure and supervise the cessation of hostilities'. He then expanded on this point: 'It

[62] S.M. Maloney, 'Die Schaffung der United Nations Emergency Force I, November 1956 bis März 1957', in Heinemann and Wiggershaus, *supra* note 1, 264–266.

[63] UN Doc. A/3302, 6 November 1956. Cf. B. Urquhart, *Ralph Bunche: An American Life* (1993), 267 and Pearson, *supra* note 26, 257, who additionally reports the following incident: 'As a footnote to the history of these times, the original draft of the report by Hammarskjöld and Bunche used the phrase "to enforce and supervise the cessations of hostilities" and it managed to slip through our revision during the early hours of 6 November. However, I spotted it an hour or so later, just as the draft was going off to be reproduced. We changed it to "to secure and supervise". Thank goodness I noticed it, because we would have soon been in the soup if this force had been charged with the job of "enforcing" anything' (at 259).

[64] Cf. Cordier and Foote, *supra* note 1, 344–351.

[65] *Ibid.*, 346.

follows from its terms of reference that there is no intent in the establishment of the Force to influence the military balance in the present conflict and, thereby, the political balance affecting efforts to settle the conflict.'[66] Furthermore, Hammarskjöld pointed out that UNEF was acting on the basis of the 'Uniting for Peace' resolution. Consequently, it could not resort to Security Council action under Chapter VII and depended on the consensus of the parties involved – in particular as regards permission for the international force to enter the operational area. There were also strict limits on the functions of the force on the ground:

> The force obviously should have no rights other than those necessary for the execution of its functions, in cooperation with local authorities. It would be more than an observers' corps, but in no way a military force temporarily controlling the territory in which it is stationed; nor, moreover, should the force have military functions exceeding those necessary to secure peaceful conditions on the assumption that the parties to the conflict take all necessary steps for compliance with the recommendations of the General Assembly.[67]

To summarise, the Secretary-General formulated five basic principles that would henceforth serve as a model for other UN peacekeeping missions:[68]

(1) The peacekeeping mission is in principle an emergency measure and limited in time.
(2) The peacekeeping mission shall be carried out with complete impartiality. Its deployment may not in any way change or prejudice longer-term political or military power relationships. Force may only be used in self-defence.
(3) The permanent members of the Security Council are excluded from supplying troops for peacekeeping missions.
(4) The peacekeeping mission shall be under the unified command of a single UN officer.

[66] Cf. *ibid.*, 347. [67] Cf. *ibid.*, 348.

[68] Cf. Fröhlich, *Political Ethics*, *supra* note 1, 154–155. Hammarskjöld was keenly aware of the fact that UNEF could become a model for the future. In 1958 he reflected on the UNEF experiences in a summary study to the General Assembly focusing 'on those principles and conclusions which emerge from a study of the operation as a whole and which might afford useful guidance for any future efforts looking towards the establishment or use of international United Nations instruments serving purposes of the kind met by UNEF'. Cordier and Foote, Vol. III, *supra* note 1, 231. Cf. also N. MacQueen, *United Nations, Peace Operations and the Cold War*, 2nd edition (2011), 41–45.

(5) The deployment of peacekeeping units depends on the consensus of the parties involved, in particular that of the respective host country.

Hammarskjöld emphasised the 'exploratory character'[69] of his report and pointed out that much would ensue as concrete steps were implemented. He also suggested that an 'advisory committee to the Secretary-General for questions relating to the operations' be established and underlined: 'If the force is to come into being with all the speed indispensable to its success, a margin of confidence must be left to those who will carry the responsibility for putting the decisions into effect.'[70]

Pearson had telephoned parts of the report to Ottawa where Prime Minister Louis St. Laurent used it in direct appeals to London pressing for an acceptance of the force and inter alia 'indicating the risk of a split in the Commonwealth'.[71] Hammarskjöld, for his part, also forwarded the report formally to Paris and London without delay. The pressure from Ottawa and elsewhere surely had its effect on the United Kingdom. The government was under enormous domestic political pressure from the opposition, and the United States continued to apply additional economic and political pressure. 6 November was election day in the United States and Eisenhower received additional support for his diplomatic course with a clear win. According to Cordier and Foote, Hammarskjöld's report arrived at just the right time, providing 'a line of retreat at a moment when the various pressures to halt the ill-started military adventure had built to overwhelming proportions'.[72] In any case, Dixon asked to see the Secretary-General on the morning of 6 November and said that the British government wanted him to publish an announcement that the UK 'will agree to stop further military operations' on the condition that Israel and Egypt have accepted an unconditional ceasefire 'and that the international force to be set up will be competent to secure and supervise' the mandate of the General Assembly resolution.[73] The threads of a solution now lay before Hammarskjöld and he followed suit: he asked to send the text of the British statement to Jerusalem and Cairo, informed ambassadors Abba Eban and Loutfi of its content and at the same time communicated the Israeli as well as Egyptian acceptance of the ceasefire to Dixon. The simultaneous declarations offered the chance to solve the diplomatic

[69] Cf. Cordier and Foote, *supra* note 1, 350.
[70] Cf. *ibid.*, 350–351.
[71] Notes, *supra* note 4, 6.
[72] Cordier and Foote, *supra* note 1, 340.
[73] Cf. Notes, *supra* note 4, 6; Cordier and Foote, *supra* note 1, 341.

dilemma of mutually exclusive conditions by the parties involved. Much to Hammarskjöld's irritation, the messages to Jerusalem and Cairo were accidently not sent to the capitals, which he only realised in the evening. He immediately contacted Eban and Loutfi since he was anxious to see that the concurring initiatives of all sides developed the planned synergy, thus leaving no vacuum that could be exploited by further unilateral conditions. His fears were justified as Cairo Radio reported a withdrawal from the Egyptian ceasefire commitment which Loutfi, however, explained to be a misunderstanding.

After the progress on the ceasefire, another problem came up. The letter from Dixon contained an important paragraph suggesting that the technicians with the Franco-British force should at least start clearing the obstacles in the Canal.[74] While this surely made sense for pragmatic reasons since Britain and France were technically best equipped to handle this issue, it again brought up the question of what kind of relationship UNEF would have to, and with, the Franco-British force. For Eden, the technical aid by British and French experts was an important aspect of face-saving. Eisenhower, however, who called Eden around noon to say how pleased he was on the acceptance of the ceasefire, advised him 'not [to] insist that he [Hammarskjöld] take them'.[75] Eisenhower's dominant fear was that the Soviet Union would still look for a chance to be part of the resolution of the crisis:

> What I want to do is this. I would like to see none of the great nations in it. I am afraid that Red boy is going to demand the lion's share. I would rather make it no troops from the big five. I would say, 'Mr. Hammarskjöld, we trust you. When we see you coming with enough troops to take over, we go out.'[76]

This, of course, was fully in line with the report that Hammarskjöld had presented. The terms of the debate had significantly shifted: Britain was no longer in a position to decide on its own. It had to take into consideration the position of the other powers involved and it even had to deal directly with the Secretary-General, who undoubtedly had become a major actor in the crisis.[77]

74 Cf. Cordier and Foote, *supra* note 1, 341.

75 Glennon, *supra* note 14, 1026. 76 *Ibid.*, 1027.

77 As E. Johnson, 'The Suez Crisis at the United Nations: The Effects for the Foreign Office and British Foreign Policy', in Smith, *supra* note 1, 165–177, has shown, this experience caused quite substantial reappraisals of the British view on the United Nations. See also

16.2.10 *Wednesday, 7 November 1956*

The idea of an international force finally gained shape through a resolution that Tunisia's representative, Mongi Slim, submitted to the General Assembly after consultations with Hammarskjöld.[78] The resolution to establish UNEF was adopted by sixty-four votes in favour, none against and twelve abstentions. The USSR declared its doubts about whether UNEF was compatible with the Charter, but chose to abstain as Egypt had voted in favour. Again, the resolution gave a specific mandate to the Secretary-General as it authorised him 'to issue all regulations and instructions which may be essential to the effective functioning of the force, following consultation with the Committee aforementioned, and to take all other necessary administrative and executive action'.[79]

The foundations which had developed from the various notes and communications were, however, still fragile. During the meeting of the General Assembly, Hammarskjöld was informed (through Burns) of the content of a speech Ben Gurion had been giving in the Knesset, stating that the armistice agreement had no validity and that there would be no stationing of UNEF on Israeli territory. In other words, the question of withdrawal was open again. Hammarskjöld decided to call Eban in an effort to, again, state the view of the General Assembly resolution that made reference to the armistice lines. In his notes he recalls:

> Mr. Eban then asked me how I envisaged the situation in case Israeli troops were to withdraw: would Egyptian troops then come up to the Demarcation Line? I replied that obviously Egyptian troops had freedom

the chapter on 'The United Nations and the Suez Crisis: British Ambivalence towards the Pope on the East River', in Wm. R. Louis, *Ends of British Imperialism: The Scramble for Empire, Suez and Decolonialization* (2006), 665–688. Although the differences with the Secretary-General from the time of the Suez crisis were eventually left behind and London defended Hammarskjöld as a person during the Congo crisis, the 1960 attack by the Soviet Union on the office of a (potentially too independently-minded and activist) Secretary-General in principle also found support on the British side. See E. Johnson, 'The British and the 1960 Soviet Attack on the Office of the United Nations Secretary-General' (2003) 14(1) *Diplomacy & Statecraft* 79.

[78] Cf. T.M. Franck, 'Finding a Voice: How the Secretary-General makes himself heard in the Councils of the Nations', in J. Makarczyk (ed.), *Essays in International Law in Honour of Judge Manfred Lachs* (1984), 484.

[79] GA Res. 1001 (ES-I), 7 November 1956.

> to move on Egyptian territory. Eban said that he felt that that would seriously complicate any acceptance on the Israeli side of withdrawal, because we might then have a renewal of incursions which would threaten Israeli lives. I considered it necessary to reply to Eban that I hoped he fully realized – and that Jerusalem fully realized – that the time was past for talks about such security problems; what we were discussing was a question which might well decide whether 'two months from now there would be any Israel at all'. He could take that as an expression of my most seriously considered opinion.[80]

Again, Hammarskjöld had strengthened his positions when, just before the telephone call with Eban, he had asked Lodge to urge President Eisenhower to send a personal message to Ben Gurion requesting immediate withdrawal. At the same time, the Afro-Asian countries had introduced another resolution calling 'upon Israel immediately to withdraw behind the armistices lines',[81] as well as calling for the UK and France to withdraw from Egyptian territory, that was adopted by sixty-five votes to one, with ten abstentions. At 10 p.m. Hammarskjöld had a long meeting in his office with Lodge and Barco, as well as Cordier and Bunche. Lodge underlined his impression that the situation in neighbouring Jordan was highly explosive for Israel and that the United States was deeply worried about the option of possible Soviet support behind provocations across the border.[82] Hammarskjöld 'said that this would indeed argue for the utmost speed' in carrying out the General Assembly resolution.[83] In a letter to Cairo from the same day, Hammarskjöld had indicated that the Force would be able to come into operation rather soon due to the help of troops from Canada, Colombia, Denmark, Finland, Norway and Sweden. He wrote:

> I therefore ask you for an immediate reply to the question whether Egypt would raise objection against participation of troops from any of

[80] Notes, *supra* note 4, 3. For a broader analysis of Hammarskjöld's perspective on the relationship between Israel and the UN as well as some insights into the personalities of the Secretary-General and the Israeli Prime Minister see M.B. Oren, 'Ambivalent Adversaries: David Ben-Gurion and Israel vs. The United Nations and Dag Hammarskjöld, 1956–1957' (1992) 27 *Journal of Contemporary History* 89, who also quotes the conversation between Hammarskjöld and Eban (at 106). E. Barak, 'Caught in the Middle: The United Nations Emergency Force, Israel, and the 1960 "Rotem Crisis"' (2006) 17 *Diplomacy & Statecraft* 393 analyses a grave incident in 1960 that also raised the question of how the Secretary-General understood the role of the UN in the face of a threat to Israel and how the Israelis perceived the UN in that crisis.

[81] GA Res. 1002 (ES-I), 7 November 1956.

[82] Glennon, *supra* note 14, 1068–1070. [83] *Ibid.*, 1069.

> the aforementioned countries in the Force to be stationed on Egyptian territory in fulfilment of the prescribed tasks.[84]

16.2.11 Thursday, 8 November 1956

At noon, Mordecai Kidron of the Israeli delegation came to see Hammarskjöld and announced that he was waiting for a message from Ben Gurion. Later on, the Israeli Foreign Minister Golda Meir sent a cable stating that 'the Government of Israel will willingly withdraw its forces from Egypt immediately upon the conclusion of satisfactory arrangements with the United Nations in connection with the emergency international force'.[85] While this statement obviously still was a little ambivalent and contained a condemnation of Egyptian-sponsored raids into Israel, Hammarskjöld took it to mean acceptance of a ceasefire and acceptance of the international force. Once again using 'publicity in support of private diplomacy',[86] he announced the Israeli commitment in a press conference to consolidate the diplomatic progress.[87] Obviously, Hammarskjöld's strong wording and the other pressure applied on Israel had had an effect. The Israeli mission had sent urgent messages to Jerusalem and Eban told Hammarskjöld that:

> he had been in constant telephone contact with Jerusalem all through the night and added that as soon as Mr. Ben-Gurion saw 'the world political context' he changed to this new line. Mr. Eban, at the same time asked me to use my information 'with one Security Council Member' and to try and prevent activities from that side. In line with this, I immediately sent to [V.V.] Kusnetzov [of the Soviet delegation] a note in which, after having told him about the Israeli message I added 'this brings the situation under full control unless unrest breaks out in the Northern part. I have had the most disturbing information on the situation in Syria. May I ask you to do what you can do in order to make us avoid renewed Fedayeen activities or anything that might disturb the extremely delicate but promising situation'.[88]

With one problem being mitigated, the next complication already appeared on the horizon since Egypt had not yet replied on the matter of Force composition.

[84] KB DHS, *Dag Hammarskjöld*, Letter to Omar Loutfi, 7 November 1956, *supra* note 3.
[85] GA Res. 3320 (XXIX), 14 December 1974.
[86] Cordier and Foote, *supra* note 1, 316. [87] Cf. *ibid.*, 359–360.
[88] Special Note 3, *supra* note 4.

16.2.12 Friday, 9 November 1956

Early in the morning, Loutfi transmitted the reply by Fawzi. Egypt needed some more clarifications and would send a number of questions via Burns. Hammarskjöld recalls:

> Loutfi added that it was partly a problem of public reactions to Canadians, as 'being under the Crown'. I replied that I must insist on Canadians. The legal objection was not valid and a refusal by Egypt on this point would be most harmful to Egypt.[89]

In his notes, Hammarskjöld underlines:

> The next days were full of steps and decisions putting the UNEF into effect. I was aiming at getting the troops in during the weekend of the 10th and 11th, feeling that the utmost haste was necessary in order to forestall a possible acceptance of volunteers by Egypt.[90]

His notes end with this entry; the Emergency Session of the General Assembly, that had declared it would remain in session until the cease-fire and withdrawal were settled, came to a close on 10 November. The first troops from Denmark entered Egypt on 15 November after a number of difficult questions had been settled. Obviously the precedent of a sovereign government admitting an international UN force onto its territory proved to be exceedingly difficult and presented a number of further challenges.

16.3 The constitutional structure of UNEF

These challenges were dealt with by the advisory committee, established by Resolution 1001 with participants from Brazil (Cyro de Freitas Valle), Canada (Lester Pearson), Ceylon (R.S.S. Gunewardene), Colombia (Francisco Urrutia), India (Arthur Lall), Norway (Hans Engen) and Pakistan (Muhammad Mir Khan).[91] The meetings of this committee were strictly confidential, but written notes are in the UN Archives.[92] They allow for a more detailed account of the creation of UNEF, Hammarskjöld's personal influence and how he approached this problem.

[89] Special Note 4, *supra* note 4. [90] Notes, *supra* note 4, 7.

[91] Cordier and Foote, *supra* note 1, 355–357.

[92] In addition to the verbatims from the UN Archives, the principal letters, cables and communications of that time find themselves in Hammarskjöld's numbered annex to his Notes from August 1957 at KB DHS (see Annexes I to XXV), *supra* note 3.

Zacher calls the committee a 'source of ideas and channel of communications',[93] a tool that Hammarskjöld had created in order to further his own style of conflict resolution. Although the meetings were confidential in principle, it was assumed that the participants informed their governments, and possibly other delegations, about the results and the need for action. For Cordier, the committee was designed to keep the policies of the Secretary-General 'on the rails'[94] of the views of Member States. Hammarskjöld clearly dominated the meetings by holding long explanations – virtually monologues – of his respective procedures. As a rule, such actions were not questioned and the committee operated on consensus rather than voting.

In the committee, it soon became apparent which members fulfilled which roles. Lall, who kept a very close eye on the interests and rights of Egypt, tended to ask the critical questions. Pearson, as a rule, presented the view of the Western states. However, there was seldom any tension. Hammarskjöld often asked his staff to supplement the political arguments with business-like progress reports. Bunche played a crucial role in this respect. After the decision of the General Assembly, Hammarskjöld had turned to him and said: 'Now, Corporal, go get me a force.'[95] Bunche's role should not be underestimated, as in 1948 he had drawn up the principles governing UNTSO that Hammarskjöld directly referred to.[96] Urquhart calls UNEF 'a force he [Bunche] had virtually created'[97] and continues: 'It was Bunche's task to transform Hammarskjöld's "metaphysical" subtleties into practical arrangements on the ground.'[98] In a private note of April 1957 which Bunche recorded on the occasion of a visit, he stated:

> Seeing UNEF in operation out here and its remarkable success, I do feel a sense of quiet pride in the knowledge, known only to a few out here, that I was primarily responsible for the organization of the force, the getting off the ground, and have been directing it from the beginning. It is, perhaps, my finest achievement, exceeding the armistice negotiations.[99]

Among other things, Bunche had to grapple with the question of how to give the force a common identification. In this context, the idea emerged

[93] M.W. Zacher, *Dag Hammarskjöld's United Nations* (1970), 184.
[94] A.W. Cordier, 'The Role of the Secretary-General', in R.N. Swift (ed.), *Annual Review of United Nations Affairs 1960–1961* (1960), 10.
[95] Rovine, *supra* note 35, 289. [96] Urquhart, *supra* note 63, 266.
[97] *Ibid.*, 285. [98] *Ibid.*, 271. [99] *Ibid.*, 297.

of painting the helmet of the soldiers in the blue of the flag of the UN.[100] At the same time, Bunche coordinated the offers and queries of Member States who wanted to join UNEF. In mid-November he remarked: 'This is the most popular army in history – an army which everyone fights to get into.'[101] UNEF, however, was far from being non-controversial and the debate inter alia centred on three aspects.

16.3.1 Composition of UNEF

One of the first issues that could have hardened suspicions of a Franco-British connotation to UNEF was the offer of the two governments to clear the Suez Canal of ships deliberately sunk to block it.[102] Experts thought it virtually impossible to clear the canal without British and French assistance. In December, the British tried to play all their cards, issuing an ultimatum stating that the international force could not use the Anglo-French equipment and heavy-lift ships at Port Said if no technicians from the two countries were involved. The importance of canal clearance for the whole operation may be derived from a cable from Dixon to Lloyd after he had presented the ultimatum to the Secretary-General: 'Hammarskjöld, I think … is on the verge of collapse. He literally burst into tears this evening when I told him of the [ultimatum].'[103] But Dixon went on to state that: 'Surprisingly enough this strange intellectual whom we have elevated into a superman is made of flesh and blood. It may sound absurd but if this man collapses or turns against us our position will become immeasureably more complicated.' Lloyd cabled back: 'You should tell him that he is the last person with whom we want to get at loggerheads.' In the end, the British ultimatum had no effect and the UN managed to rely on other

100 See Bunche's remarks in AC UNEF 14 November 1956, *supra* note 5, 27: 'I might say, in conclusion, that we are trying to give some kind of common identification to the Force so that it can be readily identified as a United Nations Force. In addition to the arm bands and shoulder patches, we are purchasing a considerable supply of what are known as helmet liners – the liners that go in the steel helmets. These were considered by the military group yesterday. They will be painted in United Nations blue. They are light in weight, they are made of plastic, and they will look quite nice when painted with United Nations blue, with the letters "UN" in white on each side and the UN seal in front. In addition we are having UN blue helmets made so that the national units, while wearing their own uniforms, will have a common headdress.'

101 AC UNEF, 14 November 1956, *supra* note 5, 29.

102 Cordier and Foote, *supra* note 1, 341.

103 Cf. Kyle, *supra* note 1, 521.

countries resulting in one of the great logistical successes of the world organisation.[104]

The same imperative to shut off national preferences and connotations applied to the problem of transporting the troops to Egypt. Hammarskjöld could not rely on US planes, although this would have been the easiest and quickest solution. To avoid political complications, Hammarskjöld (in consultation with the Americans) picked a UNEF meeting place near Naples. Most contingents were flown there in American aircraft, whence Hammarskjöld arranged for Swissair to fly them on to Egyptian territory.[105] To demonstrate his personal involvement and that of his office, Hammarskjöld accompanied the Colombian UNEF contingent to Egypt on 16 November, which underscored the international character of the force.[106] He explained this step in the committee: '[I]t would make it easier for them [the Egyptians] to understand that it was an international Force, if the Force followed, and might make them look at it in the right way.'[107]

Egypt showed itself heavily concerned with the selection of troop-contributing countries. As indicated above, Cairo had strong reservations against Canadian troops while Ottawa wanted to be part of the endeavour that it had brought into existence. Unfortunately, the Canadian Defence Ministry sought to deploy an infantry battalion with the name 'The Queen's Own Rifles',[108] thus offering a problematic allusion to the British Forces. After some irritation, Hammarskjöld was able to obtain Egyptian agreement to the inclusion of other Canadian troops as part of UNEF's air transport. Cairo did, however, also question Norwegian and Dutch troops as they represented NATO countries. Hammarskjöld referred once more to the principle underlying the General Assembly resolution, that UNEF was a genuinely international emergency force and not just a collection of national units, but in recognition of Egypt's reservations, he included Yugoslav and Indonesian contingents to prevent a Western preponderance.[109] However, the composition of UNEF was not the only new challenge in creating the force.

[104] Urquhart, *supra* note 1, 198–202.
[105] Cordier and Foote, *supra* note 1, 362.
[106] K.R. Gray, 'United Nations Notebook: The Relationship of Dag Hammarskjöld with the Press' (1987) 1 *Development Dialogue* 45.
[107] AC UNEF 14 November 1956, *supra* note 5, 25.
[108] Cordier and Foote, *supra* note 1, 370–371. See also Schulte, *supra* note 24, 66–68, who details the irritations of a Canadian contribution that went far beyond the actual name of that battalion.
[109] Cordier and Foote, *supra* note 1, 363.

16.3.2 *Nature of UNEF*

The nature of the emergency force was clearly ambivalent. On the one hand, it could not rely on the compulsory powers of Chapter VII of the UN Charter, which are only at the disposal of the Security Council. On the other hand, it was obviously more than what Chapter VI of the Charter foresees as the options for the 'pacific settlement of disputes'. Although it was a military force, it could not impose its will upon the conflicting parties, but instead relied on their consent. The Brazilian representative in the advisory committee neatly coined this ambivalence when he said: '[I] think we are in Chapter six and a half.'[110] Hammarskjöld picked up this thought and added: '[T]he trouble is that it does not give us the rights of Chapter VII, although it presents us with some of the problems of Chapter VII.'[111] This context, although under changed circumstances, is still a constant companion to UN peacekeeping forces throughout the world.[112] This special situation was of course also a consequence of the fact that it was the General Assembly, and not the Security Council, that had authorised UNEF. Although it could not block the creation of UNEF, the Soviet Union challenged the improvised mechanism for a shared financing of the mission, as it wanted to avoid a precedent for similar action of the Assembly circumventing a Soviet veto. This was to lead to a profound financial crisis in the organisation.[113]

16.3.3 *Duration of UNEF*

In outlining its own interpretation of sovereign consent, Egypt also wanted to include the option that Cairo could terminate the peacekeeping mission unilaterally. Hammarskjöld questioned this reading in an aide-memoire to Fawzi from 12 November 1956:

> I want to put on record that the conditions which motivate the consent to entry and presence, are the very conditions to which the tasks established for the Force in the General Assembly resolution, 4 November, are directed. Therefore, I assume it to be recognized that as long as the task, thus prescribed, is not completed, the reasons for the consent of the Government remains valid, and that withdrawal of this consent before

[110] AC UNEF 14 March 1957, *supra* note 5, 25.
[111] *Ibid.*
[112] Cf. Fröhlich, *Keeping Track*, *supra* note 1.
[113] Cf. Luard, *supra* note 1, 443–466.

> completion of the task would run counter to the acceptance by Egypt of the decision by the General Assembly.[114]

Thus, in Hammarskjöld's view, consent to the mission also entailed acceptance of the continued presence and activity of the force: the government undertook to accept the purpose and goal of the mission until its mandate was fulfilled. In the event of differences of opinion over the completion of the mission, the UN and Egypt could negotiate – an option that Hammarskjöld, as he explained to Fawzi, wanted to be understood as safeguarding the rights of the UN: 'We both have to reserve our freedom of action, but all the same we can go ahead hoping that the controversial situation will not arise.'[115] In the case of irreconcilable points of view, the Secretary-General would have to take the question to the General Assembly. Fawzi immediately rejected this reading, repeated the view of his government and threatened to cancel the whole undertaking if even the most minor restriction on Egypt's sovereign rights was open to debate.[116]

Hammarskjöld sought to bridge the differences with the so-called good faith agreement,[117] which would establish the procedural modalities for a UNEF withdrawal and safeguard the position of the UN in the event of unilateral termination by Egypt, without affecting Egypt's sovereignty in sensitive areas. The good faith agreement was the result of numerous drafts and diplomatic formulations of compromise that was finally accepted as an annex to Hammarskjöld's UNEF report of 20 November. The crucial passage reads:

> The Government of Egypt declares that, when exercising its sovereign rights on any matter concerning the presence and functioning of UNEF, it will be guided, in good faith, by its acceptance of General Assembly resolution 1000 (ES-I) of November 5, 1956 … The United Nations takes note of this declaration of the Government of Egypt and declares that the activities of UNEF will be guided in good faith, by the task established for the Force in the aforementioned resolutions; in particular, the United Nations, understanding this to correspond to the wishes of the Government of Egypt, reaffirms its willingness to maintain UNEF until its task is completed.[118]

[114] KB DHS, *Dag Hammarskjöld*, Aide Mémoire to Fawzi, 12 November 1956, *supra* note 3.
[115] *Ibid.*, Cable to Leary with Letter to Fawzi, 13 November 1956.
[116] *Ibid.*, Mahmoud Fawzi, Communication to Dag Hammarskjöld, 13 November 1956 and 14 November 1956.
[117] A. D'Amato, 'Good Faith' (1984) 7 *Encyclopaedia of Public International Law* 107.
[118] Cf. Cordier and Foote, *supra* note 1, 375–376.

Hammarskjöld recorded his interpretation of the text in several notes in the file on the 'Suez story'[119] and added it to a memorandum on 5 August 1957.[120] He admits that there was an 'element of gambling'[121] in the repeated queries and rejections or declarations of differences of opinion. On 16 and 17 November, Hammarskjöld negotiated with Nasser for seven hours; the latter finally made up his mind to accept the text after thrice threatening to call off the entire operation.[122] In his memorandum Hammarskjöld stresses that Egypt thereby recognised the obligation to accept the character and mandate of UNEF included in its agreement to the resolution of the General Assembly. Although a clearer formulation in terms of international law would have been desirable, it could not be realised. Time was of utmost importance for all of the problems that Hammarskjöld and the Committee dealt with. In a first assessment at a committee meeting on 19 November, Hammarskjöld presented the following balance:

> I can confirm ... that the time factor was vital ... I also concluded that legal texts of the usual nature were of little importance in a situation of the present nature, because it was, of course, the moral and political forces which decided the issue, and not this or that written word.[123]

The intermittent success and eventual dissolution of the good faith agreement is a good case in point of the ambivalent stand that Hammarskjöld took. The compromise that developed out of these considerations did not, in the end, forestall the Egyptian abrogation of the agreement in 1967 and the subsequent withdrawal of UNEF.[124] Hammarskjöld clearly seems to have been aware of this inherent fault in such a construction when in November 1956 he said: 'If we cannot base the United Nations action on a reasonable degree of good faith, then, of course, we have embarked on an extremely dangerous adventure.'[125]

[119] KB DHS, Drafts for Aide Mémoire: n.d., *supra* note 3.
[120] *Dag Hammarskjöld*, Aide Mémoire, 5 August 1957, *supra* note 3.
[121] *Ibid.*
[122] KB DHS, *Dag Hammarskjöld*, Aide Mémoire, 5 August 1957, *supra* note 3, 7–8.
[123] AC UNEF 19 November 1956, *supra* note 5, 1.
[124] Cf. Y. Tandon, 'UNEF, the Secretary-General, and International Diplomacy in the Third Arab-Israeli War' (1968) 22 *International Organization* 529. Pearson, *supra* note 26, 260–261, recalls a discussion with Hammarskjöld after Nasser had insisted on his right to bring about the withdrawal of UNEF: 'I remember reacting quite strongly, but not violently. I said, "This is going to cause trouble in the future." Hammarskjöld said: "Oh, don't worry about it, because I told him [Nasser] that condition was quite inadmissible." It did not turn out to be inadmissible eleven years later.'
[125] AC UNEF 14 November 1956, *supra* note 5, 26.

16.4 Conclusion

An adventure it was in any case. Hammarskjöld's actions were also motivated by his realisation that UNEF was a precedent for future missions and an important step in the constitutional development of the world organisation.[126] He attached great importance to the fact that UNEF 'get[s] the start it deserves and set[s] a precedent which the United Nations needs'.[127] UNEF not only established the UN peacekeeping forces but also the central role played by the Secretary-General in this context: 'He organizes the force, writes its terms of reference, appoints the commander, negotiates the necessary agreements with the parties, including the host countries, and handles numerous smaller and larger diplomatic problems connected with the mission.'[128] The series of personal mandates from the General Assembly resolutions highlights Hammarskjöld's very prominent role in establishing UNEF: 'While the original conception of the emergency force was not his, Hammarskjöld clearly was the chief agent in its construction and the formulation of its basic principles, and was of course its primary administrative officer.'[129] Urquhart records a number of qualities that Hammarskjöld displayed during the crisis and the detailed reconstruction of the days after the Israeli attack clearly give proof to each of them:

> In all this hubbub the Secretary-General must keep a clear head and a balanced picture of the situation. He must preserve an imaginative, constructive, and forward-looking approach to a constantly shifting series of problems and a kaleidoscopic panorama of changing national policies. Hammarskjöld, by his capacity for concentration and thinking ahead, was a master at this game and dominated these hectic periods by his stamina, intellectual energy, imagination, and skill in political and legal drafting and in thinking out ways around apparently insurmountable obstacles. He was instantly and instinctively aware of the ramifications and possible repercussions of any given course of action and almost automatically thought out in advance the combination of results, both good and bad, that could be expected from a particular move, as well as the

[126] Cf. M. Fröhlich, 'The Quest for a Political Philosophy of World Organization', in S. Ask and A. Mark-Jungkvist (eds.), *The Adventure of Peace: Dag Hammarskjöld and the Future of the UN* (2005), 130–145.

[127] Press Conference 12 November 1956; cf. Cordier and Foote, *supra* note 1, 367.

[128] K. Skjelsbaek and G. Fermann, 'The UN Secretary-General and the Mediation of International Disputes', in J. Bercovitch (ed.), *Resolving International Conflicts: The Theory and Practice of Mediation* (1996), 97–98.

[129] Rovine, *supra* note 35, 291.

> alternative moves that might be made ... In such circumstances only firm and unquestioned leadership can provide the impetus required to keep all the various participants moving in relative harmony and in the same direction.[130]

Pearson, in his Nobel Peace Prize speech, humbly said that Hammarskjöld deserved most credit for the establishment of UNEF.[131] UNEF was, however, not one man's achievement but was made possible inter alia by the combination of Pearson's idea, Bunche's organisational ability and Hammarskjöld's principled stand and leadership. Here was a 'dream team' of international organisation; coincidentally, all three were awarded the Nobel Peace Prize.

One crucial condition for the realisation of this innovation undoubtedly was the strong support from the United States, which can be seen not only from Eisenhower's praise of Hammarskjöld citied at the beginning. Kyle concludes that the United States had 'as a matter of conscious policy, delegate[ed] much of its policy-making ... to the Secretary-General'.[132] Washington had decided to place its cards with the UN in an effort to mitigate a major crisis in the Western alliance and to fend off Soviet influence in the Middle East. As the meeting with the American delegation in Hammarskjöld's office on 7 November illustrates, the Secretary-General closely worked with the United States, inter alia agreeing that the possible inclusion of Czechoslovakian and Romanian troops in UNEF should be denied.[133] No wonder that Under-Secretary of State Herbert Hoover, in a Meeting of the National Security Council on 8 November, praised the Secretary-General: 'Mr. Hammarskjöld', he said, had 'matured greatly in recent months. The only question seemed to be his physical endurance. He had had no sleep for three days'.[134] Secretary Hoover added that Mr Hammarskjöld seemed 'without question to be on our side'.[135] From what can be seen from the UN documents, this assessment needs to be specified in order to avoid the simple conclusion that Hammarskjöld just followed Washington's course. Hammarskjöld was on the US side as much as the US was on the UN side: they had a common interest in strengthening UN influence on the crisis. The strong and early support for the UN, in Eisenhower's view, was important in precluding the chance that the Soviet Union may have taken the lead in the UN efforts, not only branding

[130] Urquhart, *supra* note 1, 176–177.
[131] L. Pearson, *Diplomacy in the Nuclear Age* (1959), 104.
[132] Kyle, *supra* note 1, 493. [133] Glennon, *supra* note 14, 1070.
[134] *Ibid.*, 1082. [135] *Ibid.*

the UK and France as aggressors and diverting attention from Hungary, but also possibly calling for economic sanctions against Israel which may even have called for a role of the US Sixth Fleet as the only force capable of implementing such sanctions.[136] In his dealings with Britain and Israel, Hammarskjöld consciously used pressure from Washington to further the UN agenda and, in a letter to the American President from 24 November 1956, acknowledged the Americans' indispensable help.[137] The Soviet Union, on the other hand, had compromised its commitment to the UN Charter principles by the concomitant invasion in Hungary.[138] Moscow certainly had a strong influence on the development of the crisis but was not a major actor in the diplomacy leading up to the establishment of UNEF.

Kyle unambiguously judges: 'The organisation which emerged with enhanced credit from the whole crisis was the United Nations; the individual was Dag Hammarskjöld.'[139] Miller also sees the Suez crisis as 'the real turning point in Mr. Hammarskjöld's world posture': '[T]he complex of events allowed his diplomatic skills to have catalytic impact of much importance.'[140] UNEF's immediate success – a UN peacekeeping force as a theoretical and practical innovation – made the saying 'Leave it to Dag!' a slogan of international diplomacy. He took on several other critical tasks right up to the peacekeeping efforts in the Congo[141] which would also bring him into direct opposition to the Soviet Union, who dramatically had called for his resignation in the so-called troika proposal.[142] As Suez already showed, a strong Secretary-General of the United Nations is not automatically what its Member States, especially the powerful ones, want to have. The resolution of the Suez crisis left clear reservations towards Hammarskjöld on the side of the British: Kyle contrasts two assessments

[136] Cf. the detailed account from the White House's perspective in D.N. Nichols, *Eisenhower 1956. The President's Year of Crisis. Suez and the Brink of War* (2011), 218–271.

[137] KB DHS, *Dag Hammarskjöld*, Letter to Dwight D. Eisenhower, 24 November 1956, *supra* note 3.

[138] The political constellation that had made it possible to contain the Suez crisis within the framework of the United Nations also explains why it was not possible to find a similarly constructive solution for the simultaneous crisis in Hungary (Lash, *supra* note 41, 111). Here, too, Hammarskjöld had tried to establish a role for the United Nations by offering to mediate and to visit Hungary. Consistent rejection by the Soviet Union and the puppet government in Hungary made further steps – even in the General Assembly – impossible.

[139] Kyle, *supra* note 1, 558.

[140] Miller, *supra* note 1, 93.

[141] Cf. Urquhart, *supra* note 1, 545–589.

[142] Cf. Fröhlich, *Political Ethics*, *supra* note 1, 164–170.

by Pearson and Dixon. Whereas the Canadian wrote '[t]hank God we have Dag Hammarskjöld as Secretary-General … [h]e has really done magnificent work under conditions of almost unbelievable pressure',[143] the Briton, echoing earlier statements, wrote '[w]e may find it inconvenient … to have to deal with a Secretary-General who will be elevated to the status of a Pope with temporal as well as spiritual powers'.[144] In a further assessment, Dixon wrote in a secret memorandum to Selwyn Lloyd in January 1958: 'The outcome of the crisis left him [Hammarskjöld] more than a symbol or even an executive; he had become a force.'[145] Dixon's ambivalent position towards the crisis and the role of the UN here finds its expression in what one may call 'faintly disguised praise'[146] for the Secretary-General. Going beyond Dixon's assessment there are, however, strong signs of a rather profound estrangement between Hammarskjöld and the British after Suez.[147] Also the French, under General de Gaulle, showed a deep aversion towards the UN and its Secretary-General and this, again, was partly motivated by the Suez affair.

The story so far has left out the deep spiritual aspect of Hammarskjöld's personality as portrayed in his posthumously published diary *Markings*.[148] The Suez crisis was a time of particularly frequent entries, some of which dealt with the political events discussed above. In a section dated 1 to 7 November, in the midst of many reports and sometimes confusing ultimatums and consultations, Hammarskjöld wrote: 'Without our being aware of it, our fingers are so guided that a pattern is created when thread gets caught in the web.'[149] This characteristic conception of a comprehensive sense that can be manifested in personal actions is also obvious in the entry for 17 November 1956, in which he writes of the constant presence of divine will: 'My device – if any: / Numen semper adest. / In that case: if

143 Kyle, *supra* note 1, 481. 144 *Ibid.*

145 Cited in A. Orford, *International Authority and the Responsibility to Protect* (2011), 68.

146 Louis, *supra* note 77, 688.

147 Cf. *supra* note 73. E. Johnson, '"The Umpire on Whom the Sun Never Sets": Dag Hammarskjöld's Political Role and the British at Suez' (1997) 8(1) *Diplomacy & Statecraft* 249; when Dixon spoke of the British government's problems regarding its wish to use the salvage fleet, Hammarskjöld had answered rather coldly: 'In the face of such difficulties, governments sometimes fall.' See Kyle, *supra* note 1, 512.

148 Cf. Fröhlich, *Political Ethics*, *supra* note 1. On the ethical side of the UN Secretary-General see also recently K.J. Kille (ed.), *The UN Secretary-General and Moral Authority: Ethics and Religion in International Leadership* (2007).

149 D. Hammarskjöld, *Markings* (1964) (translated from the Swedish by L. Sjöberg and W.H. Auden), 140.

uneasy – why?'[150] Though it may seem astonishing that at this hectic time Hammarskjöld was writing and reflecting on sentences like these, one is compelled to the conclusion that precisely this preoccupation is a key to the intensity of his work at this time.

In an entry for 29 November, against the backdrop of his growing personal responsibility, he dwells on the question of fame and humility:

> Faulkner: Our final wish is to have scribbled on the wall 'Kilroy was here.' / The last ditch of the enemy. We can sacrifice ourselves completely to that which is beyond and above us – and still hope that the memory of our choice shall remain tied to our name or, at least, that the future generations shall understand why and how we acted. At times it seems to us that the bitterness we feel when we fail at an attempted task lies in this: that our failure will condemn our efforts themselves to oblivion. / O contradiction! O last stand! If only the goal can justify the sacrifice, how, then, can you attach a shadow of importance to the question whether or not the memory of your efforts will be associated with your name? If you do, is it not all too obvious that you are still being influenced in your actions by that vain dead dream about 'posterity'?[151]

The reference to Faulkner and the popular slogan among US soldiers in the Second World War can be most probably tied to Faulkner's speech at receiving the National Book Award for Fiction in February 1955. Faulkner had said:

> By artist I mean of course everyone who has tried to create something which was not here before him, with no other tools and material than the uncommerciable ones of the human spirit; who has tried to carve, no matter how crudely, in the tongue of the human spirit, 'Kilroy was here'.[152]

With this, notwithstanding his own references to guidance and humility in spiritual terms, one could of course see Hammarskjöld as the artist of the peaceful resolution of the Suez crisis. His means were not tangible resources of power, but rather moral force that subsequently came to be the classical rationale of numerous peacekeeping missions. In a radio message to the soldiers of UNEF at the end of 1956, Hammarskjöld said:

150 *Ibid.* 151 *Ibid.*

152 B. Erling, *A Reader's Guide to Dag Hammarskjöld's Waymarks* (1999), 168. See also the German edition of *Markings* – Dag Hammarskjöld, *Zeichen am Weg*, edited by M. Fröhlich, 2nd edition (2012), 161. It is interesting to note that the reference to Kilroy surfaced in a very direct sense when the sunken tug *Edgar Bonnet* was lifted during the salvage operations in the canal. The ship had written the very same slogan over its bridge. Hammarskjöld was present at the lifting of the ship on 25 March 1957. Cf. UN Photos 65609 and 128305.

> As members of the United Nations Emergency Force you are taking part in an experience that is new in history ... You are the front line of a moral force which extends around the world, and you have behind you the support of millions everywhere. Much will depend upon the example that this Force sets. Your success can have profound effect for good, not only in the present emergency, but on future prospects for building a world order, of which we may all one day be proud.[153]

The promise and problems of the Suez experience still accompany peacekeepers around the world today.

[153] Cordier and Foote, *supra* note 1, Vol. III, 405.

17

Breaking free

Dag Hammarskjöld, good offices and heads of international organisations

AOIFE O'DONOGHUE

17.1 Introduction

Besides being highly influential in establishing the role of heads of international organisations within international law, Dag Hammarskjöld's endeavours significantly altered the office of UN Secretary-General. In contemporary international law, heads of international organisations hold important positions. Dag Hammarskjöld's effect on the office of UN Secretary-General and, more particularly, on the good offices role of heads of international organisations, is arguably unparalleled. His impact was partly a consequence of the groundwork, at both the UN and League of Nations, of previous holders of the office of Secretary-General. Indeed Tryge Lie can be greatly credited for developing the office of UN Secretary-General. Nonetheless, these officeholders did not instigate the transformation achieved by Dag Hammarskjöld.[1] He went beyond merely carrying out the office of Secretary-General; he understood what the office could conceivably become if developed correctly and, as such, greatly expanded its remit, establishing what is recognised as the contemporary role of heads of international organisations.

Dag Hammarskjöld's impact is so potent that the role now played by heads of international organisations, and particularly the UN Secretary-General, in the contemporary international legal order would have been inconceivable before he entered office.[2] Dag Hammarskjöld advanced the

Aoife O'Donoghue is Senior Lecturer in Law, Durham Law School.

[1] Under Article 6 of the Covenant of the League of Nations the Secretary-General held a role limited to that of a purely administrative officer.

[2] J.L. Kunz, 'The Legal Position of the Secretary-General of the United Nations' (1946) 40 *AJIL* 786, at 786.

independent voice of heads of international organisations and the key role they play in conflict management and resolution. This chapter focuses on the UN Secretary-General and, more particularly, the role played by Dag Hammarskjöld in developing good offices. The purpose of this chapter is to consider Dag Hammarskjöld's impact upon the role of UN Secretary-General and good offices. This will be realised through an examination of both his good offices and those of the Secretaries-General who followed.

Holding unique positions in international law enables the heads of international organisations to engage with conflict, post-conflict and transitional states differently to other international actors. Strictly, as heads of secretariats, they are first bound by the internal rules of their organisations, second by international institutional law and third by general international law.[3] Yet, these legal parameters stop somewhat short of articulating the full extent of the role, which certain heads of international organisations, particularly UN Secretaries-General, have carved for themselves. Dag Hammarskjöld, in moving beyond the strict limits of the Charter and the role played by his predecessors at the UN and the League of Nations, set the tone for future UN Secretaries-General and arguably other heads of international organisations. A UN Secretary-General may now intervene in a conflict on a number of bases; on a UN mandate, on his own initiative independent of a mandate or, alternatively, at the request of parties. In each of these cases, the Secretary-General will either decide the form and structure of the conflict management or will be highly influential in its establishment and design. This is far beyond what was first envisaged for the UN Secretary-General.[4] Dag Hammarskjöld enabled the office of UN Secretary-General to break free from the other organs of the UN and strengthened the independent role of the office.

Despite good offices' rather nebulous legal underpinnings, beginning with the establishment of the UN, contemporary good offices have emerged as one of the foremost forms of pacific settlement. Generally speaking, contemporary good offices consist of the heads of international organisations using their position to undertake a range of dispute management practices. While states and other international actors may undertake good offices, since the establishment of the UN the heads of international organisations have become far more active in this field. This chapter considers how much this is the result of Dag Hammarskjöld's

[3] P. Sands, P. Klein and D.W. Bowett, *Bowett's Law of International Institutions* (2009), 303–314.

[4] Report of the Preparatory Commission of the United Nations (23 December 1945) Chapter VIII, section 2, paras 8–17.

actions. This examination requires an analysis of the legal structure of good offices and the UN, as well as the practice that Dag Hammarskjöld and other Secretaries-General instituted.

Ultimately, this piece assesses how much Dag Hammarskjöld can claim credit for the present-day operation of good offices and, further, what attribution should be given to him in understanding the present roles of heads of international organisations. In asking these questions, several other issues are also considered. For example, what were the legal structures for good offices that Dag Hammarskjöld worked within, how were these transformed by practice during his time in office and how much of this change has formed part of contemporary practice? Further, what insights may be garnered from the development of good offices, in relation to contemporary dispute settlement and, more importantly, the role of heads of international organisations as international actors? This chapter seeks to understand what elements of the changes brought about by Dag Hammarskjöld remain relevant today.

17.2 What are good offices?

Good offices possess no international legal definition. Rather, a multitude of various treaty definitions, General Assembly resolutions, and other documents set out its broad parameters. As one of the many methods available for the pacific settlement of disputes, good offices emerge as a practice largely associated with the heads of international organisations, particularly the UN Secretary-General.[5] Indeed, it is the practice of UN Secretaries-General which is the best guide to good offices operation in

[5] For an excellent overview of international dispute settlement see J.G. Merrils, *International Dispute Settlement* (2011) particularly with regard to good offices, 222–225, as well as L. Gordenker, *Maintenance of Peace* (1989), 144; T.M. Franck, 'The Secretary-General's Role in Conflict Resolution: Past Present and Pure Conjecture' (1995) 6 *EJIL* 360, at 360; A. Brehio, 'Good Offices of the Secretary General as Preventative Measures' (1998) 30 *NYU Journal of International Law and Politics* 589; B.G. Ramcharan, 'The Good Offices of the United Nations Secretary-General in the Field of Human Rights' (1982) 76 *AJIL* 130; id., *Humanitarian Good Offices in International Law* (1983); K.R. Simmonds, 'Good Offices and the Secretary General' (1959) 29 *Nordisk Tidsskrift International Relations* 330; T. Fischer, 'Switzerland's Good Offices: A Changing Concept 1945–2002' (Nr 37, Centre for International Studies, 2002); W.J. Dixon, 'Third-party Techniques for Preventing Conflict Escalation and Promoting Pacific Settlement' (1996) 50 *International Organization* 653; F.O. Vicuna, 'New Dispute Settlement Procedures' (1999) 31 *Studies in Transnational Legal Policy* 59; R. Probst, *'Good Offices' in the Light of Swiss International Practice and Experience* (1989); I. Johnston, 'Role of the UN Secretary-General: The Power of Persuasion Based on Law' (2003) 9 *Global Governance* 441; Report of the Secretary

the twenty-first century. UN Secretary-General Javier Pèrez de Cuéllar argued that good offices are a form of 'quiet diplomacy' and, as such, developing a legal analysis is made more difficult by the lack of documentation and muted terms of its operation.[6] The legal literature and analysis is also somewhat sparse.

Generally, good offices are a form of dispute settlement which maintains numerous techniques for resolution and is capable of evolving alongside a dispute. As such, its exact content is less important than its reliance on the office undertaking the role together with its ability to evolve with the conflict.[7] The importance of the office and the personality of the individual undertaking good offices is evident in its description. An office holder undertakes 'her' good offices, this subjectivity ties the process to the person holding the office, a point which will be returned to in the context of Dag Hammarskjöld.

Good offices developed from a narrow, state-led form of diplomacy to incorporating a broad range of pacific settlement activities. One of the key features of its evolution has been the transition from state-based, to non-state actors being the prime drivers of its operation.[8] Good offices include: facilitating talks or other procedural obligations, active participation in negotiating, implementing, adjudicating and supervising peace agreements as well as settlements involving humanitarian and human rights law, in addition to mediation or conciliation.[9] Good offices transform alongside the conflict, as they descend into violence, during the conflict and afterward, as a method of preventing and ending the violence as well as reconstructing peace including monitoring both ceasefires and peace agreements. Thus, good offices change as circumstances require.

Historically, various international and regional treaties include a rather narrow interpretation of good offices. The 1899/1907 Convention for the Pacific Settlement of International Disputes defines good offices under Article 2 '[i]n case of disagreement or dispute, before an appeal to arms, the Contracting Parties agree to have recourse as far as circumstances

General, 'In Larger Freedom: Towards Development, Security and Human Rights for All', UN Doc. A/59/2005 (2005).

6 R. Adams and B. Kingsbury (eds.), *United Nations, Divided World* (1996), 133.

7 A. O'Donoghue, 'Good Offices: Grasping the Place of Law in Conflict', Society of Legal Scholars, Legal Studies (2013), at http://onlinelibrary.wiley.com/doi/10.1111/lest.12029/pdf.

8 See Vicuna, *supra* note 5, at 60.

9 See for example the description in Ramcharan, *Humanitarian*, *supra* note 5, at 35–51, id., 'The Good Offices', *supra* note 5.

allow to the good offices or mediation of one or more friendly powers'.[10] This conception of good offices separates the process of mediation and identifies it closely with conciliation. Arguably, while maintaining a distinctive form, good offices include both mediation and conciliation, as well as other forms of dispute settlement activities.

Under Article 3 of the 1899/1907 Convention, powers that are 'strangers to the dispute' should offer their good offices on their own initiative.[11] This established a right of initiative as part of the practice of good offices. The significance of this right of initiative became evident as multilateralism evolved in the post-Charter era, particularly as, from the outset, UN Secretaries-General became involved in situations without specific mandates or invitations. Article 6 of the 1899/1907 Convention states that the practice of good offices has 'exclusively the character of advice and never has ... binding force'.[12] This non-binding character remains, unless the parties agree otherwise or the Secretary-General is acting under a Chapter VII Security Council resolution.

Various heads of international organisations employ good offices, particularly and most comparable to the UN, the Commonwealth Secretary-General and the Director General of the WTO. The Commonwealth increasingly engages in good offices; the Millbrook Commonwealth Action Programme on the Harare Declaration, 1995, the Harare Commonwealth Declaration, 1991 and the Coolum Declaration all set good offices as a priority for the Commonwealth Secretary-General.[13]

Under the dispute settlement process within the WTO, its Director General has a good offices role. Article 5 of the Dispute Settlement Understanding states that '[g]ood offices, conciliation and mediation are procedures that are undertaken voluntarily if the parties to the dispute so agree'. Under Article 5.6 the '[t]he Director-General may, acting in an *ex officio* capacity, offer good offices, conciliation or mediation with the

[10] Art. 2, 1907 Convention for the Pacific Settlement of International Disputes, is identical in both conventions.

[11] *Ibid.*, Art. 3

[12] For other examples of Treaty based good offices see 1985 Vienna Convention on the Protection of the Ozone Layer, 1513 UNTS 293, Art. 11, 1948 The American Treaty on Pacific Settlement, 30 UNTS 55.

[13] The Millbrook Commonwealth Action Programme on the Harare Declaration, 1995, Issued by Heads of Government, New Zealand, 12 November 1995; The Harare Commonwealth Declaration, 1991, Issued by Heads of Government in Harare, Zimbabwe; The Coolum Declaration, The Commonwealth in the 21st Century: Continuity and Renewal 2002, all available from the Commonwealth website, www.thecommonwealth.org.

view to assisting Members to settle a dispute'.[14] While, arguably, the UN Secretaries-General's good offices remains the most developed, the role played by both these heads of organisations suggests that good offices is now more widely regarded as part of the responsibilities of heads of certain international organisations.

17.3 UN good offices

The 'In Larger Freedom' report acknowledges the importance of:

> using the Secretary-General's Good Offices to help resolve conflicts ... but we could undoubtedly save many more lives ... I urge Member States to allocate additional resources to the Secretary-General for his good offices function.[15]

The UN Secretary-General's good offices grew out of the Charter's legal structure. Article 2(4) together with Chapters VI and VII of the Charter set the basic parameters under which pacific dispute settlement occurs. These articles are the springboards from which good offices emerged, though to fully understand its legal position, it is necessary to move beyond the Charter.[16] For example, Article 99 states that 'the Secretary-General may bring to the attention of the Security Council any matter which in his opinion may threaten the maintenance of international peace and security'.[17] This article enables a Secretary-General to independently assess whether a threat to international peace and security exists.[18] Good offices go unmentioned in the Charter, and therefore it is

[14] Under Art. 22.6 if a Panel or Appellate review is already underway, the Director General may appoint an arbitrator if disputing parties cannot agree on deadlines. 'A Handbook on the WTO Dispute Settlement System: A WTO Secretariat Publication' (2004) 94 Dispute Settlement Understanding, Annex 2 World Trade Agreement

[15] See 'In Larger Freedom', *supra* note 5, at 30.

[16] Chapter XV of the Charter sets out the functions of the Secretariat and the Secretary-General; this accompanied with Chapter VI, Chapter VII and Chapter XIV set out the dispute settlement procedures available to the UN. While there is no specific mention of good offices anywhere in the Charter, subsequent practice, including resolutions of the Security Council and General Assembly, has made it an integral part of the UN's dispute settlements measures.

[17] Kofi Annan argued that 'successive Secretary-Generals ... have invoked this article very sparingly'. See above, Chapter 2, at 40.

[18] This has since been supplemented by the General Assembly Resolutions inter alia UNGA Res. 37/10; The Manila Declaration on the Peaceful Settlement of Disputes between States (15 November 1982), UNGA Res. 43/51; Declaration on the Prevention and Removal of Disputes and Situations Which May Threaten International Peace and Security and on the Role of the United Nations in this Field (5 December 1988), UNGA Res. 50/50; United

the resolutions of the General Assembly and Security Council, coupled with practice, that require consideration.[19]

The UN Handbook on the Peaceful Settlement of Disputes defines good offices as when:

> [s]tates party to a dispute are unable to settle it directly, a third party, may offer his [or her] good offices as a means of preventing further deterioration of the dispute and as a method of facilitating efforts towards a peaceful settlement of the dispute.[20]

Further it states that, '[t]he third party exercising good offices normally seeks to encourage the parties to the dispute to resume negotiations, thus providing them with a channel of communication'.[21] This is a basic outline of what good offices encapsulates within the UN structure; albeit making no mention of involvement beyond facilitation or encouragement, it does not exclude these possibilities either.

The General Assembly Resolution on the Peaceful Settlement of Disputes between States affirms that the 'Secretary-General should make full use of the provisions of the Charter'.[22] General Assembly Resolution 43/51 also examined the good offices of the Secretary-General, stating that the 'Secretary-General if approached by a State or States directly concerned with a dispute or situation should respond swiftly by urging the States to seek a solution ... and by offering his good offices'.[23] It goes on

Nations Model Rules for the Conciliation of Disputes between States (11 December 1995) UNGA Res. 57/26, Prevention and Peaceful Settlement of Disputes (3 February 2003); Johnstone argues that UNSC Res. 1366 extends the power of Article 99 somewhat in that it enables the Secretary-General to bring to the attention of the Security Council cases of serious violations of international law. See Johnston, *supra* note 5, at 441–442.

[19] UNGA Res. 43/51 Declaration on the Prevention and Removal of Disputes and Situations Which May Threaten International Peace and Security and on the Role of the United Nations in this Field (5 December 1988); UNGA Res. 37/10 The Manila Declaration on the Peaceful Settlement of Disputes between States (15 November 1982).

[20] The United Nations Handbook on the Peaceful Settlement of Disputes Between States, UN Doc. OLA/COD/2394, para. 101.

[21] *Ibid.*, at para. 102.

[22] General Assembly Resolution 37/10, The Manila Declaration on the Peaceful Settlement of International Disputes, 15 November 1982. Part II 6. It also states in Part I, 5 that 'States shall seek in good faith ... settlement of their international disputes by any of the following means: negotiation, inquiry, mediation, conciliation, arbitration ... or other peaceful means of their own choice, including good offices'.

[23] General Assembly Resolution 43/51 Declaration on the Prevention and Removal of Disputes and Situations Which May Threaten International Peace and Security and on the Role of the United Nations in this Field, 5 December 1988, Part 20. It goes on in Part 21 to state: 'The Secretary-General should consider approaching the States ... in an

to say that 'The Secretary-General should … consider making full use of fact finding capabilities'.[24] These resolutions were followed in 1995 and 2003 by resolutions reaffirming this role.[25] The Security Council, meeting for the first time at Head of State level, also requested that the Secretary-General continue to make use of good offices.[26]

Together with more specific mandates, these resolutions establish the legal and political basis for good offices within the UN. In combination, these put beyond dispute that good offices form part of the Secretary-General's function. Thus, it is the parameters of action which are open to discussion and not good offices' legitimacy. Both the Security Council and General Assembly have utilised good offices on many occasions, some of which are explored in the next section. The Charter, resolutions and specific mandates of the Security Council and General Assembly are integral to understanding the good offices role which Secretaries-General carved for themselves.

17.3.1 Security Council mandates

Article 98 is the basis on which the Security Council uses the Secretary-General's good offices. Under this article, the Security Council can ask the Secretary-General to carry out any activities that it considers necessary. Chapters VI and VII outline the Security Council's role in maintaining international peace and security and enable it to mandate the Secretary-General to take steps necessary to carry out this function. While actions taken under Chapter VII provide a Secretary-General with particularly strong legal foundations, the manoeuvrability and independence of the Secretary-General in carrying out the role must also be carefully maintained.

In 1946 the Security Council first used the Secretary-General's good offices. The conflict centred on the presence of Soviet troops in occupation of the Northern Azeri region of Iran. Trygve Lie, already involved on his own initiative, was asked by the Security Council, in the absence of the

effort to prevent it from becoming a threat to the maintenance of international peace and security'.

24 *Ibid.*, at part 22.

25 General Assembly Resolution 50/50 United Nations Model Rules for the Conciliation of Disputes between States, 11 December 1995; GA Resolution 57/26, Prevention and Peaceful Settlement of Disputes, 3 February 2003.

26 UN Doc. S/235000, 13 January 1992, at 4.

USSR, to have all parties report to him on troop withdrawal.[27] In the same year, the Security Council asked Trygve Lie, again already engaged on his own initiative, to be involved in the Commission to settle a dispute on the northern Greek frontier between Greece and Yugoslavia.[28] These two incidences show the Security Council's early confidence in both the office of the Secretary-General and Trygve Lie as incumbent in this position.

The Security Council asked Trygve Lie to report on events in Korea.[29] These reports are key to understanding the developing character of good offices as Trygve Lie used the opportunity to make a statement on his own understanding of events as opposed to an impartial account. Franck argues that, with particular regard to Security Council mandates, such reports enable a Secretary-General to separate himself from both the disputants and the Security Council.[30] In doing so, Trygve Lie laid the foundations for the actions subsequently taken by Dag Hammarskjöld.

17.3.2 General Assembly mandates

Unlike the Security Council, the General Assembly has asked the Secretary-General to become involved in a specific conflict on very few occasions. Rather, the General Assembly has been prolific in reaffirming the importance of the Secretary-General's good offices as a key aspect of the pacific settlement of disputes.[31] In 1950 the General Assembly established the Permanent Commission for Good Offices, but this initiative was not followed by any concerted efforts to actually engage in the practice.[32] Despite the ability to give the Secretary-General whatever instruction it wishes, and the adoption of the 1950 Uniting for Peace Resolution, the General Assembly was slow to give a specific mandate.[33]

[27] SC Resolution 2, The Iranian Question, 30 January 1946.

[28] SC Resolution 15, The Greek Question, 19 December 1946.

[29] Gordenker, *supra* note 5, at 144.

[30] Franck, *supra* note 5, at 384. Reports of the Secretary-General to the Security Council since 1994 are available at the United Nations website at: www.un.org/documents/.

[31] For example, GA Resolutions 37/10 The Manila Declaration on the Peaceful Settlement of Disputes between States, 15 November 1982; GA Resolution 43/51 Declaration on the Prevention and Removal of Disputes and Situations Which May Threaten International Peace and Security and on the Role of the United Nations in this Field, 5 December 1988; GA Resolution 50/50 United Nations Model Rules for the Conciliation of Disputes between States, 11 December 1995; GA Resolution 57/26, Prevention and Peaceful Settlement of Disputes, 3 February 2003.

[32] GA Resolution 379(V) Establishment of a Permanent Commission of Good Offices, 17 November 1950.

[33] GA Resolution 377(V) United For Peace, 3 November 1950.

Trygve Lie was only set administrative tasks within dispute settlement missions rather than any separate mandate for active involvement in dispute resolution.

This lack of General Assembly activity can be explained by the more proactive role the Security Council was undertaking at the time. The Peking Formula, an initiative of Dag Hammarskjöld's explored below, is indelibly linked to the differences between Security Council and General Assembly mandates. The role of Chapter VII and its binding character differentiates the mandates of both organs and, as such, changes the relationship both have with the Secretary-General. Nonetheless, prior to Dag Hammarskjöld taking office, the General Assembly had not actively engaged the Secretary-General as a purveyor of good offices.

17.3.3 On the initiative of the Secretary-General

The Secretary-General, no matter who has held office, has always acted on his own initiative. The description of early Security Council mandates in the previous section, where Trygve Lie had, in fact, already become involved, are good examples of such activity. Trygve Lie's involvement in the Iranian question was one of the first such activities, unequivocally laying claim to the Secretary-General's ability to inquire into situations on his own initiative. The basis on which the Secretary-General becomes involved in negotiations is probably most closely linked to Article 99. To assess whether there is a threat to international peace and security the Secretary-General will, at the very least, have to investigate the circumstances. The ability of the Secretary-General to use Article 99 in circumstances where he felt there was a threat to international peace and security, aided in the development of autonomous initiatives and underpins the necessity to carry out the role as prescribed by the article, though it has been sparingly applied.

During the Korean conflict, Trygve Lie took a very public position. Luard suggests that '[i]t is arguable that he might have done better to leave the initiative more strictly in the hands of the Council and have acted … on the basis of instructions he received from the political bodies'.[34] Trygve Lie came under attack from the Soviet Union for his actions and, as a result, they refused to back him for another term in office. The United States resolved to veto any candidate other than Trygve Lie and, in the end,

[34] E. Luard, *A History of the United Nations, Volume 1: The Years of Western Domination 1945–1955* (1982), 349.

a General Assembly resolution extended Lie's term of office.[35] Thereafter, the Soviets 'consistently boycotted Trygve Lie on every occasion when he appeared'.[36] Nationalist China also refused to back Lie due to his support for communist China's representation at the UN. Thus Trygve Lie's ability to carry on good offices was radically reduced and eventually his position being untenable, hastening his retirement.

From these early episodes, what is clear is that the Secretary-General was not free to voice an unrequested opinion or become involved in a situation without being first solicited to do so or at least being ratified after he had become involved. If not, the wrath of certain members was sufficient to stop the Secretary-General from carrying out his office. From this basic outline of the circumstances in which Dag Hammarskjöld took over the role of Secretary-General and good offices, it is possible to examine the consequences of his term in office.

17.4 Dag Hammarskjöld and good offices

This section examines the good offices undertaken by Dag Hammarskjöld while he was the UN Secretary-General. Two key events, Congo and Peking hostages, are examined as essential examples of the changes brought about by Dag Hammarskjöld. The development of what was known as 'leave it to Dag' is also considered as an important feature of Dag Hammarskjöld's influence both on the role of Secretary-General and the use of the good offices.[37] 'Leave it to Dag' also highlights how much of the role of Secretary-General and good offices is linked to the personality holding the office.

'Leave it to Dag' emerged during the Suez crisis of 1956. Dag Hammarskjöld had already, before the UN asked for his involvement, held consultations in Israel and Egypt during the build-up to the Suez crisis. Subsequently, under instructions from the Security Council, Dag Hammarskjöld became embroiled in the conflict.[38] Suez is a good example of a Security Council mandate during Dag Hammarskjöld's time in office. The resolution required Dag Hammarskjöld to report on compliance with the armistice agreement and further to ensure its

[35] GA Resolution 492/(V) Continuation in Office of the Secretary-General of the United Nations, 1 November 1950.

[36] See Luard, *supra* note 34, at 352.

[37] Gordenker, *supra* note 5, at 352.

[38] SC Resolution 118 Complaint by France and the United Kingdom against Egypt, 13 October 1956; SC Resolution 119 Complaint by Egypt against France and the United Kingdom, 31 October 1956.

effectiveness. Dag Hammarskjöld played a central role in relaxing the tensions between the parties and indeed the parties were quite positive about his involvement.[39]

After the initial crisis had passed, Dag Hammarskjöld continued as a guarantor of the settlement, most probably extending the role beyond what the Security Council mandated; however, as Higgins points out, most of these resolutions tend to be vague in their exact parameters.[40] Dag Hammarskjöld's success in Suez led directly to the 'leave it to Dag' approach within the Security Council and established both Dag Hammarskjöld and the office of Secretary-General at the centre of pacific settlement of disputes; though how much this relied on Dag Hammarskjöld's personality is unquantifiable.

While it was in Suez that the confidence of UN members in Dag Hammarskjöld was established, it was in both Congo and in establishing the Peking formula that Dag Hammarskjöld pushed the basis for Secretary-General action. Both of these events moved authorisation for good offices beyond the membership and politics, and put the office of Secretary-General forward as an independent office, an international actor based within the Charter with guidance from UN organs as a secondary basis of action.

17.4.1 Congo

The conflict in Congo was a test for the UN and an indicator of the type of conflicts which would become central to its work. Congo was particularly important for Dag Hammarskjöld as he grappled not only with both conflicting parties within the country, but also with the wider interests pushing for various outcomes. Congo came to dominate his final years in office. Gordenker argues that 'nothing had more novelty than the role of the Secretary-General in organising and directing the deployment of armed battalions'.[41] Indeed, Congo was a watershed for both the UN and the office of Secretary-General.

Prior to the initial Security Council mandate, Dag Hammerskjöld used Article 99 to propose the deployment of peacekeepers in Congo.[42] The Security Council granted Dag Hammarskjöld an extremely wide and

[39] Gordenker, *supra* note 5, at 157.

[40] R. Higgins, *Problems and Process: International Law and How We Use It* (1994), 172.

[41] Gordenker, *supra* note 5, at 157.

[42] E. Luard, *A History of the United Nations*, Vol. II: *The Age of Decolonisation 1955–1965* (1989), at 220.

somewhat vague mandate, enabling him to take an extensive range of actions.[43] Dag Hammarskjöld took a very hands-on approach, which has not been replicated since. The wide remit granted by the Security Council mandate allowed Dag Hammarskjöld to react to changing events on the ground and to make decisions quickly.[44] The unfolding events in Congo are discussed in depth elsewhere (see Part III above) and, as such, this chapter will only linger upon its impact on good offices.

In describing his decision-making process, Dag Hammarskjöld outlined the legal hierarchy which a Secretary-General should follow in settling upon a plan of action. First, follow 'the principles and purposes of the Charter which are fundamental law and accepted by and binding on all States'.[45] Second, consider 'the body of legal doctrine and precepts that have been accepted by States generally and particularly as manifested in the resolutions of UN organs'.[46] Dag Hammarskjöld placed the Charter, and not the mandate given by members, either through the Security Council or General Assembly, as the first basis of his authority. This is significant in establishing the independence of the office of Secretary-General and the role maintained through good offices.

Dag Hammarskjöld argued that Member States, in signing the Charter, were binding themselves, on all occasions, to follow its precepts.[47] The hierarchy established under Article 103 of the Charter extends to the entire international legal order. Customary international law, treaty law and other secondary sources of authority complete and sustain the Charter but do not compete for power. This established a binding line of authority, which places the Charter at its apex followed by the Security Council as the organ with binding authority. Yet, even Security Council resolutions must be in compliance with the precepts of the Charter. Kofi Annan argued, confirming Dag Hammerskjöld's chain of authority, that '[a] Secretary-General must be judged by his fidelity to the principles of the Charter'.[48]

Importantly, for good offices, this line of authority establishes the independence of the UN Secretary-General as separate from other UN organs. According to Dag Hammerskjöld, when a Secretary-General is following

[43] SC Resolution 143, The Congo Question, 17 July 1960.

[44] For a full account of the Congo operation see Gordenker, *supra* note 5, at 217–282.

[45] H.K. Jacobson, *Networks of Independence: International Organisations and the Global Political System* (1979), 137.

[46] *Ibid.*, at 137. [47] Charter of the United Nations, Art. 2.2.

[48] Podium, 'Impartiality Does Not Mean Neutrality. From a Speech by the Secretary-General of the United Nations to the Council on Foreign Relations in New York', *The Independent*, 22 January 1999.

a Security Council mandate under Article 98, both the spirit of the mandate and the Charter, with the Charter as pre-eminent, must be kept in mind. Yet, if a Secretary-General judged a Security Council mandate to be outside the principles of the Charter it is not clear what options might be open to him, particularly as there is no judicial review or other similar process within the UN.

Dag Hammarskjöld's involvement in Congo led him to an impasse with the Soviet Union similar to what Trygve Lie had experienced concerning Korea. While, unlike Trygve Lie, he was appointed for a second term by the Security Council, the Soviet Union instigated a sustained plan to remove him from office, and to contemporaneously greatly reduce the power of the Secretary-General. Chairman Khrushchev stated that the

> [a]ssembly should call Mr Hammerskjöld to order, ensure that he does not misuse the position of the Secretary-General; but carries out his functions in strict accordance with the provisions of the UN Charter and the decisions of the Security Council.[49]

This mirrors comments made in 2004 by the Greek Cypriot leaders regarding Kofi Annan.[50] When a Secretary-General acts in a manner which dissatisfies some members, there is still criticism; however, following Dag Hammarskjöld, such censure is not paralysing. The Soviet Union boycotted Dag Hammarskjöld and proposed a troika office of Secretary-General.[51] This plan never obtained enough support to become a serious option, as the political hyperbole that underlined both the criticism and the troika proposal was evident. The impact upon the development of good offices of the Soviet Union's campaign is unclear as it was cut short by Dag Hammarskjöld's death. If a troika position had been created, it is possible that growth may have been stunted as the independence behind good offices would be reduced and possibly good offices may have ceased altogether.

17.4.2 The Peking formula

Dag Hammarskjöld's establishment of the 'Peking formula' was key in furthering the independence of the office of Secretary-General

[49] See Luard, *supra* note 42, at 203.

[50] Reported in *The Washington Times*, 14 June 2004 and 'Annan's Future Clouded, US Says', *The Washington Post*, 22 April 2003.

[51] J. Cockayne and D.M. Malone, 'Relations with the Security Council', in S. Chesterman (ed.), *Secretary or General? The UN Secretary General in World Politics* (2007), 69 at 75.

and developing good offices as one of its most important functions. Fundamentally, the Peking formula enables the Secretary-General to adjust a General Assembly mandate to make possible his completion of a good offices mission. If a Secretary-General receives a mandate from the General Assembly to conduct negotiations and the mandate is either restrictive or criticises one or more of the parties, the Secretary-General modifies the mandate to accommodate negotiations.

The Peking formula was established in 1954 when Dag Hammarskjöld was given a mandate by the General Assembly to negotiate the release of US aircrew hostages held in the People's Republic of China which, at that time, remained unrepresented at the UN (as Nationalist China held the seat). This last detail added to the complications in undertaking the mission. However, the biggest hindrance to resolving the situation proved to be the General Assembly's resolution.[52] In its outright condemnation of the government of the People's Republic of China for detaining the aircrew, the resolution made it highly unlikely that they would agree to negotiate for the release of the hostages under its terms.

Dag Hammerskjöld found the resolution too partisan to allow for successful dialogue. To reach a deal with the government of the People's Republic of China, he disengaged the negotiations from the very General Assembly resolution that granted his mandate. Dag Hammerskjöld assured the government of the People's Republic that their acceptance of his good offices did not imply acceptance of the UN General Assembly's censure. In disassociating himself from the resolution and taking an impartial stance he fell somewhere between a specific mandate to act and an independent initiative.

The innovation of the Peking formula should not be underestimated. The use by the General Assembly of good offices while contemporaneously accepting impartial political and diplomatic activity on the part of the Secretary-General was essential in developing the autonomy of the Secretary-General and of good offices. It is what Hammarskjöld described as having 'led to the acceptance of an independent political and diplomatic activity on the part of the Secretary-General as the neutral representative of the Organisation'.[53] This growing independence was sustained and transformed by Dag Hammarskjöld while he was in office and continued by his successors.

[52] GA Resolution 906/(IX) Complaint of Detention and Imprisonment of United Nations Military Personnel in violation of the Korean Armistice Agreement, 10 December 1954.

[53] Gordenker, *supra* note 5, at 144.

Importantly, the Peking formula is indelibly linked to a General Assembly and not a Security Council mandate thus indicating that while the Secretary-General can deviate from a mandate established by the General Assembly, this is less likely with a Security Council resolution. The authority sanctioning both organs' use of the Secretary-General comes from the same article of the Charter and this may prima facie imply that the ability to digress from a strict reading of a mandate should be cognate. Nonetheless, reading the Charter as a whole, the Chapter VII authority of the Security Council to bind members in matters of international peace and security must also be considered.[54] This supremacy appears to be the reason for the Secretary-General's stricter interpretation of Security Council resolutions, even when not adopted under Chapter VII, as opposed to the liberal interpretations of General Assembly resolutions. However, the above discussion of Dag Hammarskjöld's own view of the line of authority should also be kept in mind in considering the Peking formula.

17.5 After Dag Hammarskjöld

Discussing the legacy of Dag Hammarskjöld, Kofi Annan stated that: 'I suspect he would envy me the discretion I enjoy in deciding what to say and what topics to comment on.'[55] Kofi Annan regarded himself, the seventh Secretary-General, as having much more discretion and independence than Dag Hammarskjöld. To fully understand the impact which Dag Hammarskjöld had on good offices and the office of Secretary-General, a brief overview of the activities of the Secretaries-General who followed him is necessary. This section will outline how good offices developed after Dag Hammarskjöld's death.

Since U Thant's engagement in the dispute in 1964, Cyprus has been a re-occurring fixture of the good offices of Secretaries-General, which continues to be beyond resolution.[56] Following the Turkish invasion of 1974, Kurt Waldheim established a framework for negotiation;[57] however, as with every case since, subsequent talks stalled.[58] Boutros Boutros-Ghali held intensive negotiations in 1993.[59] This effort was welcomed

[54] UN Charter Art. 98. [55] See Chapter 2, at 40.
[56] For details see www.cyprus-un-plan.org.
[57] Report of the Secretary-General on Cyprus, 30 April 1977, SG S/12523.
[58] K. Waldheim, *The Challenge of Peace* (1980), 73.
[59] UN Doc. S/24472 of 21 August 1992.

by the Security Council but, again, was unsuccessful.[60] Kofi Annan, in his efforts to resolve the dispute, moved far beyond the traditional role of good offices to actually composing, instead of mediating, a settlement that became known as the Annan Plan. Under the Plan, if parties failed to negotiate a settlement, it was agreed to put to a resolution composed by the Secretary-General to the people by referendum.[61] Ultimately, the plan was rejected by the Greek Cypriot community.[62] In the aftermath of the failed plan, Kofi Annan decided that he had accomplished all he could at that time.[63] Negotiations have once again commenced under the current Secretary-General.[64]

From a good offices perspective, what is important is the vast independence that Kofi Annan had in devising a resolution, which was directed at individuals and not their representatives. For the first time, there was a direct line between individuals and the office of Secretary-General. This appears to be the furthest that Security Council mandated good offices have been extended. While in the Congo, Dag Hammerskjöld had the power to conduct battles on the ground, he did not have the authority to bypass the political representatives and go directly to the people. The Cypriot Security Council resolutions tend to be imprecise and no member of the Security Council has criticised a Secretary-General's actions in Cyprus, which suggests their acquiescence to his wider activities. This exemplifies just how much the role has grown, and the trust parties and the Security Council now have in the good offices of the Secretaries-General, even if some parties to the dispute have themselves criticised the Annan Plan and subsequent negotiations have yet to bear fruit.[65]

[60] SC Resolution 889 Cyprus, 15 December 1993.

[61] Text of the Annan Plan and other details are available at www.cyprus-un-plan.org.

[62] Report of the SG on his mission of Good Offices in Cyprus. 28 May 2004, S/2004/437,1.

[63] *Ibid.*, 2.

[64] 'Cyprus: Ban Calls for Decisive Steps towards Final Settlement after Intensive Talks', *UN News Service*, 25 January 2012, www.un.org/apps/news/story.asp?NewsID=41035&Cr=Cyprus&Cr1=#.

[65] Reported in *The Washington Times*, 14 June 2004: 'In a seven-page response to a highly critical report on the Greek-Cypriot attitude by Mr. Annan, Mr. Papadopoulos described proposals for better relations with the Turkish-Cypriot state as "outside the secretary-general's good offices mission" and in "direct contravention of the Security Council resolution and international law." He termed Mr. Annan's conclusions "insulting", "offensive" and "flawed" and said the United Nations was setting itself up as "judge and jury". Though given both sides agreed to let the Secretary-General put forward a settlement this seems more like political posturing given international criticism.'

The Security Council continues to rely on good offices. Its use has ebbed and flowed; for example, in the aftermath of the Cold War the Security Council's invocation of good offices diminished. Nonetheless, what is evident is how much the Security Council values good offices as a significant aspect of the Secretary-General's role.[66] In this short space, every Security Council mandate cannot be discussed; however, the continued use and support for good offices is apparent. In 1946, it was the first UN organ to entrust the Secretary-General with good offices. Although this is not surprising given the Security Council's role in the maintenance of international peace and security, it suggests an immediate recognition of its importance. The Security Council allows much latitude in these mandates. While occasionally there has been criticism, the role which Dag Hammerskjöld established allows for much independence. The Security Council readily relies on good offices and its lead gave credence to the mandates, which have followed from other UN organs.

The General Assembly continues to employ the Secretary-General's good offices. For example, over several years the General Assembly requested the Secretary-General's involvement in Cambodia.[67] In addition, variations on the Peking formula continue, for example, Javier Pèrez de Cuéllar in Afghanistan in the 1980s. The Soviet Union's veto in the Security Council left it to the General Assembly to mandate the Secretary-General's negotiations.[68] Over the following years, the Secretary-General was heavily involved. The General Assembly's resolution called for the immediate withdrawal of Soviet troops, an objectionable proposition to both the Soviet Union and the Afghan government it supported.[69] To conduct negotiations, the Secretary-General employed the Peking formula.[70] Urquhart described the Secretary-General's involvement as 'offer[ing] a compelling example of an exceedingly difficult and long step by step process of UN conflict resolution in a situation in which others could not or did not wish to act'.[71]

[66] Security Council Resolution 669 Iraq-Kuwait, 24 September 1990, 'Welcoming the Secretary-General's use of his Good Offices to advance a peaceful solution based on the relevant resolutions of the Council'.

[67] GA Resolution 34/22 The Situation in Kampuchea, 14 November 1979; GA Resolution 44/22 The Situation in Kampuchea, 16 November 1989.

[68] GA Resolution 35/37 The Situation in Afghanistan and its Implications for International Peace and Security, 20 November 1980.

[69] GA Resolution ES-6/2, 14 January 1980.

[70] UN Press Release SG/SM/4124, 20 April 1980.

[71] V. Avakov, 'The Secretary General in the Afghanistan Conflict, the Iran-Iraq War, and the Gulf Crisis', in B. Rivlin and L. Gordenker (eds.), *The Challenging Role of the UN*

Of late, the General Assembly has taken a backseat in good offices as the Security Council takes the lead in international peace and security. Though, as mentioned above, the General Assembly has continued to support the notion of good offices in the guise of broader resolutions on dispute settlement within the UN.

The Secretary-General continues to act on his own initiative. In 1962, a Yemenite *coup d'état* and the involvement of foreign forces supporting both sides of the conflict caused an escalation in violence within the country. U Thant negotiated for the dispatch of UN forces to supervise the withdrawal of foreign forces. Subsequently, he reported his activities to the Security Council, which did not debate the report, suggesting its tacit agreement to the Secretary-General acting on his own initiative.[72]

U Thant's involvement in Vietnam illustrates the pressure a Secretary-General can bring to bear upon members of the UN. Originally, U Thant expressed a wish to only hold one term of office; however, 'when he made public his reluctance, the expressions of support and confidence which his reluctance had elicited demonstrated that he too now had considerable capacity to make demands'.[73] He chose to claim a wider UN role in Vietnam. While such a demand was not popular with the United States and he had little success, unlike his immediate predecessor he did not fall out with a Major Power to such a degree that his tenure became impractical, underscoring the growing independence of the office.

Kurt Waldheim was less sure of the Secretary-General's ability to act and stated, following an unsuccessful involvement in the 1980 American hostage situation in Iran, that the 'simple truth' was that the Secretary-General 'has no executive power'.[74] This pronouncement was made despite the fact that during an earlier hostage situation in Algeria, Kurt Waldheim neither sought nor received any mandate and successfully negotiated the release of hostages. This incident also demonstrates that states are willing to respond to such activities by a Secretary-General.[75]

In 1983, Javier Pèrez de Cuéllar, with the Secretary-General of the OAS and the Contadora Group, settled various conflicts in Central and

Secretary General Making: The Most-Impossible Job in the World Possible (1993), 152 at 155.

[72] *Ibid.*, at 167. [73] U Thant, *View from the UN* (1978), 80.

[74] O. Pellicer, 'The United Nations in Central America: The Role of the Secretary General', in Rivlin and Gordenker, *supra* note 71, at 179.

[75] See Waldheim, *supra* note 58, at 179.

South America.[76] Their efforts resulted in the Arias plan, the Esquipalas Accords I and II and the Declaration of Costa del Sol.[77] His personal involvement in settling the Central American issue was pivotal, and without his intense motivation, it is doubtful that such success would have been achieved.[78] The fact that the majority of the activities undertaken were outside a Security Council or General Assembly mandate helped to cement the independent good offices role, especially when it resulted in a successful resolution.

In 1991, Javier Pèrez de Cuéllar involved himself in the Lebanon hostage situation. After several fruitless efforts by other mediators to liberate the hostages, Javier Pèrez de Cuéllar secured their release.[79] He stated that 'I have been working I don't know how many years, working quietly in order to obtain the release of all the hostages'.[80] This illustrates the low-key manner in which good offices are performed. He eventually secured the release of all the hostages in Lebanon; this is especially significant given the difficult ongoing power struggles in the area.

A more recent development has been the use of good offices outside the realm of the UN: a request by parties to a dispute or regional group, to a Secretary-General to use his good offices to resolve a dispute. Probably the most famous example is the Rainbow Warrior dispute.[81] Such requests epitomise the confidence which states place in the office of Secretary-General. This authority is distinct to that used by the Security Council or the General Assembly under the Charter. How much this authority depends on the individual personality of the incumbent or the political climate at the time is open to debate.

Under Article 100 of the Charter the Secretary-General and the Secretariat 'in the performance of their duties ... shall not receive instructions from any Government'. Acting at the request of the parties, it is possible for the activities to fall outside the duties under the Charter and, as such, grant more leeway. In acting as Secretary-General (and it is as Secretary-General that the individual has been solicited and not as a private person), he should follow first 'the principles and purposes of the Charter which are fundamental law and accepted and binding on all States'.[82] It is difficult to imagine circumstances that would permit

[76] Consisting of Colombia, Mexico, Panama and Venezuela.

[77] See Pellicer, *supra* note 74, at 177–178. [78] *Ibid.*, 181.

[79] T.M. Franck, *Fairness in International Law and Institutions* (1997), 188.

[80] 'Hostage Release: Steady Gains for the Freedom-Brokers', *Guardian*, 25 September 1991.

[81] Rainbow Warrior Dispute (1987) 26 ILM 1346.

[82] See Jacobson, *supra* note 45, at 137.

circumvention of the principles of the Charter. If such activities were in contravention of a resolution, it is very possible that the Secretary-General may be transgressing Article 100.

The Cuban Missile Crisis proffers a good example of the use by Major Powers of Secretary-General good offices. Reportedly, the

> US Assistant Secretary of State for International Organisational Affairs credits the Secretary-General with serving as a middleman in crucial parts of the dialogue between President Kennedy and Chairman Khrushchev which assistance led to a peaceful solution.[83]

U Thant was on hand to 'propose a quid pro quo between the Soviet Union and the US for simultaneous removal of missiles from Turkey and Cuba'.[84] Although this never came to pass, it suggests the faith the superpowers had in the Secretary-General's impartiality and independence, as well as his ability to act without a Council or Assembly mandate. The very fact that it was the two superpowers who had solicited the Secretary-General's aid further added, at this critical juncture, to the legitimacy of parties coming to the Secretary-General independent of a UN mandate.

During the Rainbow Warrior dispute, Javier Pèrez de Cuéller, at the request of France and New Zealand, negotiated a settlement between the two states.[85] This settlement, that looked more akin to arbitration than traditional good offices, was a departure, which, similar to the Annan Plan, illustrated the depth of authority given to Secretaries-General. Both parties agreed in advance to a binding settlement, a significant departure from traditional good offices demonstrates the change that has come about in their operation.

There are many examples of a Secretary-General embroiling himself in good offices at the request of the parties. So far, this has not led to any conflict of interest with resolutions of the UN organs, although such a conflict is not purely hypothetical. As Trygve Lie stated:

> when he agrees with us, governments tend to feel the Secretary-General is within his rights and is a good fellow besides; when his views differ from ours he is clearly exceeding his authority, his reasoning is bad and even his motives may be suspect.[86]

A Secretary-General must keep his position as an officer of the UN at the forefront of his mind, if he is not to do damage to both the office of

[83] See Franck, *supra* note 79, at 178 and see Gordenker, *supra* note 5, at 174.
[84] See Luard, *supra* note 34, at 353. [85] Rainbow Warrior Dispute, *supra* note 81.
[86] See Luard, *supra* note 34, at 346.

Secretary-General and good offices. So far all Secretaries-General have succeeded in balancing commitments to resolving conflict and to the UN. Their ability to do so is largely down to the groundwork set by Dag Hammarskjöld during his term in office.

17.6 Conclusion

It was suggested when Javier Pèrez de Cuéller took over as Secretary-General that his predecessors had created a 'dispute settlement role' whose content might be in opposition to most UN members.[87] More than any other holder of the office of Secretary-General, Dag Hammarskjöld established the dynamism and independence of the dispute settlement role identified when Javier Pèrez de Cuéller took office. Dag Hammarskjöld's impact as Secretary-General is evident in the independence of the office, the development of good offices beyond a very narrow conception, and the expansion of the role of the individual international actor. While this chapter examined this evolution only in the context of good offices, in many ways this exemplifies the strengths and difficulties associated with the office of Secretary-General and just how important Dag Hammarskjöld was to the role.

The intervention of international actors in conflict has become an accepted attribute of conflict resolution and transitions to peace. Yet, as outlined, the exact parameters of action for heads of international organisations are far from obvious. The legitimacy of the UN Secretary-General's actions emanates from the Charter and the UN organs, as well as the practice from the office. The Secretary-General is an accepted international actor and arbitrator whose involvement does not denote any acceptance of the wider UN membership's political views. Without the advances made by Dag Hammarskjöld it is unlikely that the office would have developed to the extent that Secretaries-General are free to act independently of both the members and organs of the UN.

When, as the first Secretary-General, Trygve Lie was sworn into office, the President of the General Assembly called upon him to be 'firm without intransigence … be conciliatory without weakness … impartial without exception'.[88] Trygve Lie's difficult task of laying the groundwork for the office must be given credit, particularly his perseverance in not bowing to

[87] See Adams and Kingsbury, *supra* note 6, at 148.

[88] Verbatim Record of the Twenty-Second Plenary Meeting, Installation of the SG of the UN, Saturday, 2 February 1946 at 11:00 a.m. A/PV.22.

the pressures placed upon him by members. Nonetheless, incontrovertibly it was Dag Hammarskjöld, standing fast in the Congo and during the Peking hostage situation, who firmly established that a Secretary-General was not at the whim of the powerful states or members; and further, regarding good offices, a Secretary-General works within the principles of the Charter and not the vagaries of politics. Naturally, there are legitimate criticisms of Dag Hammarskjöld's specific actions and policies. Nevertheless, his lasting legacy to those UN Secretaries-General who followed him is an office which, if used correctly, can be independent, authoritative and bring about pacific resolution to conflicts.

18

Dag Hammarskjöld's diplomacy

Lessons learned

PETER WALLENSTEEN

18.1 Hammarskjöld then, Annan later

UN Secretary-General Dag Hammarskjöld's achievements remain highly relevant in the field of international diplomacy. In his memoirs, his successor of many years later, Kofi Annan, refers to the importance of Hammarskjöld's contributions to the UN and its standing, not the least in his ambition to stabilise conflicts as early as possible.[1] When facing a new situation, Annan would say to himself 'how would Hammarskjöld have handled this?'.[2] There are lessons to be learned from Hammarskjöld as well as from Annan. This is what is discussed in this contribution.

The number of armed conflicts today is higher than during Hammarskjöld's time of the 1950s, when there were less than twenty armed conflicts going on in a particular year. Using the Uppsala Conflict Data Program definitions, the years 1953–1961 saw a total of forty-six armed conflicts. This contrasts with the post-Cold War period. Between 1989 and 2011 a total of 137 armed conflicts were waged around the world. Thirty-seven were active by 2011 and at no time did the number go below thirty. This is the world Kofi Annan had to relate to. During his ten years as Secretary-General there were seventy-six armed conflicts in the

Peter Wallensteen is Senior Professor of Peace and Conflict Research/Dag Hammarskjöld Professor of Peace and Conflict Research, Uppsala University 1985–2012. Richard G. Starmann Sr. Research Professor of Peace Studies, University of Notre Dame, Indiana, USA, since 2006. The author is grateful for comments from the editors, but remains solely responsible for the contents.

[1] K. Annan with N. Mousavizadeh, *Interventions: A Life in War and Peace* (2012), 32.
[2] K. Annan, Chapter 2 above, at 35.

world, a 50 per cent increase in the annual rate of armed conflicts from the Hammarskjöld years.[3]

Hammarskjöld's diplomacy concerned the peaceful handling of such armed conflicts. Hammarskjöld's experiences may give us insights that are also relevant in a post-Cold War period. During the 1950s, there were very few peace agreements, but Hammarskjöld excelled in solving conflicts short of war or early in their development. Since the 1990s, we have seen more peace agreements than during any period since the Second World War, as well as many early attempts at preventing conflict escalation.

Indeed, there are many similarities between Hammarskjöld and Annan. They both took over an organisation in crisis. Their moment of ascendance as the second and seventh Secretary-General, respectively, illustrates this. When the first UN Secretary-General, Trygve Lie, had to resign in the aftermath of the Korean War, Hammarskjöld replaced him; when the sixth holder of the office, Boutros Boutros-Ghali, was not elected for a second term, Annan took over his office. Hammarskjöld and Annan both spent considerable energy on repairing the standing of the UN. Both emphasised its autonomy to Major Powers. They saw similar purposes for the organisation. In Hammarskjöld's last Annual Report he spelled out that the organisation had to be understood as 'a dynamic instrument' with the aim of 'forestalling conflicts and resolving them'.[4] Annan would agree with that, but put in a broader framework that specifically referred to development, human rights and gender equality as well.[5] A major crisis for Hammarskjöld was the Anglo-French-Israeli invasion of Egypt in 1956, an event with traits similar to the US-led invasion of Iraq in 2003. Both of these events meant that founding members of the organisation acted contrary to the stipulations they themselves had written into the UN Charter. Both men also encountered direct challenges from significant circles in a permanent Member State. In Hammarskjöld's case the Soviet Union demanded in 1960 that he should resign, and for Annan the same demand was raised by a US Senator in the aftermath of the Iraq

[3] The number of conflicts during the different periods of tenure is calculated from T. Pettersson and L. Themnér, *States in Armed Conflict 2009* (2010). The data for 2011 are from L. Themnér and P. Wallensteen, 'Armed Conflict, 1946–2011' (2012) 49(4) *Journal of Peace Research* 565.

[4] A.W. Cordier and W. Foote, *Public Papers of the Secretaries-General of the United Nations, Vol. V: Dag Hammarskjöld 1960–1961* (1975), 542.

[5] Annan, *supra* note 1, 13.

invasion and the complexities of the Oil-for-Food programme.[6] Both withstood the pressure, to the benefit of the organisation.

In the following sections, we will focus on Hammarskjöld's action, studying his involvement in twenty crises during his tenure. In particular, our concern is with the type of diplomacy, the phase of the conflict and typical traits in his handling of these crises. In some instances, a comparison will be made with the experiences of Kofi Annan. The investigation has as its starting point the idea of three identifiable phases in the dynamics of a conflict.[7]

First, we point to the initial phase where the parties continue to give preference to war efforts. This is *agenda diplomacy*: getting the parties, as well as the international community, to focus on conflict resolution. In other writings, this has also been seen as the moment when a mediator enters a conflict, 'going in'.[8] Often there is limited space for peace diplomacy by third parties. The party who believes it is about to win sees no reason for negotiations. The one fearing it will lose may be more welcoming. It can be difficult to find an agreed point of entry for international mediation. The UN Secretary-General is in a legal and international position that gives more space for such action.

In the phase that follows, the primary parties can be constructively interested in finding an agreement. The hope of victory may have faded for both parties, making them willing to enter into direct or indirect contact. Some writers have referred to these as ripe moments.[9] This is seen as the phase of *agreement diplomacy*. If it works, the conflict may be terminated; if it fails, the conflict reverts back to the battlefield, and peace diplomacy has to start all over again. The number of full-scale peace agreements was low in Hammarskjöld's time, but there were other types of arrangements. In the post-Cold War period, Kofi Annan could oversee a host of deals being negotiated, sometimes with a heavy UN input (Kosovo, East Timor, Afghanistan, Sudan), and sometimes outside the UN framework (South Africa, Nepal).

In case of an agreement, there is a third phase of *implementation diplomacy*. This is the time for translating an agreed text into reality, building on the conditions that are conducive for implementation and durability of

6 *Ibid.*, at 360.

7 P. Wallensteen, 'Dag Hammarskjöld and the Psychology of Diplomacy', in P. Wallensteen (ed.), *Peace Research: Theory and Practice* (2011), 154.

8 I. Svensson and P. Wallensteen, *The Go-Between: Jan Eliasson and the Styles of Mediation* (2010).

9 W.I. Zartman, *Ripe for Resolution: Conflict and Intervention in Africa* (1989).

the agreement. Today, this is often referred to as peacebuilding, and the UN now has a special commission for this activity.

There may be different skills needed for the different phases. Agenda diplomacy has an important element of secrecy, tacit understandings and closed-door activities. Agreement diplomacy is a matter of making parties get to know each other, 'understanding' the opposing side and finding ways to overcome incompatibilities. Implementation diplomacy takes place after a deal is made. It is open, observable, but technical. It rests on long-term commitment, intimate knowledge of the actors and their priorities, attention to detail and, not least, an eye to potential spoilers.[10]

These conflict phases are not equally long, and they do not necessarily follow neatly one after each other. The distinction is still important as it provides different measures of 'success'. In the first phase, it is a matter of getting a conflict on the international agenda; in the second, it is finding an agreement; and in the third, a 'normalisation', where ultimately war is no longer the main concern.

18.2 Conflicts on the UN agenda

Hammarskjöld was a significant actor in many of the conflicts of his time. The thorough biography by Brian Urquhart opens the possibility for a closer analysis of Hammarskjöld's role as a third party.[11]

It is important to recall that the international system was highly polarised and hierarchical during the Cold War, with a constant danger of escalation from a local conflict to a nuclear confrontation. The aggressive posture of the two major protagonists coloured international relations. The post-Cold War period has other features. Most importantly, the continuous, global Major Power rivalry is not present. This does not exclude particular regionally based clashes of interest, but the fear of escalation to global nuclear confrontation is not equally prominent.

Clearly, Hammarskjöld's activities were a first expression of what we today label as the 'international community'. He was using the possibilities vested in his office. Acting for the international community means giving priority to resolutions that will benefit an entire system, not just particular actors. In the history of diplomacy there is a focus particularly

[10] S.J. Stedman, 'Spoiler Problems in Peace Processes' (1997) 22(2) *International Security* 5; S.J. Stedman, 'Conflict Prevention as Strategic Interaction: The Spoiler Problem and the Case of Rwanda', in P. Wallensteen (ed.), *Preventing Violent Conflicts* (1998), 67.

[11] B. Urquhart, *Hammarskjold* (1972, reprinted 1994).

on diplomats working from their own foreign ministries to pursue national interests. Certainly, states remain significant. The rise of the UN, international organisations and, even more recently, international non-governmental organisations, independent media and global corporations, change the state-centered world. There are now significant actors who do not have a particular state or government as their primary allegiance. Dag Hammarskjöld is a first powerful exponent of this trend, which has become more marked in the post-Cold War period.

Building on the work by Urquhart, twenty international disputes have been identified as cases of Hammarskjöld's diplomacy.[12] Many of them involved tensions between important powers, notably the US–China dispute over the airmen that had been forced to land in China. This was a crisis but not an active armed conflict, despite being an outgrowth of the Korean War and the agreed truce. The twenty crises that saw Hammarskjöld action, dealt with seven different armed conflicts or wars. His five significant Middle East diplomatic missions in the years 1956–7 were all part of one war, the one over the Suez Canal. Similarly, the one war in the Congo gave Hammarskjöld six diplomatic and military crises to handle in fourteen months, from July 1960 until his death.

We should see this against the backdrop of all the other armed conflicts going on during Hammarskjöld's eight-year tenure. There was close to forty additional conflicts. In most of these there was little or no UN activity registered. A fair number of these were crises with at least one major power involved deliberately preventing international action. The examples are cases where one party was a permanent member of the Security Council, for example France (Algeria; Indochina; decolonisation conflicts in Africa), Britain (engaged in protracted conflicts in Malaya and Kenya), China (Taiwan Straits and Tibet), the Soviet Union (the invasion of Hungary) or the United States (rebellions in Guatemala, Cuba, and coups in Latin America). National governments also prevented the UN from engaging in what they defined as internal conflicts, for example Burma, Ethiopia, India and Indonesia.

When comparing this record to the tenure of Kofi Annan, the reach of actions of the Secretary-General has been enlarged. Even so, some situations were still outside UN action, for instance involving Russia (Chechnya), Britain (Northern Ireland), India (numerous conflicts in Northeast India), Burma (regionally based conflicts), and the invasion of Iraq in 2003. However, in most other conflicts the UN Secretary-General

[12] Wallensteen, *supra* note 7, 159.

was involved early on. It is disturbing to note that some conflicts were on the list of armed conflicts during both of these periods, testifying to their intractability: Palestine, Lebanon, Congo, as well as some of the conflicts in India and Burma/Myanmar.

Looking at all twenty crises, Hammarskjöld had a large measure of success: twelve outcomes are categorised in this way. There were six clear-cut failures and two were unsolved at the time of his death. There is no record to compare this to, as no similar investigation has been made of other Secretaries-General. Still, it must be judged as remarkable. There is a consistent pattern for the failures: these were crises where Hammarskjöld tried to act but encountered firm opposition of a determined major power (the United States in Guatemala and Laos, Britain in the Middle East, France in Bizerte, the Soviet Union in Hungary and Congo 1960–1). Major power objection was not necessarily the end of crisis management, however. In several instances, it was possible for the Secretary General to overcome resistance either by mustering support from other permanent members of the Security Council or by taking the issue to the General Assembly. It is noteworthy that Hammarskjöld managed to build strong international coalitions for his actions. On this score, he was more successful than his predecessor and he may have set a pattern of action for his successors. Hammarskjöld's coalitions shifted from one issue to another. In the Suez crisis, he had the support of the Soviet Union and the United States, as well as the non-aligned countries of Europe, Asia and the Arab world. In the Congo, the backing of the newly independent African and Asian countries was important. Whether deliberate or not, he clearly acted to avoid antagonising all permanent members at the same time.

In Hammarskjöld's actions, the Middle East and Africa had the lion's share of attention. The Cold War as such was outside his range (such as conflicts over Germany, Cuba, Taiwan, Indochina and disarmament issues). This is different from the pattern of the Secretaries-General in the post-Cold War period. Their actions demonstrate the global significance of the UN. Indeed, the way the Soviet Union ended its extensive international involvement was to hand the issues to the UN. Afghanistan, Angola, Namibia, Central America and Indochina all became significant arenas for UN action. Many of these issues were solved by the mid 1990s, which is why Kofi Annan's period, beginning in 1997, marks the start of the new post-Cold War period. This is also why we find Europe higher on the UN agenda, as this time saw the breakup of Yugoslavia. In Annan's tenure this meant dealing with the crises over Kosovo and Macedonia.

The long-term peacebuilding efforts in Europe, however, have been the purview of the European Union.

The many crises of Africa were a must for the organisation, as were crises over East Timor. However, in the Middle East, the UN was largely sidelined, compared to its central role at the time of Hammarskjöld. Under US President Clinton, the Oslo process became a US-driven undertaking, where the UN could 'only watch' US actions.[13] Nevertheless, Annan worked to give a role for the UN, succeeding to create the Quartet of the United States, Russia, the EU and the UN, which became a credible diplomatic constellation.[14] Other crises in the Middle East, notably the 2003 US-led attack on Iraq, took place without a supporting UN resolution. Only gradually did the UN get involved, but the direction was set by the United States and its Iraqi allies. In the Syrian civil war in 2012, the organisation was almost paralysed. The lesson is that once Major Powers decide to keep the issues to themselves, the UN has difficulties in getting into the deliberations. This lesson could be seen already in the Cold War issues, where real peacebuilding was replaced with attempts at bilateral crisis management, and one-sided supply of weapons, assistance and diplomatic support.

Let us, finally, also note that Hammarskjöld's diplomacy to a large degree dealt with interstate relations. This could be seen in the many Middle Eastern crises, with Israel, France and Britain on one side, and Egypt on the other. His breakthrough as a crisis diplomat was in the interstate conflict between the United States and China in 1954–5, which did not escalate to an armed conflict. Similarly he did act early in some other interstate conflicts, such as Cambodia-Thailand, UK-Saudi Arabia and in the internationalised crisis over Lebanon in 1958.

This makes the heavy commitment to the crisis in the Congo very special. The crisis could have been defined as an internal affair. However, the Congolese government had asked for assistance pointing to Belgian interventions and Hammarskjöld decided that the UN should respond. The Security Council agreed. It involved a mandate which stated that the UN would not side with any of the internal actors. As these actors were increasingly in conflict, the UN situation became uniquely complex. Furthermore, it also turned into a territorial issue, as mineral-rich Katanga tried to secede, no doubt supported by international interests.[15]

[13] Annan, *supra* note 1, 254. [14] *Ibid.*, 273–294.

[15] S. Williams, *Who Killed Hammarskjöld? The UN, the Cold War and White Supremacy in Africa* (2011), 33.

Hammarskjöld faced some of the problems that later would confront his successor: can the UN intervene in internal affairs? National government consent is necessary, but does it also mean that the UN supports that particular government? What if the conflict turns into separatism, can the UN then remain completely neutral? Remarkably, Katanga was the only separatist conflict that Hammarskjöld had to deal with; all the others concerned government power or territory from a military-strategic perspective. Still, he faced some of the same dilemmas that have become particularly prominent in the post-Cold War era: should the UN support one faction against another because it happens to hold power? Should the UN act to prevent genocidal violence, or does that constitute unacceptable interference? On these counts, Kofi Annan had a different task. Most of the conflicts of his tenure were internal, some of them separatist, some even involving humanitarian concerns speaking in favour of separation (for example in Kosovo).

These are the global patterns of UN conflict engagement. When analysing *agenda diplomacy*, the focus is on the UN. There is a formal way for setting the UN agenda, whether for the General Assembly or for the Security Council. A key provision is that the dispute has to constitute a threat to 'international peace and security'. Traditionally, only interstate conflicts that might turn into war were considered. It is the external form of violence, for instance 'aggression', that determines if the conflict should be on the Council's agenda. For an 'internal' conflict to enter, it has to be seen as endangering the inhabitants of a particular country, as well as a region or the world as a whole. On this score, there is a remarkable difference between the Cold War period and the one we find ourselves in today. Humanitarian concerns brought a number of civil wars to the UN agenda after 1990. The threat of international terrorism has done the same in the post-9/11 period. The doctrine of a responsibility to protect (R2P), accepted by the General Assembly in 2005, further reinforced this and saw its first full application in Libya in 2011.

Internationally dominant actors have a greater chance of defining as well as preventing conflicts from being defined as international issues. The veto vested in the five permanent members of the Security Council gives them particular authority. At the same time, the Secretary-General has the mandate, in Article 99 of the UN Charter, to bring to the attention of the Security Council issues considered to be threatening to international peace and security. Ultimately, the resulting agenda is made by the permanent members: if they accept, a conflict enters the international agenda. In this way they can also instruct the Secretary-General to take (or not to take) action in particular questions. Agenda diplomacy is a highly intriguing subject.

In *agreement diplomacy*, negotiations between the parties are central and the role of the outsider is to promote contacts. This involves, in particular, meeting the parties face to face (shuttle diplomacy) and/or bringing the parties to the same table (conference diplomacy). Considerable attention has to be given to the building of confidence between warring sides, and with the third party. Often the third party draws on the commitment of a broader grouping of states and actors interested in an agreement. In many conflicts there may be a peace-supporting coalition. Agreement diplomacy involves working more directly with the parties in conflict.

Finally, *implementation diplomacy* enters when signed agreements are falling apart or are in danger of doing so. In this situation, the confidence between the parties is likely to erode quickly. The outside actor may be the only one defending the agreement. This is a complicated role for the third party: should the outsider uphold an agreement the signatories are no longer interested in? What to do if only one side sticks to the agreement, or if new parties with new concerns enter the situation? The diplomacy to maintain the de facto coalition which entered into an agreement is a different challenge from the other phases. Implementation diplomacy involves the recreation of a coalition, but also has to adapt to changing circumstances. Compromises may be necessary but may also contribute to the erosion of a coalition.

18.3 Lessons from UN conflict diplomacy

As could be expected, Hammarskjöld was active in all three types of diplomacy.[16] The twenty crises contain eight cases of agreement diplomacy. Following the classifications in 'success' and 'failure', his record shows the least success in agenda-setting (three out of six), most success in implementation negotiations (five out of six) and agreement diplomacy evenly split (four out of eight). The slogan of the time, 'Leave it to Dag', often referred to cases of negotiation and implementation of agreements. Agenda-setting and agreement-making are likely to attract most concern in foreign policy circles. The complexities may be larger, the fears higher, and the interests stronger. Once a settlement is concluded, the Secretary-General may have more space, the issues may appear more 'technical' and

[16] See generally Wallensteen, *supra* note 7.

thus less politicised. Getting a conflict onto the agenda of the Council may be the most controversial. It means focusing the organisation's energy with far-reaching consequences for the organisation as well as for the course of the conflict. Thus, there will be more hesitancy among the Member States. Also, of course, once a conflict is on the agenda, there are likely to be more issues to deal with, both in finding agreements and in implementing them. Agenda diplomacy is more crucial, more rare, and thus particularly interesting.

18.3.1 Agenda diplomacy

Agenda-setting is the category with the least success for Hammarskjöld. This is indicative of the constraints at the height of the bipolar Cold War period. The United States prevented the UN from acting in the conflict in Guatemala 1954 and the Soviet Union did the same when it invaded Hungary in 1956. Similarly, he was prevented from acting in Laos in 1959, at a time which saw the beginning escalation of the new Indochina war.

Hammarskjöld's most notable accomplishments in agenda diplomacy were in the Congo crisis in 1960 and in the Soviet challenge to his position as Secretary-General. Both of these remarkable instances require a closer look.

In July 1960 the former Belgian Congo became independent, which soon led to violence and intervention by Belgium, ostensibly to protect the lives of Belgian citizens but in fact attempting to take control over parts of the country. After receiving a telegram with a request for UN technical assistance, Hammarskjöld explicitly used his powers under Article 99 in the Charter to quickly convene the Council. In his statement to the Council on 13 July 1960 he described his view that the 'stopgap arrangement envisaged by the Government of the Congo is preferable to any other formula. It is, therefore my conclusion that the United Nations should accede to the request'. He then proceeded to outline the principles for a peacekeeping operation that became standard operating procedures for years to come.[17]

He also emphasised the need for speedy action. The Council was convened at 8:30 p.m. and the vote took place at about 3:20 a.m. on 14 July. Tunisia had proposed the resolution and it was passed with eight votes in favour, none against and three abstentions. Remarkably, as this was at a critical moment in the Cold War, both the United States and the USSR

[17] Cordier and Foote, *supra* note 4, at 22–23.

voted for the resolution. The other three permanent members, France, United Kingdom and Nationalist China, all abstained,[18] in effect allowing the operation to go forward. Thus, the UN embarked on a major operation that was to engage the organisation for several years, and strain the notion of peacekeeping. It also led to the loss of the creative and energetic Secretary-General fourteen months later.

The Congo operation was unique. It was a reaction to an international intervention by Belgium, but it was also an internal conflict. In fact, much of the implementation diplomacy that Hammarskjöld had to resort to concerned the internal affairs of the Congo. His 13 July statement made it clear that the operation would only use force in self-defence and not be party to internal conflicts. The complexities of Congolese politics, however, were to challenge these principles. Indeed, this has also been the case in many post-Cold War internal armed conflicts.

The second agenda issue refers to the crisis over his position in the Secretariat. After a short period, the Soviet Union grew dissatisfied with the way the Congo operation unfolded. The Soviet leader Nikita Khrushchev came to the General Assembly in New York in the autumn of 1960 and asked that Hammarskjöld be replaced by a troika: there should be three Secretaries-General and they would only be able to act when all three agreed. One was to represent the West, one the Soviet bloc and one the non-aligned. He followed up on 3 October 1960 by asking for Hammarskjöld's resignation. In a crisp, composed and sharp rejoinder, Hammarskjöld responded that the Soviet Union did not intend to replace him with someone else: 'by resigning I would, therefore, at the present difficult and dangerous juncture throw the Organizations to the winds.' Thus, he was not willing to resign but instead made clear that it was all the other nations that needed the UN for its protection. He concluded: 'I shall remain in my post during the term of office as a servant of the Organization in the interest of all those other nations as long as they wish me to do so.' The speech drew a several-minutes-long standing ovation.[19] It was a remarkable performance and the enthusiastic support for Hammarskjöld was overwhelming. This meant that he was able to prevent the Soviet Union from successfully pursuing the troika proposal. In this case, Hammarskjöld prevented a Member State from placing the issue on the agenda, although the Soviet Union kept up the pressure on him and for the idea until his death. Hammarskjöld correctly saw that this proposal would in effect paralyse the UN.

[18] *Ibid.*, at 26. [19] *Ibid.*, at 200–201.

As we would expect, the failures in agenda diplomacy were in cases close to the interests of a particular permanent member (for instance, the United States in Guatemala, the USSR in Hungary). In the case of Hungary, the new government installed after the Soviet invasion in 1956 only invited Hammarskjöld to discuss humanitarian aid, not the political and military situation. The latter was seen as an internal affair confined to the relations between Hungary and the Soviet Union. Thus, the Soviet invasion could not be brought to a decision in the Security Council, and the actions decided on by the General Assembly could not be implemented.[20] Agenda-setting, in other words, is clearly in the purview of Major Powers. It is difficult for other actors to bring matters to the Security Council. Support of the permanent members is necessary. When Hammarskjöld succeeded – as in the Congo – he had considerable support from a large coalition of African and Asian states. Their combined voting power in the UN as well as the attention to, and optimism for, decolonisation made this 'in line with the times'. Furthermore, this crisis was initially seen to be outside the Cold War, and thus his actions were, as we just saw, acceptable to the permanent members as well.

There were instances when Hammarskjöld refrained from bringing matters to the Council. One case was the war in Algeria, which France defined as an internal matter. In 1955 African and Asian countries wanted him to take up the issue. Hammarskjöld chose to follow France, even arguing that France was searching for a negotiated solution.[21] His arguments were not convincing. It is more likely that he wanted to avoid a confrontation with a permanent member of the Council, particularly as the likelihood of him achieving a result beyond a demonstration effect was small. It might also have been a balancing act and strategic calculation not to spoil relations, which were needed in support of other decisions. It did not earn him much gratitude, however. French President General Charles de Gaulle was not a friend of this international civil servant's handling of matters, but on the contrary raised obstacles both in the Congo crisis and in the conflict over Bizerte.

If there is a situation of agenda diplomacy during Kofi Annan's term of office that has parallels with the Congo, it is the crisis over East Timor. The change of government in Indonesia in 1998 opened the possibilities

[20] The Soviet Union acted in a similar way in 1979 when it invaded Afghanistan. At this time, however, it met the resistance not only from the West but also from the Muslim world. It could not prevent the appointment of a Special Representative that later became useful in negotiating the withdrawal of Soviet forces in 1988–9.

[21] Urquhart, *supra* note 11, at 309.

of a diplomatic solution to a protracted problem that was the result of Indonesia's occupation in 1975. The UN had attended to the issue at times, but Indonesia was not interested in a solution. It had a prominent place in Third World politics as well as close military ties to the United States, giving it strong international backing. Annan's diplomacy gave the UN a role in the referendum that finally took place in August 1999 on the status of East Timor. The outcome was strongly in favour of independence, sparking indiscriminate violence by pro-Indonesian militias, even threatening the UN staff on the ground. In an unusual move, Kofi Annan issued an ultimatum to the Indonesia government to restore order within forty-eight hours, otherwise the international community would have to be invited to do so. The Indonesian government chose to ask for such support and, on 15 September 1999, Council voted in favour of a UN-authorised intervention led by Australia.[22] This was a smaller operation than the Congo mission which Hammarskjöld set up, but the way the two acted is similar. They both demonstrated that political space is available for the UN Secretary-General to set the agenda for UN action. In these situations, the two acted as generals, not as 'secretaries' in the way the Soviet leader Khrushchev had preferred.[23]

18.3.2 Agreement diplomacy

There are eight cases of agreement diplomacy during Hammarskjöld's time. The Secretary-General was the architect of a number of them. There are even examples of near-agreements that potentially solved the issues of conflict. This is most evident in the Canal crisis that preceded the Suez invasion in 1956. By mid-October 1956, Hammarskjöld had secured support from Egypt for principles that largely met the conditions laid out by the users of the Suez Canal, which had been unilaterally nationalised by Egypt. Nevertheless, Britain and France moved on with their war preparations. In late October 1956 they launched an intervention, coordinated with Israel. Their UN diplomacy was actually aimed at preventing a possible agreement. It was meant to demonstrate to the public that the issues could not be handled through diplomacy. Hammarskjöld's actions threatened this strategy.[24] This illustrates a basic truth, close to a truism,

[22] Annan, *supra* note 1, at 110–112.
[23] See on this theme, S. Chesterman (ed.), *Secretary or General? The UN Secretary-General in World Politics* (2007).
[24] Urquhart, *supra* note 11, 167–169

in negotiations and diplomacy: if key parties do not want negotiations to succeed, agreements are unlikely, but they will also act so as to absolve themselves and put the blame elsewhere.

There is a similar experience for Kofi Annan in the run up to the US-led invasion of Iraq in 2003. There was a UN inspection mission in place, dealing exactly with the issue of weapons of mass destruction that the US administration said was its rationale for threatening war with the country. The UN mission actually suggested that there was a peaceful way of dealing with the issue, at a time when the US coalition had already decided that an invasion was the preferred option. The actions of the UN Secretariat seemed to threaten the legality of the action, and it became imperative to demonstrate the futility of the UN mission. That is what the Secretary of State Colin Powell attempted to do in a presentation to the Security Council on 5 February 2003. This followed on from Annan's earlier attempt to find a negotiated settlement, which actually led to an agreement on inspections into presidential palaces in Iraq in 1998, carried out in spite of American objections.[25]

Again this applies to parties that are strong enough to prevent agreement. For other actors, agreement, through the Secretary-General, may have been a preferred alternative to dealing directly with the adversary. Hammarskjöld's diplomatic breakthrough came in such a crisis, involving two strong powers, the United States and the People's Republic of China. There were no diplomatic relations between the two. The issue of US pilots held in China created tensions. It may also have been in the interest of China to use these pilots for improving its international standing. The contacts established by Hammarskjöld led to the release of the pilots in an extraordinary gesture, presented as a gift on his fiftieth birthday (29 July 1955). Hammarskjöld could use this achievement to strengthen his position. In many of the following crises he had strong public support in the United States.

18.3.3 Implementation diplomacy

Hammarskjöld became involved in implementation primarily through UN peacekeeping operations. The conditions agreed on for UNEF in Egypt became guiding principles for all peacekeeping operations during the Cold War. The withdrawal of Israeli troops from Sinai in 1957 included considerable negotiations and delicate arrangements. In both of

[25] Annan, *supra* note 1, at 325–328.

these cases, the outcome was a success for Hammarskjöld's diplomacy. It should be noted, however, that the UN was not the only actor in bringing this about. In both cases, the role of the United States was highly important.

Also in the Congo, Hammarskjöld had to solve problems of implementation of the Council's resolution. This resulted in severe crises primarily around Katanga's attempted secession. Hammarskjöld's implementation diplomacy became highly transcontinental. It involved meeting the demands of actors in the Congo, handling questions with Belgium, which had troops in the area, and finding workable formulas in New York to keep the Security Council on-board. Hammarskjöld was a master in such complex diplomacy. There is, however, one striking failure: the assassination of the first Premier Minister of independent Congo, Patrice Lumumba, in January/February 1960. It was upsetting in its brutality. Could the UN have intervened more effectively to avert this? It would have been a heavy involvement in the internal affairs of an independent country, but it may also have served to change the country's development in a different direction. Hammarskjöld's skill in managing international diplomacy encountered local actors with entirely different priorities.

Kofi Annan faced similar dilemmas. Following the US invasion of Iraq in 2003 the UN was called in, and he accepted. A sizeable mission was set up, outside the Green Zone in Baghdad, no doubt as a demonstration that it was separate from the US-led operation. It also meant that it was less well protected. On 19 August 2003 a massive bomb destroyed the headquarters killing 22 UN workers, including the chief of mission Sergio Vieira de Mello.[26] Although not part of the US mission, the UN was apparently perceived as such by some actors. The hope that the UN could act as a neutral party separated from other forces was challenged. The assassination of Lumumba led to questions about UN actions to protect him and accusations that the UN was somehow to blame; the bomb in Baghdad suggests that some blamed the UN for the war, although it had never been accepted by the Security Council or the Secretary-General. Even implementation diplomacy, in other words, is not just a matter of technical engineering, but has its political dimensions.

18.4 Success in UN crisis diplomacy

Hammarskjöld's background made him well suited to understand the significance of the power inherent in his office. His father was Prime Minister

[26] *Ibid.*, at 356.

of Sweden at a trying moment in the country's history (the First World War). Dag Hammarskjöld worked closely with Ernest Wigforss, one of the most influential men in Swedish politics in the first part of the twentieth century. Hammarskjöld himself was involved in the reconstruction of Europe after the Second World War and later became a member of the Swedish Cabinet. He was not new to power.

At the same time he was neither an admirer of power nor its humble servant. On the contrary, he knew how power could be used to serve the needs of the reformer or crisis manager. It meant knowing the direction of change and finding ways to promote your goals, without provoking unnecessary resistance.

In this regard, there are interesting parallels with Kofi Annan, also having a background in a leading family, in his native Ghana, also learning early on about the operations of political power, as well as the importance of economic development in peacebuilding.[27]

Both men would, of course, agree that 'success' in diplomacy does not mean success only for one person. Others were pushing in similar directions. This also means that 'failure' does not mean failure only for the Secretary-General. In some instances, Hammarskjöld as well as Annan were the chief negotiators, but they may not have been able to succeed, unless there had been strong support from others (for example the United States, African and Asian countries, etc.). In reality, 'success' is an achievement for a constellation of forces interested in agreement. Coalition building, in other words, was – and is – integral to the operation of the UN system. A successful Secretary-General has to be an expert at this.

Central to Hammarskjöld's success was his ability to work, at the same time, with the strongest and the weakest members of the UN system, that is both with the United States and with the newly independent states. This is remarkable as the latter often were highly critical of the United States and the West in general. It is noteworthy that Hammarskjöld repeatedly ran into conflict with the Eisenhower administration (in Guatemala 1954 and Laos in 1959) and still worked in parallel with it in other cases (the pilots in China 1954–5, Suez 1956, Congo 1960). Thus, there was flexibility on both sides, which made the relationship complex and difficult to entangle.

This is true for any Secretary-General. The United States is a founding member of the UN, it remains one of its major contributors, and it has global interests. Thus, relations with the United States are central, and indeed Kofi Annan worked hard to maintain that relationship, even in the face of

[27] *Ibid.*, at 15–27.

the Iraq War and Congressional opposition to the UN. If this was complex at the time of Hammarskjöld, it seems only to have grown more difficult.

Hammarskjöld, of course, had to also have a working relationship with the Soviet Union. It went from being positive in 1956 (in the Suez crisis, in spite of the Hungary invasion) to being extremely negative in the autumn of 1960 (after initial cooperation on the Congo operation). Annan, on the other hand, encountered Russian direct interests only in particular instances, most clearly in the Kosovo crisis of 1999, when he implicitly endorsed the NATO air strikes on Serbia after the failure of the negotiations. Although action took place without the authority of the Security Council, he argued that 'there are times when the use of force may be legitimate in the pursuit of peace'. He later even talked about humanitarian protection as an evolving international norm.[28] Russia was of a different mind but could still work with him in a negotiated ending on the 1999 Kosovo crisis, as well as in the Middle East.

For Hammarskjöld, the relations with France were negative throughout the period (Suez 1956, Bizerte 1961), although his competence and elegance should have intrigued any French leadership, not least because he advocated French authors for the Nobel Prize in literature, in his role as a member of the Swedish Academy.

These complexities contrast with the closeness Hammarskjöld had with many Third World leaders. India's Prime Minister Jawaharlal Nehru was a significant partner in many crises. The relationship was strong, but not without disagreement. The implicit coalition that maintained the UN operation in the Congo was not easy to manage but survived setbacks and turbulence. On this score, Annan demonstrates a similar pattern of working with the global South as well as with the North. During the Bush administration, following the invasion of Iraq, there was an increasing polarisation between the United States and the many other nations in the UN. Annan even comments that he found himself as a 'global interpreter, explaining the United States to the world, and the world to the United States'.[29] For the UN to function, all Member States need to be involved. The Secretary-General is key to making this work.

18.5 Features in Hammarskjöld's diplomacy

There are some features which may have been special to Hammarskjöld, notably his emphasis on travel, personal relations and coalition building.

[28] *Ibid.*, at 96–97. [29] *Ibid.*, at 3.

18.5.1 *Travel diplomacy*

The breakthrough for Hammarskjöld's diplomacy came with his visit to China in 1954. Meeting the Chinese leader Zhou Enlai paved the way for the release of the American pilots held by the People's Republic. This unexpected success took place at an early stage of his first term in office. It gave him and his office remarkable recognition and appreciation, particularly in the United States. Following this pattern, Hammarskjöld often went to the scene of a crisis and personally conducted negotiations. This was the case for the Middle East conflicts in 1956–7, where Hammarskjöld's first visit in April 1956 laid the foundation of good relations with leading personalities in the region (such as Ben Gurion and Nasser). He wanted to go to Hungary, but was denied that possibility. Hammarskjöld's diplomacy in the crisis in the Congo initially took place in New York. Thanks to his Africa tour half a year earlier, he had gained personal insights and connections, which were highly useful as the Congo crises unfolded. The first UN troops to go to Katanga in August 1960 were led by Hammarskjöld personally. His aircraft was circling around the airfield in Elizabethville while he was negotiating the landing of the UN troops with the Katangese leader, a daring case of diplomacy, not repeated by many world leaders. Indeed, it was on a trip of personal diplomacy that Hammarskjöld died.

Travel diplomacy became Hammarskjöld's trademark. It was more effective at the time than it might be today. It was not easy to travel as much as Hammarskjöld did, and leaders were not used to as many meetings as they would have today. One visit then may equal many visits today. It provided leaders an opportunity that might not come back. In today's world, with more routine travelling and more comfortable conditions, such personal diplomacy may no longer be as effective. Still, mediators testify to the importance of actually being on the ground.[30] However, today's diplomacy may be more a matter of personal conversations over a safe telephone system, rather than actually meeting in person. Kofi Annan appears constantly to have been in contact with world leaders on the phone. He reports one case where this did not work. When he suggested to Saddam Hussein that they could be in contact over the phone, Saddam responded: 'That thing, I never touch it.'[31] Certainly, more than one prominent leader had encountered phones that contained bombs. This, then, is a further argument in favour of travel diplomacy.

[30] See generally Svensson and Wallensteen, *supra* note 8.
[31] Annan, *supra* note 1, at 328.

18.5.2 Building trust

Egypt's President Nasser had never 'gone back on anything he said to me personally', Hammarskjöld said when others complained about Nasser's action.[32] He trusted that promises made to him would be kept, but it also made him convey promises to others. Deals could hinge on the ability of others to fulfil their pledges. The least that was required was that everybody understood the promises in a reasonably similar way. By establishing trustful relations, which was helped by his travel diplomacy, Hammarskjöld could be a channel for contact, but also a spider in a web. He was often the only one that maintained relationships with the opposing sides, and could deliver messages from one to the other. He was able to bring correct messages with necessary interpretations, and constructive proposals.

In the end, the trust in Hammarskjöld depended on an agreement being carried out as intended. Nasser responded to Hammarskjöld's above comment: 'I wish to maintain that record.'[33] Thus, a promise made to Hammarskjöld was a promise not broken. In an international system often described as 'anarchical', with actions only guided by 'national interest', it is enlightening to find that a promise is a promise, even though the actor to which it is given does not command an army or even represent a state. Hammarskjöld obviously established such relations with many political leaders, for example Jawaharlal Nehru, Zhou Enlai, numerous leaders in the Middle East and the King of Laos.[34] In the Lebanon crisis of 1958, Nasser made some commitments to Hammarskjöld and US intelligence confirmed that Nasser carried them out.[35] The strategy worked with the leaders Hammarskjöld encountered. It was less successful in the turbulent Congo crisis. It appeared that the political actors played according to other rules. Linnér described him as 'a nobly formed Ming vase among rough clay jars'.[36]

18.5.3 Early action

Hammarskjöld's actions in Guatemala, the Middle East in 1956 and Lebanon all aimed at preventing conflicts from escalating. Success could

[32] Urquhart, *supra* note 11, at 269. [33] *Ibid.*

[34] Urquhart, *supra* note 11, at 148, 355. [35] *Ibid.*, at 275.

[36] S. Linnér, *Dag Hammarskjöld and the Congo Crisis, 1960–61*, The Dag Hammarskjöld Lecture (2007), 26, at: www.dhf.uu.se/pdffiler/Dh_lecture_2007.pdf, accessed 11 November 2012.

be recorded. In some cases, however, Hammarskjöld was blocked by permanent members (the United States in Guatemala, Britain and France in the Middle East). The term 'preventive diplomacy' was coined by Hammarskjöld, and achieved prominence again after the Cold War.[37] The assumption was that in an early phase of a conflict, the positions of the parties have not hardened and, thus, there is more room for a conflict-solving formula. Once conflict action has set in, violence has taken place and troops are in battle, the options quickly narrow.[38] The mixed record in preventive diplomacy also indicates some of the difficulties encountered.

The following example is instructive. When Hammarskjöld discussed the situation in Guinea (Conacry) with French President de Gaulle in July 1959, arguing that the economic decline of Guinea – as predicted by de Gaulle – should be prevented through assistance, de Gaulle responded that he was 'complètement désintéressé'.[39] The hardship inflicted was seen as an instrument to bring Guinea back to the fold. Of course, the opposite remained true. Guinea became even more strongly aligned with the radical African countries.

Early action as well as travel diplomacy involved dangers to Hammarskjöld and his diplomacy. There was considerable political risk in going to Beijing in 1954 without guarantees of a successful outcome. This was amplified by the media coverage and by the difficulties in estimating what the leaders of the People's Republic of China would think of a representative from an organisation to which they did not have access. By involving himself and his office in negotiations, visits and proposals, Hammarskjöld may also have risked undermining the position he had. Failure may lead to further failure, as success may stimulate further success. He was well aware that he took a 'calculated risk', for example in Laos 1959, and in the Congo, where he was concerned about the consequences from not acting.[40] He also admitted, speaking of Congo, that 'I am not optimistic' (11 July 1960). Still he took the risks. Entering with UN troops into Katanga in August 1960 was a daring move, as was his last flight to Ndola in September 1961.[41]

[37] UN Secretary-General Boutros Boutros-Ghali took this up: UN Secretary General, *An Agenda for Peace, Preventive Diplomacy, Peacemaking and Peacekeeping* (1992), A47/277-S/2411.

[38] M.S. Lund, *Preventing Violent Conflicts: A Strategy for Preventive Diplomacy* (1996).

[39] Urquhart, *supra* note 11, 379.

[40] *Ibid.*, at 353, 389.

[41] *Ibid.*, at 394, 414, 416–427.

This was not bravery for the sake of bravery. It was the result of calculations. In a way it may reflect his earlier career as an economist, giving training in weighing pluses and minuses, pros and cons. He was, in a sense, an early user of game theory, estimating the utilities of different moves. His record suggests that he often made the correct estimates.

18.5.4 Coalition-building

Coalition-building was probably the most central element in Hammarskjöld's way of diplomacy. It meant having all parties agree on the procedure that he wanted to follow. To be efficient, this required not only that the Secretary General could operate with the Member States through their representatives in New York, but could also go directly to the political leaders in the capitals. His intensive travelling gave him such access, and this in turn gave him further access to others. Hammarskjöld could operate in a spiral of positive expectations. Others thought that he had leverage, his opinions mattered, and thus new coalitions could continuously be moulded for the issues that arose, and leverage created. The coalitions shifted over time, from the success with the American pilots in 1954–5, to the support of most Member States in the Suez crisis in 1956 and initially also in the Congo conflict. When the Soviet Union withdrew its backing, Hammarskjöld could still count on the support of the African and Asian countries.

Keeping a coalition together meant acting on several levels of diplomacy at the same time. Hammarskjöld operated in three arenas in the Congo crisis: in Congo itself, in Belgium and in the UN. These were different dynamics and only he had full insights and understanding of what went on. The interplay between what one actor did in one arena with what another did thousands of kilometres away may not have been apparent to each of the separate actors. Hammarskjöld saw the entire picture. It certainly made operations highly fragile and difficult to maintain. It required an ability to assimilate considerable amounts of information, weigh it and find imaginative ways of moving forward. In the 1950s it was a novelty to operate in such a global way. The term 'two-level games'[42] suggests that political leaders in international affairs consider their country in relation to other countries, as well as their own standing in domestic affairs. In UN politics and much of international diplomacy, this is too

[42] R.D. Putnam, 'Diplomacy and Domestic Politics: The Logic of Two-Level Games' (1988) 42(3) *International Organization* 427.

limited a perspective. There are more levels and actors to consider. There are also the internal dynamics of a great number of states (not only the Major Powers, for instance), and the politics of UN policy-making, but also the international relations entangling major powers in difficult webs of linkages and conflicts.

The way leaders handle these complexities is an increasingly urgent research task. On the one hand, there is the Hammarskjöld approach of trying to anticipate what will happen in this entire web of actors, goals and actions. This is an anticipatory and preventive strategy, which relies on information and political intuition. Another strategy is trial and error. Leaders may try a particular course of action, to see what will be the result. The approach seems to be 'if it works, it works; if it doesn't, find an excuse'. The strategy is convenient, but assumes authoritarian control over a society. It is not likely to work for a UN Secretary-General.

Furthermore, the crisis diplomacy of Kofi Annan exhibits these features, not least in marshalling international support for actions in the case of East Timor, where the UN was a definite lead actor and also could score a degree of success. His diplomacy involved the creation of an invisible coalition to support this action, as there were no pre-existing regional organisations to build on. It is an interesting case of pulling together the concerns of Australia, the United States, Malaysia, Thailand, Portugal, Indonesia and others, and without meeting the opposition of China and Russia.

18.6 The primary lesson: the integrity of the office

The standing Hammarskjöld acquired for himself and the UN at times seems to have tempted him to think of the institutions and his office as a force above the politics of others. It might be turned into an independent actor in international affairs.[43] This would be unacceptable to the majority of the Member States. In fact, Hammarskjöld was coming close to such a position in international affairs. The heated exchange between him and the Soviet leader, Nikita Khrushchev, in the autumn of 1960 on the role of the Secretary-General, had such undercurrents. The Soviet proposal for a troika replacing the Secretary-General reflected dissatisfaction with the autonomy of the office. It was a formative battle and the outcome made sure that UN integrity remained intact. Without that, his successors would not have been able to play a constructive role in international

[43] Urquhart, *supra* note 11, at 258–259.

affairs, or even use the position to develop new norms for international actions, such as the idea of a responsibility to protect. It became associated with Kofi Annan. The UN Secretary-General remains a unique post in a world of strong states. It is the only body with powers to bring up issues, negotiate their course and be part of the implementation of the resulting decisions. Hammarskjöld understood its potential and his successors, not least of all Kofi Annan, continue to build on that achievement.

19

Visions of international life

From Hammarskjöld to Annan and beyond

JAN ANNE VOS

19.1 Introduction

The tenures by Kofi Annan and Dag Hammarskjöld as, Secretary-General of the United Nations, are commonly compared and contrasted.[1] Both figures espoused visions of international life. The successive introductions by Hammarskjöld to the Secretary-General's Annual Reports to the UN General Assembly highlight institutional changes in the UN. They arguably reflect a transition from a horizontal (i.e. an intergovernmental) to a vertical (i.e. partly supranational) conception of the UN. This vision was partly shared and developed by Annan. Annan's main reform proposal, his report 'In Larger Freedom', entailed a re-thinking of UN structures. It may be read as a reformulation of the interplay between the purposes contained in Article 1 of the Charter of the UN (e.g. peace and security, democracy, human rights). In the Congo and Libya, their visions have partially been tested 'on the ground'. This practice shows that the application of this type of internationalism by the UN continues to pose dilemmas concerning the relationship between international authority and obligations of domestic authorities.

Jan Anne Vos is Director, XYNTHEZYX, Global Law Company, formerly a researcher at T.M.C. Asser Institute, The Hague.

[1] S. Meisler, *Kofi Annan: A Man of Peace in a World of War* (2007), 3–6, 147–168, 201–216, 235–252; B. Urquhart, 'The Evolution of the Secretary-General', in S. Chesterman (ed.), *Secretary or General? – The UN Secretary-General in World Politics* (2007), 15, at 19–23, 27–29; S. Tharoor, '"The Most Impossible Job" Description', in Chesterman, *ibid.*, at 33.

19.2 Framework

The Secretariat has been designated in Article 7(1) of the UN Charter as one of the principal organs of the UN. The Secretary-General is entrusted with administrative and political powers and heads the Secretariat.

The Secretary-General operates in a complex environment which is shaped by interests of other principal UN organs and UN Member States. Pursuant to Article 98 of the UN Charter, the Secretary-General shall perform such functions as may be entrusted to him by the General Assembly, the Security Council, the Economic and Social Council and the Trusteeship Council. The establishment and operation of the United Nations Emergency Force (UNEF) has shown to what extent the constitutional politics of the Secretariat may be affected by the relationship between the Security Council and the General Assembly, including the exercise of powers by the Assembly on the basis of the Uniting for Peace resolution.[2]

Article 99 of the UN Charter allocates an autonomous function to the Secretary-General: 'The Secretary-General may bring to the attention of the Security Council any matter, which in his opinion, may threaten the maintenance of international peace and security.' In international life, this provision has been developed so as to form the basis of fact-finding missions and good offices.[3] In so far as such functions are understood as emanating from inherent or implied powers, such powers must be seen as conferred by the Member States. At the same time, while such functions may be regarded as autonomous, their exercise should be directed at the activities of the Security Council.

Annan made constructive use of the dynamics of the Charter and the interplay between international peace and security and economic and social development. He argued in his report 'In Larger Freedom' that the Secretary-General, in consultation with the Director-General of the World Health Organization, might invoke powers under Article 99 of the UN Charter in order to draw to the attention of the Security Council any overwhelming outbreak of infectious disease that threatens international peace and security.[4]

[2] UN Doc. A/RES/377 (V).

[3] 'In Larger Freedom: Towards Development, Security and Human Rights for All', Report of the Secretary-General, UN Doc. A/59/2005 (2005), at para. 108.

[4] See *ibid.*, at para. 105.

But overall, the authority of the Secretary-General is based on power entrusted to him/her by UN principal organs and UN Member States. The exercise of autonomous functions is based on powers conferred by UN Member States. The mandated functions (i.e. those under Article 98), are entrusted by other UN organs.

19.3 Living constitution

In a typology of leadership styles of Secretaries-General, Kille has distinguished between managerial, visionary and strategic styles, derived from scores on six personal characteristics:

(1) responsiveness (sensitivity to context and analytical capability);
(2) belief that can influence (self-perception as capable of influencing events);
(3) need for recognition (unwillingness to control and credit);
(4) need for relationships (desire to maintain good personal relationships);
(5) supranationalism (attachment to UN values); and
(6) problem-solving emphasis (prioritising completion of tasks).[5]

According to Kille, a 'visionary style' can be associated with supranationalist thinkers who:

(1) clearly believe in their ability to influence;
(2) focus on problem-solving; and
(3) desire control over and public acknowledgement of their efforts, while remaining less sensitive to context and interaction with others.

By contrast, a 'managerial style' is characterised by:

(1) a limited belief in the ability to have influence;
(2) a strong responsiveness to conditions;
(3) the use and need of relationships in action (including balancing of interests against task completion); and
(4) a lesser emphasis on supranationalism.[6]

Based on this matrix, Kille classified Hammarskjöld's style generally as visionary. But he qualified this categorisation in light of Hammarskjöld's

[5] K. Kille, *From Manager to Visionary – The Secretary-General of the United Nations* (2006), 16–22.

[6] *Ibid.*

responsiveness, i.e. his sensitivity to context. The thrust of his vision was to direct the UN towards a cooperative international community oriented by global values.[7] This approach is conveyed in the introductions of his Annual Reports to the General Assembly, including the 1961 introduction. These reports stand as political statements.[8] In fact, taken as a whole, the successive introductions of the Annual Reports to the General Assembly reflect institutional developments which strengthen the emergence of 'vertical' (i.e. supranational) features in the conception of UN authority and working methods.[9]

In the 1953 introduction to his Report to the General Assembly,[10] Hammarskjöld depicted the work of the UN in terms of a magic triangle, consisting of the interrelated fields of security, development and cooperation. Following on, the introduction to the 1954 Annual Report focused on the actualisation of principles. The 1955 introduction highlighted quiet diplomacy as a means to enhance the usefulness of the UN. Set against the background of the so-called 'Beijing formula' in the light of the potentialities of the UN Charter, this first set of three reports may be seen as marking the expansion of the position of the Secretary-General from a conduit for consultations between (Member) States to an autonomous constitutional responsibility for the general purposes set out in the UN Charter, entailing independent rights and duties.[11]

The introduction to the 1956 Annual Report stressed the drive towards universality of the UN by means of the realisation of the right to self-determination. The 1957 introduction focused naturally on the Suez and Hungary crises and emphasised the step-by-step development of the UN Charter. The 1958 introduction was rather low-key and described, against the background of the establishment of the International Atomic Energy Agency, possible advances in disarmament and the peaceful uses of atomic energy. In this second series of three reports, self-determination, peacekeeping and the fruition of atoms for peace may be seen as filling in the security and development sides of the magic triangle, while actually downplaying a grand design for the UN.[12]

[7] *Ibid.*, 69–81. [8] *Ibid.*, at 97–99.

[9] M. Fröhlich, *Political Ethics and the United Nations – Dag Hammarskjöld as Secretary-General* (2008), 24–44.

[10] Introduction to the Annual Report of the Secretary-General on the work of the Organization, 1 July 1952–30 June 1953, 15 July 1953, UN Doc. A/2404.

[11] B. Urquhart, *Hammarskjöld* (1972), 86–131.

[12] Introduction to the Annual Report of the Secretary-General on the Work of the Organization, 16 June 1956–15 June 1957, UN Doc. A/3594/Add. 1 (1957), at 3–4: 'The

The introduction to the 1959 Annual Report put these developments in a dynamic perspective and concentrated on the cooperation side of the magic triangle. Putting forward the so-called vacuum theory, Hammarskjöld evoked the development of constitutional life.[13] The 1960 introduction extended this conception by characterising UN action as international executive authority.[14] The 1961 introduction, finally, completed this line of thought, by addressing the very structure of the UN system based on a domestic analogy. It argued that the organic growth that states had achieved internally in relation to executive action might now also be within reach for the UN.[15] This third and final set of reports, therefore, used a constitutional analogy that approximated the UN to a supranational body, i.e. an entity situated at the international plane that is endowed with the authority to create rules of public international law applying to states.[16]

These views informed Hammarskjöld's view of the role of international law and its relationship with international politics. From the perspective of the achievement of a cooperative international community, the concept of international law was to be seen as an instrument through which the sovereignty of states would increasingly be limited. From this point of view, Hammarskjöld emphasised that states should adhere more to international law and should facilitate the expansion of the jurisdiction of the International Court of Justice. International politics was accordingly seen as something against which international law should operate. As it transpires through these views, however, and as the Permanent Court of International Justice had made clear previously in the *Case of the S.S. Wimbledon*,[17] the development of rules of international law was seen, at the same time, as based on the sovereignty of states and consequently anchored in the field of international politics. The development of the cooperation side of the triangle, therefore, while bearing supranational features, remained entrenched in the field of international politics.

Charter, read as a whole, does not endow the United Nations with any of the attributes of a super-State'.

13 Introduction to the Annual Report of the Secretary-General on the Work of the Organization, 16 June 1958–15 June 1959, UN Doc. A/4132/Add. 1 (1959), at 1–4.

14 Introduction to the Annual Report of the Secretary-General on the Work of the Organization, 16 June 1959–15 June 1960, UN Doc. A/4390/Add. 1 (1960), at 2–5, 7–8.

15 Introduction to the Annual Report of the Secretary-General on the Work of the Organization, 16 June 1960–15 June 1961, UN Doc. A/4800/Add. (1961), at 1–3, 5–8.

16 I. Kant, 'Perpetual Peace: A Philosophical Sketch', in H.S. Reis (ed.), *Kant – Political Writings* (1991), 93, at 102.

17 *Case of the S.S. Wimbledon*, Judgment of 17 August 1923, Series A, No. 1, at 25.

19.4 (M)ONU(S)C(O)

The establishment and operation of the United Nations Operation in the Congo (ONUC) brought many of the threads together that were identified in the successive introductions of the Annual Reports to the General Assembly, i.e. the realisation of the right to self-determination, the consensual basis of UNEF and the characterisation of UN action as executive. Hammarskjöld explicitly invoked Article 99 of the UN Charter to bring the situation in the Congo, which had just become independent on 30 June 1960, before the Security Council.[18] On the elliptic basis of paragraph 2 of Resolution 143 (1960), ONUC was to assist the Republic of the Congo in the restoration of law and order. However, the invocation of Article 25 of the UN Charter in Resolution 146 (1960) in fact superseded this consensual basis.[19] Subsequently, ONUC's mandate was successively reinforced in paragraph 1 of Resolution 161 (1961) (preventing 'civil war') and in Resolution 169 (1961), which favoured territorial integrity over secession.

Resolution 146 was based on the assumption that Belgian troops would withdraw. It distinguished between an international situation and an internal situation. Paragraph 4 of the resolution maintained in particular that the UN would not interfere in the political conflict between the central government and the provincial government of Katanga.[20] In his Memorandum on the Implementation of paragraph 4, Hammarskjöld relied on this aspect in order to secure the deployment of ONUC in Katanga.[21] This understanding was complemented by the view that ONUC's deployment was mandatory for both the central government and the provincial government. When the constitutional crisis within the central government erupted between Kasavubu and Lumumba, this political impartiality was extended to the relationship between the Chief of State and the Prime Minister. In addition, paragraph 3 of General Assembly Resolution 1474 (ES-IV) (based on the Uniting for Peace resolution), supported this position,[22] although it did not prevent the General Assembly from siding with Kasavubu later. ONUC thus paired what appeared to be a sufficient mandate – binding in respect of both the central government

[18] See Kille, *supra* note 5, 92–95.

[19] E.M. Miller (i.e. O. Schachter), 'Legal Aspects of the United Nations Action in the Congo' (1961) 55 *American Journal of International Law* 1, at 13–15.

[20] See *ibid.*, at 15–18.

[21] G. Abi-Saab, *The United Nations Operation in the Congo 1960–1964* (1978), 37–48.

[22] See Miller (Schachter), *supra* note 19, at 18–19, 23–25.

and the provincial government – with non-interference in the political field, transplanting in this respect the principles for the establishment and operation of UNEF not only from the Middle East to Africa, but also from the international plane to the internal sphere of states.[23] As Meisler has pointed out, this tension between a hierarchical, interventionist approach, on the one hand, and a neutral peacekeeping approach, on the other hand, impeded the UN in its subsequent actions and omissions in Somalia, Rwanda and Bosnia.[24]

Ultimately, ONUC 'resolved' the situation by stressing the interplay between law and order, civil war and political conflict. Maintaining law and order sometimes required measures interfering in the political conflict, such as the closing of the airports and radio stations to the detriment of Lumumba. The political conflict formed the basis of civil war. The mandate to prevent civil war was sometimes interpreted extensively (e.g. as permission to strike Tshombe's air force) and sometimes restrictively. On the ground, political impartiality therefore had to give way to a more robust and 'interventionist' approach in the implementation of parts of the mandate. On the international plane, however, the Secretary-General remained a rival executive arm to the Security Council and lost its moorings in the political field.[25]

Indirectly, the plane crash that took place on 6 April 1994 in Rwanda brought about the type of conflict that Hammarskjöld had so anxiously sought to avoid: the Great African War (1998–2003).[26] Rwanda and Uganda sought to retain their influence in the Democratic Republic of the Congo, first directly and later through their respective proxies, the Rassemblement Congolais pour la Démocratie and the Mouvement pour la Libération du Congo.[27] The Security Council reacted by passing Resolution 1234 (1999) and, after the conclusion of the Lusaka Ceasefire Agreement, established the United Nations Organization Mission in the Democratic Republic of the Congo (MONUC).[28] While originally circumscribed as an ordinary peacekeeping mission, MONUC's mandate has gradually been brought within the ambit of Chapter VII of the UN Charter.[29] In view of the new phase reached within the Democratic

[23] See Urquhart, *supra* note 11, at 159–230, 389–456.
[24] See Meisler, *supra* note 1, at 55–124.
[25] D. Malone and J. Cockayne, 'Relations with the Security Council', in Chesterman, *supra* note 1, 69, at 71–78.
[26] See also Chapter 12, this volume.
[27] D. van Reybrouck, *Congo – Een Geschiedenis* (2011), 419–498.
[28] UN Doc. S/RES/1279 (1999).
[29] UN Doc. S/RES/1493 (2003).

Republic of the Congo, MONUC has been transformed, with effect from 1 July 2010, into the United Nations Organization Stabilization Mission in the Democratic Republic of the Congo (MONUSCO), based on Chapter VII of the UN Charter.[30] Tragically and ironically, it would appear that both successes and failures ascribed to MONU(S)C(O)[31] demarcate the disconnection between the UN, representing international society, and the internal Congolese sphere, which is seen – from the international plane – as a threat to international peace and security.

19.5 'In Larger Freedom'

In his typology of leadership styles, Kille identified an 'ideal' strategic style of a Secretary-General. He associates this strategic style with personalities who:

(1) share supranational ideals;
(2) are willing to defend the UN, while believing in their influence;
(3) are responsive to situational requirements; and
(4) show a desire to maintain good relationships.[32]

Kille adds that strategic leadership requires a relatively low need for recognition and a nuanced approach to problem-solving which balances tasks to be completed with relations to others. Based on this scale, Kille classified Annan's style as a strategic leader.[33] He points to the use of reports to guide the process of reform of the UN as a hallmark of Annan's tenure of the office of Secretary-General.[34] In particular, his report 'In Larger Freedom' contains a strategic vision for the UN which goes beyond immediate reform proposals.

The words 'In Larger Freedom' are taken from the preamble of the Charter of the UN. In the report, Annan explains that these terms were used to stress the enduring relevance and to capture the interrelation

30 UN Doc. S/RES/1925 (2010). On similarities and differences between ONUC and MONU(S)C(O), see J.-E. Wanki, 'Disarming War, Arming Peace: The Congo Crisis, Dag Hammarskjöld's Legacy and the Future Role of MONUC in the Democratic Republic of the Congo' (2011) 11 *African Journal on Conflict Resolution* 101.

31 S.P. Sheeran, 'A Constitutional Moment? United Nations Peacekeeping in the Democratic Republic of Congo' (2011) 8 *International Organizations Law Review* 55, at 59–64.

32 Kille, *supra* note 5, at 16–20, 158–165, 171–174.

33 The strategic style is a composite of the managerial and visionary styles, but it does not in itself exclude visionary aspects. *Ibid.*

34 *Ibid.*

between development, security and human rights.[35] Annan develops the idea of freedom under the umbrella of three concepts:

(1) 'freedom from want' (development);
(2) 'freedom from fear' (security); and
(3) 'freedom to live in dignity' (human rights).

The 'freedom to live in dignity' is subdivided into:

(a) the rule of law;
(b) human rights; and
(c) democracy.

By placing the notion of human rights at the centre of dignity and subsuming the areas of development and security under categories of 'freedom from want' and 'freedom from fear', the report focuses on three core themes, taken from paragraphs 1 and 3 of Article 1 of the UN Charter:

(1) Human Rights;
(2) Economic and Social Cooperation/Development; and
(3) International Peace and Security.

The report further stresses the interrelation between these fields, asserting that 'we will not enjoy development without security, we will not enjoy security without development, and we will not enjoy either without respect for human rights'.[36] The report does not expressly seek to establish a hierarchy between these fields. In fact, the idea of hierarchy seems to go against the interrelated nature of these fields. But the framing of the report appears to suggest a certain prevalence of the notion of human rights. For instance, economic and social development might be seen as an embodiment or particularisation of economic and social rights. The protection of international peace and security, in turn, might be regarded as a particularisation of civil and political rights. Such a perspective diverges from the approach adopted previously by the International Court of Justice in *Certain Expenses of the United Nations*, i.e. the Advisory Opinion which implicitly endorsed the conformity of UNEF and ONUC (propelled by Hammarskjöld) with the UN Charter. In the opinion, the ICJ argued that international peace and security retains a primary place in Article

[35] See 'In Larger Freedom', *supra* note 3, at para. 14.
[36] *Ibid.*, para. 17.

1(1) of the UN Charter, and that the realisation of other UN purposes is dependent upon the attainment of that basic condition.[37]

Annan's approach converges markedly with the magic triangle described by Hammarskjöld in the introduction to his 1953 Annual Report to the General Assembly. Both reports identify security and development as pillars of the UN system. Annan, however, substituted Hammarskjöld's focus on cooperation by reliance on human rights. Both reports stress the interrelatedness of the respective concepts, i.e. the idea that the three dimensions form a whole. In public discussion of Annan's report, the emphasis is mostly placed on the specific reform proposals contained in the report such as the development of the concept of the responsibility to protect, the transformation of the Commission on Human Rights into the Human Rights Council or the establishment of the Peace-building Commission.[38] But the most enduring significance of the report may actually lie in its vision of the purposes of the UN.

This should not detract from the more immediate practical role that Annan has played in the development of core principles. This approach marks another point of convergence between Hammarskjöld and Annan.[39] Annan strongly embraced the idea of the responsibility to protect, previously promoted by the High-level Panel on Threats, Challenges and Change. The concept corresponded to his views on intervention which he had set out in his Ditchley Lecture in 1999.[40] Annan saw one of the primary *raison d' être* of states in their duty to protect their population. He also shared the view that the responsibility to help protect the human rights and well-being of civilian populations may shift to the international community. He defended enforcement action for that purpose.[41] This vision bears synergies with Hammarskjöld's reaction to crimes unfolding in the situation in the Congo. Hammarskjöld recognised that:

(1) UN action countering crime would be covered by a mandate to maintain law and order; and
(2) that the concept of sovereignty should not be used or seen as a shield against such action.[42]

37 *Certain Expenses of the United Nations (Article 17, Paragraph 2, of the Charter)*, Advisory Opinion of 20 July 1962 [1962] ICJ Rep. 151, at 167–168.

38 A. Adebajo, 'Pope, Pharaoh, or Prophet? The Secretary-General after the Cold War', in Chesterman, *supra* note 1, 139, at 151–155.

39 I. Johnstone, 'The Secretary-General as Norm Entrepreneur', in Chesterman, *supra* note 1, 123, at 131–137.

40 See Meisler, *supra* note 1, at 171–186.

41 See 'In Larger Freedom', *supra* note 3, at para. 135.

42 For a study of the approach of Hammarskjöld towards 'humanitarian intervention', see Chapter 9, this volume.

This general development seems to be in line with the vision traced in Hammarskjöld's Annual Reports to the General Assembly. It reflects a move towards a strengthening of UN authority in the relationship between the UN and its Member States, i.e. the recognition of the use of certain top-down approaches and supranational features (the 'super-state' model). Annan called expressly for the strengthening of the rule of law – both internationally and nationally – as well as greater participation in multilateral conventions and recognition of the compulsory jurisdiction of the International Court of Justice.[43] Yet, he also continued to regard sovereign states as the basic and indispensable building blocks of the international system.[44] Taken together, these views appear to entail a basic metaphoric contradiction. Article 2(1) of the UN Charter provides that the UN is based on the sovereign equality of the Member States. That is how the UN has traditionally been seen and what makes it possible to explain the existence of the UN as an entity created by states. Many of the contemporary efforts at UN level, however, are focused on strengthening the position of the UN and reforming state structures from 'outside', and not from within. This challenges the premise that states form the basic and indispensable building blocks of the international system.

19.6 Divergence and convergence

The relationship of the UN to Member States was addressed by the ICJ in the Advisory Opinion concerning *Reparations for Injuries Suffered in the Service of the United Nations*. In this case, the Court examined the question as to whether the UN could claim compensation for injuries directly sustained by the UN Mediator in Palestine, Count Folke Bernadotte, in circumstances not dissimilar from the plane crash of Hammarskjöld at Ndola. The Court acknowledged the international personality of the UN. It engaged with the notion of 'international life'[45]

[43] See 'In Larger Freedom', *supra* note 3, at paras. 132, 136, 139.

[44] See *ibid.*, at para. 19.

[45] The term has become an established topic in ICJ jurisprudence and is commonly relied on in both public international law and international relations writings without, however, being defined. See *Legality of the Use by a State of Nuclear Weapons in Armed Conflict*, Advisory Opinion of 8 July 1996 [1996] ICJ Rep. 66, at para. 25: 'The powers conferred on international organizations are normally the subject of an express statement in their constituent instruments. Nevertheless, the necessities of international life may point to the need for organizations, in order to achieve their objectives, to possess subsidiary powers which are not expressly provided for in the basic instruments which govern their activities.'

in its opinion[46] which links international law to international politics and broader cosmopolitan goals, such as the pursuance of common values and the idea of international society. But, the Court refused to equate the UN to a 'super-state'. It held:

> [T]he Organization is an international person. That is not the same thing as saying that it is a State, which it certainly is not, or that its legal personality and rights and duties are the same as those of a State. Still less is it the same thing as saying that it is 'a super-State'.[47]

Later, the Court confirmed and expanded this view in its Advisory Opinion on the *Interpretation of the Agreement of 25 March 1951 between the WHO and Egypt*.[48]

Hammarskjöld's introductions depart partly from this conception. Both the theorisation of the UN as a constitutional body and the development of international executive authority mark a shift towards a novel conception of the UN which emancipates the organisation from state authority. This approach is in line with the conception of international organisations as governance bodies and 'constitutionalist approaches' towards international organisation.[49] But it conflicted with the constraints of the time. When Hammarskjöld's vision was tested on the ground in the Republic of the Congo, it caused tensions and conflicts with political impartiality. ONUC stopped short of interfering in the internal political conflict, even though informally it steered the resolution of the conflict towards the re-establishment of central authority,

Annan's report 'In Larger Freedom' refined thinking on the tension between external interference and domestic empowerment. It endorsed

[46] See *Reparation for Injuries Suffered in the Service of the United Nations*, *supra* note 39, at 178: 'Throughout its history, the development of international law has been influenced by the requirements of international life ... This development culminated in the establishment in June 1945 of an international organization whose purposes and principles are specified in the Charter of the United Nations.'

[47] *Reparation for Injuries Suffered in the Service of the United Nations*, Advisory Opinion of 11 April 1949 [1949] ICJ Rep. 174, at 179.

[48] The Court held that 'there is nothing in the character of international organizations to justify their being considered as some form of "super-State"'. See *Interpretation of the Agreement of 25 March 1951 between the WHO and Egypt*, Advisory Opinion of 20 December 1980 [1980] ICJ Rep. 73, at para. 37. The Court added: 'International organizations are subjects of international law and, as such, are bound by any obligations incumbent upon them under general rules of international law, under their constitutions or under international agreements to which they are parties.'

[49] B. Fassbender, 'The United Nations Charter as Constitution of the International Community' (1998) 36 *Columbia Journal of Transnational Law* 529.

the concept of responsibility to protect which seeks to strengthen both the UN and its Member States. The concept was included in the Outcome Document of the 2005 World Summit and endorsed by the Security Council and the General Assembly.[50] Subsequently, it was invoked and applied in Resolution 1973 (2011) relating to Libya. The mandate combined the protection of civilians (paragraphs 4–5) with the establishment of a no-fly zone (paragraphs 6–12). In this context, political impartiality was not considered as an obstacle to intervention, i.e. action for the protection of the civilian population against the Gaddafi government. It resulted in constitutional change,[51] i.e. the substitution of the Gaddafi government by the Transitional National Council and the re-establishment of state institutions, with assistance by the United Nations Support Mission in Libya (UNSMIL).[52]

This type of action raises challenges to the conception of UN authority. The more the UN intervenes in different types of internal political conflict (i.e. constitutional, institutional and democratic disputes) the closer it comes to the idea of a kind of 'super-state' which has been rejected in ICJ jurisprudence. In the field of territorial administration, this tendency has partially materialised: in the context of Kosovo and East Timor, the UN has in fact become a 'surrogate state', overriding domestic state structures on a transitional basis.[53] From a 'Third World' perspective, this 'supranational' conception of UN authority is actually experienced as a reality.[54]

[50] UN Doc. A/RES/60/1 (2005), at paras. 138–139.

[51] Constitutional transformation also occurred in the context of the action of the United Nations Operation in Côte d'Ivoire relating to the post-electoral crisis in Côte d'Ivoire. See UN Doc. S/RES/1528 (2004); UN Doc. S/RES/1933 (2010), para. 4; UN Doc. S/RES/1962 (2010); UN Doc. S/RES/2000 (2011), para. 6; UN Doc. S/RES/2062 (2012). The Special Representative of the Secretary-General (SRSG) certified the results of the second round of the presidential elections as determined by the Independent Electoral Commission, rather than by the Constitutional Council. The SRSG derived this competence from the Pretoria Agreement on the Peace Process in Côte d'Ivoire, the Declaration on the Implementation of the Pretoria Agreement and Security Council Resolution 1765 (2007). See Twenty-seventh progress report of the Secretary-General on the United Nations Operation in Côte d'Ivoire, UN Doc. S/2011/211, paras. 14–18, 74–75.

[52] UN Doc. S/RES/2009, para. 12; UN Doc. S/RES/2040, para. 6.

[53] For a discussion, see R. Wilde, *International Territorial Administration* (2008), C. Stahn, *The Law and Practice of International Territorial Administration* (2008). See also Chapter 21, this volume.

[54] B. S. Chimni, 'International Institutions Today: An Imperial Global State in the Making' (2004) 15 *European Journal of International Law*, 1.

In contemporary practice, there is a tension between interventionist approaches and a more 'neutral' approach to peacekeeping, as evidenced by the UN engagement in Somalia, Rwanda and Bosnia.[55] One of the most striking contrasts to the UN approach in Libya is the humanitarian action carried out by the Unified Task Force (UNITAF) in Somalia in 1992/1993. Both operations were enforcement actions under Chapter VII of the UN Charter, involving UN engagement in internal situations. Both actions involved the deployment of UN-sponsored/backed forces for purposes of the protection of elementary principles of humanity. Both operations were limited in time. UNITAF withdrew from a more or less ongoing conflict and was succeeded by the United Nations Operation in Somalia II (UNOSOM II). In its report, the Commission of Inquiry established pursuant to Security Council Resolution 885 (1993) to investigate armed attacks on UNOSOM II personnel, highlighted the difference between UNOSOM II, authorised under Security Council Resolution 814 (1993) to disarm the parties to the conflict, and traditional peacekeeping operations based on their consent.[56] It found that UNOSOM II had exceeded its mandate in the political field. It arrived at the general recommendation that the UN should refrain from undertaking further peace enforcement actions within the internal sphere of states. It noted that in cases where the UN would decide to undertake such actions, the mandate should be limited to specific objectives and use of force should only be allowed after the exhaustion of peaceful remedies.[57]

The misdirected UNOSOM II actions in Somalia had some impact on the omissions of the UN in Rwanda and Bosnia. The Report of the Independent Inquiry into the Actions of the United Nations during the 1994 Genocide in Rwanda stressed the traditional nature of both the United Nations Assistance Mission for Rwanda (UNAMIR) I – established by Security Council Resolution 872 (1993) – and UNAMIR II – established by Security Council Resolution 918 (1994) – as based on the consent of the parties.[58] The mandate to re-establish the Arusha Peace Accord rendered the UN incapable of dealing with the unfolding genocide.[59] The

[55] See Meisler, *supra* note 1, 55–124.

[56] Report of the Commission of Inquiry Established pursuant to Security Council Resolution 885 (1993) to Investigate Armed Attacks on UNOSOM II Personnel which Led to Casualties among them, UN Doc. S/1994/653, at paras. 44–45, 51–53, 188–212.

[57] *Ibid.*, at para. 270.

[58] Report of the Independent Inquiry into the Actions of the United Nations during the 1994 Genocide in Rwanda, UN Doc. S/1999/1257, at 31–32, 38–39.

[59] *Ibid.*, at 41–43.

United Nations Protection Force (UNPF/UNPROFOR) operated on the basis of a mandate (Security Council Resolution 836 (1993)), which combined traditional peacekeeping with an enforcement component. In this context, the Secretariat inferred that the use of force was restricted to self-defence. It maintained this position until after the fall of the safe areas of Srebrenica and Žepa.[60] The Report of the Secretary-General pursuant to General Assembly Resolution 53/35 ('The Fall of Srebrenica') concluded: 'Peacekeepers must never again be deployed into an environment in which there is no ceasefire or peace agreement.'[61] This experience suggested that the UN should generally refrain from interfering in internal armed conflict, be it in the form of peace enforcement or peacekeeping.

The failures of the UN in Rwanda and Bosnia led to a reconsideration of peacekeeping operations in the Report of the Panel on United Nations Peace Operations (the so-called Brahimi Report), which investigated the move from traditional peacekeeping to complex peace operations.[62] Flanked by emphases on conflict prevention[63] and peace-building,[64] the Brahimi Report analysed whether and how the UN could better operate in the internal sphere of states. It argued that complex peace operations require a reconfiguration of:

(1) the importance of the consent of the local parties;
(2) the conception of impartiality; and
(3) the modalities of the use of force.[65]

The report suggested that the requirement of consent would need to be adapted to the interests of the population, in order to prevent that a lack of or withdrawal of consent by a party to the conflict would compromise the success of the operation.[66] The report stressed that the principle of impartiality had to be interpreted in light of the humanitarian principles contained in the UN Charter, limiting divergences between UN interests and the interests of the affected populations. It also recommended operations be vested with the capability to use force commensurate with

[60] Report of the Secretary-General pursuant to General Assembly resolution 53/35 – The Fall of Srebrenica, UN Doc. A/54/549, at paras. 77–78, 452.
[61] *Ibid.*, at para. 498.
[62] Report of the Panel on United Nations Peace Operations, UN Doc. A/55/305-S/2000/809 (2000), paras. 15–28.
[63] *Ibid.*, at paras. 29–34.
[64] *Ibid.*, at paras. 35–47.
[65] *Ibid.*, at paras. 48–55.
[66] M. Fröhlich, 'Keeping Track of UN Peace-keeping – Suez, Srebrenica, Rwanda and the Brahimi Report' (2001) 5 *Max Planck Yearbook of United Nations Law* 185, at 192–211.

the execution of their mandate.[67] These recommendations have subsequently (re)shaped a number of peace operations, including MONUC and MONUSCO, which has been authorised to execute its mandate and use force against a recalcitrant faction.[68]

There has thus been a significant transformation of peacekeeping principles over time. In the context of ONUC, the UN had to cross the veil between international engagement and involvement in the internal sphere of states. The events in Somalia, Rwanda and Bosnia led to a re-thinking of UN operations in the Brahimi Report. MONUC and MONUSCO represent modern examples of complex peace operations, carried out under Chapter VII of the UN Charter. Where traditional peacekeeping is replaced by peace enforcement, the UN takes on a different identity. It takes over tasks usually reserved to its Member States. The UN complements or substitutes the authority of state actors. Yet, this enforcement mode and reliance on the responsibility to protect is not automatic but dependent on the unity of the international community. This is exemplified by the lack of consensus in the Syrian situation.[69]

19.7 Conclusion

This chapter has shown that the visions of international life expounded by Hammarskjöld and Annan have challenged some of the fundamental parameters of international law. There is an inherent tension between the growing resolution of internal constitutional, institutional and political issues at the international plane, and the assumption that states remain the basic and indispensable building block of international society. Of course, the UN Charter as such has never been 'blind' towards the internal organisation of states.[70] Moreover, interventions under concepts such as R2P, protection of civilians or maintenance of law and order are often guided by the ultimate idea of restoring or strengthening state authority. But this type of internationalism poses a dilemma for the conception of

[67] *Ibid.*, at 211–228.

[68] UN Doc. S/RES/1991 (2011); UN Doc. S/RES/2053 (2012); www.crisisgroup.org/crisiswatch, nr. 104, 1 April 2012; nr. 108, 1 August 2012.

[69] On 2 August 2012, Kofi Annan indicated that he would not seek an extension of his mission – which had resulted in a six-point proposal supported by the United Nations Supervision Mission in Syria (UNSMIS). See UN Doc. S/RES/2042 (2012); UN Doc. S/RES/2043 (2012); UN Doc. S/RES/2059 (2012). Lakhdar Brahimi was appointed as Joint Special Representative for Syria on 17 August 2012.

[70] See, e.g., Art. 2 (7) of the UN Charter.

UN authority. If states are no longer seen as the basic and indispensable building blocks of international society, it is difficult to derive the authority of international institutions from conferred powers. Article 2(1) of the UN Charter loses some if its grounding if the UN sees itself increasingly as an institution to strengthen its Member States. It is contradictory to argue that Member States build the foundation of the UN, if these very states are in fact strengthened through external action. This exercise of international authority under the auspices of peace maintenance has transformed the relationship to state authority. It has introduced vertical features through which action by international institutions prevails over Member States.

The UN Secretariat is between 'a rock and a hard place' in these institutional dynamics. The Secretary-General must balance intergovernmental and supranational interests in the exercise of his mandate. The Secretary-General is not fully independent of the Member States, but he must at the same avoid adopting positions that would make him appear dependent on Member States. Towards the end of their second terms, both Hammarskjöld and Annan experienced the consequences of this dilemma. They have been antagonised by the superpowers (i.e. the former USSR and the United States) in relation to their stance in the Congo (Hammarskjöld) and Iraq (Annan).

20

EU global peace diplomacy

Institutional framework

STEVEN BLOCKMANS

20.1 Introduction

Dag Hammarskjöld advocated a community-based vision of the United Nations (UN) in maintaining international peace and security. In his last Annual Report to the General Assembly, he argued that this objective would only be achieved on the basis of four fundamental principles, namely:

(1) equal political rights, both sovereign and individual;
(2) equal economic opportunities, through higher standards and also conditions conducive to economic and social advancement;
(3) a firm framework of the rule of law, which should underpin all activities of the international community; and
(4) the prohibition of the use of force except 'in the common interest'.[1]

These principles are at the core of the Treaty on European Union (TEU) and apply not only within the legal order of the EU, but also to the Union's

Steven Blockmans is Professor of EU External Relations Law and Governance, University of Amsterdam, Senior Research Fellow and Head of the EU Foreign Policy programme at the Centre for European Policy Studies (CEPS), and member of the governing board of the Centre for the Law of EU External Relations (CLEER). Section 20.2 draws in part on S. Blockmans and R.A Wessel, 'The European Union and Peaceful Settlement of Disputes in its Neighbourhood: The Emergence of a New Regional Security Actor?' in A. Antoniadis, R. Schütze and E. Spaventa (eds), The European Union and Global Emergencies: A Law and Policy Analysis (2011), 73–103. Section 20.3 draws on L. Erkelens and S. Blockmans, 'Setting up the European External Action Service: an Act of Institutional Balance' (2012) 8 *European Constitutional Law Review* 246–279. Section 20.4 builds on S. Blockmans, 'The European External Action Service One Year On: First Signs of Strengths and Weaknesses', *CLEER Working Paper* 2012/2.

[1] Annual Report of the Secretary-General on the Work of the Organization, 16 June 1960–15 June 1961, UN Doc. A/4800 and Add.1, 16 June 1960–15 June 1961.

external action. Article 3(5) TEU, as last amended by the Treaty of Lisbon, states:

> In its relations with the wider world, the Union shall uphold and promote its values and interests and contribute to the protection of its citizens. It shall contribute to peace, security, the sustainable development of the Earth, solidarity and mutual respect among peoples, free and fair trade, eradication of poverty and the protection of human rights, in particular the rights of the child, as well as to the strict observance and the development of international law, including respect for the principles of the United Nations Charter.

Article 21 TEU further elaborates these objectives and starts from the premise that the Union's action on the international scene:

> shall be guided by the principles which have inspired its own creation, development and enlargement, and which it seeks to advance in the wider world: democracy, the rule of law, the universality and indivisibility of human rights and fundamental freedoms, respect for human dignity, the principles of equality and solidarity, and respect for the principles of the United Nations Charter and international law.

The EU's sanguine worldview, as expressed in its constitutional objectives,[2] is therefore largely consistent with Hammarskjöld's vision of the UN. The methodology prescribed by the EU Treaty is one whereby the Union 'shall seek to develop relations and build partnerships with third countries, and international, regional or global organisations *which share the principles* referred to [above]'.[3] As such, the Union is held to promote multilateral solutions to common problems, in particular in the framework of the UN. This is especially apparent in Article 21(2)(c) TEU, which resonates the Member States' preambulary resolve to implement a Common Foreign and Security Policy (CFSP) 'in order to promote peace, security and progress in Europe and in the world'.[4] The Treaty's approach is therefore also in line with the methods advocated by Hammarskjöld to maintain international peace and security.

[2] See J. Larik, 'Entrenching Global Governance: The EU's Constitutional Objectives Caught Between a Sanguine World View and a Daunting Reality', in B. Van Vooren, S. Blockmans and J. Wouters (eds.), *The EU's Role in Global Governance: The Legal Dimension* (2013), 7–22.

[3] Art. 21(1) TEU (emphasis added).

[4] Article 21(2)c TEU: 'The Union shall define and pursue common policies and actions, and shall work for a high degree of cooperation in all fields of international relations, in order to: … preserve peace, prevent conflicts and strengthen international security, in accordance with the purposes and principles of the United Nations Charter, with the principles of the Helsinki Final Act and with the aims of the Charter of Paris, including those relating to external borders.'

However, a question which has annoyed the European Union since the launching of the CFSP at Maastricht in 1991, is whether the EU can also muster the diplomatic clout to effectively contribute to the collective security system that Hammarskjöld envisaged.[5] The CFSP is one of the Union's policy areas which suffers most from the difficulty in forging common positions, due to Member States' different historical trajectories and diverging socio-economic, political and security interests. Furthermore, until the Lisbon Treaty entered into force on 1 December 2009, the Union's diplomatic structures to engage in the realm of foreign and security policy did not amount to much more than the position of the High Representative for the CFSP, supported by his staff at the Council General Secretariat. The purview of the Commission's delegations around the globe was restricted to those competences specifically attributed to the European Community (EC): trade and, to a lesser extent, development. The Lisbon Treaty, which pivoted the EC into the EU and explicitly endowed the latter with international legal personality, has changed all that: it merged the Union's external action objectives in Articles 3(5) and 21 TEU, and re-designed the institutional framework to render the organisation's external action more coherent, visible and effective.[6]

This chapter will examine whether the EU's new institutional framework does indeed enable it to match the Lisbon Treaty's ambitions to act as a global peace broker. This chapter will first argue that the EU can be seen as an international arrangement or agency in the context of Chapter VIII of the UN Charter (Section 20.2). It will then analyse the Lisbon Treaty's new institutional architecture in the field of EU external action by examining the key (hybrid) position occupied by the High Representative of the Union for Foreign Affairs and Security Policy/Vice-President of the European Commission (HR/VP) (Section 20.3). Special attention will be paid to the European External Action Service (EEAS), the EU's new

[5] Elsewhere, I have examined the EU's practice with the use of the diplomatic instruments mentioned in Art. 33 UN Charter, which the EU – as an international actor, above and beyond its Member States – has at its disposal to engage in peaceful dispute settlement. See S. Blockmans, 'EU Global Diplomacy: Instruments to Support Status Processes', in B. Van Vooren, S. Blockmans and J. Wouters (eds.), *The EU's Role in Global Governance: The Legal Dimension* (2013), 110–125. For an account on the Union's impact on the development of substantive norms in the context of status processes, see S. Blockmans, 'EU Global Peace Diplomacy: Shaping the Law on Statehood', in D. Kochenov and F. Amtenbrink (eds.), *European Union's Shaping of the International Legal Order* (2013), 130–168.

[6] See Final Report of Working Group VII on External Action, Convention on the Future of Europe, Doc. CONV 459/02, Brussels, 16 December 2002, at 6–7.

diplomatic service which is to assist the HR/VP in his[7] functions, and its internal capacities to offer the diplomatic services mentioned in Article 33 of the UN Charter: 'negotiation, enquiry, mediation, conciliation ... or other peaceful means' (Section 20.4). The ongoing EU-facilitated dialogue between Belgrade and Priština over the status of Kosovo will be used as the first post-Lisbon case study to see whether the EU is indeed up to the task of a peace mediator (Section 20.5). The concluding observations will provide an overall assessment of the reception of Hammarskjöld's approaches towards peace diplomacy in the context of the EU's institutional setting for external action (Section 20.6).

20.2 The EU as a 'Chapter VIII' vector of peace

The above-mentioned instruments of Article 33 of the UN Charter returned in the 1970 Declaration on Principles of International Law Concerning Friendly Relations and Co-operation among States: 'states shall accordingly seek early and just settlement of their international disputes by negotiation, inquiry, mediation, conciliation, arbitration, judicial settlement, resort to regional agencies or arrangements or other peaceful means of their choice'.[8] A fuller enumeration would also include consultation and good offices.[9] Whereas the obligation to seek settlement of their disputes is directed to *states*, 'resort to regional agencies or arrangements' is *one* of the means available to them.[10] Indeed, this is where regional international organisations may come in and some constitutive treaties explicitly foresee a peaceful dispute settlement role for their organisations.[11] In Europe, the

[7] In the following, the personal nouns 'he', 'him' or 'his' will be used in references to the legal texts regarding the HR/VP. The female form of the nouns will be used when referring to the first incumbent: Catherine Ashton.

[8] UNGA Res 2625 (XXV) of 24 October 1970, UN Doc. A/8082, GA 25th session 121.

[9] See, generally, M. Shaw, *International Law* (2008), 1010–1024. See more in general, United Nations, *Handbook on the Peaceful Settlement of Disputes between States* (1992); J. Collier and V. Lowe, *The Settlement of Disputes in International Law* (1999); J. Merrills, *International Dispute Settlement* (2005); and S. Koopmans, *Diplomatic Dispute Settlement: The Use of Inter-State Conciliation* (2008). Whereas the definition of a 'dispute' is generally distinguished from that of a 'conflict', a term which is used to signify a general state of hostility between the parties, the present chapter will use the terms interchangeably, following the link provided by Art. 33 of the UN Charter which uses the concept 'disputes' also with respect to controversies in which international peace and security are at stake.

[10] On the concept of regional arrangements, see A. Abass, *Regional Organizations and the Development of Collective Security: Beyond Chapter VIII of the UN Charter* (2004).

[11] See, e.g., the Protocol Relating to the Establishment of the Peace and Security Council of the African Union, adopted on 9 July 2002. Similarly, ECOWAS, SADC, Arab League

European Convention for the Peaceful Settlement of Disputes[12] lays down the agreement that legal disputes are to be sent to the ICJ and that other disputes are to be solved through conciliation and/or arbitration.[13] The Organization on Security and Cooperation in Europe (OSCE) established a number of conventions and mechanisms related to early warning, conflict prevention and crisis management – allowing, for instance, to send observer and mediation missions to participating states. What is striking, however, is that these (pan-)European organisations and mechanisms are primarily directed at preventing or solving conflicts between members of those organisations only. As we will see below, this is different for the EU.

The question this chapter tries to answer is whether the EU possesses the diplomatic capacity to effectively engage in peaceful dispute settlement between non-Member States. Against the international legal background sketched out in this section, the question that should then be answered first is whether the EU can be seen as a regional agency or arrangement in the sense of the UN Charter and the Declaration on Friendly Relations. Without any doubt, this question should be answered in the affirmative.

Chapter VIII (Article 53) of the UN Charter allows the Security Council to 'utilize … regional arrangements or agencies for enforcement action under its authority'. According to Akehurst, 'the difference between an agency and an arrangement would appear to be that an *agency* possesses an institutional superstructure … whereas an *arrangement* does not … In other words, an agency is simply a more highly developed form of an arrangement'.[14] With regard to the EU, the existence of an 'institutional superstructure' is beyond doubt.[15] The question, however, to which extent the institutional structure may also be used to fulfil a role as 'regional agency' is less easy to answer. Whereas regarding the EU as a regional agency would explain the way in which the Union intends to attain its objectives laid down in Article 21(2)(c) TEU, the Treaty at this moment does not provide any additional clues for

and OAS proclaim themselves as a 'regional arrangement or agency'. In NATO, mechanisms have been set up to act as a regional arrangement or agency, outside of the allied territory. See G. Nolte, 'Die "neuen Aufgaben" von NATO und WEU: Völker- und verfassungsrechtliche Fragen' (1994) 95 *ZaöRv* 107. See, generally, C. Dominicé, 'Co-ordination between Universal and Regional Organizations', in N. Blokker and H. Schermers (eds.), *Proliferation of International Organizations: Legal Issues* (2001), 65–84.

12 1957, Council of Europe.

13 *UNTS* (1958), no. 320, at 243–256. See further the CSCE Convention on Arbitration and Conciliation of 1992, 32 *ILM* (1993) 553.

14 M. Akehurst, 'Enforcement Actions by Regional Organizations with Special Reference to the Organization of American States' (1967) 42 *BYIL* 177 (emphases added).

15 See also L. Vierucci, 'WEU: A Regional Partner of the United Nations?', *Chaillot Paper* No. 12 (1993), who argued that the WEU (at the time the 'military arm' of the EU) could be seen as a regional arrangement.

the Union to function as a regional agency. Neither did the TEU expressly claim to fall within the ambit of Chapter VIII of the UN Charter. On the other hand, the concept of 'regional arrangements and agencies' is not defined by the Charter, and according to UN Secretary-General Boutros Boutros-Ghali this was intentional:

> The Charter deliberately provides no precise definition of regional arrangements and agencies, thus allowing useful flexibility for undertakings by a group of States to deal with a matter appropriate for regional action which also could contribute to the maintenance of international peace and security. Such associations or entities could include treaty-based organizations, whether created before or after the founding of the United Nations, regional organizations for mutual security and defence, organizations for general regional development or for cooperation on a particular economic topic or function, and groups created to deal with a specific political, economic or social issue of concern.[16]

The Secretary-General even explicitly hinted at the possible 'emergence' of new regional arrangements in Europe.[17] In his Agenda for Peace, the UNSG thus stressed the need for flexibility in the post-Cold War era, and the purpose of establishing closer links with regional organisations was not to set forth 'any formal pattern of relationship between regional organisations and the United Nations, or to call for any specific division of labour'.[18]

The many references to the UN in the EU Treaties, including the implicit competence in Protocol 10 to act in response to a request of the UN to participate in the peaceful settlement of disputes ('the United Nations Organisation may request the Union's assistance for the urgent implementation of missions undertaken under Chapters VI'), point to new characteristics of the European Union to act as a global peace broker.[19] Based on this, as well as on the above-mentioned objectives in the EU Treaty, it would be difficult for the EU to deny that it is subject to Chapter VIII of the UN Charter.[20]

The implications of the acceptance of a role for the EU as a 'Chapter VIII organisation' are not to be disposed of too easily. According to

[16] Report of the Secretary-General, *Agenda for Peace*, UN Doc. A/47/277 – S/24111.

[17] Report of the Secretary-General on the Work of the Organisation, *Secretary Gen Rep 21*, 1990, 21.

[18] Report of the Secretary-General, *Agenda for Peace*, UN Doc. A/47/277 – S/24111, at 10.

[19] A similar competence to act 'in response to requests from the United Nations Organisation' may be found in relation to the permanent structured cooperation ex Arts. 42(6) and 46 TEU.

[20] See also N. White, 'The EU as Regional Security Actor within the International Legal Order', in M. Trybus and N. White (eds.), *European Security Law* (2007), 329–349.

Article 52 of the UN Charter, the activities of regional arrangements or agencies are to be consistent with the purposes and principles of the UN. Moreover, regional arrangements and agencies have a primary function in the pacific settlement of local disputes;[21] they shall make every effort in that respect before referring the dispute to the Security Council, but they 'have autonomy in diplomacy, in peaceful settlement, and implicitly in the case of consensual peacekeeping, subject to a reporting requirement'.[22] Currently, nothing in the EU Treaties seems sufficient to enable the EU to fulfil this task internally. The Union's policies in this area are primarily (if not exclusively) related to threats to or breaches of the peace within or by states that are *not* members of the EU. This clearly distinguishes the EU from other regional arrangements and agencies, which see as their primary task the settling of disputes among their Member States.

20.3 The High Representative: spider in the EU's institutional web of diplomacy

The post of the HR/VP is the cornerstone of the Lisbon Treaty system in the domain of EU external relations and the key innovation in the Union's conduct of foreign policy. Under the Amsterdam Treaty, it was the Secretary-General of the Council (Javier Solana) who – while exercising the function of High Representative for CFSP – assisted the rotating Presidency of the General Affairs and External Relations Council (GAERC).[23] But the rotating Council Presidency externally represented the Union in CFSP matters and remained (formally) responsible for the implementation of its decisions.[24] This construction has been fundamentally changed by the Lisbon Treaty.

In the area of CFSP, the High Representative now exercises elements of the functions which were previously carried out by the rotating Presidency, the Secretary-General of the Council in his capacity as High Representative, and the European Commissioner for External Relations. As will be explained in more detail below, the High Representative

[21] Local disputes are commonly understood as disputes exclusively involving states which are parties to the regional arrangement or agency (cf. also Arts. 34 and 35 UN Charter).

[22] Art. 54 UN Charter provides that the Security Council shall at all times be kept fully informed of activities which are undertaken or are being contemplated under regional arrangements by regional agencies for the maintenance of international peace and security. This would include all activities by the EU related to the peaceful settlement of disputes.

[23] Art. 18(3) TEU (Amsterdam).

[24] See Art. 18(1) and (2) TEU (Amsterdam).

'conducts' the Union's Common Foreign and Security Policy, presides over the Foreign Affairs Council and – as first Vice-President of the European Commission – is charged with the coordination of external relations matters falling under the competence of the Commission. This multi-hatted personality occupies a crucial leadership role for a single Union, supported by a brand-new diplomatic service.[25] Arguably, the position of the HR/VP is a strong competitor of that of the UN Secretary-General in the contest for 'the most difficult job in the world'.[26]

However, even before the Lisbon Treaty entered into force, the HR's Vice-Presidential powers had already been curtailed by Commission President designate Barroso's removal of several sections from the previous Directorate-General for External Relations (DG Relex) to other DGs: staff involved in international climate-change negotiations were moved to the new DG for climate action; the energy task-force was moved to the DG for energy; and responsibility for the European Neighbourhood Policy (ENP) was moved to DG Enlargement (DG-E).[27] Barroso maintained that these transfers were 'simply a question of strengthening the … directorates-general', but Member States' diplomats were reported to have said that the moves were 'made to insulate the units from the pull of the EEAS', whereas these diplomats believed that the EEAS was in need of staff dealing with the external dimensions of internal policies.[28] Furthermore, in striking contrast with relevant Treaty provisions, the HR/VP's actual coordinating powers within the Commission over issues pertaining to the EU's external relations have not been (fully) effectuated. The HR/

25 See P.J. Kuijper, 'Of "Mixity" and "Double-hatting", EU External Relations Law Explained', inaugural lecture, 23 May 2008 (2008), at 14. The 'single Union' refers to the merger of the former Community and the Union into one international organisation possessing a single legal personality. According to Jean-Claude Piris the HR is 'triple-hatted'. He argues that the HR also took over the function of Secretary-General of the Council/High Representative for CFSP (SG/HR). See J.-C. Piris, *The Lisbon Treaty: A Legal and Political Analysis* (2010), at 243. However, because the HR/VP is also President of the European Defence Agency and Chairperson of the board of the EU Institute for Security Studies, the term 'multi-hatting' is perhaps even more fitting.

26 According to T. Lie, the first incumbent as UNSG. See www.norway-un.org/NorwayandUN/The-Legacy-of-Trygve-Lie/Trygve-Lie-first-UN-Secretary-General-/.

27 Changes made pursuant to Art. 17(6)a and b TEU and *Political Guidelines for the next Commission*, from José Manuel Barroso, 3 September 2009. Available at: www.ec.europa.eu/commission_2010–2014/president/pdf/press_20090903_en.pdf. But, also compare Art. 248 TFEU and Art. 18(4) TEU.

28 T. Vogel, 'Turf War Continues over EU's Diplomatic Corps', *European Voice*, 11 March 2010.

VP was charged to chair a group comprising all Commissioners with substantial elements of foreign affairs in their portfolios,[29] but Barroso brought the Treaty-based coordinating powers of the HR/VP back to the College, chaired by its President, i.e. Barroso himself.[30] Thus, within the Commission, it is the President who keeps the reins in external matters. Therefore, Barroso's pre- and post-Lisbon manoeuvres have eroded the HR/VP's responsibilities as entrusted to him by the Treaty – something that Ashton has accepted in practice.[31]

In fact, such a limitation also occurred on the 'HR' side of the position. This has been mainly due to institutional and organisational changes brought about by the Lisbon Treaty. In the first place, this is a consequence of the European Council:

(1) gaining the formal status of an institution of the Union;
(2) being headed by a permanent President whose tasks include the external representation of the Union in CFSP matters, at his level and in that capacity;[32] and
(3) accruing – formal – dominance in substantive CFSP matters.[33]

And although the HR/VP takes part in the work of the European Council, he is not a formal member of it.

Second, changes in the configurations of the Council of Ministers affected the position of the HR/VP. The GAERC was split up by the Lisbon

[29] The Commissioners responsible for 'International Cooperation, Humanitarian Aid and Crisis Response', 'Development', 'Enlargement and European Neighbourhood Policy', 'Economic and Monetary Affairs' and 'Trade'.

[30] *Information Note from the President, Commissioners Groups*, SEC (2010) 475 final, Brussels, 22 April 2010. Since its creation, the group of external Commissioners has allegedly met only a handful of times, presided over by Barroso. Interviews with EU officials prior to the publication of S. Blockmans, 'Fit for Purpose? The European External Action Service One Year On', *OXFAM Briefing Paper* No. 159, 23 January 2012.

[31] See further L. Erkelens and S. Blockmans, 'Setting up the European External Action Service: an Act of Institutional Balance' (2012) 8 *European Constitutional Law Review* 246–279.

[32] Art. 15(6) TEU, the second last sentence. It is provided as well that this competence of the President of the European Council is without prejudice to those of the HR in the CFSP area.

[33] The Lisbon Treaty now specifically provides that alongside the overall task of the European Council to define the general political directions and priorities of the Union it shall lay down strategic guidelines on the Union's external action. See Art. 22 TEU, a provision that did not exist in the former TEU. See also Art. 16(6) TEU, last sentence: 'The Foreign Affairs Council shall elaborate the Union's external action on the basis of strategic guidelines laid down by the European Council and ensure that the Union's action is consistent.'

Treaty into two different configurations: the General Affairs Council (GAC) and the Foreign Affairs Council (FAC).[34] The FAC is chaired by the HR/VP and responsible for the whole of the EU's external action.[35] The GAC remains in the hands of the rotating Presidency.[36] It is up to the GAC – not the FAC – to prepare and to ensure the follow-up of the work of the European Council.[37] This means that, in principle, the strategic CFSP guidelines are prepared by the GAC. It may be that in practice, the FAC takes part in these preparations, but the formal responsibility to take a decision on draft texts before submitting them to the European Council rests on the GAC's shoulders – in liaison with the President of the European Council[38] and the Commission.[39] It may thus be concluded that the GAC is a cornerstone for the work of the European Council.[40] By contrast, the FAC has become instrumental for the European Council to elaborate upon the Union's external action within the framework of its political guidelines.

In the third place, the position of the HR within the FAC has changed and has turned into a somewhat hybrid mixture of competences of the

[34] Art. 16(6) TEU, in the second last and last sentence respectively.

[35] See Art. 2(5) of the Rules of Procedures of the Council, *OJ* 2009 L 325/35: 'The Foreign Affairs Council shall elaborate the Union's external action on the basis of strategic guidelines laid down by the European Council and ensure that the Union's action is consistent. It shall be responsible for the whole of the European Union's external action, namely common foreign and security policy, common security and defence policy, common commercial policy, development cooperation and humanitarian aid.'

[36] The HR/VP has developed a practice of asking the rotating Presidency to also chair the FAC in her absence. This constitutes a remarkable return to the pre-Lisbon situation and runs contrary to the intention to create permanency at the helm of the FAC.

[37] Art. 16(6) TEU, second sentence: 'The General Affairs Council shall ensure consistency in the work of the different Council configurations. It shall prepare and ensure the follow-up to meetings of the European Council, in liaison with the President of the European Council and the Commission.'

[38] Conversely, it is also provided that the President of the European Council ensures the preparations of the European Council on the basis of the work of the GAC. See Art. 15(6)(b) TEU.

[39] A procedure involving the FAC has been explicitly provided with regard to the preparation of the draft programme of activities of the trio of rotating Council Presidencies. See Art. 2(6) of the Rules of Procedures of the Council, *OJ* 2009 L 325/35. It shall be prepared by the three Member States with the President of the FAC (i.e. the HR) and in close cooperation with the Commission and the President of the European Council. Then the document shall be presented with a view to its endorsement by the GAC.

[40] See P. Kaczyński and A. Byrne, 'The General Affairs Council: The Key to Political Influence of Rotating Presidencies', *CEPS Policy Brief* No. 246, July 2011. The authors argue that notwithstanding the GAC's institutional key position, in practice its importance and effectiveness have withered.

former HR position (Solana) and the rotating Presidency of the former GAERC. The HR now chairs the FAC but is no longer a member of this Council configuration. The Council consists only of the representatives of the Member States at ministerial level. Pre-Lisbon, the rotating President was a *primus inter pares* of the FAC. Post-Lisbon, the HR/VP is not: he has the power to present proposals to the FAC and to conduct the Union's foreign policy, but he shall carry out that policy as mandated by the Council.[41] In other words, the HR/VP has nowadays a certain freedom of movement but only insofar as mandated by the FAC, of which he is formally not a member.

Based on the three above-mentioned points, there are sufficient grounds to support the argument that the HR side of Ashton's position has been constructed in a substantively weaker way when compared to the position under the pre-Lisbon TEU. From an institutional point of view, the FAC has become politically dependent on the European Council and is – in theory – superseded by the GAC, which is the cornerstone of the work of the European Council. From a functional point of view the HR only 'takes part' in the work of the European Council. Further, he chairs the FAC but is not a member of it and works on the basis of mandates given by its members. In other words, the HR is more than ever instrumental to the political course of EU external action, as determined by the European Council and the Council.

Overseeing the construction of the position of the HR/VP *in toto*, it may be concluded that it constitutes a genuinely new post. It may appear as a *sui generis* and therefore independent position, supported by a formidable diplomatic service;[42] but, looking through the institutional prism, the HR/VP appears to be strongly embedded within both the Commission as well as the (European) Council. On the one hand, bureaucratic moves manoeuvred Vice-President Ashton in a position of dependency within the Commission, notwithstanding the Treaty-based powers bestowed upon her. On the other hand, the Treaty-based hierarchical and mandated nature of her functional relationships with the European Council and the Council, respectively, made the HR/VP very much dependent on the intergovernmental system of EU foreign policy-making. As it stands

[41] Art. 18(2) TEU: 'The High Representative shall conduct the Union's common foreign and security policy. He shall contribute by his proposals to the development of that policy, which he shall carry out as mandated by the Council. The same shall apply to the common security and defence policy.'

[42] See Section 20.4 of this chapter.

now, this implies that those institutions will largely determine the room for manoeuvre of the incumbent of the HR/VP position.[43] The ensuing questions are then: which of these institutions pulls the HR's strings faster and harder? How will the HR/VP cope with those forces? Arguably, such a state of affairs cannot be without consequence for the institutional positioning of the EEAS and, ultimately, the coherence, visibility and effectiveness of EU external action.

20.4 The EU's new diplomatic service and toolkit for peace mediation

20.4.1 European external action service: organisation and functioning

On 1 December 2010, one year after the Lisbon Treaty entered into force, the EEAS was formally launched.[44] An initial transfer of about 1,500 staff took place on 1 January 2011, whereby the EEAS effectively began its operations.[45] The legal basis for the creation of the Action Service is surprisingly concise and open-ended. Article 27(3) TEU provides a single general procedural rule for the establishment of the EEAS, i.e. by way of a Council Decision, proposed by the HR, adopted with the consent of the Commission after having heard the opinion of the European Parliament. Functionally autonomous from the Commission and Council, and placed under the authority of the High Representative, the EEAS is a service, which has to 'assist' the HR in fulfilling his mandate.[46] But because the EEAS was subsequently also expected to 'support' the President of the European Council, the President of the Commission, and the Commission as a whole in the exercise of their respective functions in the area of external relations,[47] the task of inserting the EEAS into the

[43] Pieter Jan Kuijper concluded already in May 2008 that the loyalty of the HR/VP 'may be sorely tested'. See P.J. Kuijper, 'Of "Mixity" and "Double-hatting": EU External Relations Law Explained', inaugural lecture, 23 May 2008 (2008), at 15.

[44] See A. Rettman, 'Ashton Names EU Foreign-Service Priorities at Low-Key Launch Event', *EU Observer*, 2 December 2010.

[45] In line with Art. 7 of Council Decision 2010/427/EU of 26 July 2010 establishing the organisation and functioning of the European External Action Service, *OJ* 2010 L 201/30 (hereinafter: EEAS Council Decision). See S. Blockmans and C. Hillion (eds.), *EEAS 2.0: A Legal Commentary on Council Decision 2010/427/EU establishing the Organisation and Functioning of the European External Action Service* (2013).

[46] Art. 27(3) TEU, first sentence.

[47] Pursuant to Art. 2 EEAS Council Decision.

Union's new institutional architecture pertaining to external action was bound to be a laborious exercise.[48] On top of this, the search for a well-balanced outcome was compounded by, inter alia, the decision to transfer relevant departments (and their officials) from both the Commission and the Council General Secretariat, resulting in a substantial drain of know-how and leaving deep traces in the organisational structures of these institutions.[49]

The configuration of the initial transfer of civil servants (in headquarters and in Delegations) has meant that the organisational *ethos* was – at first – predominantly based on the administrative routines inherited from the European Commission.[50] In the short term, this required an adaptation in working methods from the experts transferred from the Council General Secretariat's DG-E (i.e. the geographical and global and multilateral elements). However, the EEAS Council Decision in some areas, most notably in crisis management, requires the prevalence of Council Secretariat routines. In the longer term it will be interesting to see how the diversity in national diplomatic cultures among temporarily seconded national experts will impact on the development of an *esprit de corps* within the EEAS.[51] Arguably, politicising parts of the external action brief previously shaped by way of the so-called 'Community method' is well underway.[52]

[48] See L. Erkelens and S. Blockmans, 'Setting up the European External Action Service: an Act of Institutional Balance' (2012) 8 *European Constitutional Law Review* 246–279.

[49] For instance in DG Development, which was subsequently merged with DG AIDCO. The move overall also implied that the responsibility of staffing the Delegations was transferred from the Commission to the EEAS. See also M. Emerson, R. Balfour, T. Corthaut, J. Wouters, P.M. Kaczynski and R.L. Thomas, *Upgrading the EU's Role as Global Actor: Institutions, Law and the Restructuring of European Diplomacy* (2011).

[50] D. O'Sullivan, 'Setting up the European External Action Service', Speech at the IIEA, Dublin, 14 January 2011, available at: www.iiea.com. See also C. Carta, *The European Diplomatic Service: Ideas, Preferences and Identities* (2011).

[51] The EEAS Council Decision stipulates that the members of the staff of the EEAS are subject to a high degree of mobility, in particular between the central administration and the Delegations. Because of this, all EEAS staff will in principle serve periodically in EU Delegations. This rotation is essential for staff to acquire experience on the ground and also to avoid an excessive identification with the interests of the states in which they are posted. Likewise, it is stated that civil servants serving in the EEAS will have the right to apply for posts in their institution of origin under the same conditions as internal candidates. It is by no means impossible that in the long term the existing links between the Action Service and the staff's institutions of origin should be weakened, thus reinforcing the functional autonomy of the EEAS.

[52] See R. Dehousse (ed.), *The 'Community Method': Obstinate or Obsolete?* (2011). Countertrends can also be observed, i.e. the 'judicialisation' of EU foreign policy and

One of the most precious assets of the EEAS is the network of EU Delegations on the ground.[53] Delegations in third countries have successfully made the transition from Commission to EU Delegations and now pack a political section (EEAS staff) and an operations section (Commission staff). Provided they are appropriately staffed, the strengthened Delegations can have a crucial threefold role:

(1) they can provide services at headquarters in Brussels with information and analysis of developments on the ground, contacts with local actors, and a reinforced outreach;
(2) they can coordinate the work of Member States' embassies (formerly a task performed by the rotating Presidency), helping Europeans 'sing from the same hymn sheet';[54] and
(3) they can represent an authoritative interlocutor to third country governments and societies in all areas of cooperation, with positive consequences on the EU's image abroad.[55]

As to the first point, the challenge in 2011 has been to radically transform the cooperation between HQ and Delegations in order to get a genuine two-way interaction right, both in terms of policy-shaping and policy execution. In taking up the permanent presidency to coordinate positions between Member States' embassies (point (2) above), the EEAS has been particularly effective in bilateral settings. A case in point is the EEAS' civilian operational coordination in response to crises like the ones in Fukushima and Libya.[56] In multilateral settings, however, there have been quite a lot of problems, not caused by the EEAS itself, but by those Member States (most vocally the United Kingdom) insisting on a strict reading of the attribution of (shared) competences under the Lisbon Treaty. Finally, on the third point, one could expect the EU Head of Mission, who brings together all aspects of EU external policies, to become the most important ambassador around in many capitals of the world because s/he has a rich

the 'developmentalisation' of security policy. I am grateful to Christophe Hillion for pointing this out to me.

[53] Currently, there are 141 EU Delegations, including the ones recently opened in Libya, South Sudan and Burma/Myanmar.

[54] Dixit Michael Mann, Catherine Ashton's spokesman. See A. Rettmann, 'Van Rompuy: EU Should Take Credit for Libya', *EU Observer*, 5 April 2011.

[55] See R. Balfour and H. Ojanen, 'Does the European External Action Service Represent a Model for the Challenges of Global Diplomacy?' (2011) 1117 *IAI Working Papers*.

[56] See S. Blockmans, 'The European External Action Service One Year On: First Signs of Strengths and Weaknesses', *CLEER Working Paper* 2012/2.

toolbox at his/her disposal and the ear of the ambassadors of EU Member States present on the ground.

According to Article 4(3) of the EEAS Council Decision, full internal coordination, i.e. between all the structures of the EEAS, shall be ensured. How this principle of internal coherence will be operationalised, however, is not entirely clear. It did not help that, in its first year of activities, the Service was not yet in a single headquarters; its people scattered over different buildings.[57] But aside from the logistics, there is a more fundamental problem of disconnect between a top-heavy management and the expert desk officers down the chain. On paper, the EEAS is there to provide expert analysis to the HR. On-the-ground presence and knowledge should beef up the Union's foreign policy aims. This is supposed to provide bottom-up coherence to EU external action, even if coherence at the very top is still missing at times. The problems that are reported concern: the difficulties of communication, a hazy chain of command,[58] as well as blurred boundaries between certain portfolios, and the sometimes late or lack of feedback from the top.[59]

These problems are compounded by a number of structural deficiencies. For instance, the institutional changes provided for by the Lisbon Treaty were introduced without the simultaneous streamlining of the distribution of competences or decision-making procedures. The Lisbon Treaty has not ended the first/second pillar dichotomy of late: CFSP and Common Security and Defence Policy (CSDP) remain located in the TEU, separate from the Union's other external relations policies in the Treaty on the Functioning of the EU (TFEU): trade, development, cooperation with third countries, humanitarian aid, relations with international organisations. Arguably, this legal and procedural partition will complicate the inter-institutional quest for an integrated approach to EU external action encompassing a security dimension. This is not helped by the fact that the organisational chart of the EEAS incorporates the split: the CSDP structures (including EUMS, CMPD, CPCC) are set apart from the directorate on global and multilateral issues and do not directly link up with the divisions on conflict prevention and security policy.[60] Relying on informal

[57] The move into the new headquarters of the EEAS on the Rond Point Schuman in Brussels, rather symbolically located in between the European Commission's Berlaymont building and the Council's Justus Lipsius building, has been completed in May 2012.

[58] See H. Mahony, 'Diplomatic Service Blues', *EU Observer*, 29 June 2011.

[59] Interviews with EU officials.

[60] Analysis based on the organisational chart of the EEAS of 1 March 2013, available at: http://eeas.europa.eu/background/docs/organisation_en.pdf.

work processes is not the most transparent, effective and durable way of coordinating and mainstreaming policy issues which once coloured everything that the EEAS was supposed to be about (cf. the tagline accompanying an earlier version of the organigramme: 'The EEAS: a service for conflict prevention, security + stability').[61] It is the Corporate Board's task to ensure internal coherence and coordination and to make sure that the global and multilateral issues are reflected in the geographical and regional concerns and vice versa. The idea is thus to 'mainstream' thematic – usually very technical – issues on a systematic basis to the geographic directorates, and that the geographic directorates treat the thematic directorates as resource bases. All the while, the Corporate Board – most notably the Deputy Secretary-General for Political Affairs – offers 'guidance' towards an integrated policy approach.

Of course, coordination within the Service is one thing. But the real litmus test is whether the EEAS will be able to provide the kind of assistance to the various political masters that it is supposed to serve, and coordinate external policies in such a way, so as to attain a higher level of visibility and effectiveness of EU external action. Arguably, it would be unfair at this early stage of its existence to deliver a full-blown value judgement of the Service's role in rendering EU foreign policy more coherent, consistent and effective. The dust still needs to settle on the Union's new diplomatic service and some open institutional issues remain. The HR provided the first deep and comprehensive review of the EEAS' organisation and functioning in July 2013.[62] The review was not accompanied by appropriate proposals for the revision of the 2010 EEAS Council Decision. However, the Council may, in accordance with Article 27(3) TEU, revise this Decision in the light of a review by the next HR at the end of 2015.[63]

20.4.2 Operational strengths and weaknesses

In operational terms, the most important test for the EEAS, as indeed the EU as a whole, is how the EU deals with its neighbouring countries.[64] According to Ashton: 'I said from the beginning that I thought how we

[61] The High Representative's draft organisational chart of 23 July 2010, on file with the author.

[62] Art. 13(3) of the EEAS Council Decision.

[63] See the conclusions of the General Affairs Council of 17 December 2013, point 11.

[64] See S. Blockmans, 'The European External Action Service One Year On: First Signs of Strengths and Weaknesses', *CLEER Working Paper* 2012/2.

operate in our neighbourhood, the effectiveness of what we did, would define the European Union into the future. And I still believe that.'[65] The EU's slow and timid response to the momentous change brought about in Tunisia and other so-called 'Arab Spring' countries has put the spotlight on the birth pains of the EEAS, which had only just become operational on 1 January 2011.[66] This was compounded by a frustration about the lack of leadership at the highest institutional levels.[67] However, after some initial hesitations and setbacks,[68] and faced with a military intervention by Member States outside of the EU framework in Libya, the EEAS reacted to events and played its role as both a policy and donor coordinator. It provided added value in terms of crisis response, democratic transformation and economic development, responding to the specific needs of each country, rather than viewing them all through the same policy lens.[69] Also, it supported wider international efforts through the use of sanctions against the Gaddafi regime in Libya and the Assad regime in Syria.[70]

[65] See 'Remarks by High Representative Catherine Ashton at the AFET Committee in European Parliament in Strasbourg, 12 December 2011', Press Release A 511/11, Brussels, 13 December 2011, at 2.

[66] Compare, for example, 'Statement by EU High Representative Catherine Ashton and European Commissioner for Enlargement Štefan Füle on the Situation in Tunisia', Press Release A 010/11, Brussels, 10 January 2011; 'EEAS Senior Officials' Mission to Tunisia', Press Release A 029/11, Brussels, 26 January 2011; and 'Statement by the EU High Representative Catherine Ashton on Tunisia', Press Release A 034/11, Brussels, 28 January 2011. See also T. Garton Ash, 'If this is Young Arabs' 1989, Europe must be Ready with a Bold Response', *Guardian*, 2 February 2011: 'What happens across the Mediterranean matters more to the EU than the US. Yet so far its voice has been inaudible.'

[67] See R. Balfour and H. Ojanen, 'Does the European External Action Service Represent a Model for the Challenges of Global Diplomacy?' (2011) 1117 *IAI Working Papers* at 2.

[68] See D. O'Sullivan, 'Setting up the European External Action Service: Part II', Speech at the IIEA, Dublin, 6 October 2011, available at: www.iiea.com, referring to the ups and downs of the EU-Tunisia Task Force and the failure of the recipients to show up at an international donor conference organised by the EEAS: 'We had to fix the car while the engine was running.' The Task Force eventually took place at the end of September and brought together the instruments of the EU and support from the EIB, the EBRD, the African Bank, the World Bank and others. EUR 4 billion of support was pledged over three years to the economy of Tunisia.

[69] Coordination, both inside the EU and with international partners, is a key element in the mandate of the new EU Special Representative for the Southern Mediterranean.

[70] For the EEAS' own appraisal, see 'One Year on from the Arab Spring – A Summary of the EU's Action – 17/12/11', available at: http://eeas.europa.eu/top_stories/2011/171211_arabsprin_en.htm, 'The EU's Response to the "Arab Spring"', MEMO/11/918, Brussels, 16 December 2011, and 'EU's Response to the "Arab Spring": The State-of-Play after Two Years', Press Release A 70/13, Brussels, 8 February 2013.

In the wider Muslim world, one can point to a number of other small successes achieved by the High Representative and the EEAS, which illustrate the added value of the Lisbon structures.[71] In 2011, the EU has taken a more central role in the Quartet efforts to get the Middle East Peace process unstuck. Of course, being a 'player' as well as a 'payer'[72] also means a heightened risk of mediatised failure. Still, the HR, supported by the EEAS and the Union's international partners, is occupying a policy space otherwise left to other members of the Quartet. Also, the HR and the EEAS managed to prevent a complete fall-out of Member States over Palestine's application for UN membership in September 2012. However, the EEAS cannot take applause for having forged a more constructive common approach to the issue of statehood of Palestine. In fact, the agreement to disagree collapsed at the end of October 2011 when Member States voted differently over the admission of Palestine to UNESCO. On a more positive note, the EU, by way of the HR and the EEAS, continues to lead on behalf of the international community (the 'E3+3', i.e. the UK, France, Germany plus the United States, Russia and China) to engage with Iran on its nuclear programme.

Though the Southern neighbourhood and the Muslim world have come into much sharper focus due to events unfolding since 2011, the EU has tried hard not to neglect its other neighbourhoods. The Eastern neighbours were taken up in the drive forward pushed by the reviewed strategy for the ENP in May 2011. Despite some regrettable steps backward in the transition to democracy in Belarus (political prisoners), irregularities during the general elections and selective justice in Ukraine (sentencing of Yulia Tymoshenko), the strategic importance of the Eastern Partnership was reinforced at the September 2011 summit at Warsaw[73], before it was dented at the November 2013 summit in Vilnius. However, the EU's half-hearted calls for respect of common values in return for closer relations ring hollow in the scramble for influence in the neighbourhood shared with Russia.

In the Western Balkans, the EEAS has helped to maintain stability, defuse tension and push forward a pro-EU agenda. Under the leadership

[71] For a review of the EU's performance in Yemen, see S. Blockmans, 'Fit for Purpose? The European External Action Service One Year On', *OXFAM Briefing Paper* No. 159, 23 January 2012.

[72] See 'Remarks by High Representative Catherine Ashton at the AFET Committee in European Parliament in Strasbourg, 12 December 2011', Press Release A 511/11, Brussels, 13 December 2011, at 4.

[73] See 'Joint Declaration of the Eastern Partnership Summit', Press Release 14983/11 (PRESSE 341), Warsaw, 30 September 2011.

of the High Representative, the EEAS is facilitating an ongoing dialogue between Serbia and Kosovo aimed at establishing relations and creating lasting stability and prosperity.[74] Ashton herself has staved off an independence referendum in Republika Srpska in 2011 and thus contributed to (short-term) stability in Bosnia and Herzegovina.[75]

Further afield, the EU has been fighting piracy and famine in the Horn of Africa, through a series of actions off the coast of Somalia and on land. A 'more integrated' EU approach to crisis response that brings together humanitarian, disaster relief, crisis management capabilities, peacebuilding and development cooperation has been hammered out in a strategy for the region.[76] A similar strategy, but more focused on security issues, has been developed for the Sahel region and is currently being implemented in Niger and Mali.[77] A more comprehensive approach, albeit workable for only a limited period of time, was endorsed for Sudan and South Sudan.[78] What transpires from the development of these (sub-)regional strategies is the effort which the EEAS, as a coordinator of external action, has put into making the different parts of the EU *famille* act in a more joined up way.

In the wake of the September 2010 European Council Summit on strategic partnerships, the EEAS has intensified its ties with strategic partners, including China, the United States, Russia, India, Brazil and South Africa, whose support and close cooperation is essential to move forward on global issues like security, trade or climate change. 'The driving force of this exercise is to beef up the way [the EU conducts its] diplomacy, by focusing more on core priorities seeking greater policy and institutional coherence and focusing on delivering more results.'[79]

At the multilateral level, the EEAS did score a small victory with the adoption on 3 May of UN General Assembly Resolution 65/275 on the

[74] See Section 20.5 of this chapter.

[75] L. Smiljanic, 'Dodik Cancels Referendum after Talks with Ashton', *Southeast European Times*, 16 May 2011.

[76] Foreign Affairs Council meeting conclusions of 14 November 2011, Press Release 16756/11 (PRESSE 422), PR CO 68.

[77] The Sahel strategy is available at the website of the EEAS: www.eeas.europa.eu/africa/docs/sahel_strategy_en.pdf.

[78] The Comprehensive Approach was neither 'adopted' nor made public for fear of backfiring on the EU and/or negatively influencing Khartoum's position towards South Sudan ahead of the latter's independence day. See 3101st Foreign Affairs Council meeting, Press Release 11824/11 (PRESSE 181), Luxembourg, 20 June 2011, at 8, point 8.

[79] D. O'Sullivan, 'Setting up the European External Action Service: Part II', Speech at the IIEA, Dublin, 6 October 2011, available at: www.iiea.com.

participation of the EU in the work of the UN.[80] The resolution, which was adopted by 180 out of 197 votes in favour after a failed attempt in September 2010,[81] sets out working modalities that allow the Union's external representatives to present the positions of the EU and its Member States at the UN. However, this does not alter the EU's observer status in the UN General Assembly. Also, the resolution does not give the EU a right to vote or to co-sponsor draft resolutions or decisions in writing. The resolution does give the EU the ability to speak early among other major groups, when speaking on behalf of the twenty-seven EU states, and invites the EU – i.e. the President of the European Council and the HR/VP – to intervene in the general debate at the opening of the General Assembly. Previously, Palestine and the Holy See were the only observers that could take the floor in that debate. In addition, the EU has obtained the right to orally present proposals and amendments, a possibility that no other observer has at its disposal, and the right to reply once to a speech regarding EU positions. What is more, the resolution also applies to the participation of the EU – i.e. the EEAS and the Commission – in the sessions and work of the UN General Assembly, its committees and working groups, in international meetings and conferences convened under the auspices of the General Assembly, and in UN conferences. However, the resolution has no direct implications for the EU's participation in the work of other bodies or multilateral fora. Thus, the resolution does not apply generally in the UN system. Nevertheless, the EEAS has already proved its added value in some of the UNGA subcommittees and in the negotiations for an Arms Trade Treaty.

What transpires from the above is that, after a series of somewhat shaky performances, the EEAS has started to perform consistently better in the Brussels arena, in the countries in which it represents the European Union, alongside the HR/VP's international counterparts, including in multilateral fora. It is by launching ideas and joining up the different strands of EU external policies and instruments that the EEAS can show its added value. An area where both the Member States and the

[80] For a critical appraisal of the EU's 'success' in pushing for the resolution, see J. Wouters, J. Odermatt and T. Ramopoulos, 'The Status of the European Union at the United Nations After the General Assembly Resolution of 3 May 2011', *GGS Opinions*, July 2011. For a more positive assessment, see P.A. Serrano de Haro 'The Participation of the European Union in the Work of the United Nations: General Assembly Resolution 65/276', *CLEER Working Papers* 2012/5.

[81] See M. Emerson and J. Wouters, 'The EU's Diplomatic Debacle at the UN: What Else and What Next?', *CEPS Commentary*, October 2010.

UN would like to see the EU play a more active (Chapter VIII) role is in peace mediation.

20.4.3 *The EU's mediation and dialogue capacities*

An overview of the EU's practice as a regional arrangement for peace reveals that, so far, the Union has been engaged in the entire spectrum of mediation, facilitation and dialogue processes mentioned in Article 33, UN Charter.[82] While in practice fact-finding, mediation, conciliation and other instruments are already an integral part of the EU's external action toolbox, the EU has so far used these diplomatic tools in a rather ad hoc fashion. Furthermore, what transpires is that such diplomatic processes are often identified with outstanding personalities who play a key and visible role. Peaceful dispute settlement is, however, a team effort, which requires substantial expertise, knowledge, technical capacity and engagement at different levels over time as well as cooperation with other actors in order to be effective and to improve its chances of success.

On the basis of a concept floated at the end of 2009, the EU aims to develop a more systematic approach to its peaceful dispute settlement efforts and to strengthen its mediation support capacity, to allow it to contribute in a more efficient and effective way of preventing and resolving conflicts.[83] It is the Union's ambition to strive to establish and promote the use of mediation as a tool of first response to emerging or ongoing crisis situations. As such, mediation could also be mainstreamed into other EU conflict prevention and crisis management activities, wherever relevant. Strengthening the Union's mediation support capacity involves: the provision of operational support to ongoing mediation and dialogue initiatives; assessment of lessons learned; identification of best practices; and, as appropriate, the development of guidelines for the EU practice in the area of mediation; developing training and capacity building in the area of mediation as well as networking and coordination with other actors in crisis management.

The response to these calls has been the creation of a Division for Conflict Prevention, Peace building and Mediation Instruments within

[82] See S. Blockmans, 'EU Global Diplomacy: Instruments to Support Status Processes', in B. Van Vooren, S. Blockmans and J. Wouters (eds.), *The EU's Role in Global Governance: The Legal Dimension* (2013), 110–125.

[83] See Council General Secretariat, 'Concept on Strengthening EU Mediation and Dialogue Capacities', doc. 15779/09, 10 November 2009.

the EEAS' Directorate for Security Policy and Conflict Prevention. With the right resources and clout, this Division could indeed contribute expertise on conflict, peace and security issues to the full range of EU policies, programmes and activities in conflict-affected countries and fragile situations by, for example, providing support to the HR and EU Special Representatives (EUSRs) in the preparation and conduct of peace negotiations, organising training on conflict and peaceful dispute settlement issues for the regional managing directorates, and using the Instrument for Stability to support mediation and conciliation efforts. Whereas there exists already a close cooperation between the EEAS' Division for Conflict Prevention, Peace building and Mediation Instruments, on the one hand, and the Commission's Foreign Policy Instruments DG (for assistance in the short-term) and DG Development Cooperation's security policy unit (for longer-term aid), on the other hand, the precise boundaries of portfolios, competences and responsibilities remain to be settled.[84] Another observation relates to the form in which the EEAS will provide mediation support. Under the Instrument for Stability, a sum of EUR 1 million was earmarked by the European Parliament in the 2011 budget, allowing the EEAS to spend EUR 600,000 in 2012 to start up a pilot project on building up the EU's own mediation support capacity. The choice to spend these funds on training, coaching, and building on best practices as a resource for EUSRs seems to indicate that the idea to set up a roster of experts in mediation processes and related thematic areas, i.e. a standing team of EU mediators, has been put on the back-burner. While understandable from a budgetary perspective, this decision does translate in the necessity to organise a proper check of the negotiation abilities of personalities before they are appointed as EUSRs with a mediation mandate. Ultimately, a combination of a training capability and a flexible and useable roster of civilian experts will be the best way forward to equip the EU with the necessary deployment mechanisms for expert mediators to assist third parties in the short run, as well as the appropriate tools (offered by the EEAS) to prepare and equip EUSRs to engage in longer-term peaceful dispute settlement.[85]

[84] This is a point of more general concern. See S. Blockmans, 'The European External Action Service One Year On: First Signs of Strengths and Weaknesses', *CLEER Working Papers* 2012/2.

[85] E.g. organising (de-)briefings to secure continuity; the ability to draw on human resources more quickly, as indeed the ability to coordinate the use of financial resources more directly; compiling lessons learnt; and drawing up analyses of the 'anthropology' of conflicts. Then EUSRs De Soto, Fouéré, Marsden and Otte expressed

When strengthening its peaceful dispute settlement capacities, the EU will arguably make best use of the resources and expertise which are already available to the EU, including its Member States, as well as with the UN, regional organisations such as the African Union and the League of Arab States, national, local and civil society actors. The initial aim for the EU is to optimise the use of existing tools and instruments in the area of peaceful dispute settlement by ensuring close cooperation and coordination, internally and with other actors, leading to coherence and complementarity. In areas where the European Union does hold considerable sway, i.e. on its outer periphery, other global actors will be expecting the Union to step up to the plate and engage in mediation efforts to peacefully resolve disputes. An example thereof is the EU facilitated dialogue between Belgrade and Priština, which followed on from the 'final status process' carried out under the auspices of the UN.

20.5 EU facilitated dialogue between Serbia and Kosovo

On 10 November 2005, the UN Security Council endorsed the Secretary-General's intention to appoint Martti Ahtisaari as his Special Envoy to lead the status process, based on guiding principles agreed to by the Contact Group: no partition of Kosovo, no union with a neighbouring state and no return to pre-1999 conditions.[86] Minority rights had to be guaranteed, peacekeeping troops had to stay and an international civilian mission – probably run by the EU – had to be put in place. It is within these parameters that the UNSG Special Envoy had to find a compromise agreement between the irreconcilable positions of Belgrade and Priština,[87] against the backdrop of a deep rift within the Security Council.[88] While the final status process was expected to last for several months, the Contact Group, together with the EU High Representative, the EU Presidency, the European Commissioner for Enlargement, NATO's Secretary-General, the UN Special Status Envoy and the Special Representative of the

these needs at a conference devoted to 'Regional Actors as Vectors of Peace: What Role for the EU?' organised by the Crisis Management Initiative, an NGO headed by Nobel Peace Prize laureate Martti Ahtisaari, at the European Parliament in Brussels on 25 April 2012.

[86] Letter dated 10 November 2005 from the President of the Security Council addressed to the Secretary-General, UN Doc. S/2005/709.

[87] The Serb 'everything but independence' *vs.* the Kosovo Albanian 'nothing but independence'.

[88] See J. Headley, 'Kosovo: Déjà vu for Russia', *Transitions Online*, 28 May 2007.

Secretary-General for Kosovo (SRSG), had expressed the belief that all possible efforts should be made to achieve a negotiated settlement before the end of 2006.[89] That deadline was pushed back after a narrow majority of the Serbian electorate in an October referendum approved Serbia's new constitution – which claims sovereignty over the province of Kosovo – and general elections were called for.

The presentation of Ahtisaari's 'Comprehensive Proposal for the Kosovo Status Settlement' was delayed until 2 February 2007 in order to avoid enflaming tension ahead of Serbia's elections on 21 January 2007.[90] Rejected in Belgrade and welcomed in Priština, Ahtisaari's draft proposed an asymmetric state with supervised independence: independence to Kosovo in all (symbols, security forces, representation in international organisations, etc.) but name; a high degree of autonomy for the Serb community, including that pertaining to healthcare, education and cultural and religious sites; and an International Civilian Mission (ICM) tasked to monitor the implementation of the status settlement, as well as – implicitly – compliance with EU standards under the Stabilisation and Association Process. The ICM, headed by the 'double-hatted' International Civilian Representative/EUSR, was intended as a leaner and 'Europeanised' version of the Office of the High Representative in Bosnia and Herzegovina, but with no less intrusive powers,[91] working in cooperation with an international military presence to ensure the security of Kosovo (provided for by NATO's KFOR)[92] and a civilian rule-of-law mission (provided for by the EU)[93] in the support of local authorities.

After almost eight years in limbo, Ahtisaari's Comprehensive Proposal provided the roadmap that led Kosovo to a peculiar form of statehood.[94] Deadly violence erupted almost instantly in Kosovo and in Belgrade

[89] Kosovo Contact Group Statement, London, 31 January 2006, available at: http://ue.eu.int/ueDocs/cms_Data/docs/pressdata/EN/declarations/88236.pdf.

[90] The version of the Comprehensive Proposal of 2 February was only briefly available at: www.unosek.org, the website of the UN Office of the Special Envoy for Kosovo. A slightly amended version of the proposal was included in the addendum to the Letter dated 26 March 2007 from the Secretary-General addressed to the President of the Security Council, UN Doc. S/2007/168/Add.1.

[91] See Art. 2 of Annex IX to the Comprehensive Proposal.

[92] See Art. 13 and Annex XI to the Comprehensive Proposal.

[93] See Art. 12 and Annex X to the Comprehensive Proposal.

[94] See M. Weller, 'Negotiating the Final Status of Kosovo' (2008) 114 *EUISS Chaillot Paper*; and J. Ker-Lindsay, *Kosovo: The Path to Contested Statehood in the Balkans* (2009).

thousands took to the streets.[95] Two weeks of intensive consultations between Belgrade and Priština at the end of February ended without success. Following a final meeting between the two parties in Vienna on 9 and 10 March 2007, Ahtisaari declared that the one-year long process of negotiations had been exhausted, leaving no common ground between Belgrade and Priština.

A last ditch effort was mounted between August and December 2007, when an international Troika consisting of representatives from the EU (Wolfgang Ischinger),[96] the United States (Frank Wisner) and Russia (Alexander Botsan-Karchenko) conducted a series of meetings with both parties. In the Troika's search for a solution, the whole range of options (including autonomy, independence, partition) was once more discussed without, however, leading to any significant evolution of the positions of the parties. While many of the discussions with the Troika were repetitive, Ischinger developed a new concept, in which both sides would preserve their legal position on Kosovo and avoid mutual recognition, while committing to an ambitious and comprehensive framework of cooperation.[97] Whereas the proposal drew considerable international interest, it did not meet enthusiasm from the two protagonists. As Lehne reports:

> At the beginning of December 2007 the Troika submitted its report to the UN Secretary-General and recognised that neither side was willing to change its position on the fundamental question of sovereignty over Kosovo. The process of negotiation had now definitely come to an end. As Security Council action remained blocked by Russia, there remained only one option to decide the status question: a declaration of independence by the Kosovo Assembly, followed by international recognition.[98]

Kosovo's Albanian-dominated parliament ultimately declared independence on 17 February 2008 and has since been recognised by more than one hundred states worldwide (among which twenty-three out of twenty-eight EU Member States). However, its statehood remains contested, in

[95] See F. Terdevci, 'Kosovo's Status: Ready to Blow', *Transitions Online*, 20 February 2007.

[96] See Council Press Release CL07–177EN, 29 July 2007, Brussels, as recalled by Stefan Lehne, 'Resolving Kosovo's Status', *OIIP Policy Paper*, June 2009, at 10.

[97] As Lehne reports, Ishinger's proposal was along the lines of the 1972 Treaty concerning the basis of relations between the Federal Republic of Germany and the German Democratic Republic, which had allowed the FRG to move towards a policy of constructive engagement with the GDR, without abandoning its position of principle on German unity.

[98] See Lehne, *supra* note 96, at 10.

particular by Serbia, Russia and China,[99] and Priština has not been able to exert control over the Serbian-dominated north.

The final status talks of 2005/7 were led by Europeans but the EU – above and beyond its Member States – only played second fiddle.[100] Stefan Lehne, appointed by the Council of the EU in November 2005, acted as EU representative to support the UN Status Envoy in the implementation of his mandate,[101] and deputised Ahtisaari on a host of occasions. The negotiations were commissioned by the Contact Group, 'a forum of big powers reminiscent of the 19th century "Concert of Powers"',[102] and carried out under a mandate provided by the UNSG. The unstoppable drift in the direction of a unilateral declaration of independence created big problems for the EU due to the differences between Member States on the recognition of statehood:

> As long as the Contact Group remained operational, the Council of the EU found it relatively easy to bridge the internal divisions by simply mirroring the Contact Group's positions in its own statements. After Ahtisaari submitted his proposal, the EU still managed to agree to support the proposal (which did not explicitly mention independence), while emphasising the need for a UN Security Council decision.[103]

After the failure of negotiations and the blockage of the Security Council, the twenty-seven EU Member States narrowly succeeded in agreeing that the question of the recognition of Kosovo would be left to the decision of the individual capitals.

> However, the EU would be united in its operational engagement, in particular in the deployment of its most ambitious civilian CSDP mission so far, EULEX Kosovo, designed to strengthen the rule of law in Kosovo. The legal decisions concerning the mission were rushed through in January and early February 2008, as the support of all the twenty-seven (in the end Cyprus abstained) would have been more difficult to achieve following a declaration of independence.[104]

[99] See C. Borgen, 'Kosovo's Declaration of Independence: Self-determination, Secession and Recognition' (2008) 12 *ASIL Insight*; and M. Weller, *Contested Statehood: Kosovo's Struggle for Independence* (2009).

[100] In areas where the dialogue had not been sufficiently substantive – for instance on the economy or on community rights – Ahtisaari relied on the expertise of relevant international organisations such as the EU, the IFIs or the Council of Europe.

[101] See Council Conclusions of 7 November 2005 in Press Release No. 13622/05 (Presse 274).

[102] S. Lehne, *supra* note 96, at 18. [103] Ibid.

[104] Ibid. Council Joint Action 2008/124/CFSP of 4 February 2008 on the European Union Rule of Law Mission in Kosovo, EULEX KOSOVO [2004] OJ L42/92. UNSC Res 1244

> The formula of diversity on recognition and unity in engagement was successful in safeguarding the EU's continued role in the management of the Kosovo issue. However, as the experience since then has shown, the policy has been far from easy to implement in practice.[105]

While the establishment of normal relations between Belgrade and Priština is still far away and Kosovo's international integration will require great efforts, Kosovo's statehood is nonetheless an irreversible fact, especially since the International Court of Justice ruled that Kosovo's unilateral declaration of independence did not violate international law.[106]

In a real tour de force, the EU's HR/VP, and her (pre-EEAS) entourage managed:

(1) to convince EU Member States in the Political and Security Committee to support a press statement welcoming the Advisory Opinion and calling upon Serbia and Kosovo to engage in a dialogue facilitated by the EU 'to promote cooperation, achieve progress on the path to Europe and improve the lives of the people';[107] and
(2) to persuade Serbia to co-sponsor a UN General Assembly resolution which welcomed the readiness of the EU to facilitate a process of dialogue between the parties.[108]

A first meeting of the dialogue foreseen in UNGA Resolution 298 was held on 8 and 9 March 2011, in Brussels. Under the chairmanship of 'EU

(1999), which provided for the interim administration by UNMIK, remained in place due to Russian resistance to other options discussed in the Security Council. UNSG Ban Ki-Moon became involved in order to break the deadlock by presenting a six-point plan to the UNSC in a letter on 12 June 2008. On 26 November 2008, the Security Council approved this proposal, which provided for the deployment of a status-neutral EULEX under a continued 'UN umbrella', with UNSC Res. 1244 staying in force. This solution had a direct and severe impact on EULEX's mandate: UNMIK would stay in Kosovo and remain the official counterpart for the Serbs. This mainly had repercussions for Kosovo's Serb-dominated north, where UNMIK would continue to play a leading role, thus increasing the risk of a de facto division of the Kosovo territory.

105 Ibid.

106 See Security Council Report A/64/881, 26 July 2010, which includes the Advisory Opinion of the ICJ of 22 July 2010 on the *Accordance with International Law of the Unilateral Declaration of Independence in respect of Kosovo*. The ICJ rendered its Advisory Opinion upon request of the UNGA in its Resolution 63/3 of 8 October 2008.

107 Declaration by High Representative for Foreign Affairs and Security Policy Catherine Ashton on behalf of the European Union on the International Court of Justice advisory opinion on Kosovo, 12516/10, PRESSE 213, 22 July 2010, Brussels. This twin-track approach was quite a feat indeed, seeing that five EU Member States did not recognise Kosovo as a sovereign and independent state.

108 A/RES/64/298, 13 October 2010.

facilitator' Robert Cooper,[109] the Serbian and Kosovo delegations reiterated their commitment to the dialogue and their willingness to continue the process. Over the course of the next twelve months, nine meetings at the level of heads of delegation and even more gatherings in various technical working groups took place, in which both sides entered into discussions on several technical issues and struck agreements in a number of areas:[110] civil registry, freedom of movement, and acceptance of university and school diplomas;[111] customs stamps and cadastral records;[112] and integrated border management (IBM).[113]

The latter agreement means that the parties will gradually set up joint, integrated, single and secure posts at all their common crossing points, and that EULEX will be present in line with its mandate. This stands in stark contrast to the situation, which prevailed five months earlier, when EU facilitator Cooper decided to postpone the talks scheduled for 20 July 'when it became clear that the Serbs were not going to budge on the customs stamps'.[114] This triggered a chain reaction, prompting Kosovo to retaliate by blocking Serbian imports, which, in turn, meant that Kosovo had to take control of the border crossings. Hooded and masked Serbs, most likely organised,[115] attacked and torched two border posts. Kosovo police officers were trying to assert, for the first time, Kosovo's authority

[109] Cooper was assisted by a Greek and an Italian colleague (both seconded national experts to the EEAS), DG Enlargement (almost every meeting was co-chaired by Pierre Morel), EU staff on the ground, a number of interested EU Member States (the big countries, Austria and Sweden), as well as the United States.

[110] In March 2013, no agreement had yet been reached in the areas of energy, telecommunications, religious and cultural heritage, and the airspace (still occupied by NATO, and five Member States which do not recognise Kosovo's statehood).

[111] Press Statement, EU facilitated dialogue: three agreements, Brussels, 2 July 2011.

[112] Press Statement, EU facilitated dialogue: Agreement on Customs Stamps and Cadastre, 13772/11, PRESSE 294, Brussels, 2 September 2011.

[113] Press Statement, EU facilitated dialogue: Agreement on IBM, 18095/11, PRESSE 473, Brussels, 2 December 2011. A technical protocol on the implementation of the IBM deal was reached on 24 February 2012. Incidentally, the acronym 'IBM' is not spelled out once in the press statements announcing the agreement. Allegedly, the fudge is meant to let Kosovo and the 22 EU Member States which recognise it read 'IBM' in the usual sense. But it lets Serbia and the five non-recognising EU Member States say it refers to 'boundary management' because the word 'border' would imply statehood. See A. Rettman, 'Ambivalent Acronym Highlights EU Problems on North Kosovo', *EU Observer*, 5 December 2012.

[114] As reported by T. Vogel, 'Border Tensions', *European Voice*, 8 August 2011. See also Press Statement, EU facilitated dialogue: next round of talks postponed, 13119/11, PRESSE 256, Brussels, 19 July 2011.

[115] See D. Carjaval, 'In Kosovo, Smuggling Fosters Unusual Ethnic Cooperation', *New York Times*, 24 October 2011, who argues that ethnic unrest on the border of Serbian and

at the border crossings. The violence left one Kosovar police officer dead and several injured. EULEX Kosovo was completely powerless. The two border points had to be taken over by French and US NATO troops – not the 'European solution' that the EEAS had in mind when it began the facilitated dialogue with Serbia and Kosovo. In the end, emergency shuttle diplomacy by the EU appears to have produced the agreement for the reopening of the border crossings, but even if implemented, the agreement does nothing to address the underlying conflict.[116]

This finding is reinforced by way of a simple asterisk in the second, arguably more crucial agreement, which was reached on 24 February 2012. In the Agreement on Regional Representation and Cooperation, both parties confirmed their commitment to the fundamental EU value of effective, inclusive and representative regional cooperation.[117] The agreement allows for Kosovo to participate and sign new agreements on its own account and to speak for itself at all regional meetings.[118] This should allow both parties to sign, for instance, the draft Transport Community Treaty, which has been hanging in limbo since negotiations closed on 21 December 2009.[119] The parties agreed that 'Kosovo*' would be the only denomination to be used and that the footnote to be applied to the asterisk would read: 'This designation is without prejudice to positions on status, and is in line with UNSC 1244 and the ICJ Opinion on the Kosovo Declaration of Independence.' The twenty-six-word footnote had required close to two-and-a-half days of almost uninterrupted negotiations to finalise. No sooner had Serbia's and Kosovo's chief negotiators found this compromise, that politicians in Belgrade and Priština began pondering the implications. The mood turned celebratory in Serbia, as these twenty-six words were enough to unblock Serbia's bid to become a candidate for EU membership, which had stalled in December 2011 when Member States demanded a more constructive Serbian attitude towards Kosovo.[120] President Boris Tadić, whose party faced general

Albanian communities in Mitrovica, Kosovo, may have been more about the protection of the illegal proceeds from smuggling.

116 See T. Vogel, 'Border Tensions', *European Voice*, 8 August 2011.

117 Press Statement, EU facilitated dialogue: Agreement on Regional Cooperation and IBM technical protocol, 5455/12, PRESSE 9, Brussels, 24 February 2012.

118 Until then, agreements had been signed by UNMIK on behalf of Kosovo.

119 See S. Blockmans and B. Van Vooren, 'Revitalizing the European "Neighbourhood Economic Community": The Case for Legally Binding Sectoral Multilateralism' (2012) 17 *European Foreign Affairs Review* 577–604.

120 The European Council, in its Conclusions of 9 December 2011, EUCO 139/1/11 REV 1, 25 January 2012, point 13, set an agreement with Priština on Kosovo's regional

elections in May 2012, decided to make an impromptu visit to Brussels when the European Council granted his country the status of candidate for EU membership.[121] In Priština, meanwhile, the mood turned sour, as the government of Hashim Thaçi had to defend itself against accusations that it had compromised Kosovo's hard-won status and that the country would now be stuck for eternity with a name issue similar to that of (the Former Yugoslav Republic of) Macedonia. The footnote would prevent Kosovo from presenting itself as a fully independent country in regional meetings: instead, its nameplate would contain a reference to UNSC Resolution 1244, which reaffirmed Serbia's sovereignty over its province (while acknowledging that Belgrade no longer had any control over the area).[122] Kosovo's chief negotiator downplayed the accusations, saying that the footnote was like 'a snowflake that will melt when the summer comes'.[123] After all, the deal had turned Kosovo into 'a full participant in its own right in regional meetings and events, and will allow for further progress to contractual relations with the EU'.[124]

What the HR and the Commission are proposing is, in effect, to apply the formula agreed in the facilitated dialogue to Kosovo's bid to join the EU.[125] This, the thinking goes, should allow Kosovo to proceed on its European integration track without requiring that all EU Member States recognise its independence:

> Kosovo will thus follow the same European course as all others in the Western Balkans, in line with its European perspective ... In this light,

representation and cooperation as one of three conditions to positively decide on candidate status. The other conditions were implementation of the IBM agreement and cooperation with EULEX Kosovo.

121 European Council, Serbia is granted EU candidate status, EUCO 35/12, PRESSE 84, Brussels, 1 March 2012. While some Member States wanted to impose new conditions, it was agreed not to and stick to European Council's earlier demands only. The conclusions of the Foreign Affairs Council to grant candidate status received a lukewarm 'endorsement' in the European Council.

122 An interpretation defended in Belgrade, where Tadic said that the deal meant that Serbia did not have to give up its claim to Kosovo in order to join the EU. 'With this agreement, the policy "both Europe and Kosovo" that I have championed has passed a historic test', Tadic said. As reported by T. Vogel, 'What's in a Name?', *European Voice*, 1 March 2012.

123 *Ibid.*

124 Statement by High Representative Catherine Ashton and Commissioner Stefan Füle on the agreements reached in the latest round of Belgrade-Pristina dialogue, A 81/12, Brussels, 24 February 2012.

125 At the same time, Belgrade's refusal to accept Kosovo as an independent state will have an increasingly negative effect on Serbia's own EU accession hopes. Everyone in Tadic's entourage should know that the 'Europe *and* Kosovo' strategy will have to be abandoned before too long.

> the Commission proposes to launch a feasibility study for a Stabilisation and Association Agreement between Kosovo and the EU.[126]

The move potentially ends Kosovo's current limbo – but only if the five EU Member States that do not recognise Kosovo go along with it. This prompted Füle to seek the political backing of the Member States for launching the feasibility study, even though he had the competence to launch the study without their consent. The General Affairs Council of 28 February 2012 merely took note of the Commission's intention in this respect.[127]

The EU facilitated dialogue and the Council's endorsement of the historic agreement of 19 April 2013 on the normalisation of relations between Serbia and Kosovo (mediated by HR/VP Ashton herself) has fostered the dangerous impression that the status quo is sustainable, at least for a few years, as long as certain practical matters are attended to.[128] There is a risk that the ongoing dialogue on the implementation of the agreement will begin to be perceived as a substitute rather than a prelude to a final political settlement on the status issue. If no settlement is reached in the forseeable future, then the EU will pay the price for kicking the can down the road in 2012.

20.6 Concluding remarks

This study has shown that Dag Hammarskjöld's approaches towards peace diplomacy are mirrored in the European Union's DNA for external action in at least three ways:

(1) the EU's sanguine worldview, as expressed in its constitutional objectives, is largely consistent with Hammarskjöld's vision of the UN's role in the realm of maintaining or restoring international peace and security;
(2) the Lisbon Treaty's prescriptions on the EU's methodology for global peace diplomacy are in line with Hammarskjöld's ideas about effective multilateralism and building partnerships; and
(3) the Union's new institutional framework for external action is designed so as to allow the EU to develop a coherent, visible and effective policy on peace diplomacy which gives hands and feet to Hammarskjöld's

126 *Ibid.*

127 Council Press release 6854/12, PRESSE 65, Brussels, 28 February 2012.

128 See S. Blackmans, 'The EU as Global Peacemaker', Inaugural Speech, University of Amsterdam, 15 November 2013.

plea for a community-based vision of the UN in maintaining international peace and security.

The establishment of the EEAS, the EU's new diplomatic service, which supports the HR, is a key institutional innovation, which ought to enable the EU to make good on its constitutional promises. Of course, the proof of the pudding is in the eating. While it is early days to render a full-blown assessment of the functionality of the Lisbon Treaty's institutional changes, the first signs from a practical implementation point to a more comprehensive, structured and measured approach to EU foreign policy-making, one designed for the longer haul, more attuned to the lengthy and demanding processes of peace diplomacy, and worthy of a Nobel Peace Prize laureate.

PART V

Re-thinking internationalism: intervention, responsibility and the politics of R2P

21

From 'conference machinery' to 'global administration'?

International executive authority beyond Hammarskjöld

CARSTEN STAHN

21.1 Introduction

Over the past decades, international law has seen a revival of international executive authority.[1] Multilateral institutions exercise roles and functions of a public nature that are not unlike those performed by non-secular entities (e.g. the Church) in previous centuries. International organisations act as service providers or defenders of 'global public goods'.[2] The focus on executive action in international law may be traced back to the nineteenth century. National administrations formed joint administrative unions[3] in order to administer resources common to several states, such as natural resources and rivers. This type of administrative cooperation was then extended to sectors such as communication (International

Carsten Stahn is Professor of International Criminal Law and Global Justice, Leiden University.

[1] In the context of international organisations, authority is associated with the capacity to 'deploy discursive and institutional resources in order to get other actors to defer judgment to them'. It encompasses different dimensions, i.e. 'legal-rational authority', founded in decision-making based on objective rules and norms (Weber), 'moral authority' and 'expert authority'. See M. Barnett, 'Humanitarianism, Paternalism and the UNHCR', in A. Betts and G. Löscher, *Refugees in International Relations* (2011), 105, at 109–110. For a study, see A. Orford, *International Authority and the Responsibility to Protect* (2011), 43 et seq., 167–178.

[2] On global public goods, see D. Bodansky, 'What's in a Concept? Global Public Goods, International Law, and Legitimacy' (2012) 23 *EJIL* 651–668; G. Shaffer, 'International Law and Global Public Goods in a legal Pluralist World' (2012) 23 *EJIL* 669–693. On the 'church' analogy, see A. Orford, 'Jurisdiction without Territory: From the Holy Roman Empire to the Responsibility to Protect' (2009) *Michigan Journal of International Law* 981.

[3] See generally, R. Wolfrum, 'International Administrative Unions', in R. Wolfrum (ed.), *The Max Planck Encyclopedia of Public International Law*, Vol. V (2012), 335–344.

Postal Union), meteorology, health or aviation. International institutions have exercised administering power over territories in the aftermath of the First World War, under the umbrella of the League of Nations (Saar, Danzig Memel, Tangier, Trieste),[4] and later in the context of the UN and other international entities (e.g. EU). Today, many international organisations act as 'global public administrations'.[5] Their actions produce direct impact on national societies. They form part of what has been labelled a common 'administrative space',[6] i.e. international regulatory structures, mechanisms and transnational networks that regulate a field of activity and set and enforce norms in the realm between international law and domestic jurisdiction.

Inside the UN, the transformation from intergovernmental structures and working methods to multilateral forms of international organisation and decision-making was deeply shaped by Hammarskjöld's tenure. He represents like hardly any other UN Secretary-General the empowerment of executive authority in international relations.[7]

Hammarskjöld was a 'realist utopian'.[8] He assumed his functions at a time where the UN was under attack by conflicting ideologies and major power interests.[9] He sought to solve conflicts in a pragmatic way, in line with the spirit and principles of the Charter. This 'principled pragmatism' is visible in his approach to the international executive function. During his tenure, and in particular in the Introduction to his 1961 Report to the General Assembly, he coined a fresh vision of international executive

[4] See generally R. Wilde, *International Territorial Administration: How Trusteeship and the Civilizing Mission Never Went Away* (2008); C. Stahn, *The Law and Practice of International Territorial Administration* (2008).

[5] See generally, M. Barnett and M. Finnemore, *Rules for the World: International Organizations in Global Politics* (2004); J.E. Alvarez, *International Organizations as Law-Makers* (2005); R. Collins and N.D. White, *International Organizations and the Idea of Autonomy: Institutional Independence in the International Order* (2011).

[6] On global administrative law, see B. Kingsbury, N. Krisch and R. Stewart, 'The Emergence of Global Administrative Law' (2005) 68 *Law & Contemporary Problems* 15; B. Kingbury and L. Casini, 'Global Administrative Law Dimensions of International Organizations Law' (2009) 6 *International Organizations Law Review* 319–358; B. Kingsbury, 'The Concept of Law in Global Administrative Law' (2009) 20 *EJIL* 23–57.

[7] See generally Orford, *supra* note 1, 42–52, 169–175; A. Orford, 'From Promise to Practice? The Legal Significance of the Responsibility to Protect Concept' (2011) 3 *Global Responsibility to Protect* 400, 413–418.

[8] See generally on 'utopia' and conflicting visions in international law, M. Koskenniemi, *From Apology to Utopia: The Structure of International Legal Argument* (2005); A. Cassese (ed.), *Realizing Utopia: The Future of International Law* (2012).

[9] See O. Schachter, 'Dag Hammarskjöld and the Relation of Law to Politics' (1962) 56 *AJIL* 4–32.

authority.[10] Many of his core reflections on the role and duties of the UN have become part of the credo of the organisation and the justification of 'international humanitarianism' more broadly. Hammarskjöld stressed the need to overcome ideological divide through action. He grounded his policies and decisions not only in institutional ethics, but in a deeply normative conception of the Charter.[11] He traced 'the beginnings of a "common law" of the United Nations' in 1955.[12] Later, he formulated an 'ideology' for UN action[13] that transcended governmental interest. He was thus both an executive agent and the anti-type of an 'administrator', i.e. an advocate and visionary.

Hammarskjöld argued that peaceful progress and steps towards the 'liquidation of the colonial system'[14] cannot be reached through the General Assembly or the Security Council alone, but require the use of independent executive authority. He recognised 'a lack of balance in the Charter':

> While great attention is given to the principles and purposes, and considerable space is devoted to an elaboration of what may be called the parliamentary aspects of the Organization, little is said about executive arrangements.[15]

Based on a dynamic reading of provisions, he concluded that such ambiguity 'does not mean the Charter in any way closes the door to such arrangements or to executive action'. He noted:

> [T]he executive functions and their form have largely been left to practice, and it is in the field of the practices of the Organization that cases may be found in light of which it is now possible to evaluate the ways in

[10] See Introduction to the Annual Report of the Secretary-General on the Work of the Organization, 16 June 1960–15 June 1961, GAOR 16th Sess. Supp No. 1A (A/4800/Add.10), reprinted in Annex 1.

[11] See Dag Hammarskjöld, 'The United Nations – Its Ideology and Activities', Address before the Indian Council of World Affairs, New Dehli, 3 February 1956; Dag Hammarskjöld, 'The Development of a Constitutional Framework for International Cooperation', Address at the University of Chicago, Chicago, 1 May 1960. See generally O. Schachter, 'The International Civil Servant: Neutrality and Responsibility', in R.S. Jordan (ed.), *Dag Hammarskjöld Revisited: The UN Secretary-General as a Force in World Politics* (1983), 39–63.

[12] See Report of Secretary-General on the Work of the Organization, 15 September 1955, GAOR 10th Sess. Supp. No. 1 (A2911), at xiiii; Dag Hammarskjöld, Introduction to the Annual Report of the Secretary-General on the Work of the Organization, 16 June 1958–15 June 1959, GAOR 14th Sess. Supp. No. 1A (A/4132/Add.1), at 3.

[13] See Ideology, *supra* note 11.

[14] See 1961 Introduction, *supra* note 10, at 7.

[15] *Ibid.*, at 5.

> which the Organization may develop its possibilities for diplomatic, political or military intervention of an executive nature in the field.[16]

Most fundamentally, Hammarskjöld defended a managerial understanding of UN authority which contrasted with its more traditional conception as intergovernmental mechanism, i.e. as a 'static conference machinery', representing the interests and 'ideologies' of its Members.[17] He argued that the organisation represents 'a dynamic instrument' through which its Members also sought 'to develop forms of executive action, undertaken on behalf of all Members', aimed at 'forestalling conflicts and resolving them ... in a spirit of objectivity and in implementation of the principles and purposes of the Charter'.[18]

This commitment to independent 'executive power' and multilateralism was meant to protect UN peace maintenance from hegemonic tendencies and domination by Great Power interests during the Cold War.[19] It paved the way for modern developments, such as the extension of Chapter VII powers in the post-Cold War era to new fields (e.g. internal armed conflict, terrorism, refugee protection, international justice), the development of new forms of UN action (e.g. thematic resolutions, individualised sanctions) and the expanding role of international executive agents in conflict resolution. But it reflects at the same time some of the dilemmas of UN authority in the twenty-first century, including ongoing institutional and systemic critiques.[20]

This chapter explores how Hammarskjöld's vision of 'international executive authority' relates to the 'past' and the 'present'. It argues that many of the dilemmas that Hammarskjöld encountered are not new, but part of a broader historical trajectory. Some of his approaches, such as his 'secular church' analogy, his constitutional vision or his plea for UN ideology may have inadvertently fuelled tensions that continue to hamper the exercise of international authority until the present. Hammarskjöld's vision of internationalism will thus need to be re-thought, in order to meet the challenges of our time.

[16] *Ibid.*, at 5. [17] *Ibid.*, at 1. [18] *Ibid.*, at 1.

[19] See Orford, *supra* note 1, at 166, arguing that 'multilateralism has been seen as a significant bulwark against a resurgence of imperialism'.

[20] See generally D. Kennedy, *The Dark Sides of Virtue* (2005), at 257–258, 340; M. Barnett and T.G. Weiss (eds.), *Humanitarianism in Question: Politics, Power Ethics* (2008); M. Koskenniemi, 'International Law and Hegemony: A Reconfiguration' (2004) 17 *Cambridge Review of International Affairs* 197–218; B.S. Chimni, 'Third World Approaches to International Law: A Manifesto' (2006) 8 *International Community Law Review* 3–17.

21.2 The status quo ante

Hammarskjöld's managerial vision of institutional institutions has been shaped by different factors: his personal background and Christian values,[21] which are reflected in his public speeches and private correspondences (e.g. with Martin Buber), and broader normative ideals that have gained ground in international law since the mid to late nineteenth century.[22] He regarded his tenure as Secretary-General as an opportunity to promote the development of a global legal order, based on principles of humanity and international organisation.[23] He integrated his moral stance and his political ideas in his public speeches and reports. He used these statements to advance debates and guide normative choices.

21.2.1 Technocracy vs. autonomy

Hammarskjöld viewed the turn to international executive authority as progress.[24] His constructivist approach towards international authority was partly a reaction to the weaknesses of the League of Nations. The League had achieved tangible results through 'technical' cooperation in economic and social matters.[25] But there was a general perception that it had failed in its core mission, i.e. to secure international peace and security through its diplomacy-based architecture.[26] Hammarskjöld sought to remedy these failures in the UN context. He based his vision of internationalism on a fundamental choice: the distinction between the

[21] See Chapters 6 and 7, this volume.

[22] On the humanist foundations of the 'Hague' and 'Geneva Law', see R. Teitel, *Humanity's Law* (2011), 23–30.

[23] On 'humanity' and international law, see Teitel, *supra* note 22; A. Peters, 'Humanity as the A and Ω of Sovereignty' (2009) 20 *EJIL* 513–544.

[24] See the famous *dictum* in the 1955 Introduction, *supra* note 12, at xi ('We have only begun to make use of the real possibilities of the United Nations as the most representative instrument for the relaxation of tensions, for the lessening of distrust and misunderstanding, and for the discovery and delineation of new areas of common ground and interest. The Organization should be more than an instrument of what may be described as Conference diplomacy').

[25] See C. Tams, 'League of Nations', in R. Wolfrum (ed.), *The Max Planck Encyclopedia of Public International Law*, Vol. VI (2012), 760, 769–770.

[26] See A. Peters and S. Peter, 'International Organizations: Between Technocracy and Democracy', in B. Fassbender and A. Peters (eds.), *The Oxford Handbook on the History of International Law* (2012), 170, 185.

'historic conference pattern' and the dynamic development of executive action.

In his 1961 Introduction to the Annual Report to the General Assembly, Hammarskjöld distinguished the 'conference concept', guided by interstate cooperation, sovereign interest and preservation of peaceful co-existence, from 'more developed and increasingly effective forms of constructive international cooperation'.[27] He rooted the conference approach in 'history and ... the traditions of national policies in the past'.[28] He associated the 'conference machinery' model with certain key features, i.e. neutrality of the organisation towards 'the direction of policies on a national or international basis',[29] reflection of the 'interests and ideologies' of Member States in UN policy,[30] a Secretariat 'composed on party-lines' mirroring interests represented in main organs,[31] and reconciliation of 'conflicts of interest or ideology' through 'debate and joint decisions'.[32] He argued that the conference approach was 'still predominant' at the time of the creation of the Charter.[33] But he claimed that the UN had grown out of 'the historic conference pattern'.[34] He deplored that 'the needs for executive action' had 'not yet attracted the attention they were to receive in response to later developments'.[35]

His new emphasis on the UN as 'dynamic instrument',[36] with 'aspects of a parliamentary or quasi-parliamentary character'[37] and 'possibilities for diplomatic, political or military intervention of an executive nature',[38] is frequently represented as a radical departure from the past. Some call it 'revolutionary'.[39] But this narrative is partly misleading. The transition may not be as clear-cut as presented. The turn to executive action is part of a longer tradition of the exercise of public authority in the context of internationalisation[40] and international administrative regimes.[41]

27 1961 Introduction, *supra* note 10, at 1.

28 *Ibid.*, at 1. 29 *Ibid.*, at 2. 30 *Ibid.*, at 1. 31 *Ibid.*, at 6 and 1.

32 *Ibid.*, at 2 and 3. 33 *Ibid.*, at 5 34 *Ibid.*, at 5. 35 *Ibid.*, at 5.

36 *Ibid.*, at 1. 37 *Ibid.*, at 3. 38 *Ibid.*, at 5.

39 See A. Orford, 'The Past as Law or History? The Relevance of Imperialism for Modern International Law', IILJ Working Paper 2012/2, at 5.

40 See generally, R. Wolfrum and J. Pichon, 'Internationalization', in R. Wolfrum (ed.), *The Max Planck Encyclopedia of Public International Law*, Vol. VI (2012), 221–227.

41 See generally S. Kadelbach, 'From Public International Law to International Public Law', in A. von Bogdandy, R. Wolfrum, J. Bernstorff, P. Dann and M. Goldmann (eds.), *The Exercise of Public Authority by International Institutions* (2010), 33, 36.

21.2.2 *Historical experiments*

International executive authority has developed incrementally over time. Precedents may be found in two contexts: (1) administrative regimes and (2) territorial administration. In these contexts, international authority was tied to 'functionalist' considerations and ideas of 'trusteeship'. Hammarskjöld's approach was partly a continuation of, and partly a reaction to, these movements.

21.2.2.1 The 'functionalist' tradition

Hammarskjöld relied on 'functionalist' arguments in order to emancipate UN authority from state interests and mitigate sovereignty conflicts.[42] He stressed cooperative elements of international organisation and the distinction between common interest (represented by the UN) and national interest. This functional vision of international organisation has its origin in administrative regimes which witnessed a rapid increase at the end of the nineteenth and the beginning of the twentieth century. Functional cooperation emerged in the context of the administration of common resources (e.g. rivers).[43] It gained additional impetus with the growing industrialisation and technological progress in the nineteenth century. International institutions assumed various functions, ranging from cooperation and coordination (e.g. commodity arrangements) to provision of services, standardisation and protection.[44] First studies on International Administrative Law emerged in the late nineteenth century.[45] Emerging international administrative institutions gave international law a new shape.[46] Functionalist consideration became embedded in the conception of international law. Arbitrators, such as Max Huber, began to argue that international law 'divides between nations the space upon which human activities are employed'.[47]

[42] See Orford, *supra* note 1, 167–172.

[43] See Wolfrum, *supra* note 3, 336–339.

[44] See Wolfrum, *supra* note 3, 342, S. Cassese, 'Administrative Law without the State: The Challenge of Global Regulation' (2005) 37 *NYU Journal of International Law & Politics* 663, 687.

[45] See L. von Stein, *Die Verwaltunslehre* (1866), 94 et seq., P.S. Reinsch, *Public International Unions: Their Work and Organization: a Study in International Administrative Law* (1911).

[46] See G. Jellinek, *Die Lehre von den Staatenverbindungen* (1882), at 159.

[47] See Island of Palmas Award (*Netherlands* v. *United States*) (1928) 2 *U.N. Repertoire International Arbitration Awards* 829, 839.

The League of Nations developed an active system of economic and social cooperation since the 1920s in areas such as communication, commerce, disease control or refugee protection.[48] This approach marks one of the most important legacies of the League. It led to an 'unprecedented' level of cooperation at the time.[49]

These types of economic and technical cooperation provided the groundwork for more ambitious projects of international cooperation.[50] But they remained largely in the shadow of broader cosmopolitan ideas, such as pleas for broader political cooperation or the creation of a federation of liberal and democratic states (*Scelles*).[51] Many administrative unions gradually developed into international organisations in the course of the twentieth century. Some of them (e.g. Universal Postal Union, International Civil Aviation Organization) became UN specialised agencies. But they have remained detached from more ambitious projects of 'political' integration embodied in multilateral and regional organisations.

Hammarskjöld's 1961 Introduction echoes some of these tensions. He remained critical of a 'technocratic' vision of international authority. He defended an autonomous conception of 'international organisation' (which he distinguished from 'technical' cooperation). But he argued at the same time that this conception was not in contradiction to state sovereignty, but located in shared interests. This strand of argument, i.e. the distinction of UN authority from state sovereignty and the focus on cooperative interests, is grounded in the tradition of international administrative regimes.

A direct precedent for Hammarskjöld's managerial vision of peace maintenance may be found in regimes of territorial administration. This type of activity has a long-standing history in international law. International agents have exercised direct and indirect forms of public authority over territory since the nineteenth century. Most of them were guided by 'functionalist' considerations.

First experiences in international administration were conducted before the First World War. Groups of states exercised regulatory or executive power over internationalised cities or strategic places for military or

48 This was foreseen in Art. 23 of the Covenant of the League. See Tams, *supra* note 25, 769.

49 *Ibid.*, at 769.

50 See Peters and Peter, *supra* note 26, at 195.

51 Scelles associated the League with the idea of 'league of the free peoples'. See D. Scelle, *Précis de droit des gens: Principes et systématique* (1932), 247 and 249.

economic purposes. Examples include the multinational administration of spaces by European powers, such as administrations of the City of Cracow (1815–46), the Island of Crete, (1897–9), Albania (1912–13) and the International Zone of Tangier (1923–57).[52] This was followed by a tradition of internationalisation of cities for the purpose of dispute settlement and neutralisation under the auspices of the League of Nations. The League exercised direct administering powers over the Saar Territory, the City of Danzig and Memel, as a result of peace settlements after the First World War.[53] The Saar and Danzig regimes count among some of the longest experiments in the history of international territorial administration. They were driven partly by strategic interests (i.e. neutralisation), and partly by national-cultural concerns (i.e. protection of minority interests).[54] The League even used territorial administration as a device of conflict management. It administered the city of Leticia in Colombia from 1933 to 1934, in order to facilitate the settlement of the territorial dispute between Colombia and Peru. This intervention marked one of the early precedents of the use of territorial administration for purposes of 'managerial' conflict resolution which became later embedded in UN practice.[55]

These experiments provided early counter-narratives to the popular conception that the exercise of international authority conflicts with sovereignty interests. They provided examples that the exercise of international authority may be justified for the maintenance of public order and stability among nations.

21.2.2.2 Trusteeship responsibility

A second tradition of administration, which preceded Hammarskjöld's conception of international executive authority, is the exercise of administering powers in the context of the Mandate system and decolonisation.

This type of administration was distinct from related administrative regimes. It was geared towards the promotion of self-rule and domestic empowerment in territories under colonial rule, i.e. the creation of

[52] For details, see Stahn, *supra* note 4, at 53–58.

[53] See generally, M. Ydit, *Internationalised Territories from the 'Free City of Cracow' to the 'Free City of Berlin'; A Study in the Historical Development of a Modern Notion in International Law and International Relations* (1815–1960); S. Ratner, *The New UN Peacekeeping: Building Peace in Lands of Conflict after the Cold War* (1995).

[54] On minority protection by the League and its failures, see J.E. Nijman, 'Minorities and Majorities', in Fassbender and Peters, *supra* note 26, 95, 111–113.

[55] See Stahn, *supra* note 4, at 236.

sovereignty.[56] International authority was justified on the basis of the concept of 'trusteeship', i.e. the exercise of governing power on behalf of and to the benefit of the people of the administered territory.[57] It was inspired by the idea to 'humanise' colonial ethics and facilitate the transition from colonial rule to self-government or independence.[58] Mandate administration remained controversial due to its paternalistic justification (i.e. the 'sacred trust of civilisation'[59]) and its questionable assumptions about progress. But it introduced new methods and means of administration, by strengthening international supervision of domestic development and settings standards and regulations for the assessment of governance and progress.

Hammarskjöld was a vivid supporter of self-determination and liberation from colonial rule.[60] He saw international executive authority as a tool to advance this cause. Mandate administration provided a precedent for some of the 'dynamic' approaches towards international organisation advocated in the 1961 Introduction. It had fundamental repercussions for the relationship between international institutions and domestic jurisdiction. It indicated that international organisations may exercise 'organising functions' in the realm of domestic societies, without inferring with state sovereignty.

This conception deviated from traditional assumptions. In the first half of the twentieth century, international law was typically regarded as neutral towards the internal organisation of states. [61] Sovereignty was

[56] For a study, see A. Anghie, *Imperialism, Sovereignty and the Making of International Law* (2004), 115–194; A. Anghie, 'Colonialism and the Birth of International Institutions: Sovereignty, Economy and the Mandate System of the League of Nations' (2002) 34 *NYU Journal of International Law & Politics* 513.

[57] For a discussion, see W. Bain, *Between Anarchy and Society: Trusteeship and the Obligations of Power* (2003); R. Wilde, 'From Trusteeship to Self-Determination and Back again: The Role of the Hague Regulations in the Evolution of International Trusteeship, and the Framework of Rights and Duties of Occupying Powers' (2009) 31 *Loyola L.A. International & Comparative Law Review* 85, 95 et seq.

[58] See A. Anghie, 'Finding the Peripheries: Sovereignty and Colonialism in Nineteenth-Century International Law' (1999) 40 *Harvard International Law Journal* 1 at 37, arguing that the Mandate system replaced 'the vulgar language of profit' with that 'of order, proper governance and humanitarianism'.

[59] See Art. 22 of the Covenant of the League.

[60] See, e.g., Address Before the Academic Association of the University of Lund, 4 May 1959, UN Press Release SG/813, 4 May 1959, at 2 ('[N]obody should forget that colonization reflected a basic approach which may have been well founded in certain limited respects, but which often mirrored false claims, particularly when it touched on spiritual development. Applied generally, it was untenable').

[61] As McNair put it: 'In consequence of its internal independence and territorial supremacy, a State can adopt any constitution it likes, arrange its administration in a way it thinks fit,

understood as a shield against international interference in the external and internal affairs of a state. The Mandate system changed this vision. It challenged the principle that state organisation is outside the ambit of international scrutiny. It allowed the League to engineer the internal sphere of domestic societies in the context of the Mandates system.

Mandate administration and international oversight of the construction of internal norms and institutions remained limited to non-sovereign entities, and mostly non-European jurisdictions.[62] But international authority was formally grounded in justifications of impartiality, welfare and social progress that remain at the heart of contemporary approaches of peace-maintenance.

Mandate administration presents some striking parallels to contemporary forms of international executive authority. The exercise of jurisdiction and government over territory by the League was dissociated from sovereign rule. Administering powers by the League were neither seen as an intrusion into sovereign interests, nor as an exercise of sovereign power by an international entity. The leading theory to justify this form of authority was that 'the doctrine of sovereignty' was inapplicable to the Mandates system. As Judge McNair put it in his Separate Opinion in the *South-West Africa* case:

> Sovereignty over a Mandated territory is in abeyance; if and when inhabitants of the Territory obtain recognition as an independent State ... sovereignty will revive and vest in the new State.[63]

This model gained ground in conceptions of UN authority after the Second World War. It contributed to the emerging assumption in the peace maintenance tradition that the exercise of territorial authority by the UN is a merely 'functional' authority, which does not confer 'sovereignty' on the organisation.[64]

Mandate administration introduced a new vision of foreign rule. It presented the exercise of administering authority by the League as a neutral and disinterested activity. The administration of territories by the Mandatory powers was supervised by an expert body of the League, the Permanent Mandates Commission (PMC) which monitored progress

enact such laws as it pleases.' See L. Oppenheim, *International Law*, edited by A. McNair (4th edition, 1928), at 250.

62 See Anghie, *Imperialism, Sovereignty and the Making of International Law*, *supra* note 56, at 145–146.

63 See Separate Opinion Judge McNair, *International Status of South West Africa*, 11 July 1950, ICJ Rep. 1950, No. 10, 128, at 150.

64 See also Orford, *supra* note 1, at 172.

on the basis of reports and questionnaires. The PMC devised a system of information-gathering and public administration, based on its mandate to protect 'the well-being and development' of 'peoples not yet able to stand by themselves'.[65] It conceived its mandate in a quasi-scientific way. It developed standards and criteria to balance conflicting interests in the 'dual mandate' to promote economic development and secure the well-being of local populations.[66] Its control and management covered areas such as public services, health care, education, labour issues (e.g. slavery) and commerce.[67] Both the assumption of neutrality and the standards and regulation-driven approach of the League towards governance represent features of administration that were later taken up by the UN in the exercise of international executive authority in the spirit of Hammarskjöld.

Trusteeship remained a dilemma in subsequent practice. The UN struggled to reconcile fiduciary rule with the principle of self-determination. Article 78 of the UN Charter made it clear that the 'trusteeship system shall not apply to territories which have become Members of the United Nations' and that such relations 'shall be based on respect for the principle of sovereign equality'.[68] But the trusteeship idea remained inherent in decolonisation missions that were exercised by the UN outside the framework of the Trusteeship System,[69] such as the United Nations Assistance Missions in Libya and Eritrea after the Second World War,[70] the role of the United Nations Council for Namibia,[71] the United Nations Temporary Executive Authority (UNTEA)[72] relating to West New Guinea or the United Nations Transitional Administration in East Timor (UNTAET).[73] It also underpinned the tradition of multidimensional peacekeeping[74] and transitional administration after ONUC, including the United Nations Missions in Somalia (UNOSOM II),[75] the United Nations Transitional Authority on Cambodia (UNTAC)[76] or the United Nations Mission in

65 See Art. 22 of the Covenant.

66 See A. Anghie, 'Time Present and Time Past: Globalization, International Financial Institutions and the Third World' (2000) 32 *NYU Journal of International Law & Politics* 243, at 280–289.

67 See generally Q. Wright, *Mandates under the League of Nations* (1930), 549–579.

68 See Art. 2(1) of the UN Charter.

69 On this, see R. Wilde, 'Trusteeship Council', in T.G. Weiss and S. Daws (eds.), *The Oxford Handbook on the United Nations* (2007), 149–159.

70 For a discussion, see Stahn, *supra* note 4, at 209–220.

71 *Ibid.*, 252–259. 72 *Ibid.*, 246–252. 73 *Ibid.*, 332–346.

74 See generally Ratner, *supra* note 53.

75 Stahn, *supra* note 4, at 259–265. 76 *Ibid.*, 269–278.

Kosovo (UNMIK).[77] In each of these contexts, the UN exercised governmental and quasi-governmental power over territory in the role of caretaker for domestic authorities. It struggled with the tension of its 'dual' mandate, i.e. to represent 'communitarian interests' enshrined in UN decisions and interests of domestic stakeholders at the same time.[78]

21.2.3 Evolution or revolution?

Hammarskjöld's ideas on the use of executive authority to protect Charter principles were thus not 'revolutionary', but grounded in previous examples and undertakings. His framing of concepts provided additional weight to certain impulses that have been inherent in the concept of 'international organisation' since the first half of the twentieth century.

Hammarskjöld was cautious to avoid pitfalls of the past. He formally dissociated international executive authority from the stigma of 'civilisation' or domination. He saw both the League of Nations and the UN as new 'machinery of international organization', vested with the purpose to 'add strength to ... the common interest ... in the tasks of peacemaking and peacebuilding'.[79] He presented executive action as a functional activity that should remain detached from 'outside influences' and be guided by 'knowledge of facts'.[80] He argued that:

> whatever development the executive activities of the organization may show in the field, there should never be any suspicion that the world community would wish or indeed, could ever wish to maintain for itself, through the United Nations, a position of power or control in a member country.[81]

He was further keen to avoid the perception that the exercise of executive authority would equate the organisation to a 'super-state'. This claim was already challenged at the time of the conception of the League of Nations.[82] Hammarskjöld argued expressly that the UN is not meant to

[77] *Ibid.*, 308–330.

[78] For a discussion, see inter alia Wilde, *supra* note 4, at 379–431; W. Bain, 'In Praise of Folly: International Administration and the Corruption of Humanity' (2006) 82 *International Affairs* 525; S. Chesterman, 'Imposed Constitutions, Imposed Constitutionalism, and Ownership' (2005) 37 *Connecticut Law Review* 947; C.E. Ford and B.A. Oppenheim, 'Neotrusteeship or Mistrusteeship? The "Authority Creep" Dilemma in United Nations Transitional Administration' (2008) 41 *Vanderbilt Journal of Transnational Law* 55–105.

[79] See 'The Element of Privacy in Peacemaking', Address at Ohio University, 5 February 1958, UN Press Release SG/656, 3 February 1958, at 24.

[80] 1961 Introduction, *supra* note 10, at 7.

[81] *Ibid.*, at 8. [82] See Peters and Peter, *supra* note 26, at 185.

serve as 'a super-state trying to impose on people any "right" way of life or any other way of life different from one freely chosen by the people'.[83] He defended the exercise of managerial powers on pragmatic grounds.

Hammarskjöld's main innovation lies in the fact that he developed a nuanced normative justification for international executive authority inside the framework of the Charter. He located international authority in contemporary Charter principles, i.e. 'rule of law', 'justice' and 'common interest'.[84] This reasoning provided a principled foundation for the exercise of public authority beyond the state. He complemented this normative vision by an institutional ethic of care and compassion. These two elements formed the basis of his approach to international 'humanitarianism'.

21.3 Hammarskjöld's conception of international executive authority

Hammarskjöld's vision departs from the position of many of his successors. He developed an inherently moral justification of internationalism, which differs from technocratic models of authority advocated in contemporary discourse. His most popular, but also most dangerous, justification is his analogy of the UN to a 'secular church'.[85] He developed this idea at start of his first term of office in 1953. Hammarskjöld conceived 'the Secretariat and the Secretary-General in their relations with the Governments as representatives of a secular "church" of ideals and principles in international affairs of which the United Nations is the expression'.[86] He added that 'those who belong to organized citizens' groups supporting the United Nations in all countries, represent this secular "church" to their respective national states'.[87]

This imagery found expression in his conception of international executive authority. Hammarskjöld's conception of international executive

[83] See 'Address by Secretary-General at Dinner in his Honor Given by the American Association for the United Nations in Cooperation with the New York University Institute for Review of United Nations Affairs at the Waldorf-Astoria', New York, 14 September 1953, Press Release SG/336, 14 September 1953, at 6.

[84] 1961 Introduction, *supra* note 10, at 2.

[85] This idea was taken up by Secretary-General Javier Pérez de Cuéllar who noted that the UN Charter presents his 'religion'. See J. James and A.R. Nafziger, 'The Functions of Religion in the International Legal System', in M.W. Janis and C. Evans (eds.), *Religion and International Law* (1999), 159.

[86] See Address, American Association, *supra* note 83, at 6.

[87] *Ibid.*, at 7.

rule was based on different dimensions of authority: (1) 'legal-rational' authority and (2) moral authority.

21.3.1 *Legal-rational authority*

Hammarskjöld developed the foundation of executive authority on the basis of rational legal rules and principles.[88] He combined arguments of consent and fiction in his justification. He argued that the articles, as well as the 'purposes and principles of the Charter', provide 'basic rules of international ethics by which all Member States have committed themselves to be guided'.[89] He justified the powers of the UN to develop new forms of executive action by way of an analogy to 'standards accepted as binding for life within States'.[90] He claimed that the framework of the Charter represents essentially 'a projection into the international arena and the international community of purposes and principles already accepted as being of national validity'.[91] He treated these 'common elements' as a basis for 'international behavior and co-operation'.[92] His methodology was thus traditional in principle. Hammarskjöld did not seek to create a new order through law. He rather sought, as Schachter aptly put it, 'to find within the limits of power the elements of common interest on the basis of which joint action and agreed standards could be established'.[93] This conception was later replicated in international legal scholarship, i.e. in the characterisation of the charter as 'world order' treaty.[94]

One of the main new elements that he introduced into the conception of organisational power was his construction of the Charter as a 'constitutional framework'.[95] This idea is not entirely new. Scholars of the Viennese School, such as Verdross, had already claimed in the inter-war period that customary law and multilateral treaties may form building blocks of a 'constitution of the international community' (*Verfassung der*

[88] See also Chapter 9, this volume.
[89] 1961 Introduction, *supra* note 10, at 1.
[90] *Ibid.* [91] *Ibid.* [92] *Ibid.*
[93] Schachter, *supra* note 9, at 7.
[94] See, e.g., C. Tomuschat, 'Obligations Arising for States Without or Against Their Will' (1993-IV) 241 *Recueil des Cours* 195, at 269, speaking of the Charter as a treaty 'intended to concretize, and elaborate on, principles which on their part are constituent elements of the international legal order'.
[95] For a general discussion, see B. Fassbender, 'The United Nations Charter as Constitution of the International Community' (1998) 36 *Columbia Journal of Transnational Law* 531–616.

Völkerrechtsgemeinschaft).[96] Moreover, individual ICJ judges had branded the Charter as a 'constitutional instrument' (*Lauterpacht*)[97] or a 'constitution of international society' (*Alvarez*)[98] in individual opinions since the 1950s. Hammarskjöld was the first UN Secretary-General who translated this conception into organisational practice. He argued that 'through its universality', the Charter represents a 'true constitutional framework for world-wide international cooperation'.[99] He used constitutional analogies to describe the powers and checks and balances between UN organs. He qualified the General Assembly as the 'nearest approximation' to a 'world parliament'.[100] He regarded the Security Council as a collective 'executive' organ,[101] the Secretary-General as a 'one man "executive" with explicit authority in the administrative field'[102] and the International Court of Justice as 'a counterpart to a national judiciary'.[103]

Hammarskjöld used this constitutional approach to support progressive development and adaptability of procedures. He made this argument expressly in his 1959 Introduction to the Report to the General Assembly. He stated:

> The statements of objectives in the Charter is binding and so are the rules concerning the various organs and their competence, but it is not necessary to regard the working methods indicated in the Charter as limitative in purpose. Thus, they may be supplemented by others under the pressure of circumstances and in the light of experience if these additional procedures are not in conflict with what is prescribed. As is well known, such an evolution has in fact taken place, and it thus recognized that such new procedures may be developed when they prove productive in practice for efforts towards the objectives of the Charter. In this respect, the United Nations, as a living organism has the necessary scope for continuous adaptation of its constitutional life to the needs.[104]

This conception opened new ways for the development of UN authority and modes of action. It provided a basis for application of dynamic legal

[96] See A. Verdross, *Verfassung der Völkerrechtsgemeinschaft* (1926), v; A. Verdross, *Völkerrecht* (2nd edition, 1950), 74. For a contemporary analysis, see A. O'Donoghue, 'Alfred Verdoss and the Contemporary Constitutionalization Debate' (2012) 32 *Oxford Journal of Legal Studies* 799–822.

[97] See Separate Opinion, J. Lauterpacht, *Voting Procedures on Questions Relating to Reports and Petitions Concerning the Territory of South-West Africa*, ICJ Rep. 1955, 67, at 106.

[98] See Dissenting Opinion, J. Alvarez, *Reservations to the Convention on the Prevention and Punishment of the Crime of Genocide*, ICJ Rep. 1951, 15, 49, 51.

[99] See Constitutional Framework, *supra* note 11, at 587.

[100] See Ideology, *supra* note 11, at 663.

[101] Constitutional Framework, *supra* note 11, at 588.

[102] *Ibid.* [103] *Ibid.* [104] 1959 Introduction, *supra* note 12, at 2.

concepts, such as teleological interpretation, 'implied powers' or subsequent practice.[105] These concepts facilitated the creative development of executive authority by the Security Council and the Secretary-General in areas such as fact-finding, peacekeeping, use of force or other areas of collective security.

Based on these normative premises, Hammarskjöld defined a list of objective considerations guiding decision-making in concrete cases. This canon includes:

(1) compliance with 'the principles and purposes of the Charter' which he considered as 'fundamental law accepted by and binding on all States';[106]
(2) respect of 'legal doctrine and precepts that have been accepted by States generally, and particularly as manifested in the resolutions of United Nations organs';[107] and
(3) application of 'constitutional means and techniques' to reduce 'the element of purely personal judgment'.[108]

These elements form the core of his legal-rational justification of UN authority.

21.3.2 *Moral authority*

Hammarskjöld backed this justification by moral considerations. He developed an institutional ideology through which he supported the role of the UN as 'an instrument of action inspired by hope'.[109] This ideology is based on three classical features of humanitarianism that have become common in UN discourse:

(1) representation of 'common interest';
(2) impartiality; and
(3) the ethics of care.[110]

[105] See K. Skubiszewski, 'Remarks on the Interpretation of the United Nations Charter', in R. Bernhardt, W.K. Geck, G. Jaenicke and H. Steinberger, *Völkerrecht als Rechtsordnung – Internationale Gerichtsbarkeit-Menschenrechte: Festschrift für Herman Mosler* (1983), 891, at 893.

[106] See 'International Civil Servant in Law and in Fact', Lecture delivered to Congregation at Oxford University, 30 May 1961, at 346.

[107] *Ibid.* [108] *Ibid.*, at 347.

[109] See Ideology, *supra* note 11, at 660.

[110] For a critique in relation to UNHCHR, see Barnett, *supra* note 1, at 112.

The first key element is the idea of commonly shared interests. Hammarskjöld was convinced that the Charter embodies universally shared values. He argued that the UN 'represents ideals at least professed by all nations'.[111] He regarded it as 'the repository and voice of a common heritage of ideals to penetrate the life of states in their international relations and to influence their conduct toward a wider realization of those ideals'.[112] He connected this role to the notion of 'international community', and an entitlement of the UN to represent this community. This 'international community' idea has a long tradition in international legal scholarship, i.e. natural law traditions and universalist approaches.[113] It received some formal backing in international law as of the late 1960s, with the emergence of concepts such as 'common heritage of mankind'[114] and obligation of states towards the international community as a whole (*erga omnes* obligations).[115]

The second yardstick of Hammarskjöld's ideology is the principle of impartiality. He argued that the UN could be entrusted with authority because of its disinterested concern for peace and its neutral civil service. He defended the ability of the UN Secretariat to stand above the ebb and flow of politics and powers. He made this argument explicit in his famous 'International Civil Servant in Law and in Fact' address, where he affirmed that 'it is possible for the Secretary-General to carry out its tasks in controversial political situations with full regard to his exclusively international obligation under the Charter and without subservience to a particular national or ideological attitude'.[116] This argument reflects the classical distinction between humanitarianism and politics in humanitarian discourse.

Hammarskjöld complemented these guiding principles by his ethics of care. He took the view that executive action in support of Charter

[111] See Address American Association, *supra* note 83, at 6.

[112] *Ibid.*

[113] See H. Mosler, 'The International Society as a Legal Community' (1974) 140 *Recueil des Cours* 1; A. Paulus, *Die Internationale Gemeinschaft im Völkerrecht* (2001); M. Koskenniemi, '"International Community" from Dante to Vattel', in V. Chetail and P. Haggenmacher (eds.), *Vattel's International Law from a XXI Century Perspective* (2011), 49–75.

[114] See generally R. Wolfrum, 'Common Heritage of Mankind', in R. Wolfrum, *The Max Planck Encyclopedia of Public International Law*, Vol. II (2012), 552–457.

[115] See ICJ, *Barcelona Traction, Light and Power Company, Limited* (*Belgium* v. *Spain*), ICJ Rep. 1970, 32.

[116] See 'The International Civil Servant in Law and Fact', Lecture delivered to Congregation at Oxford University, 30 May 1961, www.un.org/depts/dhl/dag/docs/internationalcivilservant.pdf, at 346.

principles should be based on need and circumstances, rather than identity of subject. He linked the mission of the UN to 'a philosophy of solidarity' which bears resemblance to some contemporary visions of protection (e.g. Responsibility to Protect).[117] He made this point in 1953. He stated:

> [O]rganized international cooperation as represented by the United Nations and other agencies tends to reduce, rather than increase, the burden upon any single nation in its efforts to prevent war and encourage an orderly evolution towards a more peaceful, just and prosperous world. What would otherwise be a burden on the shoulders of one, is shared by many and the equitability of the sharing is something that can be worked out.[118]

He developed his institutional ethics for civil service.[119] It relies on motives and standards of care that are typically associated with humanitarian thought.

21.4 Hammarskjöld's executive authority re-visited

Hammarskjöld's 'secular church analogy' and his dual justification of UN authority were guided by noble ideals. His rational-legal justification of UN authority was designed to overcome ideological differences and foster the emancipation of the UN from state interests. His moral ideology had a deeply humanist foundation. But both propositions contained dichotomies, blind spots and problems that have remained at the heart of UN policies and approaches since the 1950s.

21.4.1 Dichotomies

Hammarskjöld's ideology and his 'constitutional vision' of international organisation were meant to rationalise UN authority and to substitute power by a communitarian model of global order. They expanded the scope of UN action, in the name of 'shared' communalities and 'public interest'. UN agents have become actively engaged in governmental and quasi-governmental activities such as policing, security, election politics, refugee protection or political reconstruction. This extension has given rise to a number of dilemmas that are sidelined in Hammarskjöld's model. They range from questions of agency, to knowledge problems (i.e. capacity to make informed decisions) and dilemmas of control and contestation.

[117] See Chapter 23, this volume.
[118] See Address, American Association, *supra* note 83, at 4–5.
[119] See *supra* note 116, and Schachter, *supra* note 11.

21.4.1.1 Empowerment vs. disempowerment

Through his ideology and 'secular church' imagery, Hammarskjöld sought to secure greater UN autonomy from state authority. He argued that international executive authority should be expanded since the UN is 'neutral' and able to protect the welfare of people and individuals. One of the central weaknesses of his logic is that he tried to construe foundations of a secular world order based on fictional concepts.

Hammarskjöld assumed that Charter principles embrace 'common interests'. He implied the existence of the 'international community'.[120] He spent little effort to specify these concepts or ground them in practice. They remained grounded in 'faith' or 'ideology'. This rendered the UN vulnerable. The 'secular church' image implied that the UN 'is a guarantor of a truth that lies beyond the State'.[121] This claim remained suspicious in the eyes of those who have become the 'victim' of executive action and intervention.[122] Some Third World lawyers felt deceived by this logic.[123] It actually turned against the UN when states claimed some of the same principles to justify exceptions to the prerogative of the UN in the area of international peace and security, i.e. pro-democratic intervention as of the 1970s and humanitarian intervention.[124]

A similar problem arises in relation to the UN's alleged impartiality. The UN enjoys a certain degree of trustworthiness and institutional independence. But it is questionable to justify international action on the basis of its impartiality or its disinterested character. In practice, such premises often turn into fiction. In many cases, they are precluded by the very terms of the mandate which pursues particular agendas or vested interests. This has been the case in the context of the Congo. Lumumba made this clear in a letter to Hammarskjöld in which he noted:

> The resolution of July 14, 1960, explicitly states that the Security Council authorises you 'to provide the Government (of the Republic of the Congo]

120 For a similar inference, see Department of Peacekeeping Operations (DPKO), *United Nations Peacekeeping Operations: Principles and Guidelines* (2008), at 24 ('The fact that multi-dimensional United Nations peacekeeping operations enjoy a high degree of international legitimacy and represent the collective will of the international community gives them considerable leverage over the parties').

121 See Orford, *supra* note 1, at 175.

122 For TWAIL critiques, see J.T. Gathii, 'Neoliberalism, Colonialism and International Governance, Decentering the International Law of Governmental Legitimacy' (2000) 98 *Michigan Law Review* 1996.

123 See A. Anghie, 'The Evolution of International Law: Colonial and Postcolonial Realities' (2006) 27 *Third World Quarterly* 739, at 752.

124 See Orford, *supra* note 1, at 177.

> with such military assistance as may be necessary'. This text adds that you are to do so 'in consultation with' my Government. It is, therefore, clear that in its intervention in the Congo the United Nations is not to act as a neutral organisation but rather that the Security Council is to place all its resources at the disposal of my Government. From these texts it is clear that contrary to your personal interpretation, the United Nations force may be used 'to subdue the rebel Government of Katanga', that my Government may call upon the United Nations services to transport civilian and military representatives of the Central Government to Katanga in opposition to the provincial Government of Katanga and that the United Nations force has the duty to protect the civilian and military personnel representing my Government in Katanga.[125]

'Managerial' actions are not 'neutral' per se.[126] They have been branded under neutral levels, such as 'technical assistance' or executive action since Mandate administration under the League.[127] In reality, they transform political, economic, social or cultural structures of domestic societies. They are thus not 'apolitical, neutral or impartial' as implied by Hammarskjöld. The use of the 'technical' label is one of the remaining problems of the conceptualisation of executive authority. In some cases, it has effectively reduced protection or facilitated excesses of authority.[128]

Hammarskjöld's ideology has failed to articulate a convincing vision of agency.[129] Hammarskjöld's vision is based on the functionalist idea that states entrusted the UN with certain functions that are beneficial to its members.[130] He assumed that these activities represent 'community interests'. His vision clouded deeper ethical considerations of 'constituency'.

125 See P. Lumumba, *Correspondence with United Nations General Secretary Dag Hammarskjöld*, July and August 1960, 14 August 1960, at www.marxists.org/subject/africa/lumumba/1960/08/umgensec.htm. On the relationship between Hammarskjöld and Lumumba, see Chapters 12 and 13, this volume.

126 See Orford, *supra* note 1, at 193.

127 For a contemporary rendering of impartiality doctrine, see DPKO, *supra* note 120, at 33: 'United Nations peacekeepers should be impartial in their dealings with the parties to the conflict, but not neutral in the execution of their mandate. The need for even-handedness towards the parties should not become an excuse for inaction in the face of behavior that clearly works against the peace process. Just as a good referee is impartial, but will penalize infractions, so a peacekeeping operation should not condone actions by the parties that violate the undertakings of the peace process or the international norms and principles that a United Nations peacekeeping operation upholds.'

128 See Section 21.4.3.

129 For a discussion, see M. Koskenniemi, 'Projects of World Community', in Cassese, *supra* note 8, 4–13.

130 For this vision of agency, see Jan Wouters and Philip de Man, 'International Organisations as Lawmakers', in J. Klabbers and A. Wallendahl (eds.), *Research Handbook on the Law of International Organizations* (2011), 190, 199, 191.

Like other 'humanitarian' justifications, Hammarskjöld's internationalism remained relatively silent on the object of protection and its interests. Hammarskjöld was conscious of the problems of assistance. He was aware that benevolent activity may create tensions, i.e. problems of domination and feelings of inferiority by the receiving side. He acknowledged that 'it may be more difficult to receive assistance than to give it'.[131] But he ultimately accepted that the UN could speak on behalf of others. This has facilitated 'managerial action', including political reform, state reconstruction or state creation (East Timor, Kosovo) based on UN initiative.[132] In many contexts, the 'for whom' question has remained unresolved.

Issues of consent, representation of domestic interests and dependency have remained critical in the exercise of international executive authority since Hammarskjöld's experience in the Congo. On numerous occasions, international actors have claimed a need to act, even in the absence of domestic consent. They have often done so, without providing a justification as to why they are entitled to represent a general public will (e.g. emergency powers) or to substitute domestic consent. International authority is often detached from the consent of the governed and based on a fictional 'social contract'. Where consent is sought, it is frequently tied to strings and conditions (e.g. standards). This has disempowering effects.[133] Many actors in the developing world have oriented their internal organisation towards international standards in order to receive assistance or maintain access to global markets.[134]

More recently, the UN has placed greater emphasis on the need to foster 'local ownership' in constitutional assistance and peacebuilding missions. The concept features prominently in many contemporary policy documents.[135] It implies that executive action should encourage local stakeholders to take responsibility in decision-making processes and implementation of policies. It seems to leave greater space to domestic

[131] See Address Lund, *supra* note 60, at 6.

[132] Some speak of a 'revolution from above', based on moral progress. See Barnett, *supra* note 1, at 127. See also A. Orford, 'International Territorial Administration and the Management of Decolonization' (2010) 59 *ICLQ* 227, 249.

[133] For a critique, see M Ayoob, 'Third World Perspectives on Humanitarian Intervention and International Administration' (2004) 10 *Global Governance* 99, 103–104.

[134] See, e.g., A. Branch, 'Against Humanitarian Impunity: Rethinking Responsibility for Displacement and Disaster in Northern Uganda' (2008) 2 *Journal of Intervention and Statebuilding* 151–173.

[135] UN Secretary-General, *The Rule of Law and Transitional Justice in Conflict and Post-Conflict Societies*, UN Doc. S/2004/616, 23 August 2004, para. 17; UN Secretary-General, *Strengthening and Coordinating United Nations Rule of Law Activities*, UN Doc. A/66/133, 8 August 2011.

entities to determine their own destiny and make their own mistakes. But it has not brought much clarity in relation to the 'constituency' dilemma.[136] The meaning of 'local' varies according to the context and the interpreter. Sometimes, the term is equated with 'national interests' by local governments in order to maintain power. In other cases, it remains difficult to interact with 'local' stakeholders because there are conflicting views as to who 'ought to be owner'[137](e.g. Bosnia) or dominating majority interests which may polarise opinion in post-conflict societies (e.g. Iraq).

These operational problems are complemented by other dilemmas, such as the difficulties for 'outsiders' to properly interpret and decide on the choices and needs of local actors. The use of international executive authority is often branded as an instrument to enable greater freedom, protection and prosperity. But the choices made by international executive agents may diminish or pre-empt the liberty or autonomy of domestic actors to make other choices. This makes it difficult to justify benevolent agency on behalf of others.

Action on behalf of the international community and in the projected benefit for others is often justified by constructed knowledge. Decisions about conditions of social life are made in response to certain actual and real-life facts. But they rely on assumed chains of events, causality streams or predictions. This raises epistemological problems about authority. It presumes that international actors are able to make informed decisions about fundamental choices, based on their vision of reality and exposure to facts. But this very same vision is often predetermined or mediated through specific interests or channels of communication. This makes it hard to determine to what extent such decisions are grounded in facts, reliable expertise or trust, and why they ought to be followed.[138] More fundamentally, in many contexts of peacebuilding, such determinations are used to 'manage' local politics or 'engineer' the internal realm of domestic societies.[139] This poses ongoing challenges to authority and justification.

From early experiments of internationalisation to contemporary engagements, international executive authority has suffered from an

[136] See S. Chesterman, 'Ownership in Theory and in Practice: Transfer of Authority in UN Statebuilding Operations' (2007) 1 *Journal of Intervention and Statebuilding* 3, 7.

[137] See E.P. Joseph, 'Ownership is Over-rated' (2007) 27 *SAIS Review* 109, at 119.

[138] For questions in relation to 'security' determinations by the Security Council, see M. Koskenniemi, 'The Police in the Temple – Order Justice and the UN: A Dialectical View' (1995) 6 *EJIL* 325, at 343–344.

[139] For a critical analysis, see N. Bhuta, 'Democratisation, Statebuilding and Politics as Technology', in B. Bowden, H. Charlesworth and J. Farral, *The Role of International Law in Rebuilding Societies after Conflict* (2009), 38, 49 et seq.

inherent problem of justification. It carries an undeniable degree of domination, based on the idea of agency. This coercive element is implicit in the use of authority for the benefit of others, i.e. in its means and in its articulation. As Koskenniemi put it:

> If the representative of a Western nation now makes that claim of universality, it is hard to see why the non-Western world would see it differently than when it was made in the languages of Christianity, civilization, 'modernity', or 'development' (among others). The claim to speak in the voice of the 'world community' is not only an innocent statement about how the world is (or what I happen to 'feel'), but also contains the implicit claim for special authority that belongs to the one who can speak on everyone's behalf.[140]

Hammarskjöld's internationalism failed to eliminate these fears and anxieties. It explains part of the remaining resistance against the 'managerial' use of international executive authority and its 'faith'-based justification.[141]

21.4.1.2 Functionalism vs. constitutionalism

A second dichotomy in Hammarskjöld's ideology is the tension between executive power and 'constitutionalism'. Hammarskjöld used a constitutionalist argument to support 'managerial' power. He derived authority for executive action from its embedding in a 'constitutional framework'.[142] But he relied on a very thin notion of constitutionalism. His approach is marked by an implicit friction. He supported a functional approach towards executive powers based on law and the 'constitutional' features of the Charter. But he failed to take this constitutionalist argument through to the end. He omitted to treat the flipside of the expansion of international executive authority, i.e. the subordination of executive power to the constraints of law and corresponding responsibilities (e.g. accountability).

Hammarskjöld defended a 'cooperation' based approach to constitutionalism. He regarded constitutionalisation as a creative evolutionary process through which 'institutional systems for coexistence' develop into a 'constitutional system of cooperation'.[143] He perceived institutional structure as a means to an end, i.e. to facilitate effective action in support of Charter principles. He sought to 'seek the optimum balance' between autonomy and independence,[144] mostly through the lens of the interplay between state authority and UN authority.

[140] See Koskenniemi, *supra* note 129, at 10.

[141] For an illustration, see B.S. Chimni, 'A Just World Under Law: A View from the South' (2006) 100 *Proceedings of the American Society of International Law* 17–24.

[142] See Constitutional Framework, *supra* note 11.

[143] *Ibid.*, at 584. [144] *Ibid.*, at 590.

Based on this conception, he treated law as an 'enabling' mechanism, rather than as a constraint. His approach favoured 'functionalism' over 'formalism'. This reflected in his treatment of sources and his reliance on Charter principles. He defended the 'sanctity' of the Charter as an instrument. But he placed less emphasis on constraints of wording or legal checks and balances. His functionalist reading expanded the scope of 'administrative' discretion among executive agents under the Charter. The label of 'international peace and security' has been extended to an ever-growing array of functions that were not expressly contemplated by the drafters, such as peacekeeping or enforcement action by 'coalitions of the able and willing'.[145]

Hammarskjöld's reading has become symptomatic of the exercise of executive power in the UN context. The UN has never taken a strict approach towards the interpretation of its own powers under the Charter. From Hammarskjöld on, the wording and language of the Charter has been used to expand UN authority. This emphasis facilitated emancipation and development of UN policies in the area of peace and security. Executive measures such as peacekeeping or territorial administration were developed on the basis of implied powers or dynamic interpretations of the Charter.[146] Even the establishment of international criminal tribunals for Yugoslavia and Rwanda, and subsequent justice mechanisms, were justified as executive actions.[147]

This executive vision of authority coincided with interpretive freedom and judicial restraint in ICJ case-law. The *Certain Expenses* case, which arose in 1962 as a result of the deployment of ONUC by the General Assembly, illustrates this development. The ICJ defended executive discretion. The Court noted that 'each organ must, in the first place at least, determine its own jurisdiction'.[148] It established a presumption of legality in relation to UN resolutions, arguing that:

145 See generally, D. Sarooshi, *United Nations and the Development of Collective Security: the Delegation by the UN Security Council of its Chapter VII Powers* (2000).

146 See Stahn, *supra* note 4, 415–453.

147 For a validation, see ICTY, Appeals Chamber, *Prosecutor v. Tadić*, IT-94–1, Decision on the Defence Motion for Interlocutory Appeal on Jurisdiction, 2 October 1995, para. 44 ('It does not follow from the fact that the United Nations has no legislature that the Security Council is not empowered to set up this International Tribunal if it is acting pursuant to an authority found within its constitution, the United Nations Charter. As set out above we are of the view that the Security Council was endowed with the power to create this International Tribunal as a measure under Chapter VII in the light of its determination that there exists a threat to the peace'). For a discussion, see J. Alvarez, 'Nuremberg Revisited: The Tadić Case' (1996) 7 *EJIL* 245.

148 See ICJ, *Certain Expenses of the United Nations (Article 17, paragraph 2, of the Charter)*, ICJ Reports 1962, p. 168.

> when the Organization takes action which warrants the assertion that it was appropriate for the fulfillment of one of the stated purposes of the United Nations, the presumption is that such action is not *ultra vires*.[149]

In 1970, this approach was confirmed in the *Namibia* case, where the Court noted:

> A resolution of a properly constituted organ of the United Nations which is passed in accordance with that organ's rules of procedure, and is declared by the President to have been so passed, must be presumed to be validly adopted.[150]

These verdicts present the 'highpoint of the functional necessity approach that dominated the UN for much of its life'.[151]

Later, this vision has come under challenge. Executive organs, such as the Security Council or the Secretary-General, have used their autonomy and executive discretion to expand their scope of activities. They developed new forms of executive action with direct impact on individuals (e.g. sanctions, international courts and tribunals) or legislative elements.[152] In particular, the Security Council used Chapter VII powers to adopt 'law making or law-determining measures'.[153] This led to a 'constitutional crisis' in the 1990s. The 'functionalist' logic created an 'interpreter' problem. UN organs became the guardians of their own space. This extension of authority posed legality and legitimacy questions in relation to the compatibility of UN executive action with Charter principles and limits of the UN.

This problem became apparent in the *Lockerbie* case, when the legal boundaries of Security Council Resolutions were tested in ICJ jurisprudence.[154] The Council had used its authority under Chapter VII to request the surrender of alleged perpetrators of the Lockerbie bombing for trial before Scottish Courts in the Netherlands. This request stood in contrast to Libya's option to extradite or prosecute under the 1971 Montreal

149 *Ibid.*

150 See ICJ, Advisory Opinion, *Legal Consequences for States of the Continued Presence of South Africa in Namibia (South West Africa) notwithstanding Security Council Resolution 276 (1970)*, ICJ Reports 1971, p. 22, para. 20.

151 See N.D. White, 'Decision-Making', in Klabbers and Wallendahl, *supra* note 130, 225, 226.

152 For an analysis, see E. Rosand, 'The Security Council as "Global Legislator"' (2004) 28 *Fordham International Law Journal* 542–590; S. Talmon, 'The Security Council as World Legislature' (2005) 100 *AJIL* 175–193.

153 For a critique, see G. Arrangio-Ruiz, 'On the Security Council's "Law Making"' (2000) 83 *Revista Di Diritto Internazionale* 609, 723.

154 ICJ, *Questions of Interpretation and Application of the 1971 Montreal Convention arising from the Aerial Incident at Lockerbie (Libyan Arab Jamahiriya v. United Kingdom and*

Convention for the Suppression of Unlawful Acts against the Safety of Civil Aviation.[155] The Court affirmed its jurisdiction[156] and implicitly subjected Chapter VII considerations to legal interpretation. But it failed to engage deeply with the Charter's architecture. The judgment marked a 'test case for the rule of law in the international legal order of the United Nations'.[157] It triggered a whole range of scholarship on the 'constitutionalisation' in the framework of the UN Charter.[158]

The idea of a demarcated 'separation of powers' in the UN system was taken a step further in the jurisprudence of international criminal tribunals. Both the ICTY and ICTR were asked to examine the legality of their establishment under the executive powers of the Security Council, based on motions of defendants. The ICTY put clear limitations to the exercise of international executive authority in *Tadić*. It noted:

> It is clear from th[e] text [of Article 39] that the Security Council plays a pivotal role and exercises a very wide discretion under this Article. But this does not mean that its powers are unlimited. The Security Council is an organ of an international organization, established by a treaty which serves as a constitutional framework for that organization. The Security Council is thus subjected to certain constitutional limitations, however broad its powers under the constitution may be. Those powers cannot, in any case, go beyond the limits of the jurisdiction of the Organization at large, not to mention other specific limitations or those which may derive from the internal division of power within the Organization. In any case, neither the text nor the spirit of the Charter conceives of the Security Council as *legibus solutus* (unbound by law).[159]

This jurisprudence paved new grounds in the theorisation of UN authority.[160] It illustrated the need for a thicker vision of 'constitutionalism' than

Libyan Arab Jamhiriya v. United States of America), Judgment of 27 February 1998, ICJ Rep. 1998, 9.

155 See Convention for the Suppression of Unlawful Acts Against the Safety of Civil Aviation, 23 September 1971, 974 UNTS 177. For a discussion, see M. Plachta, 'The Lockerbie Case: The Role of the Secutity Council in Enforcing the Principle Aut Dedere Aut Judicare' (2001) 12 *EJIL* 125–140.

156 See ICJ, *supra* note 154.

157 See B. Martenczuk, 'The Security Council, the International Court and Judicial Review: What Lessons from Lockerbie?' (1999) 10 *EJIL* 517, 546.

158 See M. Herdegen, 'The "Constitutionalization" of the UN Security System' (1994) 27 *Vanderbilt Journal of Transnational Law* 135; G.R. Watson, 'Constitutionalism, Judicial Review, and the World Court' (1993) 34 *Harvard International Law Journal* 1.

159 See Tadić, *supra* note 147, para. 28.

160 For a follow up in the context of the Special Tribunal for Sierra Leone, see J. Alvarez, '*Tadić* Revisited: The *Ayyash* Decisions of the Special Tribunal for Lebanon' (2013) 11 *Journal of International Criminal Justice* 291–302.

Hammarskjöld's model.[161] It made it clear that the 'constitutionalist' analogy in the UN context cannot be modelled after the 'domestic analogy'. It accepted the premise that constitutionalism in the UN context is not based on a full-fledged 'separation' of powers, but grounded in the concept of checks in balances, i.e. ideas of 'responsive', 'transparent' and 'accountable authority'. The question as to 'who guards the guardians' became an issue in the justification of international authority.[162]

Calls for greater accountability were partially accommodated in 'functionalist terms'. The Security Council established committees to supervise the application of UN sanctions, including de-listing procedures.[163] It established an Informal Working Group on International Tribunals. But other suggestions to fill accountability gaps, such as the pleas for the institution of 'Transitional Administration Committees'[164] were not taken on board. The 'constitutionalist' vision remains thus incomplete. Accountability has remained partial.

21.4.2 Blind spots

This result is partly a consequence of 'blind spots' in Hammarskjöld's ideology. Hammarskjöld pointed out that the philosophy of Charter is not only related to 'peace' but also to concept of 'justice'. But he failed to contemplate the implications of the concept of 'justice' for the legal order of the UN. His vision remained focused on order, executive power and discretion. 'Order' and 'justice' were seen as tools for peace maintenance. This focus represents the thinking at the time of the drafting of the Charter.[165] The UN Charter mentions 'justice' in the context of

[161] See, e.g., E. de Wet, 'The Constitutionalization of Public International Law', in M. Rosenfeld and A. Sajó (eds.), *The Oxford Handbook of Comparative Constitutional Law* (2012), 1209–1229.

[162] See, e.g., G. Verdirame, *The UN and Human Rights: Who Guards the Guardians?* (2012); H. Nasu, 'Who Guards the Guardian? Towards Regulation of the UN Security Council's Chapter VII Powers through Dialogue', in J. Farrell and K. Rubenstein, *Sanctions, Accountability and Governance in a Globalised World* (2010), 123–142.

[163] On Security Council Committees, see generally www.un.org/sc/committees/.

[164] See, e.g., S. Chesterman, *You, The People: The United Nations, Transitional Administration and State-Building* (2004), 152, 240; E. De Wet, 'Direct Administration of Territories by the United Nations and Its Member States in the Post Cold War Era: Legal Bases and Implications for National Law' (2004) 8 *Max Planck Yearbook of United Nations Law* 291, 339.

[165] See Koskenniemi, *supra* note 138, 225.

the 'peaceful settlement of disputes'.[166] It fails to mention it in the context of collective security. This disregard represents one of the weaknesses of Hammarskjöld's ideology. He failed to take humanist thought and constitutionalist theory through to the end. A consequential reading of Charter principles would have implied a greater focus on human rights protections and its consequences for public authority. Hammarskjöld's state-centric focus silenced these dimensions. It devoted little attention to institutional and formal dimensions of justice.

Hammarskjöld's vision disregarded the role of Courts as agents of justice or humanisers. He recognised that 'the development and acceptance of international law impartially administered by judicial tribunals is essential to progress towards a more just and peaceful international order'.[167] But he failed to present a 'constitutionalist' vision of judicial authority in the framework of the Charter. Based on the 'Nuremberg' experience,[168] the formulation of principles by the General Assembly in 1946[169] and human rights instruments,[170] there was a historical momentum to develop the concept of international criminal justice, and its implications for individuals. Hammarskjöld remained silent on this. It took several decades until the concept of 'justice' was (re-)connected to human rights[171] and institutionalised in UN practice.

Hammarskjöld's conception of executive authority left limited structural room for accountability mechanisms. His ideology operated on the basis of fundamental assumptions and hypotheses.[172] He argued in terms of binaries and models of trust, i.e. a logic that it is better to have a UN than not. He openly branded the UN as a 'symbol of faith'.[173] He presented UN peace operations as neutral operations, detached from domestic ideologies. Formal concepts of accountability did not gain

166 Art. 1(1) UN Charter.

167 See Introduction 1959, *supra* note 12, at 4.

168 See generally G. Mettraux (ed.), *Perspectives on the Nuremberg Trial* (2008).

169 In Resolution 95 (I), dated 11 December 1946, the General Assembly affirmed the principles of international law recognised by the Charter of the Nuremberg Tribunal and the judgment of the Tribunal.

170 E.g. the Universal Declaration on Human Rights, adopted 10 December 1948. See generally W. Schabas, *The Universal Declaration of Human Rights: The Travaux Préparatoires* (2013).

171 See W. Schabas, *The Three Charters: Making International Law in the Post-War Crucible*, Inaugural Lecture Leiden University (2013), at www.mediafire.com/view/?p7zisqsup89ay0h.

172 See, e.g., American Association Address, *supra* note 83, at 5 ('As you all know, the United Nations Charter is based on what I may call a working hypothesis').

173 See Ideology, *supra* note 11, at 659.

much ground, although they are a core element of administrative rule.[174] His ideology turned a 'blind eye' on the impact on individuals. They were not part of the picture. They were treated as objects, rather than subjects, of international law.

This focus has become entrenched in UN practice. Hammarskjöld's 'secular church' vision of UN authority neglected the prospect of abuses of authority by UN organs, and its potential impact on individuals. Based on their conception of impartiality, UN actors developed a 'clean' and 'neutral' space of operation in their actions in which there is hardly any designated space for accountability.[175] The idea that the expanding realm of UN might restrict or violate human rights protections was not seriously contemplated.[176] UN authority remains dominated by 'functional immunities' that are stretched to their limits, or occasionally treated as 'absolute immunities'.[177] There was a lack of remedy against sexual abuses by peacekeepers.[178] Sanctions were branded as 'preventive', rather than 'repressive', measures, and thus subjected to limited due process considerations. The idea of individual petitions which was inherent in the UN Trusteeship System[179] was long ignored. This vision is only gradually corrected.[180] The idea of responsibility for action is reflected in projects, such as the ILC articles on the responsibility of international organisations[181] and zero-tolerance models on sexual exploitation and abuse.[182] In some areas, UN authority is further subject to new forms of

[174] See Orford, *supra* note 1, at 204.

[175] For a critique, see D. Chandler, *Empire in Denial: The Politics of Statebuilding* (2006).

[176] See F. Mégret and F. Hoffmann, 'The UN as a Human Rights Violator? Some Reflections on the United Nations Changing Human Rights Responsibilities' (2003) 25 *Human Rights Quarterly* 314; Verdirame, *supra* note 162, 91–142.

[177] See Stahn, *supra* note 4, at 587–598.

[178] See G. Simm, *Sex in Peace Operations* (2013), 77–87, 158–177.

[179] See Rule 81 of the Rules of Procedure of the Trusteeship Council.

[180] For a criticism of UNMIK, see European Commission For Democracy Through Law, Opinion on Human Rights in Kosovo: Possible Establishment of Review Mechanisms, Opinion No. 280/2004 (CDL-AD (2004)033), 11 October 2004, available at: www.venice.coe.int/docs/2004/CDL-AD(2004)033-e.asp.

[181] See ILC, Draft Articles on the Responsibility of International Organizations (2011), adopted by the ILC at its sixty-third session in 2011, at: http://untreaty.un.org/ilc/texts/instruments/english/draft%20articles/9_11_2011.pdf. See generally M. Ragazzi, *The Responsibility of International Organizations* (2013).

[182] UN Secretariat, 'Secretary General's Bulletin: Special Measures for Protection from Sexual Exploitation and Sexual Abuse', 9 October 2003, ST/SGB/2003/13; UN GA, 'A Comprehensive Strategy to Eliminate Future Sexual Exploitation and Abuse in United Nations Peacekeeping Operations', 24 March 2005, A/59/710.

accountability, such as control by ombudspersons (e.g. in the context of sanctions)[183] or human rights review (e.g. Kosovo).[184]

21.4.3 Unintended consequences

Hammarskjöld's vision of internationalism has produced some unintended side effects. His commitment to 'executive' authority opened the way for new institutional forms of action and new modalities. But it also created new dilemmas, in particular in relation to transparency, control and legitimacy of authority. It facilitated broad reliance on delegated power in the UN context, and occasionally excessive use of authority.

21.4.3.1 Decentralisation and its effects

Hammarskjöld's vision of diplomacy and his focus on technical assistance led to proliferation of executive agents, including greater reliance on UN Special Representatives and Special Envoys.[185] The Charter does not provide express authority for these functions. Special Representatives emerged incrementally in the UN context, based on reliance on executive power for peace maintenance. Representatives of the Secretary-General were used since the late 1940s for political functions in the context of peacekeeping and mediation.[186] Under Hammarskjöld, they also became

[183] On 17 December 2009, the Security Council adopted UN Security Council Resolution 1904 which established the Office of the Ombudsperson to assist the Sanctions Committee in its consideration of delisting requests under the '1267 sanctions regime'. For a discussion, see S.E. Eckert and T.J. Biersteker, 'Due Process and Targeted Sanctions: An Update of the "Watson Report"' (2012), at: www.watsoninstitute.org/pub/Watson%20Report%20Update%2012_12.pdf. On Kosovo, see UNMIK, *Regulation on the Establishment of the Ombudsperson Institution in Kosovo*, UNMIK/REG/2000/38, 30 June 2000.

[184] See Kosovo Human Rights Advisory Panel, established by UNMIK Regulation No. 2006/12 of 23 March 2006 on the Establishment of the Human Rights Advisory Panel, amended by Regulation No. 2007/3 of 12 January 2007. The Panel is entitled to examine complaints of alleged human rights violations committed by or attributable to UNMIK. For a discussion, see Venice Commission, 'Opinion on the Existing Mechanisms to Review the Compatibility with Human Rights Standards of Acts by UNMIK and EULEX in Kosovo', adopted by the Venice Commission at its 85th Plenary Session (Venice, 17–18 December 2010), CDL-AD(2010)051, at: www.venice.coe.int/webforms/documents/?pdf=CDL-AD(2010)051-e.

[185] See generally C. Peck, 'Special Representatives of the Secretary General', in D.M. Malone (ed.), *The UN Security Council: From the Cold War to the 21st Century* (2004), 325–339; M. Fröhlich, 'The Special Representatives of the United Nations Secretary-General', in B. Reinalda (ed.), *Routledge Handbook of International Organization* (2013), 231–242.

[186] For instance, Count Folke Bernadotte was appointed by the General Assembly to mediate the Arab-Israel conflict.

involved in peacebuilding.[187] Hammarskjöld's practice set off a whole trend of deployment of Special Representatives, which culminated in the exercise of governmental authority in the context of transitional administration.[188] Numbers have increased significantly. In 1980, there was only a small number of SRSGs, i.e. a dozen. In 2010, there were more than ninety.[189]

This development was promoted by Boutros Boutros-Ghali and Kofi Annan in the post-Cold War era. They made UN diplomacy and peace operations a 'core business' of the UN.[190] They charged Special Representatives with a broader array of diplomatic and managerial functions, i.e. brokering and implementing peace accords, managing peacekeeping or peacebuilding missions, or serving as transitional administrators.[191]

This increase of functions under the realm of the executive rule has led to complex power structures and models of delegation. The typical framework is described in the UN Handbook on Multidimensional Peacekeeping as follows:

> The command of peacekeeping operations is vested in the Secretary-General under the authority of the Security Council. The Secretary-General, in turn, has delegated the overall responsibility for the conduct and support of these missions to the Under-Secretary-General for Peacekeeping Operations. The Secretary-General also, with the consent of the Security Council, appoints a Special Representative of the Secretary-General (SRSG), who serves as Head of Mission and is responsible for implementing the mission's mandate. The SRSG reports to the Secretary-General through the Under-Secretary-General for Peacekeeping Operations.[192]

This authority structure has raised problems of transparency and attribution of conduct. Typically, the SRSG enjoys a wide degree of delegated

[187] One of the earliest examples is the deployment of Adrian Pelt to Guinea-Bissau who was vested a technical assistance mandate under Hammarskjöld in 1959. See Fröhlich, *supra* note 185, at 232.

[188] *Ibid.* [189] *Ibid.*, at 236.

[190] On multidimensional peacekeeping as 'core business', see DPKO, *supra* note 120, at 21–22.

[191] *Ibid.*, at 22 ('In exceptional circumstances, the Security Council has also authorized multi-dimensional United Nations peacekeeping operations to temporarily assume the legislative and administrate functions of the State, in order to support the transfer of authority from one sovereign entity to another, or until sovereignty questions are fully resolved (as in the case of transitional administrations), or to help the State to establish administrative structures that may not have existed previously').

[192] See DPKO, *Handbook on United Nations Multidimensional Peacekeeping Operations* (2003), www.peacekeepingbestpractices.unlb.org/Pbps/library/Handbook%20on%20UN%20PKOs.pdf, at 9

authority 'to set the direction of the mission and to lead its engagement with the political process on the ground'. [193] This implies that main operational steps are only subject to rudimentary control by the Security Council. The main channel of communication is reporting by the SRSG. Control by the Council is political or indirect, i.e. through decisions on the terms of extensions of the mandate. Managerial aspects are left in the hands of the SRSG.

This structure creates considerable gaps between formal authority and reality on the ground. Moreover, it has de facto limited the space of effective remedies. Acts carried under UN control are typically attributed to the UN.[194] But the UN only accepts responsibility for acts carried out in an official or operational context.[195] This implies that certain gross violations, i.e. acts of sexual abuse by peacekeepers, are not attributed to the UN, but Member States.[196] In the UN system, compensation for human rights abuses by the UN is typically limited to personal injury and property damage (i.e. not extended to human rights violations as such[197]), and it excludes cases of operational necessity. There is no general judicial or quasi-judicial body for claims arising in the context of peace operations.[198] This gap compromises the chances of effective accountability.

The situation is even more complicated in cases of UN mandated enforcement operations.[199] In such instances, civil/administrative functions are typically assumed by UN bodies, while military functions are exercised by regional organisations or operating states. This type of delegation has led to situations in which Member States were cleared of responsibility due to fictive ultimate UN control, while remedies against

[193] DPKO, *supra* note 120, at 68.

[194] See generally K.M. Larsen, 'Attribution of Conduct in Peace Operations: The "Ultimate Authority and Control" Test' (2008) 19 *EJIL* 509.

[195] On UN practice, see B. Kondoch, 'The Responsibility of Peacekeepers, Their Sending States, and International Organizations', in T. Gill and D. Fleck (eds.), *Handbook of the International Law of Military Operations* (2010), 515, 524.

[196] See T. Gill, 'Legal Aspects of the Transfer of Authority in UN Peace Operations' (2011) 42 *Netherlands Yearbook of International Law* 37, 56.

[197] On the UN Third Party Claims Process, see GA Res. 52/247 of 17 July 1998. On the controversy on its application in the context of transitional administration, see Venice Commission, *supra* note 184, paras 45–46. The UNMIK Human Rights Advisory Panel requested 'adequate compensation for non-pecuniary damage' in several cases.

[198] See Gill, *supra* note 196, at 65, suggesting a 'standing UN claims Tribunal with jurisdiction to consider questions of breach of obligation committed within the context of UN Peace Operations'.

[199] See generally N. Blokker, 'Is the Authorization Authorized? Powers and Practice of the UN Security Council to Authorize the use of Force by "Coalitions of the Able and Willing"' (2000) 11 *EJIL* 541–568.

the UN remained illusory due to the lack of a forum to bring claims.[200] Breaches were thus addressed through voluntary compensation, rather than formal acknowledgement of responsibility.[201] This stands in contradiction to the humanitarian ethos of peace operations.

The mixture of civilian and military authority in peace operations has created challenges for executive authority. It has involved the Secretariat to a greater extent in problems of military operation. This has had some detrimental side effects. It challenged the perception of the UN as impartial actor and associated the Secretariat with some of the tragedies and failures of intervention. This became evident in contexts such as Somalia,[202] Iraq or Afghanistan where UN assistance missions became the object of attack. These legitimacy dilemmas mark the flipside of the extension of executive authority. They require new strategies, in order to maintain 'faith' in UN action. It is not enough to rely on 'formal legitimacy', i.e. legitimacy derived from the mandate or the representation of 'communitarian interests'. What counts is 'the perceived legitimacy on the ground'.[203] This needs to be built and 'earned'.

21.4.3.2 Excesses of authority

Hammarskjöld's 'secular church' analogy implied certain assumptions about UN authority and its relationship to states that have become critical, and that may have facilitated excesses of authority. Hammarskjöld rightly claimed that 'no nation or group of nations can base its future on a claim of supremacy'.[204] But he failed to think this claim through with respect to the UN itself. As Orford notes, Hammarskjöld:

> represented international politics as a dualist system in which the world could be neatly divided between states on the one hand and the 'secular

[200] See European Court of Human Rights, Grand Chamber, *Behrami v. France; Saramati v. France*, Appl. 71412/01 and 78166/01, 2 May 1997. For a discussion, see C.A. Bell, 'Reassessing Multiple Attribution: The International Law Commission and the Behrami and Saramati Decision' (2010) 42 *NYU Journal of International Law and Politics* 501; A. Sari, 'Jurisdiction and International Responsibility in Peace Support. Operations: The Behrami and Saramati Cases' (2008) 8 *Human Rights Law Review* 151–170.

[201] See Gill, *supra* note 196, at 54.

[202] See Report of the Commission of Inquiry Established Pursuant to Security Council Resolution 885 (1993) to Investigate Armed Attacks on UNOSOM II Personnel which Led to Casualties among Them, UN Doc. S/1994/653 of 1 June 1994, para. 93, noting that 'while UNOSOM II was charged with the responsibility of assisting the Somali people in the rehabilitation of their political institutions at the local, regional and national levels its approach in carrying out this mandate ... was increasingly alienating the USC/SNA, which likened this approach to "trusteeship" or "colonization"'.

[203] See DPKO, *supra* note 120, at 36.

[204] See Address Lund, *supra* note 60, at 4.

> church' of the UN on the other. Each had its own sphere of jurisdiction – states were responsible for issues of national interest, while the UN was responsible for issues of international peace and security.[205]

This model contrasts with a longer tradition in international law that regards sovereignty as a social function and states as 'trustees of humanity'.[206] Hammarskjöld's imagery may have overstated the role of the UN. This dualism was used to promote the superiority of UN structures in some contexts, or to override domestic jurisdiction in the name of the UN on behalf of alleged 'community interests'. One of the most flagrant examples is the exercise of governing powers by the UN in the context of transitional administration. These exercises of authority were branded as functional undertakings, i.e. as examples of executive rule.[207] But they were far more than emergency measures or temporary replacements of authority. In some situations, the UN performed core functions of 'the state', as a substitute to domestic authority (West New Guinea, Namibia, Somalia, Cambodia, Eastern Slavonia). In other situations, it became active in nation-building and virtually created 'the state' (East Timor, Kosovo). International authority was used to override domestic legislation, governmental acts or domestic constitutions. The UN even acted as quasi 'pouvoir constituent' by creating constitutional frameworks (East Timor, Kosovo).[208] These exercises transformed the UN into a surrogate state, under the umbrella of peace maintenance.[209] The UN replaced all previous state structures, and accumulated all functions of state authority (executive, legislative and judicial functions) under its own jurisdiction. It failed to institute a corresponding separation of powers or an accountability structure towards the governed population.[210] Review of UN regulations was carried by the UN Secretariat in New York, and in particular, by the Office of Legal Affairs, which examined

[205] Orford, *supra* note 1, at 174.

[206] See E. Benvenisti, 'Sovereigns as Trustees of Humanity: The Concept and its Normative Implications' (2013) 107 *AJIL* 295.

[207] This is reflected in labels, such as UNTEA (United Nations Temporary Executive Authority), UNTAC (United Nations Transitional Authority in Cambodia), UNTAES (United Nations Transitional Administration for Eastern Slavonia), UNMIK (United Nations Mission in Kosovo).

[208] See, e.g., M. Riegner, 'The Two Faces of the Internationalized *pouvoir constituant*: Independence and Constitution-Making Under External Influence in Kosovo' (2013) 3 *Göttingen Journal of International Law* 1035–1062.

[209] For a comparison to a kingdom, see J. Chopra, 'The UN's Kingdom of East Timor' (2000) 42 *Survival* 27.

[210] For a critique, see J. Chopra, 'Building State Failure in East Timor' (2002) 33 *Development and Change* 979, 990.

the compatibility of UN action with the underlying mandate and international legal standards.[211]

In official UN doctrine, the organisation downplayed the sovereign-like nature of its activity. It was taken for granted that the UN was entitled to shape domestic legislation and authority. This is reflected in the 'job description' of a 'transitional administrator' in the *Handbook on Multidimensional Peacekeeping*. It presents 'transitional administration' as a technical activity, without problematising the underlying assumptions. It states:

> As the head of an interim or transitional administration, the SRSG is directly responsible for governmental functions and is accountable to both the local population and to the Secretary-General. The SRSG holds full executive and sometimes legislative authority, even during the transition period, when selected functions are being devolved to local authorities …
>
> Vested with legislative authority, the SRSG is responsible for building up a legal and regulatory framework. With the legal adviser as focal point, the mission prepares legislation for promulgation by the SRSG, which may be subsequently published in an official gazette. The mission may also interpret local laws, assess their compliance with international laws and human rights standards and principles, and modify them as appropriate. The SRSG may exceptionally use executive orders and decrees to promote the rule of law, including provisions for the deployment of international judges and prosecutors …
>
> Local authorities, or self-proclaimed representatives, may have already set up pseudo administrative structures that challenge the authority of the SRSG. The SRSG will have to impose authority on them from the outset and continue to ensure that parallel administrative structures do not compete with the authority of the UN bodies. These parallel structures may or may not have the support of the local population. The SRSG needs to convince the local population and local leaders that cooperation with the UN administration is in their best interests. In cases where there is a threat to security or law and order, the SRSG, in consultation with Headquarters, must be prepared to use military or police force in accordance with the mission's rules of engagement.[212]

In this context, the label of administration has thus clearly been used to mask the 'rationale', i.e. societal transformation through UN rule. This type of authority was presented as a 'disinterested' and 'heroic' exercise of

[211] See R. Caplan, 'The Security Council and the Administration of War-Torn and Contested Territories', in V. Lowe, A. Roberts, J. Welsh and D. Zaum (eds.), *The United Nations Security Council and War* (2008), 564, 573.

[212] See DPKO, *supra* note 192, at 19–20.

power. It turned the UN de facto into a 'secular church', i.e. an 'untouchable' actor removed from state jurisdiction and accountability.

Hammarskjöld's institutional ethics did not prevent such excesses. The UN deviated from this approach only gradually through pressure from outside, i.e. civil society, domestic actors and other institutions (e.g. OSCE, Council of Europe). The basic principle, which ought to apply to such types of international executive authority was formulated by the European Commission for Democracy Through Law (Venice Commission). It stated:

> when an international organisation carries out executive functions that are similar to those of a state, it must not be exempted from any independent legal review, in particular a system of independent review of conformity with international human rights standards.[213]

There is thus an acknowledged need for greater checks and balances and for a re-thinking of the concept of agency. The more and the longer the UN exercises governing functions in a territory, the more it should open itself to consultative approaches and accountability towards domestic constituencies, either through international mechanisms or domestic forms of control.[214] Individuals must, in particular, have the possibility to have access to justice and challenge decisions of international authorities. Responsibility and accountability are part and parcel of executive authority. They should equally apply to UN authority in the twenty-first century.

21.5 Conclusion

Hammarskjöld provided new ground for international executive authority. He developed ideas that were inherent in international society. Core features of his conception of the UN remain embedded in its contemporary architecture, i.e. its institutions, operational principles and ethical standards. Many of his ideas were virtually translated into a 'business' manual for UN practice in the second half of the twentieth century. This has enabled greater space for action in support of Charter principles. But

213 Venice Commission, Opinion on the Existing Mechanisms to Review the Compatibility of Acts by UNMIK and EULEX in Kosovo, CDL-AD(2010)051, 21 December 2010, para. 48; see also CDL(2004)033, para. 91 ('UNMIK and KFOR carry out tasks which are certainly more similar to those of a State administration than those of an international organisation proper. It is unconceivable and incompatible with the principles of democracy, the rule of law and respect for human rights that they could act as State authorities and be exempted from any independent legal review').

214 See Stahn, *supra* note 4, 761–763.

it has also facilitated tensions that are inherent in international humanitarianism. Hammarskjöld assumed a concept of agency, i.e. a representation of common interests through UN structures, that requires better grounding and greater caution.

Past decades have shown that international authority has retained certain authoritative features and traces of benevolent stewardship that need to be re-thought. The acceptance of UN authority remains based on basic forms of state consent and 'faith' in the UN as an institution. The 'secular church' analogy may have supported this development. It left space to privilege 'function' over 'form' in executive action. It allowed interpreters to mix moral and positivist considerations in the justification of choices.[215] Moreover, it indirectly encouraged a 'heroic' perception of UN authority that absolved the organisation from 'fault' and sanction. Protection turned partly into domination.

A modern ethics of protection requires different language, more modesty, and greater attention to the wishes, needs and experiences of societies and people affected by international executive rule. This might not help the UN to meet all of its ambitions, but it would at least allow it to 'fail better'.[216]

Hammarskjöld may be credited with many concrete influences on contemporary practice (e.g. prevention, personalised diplomacy, decentralisation of authority). His ideology shaped the way for new approaches. Among his many principles, two ideas may stand out, that are most relevant to human security as it is understood today. These are (1) his commitment to solidarity as a concept,[217] and (2) his early understanding of 'justice' as 'social justice'.[218] Both of them remain at the heart of contemporary responses to conflict.

[215] See also Orford, *supra* note 1, at 174, speaking of the risk of 'split loyalties'.

[216] See S. Chesterman, Keynote Address 'Statebuilding and International Law', 22, at: www.westminster.ac.uk/__data/assets/pdf_file/0003/81588/Chesterman.pdf.

[217] See Chapter 23, this volume.

[218] See Chapter 14, this volume.

22

Hammarskjöld and international executive rule

A third world perspective on international law

VIJAYASHRI SRIPATI

The United Nations has traditionally been involved in supporting constitution-making processes in a number of countries ... Given the crucial role constitution-making processes can play in *building sustainable peace and supporting democratic transitions*, the development of a coherent, norms-based approach for the Organization's engagement in this area continues to be of great importance.

... Constitution-making processes are a central aspect of democratic transitions, peace-building, and state-building. For the UN, constitution-making is a broad concept that covers the process of drafting and substance of a new constitution, or reforms of an existing constitution. Both process and substance are critical for the success of constitution-making. The design of a constitution and its process of development can play an important role in peaceful political transitions and post-conflict peace consolidation. It can also play a critical conflict-prevention role. Constitution-making presents moments of great opportunity to create a common vision of the future of a state, the results of which can have profound and lasting impacts on peace and stability.

United Nations, Guidance Note of the Secretary-General, 3 June 2009

22.1 Introduction

Why does the UN push for constitutional assistance[1] today – in a post-colonial era? Look back fifty years, to June 1960, when the organisation

Vijayashri Sripati is a post-doctoral fellow, University of Toronto. A special thanks to Carsten Stahn, Henning Melber and David Cameron for their advice and support.

[1] United Nations, *Guidance Note of the Secretary-General*, 3 June 2009 [emphasis added]. See also, 2012 *Preventive Diplomacy: Delivering Results, Report of the Secretary-General*, UN Doc. S/2011/552, paras. 4–6 (26 August 2011).

was engaged in the UN Operation in the Congo (ONUC).[2] As Congo – just independent – cracked up from a constitutional breakdown, ONUC assumed governmental functions directly to fill the vacuum, sometimes even overriding the views of the Congolese.[3] A team of four experts sculpted Congo's new federal constitution.[4] Finally, it ended the secession of the cobalt and copper-rich province Katanga.[5] The first two allied 'international executive actions' were developed as preventive diplomacy measures by the former UN Secretary-General, Dag Hammarskjöld.[6] Now review the rationale he offered: maintenance of peace and security in Congo.[7] Indeed, United Nations Constitutional Assistance (UNCA) belongs to a body of practices stemming from 'international executive rule' (IER).

Those practices initially comprised fact-finding and (international) territorial administration (hereinafter ITA) developed to meet the challenges posed by newly decolonised states.[8] The post-Cold War era witnessed a newer one: peacebuilding. It covered an array of activities globalising neoliberal norms shrouded under neutral sounding programmes such as the rule of law (ROL) programmes, judicial reform and security sector reform.[9] They attacked the 'deep-rooted' political and socio-economic causes of conflict. They ostensibly aimed at preventing conflict and building peace.[10] Most recently, IER ballooned with the addition of UN

[2] See generally, UN Operations in the Congo (ONUC) online: www.un.org/Depts/DPKO/Missions/onuc.htm.

[3] See S. Ratner, *The New UN Peacekeeping: Building Peace in Lands of Conflict after the Cold War* (1995), 105–109.

[4] See C. Young, *Politics in the Congo: Decolonization and Independence* (1965), 335–338.

[5] *Ibid.*, at 343, 387.

[6] See A. Orford, *International Authority and the Responsibility to Protect* (2006), 42–43, 69–90; see also, 2012 *Preventive Diplomacy: Delivering Results, Report of the Secretary-General*, Introduction, para. 1 (26 August 2011) (describing preventive diplomacy as 'an integral part of broader conflict prevention efforts' that 'refers specifically to diplomatic action taken, at the earliest possible stage, to prevent disputes from arising between parties, to prevent existing disputes from escalating into conflicts and to limit the spread of the latter when they occur'), *ibid.*

[7] *Ibid.*, at 30. [8] *Ibid.*, at 1, 42–43.

[9] See generally B. Boutros-Ghali, *Agenda for Peace* (1992); see also, UN, 'Secretary-General's Guidance Note: UN's Approach to Rule of Law Assistance' (undated); for the deeper implications about the UN's ROL programmes see K. Boon, 'Open for Business: International Financial Institutions, Post-Conflict Economic Reform and the Rule of Law' (2006) 39 *NYU Journal of International Law & Politics* 513.

[10] See generally R. Mani, 'Peaceful Settlement of Disputes and Conflict Prevention', in T.G. Weiss and S. Daws (eds.), *Oxford Handbook on the United Nations* (2006), 300.

Parliamentary Support (UNPS).[11] Today, IER stands systematised by the UN.

This chapter analyses UNCA, the earliest expression of IER, from a 'Third World Approaches to International Law' (TWAIL) perspective.[12] It draws on a colonial analogy. The TWAIL movement birthed from the realisation that mainstream international law stems from colonial roots.[13] TWAIL advocates many principles or tenets.[14] Its key tenet questions the West's hegemonic hold over the Third World by casting it as the 'savage' or inferior 'other'. TWAIL implicates international law in creating and sustaining these relations rooted in domination and subordination.[15] This chapter suggests that UNCA playing out in the politically and economically weaker sections of the globe manifests those unequal relations – and colonial continuities. Drawing purposive connections between the international law goals proffered by internationals like Hammarskjöld and the civilised standards put forth by colonial administrators, it will identify the colonial continuities in UNCA.

22.2 International executive rule and shadows of the past

Some of the roots of IER may be traced back to the heritage of colonial rule. Internationalised constitution making occurred during European

[11] UNDP, 'Fast Facts: Parliamentary Development' (UNDP, 2011) at: www.undp.org/content/dam/undp/library/corporate/fast-facts/english/FF-Parliamentary-Development.pdf (boasting that 'the UNDP supports one in three national parliaments globally, including parliaments in 28 African countries').

[12] For a lucid analysis of the salient features of TWAIL see M.D. Santos, *Human Rights and Migrant Domestic Work: A Comparative Analysis of the Socio-Legal Status of Filipina Migrant Domestic Workers in Canada and Hong Kong* (2006), 46–47.

[13] See, e.g., A. Anghie, *Imperialism, Sovereignty and the Making of International Law* (2005); A. Anghie, 'Colonialism and the Birth of International Institutions: Sovereignty, Economy, and the Mandate System of the League of Nations' (2001) 34 *NYU Journal of International Law & Politics* 513. See also G. Gong, *Standards of Civilization* (1984). For a crisp account of constitutional democracy's imperial roots see J. Tully, 'Modern Constitutional Democracy and Imperialism' (2008) 46 *Osgoode Law Journal* 461.

[14] See Santos, *supra* note 12, at 47.

[15] *Ibid.* For TWAIL works fleshing out these particular principles see Anghie, *Imperialism*, *supra* note 13; Anghie, 'Colonialism and the Birth of International Institutions', *supra* note 13; R. Wilde, *International Territorial Administration: How Trusteeship and the Civilizing Mission Never Went Away* (2008); M. Mutua, 'What is TWAIL?' (2000) 94 *American Society of International Law Proceedings* 31; M. Mutua, 'Savages, Victims, and Savior: The Metaphor of Human Rights' (2001) 42 *Harvard International Law Journal* 201; V. Sripati, 'The UN's Role in Post-conflict Constitution-making Processes: TWAIL Insights' (2008) 10 *International Community Law Review* 411; V. Sripati, *UNCA: A TWAIL Perspective*, Doctoral Dissertation, Osgoode Hall Law School (December 2010).

colonialism and the League of Nations' (LON) Mandates System and the UN Trusteeship Systems.[16] Historically, as a colonial activity, constitution-making stemmed essentially from the administration of distinct territorial units by foreign states (foreign territorial administration) or by an international organisation.[17] It rarely occurred in isolation.[18] Colonials legitimised colonialism partly through the 'civilising mission' argument, which suggested that a 'period of political dependence or tutelage was necessary for uncivilized societies to advance to the point where they were capable of sustaining liberal institutions and self-government'.[19] The differences in the 'level of civilisation' between the colonials and the natives in turn spurred the conceptualisation and discriminatory treatment of the latter as (native) 'ward', based on their separation from the (colonial) 'guardian'. 'Geographical distinctiveness' meant dominance and control tied up with difference and separation.[20]

The LON Covenant tasked the Mandates System with two goals: protecting native peoples from exploitation; and promoting their well-being and development.[21] In practice, this equated to the mandatory powers civilising the natives, manufacturing their sovereignty by creating the political, social and cultural fabric of the state and promoting self-government.[22] As Anghie points out, Article 22 of the LON Covenant denoted 'trusteeship with independence as the goal of the trust'.[23] How did the mandatory powers free their mandates? By imposing a constitution.[24]

[16] Overall, colonial constitutional reform (including decolonisation culminating in the imposition of a constitution) was not understood to be uniform in the manifestations of colonialism carried out by different European colonial powers. See, e.g., D. Rothermund, 'Constitution-Making in the Process of Decolonization', in G. Tarabout and R. Samaddar (eds.), *Conflict, Power, and the Landscape of Constitutionalism* (2008), 14–26.

[17] See C. Stahn, *The Law and Practice of International Territorial Administration: Versailles to Iraq and Beyond* (2008), at 175.

[18] Indeed, as we have seen, ONUC's constitutional assistance flowed from its territorial administration of Congo.

[19] See M. Kohn, 'Colonialism' (1 May 1996) in *Stanford Encyclopedia of Philosophy*, at: http://plato.stanford.edu/entries/colonialism/.

[20] See Wilde, *supra* note 15, at 333.

[21] See Art. 22, 1919 Covenant of the League of Nations, at: 'Yale Law School, Lillian Goldman Law Library, The Avalon Project – Documents in Law, History and Diplomacy', http://avalon.law.yale.edu/20th_century/leagcov.asp.

[22] Anghie, 'Colonialism and the Birth of International Institutions', *supra* note 13, at 513, 515, 569.

[23] *Ibid.*, at 513 at 525 (quoting Hall).

[24] See, e.g., N. Brown, 'Constitutionalism, Authoritarianism, and Imperialism in Iraq' (2005) 53 *Drake Law Review* 923 (analysing the imposition of Iraq's first constitution by its mandatory power – Great Britain).

In addition, constitution making in the Mandates System and UNCA is tied up with the shaping of sovereignty. For example, the mandatory powers 'manufactured' sovereignty out of backward peoples.[25] Likewise, UNCA operates to strengthen state sovereignty. Akin to the Mandates System, the Trusteeship System was rooted in the notion of 'trust'.[26] Since it was responsible for furthering the 'progressive development of trust territories towards self-government or independence',[27] the UN engaged with constitution-making. For example, the UN pushed for Nauru's independence from Australia and was tangentially involved in the making of its constitution.[28]

Colonial powers justified colonialism, that is, administering foreign territories and, in particular, imposing constitutions, on the basis of the principle of trusteeship.[29] Edmund Burke first articulated the trusteeship principle in 1783, to justify the colonisation of India – and by extension, the creation of the British Empire.[30] According to this principle, the 'colonial peoples were the beneficiaries, the colonial power the trustee and there was no third party involved in the relationship'.[31] This doctrine ultimately drove and underpinned many if not all forms of colonialism.[32] After the Second World War, the victorious colonial powers legalised the international trusteeship principle in the UN Charter.[33]

The civilised standards were a method used by (European) states in the eighteenth century to divide the world into 'civilised' and uncivilised peoples. On that basis, they excluded many non-European societies from membership in the international society of states.[34] Rooted in Christian

[25] See Anghie, 'Colonialism and the Birth of International Institutions', *supra* note 13, at 516.

[26] See UN Charter, Chapter XII, International Trusteeship System.

[27] See UN Charter, Chapter XII, International Trusteeship System, Art. 76(b).

[28] See K. Le Roy, *Nauru Constitutional Review: Background and Discussion Paper* 10–11 (June 2006). Nauru was an UN Trust Territory, administered by Australia.

[29] This principle helps to conceptualise the relationship between the foreign actor administering a territory and its people 'as one of a trustee/guardian state and the beneficiary/ward territory'. The guardian state is controlling and administering the beneficiary/ward territory, acting on behalf of the latter entity – the 'sacred trust of civilization' or the 'civilizing mission'. See Wilde, *supra* note 15, at 318, 333.

[30] *Ibid.*, at 319; see A. Porter, 'Trusteeship, Anti-Slavery, and Humanitarianism', in A. Porter, *The Oxford History of the British Empire: The Nineteenth Century*, Vol. IV (1999), at 198, 198–199.

[31] B. Simpson, *Human Rights and the End of Empire: Britain and the Genesis of the European Convention* (2001), 290.

[32] See Wilde, *supra* note 15, at 319.

[33] See R. Wilde, 'Trusteeship Council', in Weiss and Daws, *supra* note 10, at 149, 150–151.

[34] See Gong, *supra* note 13, at 14–15.

mores, these standards[35] underpinned the use of colonialism, and the Mandates System and Trusteeship System. In short, colonial powers justified using these three institutions for achieving ostensible purposes: civilised standards. These standards comprised basic governmental institutions and public bureaucracy, particularly, the ability to guarantee basic rights, i.e. life, dignity and property, and especially that of foreign nationals and a judicial system.[36] Published legal codes, adherence to the rule of law, free markets, that is, the capacity to honour contracts in commerce and capital exchange, and adherence to 'civilised' norms and practices constituted the remaining standards.[37]

Western constitutional democracy topped the civilised standards.[38] Colonials promoted it as the 'universal legal order'.[39] They delegitimised existing non-Western 'customary' legal systems, plausibly by considering and 'calling Western legal orders mostly formal and non-Western mostly "customary", and ranking modern Western law as superior and more "advanced"'.[40] Consequently, peoples inhabiting non-Western legal systems were deemed uncivilised and denied protection by international law.[41] In this way, international law sanctioned colonialism.[42] Colonials used Western constitutional democracy in establishing political control and civilising their colonies.[43] In fact, imposing the Western constitutional form was a key obligation associated with colonial trusteeship. Constitutional democracy was, therefore, implicated in the civilising mission.[44]

Civilising backward peoples by imposing Western constitutional forms continued during the Mandates and Trusteeship Systems. For instance, Britain installed a puppet, King Faisal, in Iraq (its mandate) under the condition that he would head a 'constitutional, representative, and democratic' government, 'limited by law'.[45] It therefore, imposed a constitution

35 *Ibid.*, at 3, 11–21 (defining the standard of civilization as an 'expression of assumptions, tacit and explicit, that distinguished those that belong to a particular society from those that do not').

36 *Ibid.*, at 14–15. 37 *Ibid.* 38 See Tully, *supra* note 13, at 466.

39 *Ibid.* 40 *Ibid.* 41 *Ibid.*

42 *Ibid.* See also, generally Anghie, *Imperialism and the Making of International Law, supra* note 13.

43 See also M.W. Doyle, *Imperialism and Empire* (1986), 44–45. For a comprehensive account teeming with examples see J. Dupont, *Common Law Abroad: The Common Law Abroad: Constitutional and Legal Legacy of the British Empire* (2001).

44 See Tully, *supra* note 13.

45 See N. Brown, 'Constitutionalism, Authoritarianism, and Imperialism in Iraq' (2005) 53 *Drake Law Review* 923.

on Iraq drawn up to its own 'liking'.[46] British officials in Baghdad drafted the constitution, which after vetting by the colonial office in London, came into force.[47] As previously outlined, Australia freed Nauru, by imposing a Western-style constitution.

Free markets or commerce, the second civilised standard, is entwined tightly with the first. A written constitution anchoring an independent judiciary based on the rule of law governed a 'civilised' state. It therefore enjoyed the capacity of honouring contracts in commerce and capital. Colonial powers privatised and pried open colonial resources for trade, (foreign) investment, and maximising profits by imposing (European) contract law and labour regulations. They initially prized open colonial markets to European traders since it benefited the economies of both the metropolitan states and the colonies.[48] However, by the late nineteenth century, they used trade and commerce to *civilise* backward peoples.[49]

Colonials were guided by economic purposes in shaping political institutions. For example, the rule of law promotion in the mandates tied up with achieving broader economic purposes.[50] Consequently, although the Mandatory powers ostensibly operated to free backward peoples, they shackled them to newer ones. As Anghie states, 'the domination of economics resulted in what may be termed provisionally the "economization of government" or the "economization of sovereignty"'.[51]

The open door policy, or the policy of prying open colonies' markets for the benefit of both colonial powers and other states, found expression in the UN Charter.[52] Elastic and multidimensional, good governance, the next standard, was famously associated with the civilising mission. It embraced the construction of railways and public buildings, rule of law promotion, private property rights, free trade, popular consent

[46] *Ibid.*, at 926–928. [47] *Ibid.*

[48] See Anghie, *Imperialism and the Making of International Law*, *supra* note 13, at 90, 97 and 141–144.

[49] See Anghie, 'Colonialism and the Birth of International Institutions', *supra* note 13, at 592; M. Lynn, 'British Policy, Trade, and Informal Empire in the Mid-Nineteenth Century', in A. Porter and W.R. Louis (eds.), *The Oxford History of the British Empire: Volume III: The Nineteenth Century* (1999), 101, 113.

[50] See Anghie, 'Colonialism and the Birth of International Institutions', *supra* note 13, at 608–609.

[51] *Ibid.*

[52] See Wilde, *supra* note 15, at 330; UN Charter, Art. 76(d) (open door policy): 'The Administering authorities in Trust Territories were obliged ... to ensure equal treatment in social, economic, and commercial matters for all Members of the United Nations and their nationals and also equal treatment for the latter in the administration of justice.'

to government and state-driven socio-economic change.[53] Since the 'B' class Mandate Agreements called for providing 'good governance',[54] the Mandatory powers protected the peoples from slave trade, the arms trade and liquor traffic and prevented the militarisation of the territories.[55] From the mid 1930s, good governance's definition expanded. From denoting 'a simple belief in … "minimum" governance it spelt an extraordinary commitment to *social engineering and constitutional change*'.[56] By the 1940s, it stood for wholesale socio-economic change. During that period, labelled as 'Westernisation' or 'modernisation', it envisaged an ambitious role for the state in politico-economic governance.[57] In 1945, when the UN birthed, good governance, understood as a 'state-based project of socio-economic engineering', spawned ideas of international development that Western powers and IFIs embraced.[58]

22.3 International executive rule and Congo's constitutional past

The 1950s echoed with the clang of African states tugging at their colonial chains. Dag Hammarskjöld rose to head the UN as its second Secretary-General during this period. He perceived decolonisation as throwing up many challenges. Finding Africa potentially a vortex for Cold War politics, he perched 'maintaining order' and 'protecting life' there topmost among the UN's responsibilities.[59]

Was the UN suited to fulfil these responsibilities? Yes. According to Dag Hammarskjöld, its independence, neutrality and impartiality made it so.[60] Nevertheless, achieving them called for a dynamism that the glacial 'conference approach' stymied.[61] The exercise of 'executive rule' by the UN offered new prospects. Hammarskjöld, therefore, advocated that the UN should embrace it.[62] IER practices have spread because they flow

[53] See P. Burroughs, 'Imperial Institutions and the Government of Empire', in Porter and Louis, *supra* note 49, at 170–175.

[54] Wilde, *supra* note 15, at 331, n. 165.

[55] *Ibid.*, at 330–332.

[56] V. Hewitt, 'Empire, International Development and Good Government', in M. Duffield and V. Hewitt, *Empire, Development & Colonialism – The Past in the Present* (2009), 30 at 30.

[57] *Ibid.*, at 34.

[58] *Ibid.*, at 35–36 ('Post-war conceptions of international development and industrialization were the direct legatees of Britain's state-based project of socio-economic engineering').

[59] See Orford, *International Authority*, *supra* note 6, at 5.

[60] *Ibid.* [61] *Ibid.* [62] *Ibid.*

from operationally oriented documents – not doctrinal elaborations.[63] The UN incorporated practices and modalities into Security Council mandates, practice notes, guidance notes, rules of engagement, and instruction manuals.[64] Hammarskjöld considered these 'texts' fit to guide future operations as well.[65] According to Hammarskjöld, the UN could insert its neutral presence to fill the political vacuum caused, for instance, by a temporary crisis of authority within a territory.[66] Therefore, where a new post-colonial government collapsed, the UN displaced local actors to carry out governance. It mediated between warring groups to simmer down conflict. Moreover, it drafted a new constitution to restore order.[67] Indeed, according to him, Africa's vulnerability to 'new … forms of predominance and influence' impelled the UN to usurp these functions.[68] Consider his comments that the UN must:

> *support policies aiming at independence, not only in the constitutional sense but in every sense of the word*, protecting the possibilities of the African peoples to choose their own way without undue influences being exercised and without attempts to abuse the situation. This must be true in all fields – the political, the economic, as well as the ideological – if independence is to have a real meaning.[69]

Freed from the big power struggles over ideology and influence and devoid of personal ambition, the UN could offer its services without crushing the 'free choice of … peoples'.[70] Guided by these notions, he initiated ITA and UNCA in Congo. A quick peep into Congo's troubled constitutional past will help contextualise its constitutional breakdown and ONUC's constitutional assistance.

When Leopoldville convulsed with riots in January 1959, Belgium tinkered with the colonial framework, opening up narrow political space for the Congolese.[71] Therefore, the Belgian Governor-General continued

[63] *Ibid.*

[64] *Ibid.*, at 5; see also V. Sripati, 'UN Constitutional Assistance Projects in Comprehensive Peace Missions: An Inventory 1989–2011' (2012) 19(1) *International Peacekeeping* 93, at 95.

[65] Orford, *supra* note 6, at 5. [66] *Ibid.* [67] *Ibid.*

[68] *Ibid.*, at 5, n. 14. See also *Introduction to the Annual Report of the Secretary-General on the Work of the Organization*, UN Documents, Suppl. No. 1A, A/4390/Add.1, 2 (1960).

[69] *Ibid.* [70] *Ibid.*

[71] R.E. Lester and M. Schipper, 'Confidential U.S. State Department Central Files' – Congo 1960 – Jan. 1963, vii (2002), at: http://academic.lexisnexis.com/documents/upa_cis/11275_CFCong60-63IntFor.pdf. See generally H. Karan Jacobson, 'ONUC's Civilian Operations: State-Preserving & State-Building' (1964) 17(1) *World Politics* 75.

to reign supreme.[72] Embittered with Belgium's cosmetic changes, the Congolese ratcheted up their revolt.[73] Consequently, in January 1960 Belgium cobbled together a 'Round Table Conference' (hereinafter Brussels Conference), which announced independence for the Congo on 30 June.[74] The *Loi Fondamentale* (Fundamental Law) adopted by the Brussels Conference duplicated the Belgian constitution.[75] It divided power at three levels: between the Head of State (titular head) and the Prime Minister, exercising actual powers; between the Senate and the Chamber of Representatives; and between the central government and the provinces.[76] Signs of a conflict flaring up over jurisdiction lurked here.[77]

The parliamentary elections of May 1960 resulted in a coalition government patched together with Lumumba (Prime Minister) and Kasavubu (President) as its head.[78] Mobutu headed the *force republique* that soon turned into the national army.[79] During colonial rule, Brussels controlled the central bank and many 'para-statal' agencies providing electricity and transport in Congo.[80] Belgium left this issue unresolved.[81] Therefore, when the Republic of Congo (as it was then known) burst free, this matter along with other ethnic-regional issues dominated the political climate.

Meanwhile, in July 1960, soldiers of the national army revolted against their Belgian commander's persistent refusal to Africanise the officer corps.[82] They also demanded higher wages.[83] Lumumba's government yielded to their demands.[84] His approach to social demands rattled Belgium because the latter continued to exploit Congo for its minerals and other wealth.[85] It therefore invaded the Congo by entering the resource-rich province Katanga on 10 July 1960.[86] A day later Katanga seceded.[87] Belgium airbrushed its invasion with the ostensible purpose of protecting European and other human lives.[88] Repudiating Belgium's hollow rhetoric, Lumumba sought UN military aid to protect Congo.[89] He characterised the unsolicited Belgian military intervention as 'external aggression'

[72] Lester and Schipper, *supra* note 71, at vii.
[73] *Ibid.* [74] *Ibid.* [75] *Ibid.*, at viii. [76] *Ibid.* [77] *Ibid.*
[78] *Ibid.* Lumumba headed the Congolese National Movement (MNC) party and Kasavabu headed the ABAKO party. Only in Orientale province did the MNC win a solid majority. 'Katanga was split between separatists identified with Tshombe's CONAKAT Party and "Unitarists"', *ibid.*
[79] *Ibid.* [80] See Orford, *supra* note 6, at 72. [81] *Ibid.*
[82] See Lester and Schipper, *supra* note 71, at viii.
[83] See Orford, *supra* note 6, at 30.
[84] *Ibid.*, at 70. [85] *Ibid.* [86] *Ibid.*, at 72. [87] *Ibid.*
[88] *Ibid.* [89] *Ibid.*, at 71.

and a 'threat to international peace'.[90] 'Avoiding any legal characterization of the situation in the Congo',[91] Hammarskjöld, however, concluded that the presence of Belgian troops threatened international peace.[92] These circumstances sparked ONUC, a Security Council mandated peace operation for the Congo in July 1960.[93] According to the UN:

> The initial mandate of ONUC was to ensure the withdrawal of Belgian forces from the Republic of the Congo, to assist the Government in maintaining law and order and to *provide technical assistance*. The function of ONUC was subsequently modified to include maintaining the territorial integrity and political independence of the Congo, preventing the occurrence of civil war and securing the removal from the Congo of all foreign military ... not under the UN command, and all mercenaries.[94]

Constitutions are 'power maps'. And constitution-making is quintessentially a *political* and sovereign act. Therefore, UNCA can never equate to mere technical assistance. The UNCA moment in Congo illustrates this.

The constitutional crisis erupted on 5 September 1960 when Kasavabu dismissed Lumumba.[95] Although Congo's parliament supported Lumumba and voted to reinstate him as the Prime Minister, Hammarskjöld interpreted Congo's *Loi Fondamentale* (constitution) and the mandate given to him to decide that he had to act on his own responsibility.[96] He judged Kasavabu's revocation to be constitutional and told the Security Council about his decision.[97] This consequently blocked Lumumba's opportunity to stage an immediate counter-coup.[98] Hammarskjöld concluded that 'there was nobody, really nobody, with whom they could consult without prejudging the constitutional issue'.[99]

Meanwhile, within a week, Mobutu switched to the Kasavabu side. 'Neutralising' the Chief of State, the Prime Minister, and the parliament, he designated a student-composed caretaker government (*College des Commissaires*) to run the country until the end of the year.[100] Thus, two

[90] *Ibid.*, at 71 and 73 (quoting from the cable dated 12 July 1960).

[91] *Ibid.*, at 74. [92] *Ibid.*, at 75.

[93] See Security Council Resolution 143 (1960), UN Doc. S/4387, 14 July 1960. The Resolution called for the withdrawal of Belgian troops.

[94] See ONUC details, *supra* note 93.

[95] Lumumba's position was tenuous. Teaming up with smaller parties, his Congolese National Movement (MNC) enjoyed only a slim majority of seats in both chambers. Lester and Schipper, *supra* note 71, at viii.

[96] See Orford, *supra* note 6, at 82.

[97] See Young, *supra* note 4, at 328. [98] *Ibid.*

[99] See Orford, *supra* note 6, at 82–83, quoted on page 83.

[100] *Ibid.*, at 83. See also Young, *supra* note 4, at 329.

months after Lumumba's dismissal (the first breakdown), the constitutional parliamentary government created by the *Loi Fondamentale* collapsed.[101] In addition, by the end of 1960, the Congo had split into four autonomous fragments. With the three major conflicting groups (owning their own armies) receiving international support, Congo's conflict stood wholly internationalised.[102]

Initially supportive of Kasavabu, the UN now 'retreated to a position of neutrality'.[103] It remained non-committal about either party.[104] As far as civilian operations were concerned, it teamed up with the de facto authorities.[105] Hammarskjöld saw in the 'vacuum' created by the governmental collapse, the 'special possibilities and responsibilities of the Organization'.[106]

Therefore, ONUC carried out key political tasks. For instance, allying with the International Monetary Fund, it installed the Monetary Council as a step towards creating a National Bank.[107] Gradually, it also helped glue the conflicting groups. In this way, it pushed parliament to reconvene in isolation at Lovanium University in July 1961.[108] Not all groups attended though. However, parliament consented to a government led by Cyrille Adoula as Lumumba's successor.[109] With this, the UN helped restore the constitutional order that had begun to collapse on 5 September 1960. However, the South Katangese secessionist forces still simmered with discontent.[110]

In 1962, building on IER initiated by the late Hammarskjöld, ONUC confronted Congo with a 'comprise formula'. It consisted of a guaranteed federal constitution prepared by UN experts coupled with a threat of heaping Katanga with economic sanctions lest it fail to drop its secessionist plans.[111] Consequently, on 14 January 1963, Moïse Tshombe, the Katangese leader, announced jettisoning his secessionist plans.[112] Meanwhile, ONUC's expert team headed by T.O. Elias completed the draft constitution, which guided the Congolese in shaping their final one.[113] Congo's 1964 federal constitution replicated the UN draft constitution.[114]

[101] Young, *supra* note 4, at 326. [102] *Ibid.*, at 331–332.

[103] *Ibid.*, at 330. [104] *Ibid.*

[105] Orford, *supra* note 6, at 83. [106] *Ibid.*, at 84.

[107] Young, *supra* note 4, at 334. [108] *Ibid.*, at 337.

[109] *Ibid.*, at 338. [110] *Ibid.*, at 340–341.

[111] *Ibid.*, at 342. These two specific proposals 'were not negotiable'. *Ibid.* The UN Plan was prepared on the watch of then Secretary-General, U Thant, who succeeded Hammarskjöld. Dag Hammarskjöld died in a plane crash on 18 September 1961.

[112] *Ibid.* In fact, beginning on 28 December 1962 itself, the UN flexed its military muscles in bringing Jadotville under its control. On 3 January 1963 Jadotville fell. *Ibid.*, at 342–343. Shortly thereafter, the UN stamped out Katanga's secession.

[113] *Ibid.*, at 340–344, 530–531. [114] *Ibid.*, at 531. It only omitted the word 'federal'.

Constitution-making expresses the right to self-determination. Hammarskjöld supported this goal. Was he then suggesting that Congo was not a free territory and the Congolese were no longer sovereign in a formal sense? No. He simply dismissed the Lumumba government as a 'clumsy, inadequate government that does not do the proper thing'.[115] He rationalised ITA and UNCA as *temporary* practices under the umbrella of the UN's supposed neutrality. In addition, 'he was committed to bringing the underdeveloped countries into the world market in the proper way'.[116] His statement to the Security Council, made within two months of Congo gaining freedom and at the height of the constitutional crisis, illustrates his economic thinking:

> Members will have gathered from the report that, in spite of the great natural resources of the country, the financial situation is one of bankruptcy. True, there are financial assets, but they are hopelessly insufficient.
>
> In this situation spokesmen of the central government speak about the assistance rendered by the international community through the United Nations as if it were an imposition and treat the Organization as if they had all rights and no obligations. They seem to believe that the independence of the Republic of the Congo, in the sense of the international sovereignty of the state which everybody respects, means independence also in a substantive sense of the word which, in our interdependent world of today, is unreal even for a country living by its own means and able to provide for its own security and administration.
>
> A government without financial means is dependent on those who help it to meet its needs. It may depend financially on another state, or group of states, and thereby tie its fate to that of the donors. Or it may depend on the international community in its entirety, represented by the United Nations, and so remain free. There is no third alternative this side of a complete breakdown of the state through inflation or a speedy disintegration of all social and economic services.
>
> These are the hard facts which should be remembered when the relations of the United Nations with the central government are discussed.[117]

22.4 UNCA in the post-Cold War era

Since 1989, the Security Council initiated fourteen peace operations – with UNCA mandates – spanning Asia, Africa, the Middle East and Eastern Europe.[118] In 1989, it mandated UNCA to assist Namibia,

[115] See Orford, *supra* note 6, at 86. [116] *Ibid.*
[117] *Ibid.*, at 85–86 [emphasis added]. [118] See Sripati, *supra* note 64, at 93.

colonised by South Africa, in its transition to freedom.[119] It authorised UN Territorial Administration and UNCA in East Timor in the same context: decolonisation.[120] It deployed UNCA to end conflict and build peace in Cambodia[121] and in five 'post-conflict' African states: Sudan, Rwanda, Burundi, Somalia and the Democratic Republic of the Congo (DRC).[122] In 2001, Al-Qaeda, harboured by the Taliban in Afghanistan, orchestrated a terrorist attack in the United States. Consequently, the Security Council introduced UNCA initially in Afghanistan and later in Iraq (following its occupation by the United States) to uproot bad governance from these 'failed states'.[123]

In 2007, the Security Council deployed UNCA to shape an inclusive society in Nepal, reeling from a decade-long civil war led by the Maoists.[124] It authorised UNCA in Kosovo to 'promote self-government for the people of Kosovo *within* the Federal Republic of Yugoslavia' and facilitate a process designed 'to determine its future political status'.[125] In 2010, it mandated UNCA in South Sudan that declared independence, splitting from the Northern part of Sudan.[126] Most recently, the Security Council authorised UNCA in Libya to consolidate the democratic impulses of the Arab uprisings following the toppling of Colonel Gaddafi.[127]

UNCA's trajectory in the post-Cold War era illuminates its deeper implications: first, it played out in eleven *sovereign independent* Third World states. Next, it occurred in states clustered under the International Financial Institutions' (IFIs) Heavily Indebted Countries (HIDCs) and the UN's Least Developed Countries (LDCs) categories.[128] Finally, it cropped up under varied contexts. However, the Security Council, in all the fourteen states, deployed it for a broader common purpose: to prevent conflict and build peace.[129]

[119] *Ibid.*, at 97–98. [120] *Ibid.*, at 103. [121] *Ibid.*, at 102–103.

[122] I have not listed the states either in alphabetical or chronological order. *Ibid.*, at 100 (Sudan), 98–99 (Rwanda), 99–100 (Somalia) and 95–97 (Burundi). For UNCA in the DRC see Sripati, *UNCA*, *supra* note 15, at Chapter III, 95, n. 3.

[123] *Ibid.*, at 101–102 (Afghanistan) and 106–107 (Iraq).

[124] *Ibid.*, at 103–104. [125] *Ibid.*, at 104–105. [126] *Ibid.*, at 100–101.

[127] *Ibid.*, at 108, n. 15. See also Security Council Resolution 2009, S/Res/2009 (16 September 2011), at para. 12(b) (mandating the UN Support Mission in Liberia [UNSMIL] with UNCA responsibilities).

[128] See UNDESA, 'LDCs: The Criteria for Identifying Least Developed Countries' (undated), available at: www.un.org/en/development/desa/policy/cdp/ldc/ldc_criteria.shtml.

[129] Barring Kosovo, Namibia and East Timor, the remainder of the fourteen UNCA-recipients are sovereign independent states. See, e.g., Report of the Secretary-General, 'The Causes of Conflict and the Promotion of Durable Peace and Sustainable Development in

The UN Charter mandates the UN to settle disputes peacefully.[130] However, it nowhere refers to conflict prevention and preventive diplomacy. Why then did the UN shift its energies to 'conflict prevention'? In the late 1980s, conflict erupted in fourteen African states rippling across the entire continent.[131] Those conflicts killed and maimed thousands, and forced many more to flee.[132] According to the UN, these horrors impelled it to move from a 'culture of reaction' to a 'culture of conflict-prevention'.[133] They pushed the UN to attack the 'root causes of conflicts', or, conversely, 'threats to peace'.[134]

What were those threats? 'Bad' or 'failed' governance topped the list.[135] In the early 1990s, 'bad' or 'failed' governance became almost synonymous with African governance, or more broadly Third World governance. It stood for political leaders disrespecting their constitutions; rigging elections to hold onto power; disallowing dissent by imprisoning political opponents; looting treasuries and funnelling public money into private accounts; corrupting public servants, judges and elected officials; and eviscerating agencies of accountability and transparency to the point that they can no longer prevent abuses.[136]

In the mid 1990s, a new 'threat' cropped up: the mismanagement of the environment and natural resources. Brimming with oil, coltan, diamonds, gas and other natural resources, Sudan, Liberia, Angola, the DRC, Sierra Leone and Cotê d'Ivoire hold the potential for prosperity. However, according to the UN Environment Programme (UNEP), these resources fuelled conflict.[137] For instance, dazzled by Sierra Leone's diamond fields, Liberian warlord Charles Taylor, lurking across the border, stoked the then ongoing Sierra Leonean civil conflict.[138] To capture control over these lucrative resources, he initially pumped Sierra Leone's rebel group, the Revolutionary United Front (RUF) based in Monrovia (Liberia), with money, arms and his own troops.[139] Ultimately, in 1991, he orchestrated its invasion of Sierra Leone, wrecking its peace and leaving

Africa', UN Doc. A/52/871 – S/1998/318, para. 29 (13 April 1998); see generally, Boutros-Ghali, *supra* note 9; Mani, *supra* note 10, at 311–313.

130 UN Charter, Art. 1(1).

131 See Report, *supra* note 129, para. 4. 132 *Ibid.*

133 *Ibid.*, at 65. See also, Report of the Secretary-General, 'Prevention of Armed Conflict', UN Doc. A/55/985-S/2001/574, executive summary (7 June 2001).

134 See Report, *supra* note 133. 135 See Report, *supra* note 129, at paras. 12–13.

136 *Ibid.*, at paras. 12, 77, 81–82, 97.

137 UNEP, *From Conflict to Peace Building: The Role of Natural Resources and the Environment* (2009), at 5.

138 *Ibid.*, at 10. 139 *Ibid.*

over two million dead. The war also displaced millions and left scores maimed and raped.[140]

From the neoliberal political economy standpoint, securing ownership and property rights in natural resources is critical to attracting international investors and capital.[141] Muddied laws and regulations deter potential investors.[142] According to the World Bank, unclear provisions on ownership rights for diamonds in Angola had created a perception of it as a 'high-risk location', repelling foreign investors.[143] In a series of resolutions, the Security Council therefore began to address natural resource governance.[144] It also called upon peace operations to build state capacity to use and share natural resources fairly and sustainably.[145]

According to the World Bank's *World Development Report*, institutionalisation of market forces, economic liberalisation, public–private partnerships and enforcement of contracts require a clean state – bereft of corruption.[146] Programmes designed to eliminate barriers to corruption, promote transparency and accountability in public administration, and enhance a state's administrative capacity, therefore, soon merged into the UN's peace-making, peacebuilding, and constitutional assistance programmes.[147] Anti-corruption and good governance provisions showed up in peace agreements concluded for Burundi, Liberia, Guatemala, El Salvador and Sierra Leone because of the World Bank.[148] Corruption

140 *Ibid.*

141 See N. Haysom and S. Kane, 'Briefing Paper: Negotiating Natural Resources for Peace: Ownership, Control and Wealth-sharing' (2009), 12; World Bank, 'Angola: Economic Memorandum: Oil, Broad-based Growth and Equity' (2006); see also S. Gill, 'New Constitutionalism, Democratization and Global Political Economy' (2007) 10 *Pacifica Review: Peace, Security & Global Change* 23, at 25.

142 *Ibid.* 143 *Ibid.*

144 For a list of Security Council resolutions relating to natural resources and conflict, see Security Council Report, *Natural Resources and Conflict*, available at: www.securitycouncilreport.org; see, e.g., Security Council Resolution, UN Doc. S/Res/1509 (19 September 2003) (authorising UN Mission in Liberia to assist the transitional government in administering natural resources).

145 See, e.g., Security Council Resolution, UN Doc. S/Res/1509 (19 September 2003) (authorising UN Mission in Liberia to assist the transitional government in administering natural resources in Liberia); UN Dept. of Press Information, 'Security Council Underscores Need for Peacekeeping Mandates to Consider Helping States Prevent Illegal Exploitation of Natural Resources from Fuelling Conflict' (25 June 2007); see also UNEP's recommendation in UNEP, *supra* note 137 at 5 (para. 4).

146 See Gill, *supra* note 141, at 32.

147 See Report, *supra* note 129, paras. 75–76, 81; for details about anti-corruption provisions in UN-assisted constitutions see Sripati, *UNCA*, *supra* note 15, at Chapter 4.

148 See B. Spector, *Negotiating Peace and Confronting Corruption: Challenges for Post-Conflict Societies* (2010), 149–169.

also gained traction since it was portrayed as hindering today's 'civilised' financial standards: privatisation, liberalisation and allied practices.[149] In 1999, Michael Camdessus, then IMF Director, offered the first stirrings of that view:

> A consensus is clearly crystallizing ... on the need to establish at the international level the discipline that has progressively come to prevail in domestic markets ... that governments had not devoted enough attention in order to secure such a *civilized environment* ... Consequently, tremendous effort is under way to establish *standards and codes of good practice at the international level* that build on and offer the potential to globalize the standards that exist *within the most advanced nations*.[150]

Contributing to this discourse, the UN conjured the spectre of corruption breeding conflict, producing an inhospitable environment for 'enacting needed reforms' such as privatisation and fiscal consolidation, and hindering sustainable development.[151] Above all, it portrayed corruption as an obstacle to achieving the 'international ideals of the free market, rule of law, democracy and broad prosperity'.[152]

During the late 1990s, images of mass rapes in Africa and the Balkans, and the Taliban executing Afghan women cowering under blue burqas streamed across the UN radar screen. They exposed a new threat: gender discrimination.[153] The UN Secretary-General and the Security Council, backed by US policy-makers, therefore added fresh energy to eliminating it. Connecting the dots between discrimination and conflict, the UN urged national stakeholders to tap into women's peacebuilding potential.[154] The Security Council's 1325 Resolution extolled a new 'participatory' standard for making constitutions: rope women into making peace and creating constitutions outlawing gender discrimination.[155]

149 See G. Gong, 'Standards of Civilization Today', in M. Mozaffari (ed.), *Globalization & Civilization* (2002), 77 at 91.

150 M. Camdessus, *From Crisis to a New Recovery: Excerpts from Selected Addresses* (1999), vi.

151 See Report, *supra* note 129, at para. 82.

152 UN Office for Drug Control and Crime Prevention, *Global Programme against Corruption – Anti-Corruption Tool Kit, Foreword* (unnumbered page) (2002), www.unodc.org/pdf/crime/toolkit/f1tof7.pdf.

153 See Report, *supra* note 129, at para. 89.

154 Security Council Resolution 1325 (2000), UN Doc. S/Res/1325 (2000) (31 October 2000); United Nations, *Women, Peace and Security*, Study submitted by the Secretary-General pursuant to Security Council Resolution 1325 para. 10 (United Nations, 2002), available at: www.un.org/womenwatch/daw/public/eWPS.pdf.

155 Security Council Resolution 1325 (2000), UN Doc. S/Res/1325 (2000), 31 October 2000; for the UN's transparent, inclusive and participatory constitution-making standard,

Meanwhile, other issues widened the 'threats to peace' definition. What were they? In the wake of 9/11, terrorism, defined as violent conflict, became the new threat.[156] It sparked the UN's counter-terror campaign. The UN cast building state capacity in countering terrorism as a conflict-prevention measure.[157] It therefore put this strategy at the top of its counter-terror agenda.[158] Sexual violence and the rape of children appeared next. The Security Council affirmed violations of children's rights as a peace and security concern.[159] Consequently, international standards for protecting children in armed conflict evolved, sparking child protection provisions in peace agreements.[160] They also triggered guidelines relating to children for constitution-making and constitutional content.[161] Backed by US Secretary of State Hillary Clinton, sexual violence against women showed up on the plank of threats.[162]

see UNCA Guidance note, *supra* note 1, at 4. See also V. Sripati, 'UNCA: Making New Additions to the Standards of Civilization?' ASIL Int'l Org. Newsletter 3 (Summer 2009) [abstract].

156 See United Nations, 'Fact Sheet: UN Action to Counter Terrorism', March 2009, at 5–6. See also, Report of the Secretary-General, 'United Nations Global Counter-Terrorism Strategy: Activities of the United Nations System in Implementing the Strategy', UN Doc. A/64/818 11–17 (17 June 2010).

157 See 'UN Action to Counter Terrorism', at: www.un.org/terrorism/. See UNGA Res. UN Doc. UNGA/Res./60/288 (A/60/L.62), A/RES/60/288 (20 September 2006); Helping Member States to Counter Terrorism, at: www.un.org/terrorism/makingadifference.shtml; Report of the Secretary-General, 'High-Level Panel on Threats, Challenges and Change, A More Secure World: Our Shared Responsibility' (2004), para. 1 s. 48(d); 'In Larger Freedom: Towards Development, Security and Human Rights for All', Report of the UN Secretary-General, UN Doc. A/Res/59/2005, §III 'Freedom from Fear', para. 74–75; §III B, para. 87–88 (21 March 2005).

158 See United Nations, 'Fact Sheet', *supra* note 156; see generally, Report of the Secretary-General, 'Strengthening the United Nations Crime Prevention and Criminal Justice Programme, in Particular its Technical Cooperation Capacity', UN Doc. A/60/131 (25 July 2005).

159 See, e.g., Security Council Resolution 1379 (2001), UN Doc., S/Res/1379 (2001); Security Council Resolution 1460 (2003), UN Doc., S/Res/1460 (2003), Security Council Resolution 1612 (2005), UN Doc., S/Res/1612 (2005).

160 For peace accords that do contain references to children, see e.g. Lome Peace Accord on Sierra Leone (1999); Arusha Accord on Burundi (2000); Accra Peace Agreement on Liberia (2003); Comprehensive Peace Agreement on Sudan (2005); Darfur Peace Agreement (2006). For standards relating to children's rights in constitutions see UNCA Guidance Note, *supra* note 1, at 2–3.

161 See UNCA Guidance Note, *supra* note 1, at 4; see *infra* discussion on the UN's good constitution.

162 See Security Council Resolution, 1820 (2008), UN Doc. S/RES/1820 (2008), paras. 4, 12 and 13.

Deployed by the UN to counter these threats, UNCA expanded during the post-Cold War era.[163] However, it received scarce scholarly attention as a stand-alone theme.[164] For example, Anne Orford does not engage intensively with UNCA in her discussion of IER practices initiated by Hammarskjöld.[165] Steven Ratner is one of the few scholars acknowledging that complex international peace operations enjoy a long history. He situates ONUC in the 'old' era of peacekeeping, explaining it (peacekeeping) 'in terms of earlier efforts at the "new" paradigm'.[166] He mentions ONUC's constitutional assistance in passing, entwining it with his broader discussion about the different generations through which peacekeeping has supposedly evolved.[167] The UN has neglected to map its constitutional assistance projects in peace operations and the development assistance context. Therefore, UNCA's trajectory remains shrouded.[168]

As I previously demonstrated through my UNCA inventory,[169] ONUC's constitutional assistance is not an entirely 'new' phenomenon.[170] In fact, in 1951, before ONUC wrote Congo's constitution, the UN Commissioner, Adrian Pelt, assisted Libya's Transitional National Assembly in drafting Libya's first constitution.[171] I therefore suggest that 1989 merely signals a particular moment of UNCA's rejuvenation.

[163] For the expansion in the UNCA agenda and activities during the post-Cold War era, see Sripati, *supra* note 64, at 112–113.

[164] For a lone comprehensive analysis of UNCA, see Sripati, *UNCA*, *supra* note 15. For a shorter work discussing constitutional assistance under external (including the UN's) influence see P. Dann and Z. Al-Ali, 'The Internationalized Pouvoir Constituant: Constitution-Making under External Influence in Iraq, Sudan and East Timor' (2006) 10 *Max Planck Yearbook of United Nations Law* 423. For a work on international territorial administration discussing externally driven constitution-making see Stahn, *supra* note 17.

[165] See Orford, *supra* note 6, at 5.

[166] See Ratner, *supra* note 3, at Chapter 4. I borrow this phrase from Wilde, *supra* note 15, at 276.

[167] See Ratner, *supra* note 3, at 105.

[168] In these circumstances, the UN's discourse about using UNCA 'proactively' to combat 'newer threats and newer areas', such as 'constitutional crises', remains misleading. See Report, *supra* note 1.

[169] See Sripati, *supra* note 64.

[170] See Sripati, *UNCA*, *supra* note 15, at Chapter 3. For Ban Ki-moon's comments that today the UN pursues 'proactive' preventive diplomacy to meet 'new challenges' in 'newer areas' such as 'constitutional crises', *see* Report, *supra* note 1.

[171] See A. Pelt, *Libyan Independence and the United Nations: A Case of Planned Decolonization* (1970).

That rejuvenation arose from the UN straying from its explicit Charter mandate of peaceful settlement of disputes towards a broader goal: 'conflict prevention' – backed up by a broader definition of 'threats to peace'. UNCA represents a continuum of internationalised constitution-making (representing varying degrees of external domination and influence in constitution-making) comprising (post-renaissance European) colonialism, the League of Nations' Mandates System, and the UN Trusteeship System.

22.5 UNCA revisited

The UN approach towards UNCA is shaped by antinomies. The UN argues that the 'primary responsibility for conflict prevention rests with national governments'.[172] and that it is incumbent on domestic authorities to create a good constitution.[173] However, it considers failed or post-conflict states experiencing a history of authoritarianism and exclusion as insufficiently experienced in democratic practices and lacking knowledge, expertise and institutional support to sculpt it.[174] It considers its main role as:

> Principally to assist national governments and their local counterparts in finding solutions to their problems by offering support for the *development of national and regional capacities for ... conflict prevention and long-term peacebuilding.*[175]

The UN pitches UNCA as building state capacity in conflict prevention. It deploys it as part of its 'broader, nationally-owned strategies to promote peace'.[176] ONUC wrote Congo's constitution. This may have set in motion a broader trend. Building on Hammarskjöld, Secretary-Generals expanded the UNCA *practice* in the post-Cold War era. From 1989 to 2009, the UN pushed more than a dozen post-conflict states to forge peace, by creating a *new good constitutional order.* Post-conflict peace agreements concluded in the DRC, Sudan, Nepal, Rwanda, Burundi, Somalia, Cambodia and Afghanistan[177] envisaged a new political order

[172] See Report, *supra* note 133, executive summary.

[173] See ROL Guidance Note, *supra* note 9; UNCA Guidance Note, *supra* note 1.

[174] The array of UNCA activities sheds light on the challenges perceived by the UN regarding local constitution-making and constitutional content. For a comprehensive inventory of UNCA activities see Sripati, *supra* note 64, at 112–113. See also Boutros-Ghali, *supra* note 9, at para. 9.

[175] See Report, *supra* note 133, para. 12.

[176] See Report, *supra* note 1, Summary.

[177] See V. Sripati, 'Table 5: UNCA Implements Peace Agreements Mandating the Making of a New Constitution' [unpublished manuscript on file with the author].

based on a new constitution, conforming to UN criteria. Moreover, those peace processes were sponsored either by the UN on its own or allying with a regional organisation. Finally, all those peace agreements designated the UN to assist in implementing them.[178]

Most recently, the UN, backed by the United States and teaming up with the Gulf Cooperation Council, pushed Yemen to conclude the Gulf Cooperation Council Agreement (hereinafter GFC Agreement). The GFC Agreement concluded in November 2011 mandates a new constitution for Yemen.[179] These cumulative actions consolidated the UNCA repertoire. They built up the UNCA practice. However, it was not until almost two decades later that the UN translated UNCA actions into strategy. In 2006, the Secretary-General's Executive Committee formally endorsed UNCA as a conflict-preventive activity.[180] Three years later, the Secretary-General released a guidance note, explaining UNCA's key policy function: standard-setting.[181] Subsequently, guidance notes transmitting allied IER practices such as promoting the rule of law, National Human Rights Institutions, transitional justice, and children's rights cluttered the UN's smorgasbord.[182] This momentum at the policy-making front rippled outward to strengthen the institutional basis for, as well as the UN's capacities in, constitutional assistance. The UN created the Peace-building

[178] See Sripati, *supra* note 64.

[179] See UNDP, 'UNDP Backs Yemen Elections', in *UNDP Washington Update 2* (March 2012) (affirming the making of a new Yemeni constitution and its ratification through a constitutional referendum and the UN's forthcoming constitutional assistance). The constitution-making process was meant to conclude in late 2013, enabling general elections to take place before mid 2014. See also Remarks of Hillary Clinton, US Secretary of State, 'Signing of GCC-Brokered Agreement in Yemen', 23 November 2011, at: www.state.gov/secretary/rm/2011/11/177749.htm (affirming 'the United States, in coordination with our international partners, will continue to closely monitor and support Yemen's political transition'). For the UN's translation of the agreement, see 'GFC Initiative for Yemen' reprinted in I. Sharqieh, 'A Lasting Peace? Yemen's Long Journey to National Reconciliation', Appendix I, Brookings Doha Center Analysis Paper No. 7, February 2013. For the requirement to make a new constitution see *ibid.*, para. 6.

[180] See Report of the Secretary-General, 'Progress Report on the Prevention of Armed Conflict', UN Doc. A/60/891 (18 July 2006), at para. 91 (mentioning the creation of the Policy Committee in 2005); 'Security Council Report Special Report No. 2', at 2 (5 October 2007) at: www.securitycouncilreport.org (reporting that an 'internal' policy paper on constitutional reform and constitution-making was awaiting approval by the UN Secretary-General's Policy Committee).

[181] See UNCA Guidance Note, *supra* note 1.

[182] See Guidance Note of the Secretary-General – UN Approach to Justice for Children (2008); UN-OHCHR, Guidance Note on National Human Rights Institutions and

Commission (PBC)[183] and the Mediation Support Unit (MSU) (within the Department of Political Affairs – DPA) vesting them with UNCA responsibilities. Comprising experts in constitutional law, ceasefires and transitional justice, the MSU stands ready for deployment into conflict zones to help resolve crises. Interestingly, and significantly, UNCA stands systematised today. Consider this statement by the UN:

> The United Nations has been involved in a number of constitution-making processes. In recent years, these have included Cambodia, Timor-Leste, Afghanistan, and Iraq. The Organization *is likely to be called upon in the future to assist other countries* in their constitution-making processes.[184]

In 1960, Hammarskjöld operationalised IER based on the UN's neutrality and impartiality and the temporary quality of those practices. In addition to the justifications offered by Hammarskjöld, the UN based its constitutional assistance on supposed state consent[185] and the doctrine of 'strengthening state sovereignty'.[186] It suggests that requests by states for such assistance triggers UNCA.[187] This conceals more than it reveals.

22.5.1 International law, policy implementation and good governance

Hammarskjöld offered a way of thinking about IER – UNCA. He situated it in the Charter framework. He used it as a preventive diplomacy tool to eliminate the 'root causes of conflict', arguing that 'we have only begun to explore the full potentialities of the United Nations as an instrument for multilateral diplomacy, especially the most useful combinations of public discussion on the one hand and private negotiations and mediation on the other'.[188] He thus paved the way for his successors to unleash those full

Transitional Justice (United Nations, September 2008); UN, Guidance Note of the Secretary-General on Democracy (United Nations, undated); UN-DPA, Guidelines for Mediators Relating to Conflict Related Sexual Violence in Conflict and Peace Agreements (UN-DPA, Policy and Mediation Division, 2012).

183 The PBC was established in 2005 as a subsidiary body of the Security Council. See generally: 'Peacebuilding Commission', at: www.pbc.org.

184 See UNCA Guidance Note, *supra* note 1, at 3.

185 *Ibid.*

186 See Sripati, *UNCA*, *supra* note 15, at Chapter 6. For statements about 'strengthening state sovereignty', see Report of the Secretary-General, 'Implementing the Responsibility to Protect', UN Doc. A/63/677, para. 10(a) (12 January 2009); Report, *supra* note 91, para. 6 (Executive Summary).

187 See UNCA Guidance Note, *supra* note 1, at 1.

188 See Report, *supra* note 1, at 1 ('The UN dedicates this report to the memory of former Secretary-General, Dag Hammarskjöld').

potentialities. It is thus no wonder that UN policy-makers acclaim him as the 'hero' of the preventive diplomacy story.[189] Following Hammarskjöld's example, UNCA is now part and parcel of a 'conflict preventive' activity in the UN peace and security system.[190]

In 1992, Boutros Boutros-Ghali built on Hammarskjöld's IER *practices*. By connecting the dots between peace, development and democracy,[191] he underscored the importance of *democratising* states in order to prevent conflict. This idea shone the spotlight on the significance of sound internal governance.[192] By extension, it strengthened the legitimacy of UNCA as capacity building.[193] Consider this passage from his *Agenda for Peace*:

> There is a new requirement for technical assistance which the United Nations has an obligation to develop and provide when requested: support for the transformation of *deficient* national structures and capabilities, and for the strengthening of new democratic institutions.[194]

Commencing from where Boutros-Ghali left off, Kofi Annan pushed for a broader and more comprehensive idea of 'conflict prevention'.[195] Conflict prevention so understood 'takes peaceful settlement of disputes one step farther by addressing *both the immediate and root causes of conflict*'.[196] He broadened and categorised preventive diplomacy approaches into 'structural prevention' and 'operational prevention'.[197] 'Structural prevention' seeks to 'transform the underlying characteristics of groups, states, and regions that increase their risk of violent conflict'.[198] Operationally, it translated into building sustainable in-country capacity to prevent violent conflicts. In addition, it accrued to all UN agencies.[199]

Accordingly, the UNDP linked speeding up socio-economic development with conflict prevention. Under this paradigm, violent conflict is understood to arise because 'respect for the rule of law breaks down as a result of unsound or ineffective legal or constitutional systems'. Therefore, it offered constitutional support to speed up the achievement

189 See B. Ramcharan, *Preventive Diplomacy at the UN* (2008), xv (Foreword) [emphasis in the original title].

190 See Report, *supra* note 138, at Annex B, 'Review of the UN System Capacity for Conflict Prevention: Key Findings'.

191 See Boutros-Ghali, *supra* note 9, at para. 59.

192 *Ibid.* 193 *Ibid.* 194 *Ibid.*

195 See Report, *supra* note 180, at Summary and Annex.

196 See Mani, *supra* note 10, at 300, 301. 197 See Report, *supra* note 133.

198 See Mani, *supra* note 10, at 301. 199 *Ibid.*

of development.[200] It used two ostensibly technocratic processes, the UN Development Assistance Frameworks (UNDAF) and Poverty Reduction Strategy Papers (PRSP), to lever its constitution support. However, it branded support as broader conflict prevention.[201] In this way, it helped produce the good constitution embodying international human rights and standards set by the IFIs: free markets and anti-corruption commissions. Consider the communalities in UNDP-assisted constitutional processes and constitutions of Togo, Nauru, Bhutan, Malawi, Maldives and Solomon Islands.[202] Through these structures, the UN projected good governance into the development assistance world. If, despite systemic and structural measures, conflict still confronts a state, the Security Council and the Secretary-General deploy 'operational prevention' measures.[203] These measures refer to those applicable 'in the face of immediate crisis'.[204] They include UNCA.

As an activity, UNCA falls within the Secretary-General's 'good offices'. The Secretary-General may therefore use it to resolve constitutional disputes.[205] According to the Secretary-General:

> My predecessors and I have provided our good offices in a wide range of situations and on countless occasions, offering an avenue for the resolution of inter-state wars, intra-state wars, border disputes, maritime disputes, *constitutional disputes*, electoral disputes, questions of autonomy and independence, hostage crises and a vast range of other disagreements and problems. My good offices are always at the disposal of Member States, especially in cases where my envoys or I could help to avoid the outbreak of conflict.[206]

Secretary-General Kofi Annan used his good offices to push Nepal's conflicting parties towards eschewing violence and concluding peace.[207] It culminated in the creation of the UN Mission in Nepal (UNMIN)

[200] UNDP Democratic Governance Group and Bureau for Development Policy, *Elections and Conflict Prevention: A Guide to Analysis, Planning and Programming* (undated) at: 'UNDP Oslo Governance Center', www.undp.org/oslocentre/; in November 2000, the UNDP adopted a conflict prevention strategy devoting 20 per cent of its track 3 funding for 'preventive and curative activities'. See *Role of UNDP in Crisis and Post-Conflict Situations*, UN Doc. D/P/2001/14, paras. 58, 4–15 (November 2000).

[201] See Sripati, *UNCA*, *supra* note 15, at Chapter 2. The PRSPs articulate the economic and social poverty-reduction programmes that countries seeking debt relief under the Heavily Indebted Poor Country debt reduction process (HIPC) must produce. The World Bank and the IMF started them in 1999. *Ibid.*

[202] See Sripati, *supra* note 64, at 97.

[203] See Mani, *supra* note 10, at 311, 312.

[204] *Ibid.*

[205] See UN Charter, Art. 99.

[206] See Report, *supra* note 180, para 32.

[207] United Nations, The United Nations and Nepal's peace process 5 (Preface).

to assist the Nepalese to forge an 'inclusive, transparent and participatory constitution-making process in 2008'.[208] UNMIN assisted Nepal in holding elections for its Constituent Assembly. According to the UN Secretary-General:

> The work of the [UNMIN] Gender Affairs Section has continued to focus primarily on the Constituent Assembly and the role of its elected women members. Approximately one third of the 575 members of the Assembly are women, making Nepal fourteenth out of 135 countries ranked according to the number of women in their elected national parliaments.[209]

In simple terms, the Secretary-General ostensibly uses UNCA to resolve crises having constitutional implications. UNCA's 'operational (conflict) prevention' function then lies in encouraging political dialogue among conflicting groups and creating a climate conducive to the peaceful settlement of disputes by citizens. It also ostensibly reduces conflict by spiking up the number of women and indigenous groups at constitutional roundtables, allowing them to articulate their demands and grievances, guiding and educating them in articulating how the (new) draft constitution could advance their interests, and empowering them to exercise their choice. Most recently, Ban Ki-moon announced the UN's 'proactive' preventive diplomacy to meet 'new challenges' thrown up by 'newer areas' such as 'severe constitutional crises ranging from unconstitutional changes of government to violent electoral disputes'.[210] According to his report, the UN confronts these crises with a 'wider range of tools' such as UNCA.[211]

Consider the UN's 'proactive' preventive diplomacy efforts in Guinea.[212] Following the constitutional coup in Guinea, the UN pushed Guinea's conflicting parties to agree to restore constitutional order in tune with the principles of 'good governance'.[213] The new constitution adopted by Guinea's ad hoc parliamentary body, the National Council of Transition,

[208] See Security Council Resolution 1740 (2007), UN Doc. S/Res/1740 (2007); UNCA Guidance Note, *supra* note 1, at 4.

[209] See Report of the Secretary-General on the request of Nepal for United Nations assistance in support of its peace process, UN Doc. S/2008/454, para. 35 E, Gender, social inclusion and child protection (10 July 2008).

[210] See Report, *supra* note 1, paras. 1, 4 and 35.

[211] *Ibid.*, at paras. 4 and 35.

[212] For basic facts relating to the conflict see C.T. Call, *UN Mediation and the Politics of Transition after Constitutional Crises* (2012); Department of Political Affairs, Multi-year appeal (2012 update); Report, *supra* note 1, at para. 24.

[213] See preamble, The Ouagadougou Peace Agreement (15 January 2010) [on file with the author].

in April 2010,[214] conforms to the UN's standards.[215] For example, it anchors a national human rights commission and pledges to root out corruption through appropriate anti-corruption institutions.[216] In this way, the UNCA engine chugs across the entire conflict prevention spectrum conveying international human rights and IFIs' financial standards in post-conflict and other states. To use UN jargon in translating this phenomenon, UNCA remains relevant across the full conflict prevention spectrum from 'structural prevention' to 'operational prevention', and the 'proactive prevention' spheres. Figure 22.1 (see Annex to this chapter) captures how the UN fits UNCA into the Charter framework.

Hammarskjöld's successors used his preventive diplomacy legacy to catapult a conflict-prevention tool: the good constitution.

22.5.2 Good constitution = good governance?

According to the UN, a good constitution radiates good governance. It is a people's constitution. Its inclusive process draws in women, children and indigenous groups historically shut out from constitution making.[217] It breeds national ownership and respect for the rule of law.[218] Therefore, in a state enjoying good governance, no person or institution can force a child to slave in mines and shafts, sift pans for gemstones or slosh in the mud searching for surface diamonds.[219] By pushing local stakeholders towards such standards, UNCA promotes international law relating to children, women and indigenous groups.

A good constitution also outlaws terrorism. In this way, it prevents violent conflict. Consider the anti-terror provisions in the UN-assisted constitutions of Iraq, Afghanistan and Bhutan.[220] These provisions have spawned national legislation combating allied offences such as money

[214] See Human Rights Watch, 'Guinea – Country Summary' 1–2 (January 2011).

[215] See *infra* discussion on the salient features of a good constitution.

[216] For criteria for a good constitution see ROL Guidance Note, *supra* note 9, at 4. For compliance with UN's standards see 'Constitution of 7 May 2010 (Guinea)', Art. 146–147 [NHRI] and preamble (anti-corruption); right to property (Art. 13), environmental rights (Art. 16).

[217] See UNCA Guidance Note, *supra* note 1, at 4. [218] *Ibid.*

[219] See *Report of the Secretary-General on Children and Armed Conflict*, UN Doc. S/2010/577 (9 November 2010) at paras. 21, 30, 35 and 54.

[220] See, e.g., Constitution of the Islamic Republic of Afghanistan (2004), in G. Flanz and R. Grote (eds.), *Constitutions of the Countries of the World* (Vol. II), preamble & Ch. 1, Art. 7; The Constitution of the Republic of Iraq (2005), in *ibid.*, Vol. IX; The Kingdom of Bhutan Constitution (2008), in *ibid.*, Vol. II Art. 8(5).

laundering, smuggling in narcotics, drugs and arms.[221] Next, a good constitution embeds international environmental rights and mechanisms halting the illegal extraction of high-value natural resources such as coltan, gold, copper and other minerals.[222] It offers means for fairly sharing oil, thereby preventing conflict in supposedly divided societies with antagonistic communities.[223] Consider the natural resource governance and environmental protection provisions showing up in the UN-assisted constitutions of Iraq, Bhutan, Kosovo and Afghanistan.[224]

Consider also the role of UN experts. They advise stakeholders on strengthening their weak rule of law institutions, clarifying their laws and allocating power to manage and develop the collection and sharing of natural resources.[225] These UNCA activities are explained as promoting international environmental rights, positively influencing the distribution of natural resources and speeding up the achievement of sustainable development, a Millennium Development Goal.

A good constitution promotes free markets – an international ideal. UNCA carried this initiative forward. Market economy provisions and allied institutions (anti-corruption commissions) show up in the constitutions of the DRC, Sudan, Malawi, Bhutan, Kosovo, Rwanda, Somalia, Burundi, Maldives and Afghanistan.[226] Anti-corruption commissions control the financial industry, infusing transparency and erecting barriers to corruption.[227] A transparent and corruption-free polity in turn helps attract big foreign capital. Foreign companies invest resources for instance in agriculture, mineral and fuel production, creating value shared among their investors, the managers and employees, ultimately spurring the recipient state's economic growth. Robust economic

[221] See Bhutan's Anti Money Laundering Act, at: www.unodc.org/pdf/india/publications/south_Asia_Regional_Profile_Sept_2005/09_bhutan.pdf; Iraq Anti Money Laundering Law (2004).

[222] See UNEP recommendations, *supra* note 137, at 5.

[223] See Haysom and Kane, *supra* note 141, at 12–13.

[224] See e.g. Constitution of the Islamic Republic of Afghanistan (2004), in Flanz and Grote, *supra* note 221 (Vol. II) pmbl, Art. 15 and 20. See The Kingdom of Bhutan Constitution (2008), *ibid.*, at 1–39; The Constitution of the Republic of Iraq (2005), *ibid.*, at Art. 7 ['Values'] and 52.

[225] See Haysom and Kane, *supra* note 141, at 5–13.

[226] For details about market economy provisions and anti-corruption commissions in UN-assisted constitutions, see Sripati, *UNCA*, *supra* note 15, at Chapter 4.

[227] R.E. Messick, 'Judicial Reform: The Why, the What, and the How', Prepared for Delivery at a conference on Strategies for Modernizing the Judicial Sector in the Arab World, 15–17 March 2002, Marrakech, Morocco.

growth ripples outward promoting global macroeconomic stability and preventing financial destabilisation.

In these multiple ways, UNCA ostensibly serves to eliminate threats or to prevent conflict. The UN portrays it as simultaneously implementing:

(1) democracy, the rule of law and human rights, including gender equality, women's right to political participation and indigenous rights;
(2) the international ideals of free markets and economic prosperity; and
(3) sustainable development.

In short, UNCA promotes good governance. But viewing UNCA as an international law and policy-implementing mechanism removes it from its broader historical setting. It is useful to broaden the analytical framework and explore some of the synergies between historical approaches (see Section 22.2) and modern UNCA practice.

22.6 Identifying the colonial continuities in UNCA

UNCA is partly rooted in the tradition of the 'civilising mission', and partly a development thereof. Remarkable parallels exist between 'good governance' used by the World Bank within the neoliberal paradigm from the 1990s onwards and the term's formulation and usage by British authorities in the early twentieth century.[228] Parallels also exist in the term's trajectory towards an expansive social and institutional notion of development in each of these periods.[229]

'Civilised' normative practices (rooted in Christianity) constituted the last standard of civilisation.[230] *Sati*, polygamy and slavery were considered 'uncivilised'. Therefore, they had to be outlawed.[231] Consider the abolition of the Indian practice, *Sati*, in colonial India. No act provided more moral justification for colonisation than the outlawing of *Sati* by Lord William Bentinck in 1829. 'White men' are protecting 'brown women from brown men'[232] – this phrase by Gayatri Spivak best captures the

[228] *Ibid.*, at 37.

[229] *Ibid.* See also V. Hewitt, 'A Cautionary Tale: Colonial and Post-Colonial Conceptions of Good Government and Democratization in Africa' (2006) 44 *Commonwealth & Comparative Politics* 41.

[230] Gong, *supra* note 13, at 16. [231] *Ibid.*

[232] See C. Midgely, *Feminism and Empire: Women Activists in Imperial Britain, 1790–1865* (2007), 66 (quoting G. Spivak).

idea and ostensible goal underpinning British colonisers' actions. It also reveals how, by casting colonised Indian women as victims of barbaric practices, the British justified colonising India.

UNCA's standards resonate in nineteenth-century civilised standards: the Western constitution (based on the rule of law, anchoring an independent judiciary, human rights, and rule of law institutions), free markets and good governance (tied to achieving a particular form of political economy) and norms and practices impacting women's emancipation. One can draw a straight line between the civilised financial standards (free markets) prescribed by the IFIs and the type of political institutions (independent judiciaries and anti-corruption commissions) they advocate for producing and sustaining their specific development policies. In other words, as was the case during various forms of colonialism, rule of law promotion today is not ideologically neutral. It ties up with achieving a specific kind of political economy, that is, a neoliberal economy. IFIs' conditionality comes masked as neutral international financial standards required for good economic governance. The UN allies with IFIs in promoting them as good governance. I suggest that UNCA's 'transparent, inclusive, and participatory constitution-making' adds a new standard to nineteenth-century civilised standards.

22.7 Conclusion

UNCA has now existed for several decades. It has essentially materialised in the LDCs – the more impoverished and politically weaker sections of the globe. Most significantly, it has come to stay.[233] This is clearly illustrated by the case of the Congo. After enduring two decades of debilitating dictatorship and violence, Congo experienced a second round of UN intervention in the late 1990s.[234] After concluding a UN-brokered peace agreement in 2003 and bowing to IFIs' dictates, Congo wrote a new

[233] See UNCA Guidance Note, *supra* note 1, at 4.

[234] See The United Nations Organization Mission in the Democratic Republic of the Congo (MONUC) established by Security Council Resolution 1258 (1999), UN Doc. S/Res/1258 (1999). Following Congo's conclusion of the all-inclusive peace accord in 2002, MONUC, an observer mission, morphed into a multidimensional peace-building operation with a robust mandate. See Security Council Resolution 1493 (2003), UN Doc. S/Res/1493 (2003).

constitution in 2005 – with MONUC's guidance.[235] MONUC signalled the transition from peacekeeping to state-building. This shift makes it impossible to preserve neutrality, as suggested.

Congo's situation, emblematic of other UNCA recipient-states, points to the salience of the end game of UNCA.[236] Indeed, Hammarskjöld presciently alluded to Congo's vulnerability at the height of its constitutional crisis. He said:

> They seem to believe that the independence of the Republic of the Congo … means independence also in a substantive sense of the word which, in our interdependent world of today, is unreal even for a country living by its own means and able to provide for its own security and administration.[237]

Given that it is enmeshed with conditions and other forms of standard-setting, how does the UN envisage making the achievements of its constitutional assistance, if any, sustainable? Has it coined a coherent 'exit strategy' for UNCA? Does it envisage institutional support for UNCA states-recipients in the post-constitution stage? Like many other aspects of UNCA, the UN neglects to articulate a coherent 'exit strategy' for UNCA. It merely concedes that 'following up' on its constitutional assistance demands 'substantial financial and human resources'.[238] These questions, however, bear directly on matters of public policy and demand attention.

Regrettably, UNCA – let alone the subject of its 'exit strategy' – remains a 'sleeping beauty'. Trapped in the 'post-conflict' and/or 'how to do it better' (technocratic appraisals) brackets, it has escaped full bloom as a distinct field fit for sustained critical analysis.

235 See Sripati, *UNCA*, *supra* note 15, at Ch. 3. During the transitional government period, the President of Congo, President Joseph Kabila liberalised domestic political activity and carried out economic reforms prescribed by the World Bank and IMF.

236 See generally R. Caplan, *Exit Strategies and State Building* (2012).

237 See Orford, *supra* note 6, at 86 [quoting Hammarskjöld].

238 See UNCA Guidance Note, *supra* note 1, at 5.

Annex

<table>
<tr><th rowspan="2">UN organs responsible for peaceful settlement of disputes and conflict prevention</th><th colspan="2">Peaceful settlement of disputes intertwines with conflict prevention</th><th rowspan="2">Measures [inclusive list]</th><th rowspan="2">'Conflict preventive' tool</th></tr>
<tr><th>Peaceful settlement of disputes</th><th>Conflict prevention 'Takes peaceful settlement of disputes one step farther by addressing both the immediate and root causes of conflict'</th></tr>
<tr><td>General Assembly</td><td rowspan="3">Peaceful settlement of disputes</td><td rowspan="3">[Conflict] 'operational prevention'*</td><td>UNGA resolutions</td><td>UNGA endorsed UNCA</td></tr>
<tr><td>Security Council</td><td>Comprehensive peace missions</td><td>UNCA promotes the 'good' constitution</td></tr>
<tr><td>Secretary-General</td><td>Negotiation; preventive diplomacy: mediation including 'good offices'; fact-finding; and conciliation</td><td>UNCA promotes the 'good' constitution</td></tr>
<tr><td>All UN agencies including UNDP, ECOSOC, and UNDESA</td><td>Not applicable</td><td>[Conflict] 'Structural Prevention'**</td><td>Development and governance programmes including CCA/UNDAF*</td><td>UNCA promotes the 'good' constitution</td></tr>
</table>

Figure 22.1 Situating United Nations Constitutional Assistance (UNCA) in the Charter framework

Source: Created by author. R. Mani, 'Peaceful Settlement of Disputes and Conflict Prevention', in T.G. Weiss and S. Daws (eds.), *Oxford Handbook on the United Nations* (2006), at 300, 314.

Acronyms: Common Country Assessments (CCA) & UN Development Assistance Framework (UNDAF); Department of Political Affairs (DPA); UN Development Programme (UNDP); Economic and Social Council (ECOSOC); UN Department of Social and Economic Affairs (UNDESA); UN General Assembly (UNGA).

* Refers to those 'measures applicable in the face of immediate crisis'.

** Seeks to transform the underlying 'characteristics of groups, states, and regions that increase their risk of violent conflict'.

23

Who cares?

Dag Hammarskjöld and the limits of responsibility in international law

J. CRAIG BARKER

Isn't the fulfilment of our duty towards our neighbour an expression of our deepest desire? It very well may be. In any case, why torture ourselves in order to hurt others.[1]

Assenting to his possibility – why? Does he sacrifice himself for others yet for his own sake – *in megalomania? Or does he realize himself for the sake of others? The difference is that between a monster and a man. 'A new commandment I give unto you: That you love one another.'*[2]

Dag Hammarskjöld

23.1 Introduction

Dag Hammarskjöld was a deeply spiritual and caring man. His writings in his private diary, published posthumously as *Markings*, reflect the life of a man dedicated to self-sacrifice in service of others. This 'spiritual memoir' betrays the inner turmoil of such sacrifice and his dedication to faith.[3] It represents the private thoughts of an individual who was committed

J. Craig Barker is Professor of Law, Centre for Responsibilities, Rights and the Law, School of Law, Politics and Sociology, University of Sussex.

[1] D. Hammarskjöld, *Markings* (1965 and 2006), 14. [2] *Ibid.*, at 69.

[3] Hammarskjöld's faith was a faith in God, but his faith was a tolerant one. When asked once why the UN Charter did not contain any reference to God, he drew attention to the Preamble of the Charter 'where the nations express their faith in the dignity and worth of the human person' and pledge themselves 'to practice tolerance and live together in peace with one another as good neighbours'. He felt sure that this was a recognition of 'the will of God: that we should love our neighbours as ourselves'. D. Hammarskjöld, 'Address before the Second Assembly of the World Council of Churches, Evanston, Illinois, 20 August 1954', in W. Foote (ed.), *The Servant of Peace: A Selection of the Speeches and Statements of Dag Hammarskjöld, Secretary-General of the United Nations 1953–1961* (1962), 56. See also Chapter 9, this volume.

to work for others. According to Hammarskjöld himself, he inherited 'a belief that no life was more satisfactory than one of selfless service to your country – or humanity'.[4] And it was to humanity that Hammarskjöld dedicated himself. He was truly a 'servant of peace'.[5]

Hammarskjöld was, additionally, a responsible man both in private and in his public role. He believed fervently in 'the moral sovereignty of the responsible individual' as well as the importance of integrity and personal ethics.[6] He believed in the independence and international responsibility of the international civil servant as well as the personal responsibility of the Secretary-General.[7] He worked to develop the legal and political responsibilities of the United Nations (UN) Secretariat as well as that of the UN itself.[8] But Hammarskjöld was not only concerned with these narrow concepts of political and legal responsibility, he was concerned also with the broader responsibilities of the international community, not only to states, but also individuals, particularly through the securing of peace and human rights. His work in developing the executive role of the United Nations contributed to many innovations in UN practice, such as UN diplomacy and peacekeeping, as well as, ultimately, to the development of the concept of responsibility to protect. Hammarskjöld did not engage directly in his speeches and writings with the concept of responsibility, but the latter was at the heart of his personal and political philosophy.[9]

This chapter is focused, in particular, on the importance of the concept of responsibility in international legal discourse. It will first analyse the traditional approach to responsibility and its purported 'radical reconceptualisation' around the idea of objective state responsibility. The chapter will then consider the recent rise of responsibility discourse in international law, focusing in particular on the significance of responsibility to protect. It will be argued that responsibility to protect is best understood through the lens of existing responsibility regimes in international law. Thereafter, drawing on insights from analyses of responsibilities within domestic law, in particular in relation to the notion of family responsibility, the chapter will highlight the importance of prospective

[4] Hammarskjöld, *supra* note 1, at vii.

[5] See Foote, *supra* note 3. See also Bring, *supra* Chapter 9, this volume.

[6] D. Hammarskjöld, 'International Service', in Foote, *supra* note 3, at 83.

[7] D. Hammarskjöld, 'The International Civil Servant in Law and in Fact', in Foote, *supra* note 3, at 331–337.

[8] *Ibid.*

[9] For a fuller discussion of Hammarskjöld's personal and political philosophy, see further Chapter 9, this volume.

responsibilities and the question of what it means to be responsible in the context of international relations. Finally, the chapter suggests that one possible approach to strengthening responsibility in international law is to recognise the relational foundations of the concept of responsibility and relate this to the moral framework of the ethic of care.

23.2 'Responsibility' in international law

The concept of responsibility is the subject of considerable historic and contemporary discourse across a range of disciplines, including philosophy, political science and law. Within legal discourse, the concept of responsibility is most commonly bound up with the concept of liability. Thus, according to Peter Cane, 'as a first reaction one might be tempted to say that "responsibility" is not a legal concept at all'.[10] 'Liability' comes much more readily to the legal mind than 'responsibility'.[11] In this way, 'responsibility' is perceived of as a historic notion of answerability for past events, deriving as it does from the Latin *respondeo*, meaning, 'I answer'.[12]

23.2.1 The traditional definition of international responsibility

The linking of responsibility to historic liability is particularly apparent in international legal discourse. International law has long been criticised as lacking the necessary secondary rules to transform it from a system of rules into a fully functioning legal system.[13] The development of the rules of state responsibility have been characterised, most notably by the International Law Commission when drafting its articles on state responsibility, as an attempt to:

> define those rules which, in contradistinction to the 'primary' rules may be described as 'secondary', inasmuch as they are aimed at determining the legal consequences of failure to fulfil obligations established by the 'primary' rules. Only the 'secondary' rules fall within the actual sphere of responsibility for internationally wrongful acts.[14]

[10] P. Cane, *Responsibility in Law and Morality* (2003), 1. [11] *Ibid.*
[12] J. Lucas, *Responsibility* (1993), 5.
[13] See, in particular, H. Hart, *The Concept of Law* (1961 and 1994), 95 and 213–237.
[14] International Law Commission, 'Draft Articles on the Responsibility of States for Internationally Wrongful Acts with Commentaries', *Yearbook of the International Law Commission, 2011*, Vol. II, Part Two, UN Doc. A/66/10.

The criticism that international law lacks secondary rules has been addressed not only through the codification of the rules on state responsibility but also in relation to diplomatic protection, the responsibility of international organisations, as well as more specific projects on 'liability' for trans-boundary harm.[15] Similarly, the development of new courts and tribunals has provided the institutional framework for the determination of responsibility in international law.[16]

In a recently published analysis of *The Law of International Responsibility*, the authors highlight the many recent developments in international law concerning the entire field of international responsibility, which regulates not only states but also the broad range of actors encompassed within the international legal system,[17] including, most notably, international organisations[18] and individuals.[19] Accordingly, the book purports to examine 'many aspects of international responsibility which may arise in a multifaceted legal system'.[20] For the authors, generally speaking, international responsibility is co-extensive with liability, the word responsibility being a reflection of how the concept of liability is understood in non-English translations of liability. Thus:

> these rules [of state responsibility] have been progressively developed by the [International Law Commission] under the English rubric of 'liability'; in all other official languages of the United Nations they are covered under the same wording as the consequences of wrongful acts (e.g., *responsibilité, responsabilidad*).[21]

[15] J. Crawford, A. Pellet and S. Olleson, 'Preface', in J. Crawford, A. Pellet and S. Olleson (eds.), *The Law of International Responsibility* (2010), at v.

[16] See, for example, S. Linton and F. Tiba, 'The International Judge in an Age of Multiple International Courts and Tribunals' (2009) 9 *Chicago Journal of International Law* 407.

[17] See, Crawford *et al.*, *supra* note 15.

[18] See, International Law Commission, 'Draft Articles on the Responsibility of International Organisations', *Yearbook of the International Law Commission, 2011*, Vol. II, Part Two, UN Doc. A/66/10. See also, A. Pellet, 'The Definition of Responsibility in International Law', in Crawford *et al.*, *supra* note 15, 3 at 6–7.

[19] The question of responsibility of individuals is largely, if not exclusively, dealt with as a matter of international criminal law. See A. Pellet, 'The Definition of Responsibility in International Law', in Crawford *et al.*, *supra* note 15, 3 at 7–8. See, generally, A. Cassese, *International Criminal Law* (2008); and R. Cryer, H. Friman, D. Robinson and E. Wilmshurst, *An Introduction to International Criminal Law and Procedure* (2010).

[20] Crawford *et al.*, *supra* note 15.

[21] *Ibid.*, at vi.

23.2.2 *Responsibility and legality: the emergence of objective responsibility in international law*

It is important to recognise that the law on international responsibility has undergone significant development in recent years and now includes 'rules applying to liability for activities which are not prohibited under international law but which may entail special consequences both on the ground of prevention and of compensation'.[22] In his opening chapter of *The Law of International Responsibility* defining responsibility in international law, Alain Pellet emphasises the 'objectivization of international responsibility'[23] by questioning the traditional definition of responsibility which he considers has been subject to a 'radical reconceptualization'[24] through 'the exclusion of damage as a condition for responsibility'.[25] The resulting regime, while primarily directed at liability for injury, recognises that 'responsibility can arise regardless of legal injury of any particular state'.[26] The impact of this development cannot be underestimated. It potentially transforms the notion of responsibility from a private law analogy of rights and duties between individual states to a more structural process involving the responsibility of states, or other actors, to a larger group of states or, more obviously, to the international community. As Koskenniemi puts it, 'is the proper analogy with domestic private law or domestic public law?'[27]

The potential transformation of the law of state responsibility from a purely private law model to a model that is capable of undertaking functions of a more public law nature has been commented upon by André Nollkaemper. For Nollkaemper, the traditional law of state responsibility is more concerned with protection of subjective rights than with illegality. Thus, 'acts that transgress the legal power of a state, yet do not cause legal injury to another state, generally have not been treated as issues of international responsibility'.[28] However, the removal of the requirement of injury, coupled with the recognition of the existence of *erga omnes* obligations and *jus cogens* norms, has opened up the possibility of a state invoking the responsibility of another state for a breach of an obligation

[22] *Ibid.*, at v–vi. [23] Pellet, *supra* note 19, at 8.

[24] *Ibid.* [25] *Ibid.*, at 9.

[26] A. Nollkaemper, 'Costitutionalization and the Unity of the Law of International Responsibility' (2009) 16 *Indiana Journal of Global Legal Studies* 535, at 546.

[27] M. Koskenniemi, 'Doctrines of State Responsibility', in Crawford *et al.*, *supra* note 15, 45 at 47.

[28] Nollkaemper, *supra* note 26, at 543.

owed to the international community as a whole.[29] The development of state responsibility in relation to serious violations of peremptory norms of general international law is particularly important in this regard, in that the law requires all states to cooperate to bring such breaches to an end and not to recognise as lawful a situation created by a serious breach.[30] Nollkaemper concludes that:

> The removal of the concept of legal injury, the recognition of the rights of all states to invoke responsibility in case of breached norms protecting the collective interest, and the formulation of obligations on all states to respond to a serious breach of peremptory norms, have added a stronger constitutional nature to the law of responsibility. This strengthens the organizational power of the law of responsibility, adds to its power to control illegal acts, and at the same time reflects and contributes to the recognition of public interest norms in international law.[31]

The development of the law of international responsibility to include not only bilateralism but also to recognise community interests has given rise to serious debate about the unity of responsibility in international law. For Pellet, the unity of the notion of international responsibility cannot be re-established given the different foundations of the different forms of accountability in the international legal order. Nollkaemper, on the other hand, argues that international law does not distinguish between various types of responsibility, such as 'contractual or tortious responsibility, or between civil, criminal or other forms of public law responsibility'.[32] Furthermore, for Nollkaemper, 'the various forms of responsibility (strict liability, ordinary wrongs, wrongs arising out of serious breaches of peremptory norms) are subject to the same general principles of responsibility, and that they form a relatively coherent whole'.[33] More importantly, for present purposes, it is submitted that what ensures the unity of analysis and understanding of responsibility in contemporary international law

[29] See Article 48 of the Articles on Responsibility of States for Internationally Wrongful Acts 2001, which permits states other than an injured state to invoke the responsibility of another state, but only where the obligation is owed to a group of states including the invoking state, or where the obligation breached is owed to the international community as a whole. International Law Commission, *supra* note 14, at 142. See also, Article 42 of the Draft Articles on Responsibility of International Organisations 2011. International Law Commission, *supra* note 18, at 132.

[30] See, Article 41 of the Articles on Responsibility of States for Internationally Wrongful Acts 2001. International Law Commission, *supra* note 14, at 131.

[31] Nollkaemper, *supra* note 26, at 549.

[32] *Ibid.*, at 552–553. [33] *Ibid.*, at 553.

is that it remains essentially historic and focused on the idea of breach. Pellet summarises the position as follows:

> The international law of responsibility has distanced itself from the 'civil law' model which previously characterized it, and no longer solely plays the role of a compensatory mechanism, to which it was for a long time confined. It is now also, and perhaps principally, a mechanism having as its function the condemnation of *breaches* by subjects of international law of their legal obligations and the restoration of international legality, respect for international law being a matter in which the international community as a whole has an interest (emphasis added).[34]

23.3 Emerging discourses of responsibility in international law

In differentiating between the extreme positions that '*all* responsibility exists in individual state-to-state relationships' and 'the opposite view that *all* responsibility involves a breach of the objective legal order', Koskenniemi has identified that 'a more or less vaguely articulated moral cosmopolitanism has been an indissociable part of the 20th century academic international law'.[35] This idea of moral cosmopolitanism has contributed to the increased assertion of broader notions of responsibility in international law. In June 2004, the notion of 'shared responsibility' was placed at the heart of the United Nations Secretary-General's High Level Panel Report on Threats, Challenges and Change entitled 'A More Secure World: Our Shared Responsibility'.[36] Recent academic literature has sought to draw on the concept of 'shared' or 'global' responsibility in relation to discourse around a number of sub-fields of international law including, most notably, human rights.[37] Arguably the most controversial example of this 'rise of responsibility' in recent years has revolved around the concept of the responsibility to protect. This concept will provide the focus for the following section of this chapter not only because of the controversy surrounding it, but also because the development of the concept can be traced back to the work of Dag Hammarskjöld in his exposition of the notion of international executive authority and is, accordingly, of particular importance to this volume.

[34] Pellet, *supra* note 19, at 15. [35] Koskenniemi, *supra* note 27, at 48.

[36] Report of the High-level Panel on Threats, Challenges and Change, A More Secure World: Our Shared Responsibility, UN Doc. A/59/565 (2004).

[37] See, for example, A. Kuper, *Global Responsibilities: Who Must Deliver on Human Rights* (2005); and M. Salmon, *Global Responsibility for Human Rights* (2007).

23.3.1 The responsibility to protect

The importance of the work of Dag Hammarskjöld to the development of the idea of responsibility to protect has been fully illustrated in this volume (Chapter 9) and elsewhere. In an address entitled 'Human Rights and the Work for Peace' delivered to the Fiftieth Anniversary Dinner of the American Jewish Committee in April 1957, Hammarskjöld told his audience that:

> The work for peace is basically a work for the most elementary of human rights: the right of everyone to security and to freedom from fear. We, therefore, recognize it as one of the first duties of a government to take measures in order to safeguard for its citizens this very right. But we also recognize it as an obligation for the emerging world community to assist governments in safeguarding this elementary human right without having to lock themselves behind the wall of arms.[38]

Although Hammarskjöld did not refer directly to the concept of responsibility, inherent within this quote are two notions of responsibility: the notion of 'sovereignty as responsibility', and the idea of the broader responsibility of the international community to assist governments in the fulfilment of their primary responsibility. These two principles constitute the two basic pillars of the concept of responsibility to protect.

It is worth noting Hammarskjöld's use of the word 'assisting' in the quoted passage. Hammarskjöld did not envisage a role for the international community in intervening in states that were not securing the protection of their civilians but was asserting, rather, an 'obligation' on the international community, primarily through the United Nations, to assist states in providing for the security and protection from fear of their populations. Hammarskjöld's use of the words 'duty' and 'obligation' in this passage is also interesting. Although a firm believer in the rule of law, he was, however, conscious of the limits of international law, which he described elsewhere as embryonic and in need of significant strengthening.[39] Nevertheless, in presenting the duty of governments and the obligation of the world community in such terms, he was asserting a putative rule of international law based around the responsibility of both governments and the international community to protect civilians. He

[38] D. Hammarskjöld, 'Human Rights and the Work for Peace', in Foote, *supra* note 3, 126 at 127.

[39] See, D. Hammarskjöld, 'The Development of a Constitutional Framework for International Cooperation', in Foote, *supra* note 3, at 251.

recognised the difficulties in developing these new 'rules' of international law based on peace and human rights. Indeed, he acknowledged that the endeavour 'may seem hopeless'.[40] Nevertheless, he was certain about the need to assert the law of the future, arguing that 'it would be treason to the future not to state the law simply because of the difficulties of the present'.[41] The obvious question concerns the extent to which international law has managed to live up to Hammarskjöld's expectations.

The concept of responsibility to protect was formally proposed in 'The Responsibility to Protect: The Report of the International Commission on Intervention and State Sovereignty' (ICISS) in 2001. It has been the subject of considerable academic and practical debate since then. It has been strongly endorsed in a number of subsequent reports and international instruments and has arguably moved from the status of an idea to an operational process. However, recent experiences in Libya and Syria have called into question both its conceptual significance and its practical relevance. More importantly for the present discussion, the legal status of the concept remains unsettled. In particular, the assertion by Gareth Evans, that the responsibility to protect might ultimately become a rule of customary international law, seems remote.

23.3.2 The normative status of the responsibility to protect

One of the most useful analyses of the normative status of the responsibility to protect is provided by Carsten Stahn.[42] Stahn has suggested that the idea of shared responsibility for the protection of civilians can be described in five propositions, each of which enjoys different levels of support. These are, first, that 'the host state has a duty to protect civilians on its territory'; second, that 'states failing the duty to protect have a weak sovereignty defence'; third, that 'foreign entities may intervene non-forcibly'; fourth, that 'foreign states may intervene forcibly'; and finally 'that foreign entities have a positive duty to act'.[43] Stahn makes clear that each of these propositions can be seen on a sliding scale of acceptance with the greatest support around the first proposition and the least, if any, around the last.[44]

It is submitted that the idea of 'responsibility' that is at the heart of this analysis is primarily one concerning liability-based responsibility and the

[40] Hammarskjöld, *supra* note 38, at 127. [41] *Ibid.*

[42] C. Stahn, 'Responsibility to Protect: Political Rhetoric or Emerging Legal Norm?' (2007) 101 *American Journal of International Law* 99.

[43] *Ibid.*, at 118–120. [44] *Ibid.*

extent of permitted responses to a breach of the primary responsibility of the host state to protect civilians on its territory. This primary duty, referred to as 'sovereignty as responsibility', will be considered later in this chapter. Stahn's remaining propositions constitute examples of possible countermeasures in response to a breach of that primary duty to protect. The legal basis for such countermeasures is contained in Article 54 of the Draft Articles on the Responsibility of States for Internationally Wrongful Acts with Commentaries, which provides that states other than an injured state may take lawful countermeasures against a breaching state to ensure cessation of the breach. This right to take countermeasures is directly linked to Article 48, paragraph 1 of those Articles.

If understood in this way, the argument about the normative status of the responsibility to protect could be considered as a reframing of the debate about the existence, or otherwise, of state responsibility for international crimes.[45] This is supported by the decision in the World Summit Outcome to limit the ambit of the responsibility to protect to four situations involving genocide, crimes against humanity, ethnic cleansing and war crimes, which constitute both crimes subject to individual criminal responsibility, and, for the most part, *jus cogens* norms. It is further supported by the direct linkage, in the discourse of responsibility to protect, between breach of the primary duty of protection and the jurisdiction of the International Criminal Court in respect of the individual criminal responsibility of state officials who are accused of committing the relevant crimes.[46]

This understanding of responsibility to protect as an example of liability responsibility is well illustrated by the example of the international response to the Libyan situation in the summer and autumn of 2011. It is apparent that even in relation to the 'commonly accepted proposition' of the responsible state attending to the needs and protection of its citizens, Libya has been allowed, over many years, to ignore its obligations under international law in relation to human rights protection and indeed in relation to its engagement in criminal activities directed against its citizens.[47] The Gaddafi regime could not ultimately rely on the sovereignty defence and yet the sovereignty of Libya remains intact and is cited as the

[45] For a critical review of the controversy over state responsibility for international crimes see Koskenniemi, *supra* note 27, at 48–49.

[46] See, for example, UN Doc. S/Res/1970 (2011).

[47] See, for example, the response of the United Nations Human Rights Committee to the fourth periodic review submitted by Libya (UN Doc. CCPR/C/LBY/4 (2007)) that was highly condemnatory of Libya's repeated failure to implement its previous recommendations. UN Doc. CCPR/C/LBY/CO/4 (2007).

primary justification for the cessation of UN action in Libya, in spite of questions being raised as to the activities of Transitional National Council forces dealing with detained Gaddafi loyalists. The 'intervention' in Libya was dependent upon a UN Security Council (UNSC) resolution – a good thing, one might say – as opposed to unilateral military action. But what led the UNSC to back the necessary resolution? Was it the need to protect the citizens of Benghazi? Yes to some extent, but it also depended on the support of the key regional body, the Arab League, as well as the almost depraved level of rhetoric from Gaddafi himself who threatened to hunt down like dogs those who opposed him and to wipe them out. Crucially, the result of intervention was nothing more than a holding to account of Gaddafi and his supporters. This was, in effect, the ultimate form of liability responsibility for the crimes of the Gaddafi regime, with the individual criminal responsibility of the key member of that regime being pursued under the rubric of international criminal law.

An alternative understanding of the meaning of responsibility within responsibility to protect is provided by Anne Orford. According to Orford, responsibility to protect should best be understood as 'a form of law that confers powers "of a public or official nature" and that allocates jurisdiction'.[48] Thus the 'responsibility' element of responsibility to protect becomes a question of public law relating to the allocation of responsibility between different actors. In making this argument, Orford draws directly on Hart's distinction between law that confers powers and law that imposes duties, as well as on Nollkaemper's constitutionalisation analysis referred to earlier in this chapter, to conclude that: 'The vocabulary of "responsibility" works here as a language for conferring authority and allocating powers rather than as a language for imposing obligations and commanding obedience.'[49]

Orford's analysis is to be welcomed, not least on the basis that it recognises Hammarskjöld's role in developing the powers of international executive action under the UN Charter and based on Articles 97–101 of the UN Charter.[50] For Orford, the development of international executive action by the United Nations occurred in practice during the process of decolonisation and beyond, but without the normative framework that the responsibility to protect now provides.[51] Building on the works of Thomas

[48] A. Orford, *International Authority and the Responsibility to Protect* (2011), 25.

[49] *Ibid.*, at 26. [50] See *ibid.*, 'Introduction'.

[51] Thus, according to Orford: 'Over time, the practices of executive action initiated by Hammarskjöld have led to the creation of a new form of administrative rule. As that form of rule began to be consolidated and centralised, it began to seem necessary to develop a

Hobbes and Carl Schmitt, Orford argues that the conceptual foundation for this new authority is not to be found in any framework of responsible behaviour but is, rather, grounded on the capacity to guarantee security and protection. While she recognises and details the authoritarian potential of the turn to protection, she argues, from a more optimistic perspective, that regarding responsibility to protect as the basis for international executive action provides a lens through which to assess and control the practice of international executive action.[52]

Unfortunately, the recent experience, of attempts by the international community to deal with repeated attacks on civilian populations and the apparently unrestrained commission of war crimes and crimes against humanity in Syria by Syrian government authorities, appears entirely to have undermined the concept of responsibility to protect. Like Libya, Syria has been allowed for many decades to ignore its human rights obligations.[53] In the face of massive human rights violations, the failure of the UN Security Council to pass a resolution supporting a military intervention against, or even a resolution condemning, the actions of the Syrian government appears to undermine the whole focus of the responsibility to protect.[54] It certainly goes against the claims of many that the introduction of a responsibility to protect would avoid situations akin to Rwanda, Srebrenica and Kosovo arising in the future where the international community had to sit back and watch atrocities taking place without being able to do anything about it. To be sure, regarding the responsibility to

full conceptualisation of the normative basis for executive authority … The responsibility to protect concept can best be understood as offering a normative grounding to the practices of international executive action that were initiated in the era of decolonisation and that have been gradually expanding ever since.' Orford, *supra* note 48, at 10–12.

52 *Ibid.*, at 210.

53 See, the response of the United Nations Human Rights Committee which condemned the failure by Syria to implement its previous recommendations on the occasion of the submission by Syria of its third periodic review to the UNHRC in 2004. UN Doc. CCPR/CO/84/SYR (2005).

54 On 4 October 2011 the UN Security Council voted on draft resolution S/2011/612. The draft was vetoed by China and the Russian Federation, and Brazil, India, Lebanon and South Africa abstained. UN Doc. S/PV.6627 (2011). On 4 February 2012 the UN Security Council voted on draft resolution S/2012/77. This second resolution, which took place at the time of the attack on the city of Homs was vetoed by China and the Russian Federation, while all of the other members of the Security Council voted in favour of the resolution. UN Doc. S/PV.6711 (2012). On 19 July 2012, the UN Security Council voted on draft resolution S/2012/538. This third draft resolution was vetoed by China and the Russian Federation, with Pakistan and South Africa abstaining. UN Doc. S/PV.6810 (2012). On the destruction of Syria's chemical weapon's programme, see Resolution 2118 (2013) of 27 September 2013.

protect as a mechanism for the allocation of responsibilities strengthens the claim of the United Nations to involve itself in the dispute. However, without the required institutional power to operationalise the responsibility to protect and overcome the sovereignty claims of Syria, it is questionable how responsible the responsibility to protect is.

Furthermore, the notion of responsibility in the context of both Libya and Syria appears increasingly complex and gives rise to conflicting responsibilities. In terms of the possibility of intervention, to prevent genocide, crimes against humanity, ethnic cleansing or war crimes, any sense of there being a 'responsibility' is wholly undermined by the legal prohibition against intervention, except where authorised by the United Nations Security Council. In the case of Libya, many factors rather fortuitously came together to bring about the passing of UNSC Resolution 1373, which 'legalised' the NATO-led intervention in that state. However, drawing on the assertions made above, it is at least questionable whether the primary motivation for NATO's intervention in Libya constituted an example of the prospective shared responsibility of the international community to protect Libyan nationals. It was, instead, an example of retrospective liability responsibility designed to punish (and ultimately to depose) the Gaddafi regime. In the case of Syria, the effect of the failure of the Security Council to pass a resolution authorising intervention was to ensure that the *legal* responsibility on states and other international actors was *not* to intervene, even in the face of substantial human rights violations taking place against the civilian populations of parts of Syria. To this extent, it might reasonably be argued that international law, far from providing a normative framework for the development of a responsibility to protect, in fact constitutes a significant barrier to the implementation of the concept.

So where does this leave the broader notion of 'responsibility' in international law? In a trenchant critique of the concept of responsibility in his 2007 book, *Law and Irresponsibility: On the Legitimation of Human Suffering*, Scott Veitch argues generally that far from providing for responsible behaviour, law generally, and international law in particular, legitimates human suffering. In what is an extremely challenging and uncomfortable analysis, Veitch cites a range of examples of where international law legitimates human suffering, including, for example, the sanctions regime, as well as the failure of international law to deal with gross violations of human rights.[55] The use of force in international law is

[55] S. Veitch, *Law and Irresponsiblity: On the Legitimation of Human Suffering* (2007), 2.

capable of providing great misery and even in the aftermath of the 'successful' Libyan intervention, the cost to human life remains unclear. Iraq and Afghanistan provide two recent examples of the suffering caused by arguably 'responsible behaviour'. On the other hand, the failure to intervene in Syria has arguably caused greater suffering than intervention would have done. Thus, the idea of responsibility has, at best, failed to provide any answers; at worst, it has proliferated suffering, particularly in the decolonised world.

For Veitch, the concept of responsibility is one that has no core meaning and indeed is fragmented and always has been so.[56] Each invocation of responsibility involves particular forms and functions that are not subject to philosophical inquiry and which are subject to manipulation.[57] Thus, Veitch argues that far from organising responsibility, 'legal institutions are centrally involved in organising irresponsibility'.[58] He continues:

> In order to understand the asymmetries between suffering and the ability to establish responsibility for it, we must understand how these very 'technologies of responsibility' themselves, as part of the broader social forms of power, also provide some of the major resources through which dispersals and disavowals of responsibility in society can occur. It is through analysing the complicitous relationship with these broader forms of power – in their diversions and distinctions, their priorities and interests – that we will come to a fuller understanding of the proliferation of irresponsibilities in the rise of responsibilities.[59]

23.4 Re-imagining 'responsibility' in international law

In light of this analysis, it might seem prudent to assert simply that international law should steer clear of a 'responsibility' discourse, both generally and more specifically in relation to the responsibility to protect. On the contrary, however, it will be argued here that a 'responsibility' discourse has an important role to play in the future development of international law, especially beyond the traditional focus of responsibility as liability. Rather than being concerned with the question of liability or the distribution of responsibilities in international law, the focus here will be on the role of law in securing responsible behaviour.

In pursuing the question of how to secure responsible behaviour, many scholars are willing to look beyond the admittedly substantial empirical evidence that states only act in rational self-interest, to look

[56] *Ibid.*, at 38. [57] *Ibid.*, at 39–40. [58] *Ibid.*, at 1. [59] *Ibid.*, at 41.

to the possibilities for states and the international community to take responsibility for the well-being of others. Communitarian scholars, such as Amitai Ezioni, look to the shared norms and social values of communities, including the international community of states.[60] This is taken a stage further by scholars concerned with the notion of solidarity, including Ronald St John Macdonald[61] and Karel Wellens[62] who argue that solidarity is a fundamental principle of cooperation in international law 'which identifies as the goal of joint and separate state action an outcome that benefits all states or at least does not gravely interfere with the interests of other states'.[63] This is further developed by Laurence Boisson de Chazournes who defines solidarity as 'a form of help given by some actors to other actors in order to assist the latter ... to recover from a critical situation',[64] and asserts that solidarity and responsibility to protect can be regarded as 'matched notions'[65] that are intertwined. Indeed she asserts that 'the notion of responsibility to protect ... [can] be considered as one of the forms that international solidarity can take'.[66] However, even if solidarity can properly be regarded as a structural principle of international law,[67] it is not yet itself a positive obligation of international law, but rather a moral obligation.[68] Accordingly, it adds little to the sense of there being a legal obligation on states, either to act in solidarity with one another or to act responsibly towards one another.

Of course, many positive rules of international law are aimed at securing responsible behaviour in international relations, for example through the development of human rights, humanitarian law, international

[60] See A. Etzioni, *New Communitarian Thinking: Persons, Virtues, Institutions and Communities* (1995).

[61] See R. St. John Macdonald, 'Solidarity in the Practice and Discourse of Public International Law' (1996) 8 *Pace International Law Review* 259.

[62] See K. Wellens, 'Solidarity as a Constitutional Principle: Its Expanding Role and Inherent Limitations', in R. St. John Macdonald and D. Johnston (eds.), *Towards World Constitutionalism: Issues in the Legal Ordering of the World Community* (2005), 775; and K. Wellens, 'Revisiting Solidarity as a (Re-)Emerging Constitutional Principle: Some Further Reflections', in R. Wolfrum and C. Kojima (eds.), *Solidarity: A Structural Principle of International Law* (2010), 3.

[63] R. St. John Macdonald, *supra* note 61, at 259–260.

[64] L. Boisson de Chazournes, 'Responsibility to Protect: Reflecting Solidarity?', in R. Wolfrum and C. Kojima (eds.), *Solidarity: A Structural Principle of International Law* (2010), 93 at 94.

[65] *Ibid.*, at 102. [66] *Ibid.*

[67] See UN Doc. A/RES /151 (LVI) and UN Doc. A/RES/213 (LVII).

[68] Boisson de Chazournes, *supra* note 64, at 95.

environmental law and international criminal law. On the other hand, the practice of international law remains firmly state-centric, having at its core the notion of state sovereignty.[69] This has always caused difficulty in international law in relation to the balancing of state interests with both the interests of individual human beings as well as the interests of the international community. In this final section it will be argued, first, that international law has an important role in determining and delimiting prospective or future responsibilities, especially those relating to the protection and security of human beings. Second, it will be argued that the moral theory of ethics of care should be considered as a possible basis for the development of international law relating to the future responsibilities of the international community.

23.4.1 The importance of prospective responsibility

In a seminal article, H.L.A. Hart proposed a taxonomy of responsibilities which included not only liability responsibility, which he considered as being 'the primary sense of responsibility', but also other senses of responsibility, 'variously derived from this primary sense of liability-responsibility', which include role responsibility, causal responsibility and capacity responsibility.[70] Causal and capacity responsibility are directly linked to liability responsibility insofar as the idea of being '"responsible for" should be used to signify causal connection and the possession of these capacities outside contexts of blame and punishment',[71] or, in other words, outside the context merely of liability, but inherently linked to it. However, the notion of role responsibility seems to suggest something separate from liability responsibility. It suggests that responsibility can be prospective as well as historical. Thus, according to Hart:

> whenever a person occupies a distinctive place or office in a social organisation to which specific duties are attached to provide for the welfare of others, or to advance in some specific way the aims or purposes of the organisation, he is properly said to be responsible for the performance of those duties or doing what is necessary to fulfil them.[72]

[69] See *Jurisdictional Immunities of the State (Germany* v. *Italy: Greece intervening)*, Merits, Judgment of 3 February 2012 (not yet published) (Judge Trinidade, Dissenting Opinion).

[70] H. Hart, 'Varieties of Responsibility' (1967) 83 *Law Quarterly Review* 346, at 363.

[71] *Ibid.* [72] *Ibid.*, at 347.

The problem here is in distinguishing specific legal duties, linked to a particular role, from what might be considered as the 'responsibilities' of a particular role. Hart indicates that he thinks, though he is admittedly not sure, that what distinguishes duties from responsibilities is that the latter are 'duties of a relatively complex or extensive kind, defining a "sphere of responsibility" requiring the exercise of discretion and care usually over a protracted period of time'.[73]

In the context of the present discussion, it seems clear that Orford's analysis of responsibility to protect as a mechanism for the conferring authority and allocating powers is a prime example of role responsibility insofar as it assigns responsibilities[74] between states, who are 'responsible for their own citizens and populations' and the United Nations, 'which is responsible for the international community as a whole'.[75] As noted above, according to Orford, the determinant factor in terms of securing responsible behaviour is the ability to provide protection and security. For Hart, the mere delimitation of responsibilities appears to be sufficient to secure responsible behaviour in so far as a responsible person is one who takes his role seriously, thus he asserts that:

> A 'responsible person,' 'behaving responsibly' (not 'irresponsibly') requires for their elucidation a reference to role-responsibility. A responsible person is one who is disposed to take his duties seriously; to think about them, and to make serious efforts to fulfil them. To behave responsibly is to behave as a man would who took his duties in this serious way.[76]

But is this enough? Cane too draws a distinction between historic responsibility covering ideas such as answerability, accountability and liability, and what he refers to as 'prospective responsibility' which encompasses the 'roles and tasks [that] look to the future, and establish obligations and duties'.[77] Cane considers prospective responsibility to be a much more important element in the concept of legal responsibility than does Hart. For Hart, prospective responsibility is merely a mechanism leading to the attribution of primary responsibility, that is, liability. Thus, he concludes his article by noting that:

73 *Ibid.*

74 D. Miller, 'The Responsibility to Protect Human Rights', in L. Meyer (ed.), *Legitimacy, Justice and Public International Law* (2009), 232 at 235.

75 Orford, *supra* note 48, at 27.

76 Hart, *supra* note 70, at 348.

77 Cane, *supra* note 10, at 31.

> Role responsibility is perhaps less directly derivable from the primary sense of liability-responsibility: the connection is that the occupant of a role is contingently responsible in the primary sense if he fails to fulfil the duties which define his role and which are his responsibilities.[78]

Cane is critical of this limited understanding of the importance of prospective responsibility.

Cane argues that prospective responsibilities can be divided into two categories: 'productive' responsibilities that are directed to the production of good outcomes; and 'preventive' responsibilities directed to the prevention of bad ones, with this latter category possibly including 'protective' responsibilities.[79] In relation to all of these categories of prospective responsibilities, Cane accepts that 'the idea of responsibility does not provide a complete conceptual apparatus for analysing the law's productive, preventive and protective functions', but that concepts such as rights and powers are also required.[80] Nevertheless, he argues that this does not mean that prospective responsibility is less valuable than historic responsibility, and, in fact, that historic responsibility is dependent upon prospective responsibility.[81]

According to Cane, the failure of responsibility narratives that focus primarily on historic responsibility is that they pay insufficient attention to the law-making institutions and, thus, 'the facilitation of cooperative and productive behaviour'.[82] As he notes: 'A well-functioning and successful legal system is one in which non-compliance with prospective responsibilities, and hence occasions for the imposition of historic responsibility, are minimised.'[83] Crucially, for Cane, it is at the level of law-making that the lack of responsibility is most apparent. As Cane notes of law generally, '[responsibility] is rarely an "active ingredient" in legal rules'.[84] This is particularly the case in relation to international law, especially in relation to the idea of sovereignty as responsibility.

[78] Hart, *supra* note 70, at 364.

[79] Cane, *supra* note 10, at 31–32. [80] *Ibid.*, at 34.

[81] Cane notes that 'there is an important sense in which historic legal responsibility is parasitic on and subsidiary to prospective legal responsibility. Historic responsibility enforces, reinforces and underwrites prospective responsibility. Historic responsibility is not an end in itself, but only a means to the various ends the law seeks to further by creating and imposing prospective responsibilities. Historic responsibility, we might say, is the pathological form of legal responsibility'. *Ibid.*, at 35.

[82] *Ibid.*, at 34. [83] *Ibid.*, at 35. [84] *Ibid.*, at 1.

23.4.2 *'Sovereignty as responsibility' as an example of prospective responsibility?*

The International Commission on Intervention and State Sovereignty recognised the importance of state sovereignty to narratives of international law when first proposing the concept of responsibility to protect. It sought to reformulate sovereignty into two concepts revolving around the idea of responsibility, noting that:

> sovereignty implies a dual responsibility: externally – to respect the sovereignty of other states, and internally, to respect the dignity and basic rights of all the people within the state. In international human rights covenants, in UN practice, and in state practice itself, sovereignty is now understood as embracing this dual responsibility. Sovereignty as responsibility has become the minimum content of good international citizenship.[85]

If this is correct, then, as suggested above in relation to the Libya intervention, sovereignty as responsibility may constitute the primary rule of international law, or at least its component parts may collectively constitute primary rules of international law, from which liability responsibility might flow. However, given the atrocities committed in Libya and Syria, as well as the many other human rights atrocities committed by governments against their citizens that occur around the world on a regular basis, it is questionable whether there is, indeed, any acceptance of this reformulation of sovereignty as responsibility. Indeed, far from supporting the idea of an existing or even emerging norm of sovereignty as responsibility, state practice around the concept of responsibility to protect appears significantly to limit the key foundational principle of sovereignty as responsibility. This is most clearly apparent from the wording of the World Summit Outcome in 2005, subsequently considered by the UN General Assembly. Paragraph 138 of that document, which has somewhat tersely been described by Gareth Evans as 'quite strong',[86] far from endorsing the idea of sovereignty as responsibility, accepts a fundamentally more limited commitment in the following terms:

[85] International Commission on Intervention and State Sovereignty 2001. The Responsibility to Protect. Available at: http://responsibilitytoprotect.org/ICISS%20Report.pdf (ICISS Report).

[86] G. Evans, 'From Humanitarian Intervention to The Responsibility to Protect' (2006) 24 *Wisconsin International Law Journal* 703, at 715

> Each individual State has the responsibility to protect its populations from genocide, war crimes, ethnic cleansing and crimes against humanity. This responsibility entails the prevention of such crimes, including their incitement, through appropriate and necessary means. We accept that responsibility and will act in accordance with it.[87]

It is clear from this language that states were unwilling to commit to anything more than a responsibility to protect populations from the four listed crimes. Although the resolution refers to the prevention of these crimes, it is only genocide which clearly includes within its legal parameters, any form of duty to prevent. It is of course possible to argue that, although the World Summit Outcome takes the form of a General Assembly resolution, it is, nevertheless, evidence of customary international law and is therefore sufficient to infer an obligation on states to prevent war crimes, ethnic cleansing and crimes against humanity as well. In terms of there being an obligation on states not to commit these crimes, the International Court of Justice accepted in the *Bosnian Genocide Case* that 'the obligation to prevent genocide necessarily implies the prohibition of the commission of genocide [by states]'.[88] The logic of this analysis should equally apply to the other three crimes, if a legal obligation to prevent can be established. But this is not the key issue for the purposes of this present argument. The key issue concerns the fact that the approval of the concept of sovereignty as responsibility accepted by states in the World Summit Outcome falls significantly short of the notion of sovereignty as responsibility envisaged in the Report of the International Commission on Intervention and State Sovereignty, which had been proposed a mere four years earlier.

To be sure, the concept of sovereignty as responsibility had been mooted before the invocation of the concept by the ICISS. Francis Deng and his colleagues at the Brookings Institute had developed the concept during the 1990s and produced a book in 1996.[89] It would seem from the ICISS report that much of their thinking was significantly influenced by this work. However, the ideas in the book not only appear aspirational, they in fact conflict with existing and long established rules of international law. Thus, the assertion that 'sovereignty carries with it responsibilities for the

[87] UN Doc. A/RES/1 (LX).

[88] *Application of the Convention for the Prevention and Punishment of the Crimes of Genocide (Bosnia-Herzegovina* v. *Serbia and Montenegro)*, Merits, Judgment of 26 February 2007, [2007] ICJ Rep. 43, para. 166.

[89] For the notable exception here, see F. Deng, D. Rothchild, I.W. Zartman, S. Kimaro and T. Lyons, *Sovereignty as Responsibility: Conflict Management in Africa* (1996).

population' may be generally recognised, but the assertion arising therefrom that 'it is from this acceptance that the legitimacy of a government derives' is of questionable validity in international law.[90] Similarly, the assertion that 'the validity of sovereignty must be judged by reasonable standards of how much of the population is represented, marginalized or excluded'[91] is not supported by existing rules of international law dealing with matters of statehood and recognition (although some developments towards such a position are visible). Finally, by way of example, the call for the dominant power or authority in a state to 'assume responsibilities that transcend parochialism or exclusive national interests ... and serves the broader interests of the community'[92] would be better secured by the development of relevant laws supporting such an aspiration.

This is not to suggest that international law is incapable of responding to calls such as these; it is merely to point out, in support of Cane's assertion, that insufficient attention has been paid so far to the development of prospective responsibilities in international law that support the notion of sovereignty as responsibility. Of course one might argue that the combination of primary and secondary rules in any legal system, including international law, may be enough to secure responsible behaviour. Thus, the primary rules provide for the desired outcome while the law of secondary rules provides for liability in the event of a breach or, where appropriate, non-breach, whether through act or omission. The combination of the two serves as a facilitator of responsible behaviour, or at least behaviour that is in compliance with the legally agreed expectations. Merely signing up to international agreements may be enough. Additionally, a range of 'responsibility mechanisms' already exists in international law. These include diplomatic methods, such as negotiation – states holding each other to account by reference to legal obligations often before the violations occur – as well as other, more centrally organised governance mechanisms, such as, the various human rights bodies associated with the monitoring of the implementation of key human rights conventions.

A particularly important development in this regard is the creation of the system of universal periodic review.[93] According to the UN website:

> The UPR [Universal Periodic Review] is one of the key elements of the new Council which reminds States of their responsibility to fully respect and implement all human rights and fundamental freedoms. The ultimate

[90] *Ibid.*, at 32. [91] *Ibid.* [92] *Ibid.*, at 33.
[93] See UN Doc. A/RES/251 (LX).

aim of this new mechanism is to improve the human rights situation in all countries and address human rights violations wherever they occur.[94]

Although directed to addressing human rights violations, the process is prospective in so far as it does not wait for such violations to occur. Accordingly, one way to address the perceived limitations of responsibility, and, in particular, prospective responsibility in the context of international law, is through the further development of governance mechanisms such as these.

Nevertheless, although many rules and processes exist in international law aimed at ensuring a minimum level of human rights protection in all states, it remains the case that international law is extremely limited in the ways in which it can ensure that states comply with human rights norms, even the most basic norms of security and protection from fear enunciated by Hammarskjöld. Ten years after the creation of the responsibility to protect, the central component of sovereignty as responsibility has yet to be fully analysed and theorised. This chapter is, to some extent, a call for work on the concept of sovereignty as responsibility to become a much more important and focused discourse in international law.

23.4.3 'Responsibility' and the ethic of care

As has been noted above, the concept of responsibility is not unique to international law. It is a concept that has been explored and analysed in many different areas of domestic law, most notably in the realm of criminal law, but increasingly also in other areas of domestic law that are, in a similar way to international law, seeking to move away from the idea that responsibility is best understood as a form of liability. One area in which this has been most apparent has been in the area of family law.

Family scholars have, for some time, sought to re-direct the law from a 'rights'-based model to one based on responsibility and connection.[95] Thus, according to Katherine Bartlett, writing in the context of parenthood, 'the law should focus on parental responsibility rather than reciprocal "rights" and express a view of parenthood based on the cycle of gift rather than the cycle of exchange'.[96] The positive conception of

[94] See www.ohchr.org/en/hrbodies/upr/pages/uprmain.aspx.

[95] See, for example, K. Bartlett, 'Re-Expressing Parenthood' (1988) 98 *Yale Law Journal* 293.

[96] *Ibid.*, at 295. According to Bartlett, the parents-as-exchange model is premised on the notion that 'Parents have rights with respect to their children in exchange for the performance of their parental responsibilities. As in the case with other individual rights

responsibility as involving both obligation and freedom to act is highlighted by Bartlett in the following way:

> [R]esponsibility means more than fulfilling some precise set of predefined role requirements. A responsible person cares not only about doing 'her part' (or 'his part') in a limited sense, but also about outcome, and is disposed toward expanding or perhaps re-defining the demands of role as necessary to accomplish that outcome. Responsibility, in other words, is a self-enlarging, open-ended commitment on behalf of another.[97]

Scholars concerned with the concept of responsibility in family law, have highlighted the importance of considering responsibility as a relational concept. Thus, according to Bartlett:

> [a]lthough some notions of social responsibility have associated duty or obligation with individual autonomy, responsibility … is grounded in relationship rather than autonomy. Responsibility describes a certain type of connection that persons may experience in their relationships with one another.[98]

Drawing on Cane's insight that responsibility 'concerns the three-way relationship between agents, "victims" and the wider community',[99] three leading family law scholars have, more recently, argued that 'there is much for the family lawyer to consider in an approach that sees responsibility as prospective, contextual and relational'.[100] Taking this a stage further, these and other family law scholars have pointed to the importance of care as an element in the conceptualisation of responsibility within families.[101] Bringing the idea of responsibility as a relational concept together with the importance of the caring, Jo Bridgeman has suggested that 'we can understand, conceptualize and develop a discourse of responsibility in relationships and within family life through a conceptual framework

claims, parents asserting rights to children tend to emphasise what is due to them rather than what they owe to others … The rights generated within this view stress entitlement over responsibility, autonomy over connectedness, self over others'. *Ibid.*, at 297–298.

[97] *Ibid.*, at 199. [98] *Ibid.*, at 299.

[99] Cane, *supra* note 10, at 56.

[100] J. Bridgeman, H. Keating and C. Lind, *Responsibility, Law and the Family* (2008), 6.

[101] See, for example, J. Eekelaar, 'Are Parents Morally Obliged to Care for their Children?' (1991) 11 *Oxford Journal of Legal Studies* 340. See also, J. Tronto, *Moral Boundaries: The Political Argument for an Ethic of Care* (1993); M. Maclean and J. Eekelaar, *The Parental Obligation* (1997); M. Fineman, *The Autonomy Myth: A Theory of Dependency* (2004); Bridgeman *et al.*, *supra* note 100; and, C. Lind, H. Keating and J. Bridgeman, *Taking Responsibility, Law and the Changing Family* (2011).

of relational responsibilities, derived from the feminist ethic of care'.[102] If the use of the concept of responsibility in international law is to move beyond the historic notion of liability and is to be more productive than merely existing as a tool for the development of prospective responsibility mechanisms, then international lawyers might draw on these insights from domestic law and pay more attention to the relational aspects of responsibility.

The moral theory of ethic of care developed as a feminist alternative to dominant moral approaches, such as Kantian moral theory, utilitarianism or virtue ethics.[103] For Carol Gilligan, the ethic of care signifies 'the different voice of women', as does 'the tie between relationship and responsibility'.[104] More controversially, for Sara Ruddick, the idea of caring is best symbolised through 'the work of mothering'.[105] It is centrally focused on 'the compelling moral salience of attending to and meeting the needs of particular others for whom we take responsibility'.[106] Furthermore, according to Held:

> Among the characteristics of the ethics of care is its view of persons as rational and interdependent … the ethics of care sees persons as enmeshed in relations with others. It pays attention primarily to relations between persons, valuing especially caring relationships … but the ethics of care is not limited to such contexts. It understands how our ties to various social groups and our historic embededness are also part of what makes us who we are.[107]

The theory has often been conceptualised as an alternative to ethics of justice, although it has been highlighted that both justice (dealing with questions of equality and inequality) and care (dealing with questions of attachment and detachment) can arise in any context.[108] The theory has

[102] J. Bridgeman, 'Parental Responsibility, Responsible Parenting and Legal Regulation', in Bridgeman *et al.*, *supra* note 100, 234 at 243.

[103] V. Held, *The Ethics of Care* (2006), 3–4.

[104] C. Gilligan, *In a Different Voice: Psychological Theory and Women's Development* (1982), 173

[105] S. Ruddick, *Maternal Thinking: Towards a Politics of Peace* (1989), *passim*.

[106] Held, *supra* note 103, at 10. [107] *Ibid.*

[108] G. Clement, *Care, Autonomy, and Justice: Feminism and the Ethics of Care* (1996), 1. Carol Gilligan notes that, 'All human relationships, public and private, can be characterized *both* in terms of equality and in terms of attachment, and … both inequality and detachment constitute grounds for moral concern. Since everyone is vulnerable both to oppression and to abandonment, two moral visions – one of justice and one of care – recur in human experience. The moral injunctions, not to act unfairly toward others, and not to turn away from someone in need, capture these different concerns'. C.

been criticised by some feminists on the grounds that 'the ethics of care amounts to a resuscitation of traditional stereotypes of women, stereotypes which are used to rationalize the subordination of women'.[109] On the other hand, as Clement makes clear, while use of the ethic of care can be 'distorted … we can look for the moral and political possibilities implicit in the ethic of care while actively addressing its dangers'.

The idea of ethic of care being limited to motherhood and, indeed, to women, has been gradually discarded, partially as a response to the feminist criticisms outlined above. Similarly, the focus of the ethic of care has moved away from the personal and parochial in order to address large-scale social or global problems.[110] Thus, according to Held, '[the ethic of care] has been developed as a moral theory relevant not only to the so-called private realms of family and friendship but to medical practice, law, political life, the organization of society, war and international relations'.[111] Similarly, Fiona Robinson has argued that the values of a 'critical ethics of care' are relevant not only 'to small-scale or existing personal attachments but to all levels of social relations and, thus, to international or global relations'.[112] Building on this assertion, Robinson has applied the ethic of care directly to humanitarian intervention.[113] More recently, Daniel Engster, although rather surprisingly not referring directly to responsibility to protect, has provided an analysis of the relevance of 'care theory' to that concept and, in particular, the 'residual responsibility' of the international community to secure the rights of people within states that have failed in their primary duty to do so.[114] Thus, he asserts

Gilligan, 'Moral Orientation and Moral Development', in E. Kittay and D. Meyers (eds.), *Women and Moral Theory* (1987), 20.

109 Clement, *supra* note 108, at 6.

110 F. Robinson, *Globalizing Care: Ethics, Feminist Theory and International Relations* (1999), 2.

111 Clement, *supra* note 108, at 9.

112 Robinson, *supra* note 110, at 2. 113 *Ibid.*, at 142–146.

114 D. Engster, *The Heart of Justice* (2007), 166. Engster moves beyond the feminist foundations of ethic of care and has conceptualized ethic of care or 'care theory' as a reciprocal concept built upon shared needs and experiences. Thus, according to Engster: 'We all make (or at least have made or will make) claims on others to help us survive, develop and function. No one could survive, develop or function during infancy, grave illness, disability, frail old age, or other periods of particular hardship without the care of other human beings. We all further depend on the care of others to sustain the social network that we require to survive and function. In attempting to justify our claims for care on others, we have all implicitly appealed to the general moral principle that capable individuals should care for individuals in need when they are able to do so. Because we have all necessarily appealed to this moral principle, we may all be said to recognize it

that '[u]nder care theory, individuals and governments have a responsibility to provide resources and other forms of support to distant people when distant peoples and their governments are unable to support their survival, development and functioning by their own means'.[115]

Of course it may be that proponents of the ethic of care expect too much of governments and their leaders. In setting up care and responsibility in this way, the suggestion is that there is a universal obligation on states to intervene, by whatever means possible, to provide for the survival, development and functioning of distant others. This does little to advance us beyond the narrow conceptualisation of responsibility and, in particular, responsibility to protect as it is currently understood. Indeed, it is probably the case that, in its current state of development, it is unrealistic to expect the ethics of care to be taken seriously in international law discourse. Thus one response to this discourse is simply to assert that states are rational self-interested actors and to expect more of them is folly, as is asserted by Jack Goldsmith and Eric Posner, among many others.[116] If this is right, then not only the ethic of care but also the concept of responsibility itself is truly limited in international law. On the other hand, it is clear that the notion of taking responsibility for others and the idea of caring for those in need underpinned the thinking of the developers of the responsibility to protect concept as it also underpins the thinking of many other scholars and practitioners within the realm of international law and international relations more generally. Most notably, for present purposes, it is clear that Dag Hammarskjöld cared. He cared about the plight of individuals in war-torn countries and was clear about the responsibility of the international community to help those in need, particularly those whose own government was unable to provide security and human rights.

Responsibility and the ethic of care are not the panacea to the world's troubles. They cannot, and indeed, can never be seen as the basis of international legal obligations to intervene in every case of state failure to protect their citizens, not least because in many cases, the responsible thing to do might be not to intervene, particularly if this involves military

as valid; and if we all recognize this principle as valid, then we should – out of a sense of consistency and morality – recognize and respond to the claims of other individuals in need for care when we can help them. We behave hypocritically and inconsistently when we refuse to care for individuals whom we are capable of helping and violate our own implicit moral beliefs.' *Ibid.*, at 166.

115 *Ibid.*, at 171.

116 See, generally, J. Goldsmith and E. Posner, *The Limits of International Law* (2005).

intervention. Furthermore, as noted above, the ethic of care is not without its critics, nor indeed without its dangers. Specifically, the ethic of care, if misused, can be seen as paternalistic, if not imperialistic. It is therefore important in developing a discourse of responsibility and care that these dangers are identified and addressed in order to ensure that 'morally admirable impulses to help are not naïve and misplaced but do lead to effective care'.[117] Nevertheless, notions of responsibility and the ethic of care can provide a lens through which to further develop international law, particularly in the face of massive human rights atrocities and the violation of established international criminal law norms. From the perspective of the development of international law more specifically, regarding responsibility as a relational concept derived from the ethic of care provides a framework for the further development of prospective responsibilities.

As well as being a relational concept, responsibility is also, as a result, multi-layered. Thus, where no relationship exists between individuals or states, then responsibility can legitimately be considered to be lower than where a relationship is apparent. If we are properly to speak about responsibility in international law there are many questions that we must address. For example, what responsibilities do we in fact owe to distant others? What is the basis of those responsibilities? On what basis can those responsibilities be established in morality or, indeed, in law? What is the role of law in strengthening such responsibilities? In the case of the responsibility to protect, we should seek to move away from the idea of a single responsibility and consider in more depth specific responsibilities inherent in the concept. For example, does the responsibility of the international community actually mean the responsibility of a specific organisation such as the UN? What are the responsibilities of individual states in this context? In particular, and in light of the experiences in Libya and Syria, what are the responsibilities, if any, of the permanent five members of the UNSC? It is not intended here to address these specific questions. Rather the intention is to highlight the limits of the present responsibilities discourse and call for further analysis of what actually is meant by the concept of responsibility in international law.

[117] Held, *supra* note 103, at 165.

23.5 Conclusion

The concept of 'responsibility' is at the heart of international law. However, it is generally regarded as a mode of securing liability or as a mechanism for the allocation of responsibilities within international law. This chapter, by analysing the emerging discourses of 'responsibility' in international law, in particular the concept of responsibility to protect, has imagined a broader role for the concept of responsibility in international law. Drawing on discourses in family law and feminist scholarship around the ethic of care, it has been argued that if responsibility is to move from the historic to the prospective, in terms of securing responsible behaviour, more attention should be paid to the role of responsibility as a relational concept giving rise to various levels of responsibility. These levels of responsibility can be strengthened by the development of prospective obligations within the law, but also depend on moral commitment.

Throughout this chapter, reference has been made to the ideas and work of Dag Hammarskjöld. Hammarskjöld would have recognised the significant developments in international legal discourse since 1961 and would have been pleased by the continued relevance and importance of the UN as an actor within international relations. Nevertheless, he would be disappointed at how little had changed in relation to the specific development of the responsibilities of both states to their own citizens and the residual responsibility of the international community for the protection of citizens not protected by their own governments. The purpose of this chapter has been to highlight the limitations of the concept of responsibility in international law as well as the need for further development of a number of elements of responsibilities discourse in international law. They relate particularly to the attempt to reconfigure sovereignty, from 'sovereignty as control' to 'sovereignty as responsibility', and the conceptualisation and development of the broader responsibility of the international community to support the survival, development and basic functioning of all citizens. It is asserted that one way to address these limitations is to analyse and conceptualise responsibility in international law through the lens of the ethic of care.

24

Libya, intervention and responsibility

The dawn of a new era?

FRANCIS KOFI ABIEW AND NOEMI GAL-OR

24.1 Introduction

Previous chapters (e.g. Chapters 9, 10 and 23) have examined the link between Dag Hammarskjöld, intervention and the Responsibility to Protect (R2P). This chapter examines a contemporary example of the tension between the protection of human rights and military action, namely the international response to Libya, and its implications.

The popular revolutions sweeping across North Africa and the Middle East in recent times give pause for thought and raise numerous questions relating to governance and the shaping of the future of the entire region. Even as the situations in Egypt, Yemen, Bahrain and Syria remain tenuous and seem to take a turn for the worse with brutal crackdowns, particularly troubling has been the situation in Libya, which Fouad Ajami describes as a 'penal colony' run by Gaddafi for the past forty-two years.

The contagion effect of protests in Tunisia and Egypt saw the Libyan people similarly embark on protests denouncing and demanding the departure of Colonel Muammar Gaddafi from power. Instead of responding to the peaceful demonstrations by meeting the legitimate aspirations and demands of his people, he chose further repression that signalled going down a one-way street of brutally killing his own people.[1] The Colonel's aggressive military campaign against the protesters resulted in the scattered opposition metamorphosing into a revolt against his regime; the emerging Libya Transitional National Council, the rebel group, then took over a few towns with intentions of marching on Tripoli.

Francis Kofi Abiew is Professor at the Department of Political Science, Kwantlen Polytechnic University, Vancouver. Noemi Gal-Or is Professor at the Department of Political Science, Kwantlen Polytechnic University and Director of the University's Institute for Transborder Studies.

[1] SC Res. 1970 (2011), UN Doc. S/RES/1970 (2011).

Ultimately, the Gaddafi regime began a campaign of brutal crackdown, notably including assaults from the air, re-capturing those cities. As the Gaddafi forces, which included mercenaries, edged closer to the city of Benghazi, the rebel stronghold, there were calls from both inside and outside Libya to impose a 'no-fly zone' over Libya to forestall a debacle, given the utterances of Gaddafi himself that he would show the residents of Benghazi who opposed him no mercy and no pity. In the context of these developments,[2] the United Nations (UN) Security Council, on 17 March 2011, passed Resolution 1973[3] which authorised the use of military force. Consequently, acting on this resolution, coalition forces including the United States, France, the UK, Canada and Italy, with the support of the Arab League and African Union,[4] on 19 March 2011, began initial air strikes and the launching of tomahawk missiles against Libya in an action dubbed 'Operation Odyssey Dawn' to implement the no-fly zone. The command and control of the mission was subsequently transferred to the North Atlantic Treaty Organisation (NATO) which took over and carried on with operation 'Unified Protector'. In the wake of over 26,500 sorties, including over 9,700 strike sorties,[5] and facilitating the rebel's ground combat, Gaddafi's forty-two-year regime was finally toppled, culminating in his death on 20 October 2011.[6] The struggle to liberate Libya concluded decidedly faster than anticipated, yet has still to translate into a safe, just and stable regime for all Libyans.

However, besides the geopolitical ramifications of the UN-authorised NATO military action, two questions of cardinal significance have emerged in juxtaposition as never before: how should the UN implement

[2] On 12 March 2011, the Arab League adopted a resolution calling on the UN Security Council to impose a no-fly zone over Libya. Reuters, 12 March 2011, http://uk.reuters.com/article/2011/03/12/uk-libya-idUKLDE71Q0MP20110312. The African Union opposed this approach: 'African Union Rejects Foreign Military Intervention in Libya', 12 March 2011, MYWEKU, www.myweku.com/2011/03/african-union-rejects-foreign-military-intervention-in-libya/.

[3] SC Res. 1973 (2011), UN Doc. S/RES/1973 (2011) (ten in favour to none against, with five abstentions – Brazil, China, Germany, India, Russian Federation).

[4] African Union, Peace and Security Council 268th Meeting, Addis Ababa, Ethiopia, PSC/PR/BR.1/(CCLXViii), 23 March 2011, www.au.int/en/sites/default/files/268th_FINAL_Press_Statement_-_Libya__EN.pdf.

[5] 'Operation Unified Protector Final Mission Stats. 02 November 2011', NATO, www.nato.int/nato_static/assets/pdf/pdf_2011_11/20111108_111107-factsheet_up_factsfigures_en.pdf [hereafter: NATO Final Mission Stats].

[6] G. Galloway, 'Canada Begins to Wind Down Mission in Wake of Gadhafi's Demise', *Globe and Mail*, 20 October 2011, www.theglobeandmail.com/news/politics/ottawa-notebook/canada-begins-to-wind-down-mission-in-wake-of-gadhafis-demise/article2208072/.

its Article 1 Charter mandates to 'maintain international peace and stability' and solve 'international problems of... [a] humanitarian character', in addition to 'promoting and encouraging respect for human rights and fundamental freedoms'? And, is it suitably placed to do so? Furthermore, in the context of events that happened on the ground, is the adoption of Security Council Resolution 1973 (2011) a classic case of humanitarian intervention? Or alternatively, is it the first demonstration of a decade long 'emerging' norm of a duty to protect civilians, triggered by threats to 'human security', namely R2P? This is more than a semantic distinction, because should it be considered the latter, a legal precedent will be established.[7]

24.2 Libya and humanitarian intervention

There is no doubt that the reaction to events in Libya represents indeed a classic case of humanitarian intervention given the references to the gross and systematic violation of human rights, coupled with the fact that the situation continues to constitute a threat to international peace and security. Humanitarian intervention understood in customary international law may be defined as:

> the reliance upon force for the justifiable purpose of protecting the inhabitants of another state from treatment which is so arbitrary and persistently abusive as to exceed the limits of that authority within which the sovereign is presumed to act with reason and justice.[8]

Alternatively, it refers:

> primarily to forcible means employed by a state, group of states, an international or regional organization, or humanitarian agencies with the aim (or at least one of its principal aims) of ending egregious human rights violations perpetrated by governments, or preventing or alleviating human suffering in situations of internal conflict.[9]

[7] It must be stressed here that this chapter is not about the law of armed conflict nor about the ethics of humanitarian intervention and R2P. Rather, it is about the distinction – made by the protagonists of the R2P that the terms of the debate must be changed from the humanitarian intervention right based language to R2P's emphasis on duty – and whether this difference is appropriate in the case of the Libya intervention.

[8] E. Stowell, *Intervention in International Law* (1921), 53.

[9] F. Abiew, *The Evolution of the Doctrine and Practice of Humanitarian Intervention* (1999), 18.

Tesón, for example, defines it as the 'proportionate transboundary help, including forcible help, provided by governments to individuals in another state who are being denied basic human rights and who themselves would be rationally willing to revolt against their oppressive government'.[10] These definitions do overlap in significant respects in providing a basic understanding of the employment of the term by scholars, in the sense that it is generally an act performed for the purpose of compelling a sovereign to respect fundamental human rights in the exercise of its sovereign prerogatives.[11] Thus, the classical notion of humanitarian intervention involves the threat or use of armed force in a state without the consent of its authorities, and with the purpose of preventing widespread suffering or death among the inhabitants. Rather confusingly, in the 1990s, a broader and less precise notion of the term was articulated by some relief agencies and writers that involved humanitarian action in complex emergencies not necessarily encompassing use of armed force, and not necessarily against the will of the target state.[12] Understandably, this was a reaction to the changing international security environment that witnessed civil wars and internal violence perpetrated on a massive scale. Civilians were often caught in the throes of such violence and desperately needed assistance in whatever form. One could characterise this as humanitarian action or humanitarian access in contrast to the classical or narrow meaning of the term.

In this context, Security Council Resolution 1973 (2011) and the subsequent NATO military action[13] speak volumes for the legality and moral legitimacy of primarily protecting the Libyan people. By a vote of ten in favour with five abstentions, the Council expressed 'grave concern at the deteriorating situation, the escalation of violence, and the heavy civilian casualties', while 'condemning the gross and systematic violation of human rights, including arbitrary detentions, enforced disappearances, torture and summary executions'. It deplored 'the continuing use of mercenaries by the Libyan authorities' and also expressed 'its determination

[10] F. Tesón, *Humanitarian Intervention: An Inquiry into Law and Morality* (1988), 5. In a frequently used definition, 'the theory of intervention on the ground of humanity ... recognizes the right of one state to exercise international control over the acts of another in regard to its internal sovereignty when contrary to the laws of humanity'. Quoted in Stowell, *supra* note 8, at 53.

[11] See for example, M. Ganji, *International Protection of Human Rights* (1962), 9.

[12] A. Roberts, 'The So-Called Right of Humanitarian Intervention' (1999) 13 *The University of Melbourne, Trinity Papers* 3, at 4–5.

[13] Consisting of NATO's deployment of more than 2,500 air, ground and maritime movements into Libya. NATO Final Mission Stats, *supra* note 5.

to ensure the protection of civilians and civilian populated areas and the rapid and unimpeded passage of humanitarian assistance and the safety of humanitarian personnel'. Furthermore, it demanded an immediate ceasefire in Libya, including an end to the current attacks against civilians, which it said might constitute 'crimes against humanity' and imposed a ban on all flights in Libya's airspace – a no-fly-zone – in addition to tightening sanctions on the Gaddafi regime and its supporters.[14] Ultimately, the Council determined that the Libyan situation 'continues to constitute a threat to international peace and security' and 'acting under Chapter VII of the Charter of the United Nations ... authorizes Member States ... acting nationally or through regional organizations or arrangements ... to take all necessary measures ... to protect civilians under threat of attack in the [country], including Benghazi, while excluding a foreign occupation force of any form on any part of Libyan territory' – requesting them to immediately inform the Secretary-General of such measures.[15]

The legal and moral case for the military intervention to protect civilians in Libya is compelling, and the swift manner in which Resolution 1973 was passed is certainly commendable in terms of the Council's responsibilities regarding the protection of human rights. The legality of the action is grounded in the Charter principles for the protection of human rights. One of its fundamental purposes, as stated in Article 1(3), is 'promoting and encouraging respect for human rights'. Similarly, by Article 55, the Members of the UN reaffirm a commitment to promoting universal respect for, and observance of, human rights and fundamental freedoms for all. Under Article 56, all Members of the UN 'pledge themselves to take joint and separate action in cooperation with the Organization for the achievement of the purposes set forth in Article 55'.

Despite the differing views on their legal effect, the actual practice of the UN has been that it has not been prevented from investigating, discussing and evaluating human rights violations and even taking military action, where necessary, as evidenced in the 1990s, despite the numerous constraints which the organisation has been facing.[16] The Charter provisions relating to human rights represent binding legal obligations for all

[14] www.un.org/News/Press/docs/2011/sc10200.doc.htm. The five abstentions are Brazil, China, Germany, India and Russia. For a summary of debates in support of, and reservations, expressed by states at the Security Council before adoption of the Resolution, see *ibid.*

[15] *Ibid.*

[16] See generally the discussion in Abiew, *supra* note 9, at 75–90 (on the internationalisation of human rights).

states, and their cumulative effect is that intervention to prevent human rights abuses is valid. While it may be doubtful whether states can be called to account for every alleged violation of the general Charter provisions, there is little doubt that 'responsibility exists under the Charter for any substantial infringement of the provisions, especially when a class of persons, or a pattern of activity are involved'.[17]

Second, and apart from noting the widespread and systematic attacks against civilians which by themselves would be grounds for action under the Charter (i.e. strictly internal human rights violations without transboundary effects), the Security Council also explicitly condemned 'the gross and systematic violations of human rights' which it determined 'continue to constitute a threat to international peace and security'[18] and grounded the authority to act under Chapter VII of the Charter. Thus, additionally, the human rights violations in Libya were linked to threats to the peace. This is evident in the massive refugee flows that may result in the further destabilisation of neighbouring countries such as Egypt and Tunisia, which themselves had undergone their own internal turmoil. The Security Council, responsible for maintaining international peace and security, was thus justified in authorising 'all measures necessary'[19] in remedying this situation.

Actual military intervention, however, was possible in large part, because of the willingness of the major powers, particularly the United States, to take immediate military action, and subsequently transferring command and control of the operation to NATO. The justification for military action to redress gross, widespread and systematic violation of human rights was imperative. As acknowledged by US President Barack Obama, British Prime Minister David Cameron, and French President Nicholas Sarkozy in an unprecedented joint letter to several major newspapers on Libya:

> [w]e must never forget the reasons why the international community was obliged to act in the first place. As Libya descended into chaos with Colonel Gaddafi attacking his own people, the Arab League called for action. The Libyan opposition called for help. And the people of Libya looked to the world in their hour of need. In an historic resolution, the United Nations Security Council authorized all necessary measures to protect the people of Libya from the attacks upon them. By responding immediately, our countries halted the advance of Gaddafi's forces. The bloodbath that he had promised to inflict on the citizens of the besieged city of Benghazi has

[17] I. Brownlie, *The Principles of Public International Law* (1990), 570.
[18] *Supra* note 3. [19] *Ibid.*

> been prevented. Tens of thousands of lives have been protected. But the people of Libya are suffering terrible horrors at Gaddafi's hand's each and every day. His rockets and his shells rained down on defenseless civilians in Ajdabiya. The city of Misrata is enduring a medieval siege as Gaddafi tries to strangle its population into submission. The evidence of disappearances and abuses grows daily. Our duty and our mandate under UN Security Council 1973 is to protect civilians, and we are doing that. It is not to remove Gaddafi by force. But it is impossible to imagine a future for Libya with Gaddafi in power. The International Criminal Court is rightly investigating the crimes committed against civilians and the grievous violations of international law. It is unthinkable that someone who has tried to massacre his own people can play a part in their future government. The brave citizens of those towns that have held out against forces that have been mercilessly targeting them would face a fearful vengeance if the world accepted such an arrangement. It would be an unconscionable betrayal.[20]

Thus, the principal moral and legal justification, as well as the motive, of the mission is clear and consequently valid under the Charter and in customary international law. This is consistent with Hugo Grotius' recognition of the importance that the law governing every human society be limited by a widely recognised principle of humanity.[21] In the Libyan context, the Security Council demanded an immediate ceasefire, including an end to the current attacks against civilians which it said might constitute 'crimes against humanity', and referred the situation in that country since 15 February 2011 to the Prosecutor of the International Criminal Court for possible prosecution of those found complicit in attacks targeting civilians, and ensuring that they were held accountable. Also, if a sovereign, although exercising his rights, acts contrary to the rights of humanity by grievously ill-treating his own subjects, the right of intervention may be lawfully exercised. In his oft-quoted words, Grotius asserts that:

> [t]here is also another question, whether a war for the subjects of another be just, for the purpose of defending them from injuries of their ruler. Certainly it is undoubted that ever since civil societies were formed, the rulers of each claimed some especial rights over his own subjects … [But] … [i]f a tyrant … practices atrocities towards his subjects, which no just man can approve, the right of human social connexion is not cut off in

[20] 'Obama, Cameron, Sarkozy Joint Letter on Libya (Full Text)', 15 April 2011, *International Business Times*, www.ibtimes.com/articles/134765/20110415/libya-obama-uk-nato-cameron.htm.

[21] See Abiew, *supra* note 9, at 35 (and the notes cited therein).

> such a case … [I]t would not follow that others may not take up arms for them.[22]

To further buttress the dimension of moral legitimacy in this case, where the state is guilty of gross and persistent human rights abuses, the consent of the governed can no longer be presumed. Legitimacy in this regard will mean that a government should respect the human rights of its citizens. Where the opposite happens, non-intervention will no longer be morally required. And the government would have lost its moral authority to demand that external actors remain uninvolved in its internal affairs. From an ethical viewpoint, governments are domestically and internationally mere agents of the people. Consequently, their international rights derive from the rights of the citizens who inhabit and constitute the state.[23]

In sum, humanitarian intervention is a short-term palliative measure that involves the use of military force to prevent or remedy egregious or large-scale human rights violations as the Libyan intervention is designed to do, and further consistent with the exclusion of a foreign occupation force, as provided for in Security Council Resolution 1973 (2011). This type of action may have facilitated the Libyans taking charge of their own affairs in fulfilling their legitimate aspirations of freedom and getting rid of the tyrant.

By comparison, R2P is much broader. It consists of prevention, reaction and rebuilding, hence of a long-term outlook. Some commentators have been quick to maintain that such is indeed the nature of Resolution 1973. They find the wordings 'responsibility of the Libyan authorities to protect the Libyan population', 'that parties to armed conflicts bear the primary responsibility to take all feasible steps to ensure the protection of civilians', and the human rights language mentioned in the World Summit Outcome Document, to be consistent with the first ever executive articulation of R2P, the essence of which is that the state and the community of states have a duty rather than merely a right to protect. So, is the world witnessing a UN renaissance à la R2P? It is doubtful that this is the case

[22] Quoted in *ibid*. Similarly, Vattel notes that 'if the prince, attacking the fundamental laws, gives his people a legitimate reason to resist him, if tyranny becomes so unbearable as to cause the Nation to rise, any foreign power is entitled to help an oppressed people that has requested assistance'. Quoted in *ibid*., at 36. Thus, the sovereignty or independence of states stops where it is violated beyond the point of tolerance.

[23] See M. Walzer, *Just and Unjust Wars* (1977), 101–108; J. Donnelly, 'Human Rights, Humanitarian Crisis, and Humanitarian Intervention' (1993) 48 *International Journal* 607, at 615–616.

since the conjunction of critical factors that should prompt invocation of military intervention grounded in either humanitarian intervention or R2P has been conspicuously absent in the worsening case of the Syrian civil war.

24.3 Libya and R2P

When, in 2005, the UN General Assembly endorsed the R2P[24] as the international community's responsibility to collectively protect civilian populations, it sought to establish a respective obligation concerning four specific categories of atrocities to which a state's new international *positive* legal duty applies: genocide, crimes against humanity, ethnic cleansing and war crimes. The UN presumed buy-in[25] to the R2P idea was therefore notably distinct from the concept created in 2001,[26] coming on the heels of NATO's military intervention in Kosovo, as well as the interventions in Rwanda, Bosnia and Somalia purportedly on humanitarian grounds. It considerably shrinks the framework of what was originally conceived by the ICISS drafters as requiring protection, namely *human security* as an 'indivisible'[27] condition. The ICISS Report, which coined the term, succinctly states that '[t]he substance of the responsibility to protect is the provision of life-supporting protection and assistance to populations at risk',[28] and elaborates that:

> [t]he emerging principle in question is that intervention for human protection purposes, including military intervention in extreme cases, is supportable when major harm to civilians is occurring or imminently apprehended, and the state in question is unable or unwilling to end the harm, or is itself the perpetrator.[29]

[24] 2005 World Summit Outcome, GA Res. 60/1, 16 September 2005, UN Doc. A/RES/60/1 (2005) [hereafter: World Summit].

[25] Endorsed neither in a separate nor legally binding instrument.

[26] International Commission on Intervention and State Sovereignty (ICISS), *The Responsibility to Protect* (2001) [hereafter: ICISS Report]. See also the comprehensive discussion in T. Weiss and D. Hubert (eds.), *Bibliography, Background: Supplementary Volume to the Report of the International Commission on Intervention and State Sovereignty* (2001); and L. Axworthy and A. Rock, 'R2P: A New and Unfinished Agenda' (2009) 1 *Global Responsibility to Protect* 54.

[27] ICISS Report, *ibid.*, at para. 1.21 [emphasis added]. 'Human security means the security of people – their physical safety, their economic and social well-being, respect for their dignity and worth as human beings, and the protection of their human rights and fundamental freedoms.' *Ibid.*, at para. 2.21.

[28] *Ibid.*, at para. 2.32.

[29] *Ibid.*, at para. 2.25. Compared with humanitarian intervention anchored in the UN Charter as discussed in Part 2 above, both concepts of human security and R2P (the

However, the language of the UN R2P is significantly more constrained. The World Summit Outcome Articles 138 and 139[30] reaffirm extant state responsibility incurred for international crimes (invoking extra-territorial universal jurisdiction as of a state's right) and elucidate the spectrum of the responsibility, respectively. While indeterminately instructing collective sanction against a manifestly defaulting state, the General Assembly's consequent recommendation can be construed as broader (more permissive) than prevalent international legal regimes (international human rights law (IHRL), the law of armed conflict,[31] and international criminal law) for the two Articles are mute as to the ascertainment of the duty and its implementation.

latter including state failure as a cause of the suffering of the population, and the state's unwillingness or inability to halt or avert it, as giving rise to a duty to protect the affected population by means of military intervention) enjoy a strikingly shorter history of norm creation and hence at best represent law in its creation – in transition from soft to hard law. In any event, it would be an exaggeration to impute to these concepts the status of customary law.

[30] '138. Each individual State has the responsibility to protect its populations from genocide, war crimes, ethnic cleansing and crimes against humanity. This responsibility entails the prevention of such crimes, including their incitement, through appropriate and necessary means. We accept that responsibility and will act in accordance with it. The international community should, as appropriate, encourage and help States to exercise this responsibility and support the United Nations in establishing an early warning capability. 139. The international community, through the United Nations, also has the responsibility to use appropriate diplomatic, humanitarian and other peaceful means, in accordance with Chapters VI and VIII of the Charter, to help to protect populations from genocide, war crimes, ethnic cleansing and crimes against humanity. In this context, we are prepared to take collective action, in a timely and decisive manner, through the Security Council, in accordance with the Charter, including Chapter VII, on a case-by-case basis and in cooperation with relevant regional organizations as appropriate, should peaceful means be inadequate and national authorities are manifestly failing to protect their populations from genocide, war crimes, ethnic cleansing and crimes against humanity. We stress the need for the General Assembly to continue consideration of the responsibility to protect populations from genocide, war crimes, ethnic cleansing and crimes against humanity and its implications, bearing in mind the principles of the Charter and international law. We also intend to commit ourselves, as necessary and appropriate, to helping States build capacity to protect their populations from genocide, war crimes, ethnic cleansing and crimes against humanity and to assisting those which are under stress before crises and conflicts break out.' World Summit, *supra* note 24 [emphasis added].

[31] For an argument that international humanitarian law (IHL) provides for a positive duty see, L. Condorelli and L. Boisson de Chazournes, 'Quelques remarques à propos de l'obligation des Etats de "respecter et faire respecter" le droit international humanitaire "en toutes circonstances"', in C. Swinarski (ed.), *Studies and Essays on International Humanitarian Law and Red Cross Principles in Honour of Jean Pictet* (1984), at 17–35. For an argument that positive primary and secondary obligations in both IHL and IHRL

For the purpose of evaluating whether Resolution 1973 and its implementation represent the advent of R2P as a moral norm, we apply the narrow UN version of R2P as the authoritative rule to determine whether a 'cause of action' for the military intervention in Libya exists. In order to assess whether the Libya case suggests the development of a respective new UN operative principle we employ elements of the 'test'[32] developed by the ICISS, summarily articulated in the report's synopsis, and elaborated on the document. Especially relevant to this part of our discussion are therefore the principles articulated under the heading of 'The Responsibility to Protect: Principles for Military Intervention'.

Undoubtedly, in the preamble, Security Council Resolution 1973 (2011) speaks the language of R2P:

> *Reiterating* the responsibility of the Libyan authorities to protect the Libyan population and reaffirming that parties to armed conflicts bear the primary responsibility to take all feasible steps to ensure the protection of civilians ...
>
> *Considering* that the widespread and systematic attacks currently taking place in the Libyan Arab Jamahiriya against the civilian population may amount to crimes against humanity ...
>
> *Determining* that the situation in the Libyan Arab Jamahiriya continues to constitute a threat to international peace and security.

It can therefore be read as applying Article 138,[33] which contemplates prevention of anticipated crimes – here crimes against humanity, which the UN suspected had already been committed in Libya, and representing a threat to international peace and security – as triggering R2P's operation by summoning the international community to the task. According to the ICISS's priorities, the responsibility to prevent represents the primary element of R2P; 'the single most important dimension of the responsibility to protect', and 'should always be exhausted before intervention is contemplated, and thus more commitment and resources must be devoted to

have long been recognised, see *Final Report on the Impact of International Human Rights Law on General International Law. Draft Report*, in International Law Association, International Human Rights Law and Practice, Rio de Janeiro Conference (2008), at 14.

[32] Since the synopsis is not formulated as a test, and some of its components are more general while others are more specific and detailed, we employ the most explicit elements. Should Res. 1973 and its implementation be found to reflect an overall tendency and pattern of consistent adherence to the principles, then this may be interpreted as indicative of the development of a new and R2P-guided modus operandi.

[33] ICISS R2P activation is conceptualised as a set of three responsibilities (pillars) consisting of prevention, reaction and rebuilding.

it'.[34] Similarly, Article 139 qualifies the implications of Article 138's finding of R2P, and mirrors the ICISS priority. Accordingly, the international community has declared itself to be 'prepared to take collective action' provided 'peaceful means be inadequate'. Therefore, the question that arises is whether Resolution 1973 was adopted subsequent to the failure of all other means.

At the time Resolution 1973 was adopted – some three weeks after Security Council Resolution 1970 (2011), the latter motivated by a reaction to the atrocities visited upon peaceful Libyan protestors by their own government – rebel forces had already formed and taken control of parts of Eastern Libya. By then, some observers concluded, the situation had escalated and transformed into a 'full-scale civil war'.[35] Accordingly, rather than prevention, Resolution 1973 refers to – and hence should be measured against – the second pillar, namely the reaction responsibility of R2P.

Whichever of the two responsibilities might have been triggered at this stage, it became plainly evident that during the unfolding of the events since their February debut and into March 2011, the trigger of 'shocking the world's conscience' came into play, prompted by the humanitarian calamity in Libya. In comparison with the two precedent instances of the unfolding Arab uprisings – the precipitated escape of the Tunisian leader away from his enraged citizenry, and the then largely peaceful protest in Egypt (referred to as 'the First Revolution') – abhorrence at Gaddafi's crackdown on his citizens positioned Libya on a different moral scale altogether. However, only part of world public opinion[36] had reached the threshold set by the ICISS – that the decision to intervene must be made only in the extreme case amounting to 'shock[ing] the conscience of mankind'.[37] Indeed, the observation that 'the war in Libya is a creation of the liberal intellectuals – just as the war in Iraq was a creation of the neo-

[34] ICISS Report, *supra* note 26, at para. 4(a).

[35] The International Crisis Group insisted that 'the popular protest movement and Qaddafi's regime followed the logic of civil war from a very early stage. This owes a great deal to the country's history and chiefly to the peculiar character of the political order Colonel Qaddafi and his associates set up in the 1970s'. 'Popular Protest in North Africa and the Middle East (V): Making Sense of Libya', No. 107 *Middle East/North Africa Report*, 6 June 2011, www.crisisgroup.org/en/regions/middle-east-north-africa/north-africa/libya/107-popular-protest-in-north-africa-and-the-middle-east-v-making-sense-of-libya.aspx [hereafter: ICG June 6 Report].

[36] Evidently, only part of it and chiefly in sectors of the open societies of the Western liberal democracies.

[37] ICISS Report, *supra* note 26, at para. 4.13.

conservatives',[38] is not so far-fetched. A concerted persuasion effort was required to win over a hesitant and reluctant US President Barack Obama and secure a Security Council Chapter VII resolution. Susan Rice, the President's Ambassador to the UN, Samantha Power, his aide and Director of Multilateral Affairs at the National Security Council, Hillary Clinton, his Secretary of State, and Anne-Marie Slaughter, the President's former State Department Policy Planning Chief[39] joined in this endeavour. The condition of the just cause threshold,[40] which demands large-scale loss of life, could not be verified although the exhortations of Gaddafi suggested inflicting such harm. However, this coming together of minds may satisfy the collective 'right intention' – a precautionary principle of R2P, stipulating that '[t]he primary purpose of the intervention, whatever other motives intervening states may have, must be to halt or avert human suffering'.[41] Indeed, that 'right intention is better assured with multilateral operations, clearly supported by regional opinion and the victims concerned'[42] was then to follow.

One should however not overlook the fact that other opinions were seeking to discredit this 'right intention' by casting Resolution 1973 in a different light. As expected, the question of legitimacy of the intervention in Libya has been brought to the fore, especially in relation to the broadening of the mission beyond strict and immediate protection of the civilian population. At its extreme, the military intervention in Libya was interpreted as a selfish national interest-driven endeavour couched in 'mission civilisatrice' rhetoric, hence '[o]ne cannot understand the military intervention and the discourse being formed around it outside its corresponding history, which is the colonial civilising mission – the White Man's burden'.[43] Then, it would certainly be a far cry from humanitarian intervention and R2P. On the other end of the spectrum is the effort to ascertain whether Muammar Gaddafi was a legitimate, even legal, target for

[38] M. Wente, 'Blame R2P: The Intellectuals Go to War', *Globe and Mail*, 26 March 2011; see also K. Anderson, 'Strategic Ambiguity and Libya', *Opinio Juris*, 22 March 2011, www.opiniojuris.org.

[39] On 24 February 2011, Anne-Marie Slaughter called for international intervention on behalf of the Libyan people. J. Rogin, 'Anne-Marie Slaughter Tweets Call for Intervention in Libya', *Foreign Policy*, 24 February 2011.

[40] *Ibid*., at para. 1(a).

[41] ICISS Report, *supra* note 26, Synopsis, The Responsibility to Protect: Principles for Military Intervention.

[42] *Ibid*.

[43] H. Yucesoy, 'European Intervention in Libya Sounds Like a Re-Emergence of the 19th-Century Colonial Mentality, Scholar Says', *Al Jazeera*, 20 March 2011, http://english.aljazeera.net/indepth/opinion/2011/03/20113319222581597.html#; R. Shrum, 'It Really

assassination,[44] or, for instance, whether arming the Libyan rebel forces had run counter to Resolutions 1970 and 1973 arms embargo stipulations,[45] to name a few.[46] Obviously, a unanimous stance on such issues of legitimacy is unlikely, and practicality commands reaching some form of consensus.[47] This was indeed how Resolution 1973 was adopted, namely with several abstentions. For the purpose of the R2P test, however, right intention represents only one out of the four precautionary principles – last resort, proportional means, and reasonable prospects. On these remaining three, the record of Resolution 1973 and its implementation remains wanting.

Does the resolution satisfy the ICISS precautionary principle of last resort? Article 139 makes military intervention dependent on 'a timely

Is About Regime Change in Libya', *The Week*, 24 March 2011, http://theweek.com/bullpen/column/213526/it-really-is-about-regime-change-in-libya.

[44] K. Anderson, 'Can the Coalition Lawfully Target Gaddafi?', *Opinio Juris*, 23 March 2011; and M.M. Lewis, 'How Should the Conflict in Libya Be Categorized?', *Opinio Juris*, 30 March 2011, both at http://opiniojuris.org.

[45] 'The effect of this would be that assistance to the rebels is only permitted in order to protect civilians or civilian populated areas. It is not permitted to assist the rebels in order to achieve the goal of overthrowing the Gaddafi government. The view may be taken that removing Gaddafi's government is what is necessary to carry out the mandate. This is a possible view but I think it goes too far. Civilian protection may be achieved by a stalemate in Libya with Gaddafi in control of the areas he currently controls and the rebels in control of the areas they control. As far as I know (and I may be wrong) there is no allegation that the civilians in Western Libya are currently in need of protection. Of course this may change, but if it doesn't, then what is required to achieve the mandate of civilian protection and protection of civilian populated areas is that Gaddafi's forces must not be allowed to take the towns and cities he has lost. Achieving that mandate does not require removing Gaddafi from control of the areas he currently controls. Now, this is incredibly messy politically. That may well be so, but a stalemate would protect civilians. So it may be lawful to assist the rebels to defend the areas they hold but not to assist them to advance on other towns. Indeed the rebels advancing on towns and cities controlled by Gaddafi is a threat of attack on civilian populated areas which UN States have a mandate to stop and prevent (though not required to do so). Also, for the reasons outlined in this paragraph, providing close air support for rebels to advance goes beyond the mandate in SC Res 1973.' D. Akande, 'Does SC Resolution 1973 Permit Coalition Military Support for the Libyan Rebels?', *EJIL:Talk!*, 31 March 2011, www.ejiltalk.org/does-sc-resolution-1973-permit-coalition-military-support-for-the-libyan-rebels/#more-3199.

[46] These are only two examples out of the larger debate concerning the legal interpretation of Res. 1973, which, in addition, have tended to compound the *jus ad bellum* with *jus in bello* questions, a subject too broad to be broached in this chapter.

[47] Initially abstaining from the resolution and later criticising its execution, Russia has changed course when, at the 27 May 2011 G-8 Summit in Deauville, it joined the legitimising group. S. Shuster, 'What Mediating in Libya Could Cost Medvedev', *Time.CNN*, 1 June 2011, www.time.com/time/world/article/0,8599,2075007,00.html.

and decisive manner, through the Security Council, in accordance with the Charter, including Chapter VII', and conditions the escalation of means of R2P operationalisation on the manifest failure of the state to protect its civilians. Although the latter part of the condition undoubtedly applies, the former begs closer attention. In this regard, Article 139 adds, such R2P action must be taken 'on a case-by-case basis and in cooperation with relevant regional organizations as appropriate'.

Although joining the President's 'four Musketeers' in ringing the alarm bells,[48] positions taken by pundits reveal profound disagreement as to the urgency of intervention, hence the determination that the last resort principle had been satisfied. According to Louise Arbour,[49] by adopting Resolution 1973, the Security Council jumped the gun, failing to wait for other means to be exhausted:

> I think to look exclusively at the military options is a form of escalation that is not prudent. The African Union had already launched a negotiation initiative, dispatched a mission, the secretary general has a special envoy so I think diplomatic initiatives have to continue to be pursued. First to cease all combat operations and to try to find a form of accommodation that would bring democratic space into Libya.[50]

Similarly, the African Union joined the military option advocacy very reluctantly,[51] in fact, only after having been at pains to avert Resolution 1973 close to the date of its adoption.[52] To be sure, when compared with UN hesitance concerning countries where other similar atrocities (albeit not by a state's air force) have been committed, the organisation's treatment

[48] US Secretary of Defense, Robert Gates, was critical of a no-fly zone strategy and had opposed US involvement in Libya prior to the adoption of Res. 1973. 'Defense Secretary: Libya Did Not Pose Threat to U.S., Was Not "Vital National Interest" to Intervene', *ABC News*, 27 March 2011, http://blogs.abcnews.com/politicalpunch/2011/03/defense-secretary-libya-did-not-pose-threat-to-us-was-not-vital-national-interest-to-intervene.html.

[49] President of the International Crisis Group, former United Nations High Commissioner for Human Rights, former Justice of the Supreme Court of Canada, and former Chief Prosecutor of the International Criminal Tribunal for Yugoslavia. 'Open Letter to the UN Security Council on the Situation in Libya', International Crisis Group, 16 March 2011, www.crisisgroup.org.

[50] L. Davidescu, 'Interview with Louise Arbour', *Euronews*, 21 March 2011, www.euronews.net/2011/03/21/international-crisis-group-warns-of-libya-splitting/.

[51] Albeit for reasons different than Arbour's. Notably, Gaddafi became the organisation's head only two years earlier.

[52] 'Reaffirms its strong commitment to the respect of the unity and territorial integrity of Libya, as well as its rejection of any foreign military intervention, whatever its form ... The African Union failed to back up its strong words of condemnation from the African Union's Peace and Security Council's 265th meeting with any credible action to halt the violence, which necessitated Resolution 1973, and in effect failing in a key

of Libya stands as a unique exception. At the backdrop of years' long inaction regarding the lot of Zimbabweans,[53] which to this date has not produced any R2P resolution let alone any less comprehensive and intrusive initiative; or, the dragging reaction to the results of the 28 November 2010 elections in Ivory Coast;[54] and lastly, the more recent and post-Libya intervention atrocities committed by the Syrian government amounting to a conduct equally 'shocking the world's conscience' but which has so far resulted in only a limited UN reaction[55] (to mention a few R2P candidate

objective to defend the Libyan state'. 'African Union and Failed Diplomacy In View Of UNSC Resolution 1973', *The Sun –Cameroon*, 26 March 2011, http://the-news-from-cameroon.com/article.php?article_id=1864. This is an excerpt from a letter by Jean Ping, Chairperson of the Africa Union Commission, expressing his personal dissatisfaction at the African Union's change of position regarding military intervention in Libya. See also 'African Union Demands "Immediate" Halt to Libya Attacks', 19 March 2011, AFP, www.google.com/hostednews/afp/article/ALeqM5i-8HhcGv5ZC4Cfeq421M_omVVpvA?docId=CNG.1411cd01df64d8f14a45e3962493fb9a.d1; G. Grant, 'Libya and the African Union: Right in Principle, Wrong in Practice', *The Telegraph*, 12 April 2011, www.telegraph.co.uk/news/worldnews/africaandindianocean/libya/8445465/Libya-and-the-African-Union-Right-in-Principle-Wrong-in-Practice.html.

53 Zimbabwean President Robert Mugabe is quoted as bragging that 'I have degrees in violence' (G. Galloway, 'Zimbabwean Activist Refuses to Buckle', *Globe and Mail*, 1 June 2011, at A14), serving to show that Colonel Gaddafi is not alone in exhorting verbal diatribes against his people.

54 Seven particular UN Security Council resolutions running back to 2000 up to SC Res. 1975 (2011) of 30 March 2011 (dealing with various manifestations of international crimes in Ivory Coast, and referring also to the use of mercenaries) serve as an appropriate yardstick to measuring 'last resort':

> 6. Recalls its authorization and stresses its full support given to the UNOCI, while impartially implementing its mandate, *to use all necessary means to carry out its mandate to protect civilians under imminent threat of physical violence*, within its capabilities and its areas of deployment, including to prevent the use of heavy weapons against the civilian population and requests the Secretary-General to keep it urgently informed of measures taken and efforts made in this regard. [Emphasis added]

Note, however, the explanation for reaching the 'last resort' conclusion: 'UN diplomats and analysts said on Tuesday that the organisation's intervention in Ivory Coast was part of a fundamental political shift in which military action against Libya – backed by two Security Council resolutions and the vocal support of the Obama administration – had provided an important spur.' D. Bilefsky, 'Strikes on Ivory Coast Reveal UN Political Shift', *Sydney Morning Herald*, 7 April 2011, www.smh.com.au/world/strikes-on-ivory-coast-reveal-un-political-shift-20110406–1d4k1.html.

55 A 2011 report notes that '[t]he substantial body of evidence gathered by the commission indicates that these gross violations of human rights have been committed by Syrian military and security forces since the beginning of the protests in March 2011. The commission is gravely concerned that crimes against humanity have been committed in different

cases), the urgency of Resolution 1973 on Libya is indeed outstanding. With only Resolution 1970 of 26 February 2011 and the puzzling Security Council Resolution 1738 (2006) condemning attacks against journalists in conflict situations albeit without any mention of Libya, a strikingly short history of attempts at the peaceful diffusion of the Libyan conflict precedes the R2P resolution. Certainly, this raises doubts as to whether the ICISS last resort principle, stipulating that '[m]ilitary intervention can only be justified when every non-military option for the prevention or peaceful resolution of the crisis has been explored, with reasonable grounds for believing lesser measures would not have succeeded',[56] has indeed been complied with.

The ICISS Report in paragraph 4.39 demands that a minimum scale, duration and intensity of 'the planned military intervention should be the minimum necessary to secure the humanitarian objective in question'. Adhering to this precautionary principle of proportional means might have been exactly what the Security Council intended to achieve when authorising the Member States to discharge their R2P duty and 'take all necessary measures to enforce compliance with the ban on flights', to coordinate their activities with the Secretary-General, and to inform the Secretary-General and the New Sanctions Committee (which was established in paragraph 24 of Resolution 1970), and provide for an assessment process (paragraph 24 of Resolution 1973). This open-ended formulation – most likely due to a combination of the urgency felt in coming to the protection of the Libyan population as well as the intention to avoid tying the hands of the Member States in pursuance of the military intervention – attracted diverging constructions. Indeed, several observers had noted early into the mission[57] that the indeterminate language – the resolution's 'strategic ambiguity'[58] – would invite unintended interpretations and consequences. As is now fully clear, the mandate of

locations in the Syrian Arab Republic during the period under review'. UN Human Rights Council, 'Report of the Independent International Commission of Inquiry on the Syrian Arab Republic', UNGA A/HRC/S-17/2/Add.1, 23 November 2011. For a condamnation of the use of chemical weapons, see Resolution 2118 (2013) of 27 September 2013, para. 2.

[56] ICISS Report, *supra* note 26, at para. 2(B).

[57] A. Orford, 'What Kind of Law is This?', 29 March 2011, www.lrb.co.uk/blog/2011/03/29/anne-orford/what-kind-of-law-is-this/; D. Akande, 'Does SC Resolution 1973 Permit Coalition Military Support for the Libyan Rebels?', *EJIL:Talk!*, 31 March 2011; M.N. Schmitt, 'Wings over Libya: The No-Fly Zone in Legal Perspective' (Spring 2011) 36 *Yale Journal of International Law Online*, at 45–58.

[58] That 'it [Resolution 1973] was almost certainly drafted precisely to that ambiguous end. The upside, of course, is that it provides an avenue by which parties can move forward. The downside, equally obviously, is that precisely that features that make ambiguity

Resolution 1973 has 'morphed' into regime change; other hidden mandates, for instance, 'sending' a warning message to Arab dictators,[59] exceeded the contemplated minimum. Certainly, the fact that Resolution 1973 gives room to adjusting the initial goals of protection of the civilian population to effecting regime change runs counter to the R2P precautionary approach requirement that '[t]he effect on the political system of the country targeted should be limited'.[60] This may even turn out to be counter-productive to efforts to solidify the R2P norm for it could deter governments which would, understandably, consider themselves as the next 'ducks in the row'.

The precautionary principle of reasonable prospects demands that:

> [m]ilitary action can only be justified if it stands a reasonable chance of success, that is, halting or averting the atrocities or suffering that triggered the intervention in the first place. Military intervention is not justified if actual protection cannot be achieved.[61]

Several issues cast doubt on the adherence to this principle in the implementation of Resolution 1973. For once, it is questionable whether arming what initially were peaceful civilian protestors who organised into armed and war-fighting opposition rebels matches the humanitarian objective of protection of civilians, or rather crosses the line from emergency protection and into taking sides in what would become a full-fledged civil war.[62] In this regard, Louise Arbour's observation early into the intervention foretells the derailment which the open-ended Resolution 1973 enabled:

> The perception of a Western, even a legal Security Council approved military operation transforms the conflict from a national insurgency into an international war opposing the West to Libyans. And in the same way, even more troubling is a possibility that this could lead to a de facto splitting of Libya between the east, which will be controlled and supported by the rebels and the west part of the country, with Tripoli at the centre, that

attractive in the short run are the features that cause it to come-a-cropper in the longer run'. Anderson, *supra* note 38.

[59] M. Zenko, 'Think Again: Libya', *Foreign Policy*, 28 April 2011, www.foreignpolicy.com/articles/2011/04/28/think_again_libya?print=yes&hidecomments=yes&page=full.

[60] ICISS Report, *supra* note 26, at para. 4.39.

[61] *Ibid.*, at para. 4.41.

[62] See also M. O'Connell, 'The Missing Peace', in *IntLawGrrls Voices on International Law, Policy, Practice*, 21 April 2011, IntLawGrrls.blogspot.com; M. Doyle, 'The Folly of Protection: Is Intervention against Qaddafi's Regime Legal and Legitimate?', *Foreign Affairs*, 20 March 2011, www.foreignaffairs.com.

> will continue to be under Gaddafi's control. And this could lead to a very prolonged and painful stalemate.[63]

Certainly, these words underscore the principle's cautioning that:

> [m]ilitary intervention is not justified … if the consequences of embarking upon the intervention are likely to be worse than if there is no action at all. In particular, a military action for limited human protection purposes cannot be justified if in the process it triggers a larger conflict.[64]

The ICISS 'test's' insistence on the 'right authority'[65] features as the condition most conspicuously complied with by Resolution 1973. Diametrically opposed to the UN unauthorised NATO humanitarian intervention in Kosovo, in the Libya case, the UN authority is formally and plainly established.[66] But this is indeed the exception. As with the precautionary principles, so concerning the ICISS operational principles, the implementation of Resolution 1973 once again demonstrates inconsistency between rule and reality. A cursory reading of Resolution 1973 and its implementation suffices to show that both fail to adhere to at least three out of the five operational principles. A resolution which 'contains many ambiguities'[67] is anathema to the requirement for '[c]lear objectives; clear and unambiguous mandate at all times; and resources to match'.[68] Adopting an expansive construction of Resolution 1973 to include regime change[69] and respectively altering course during its implementation defeats the operational principle which calls for '[a]cceptance of limitations, incrementalism and gradualism in the application of force, the objective being protection of a population, not defeat of a state'.[70] Equally, the reluctance

63 Davidescu, *supra* note 50.

64 ICISS Report, *supra* note 26, at para. 4.41.

65 'A. There is no better or more appropriate body than the United Nations Security Council to authorize military intervention for human protection purposes. The task is not to find alternatives to the Security Council as a source of authority, but to make the Security Council work better than it has'. ICISS, Synopsis, (3) Right Authority.

66 However, contrast Schmitt arguing that '[i]n terms of geographical coverage, scope of the ban, and *enforcement authorization*, it is much broader than any previous no-fly zone', (*supra* note 57, at 46, emphasis added) with Orford who doubts the foundational validity of this authority and decries that '[t]he bombing of Libya in the name of revolution may be legal, but the international law that authorises such action has surely lost its claim to be universal'. *Supra* note 57.

67 Davidescu, *supra* note 47.

68 ICISS Report, *supra* note 26, Synopsis, para. 4(A).

69 'The NATO mission in Libya is now expressly about ending the 42-year rule of the dictator Moammer Gadhafi'. Comment. 'Regime Change Needs A Debate', *Globe and Mail*, 31 May 2011, at A12.

70 ICISS Report, *supra* note 26, Synopsis, para. 4(C).

to engage in ground combat,[71] which is met in the resolution's explicit prohibition on 'foreign occupation force of any form on any part of Libyan territory' (instructed by the recent history of foreign military and humanitarian interventions), appears to run counter to R2P's operational principle that 'force protection cannot become the principal objective',[72] and that:

> Any new approach to intervention on human protection grounds needs to meet at least four basic objectives:
>
> - to establish clearer rules, procedures and criteria for determining whether, when and how to intervene;
> - to establish the legitimacy of military intervention when necessary and after all other approaches have failed;
> - to ensure that military intervention, when it occurs, is carried out only for the purposes proposed, is effective, and is undertaken with proper concern to minimize the human costs and institutional damage that will result; and
> - to help eliminate, where possible, the causes of conflict while enhancing the prospects for durable and sustainable peace.[73]

The foregoing analysis applied the World Summit Articles 138 and 139 and the threshold requirements established in the ICISS report as a test to identifying situations that trigger the R2P, and a measure to ascertaining whether just and legal means were employed to discharge the ensuing duty in the case of UN Security Council Resolution 1973 (2011) authorising military intervention in Libya. While the tenor of the resolution accords with the World Summit articles and with the essence of the R2P idea, we find that the operationalisation of the duty into a UN R2P mission remains wanting. If so, will this first attempt to speak and do R2P also be the last? Or, does it represent the first baby-step of a yet-to-evolve new UN principle?

71 'In reality, the tactic [no-fly zone] was selected not for its effectiveness at eliminating airstrikes (which it did), but rather because it required the least commitment.' Zenko, *supra* note 59. See also, M. O'Hanlon, 'Winning Ugly in Libya', *Foreign Affairs*, 30 March 2011, www.foreignaffairs.com.

72 US Congress, Resolution Declaring that the President Shall Not Deploy, Establish, or Maintain the Presence of Units and Members of the United States Armed Forces on the Ground In Libya, and for Other Purposes. 112th Congress 1st Session F:\M12\Boehne\Boehne_002.Xml, June 2, 2011, F:\Vhlc\060211\060211.193.Xml, http://rules.house.gov/Media/file/PDF_112_1/Floor_Text/BOEHNE_002_xml%281%29.pdf.

73 ICISS Report, *supra* note 26, at 14/70.

24.4 Conclusion

An important lesson worth noting so far from the Libyan case-study points to the fact that once the 'do the right thing' was initiated, it is the long-term 'endgame' that raises a number of imponderables. Is there a danger that by authorising such a broad mandate, Resolution 1973 also opened the slippery slope to 'do anything'? And if so, what are the consequences of survival for humanitarian intervention and its 'ambitious sibling' R2P? Is the UN mandated military intervention the first ever but also the last military R2P operation? Will the world experience a retraction in foreign military involvement in domestic strife and leave innocent civilians to fend for themselves when facing corrupt and vicious leaders? It is imperative that the foreign and security policies of governments recognise the framing of humanitarian initiatives in their overall strategies as consistent with their broad national interest considerations. While humanitarian intervention might be one of the kits in the toolbox in this context, it should also be noted that it is a short-term palliative measure, as we indicated earlier, to remedy egregious human rights violations. If R2P is to be invoked in such situations, then the need for marshalling the political will to undertake the more ambitious tasks of rebuilding/reconstruction will be a *sine qua non*.[74]

As we write, the UN intervention in Libya has been competing (increasingly less successfully) with Yemen, Syria, Bahrain, Egypt, and the trailing and prolonged Syrian turmoil for the world's attention. Yet unlike the overwhelming moralist outcry which engulfed world public opinion at the sight of the atrocities committed by Gaddafi,[75] an undertaking similar to Resolution 1973 has not yet followed suit and is unlikely to.[76] In this chapter, we set out to examine whether Resolution 1973 represents the first demonstration of what protagonists have claimed to be a decade-long 'emerging' norm of Responsibility to Protect triggering an international

[74] For a general overview of the distinction between the concepts of humanitarian intervention and the responsibility to protect, see for example, F. Abiew, 'Humanitarian Intervention and the Responsibility to Protect: Redefining a Role for "Kind-Hearted Gunmen"' (2010) 29(2) *Criminal Justice Ethics* 93.

[75] And what has become a prolonged intervention, see 'NATO's Libya Mission gets Extension', *SETimes.com*, 2 June 2011, www.setimes.com/cocoon/setimes/xhtml/en_GB/features/setimes/features/2011/06/02/feature-02; it is unclear at the moment whether a second extension will be authorised.

[76] Although a brutal Syrian crackdown on civilian demonstrating protestors has been taking place since mid-March 2011. As mentioned earlier, the tone of the international outcry has so far been significantly less forceful compared to the Libyan calamity.

duty to protect civilians. We also indicated that, if so, the Libya mission would establish a legal precedent. Our systematic examination of the Summit Outcome Articles 138 and 139 along with the application of the ICISS 'test' found that, indeed, the purposive element of the R2P has been adhered to. An R2P guided by deep humanitarian concern – reflected in the language of Resolution 1973 – appears to have kindled the process. Nevertheless, the rules or standards of the test listed in the ICISS report under the headings of core principles – especially the elements, priorities, and the principles for military intervention – still leave much to be desired. Furthermore, the termination of paragraphs 4 and 5 of Resolution 1973 by the subsequent UN Security Council Resolution 2016[77] of 26 October 2011 ending NATO's civilian protection mandate, blows up in the face of R2P. It sweepingly tears out the heart of the third pillar – a crucial part of R2P vocabulary and express ethos – from the UN's Libya action. The establishment of the United Nations Support Mission in Libya (UNSMIL), in paragraph 12 of Security Council Resolution 2009[78] of 16 September 2011, cannot compensate for this void. Consequently, the 'report card' of Resolution 1973 and its implementation is too meagre to serve as a legal – if only practice oriented – precedent.

Critics of the operation have been offering various perspectives of appraisal. Illustrations of comparable UN 'rescue' operations include likening the Libya case to the 1992–5 Somalia military intervention, a disappointing mission which left little imprint if any on a failed state which has continued to be 'perpetually on the brink of humanitarian catastrophe'.[79] Similarly, in spite of ten years of UN comprehensive peace and development operations in Afghanistan, the International Security Assistance Force (ISAF) operations have barely rattled the country out of its chronic political instability and human insecurity.[80] And in Kosovo, political stabilisation did materialise but at the high cost to human life following the accidental bombing of refugees by the protecting NATO forces.[81] Another assessment of the Libya mission presents the findings of studies showing that foreign intervention aimed at encouraging democratic reform

[77] SC Res. 2016 (2011). UN Doc. S/RES/2016 (2011).

[78] SC Res. 2009 (2011). UN Doc. S/RES/2009 (2011). UNSMIL was established as a mission under the leadership of a Special Representative of the Secretary-General for an initial period of three months, with the mandate of assisting and supporting Libyan national regime building efforts.

[79] G. York, 'Somalia, 1992 – Libya 2011: Are They Really As Different As We Imagine?', *Globe and Mail*, 7 May 2011, at F6.

[80] *Ibid.* [81] *Ibid.*

have routinely proven unsuccessful in effecting democratisation.[82] This we find to be a peculiar argument, for humanitarian intervention or R2P only, both apolitical in nature, and not democratisation, are listed among the objectives of Resolution 1973.[83] Further, the same studies maintain that foreign intervention designed to oust an incumbent regime and intent on having it replaced with a new government – indeed, an objective which represents the subsequently expanded mandate of Resolution 1973 – typically tends to foster civil strife.[84] Again, as noted here, such considerations shift the focus away from the essence of the resolution and, *a fortiori*, from its explicit message that the intervention in Libya represents a case of humanitarian intervention, even R2P. In this context, the recent decision of the Arab League to suspend Syria from the organisation's membership might be interpreted as a powerful R2P step.[85] To be sure, such a step represents a measure that the UN might wish to consider (for itself or as a recommendation to regional organisations) where R2P is being invoked. Suspension of membership,[86] a provision stipulated in Article 5 of the UN Charter, might prove effective as an escalating measure in the peaceful means employed and preceding, and potentially averting the need for, humanitarian intervention.

Yet, we are not holding our breath. What had begun in mid-March 2011 as a set of serious disturbances in one city in Syria inspired by, and mirroring, the regional 'Arab Spring' turmoil, has now escalated into a civil war, unwrapping old sectarian animosities, attracting Islamist undercurrents, begetting brutal suppression by the regime, and arguably, threatening to engulf the entire region, and even beyond that, in war. Under these circumstances, one might consider the threat to international peace and

[82] S.M. Walt, 'Social Science and the Libyan Adventure', *Foreign Affairs*, 24 March 2011, http://walt.foreignpolicy.com/posts/2011/03/24/social_science_and_the_libyan_adventure.

[83] In March 2011, democratisation was declared as a goal by the Libyan rebel Interim Transitional National Council (TNC). International Crisis Group, 6 June 2011 report, *supra* note 49, at 26.

[84] *Ibid.*

[85] 'The league's decision on Libya was half-hearted and without unanimity, and was soft-pedalled immediately afterward by then-secretary-general Amr Moussa. The decision on Syria was strikingly different, with 18 of 22 Arab states voting for the Syrian suspension … It's now permissible for Arab states to meddle in the internal affairs of other Arab states, when there's a clear moral or political reason to do so that reflects the sentiments of a majority of Arab public opinion.' R. Khouri, 'The Arab League Awakening', *Globe and Mail*, 15 November 2011.

[86] For an extensive analysis see, N. Gal-Or, 'Trusteeship, Suspended Sovereignty, and Enforcement of UN Membership Duties: Governance in Times of Peril' (2011) 2(3) *Journal of International Organization Studies* 44.

stability more acute than in the case of Libya. However, unlike the Libyan precedent, a repeat show of R2P resolve on the part of the international community is glaringly absent; two of the ascending superpowers, Russia and China, have been decidedly challenging the doctrine.[87]

The above examination serves to show that the compelling sincerity of the R2P advocates pressing for the adoption of Resolution 1973 and its implementation, failed to attract both political, and only modest polemic, attention. R2P is not referred to in name even in the extensive 6 June 2011 report on Libya of the International Crisis Group[88] – a non-governmental organisation set up by the ICISS Co-Chair (Gareth Evans), dedicated to R2P promotion. Indeed, while the legality, legitimacy, rationality and practicality of the extension of the fighting operations were being debated (in other words, during the implementation of R2P's second pillar), consideration was also being given to the third and final pillar. Arrest warrants were issued by the International Criminal Court against Gaddafi and others.[89] Following the arrest of Saif al-Islam Gadhafi and Abdullah Al-Senussi[90] the admissibility of the court's jurisdiction was challenged by the Libyan government. Furthermore, the Commission of War Crimes and Crimes Against Humanity by Government and Rebel Troops Alike,[91] established by the three-member Libya Commission appointed by the UN Human Rights Council, has declared a guilty finding for both sides – the now old regime and the then rebels. The moral imperative that has been the driving force of the mission has all but evaporated. Political (national, alliance and international) considerations have come to dominate the mission's agenda, while a concurrent formalist legal analysis of the international law of armed conflict has been dominating academic and legal professional internet fora.

[87] Delving into a study of the status of the R2P post-Syria is beyond the scope of this chapter. For a recent comparative analysis of the application of R2P to Libya and Syria see S. Zifcak, 'The Responsibility to Protect after Libya and Syria' (2012) 13 *Melbourne Journal of International Law* 1.

[88] *Ibid.* Equally, R2P is not referred to expressly in 'Appendix B About The International Crisis Group', *ibid.*, at 32, which may be the reason for changes made in the organisation in the course of its development. Exploring this matter is however beyond the scope of our chapter.

[89] International Criminal Court, ICC-01/11-4-Red 16-05-2011 1/23 SL PT, 16 May 2011.

[90] D. Amann, '… further from ICC …', *IntLawGrrls*, 23 November 2011, http://intlawgrrls.blogspot.com/2011/11/further-from-icc.html.

[91] 'Libya Conflict: UN Accuses Both Sides of War Crimes', *BBC News*, 1 June 2011, www.bbc.co.uk/news/world-africa-13622965.

The upshot is that, akin to preceding peacekeeping missions and other engagements generically referred to as peace operations, the UN NATO-led intervention in Libya has so far (unless a dramatic turnabout occurs) been unsuccessful in creating even a skeletal model for the more comprehensively articulated R2P. The record of the pre-Resolution 1973 R2P advocacy campaign and the text of the resolution itself will certainly serve pundits in their forthcoming debate of R2P: does the Libya experience indeed confirm that a new international norm, the R2P, had been formed and that an emerging universal endorsement of a *duty* to protect had now crystallised? Another outcome, not to be discounted, is that perhaps, and hopefully, this experience (experiment?) will generate re-assessments, refinement and adjustments of modes of engagement in peace operations so as to accord with R2P's noble imperative. Whether the cost in human lives was worth it would always remain a nagging question.

25

The Arab Uprising and the rise and fall of international human rights

LOUISE ARBOUR

25.1 Introduction

The Arab Uprising heralded a time of much promise for the people of the Arab world to obtain the full enjoyment of their rights as citizens, primarily because they were forcefully and loudly claiming those rights. However, the response by national governments, most notably in Syria and Bahrain, the resurgence of popular protests in Egypt, the apparent disengagement of much of the international community after NATO action in Libya, and the fraying consensus among those still engaged, suggests these hopes may have been premature.

Anyone commenting on these unfolding events would be wise to do so modestly, prudently and with an open mind. There are similarities but also many significant differences between the various uprisings, and between their transformative potential. Continued violence and military dominance in Egypt; a civil war, with international involvement, in Libya; the sectarian undertone of the government's crackdown on protesters in Bahrain; the multiplicity of actors in Yemen and the Assad regime's brutal and wide-scale repression in Syria make these more complex, less predictable and, in the cases of Syria and Bahrain, potentially more significant in the broader regional context than many observers first realised.

Yet they still have much in common, especially the tangible demonstration of the idea that rights withheld will not only be claimed, but, if necessary, forcibly taken. That idea, of course, lies at the heart of the Universal Declaration of Human Rights[1] and the international human

Louise Arbour is President and CEO of the International Crisis Group.

[1] See Universal Declaration of Human Rights, GA Res. 217A (III), UN Doc. A/810 at 71 (1948), para. 3 of the Preamble ('it is essential, if man is not to be compelled to have

rights regime. To a considerable extent, the people of Tunisia, Egypt, Libya, Syria and elsewhere have attempted to reclaim from their authoritarian rulers the basic right to self-determination which encompasses all their fundamental human rights and freedoms, under the unifying idea that they are entitled to control their own destiny. This is the basic proposition not only of the UN Charter,[2] but also of the two human rights Covenants – on Civil and Political Rights (the ICCPR) and on Economic, Social and Cultural Rights (ICESCR).[3]

In exercising their right to self-determination, and in claiming rights withheld, the people of North Africa and the Middle East have shattered many myths. Personal leadership, often viewed as key to national uprisings, was of minimal importance. In fact leadership was diffuse, or barely required at all, in Tunisia and Egypt. Similarly, the primacy of an agenda-setting nation or nations was rebuked. The Arab Uprising movements were indigenous, taking the international community and even neighbours by surprise, rather than the product of outward encouragement. The Israeli-Palestinian conflict, often presented as central to the region's politics, appeared to play little part in propelling protests. Demonstrators instead focused mostly on corrupt governance and lack of opportunity, and while the position of Mubarak, for example, on the Israel-Palestinian conflict may have been unpopular, policies on Israel did not take centre stage. The more nebulous concept of the enduring stability of authoritarian regimes was also overturned. Even the most deeply entrenched regimes, such as that of Gaddafi, have not proven immune to popular protest or able to survive it for long.

On the other hand, the uprisings have created their own new mythology: that of the revolutionary impetus provided by the new social networks. The Second World War was said to be the war of the radio; the Vietnam War of television; the first Gulf War of CNN and the rolling news networks; the wars in Iraq, Afghanistan, and the civil conflicts in Iran, Sri Lanka and Thailand were the battles of the internet era. The Arab Uprising, meanwhile, was interpreted by many as driven by Twitter

recourse, as a last resort, to rebellion against tyranny and oppression, that human rights be protected by the rule of law').

2 Article 1(2): 'The purposes of the United Nations are … To develop friendly relations among nations based on respect for the principle of equal rights and self-determination of peoples, and to take other appropriate measures to strengthen universal peace.' 1945 Charter of the United Nations, 1 UNTS 16.

3 See ICCPR and ICESCR common Article (1): 'All peoples have the right of self-determination. By virtue of that right they freely determine their political status and freely pursue their economic, social and cultural development.'

and Facebook. But while these instruments facilitated the unfolding of the movements – in particular in mobilising protesters – and while they have become a powerful means of transmitting the voice of civil society, they do not make revolutions: injustice does. Continued and entrenched injustice, the denial of rights and the subversion of the rule of law drove the Arab Spring uprisings much more than online social networks.

In that sense the events in Tunisia, Egypt, Libya, Yemen, Bahrain, Jordan, Syria and similar events that could take place elsewhere in the region looked, at least initially, to represent the first revival of a genuine international human rights agenda, characterised, at it should be, by people feeling empowered to claim their universal rights in revolt against injustice. They may not cast it that way, but what protesters and insurgents have in common is rebellion not just against political repression, but against that combined with unconscionable economic inequities, themselves rooted in corruption rather than in any claim of merit. It is tempting to downplay the significance of one or the other factor, but it is truly their combination that is lethal to oppressive regimes.

The Arab Uprising has demonstrated what authoritarians have always worked hard to deny: the universality and indivisibility of human rights. While occupying a seat in the Human Rights Council, representatives of these very regimes – Egypt probably being the foremost example – purported to champion human rights, but recast these rights in what they said was a culturally sensitive context. This allowed them, for instance, to reject, as exclusively Western, the idea of gender equality, as well as deny the most basic political rights and freedoms. Rather, they claimed to champion economic and social rights, and the right to development, in an effort to shame Western countries, most of which while not recognising the latter had, in fact, acted upon the former to a far greater degree.

Yet, the response of regional actors, the Arab League in particular, may suggest some movement towards the embracing of common humanitarian goals. The Arab League's resolution calling for a no-fly zone over Libya and the, at least initial, support of key African states for action to halt Gaddafi, paved the way for Chapter VII action by the Security Council.[4] The Arab League's series of resolutions on Syria, calling for an end to the regime's repression, imposing sanctions, and establishing a monitoring group, suggests at least the kernel of willingness to take humanitarian

[4] A number of states, particularly European, said the backing of the Arab League would be crucial to their decision on the establishment of a no-fly zone.

imperatives seriously and respond to the gravest abuses of civil and political rights.[5]

In their rebellion against tyranny, the people of North Africa and the Middle East have not only shown the mediocrity of their systems of governance but underscored the poverty of the international framework of human rights protection. International human rights law imposes a series of obligations on states for the benefit of individual rights-holders.[6] What the international human rights system does not provide is an adequate forum for the enforcement of these rights. In contrast to the Inter-American, European and African human rights systems, the international human rights machinery includes no independent court – there is no International Human Rights Court, for example. Instead, the Human Rights Council is tasked with handling the relationships between rights-holders and states.

It seems self-evident that states, as primary duty-bearers, should not have the monopoly on the adjudication of whether they adequately discharge their own obligations. In democratic national systems, in fact in almost all legal regimes, democratic or not, this is what *courts* do, for better or worse. In their ideal form, courts are fully independent organs of governance, tasked with adjudicating disputes between rights-holders and duty-bearers. Political co-option of courts brings with it severe operational, ethical and conceptual problems. The Human Rights Council, as a forum of states that purports to be guided by legal principles, remains nevertheless a fundamentally political body that does not come close to the independence of a properly functioning court.

The body of human rights law that the Human Right Council is designed to protect and promote deals with issues that are at the heart of the relationship between a government and its people. Not surprisingly, states on the whole do not welcome that kind of external scrutiny. For the most part they are either deferential to other states, hoping for the same treatment when their turn comes, or they side with their friends, for the same unprincipled reasons.

[5] See, for example, Resolution 7442 of the Arab League (27 November 2011) establishing sanctions. English text at www.openbriefing.org/regionaldesks/middleeast/resolution7442/.

[6] Human rights have long been divided into those that are framed negatively – i.e. require the state to refrain from certain actions such as torture, arbitrary arrest and extrajudicial executions – and those framed positively, requiring state action rather than inaction, such as those rights requiring states to provide adequate standards of health, education and shelter, as well as political participation and basic freedoms.

Yet in the case of Libya, both the Human Rights Council and the Security Council embraced a surprisingly robust series of measures that appeared to prioritise human protection over state sovereignty. Security Council Resolution 1973 authorised the use of force against the wishes of a functioning state in order to protect civilians.[7] The apparent success of humanitarian principles and of the responsibility to protect doctrine was, however, short-lived. Shortly after NATO's intervention in Libya, attention switched to unfolding events in Syria, where the Security Council's inaction contrasts starkly to the unprecedented speed of its response to Libya.

The case of Libya does, however, at least require of us a closer examination of two related modes of protection used by the Human Rights Council and the Security Council. The first is the use of international military action as the intervention of last resort under the principle of responsibility to protect – what some call the waging of humanitarian wars or the duty (or right) of humanitarian intervention. The second is the use of individual criminal responsibility under international law to respond to civil wars or repression. Both, in their own ways, focus on the protection of civilians at great risk from their own governments. Both ostensibly rest on humanitarian and legal concerns rather than on political ones. Both represent an erosion of state sovereignty in favour of a larger concept of human security. Both arose in response to the abysmal moral failures of the 1990s, epitomised by the genocide in Rwanda and the ethnic cleansing in the former Yugoslavia; and both have enjoyed increasing, but not by any measure universal, support in recent years. Both are, however, highly vulnerable to corruption or perversion by politics, and yet both inevitably apply in intensely political environments.

On 25 February 2011, the United Nations Human Rights Council adopted Resolution A/HRC /S-15/L.1 in response to the uprising in Libya, and in particular to the brutal repression that the Gaddafi regime launched to crush it.[8] The Human Rights Council used exactly the kind of language that you would expect to hear from a body entrusted with the promotion and protection of human rights worldwide. It strongly condemned the gross human rights violations perpetrated in Libya,

[7] The UN Security Council has authorised peacekeepers to use 'all necessary measures' to protect civilians in the context of non-functioning states, such as Somalia, and in states where consent has been given. For the Libyan mandate, see para. 4 of SC Res. 1973 (2011), UN Doc. S/RES/1973 (2011).

[8] See Human Rights Council Resolution A/HRC/S-15/L.9 on the Situation of human rights in the Libyan Arab Jamahiriya, 25 February 2011.

including indiscriminate armed attacks against civilians; called on the government to meet its responsibility to protect its population; urged the Libyan authorities to respect the popular will, aspirations and demands of its people; and recalled the importance of accountability and the need to fight impunity. On that basis, the Human Rights Council decided to dispatch an independent, international commission of inquiry to investigate all alleged violations of international human rights law and, where possible, make recommendations on accountability measures.

After originally peaceful protests, met by violent state repression, morphed into an armed insurgency and the situation in Libya worsened, the Security Council adopted, on 26 February, Resolution 1970 imposing sanctions on Libya and referring the case to the International Criminal Court (ICC).[9] On 17 March it adopted Resolution 1973 imposing a no-fly zone and authorising 'all necessary measures' short of occupation to protect civilians in Libya.[10]

It's fair to say that this is in stark contrast to the resolution adopted by the Human Rights Council at the end of the war in Sri Lanka in May 2009,[11] when the government of Sri Lanka inflicted a final defeat on the Tamil Tigers, or LTTE, after decades of bloody warfare. In that resolution, the Human Rights Council welcomed the efforts of the government of Sri Lanka to bring permanent peace to the country, and condemned all attacks by LTTE on civilian populations. It made no reference to the gross violations of human rights and international humanitarian law that had been perpetrated by the government forces, instead welcoming the government's continued commitment to the promotion and protection of all human rights. Yet the last few months of the war saw several thousand civilians subjected to indiscriminate armed attacks by government forces in specially created 'no-fire zones' in which they had sought protection and medical treatment, and an estimated 30,000 civilians were killed in a few months of operations on the beaches of Sri Lanka. Sufficient evidence existed to merit, at the very least, an independent investigation into whether the government of Sri Lanka and its security forces committed war crimes and crimes against humanity.

This response, woefully demonstrating the double standards inherent in much of the Human Rights Council's work, was particularly striking

[9] SC Res. 1970 (2011). UN Doc. S/RES/1970 (2011).

[10] See *supra* note 7.

[11] See Human Rights Council, Res. S-11/1 *Assistance to Sri Lanka in the Promotion and Protection of Human Rights*, 26 May 2009.

since the Council had just dispatched a Commission of Inquiry to look at possible violations of the same body of law, during more or less the same period of time, in relation to the Israeli war in Gaza, where some 1,300 people were killed. These double standards in the application of international justice are even more evident in the Security Council, which was never even seized of the matter in relation to Sri Lanka, and which made no ICC referral in the case of either Sri Lanka or the Gaza war. The ICC has also been accused of selectivity in the cases it pursues and prioritises.[12]

The UN action in Libya can also be contrasted with its response to the Syrian uprising and repression that followed. Considering the case of Syria, which soon after Libya experienced an uprising of its own, it is unlikely that UN action on Libya evidenced the shift many had hoped for. There are no signs that the Security Council intends to intervene, at least in military terms, to prevent the continuation of human rights violations committed by the Assad regime. In August 2011, the Security Council issued a statement expressing 'grave concern' over the situation in Syria, acknowledging 'widespread violations of human rights and the use of force against civilians by Syrian authorities', and calling for an immediate end to all violence. Notably, rather than calling for sanctions or outside intervention, the Security Council chose to '[reaffirm] its strong commitment to the sovereignty, independence, and territorial integrity of Syria … [and stress] that the only solution to the current crisis in Syria is through an inclusive and Syrian-led political process'.[13]

Nor, however, has the political and social upheaval in Tunisia, Egypt, Bahrain and other Middle Eastern and North African countries heralded a new dawn in international justice and human rights protection – as some hoped. Rather, the intervention in Libya may not have marked a moment of fundamental change in international politics, but rather the high-water mark of intervention to protect civilians, followed by a swift retreat and retrenchment to concepts of state sovereignty and reluctance to intervene, particularly militarily, in the internal affairs of another state.

Russia and China abstained from Security Council Resolution 1973 on Libya, later alleging that NATO had exceeded its mandate, effectively interpreting its responsibility to protect as authorisation to enact regime

[12] On the 2009 attempt by the Palestinian Authority to seize the ICC Prosecutor of the matter, see the decision of the Prosecutor dated 3 April 2012, at www.icc-cpi.int/NR/rdonlyres/9B651B80-EC43-4945-BF5A-FAFF5F334B92/284387/SituationinPalestine030412ENG.pdf.

[13] See Statement by the President of the Security Council S/PRST/2011/16, dated 3 August 2011.

change. On 5 October 2011 they vetoed a much watered-down European-drafted resolution condemning the Syrian regime's violent crackdown on protesters, arguing that the resolution contained no provision against military intervention in Syria.[14] Though their concerns were likely primarily based on a desire to shore up traditional state sovereignty, the abstentions of Brazil, India and South Africa can be more directly pinned on NATO's actions in Libya and a desire to constrain any possible military intervention. Thus the Libyan intervention may in fact have harmed the doctrine, calling into question the feasibility of future interventions. The lack of unanimous authorisation to use force in the case of Libya also illustrated deep divisions within the UN, notably between the P3 and the BRICS (Brazil, Russia, India, China and South Africa), divisions which appear only to have deepened as the Syrian crisis unfolded.

As they currently stand, and at their sharpest edges, the responsibility to protect and international criminal justice cannot be sheltered from political considerations when they are administered by the quintessential political body: the Security Council.[15] I have long advocated a separation of the justice and political agendas, and would prefer to see an International Criminal Court that has no connection to the Security Council. But such separation is neither the case nor the trend.[16] As for the responsibility to protect, it is clear that military intervention for the protection of civilians must come with a Council mandate.[17] The tangling of international law and international politics is inevitable, but the focus should be on how best to protect the rule of law and the requirements of justice from extraneous political considerations.

[14] The original draft included a reference to sanctions against the Assad regime. This was changed to 'targeted measures' in an effort to accommodate objections from Russia and China.

[15] In a keynote address to the November 2011 mid-year meeting of the American Society for International Law (ASIL), former ICC Prosecutor Luis Moreno-Ocampo admitted that the Security Council's selectivity in referring country situations to the ICC was dictated largely by geopolitical considerations.

[16] As things currently stand, the Security Council may: under Article 13(b) of the Rome Statute refer a country situation to the ICC under Chapter VII of the UN Charter; under Article 16 defer an investigation or prosecution for a period of twelve months on the basis of a resolution adopted under Chapter VII of the UN Charter; and under Article 87(7) act to enforce cooperation with the Court in cases where initial referral has originated from the Security Council. Security Council Resolution 1593 (March 2005) referring the situation in Darfur to the ICC marked the first instance of Security Council referral – Libya was the second.

[17] See World Summit Outcome Document, 15 September 2005, para. 139.

The ultimate form of protection of civilians lies in the prevention, mitigation and resolution of deadly conflict. This can be achieved primarily by political initiatives and the development of systems of good governance. Nevertheless, humanitarian considerations play a large role, as do issues of responsibility and accountability. Indeed the Responsibility to Protect doctrine includes – in line with the Genocide Convention – an obligation to punish when prevention has failed.[18] The pursuit of peace, safety and justice must therefore be choreographed to maximise the saving of civilian lives. And this, in turn, requires preserving to the maximum the integrity of all three processes: humanitarian, judicial and political.

25.2 Responsibility to protect and the requirement of proportionality

The responsibility to protect, a significant transformation of the preceding right of intervention and a relatively new normative construction, asserts that states have a responsibility to protect their people from mass atrocities and that, if a state is unwilling or unable to do so, the responsibility falls onto the international community, acting through the United Nations, to extend that protection.[19]

The doctrine was slow to take root, from its first articulation in the 2001 Canadian-sponsored International Commission on Intervention and State Sovereignty.[20] This may have been due to the release of the Commission's report barely a month after 11 September 2001, when international attention was shifting from the humanitarian issues that had dominated the 1990s to the emerging 'war on terror'. Maybe fearful of the resistance by the strong adherents to the shield of state sovereignty, many proponents of the doctrine chose to emphasise the state, rather than the international, responsibility. They also downplayed its more intrusive aspect, that of military intervention, rather emphasising softer preventative measures in the hope of gaining broad acceptance among UN Member States. This was largely successful, as evidenced by the language of the 2005 World

[18] *Ibid.*, at para. 138.

[19] Mass atrocities were originally expressed in terms of genocide, war crimes, crimes against humanity and ethnic cleansing. For a discussion, see also L. Arbour, 'The Responsibility to Protect as a Duty of Care in International Law and Practice' (2008) 34 *Review of International Studies* 445.

[20] See Report of the International Commission on Intervention and State Sovereignty, *The Responsibility to Protect*, December 2001, at http://responsibilitytoprotect.org/ICISS%20 Report.pdf.

Summit Outcome Document and many subsequent references in UN documents, at least to the state responsibility aspect of the doctrine. Its most notable application came in Resolution 1973 authorising military intervention in Libya, despite the omission of the actual words 'responsibility to protect' – words which, in the case of action against Libya, were only ever used in Resolution 1970 in relation to Libya's own responsibilities towards its people. [21]

However, the years of emphasis on anything but military action left the application of that part of the principle – the most difficult part – underdeveloped. In the report of the International Commission that articulated the R2P principle, military intervention is advocated not only as a last resort but also after a series of checks. The report suggests that 'for military action ever to be defensible the circumstances must be grave indeed', adding that 'less intrusive and coercive measures should always be considered before more coercive and intrusive ones are applied'.[22] Importantly, the Commission elaborated a six-step process to be followed when international military intervention is being considered. What the Libya case illustrated is that when such protocols are not well developed, and when time is of the essence, crucial steps may be overlooked. The most important one, in my view, is not only that military action should be a last resort, but that proportional means be applied, not only when planning the scale, duration and intensity of the intervention, but on an ongoing basis to individual military actions, in line with humanitarian law.

In order to justify military intervention, the threat to civilian lives must be demonstrably grave and imminent.[23] If this test is satisfied, the international community must ensure that less intrusive means have either been tried and failed, or are unlikely to succeed. Finally, the negative consequences or 'collateral damage' of military action must not outweigh the anticipated benefits. This principle traces the requirements of international humanitarian law, which accepts certain civilian losses and damage as incidental consequences of lawful operations, but is wider. In the context of international military intervention under the responsibility to protect, arguably the negative consequences should be assessed more

[21] See the preamble of SC Res. 1970, *supra* note 9.

[22] See International Commission on Intervention and State Sovereignty, *The Responsibility to Protect*, para. 4.1 et seq.

[23] This standard reflects the customary international law test of 'necessity' – the peril must be both grave and imminent. See, inter alia, Article 33 of the International Law Commission's Draft Articles on State Responsibility.

broadly. For example, the likelihood of military action triggering a wider regional armed conflict could militate against the proposed intervention.

Each step would have to be based on credible evidence, not mere assumptions, and crucially they must be applied in an ongoing manner. Some would argue that as Gaddafi's troops advanced on Benghazi, with the declared intention of showing 'no mercy', there was inadequate time for such a comprehensive assessment of the necessity of military action, and of the proportionality of proposed measures. This line of reasoning must be flatly rejected. There had been discussion of a no-fly zone significantly in advance of Gaddafi reaching Benghazi. The effectiveness of such a measure had to be assessed, as did the need for more expansive actions; and their consequences, both operational and political, should have been put into the balance, publicly, well before five minutes to midnight.

Even very late in the process, and in circumstances of extreme urgency, complex and difficult decisions undoubtedly can and must be made within a clear framework. It may appear callous to weigh the imminent potential loss of civilian lives against other considerations, such as the potential larger loss of lives associated with prolonged military engagement, or a reduction in the possibility of ending the war altogether. But this is precisely what must be done, governed by a pre-established policy framework that will prevent, literally, people shooting from the heart.

Once the intervention takes place, the modes of operation and need to maintain, reduce or escalate military action must be assessed, against the same criteria of necessity and proportionality as required by international humanitarian law,[24] on an ongoing basis. Similarly, each military action must be assessed in terms of proportionality under international humanitarian law, in order to minimise civilian damage. This is where the intervention in Libya struggled with conceptual difficulties. Security Council Resolution 1973 authorised 'any necessary measures' to protect civilians.[25] It assumed, not unreasonably, that Gaddafi posed a threat to his citizens – indeed, he posed such a threat for many of his forty-plus years in power. Logic would suggest that only Gaddafi's removal from power in Libya could have ensured the safety of not only those Libyans who took up arms against the regime, but also of civilians likely to be subjected to retaliation by Gaddafi, should he manage to crush the rebellion. Yet, far

[24] The proportionality rule refers to the expected, rather than actual, civilian loss and military advantage, and it therefore is a subjective one: expected civilian losses should not be excessive in relation to the anticipated military advantage. See Article 51(5)(b) and Article 57(2)(a)(iii) and (b) Additional Protocol I to the Geneva Conventions (API).

[25] See para. 4 of SC Res. 1973, *supra* note 7.

from embracing that logic overtly, and under the permissive principle of the Responsibility to Protect doctrine, Western leaders acting under the Security Council Resolution insisted repeatedly that, on the one hand, the bombing was not about regime change but, on the other, that it can only end once the regime has changed. As talk of arming the rebels intensified, as the civil war deepened, and as discussions developed as to what, precisely, constitutes a 'foreign occupation force of any form', humanitarian principles and political objectives were increasingly blurred, to the detriment of both.

25.3 International criminal justice and the independence of the ICC

The 26 February 2011 Security Council decision to refer the situation in Libya to the International Criminal Court is, however, significant for a number of reasons. First, it marks only the second time that the Council has made such a referral – the first occasion coming in a 2005 resolution on Darfur[26] – and the first time that a referral has been unanimously accepted. China and the United States, both of whom abstained on the Darfur resolution, voted in favour.

Second, the Libya referral is noteworthy for the speed with which it was made. In the case of Darfur, the Security Council first established an International Commission of Inquiry to investigate the situation, which worked for three months between October 2004 and January 2005. A further two months passed before the Security Council referral – which eventually included a mandate to investigate events going back to 1 July 2002 – the date on which the Court's jurisdiction began. In short, given that the Darfur conflict began in earnest in early 2003, it took two years and an international inquiry before the Security Council made its referral. Another two months would pass before the ICC formally opened its investigation, and several years before indictments were confirmed.

In comparison, the Libya process progressed at great speed. The decision to refer the situation to the ICC was taken less than two weeks after Gaddafi's crackdown began, and without waiting for the results of a Human Rights Council inquiry, announced just the day before. The ICC also seemed similarly keen to forge ahead: on 2 March, the Prosecutor announced that, following a preliminary investigation, he believed that

[26] See SC Res. 1593 (2005), UN Doc. S/RES/1593 (2005).

there was sufficient evidence to begin a full-scale investigation.[27] The speed of this response is unprecedented: it normally takes months for a preliminary investigation to be concluded – in this case, it took only four days. Then on 16 April, the Prosecutor made a public announcement that he has evidence showing that Gaddafi personally ordered attacks on unarmed civilians.[28] On 27 June 2011, Pre-Trial Chamber I issued three arrest warrants for Muammar Gaddafi, his son Saif, and Abdullah Al-Senussi, Head of Military Intelligence.[29] Muammar Gaddafi's death was confirmed by the National Transitional Council (NTC) in October 2011, but his son Saif has been arrested, and the Libyan Transitional Council has requested that he be tried in Libya.

Third, this decision to initiate an investigation came at a time when the role of the ICC is under scrutiny elsewhere. The Kenyan government in 2011 launched a campaign to suspend the Court's investigation of the 2007–8 post-electoral violence that claimed almost 1,300 lives, arguing that the case could trigger political turmoil in the country. The campaign received strong endorsement from the African Union, though the bid was flatly rejected by the Security Council. The strength of African support for the Kenyan position raises serious questions about the role of the ICC, questions unlikely to be answered solely by the appointment of Gambian national Fatou Bensouda as Prosecutor.

Further questions have been raised in relation to the case against Sudan's President Omar al-Bashir. Despite having been indicted in July 2009,[30] al-Bashir has received the backing of both the Arab League and the African Union. ICC member states Kenya, Chad, Djibouti and Malawi have all welcomed him on their national territory, despite the outstanding arrest warrant. Post-Gaddafi Libya also welcomed the Sudanese Head of

[27] See ICC, Press Release, 'ICC Prosecutor to Open an Investigation in Libya', 2 March 2011, at www.icc-cpi.int/menus/icc/situations%20and%20cases/situations/icc0111/press%20 releases/statement%20020311.

[28] See Office of the Prosecutor, Prosecutor's Application Pursuant to Article 58 as to Muammar Mohammed Abu Minyar GADDAFI, Saif Al-Islam GADDAFI and Abdullah AL-SENUSSI, ICC-01/11–4-Red, 16 April 2011, at www.icc-cpi.int/en_menus/icc/situations%20and%20cases/situations/icc0111/court%20records/filing%20of%20the%20 participants/office%20of%20the%20prosecutor/Pages/4.aspx.

[29] See Pre-Trial Chamber, Decision on the 'Prosecutor's Application Pursuant to Article 58 as to Muammar Mohammed Abu Minyar GADDAFI, Saif Al-Islam GADDAFI and Abdullah AL-SENUSSI', 27 June 2011, at www.icc-cpi.int/iccdocs/doc/doc1099314.pdf.

[30] See ICC, Pre-Trial Chamber I, Warrant of Arrest for Omar Hassan Ahmad Al Bashir, 4 March 2009, at www.icc-cpi.int/iccdocs/doc/doc639078.pdf; Second Warrant of Arrest for Omar Hassan Ahmad Al Bashir, 12 July 2010, at www.icc-cpi.int/iccdocs/doc/doc907140.pdf.

State – though admittedly Libya is not party to the Rome Statute. The situation was further complicated in 2011 when reports emerged that several states, including France and the United States, had in 2008 considered supporting a deferral of al-Bashir's indictment, in return for his cooperation on the secession of South Sudan, and possibly on a final peace agreement with the rebels in Darfur.[31] In the light of these developments, it is perhaps all the more surprising that three African states sitting on the Security Council – South Africa, Gabon and Nigeria – voted in favour of the Libya referral.

The increasing entanglement of justice and politics is unlikely to be good for justice in the long run. Rendering criminal pursuits subservient to political interests by, for example, activating and withdrawing cases as political imperatives dictate, is unlikely to serve the interests of the ICC which must above all establish its credibility and legitimacy as a professional and impartial substitute for deficient national systems of accountability. Partnership with the Security Council, provided for by Article 13(b) of the Rome Statute, is unlikely to prove to be the best way to attain these objectives.

25.4 Conflict prevention as the overarching objective

Humanitarian objectives are critical to the protection of civilians during armed conflicts, and more broadly at times of civil unrest, or during waves of criminality or terrorism, particularly when states of emergency and intense forms of repression are employed. Judicial objectives may also play a role in restraining those with power from the worst excesses. But, in reality, those are for the most part backward-looking tools, rather than forward-looking. When the stakes are high and the institutions weak, deterrence can be easily overrated. In short, ultimate protection must surely come from the prevention and peaceful resolution of conflicts and the application of the rule of law.

These are not distant lofty objectives. They can be pursued both domestically and internationally, and they require awareness of the early indicators of danger and political will to intervene in a preventive fashion. This is currently severely lacking in the international institutional system.

[31] For an analysis of positions of Council members, see War Crimes Research Office, 'The Relationship between the International Criminal Court and the United Nations' (August 2009), at 22–27, at www.wcl.american.edu/warcrimes/icc/documents/WCRO_Report_on_ICC_and_UN_August2009.pdf.

Properly conceived, the Human Rights Council could and should act as the forum of choice for the prevention of deadly conflict. Few of the catastrophic attacks on civilians in recent times have not been preceded by increasingly serious violations of human rights. By the time the Security Council can act on a threat to international peace and security, the situation has usually degenerated to the point of calling for coercive measures. But earlier on, other forms of prevention might have been helpful.

Consider the case of Libya. The Human Rights Council examined the case of Libya under the Universal Periodic Review (UPR) in November 2010. While the massive protests that shook North Africa were not easily predictable last fall, the comments made regarding Libya's human rights performance were hardly indicative of what we are now hearing of the homicidal nature of the Gaddafi regime. The report of the UPR proceedings[32] notes that forty-six delegations made comments. Several noted with appreciation Libya's commitments to upholding human rights. Qatar, for instance – foremost in supporting the rebels in their efforts to oust Gaddafi – praised Libya's legal framework for human rights protection. Australia and Canada welcomed improvements in human rights protection in Libya before expressing some concerns regarding specific issues. Numerous recommendations were made and accepted by Libya, ranging from adopting legislation to abolish torture to adopting a national strategy to combat discrimination against women. Nothing in that document gives any serious reason to believe that the Libyan population had cause to rise in rebellion against oppression, nor that such an uprising would be met by deadly force and illegal reprisals.

25.5 Conclusion

Ongoing events in North Africa and the Middle East are simultaneously the inspiring story of ordinary people taking back their dignity from those who oppressed and exploited them, and, overall, a disheartening tale of ongoing and continual repression, the denial of rights, and subversion of the rule of law. How successful attempts by ordinary citizens to claim their rights will be in the long term remains to be seen. Many of the grievances were economic; but the responses have largely been political or security-focused – indeed, economies appear still to be sliding. Reforms, where they are undertaken, may end up cosmetic and deceptive.

[32] See Human Rights Council, A/HRC/16/15, 4 January 2011.

More broadly, we must ask whether we are encountering a new form of conflict, characterised by its popular, national character, with people rising to overturn abusive authoritarian regimes, with, at least on the surface, no political ideology other than rebellion against economic and political injustice. The speed at which the idea of popular empowerment, in the face of apparently impregnable fortresses of power, has taken place, may signal a new era in power dynamics.

What will the reconstruction chapters look like? Will this be a new era of constitutionalism, of rule of law? Will democracy completely redefine itself, particularly in cases where dictators had been elected? Or are we likely to enter a world of truly failed states, with authority so repudiated that no new form of credible governance can emerge? Is post-authoritarianism likely to be like post-colonialism, with a generation in danger of mimicking the politics of the abusers?

The 2011 World Bank Development Report on Conflict, Security and Development[33] is timely; it emphasises justice and jobs as key to security, and institutions as its guarantor. It also stresses that institution-building takes time and money; decades, not months, and certainly more than the 1 per cent of USAID money allocated to rule-of-law support in Afghanistan in fiscal years from 2002 to 2007.[34] The mere fact that the Bank undertook that study is significant. Will others follow suit? Was the Security Council revolutionised by its willingness to embrace and apply the doctrine of R2P and referrals to the ICC in the case of Libya, or does the case of Syria represent a repudiation of the R2P doctrine and re-entrenchment of state sovereignty?

Will the upheaval caused by the Arab Uprising translate into an understanding by states that the application of international law and good international citizenship is in their national interest? Or does the inaction on Syria signal a quick return to the dichotomy between values and interests? As yet, the answer is unclear. It may all depend, in the end, on whether people will insist on being masters of their own destiny. When they do, they are unstoppable. If anything, they are contagious. And they are claiming nothing more than their human right to be protected under the rule of law.

[33] See World Bank, *The World Development Report 2011: Conflict, Security and Development*, at http://wdr2011.worldbank.org/sites/default/files/pdfs/WDR2011_Full_Text.pdf.

[34] See also 'Afghanistan: Budget and Obligations', USAID, at http://afghanistan.usaid.gov/en/Page.Budget.aspx.

PART VI

Hammarskjöld's credo

Annex 1

The Secretary-General's Annual Report to the General Assembly of the United Nations, Introduction, 17 August 1961

This turned out to be the last of Hammarskjöld's annual statements on the role and future of the United Nations given in his introductions to the Secretary-General's Annual Reports to the General Assembly. As in his Oxford University lecture on 30 May 1961, he pointed out to member governments that they were confronted with a choice between two views of the United Nations – either a 'static conference machinery' or a 'dynamic instrument' of evolution toward more effective forms of international cooperation. This last introduction was Hammarskjöld's definitive statement of the reasons, as he saw them, why the second alternative should be pursued. After dictating it he took the draft to Cordier with the remark, 'I don't see what I can write after this one.' Though completed on 17 August, it was not distributed to delegations and released to the press until 24 August.[1]

I

Debates and events during the year since the publication of the last report to the General Assembly have brought to the fore different concepts of the United Nations, the character of the Organization, its authority, and its structure.

On the one side, it has in various ways become clear that certain Members conceive of the Organization as a static conference machinery for resolving conflicts of interests and ideologies with a view to peaceful co-existence, within the Charter, to be served by a Secretariat which is to be regarded not as fully internationalized but as representing within its ranks those very interests and ideologies.

Other Members have made it clear that they conceive of the Organization primarily as a dynamic instrument of Governments through which they, jointly and for the same purpose, should seek such reconciliation but through which they should also try to develop forms of executive action, undertaken on behalf of all Members, and aiming at forestalling conflicts and resolving

[1] The text of the Introduction is taken from A.W. Cordier and W. Foote, *Public Papers of the Secretaries-General of the United Nations, Vol. V: Dag Hammarskjöld 1960–1961* (1975).

them, once they have arisen, by appropriate diplomatic or political means, in a spirit of objectivity and in implementation of the principles and purposes of the Charter.

Naturally, the latter concept takes as its starting point the conference concept, but it regards it only as a starting point, envisaging the possibility of continued growth to increasingly effective forms of active international cooperation, adapted to experience, and served by a Secretariat of which it is required that, whatever the background and the views of its individual members, their actions be guided solely by the principles of the Charter, the decisions of the main organs, and the interests of the Organization itself.

The first concept can refer to history and to the traditions of national policies of the past. The second can point to the needs of the present and of the future in a world of ever-closer international interdependence where nations have at their disposal armaments of hitherto unknown destructive strength. The first one is firmly anchored in the time-honoured philosophy of sovereign national States in armed competition of which the most that may be expected in the international field is that they achieve a peaceful co-existence. The second one envisages possibilities of inter-governmental action overriding such a philosophy, and opens the road towards more developed and increasingly effective forms of constructive international co-operation.

It is clearly for the Governments, Members of the Organization, and for these Governments only, to make their choice and decide on the direction in which they wish the Organization to develop. However, it may be appropriate to study these two concepts in terms of the purposes of the Organization as laid down in the Charter and, in this context, also to consider the character and the significance of the decisions of the Organization as well as its structure.

II

The purposes and principles of the Charter are set out in its Preamble and further developed in a series of articles, including some which may seem to be primarily of a procedural or administrative nature. Together, these parts of the Charter lay down some basic rules of international ethics by which all Member States have committed themselves to be guided. To a large extent, the rules reflect standards accepted as binding for life within States. Thus, they appear, in the main, as a projection into the international arena and the international community of purposes and principles already accepted as being of national validity. In this sense, the Charter takes a first step in the direction of an organized international community, and this independently of the organs set up for international co-operation. Due to different traditions, the state of social development and the character of national institutions, wide variations naturally exist as to the application in national life of the principles reflected in the Charter, but it is not too difficult to recognize the common elements behind those differences. It is therefore not surprising that such principles of national application could be transposed into an agreed basis also for international behaviour and co-operation.

In the Preamble to the Charter, Member nations have reaffirmed their faith 'in the equal rights of men and women and of nations large and small,' a principle which also has found many other expressions in the Charter.

Thus, it re-states the basic democratic principle of equal political rights, independently of the position of the individual or of the Member country in respect of its strength, as determined by territory, population or wealth. The words just quoted must, however, be considered as going further and imply an endorsement as well of a right to equal economic opportunities.

It is in the light of the first principle that the Charter has established a system of equal votes, expressing 'the sovereign equality of all its Members', and has committed the Organization to the furtherance of self-determination, self-government and independence. On the same basis, the Charter requires universal respect for and observance of human rights and fundamental freedoms for all 'without distinction as to race, sex, language or religion'.

It is in the light of the latter principle – or, perhaps, the latter aspect of the same basic principle – that the Charter, in Article 55, has committed the Members to the promotion of higher standards of living, full employment and conditions of economic and social progress and development as well as to solutions of international economic and related problems. The pledge of all Members to take joint and separate action, in cooperation with the Organization, for the achievement of these purposes has been the basis for the far-reaching economic and technical assistance channelled through or administered by the Organization, and may rightly be considered as the basic obligation reflected also in such economic and technical assistance as Member Governments have been giving, on a bilateral basis, outside the framework of the Organization.

It would seem that those who regard the Organization as a conference machinery, 'neutral' in relation to the direction of policies on a national or international basis and serving solely as an instrument for the solution of conflicts by reconciliation, do not pay adequate attention to those essential principles of the Charter to which reference has just been made. The terms of the Charter are explicit as regards the equal political rights of nations as well as of individuals and, although this second principle may be considered only as implicit in the terms of the Charter, they are clear also as regards the demand for equal economic opportunities for all individuals and nations. So as to avoid any misunderstanding, the Charter directly states that the basic democratic principles are applicable to nations 'large and small' and to individuals without distinction 'as to race, sex, language and religion', qualifications that obviously could be extended to cover other criteria such as, for example, those of an ideological character which have been used or may be used as a basis for political or economic discrimination.

In the practical work of the Organization these basic principles have been of special significance in relation to countries under colonial rule or in other ways under foreign domination. The General Assembly has translated the principles into action intended to establish through self-determination a free and independent life as sovereign States for peoples who have expressed in democratic forms their wish for such a status. Decisive action has in many cases been taken by Member Governments, and then the United Nations has had only to lend its support to their efforts. In other cases, the main responsibility has fallen on the Organization itself. The resolution on colonialism, adopted by the General Assembly at its fifteenth session, may be regarded as a comprehensive re-statement in elaborated form of the principle laid down in the Charter. Results of developments so far have been reflected in the birth of a great number of new national States and a revolutionary widening of the membership of the Organization.

The demand for equal economic opportunities has, likewise, been – and remains – of special significance in relation to those very countries which have more recently entered the international arena as new States. This is natural in view of the fact that, mostly, they have been in an unfavourable economic position, which is reflected in a much lower *per capita* income, rate of capital supply, and degree of technical development, while their political independence and sovereignty require a fair measure of economic stability and economic possibilities in order to gain substance and full viability.

In working for the translation into practical realities in international life of the democratic principles which are basic to the Charter, the Organization has thus assumed a most active role and it has done so with success, demonstrating both the need and the possibilities for such action.

Further, in the Preamble to the Charter it is stated to be a principle and purpose of the Organization 'to establish conditions under which justice and respect for the obligations arising from treaties and other sources of international law can be maintained'. In these words – to which, naturally, counterparts may be found in other parts of the Charter – it gives expression to another basic democratic principle, that of the rule of law. In order to promote this principle, the Charter established the International Court of Justice, but the principle permeates the approach of the Charter to international problems far beyond the sphere of competence of the Court. As in national life, the principle of justice – which obviously implies also the principle of objectivity and equity in the consideration of all matters before the General Assembly or the Security Council – must be considered as applicable without distinction or discrimination, with one measure and one standard valid for the strong as well as for the weak. Thus, the demand of the Charter for a rule of law aims at the substitution of right for might and makes of the Organization the natural protector of rights which countries, without it, might find it more difficult to assert and to get respected.

The principle of justice can be regarded as flowing naturally from the principles of equal political rights and equal economic opportunities, but it has an independent life and carries, of itself, the world community as far in the direction of an organized international system as the two first-mentioned principles. It has deep roots in the history of the efforts of man to eliminate from international life the anarchy which he had already much earlier overcome on the national level, deeper indeed than the political and economic principles which, as is well known, were much later to get full acceptance also in national life. Long before the United Nations and long before even the League of Nations, Governments were working towards a rule of justice in international life through which they hoped to establish an international community based on law, without parliamentary or executive organs, but with a judicial procedure through which law and justice could be made to apply.

The Charter states and develops the three principles mentioned here as a means to an end: 'to save succeeding generations from the scourge of war'. This adds emphasis to the concept, clearly implied in the Charter, of an international community for which the Organization is an instrument and an expression and in which anarchic tendencies in international life are to be curbed by the introduction of a system of equal political rights, equal economic opportunities and the rule of law. However, the Charter goes one step further, drawing a logical conclusion both from the ultimate aim of the Organization and from the three principles. Thus, it outlaws the use of armed force 'save in the common interest'. Obviously, the Charter cannot, on the one side, establish a rule of law and the principle of equal rights for 'nations large and small', and, on the other hand, permit the use of armed force for national ends, contrary to those principles and, therefore, not 'in the common interest'. Were nations, under the Charter, to be allowed, by the use of their military strength, to achieve ends contrary to the principle of the equality of Members and the principle of justice, it would obviously deprive those very principles of all substance and significance. One practical expression of this approach, which may be mentioned here, is that the organs of the United Nations have consistently maintained that the use of force, contrary to the Charter as interpreted by those organs, cannot be permitted to yield results which can be accepted as valid by the Organization and as establishing new rights.

In the Charter, the right to the use of force is somewhat more extensive than may seem to be the case from a superficial reading of the phrase 'save in the common interest'. Thus, apart from military action undertaken pursuant to a decision of the Security Council for repression of aggression – that is, for upholding the basic Charter principles – the Charter opens the door to the use of armed force by a nation in exercise of its inherent right to resist armed attack. This is a point on which, both in theory and in practice, the development of international law is still at a very early stage. As is well known, no agreement has been reached on a definition of aggression, beyond that found in Article 2, paragraph 4, of the Charter, and the Organization has several times had to face situations in which, therefore, the rights and wrongs in a specific case of conflict have not been clarified. It would be a vitally important step forward if wider agreement could be reached regarding the criteria to be applied in order to distinguish between legitimate and illegitimate use of force. History is only too rich in examples of armed aggression claimed as action in self-defence. How could it be otherwise, when most cases of armed conflict are so deeply rooted in a history of clashes of interests and rights, even if, up to the fatal moment of the first shot, those clashes have not involved recourse to the use of armed force?

In recognition of this situation and in the light of historical experience, the Charter makes yet another projection into international life of solutions to conflicts tested in national life, and establishes the final principle that the Organization shall 'bring about by peaceful means and in conformity with the principles of justice and international law, adjustment or settlement of international disputes or situations which might lead to a breach of the peace'. This principle, as quoted here from Article 1 of the Charter, is further developed specifically in Article 33, which requires parties to any dispute, the consequence of which is likely to endanger the maintenance of international peace and security, to 'seek a solution by negotiation, enquiry, mediation, conciliation, arbitration, judicial settlement, resort to regional agencies or arrangements, or other peaceful means of their own choice'. It is in this sphere that the Security Council has had, and is likely to continue to have, its main significance, both directly as a forum before which any dispute threatening peace and security can be brought up for debate and as an organ which directly, or through appropriate agents, may assist the parties in finding a way out and, by preventive diplomacy, may forestall the outbreak of an armed conflict. It seems appropriate here to draw attention especially to the right of the Security Council under Article 40 to 'call upon the parties concerned to comply with such provisional measures as it deems necessary or desirable' for the prevention of any aggravation of a situation threatening peace and security, and to the obligation of Members to comply with a decision on such measures.

It is in the light of the approach to international co-existence in our world today, which is thus to be found in the Charter, that judgement has to be passed on the validity of the different conceptions of the Organization which in recent times have become increasingly apparent. As already pointed out, the basic principles regarding the political equality of nations and their right to equal economic opportunities are difficult to reconcile with the view that the Organization is to be regarded only as a conference machinery for the solution, by debate and joint decisions, of conflicts of interest or ideology. It seems even more difficult to reconcile these principles with a view according to which equality among Members should be reflected in the establishment of a balance between power-blocs or other groupings of nations. The same difficulty is apparent as regards the principle of justice and the principle prohibiting the use of armed force. It is easier to apply the conference concept to the principle of prevention of conflict through negotiation, but also on this point the difficulties become considerable if it is recognized that such solutions as may be sought by the Organization should be solutions based on the rules of equality and justice.

III

The General Assembly, the Security Council, and other collective organs of the United Nations have features in common with a standing international diplomatic conference, but their procedures go beyond the forms of such a conference and show aspects of a parliamentary or quasi-parliamentary character.

While decisions of a conference, in order to commit its participants, must be based on their subsequent acceptance of the decisions, the organs of the United Nations act on the basis of voting, with the decisions being adopted if supported by a majority. However, the decisions of the Assembly have, as regards Member States, only the character of recommendations (except for financial assessments and certain other types of organizational action) so that obligations like those arising out of an agreement, coming into force after a conference, do not normally flow from them. But although the decisions, legally, are only recommendations, they introduce an important element by expressing a majority consensus on the issue under consideration.

Naturally, such a formula leaves scope for a gradual development in practice of the weight of the decisions. To the extent that more respect, in fact, is shown to General Assembly recommendations by the Member States, they may come more and more close to being recognized as decisions having a binding effect on those concerned, particularly when they involve the application of the binding principles of the Charter and of international law.

Both those who regard a gradual increase in the weight of decisions of the General Assembly as necessary, if progress is to be registered in the direction of organized peaceful co-existence within the Charter, and those who oppose such a development, have to recognize that, with certain variations in individual cases, the practice still is very close to the restrictive Charter formula. Experience shows that even countries which have voted for a certain decision may, later on, basing themselves on its character of merely being a recommendation, refuse to follow it or fail to support its implementation, financially or in other respects.

What has been said applies generally to the collective organs of the Organization, but, as is well known, the Charter has gone one step further beyond the conference concept, in the direction of the parliamentary concept, in the case of the Security Council. In Article 25, Member States of the United Nations have agreed to 'accept and carry out the decisions of the Security Council in accordance with the present Charter', thus, by agreement, making the decisions of the Council mandatory, except, of course, when such decisions take the form of 'recommendations' within the terms of Chapter VI or certain other articles of the Charter. They have further, in Article 49, undertaken to 'join in affording mutual assistance in carrying out the measures decided upon by the Security Council'.

This agreed mandatory nature of certain Security Council decisions might have led to a demand for unanimity in the Council, a unanimity which was the rule for the Council of the League of Nations. Even so, however, the arrangement would have gone beyond the conference principle with its requirement that no decision reached in an international organ should be binding on an individual Member short of his agreement. With the present arrangements, requiring a majority of seven and the concurring votes of the permanent Members, a bridge between the traditional conference approach and a parliamentary approach is provided by the commitment in Article 25 to agree to the carrying out of the decisions in the Council which should be considered as giving the Council its authority by general delegation as indeed stated in Article 24, paragraph 1.

What clearly remains within the Council of the traditional conference and agreement pattern is the condition that its decisions of a non-procedural character must be supported by the unanimous vote of the five permanent Members, thus avoiding for those Members the risk of being bound by a decision of the Council which has not met with their agreement. It may be observed that this special position for the permanent Members, apart from other reasons, has the justification that, without such a rule, the other Members of the Organization, in complying with a Security Council decision, might find themselves unwillingly drawn into a Big-Power conflict.

In spite of the delegated authority which the Council may be considered as exercising, and the condition that decisions must be agreed to by the permanent Members, the experience of the Organization, as regards the implementation of Council decisions, is uneven and does not indicate full acceptance in practice of Article 25. In this case also, examples can be given of a tendency to regard decisions, even when taken under Chapter VII, as recommendations binding only to the extent that the party concerned has freely committed itself to carry them out; there is here a clear dichotomy between the aims of the Charter and the general political practice at its present stage of development. Such cases refer not only to Members outside the Council, or, perhaps, Members inside the Council, who have not supported a specific decision, but also to Members within the Council who have cast their votes in favour of a decision but who later on are found to reserve for themselves at least a right to interpret the decision in ways which seem to be at variance with the intentions of the Council. The ambiguity of this situation emerges with special force in cases where such attitudes have been taken by permanent Members of the Council, who are considered to shoulder the responsibility for the maintenance of peace and security which is reflected in the special position they hold within the Council. Obviously, the problem whether the intended legal weight is given to decisions of the Security Council arises in practice not only in cases of non-compliance but also in cases of a refusal to shoulder the financial consequences of a decision of the Council.

These observations – which have been limited to a reminder of the Charter rules and a factual reminder also of the experiences in practice – point to a situation which in any evaluation of the United Nations must be given the most serious consideration by Members. For the judgement on the various concepts of the United Nations which are put forward, it is one thing to note what the Charter stipulates; it is an entirely different but ultimately more important question as to what the situation is in practice and what, in fact, is the weight given to decisions of the Organization when they go beyond the conference pattern of agreement.

For those who maintain the conference concept of the Organization, it is natural to side-step the mandatory nature of decisions by the Security Council. For those who take a different view, it is equally natural and essential to work for a full and general acceptance of the Charter rules. Were those to be right who hold that the Charter on the points discussed here, and, maybe, also as regards the five basic principles discussed in the first part of this Introduction, is ahead of our time and the political possibilities which it offers, such a view still would not seem to justify the conclusion that the clear approach of the Charter should be abandoned. Rather, it would indicate that Member nations jointly should increase their efforts to make political realities gradually come closer to the pattern established by the Charter.

In the light of such considerations, the significance of the outcome of every single conflict on which the Organization has to take a stand, and the weight given to its decisions in such a conflict stand out very clearly. A failure to gain respect for decisions or actions of the Organization within the terms of the Charter is often called a failure for the Organization. It would seem more correct to regard it as a failure of the world community, through its Member nations and in particular those most directly concerned, to cooperate in order, step by step, to make the Charter a living reality in practical political action as it is already in law.

Were such co-operation, for which the responsibility naturally rests with each single Member as well as with all Members collectively, not to come about, and were the respect for the obligations flowing from Article 25 of the Charter, to be allowed to diminish, this would spell the end of the possibilities of the Organization to grow into what the Charter indicates as the clear intention of the founders, as also of all hopes to see the Organization grow into an increasingly effective instrument, with increasing respect for recommendations of the General Assembly as well.

What this would mean for the value of the Organization as protector of the aims, principles and rights it was set up to further and safeguard, is obvious. The effort through the Organization to find a way by which the world community might, step by step, grow into organized international co-operation within the Charter, must either progress or recede. Those whose reactions to the work of the Organization hamper its development or reduce its possibilities of effective action, may have to shoulder the responsibility for a return to a state of affairs which Governments had already found too dangerous after the First World War.

IV

The growth of the United Nations out of the historic conference pattern – which, as observed earlier in this Introduction, at all events naturally remains the starting point in all efforts of the Organization – is clearly reflected in what, in the light of experience, may seem to be a lack of balance in the Charter. While great attention is given to the principles and purposes, and considerable space is devoted to an elaboration of what may be called the parliamentary aspects of the Organization, little is said about executive arrangements. This does not mean that the Charter in any way closes the door to such arrangements or to executive action, but only that, at the stage of international thinking crystallized in the Charter, the conference approach still was predominant, and that the needs for executive action, if the new Organization was to live up to expectations and to its obligations under the Charter, had not yet attracted the attention they were to receive in response to later developments.

The key clause on the executive side may be considered to be Article 24 in which it is said that 'in order to assure prompt and effective action by the United Nations, its Members confer on the Security Council primary responsibility for the maintenance of international peace and security'. On that basis the Security Council is given the right, under Article 29, to establish such subsidiary organs as it deems necessary for the performance of its functions, the right under Article 40 to decide on so-called provisional measures, the right to use, for the purposes of the Charter, under certain conditions, armed forces made available to the Council, the right under Article 48 to request from Governments action on the Council's behalf, as well as the right to request of the Secretary-General to 'perform such … functions as are entrusted to him' by the Council.

The various clauses here briefly enumerated open a wide range of possibilities for executive action undertaken by, and under the aegis of, the Security Council. However, no specific machinery is set up for such action by the Council, apart from the Military Staff Committee, with planning responsibilities in the field of the possible use of armed force by the Security Council under Chapter VII of the Charter. In fact, therefore, the executive functions and their form have been left largely to practice, and it is in the field of the practices of the Organization that cases may be found in the light of which it is now possible to evaluate the ways in which the Organization may develop its possibilities for diplomatic, political or military intervention of an executive nature in the field.

The forms used for executive action by the Security Council – or when the Council has not been able to reach decisions, in some cases, by the General Assembly – are varied and are to be explained by an effort to adjust the measures to the needs of each single situation. However, some main types are recurrent. Subcommittees have been set up for fact-finding or negotiation on the spot. Missions have been placed in areas of conflict for the purpose of observation and local negotiation. Observer groups of a temporary nature have been sent out. And, finally, police forces under the aegis of the United Nations have been organized for the assistance of the Governments concerned with a view to upholding the principles of the Charter. As these, or many of these, arrangements require centralized administrative measures, which cannot be performed by the Council or the General Assembly, Members have to a large extent used the possibility to request the Secretary-General to perform special functions by instructing him to take the necessary executive steps for implementation of the action decided upon. This has been done under Article 98, as quoted above, and has represented a development in practice of the duties of the Secretary-General under Article 97. The character of the mandates has, in many cases, been such that in carrying out his functions the Secretary-General has found himself forced also to interpret the decisions in the light of the Charter, United Nations precedents and the aims and intentions expressed by the Members. When that has been the case, the Secretary-General has been under the obligation to seek guidance, to all possible extent, from the main organs; but when such guidance has not been forthcoming, developments have sometimes led to situations in which he has had to shoulder responsibility for certain limited political functions, which may be considered to be in line with the spirit of Article 99 but which legally have been based on decisions of the main organs themselves, under Article 98, and thus the exclusive responsibility of Member States acting through these organs. Naturally, in carrying out such functions the Secretariat has remained fully subject to the decisions of the political bodies.

This whole development has lately become a matter of controversy, natural and, indeed, unavoidable in the light of differences of approach to the role of the Organization to which attention has been drawn earlier in this Introduction. While the development is welcomed by Member nations which feel a need of growth as regards the possibilities of the Organization to engage in executive action in protection of the Charter principles, it is rejected by those who maintain the conference concept of the Organization. The different opinions expressed on the development are only superficially related to this or that specific action and the way in which it is considered to have been carried through. They are also only superficially related to the choice of means used for translating decisions into action. The discussion regarding the development of executive functions is basically one confronting the same fundamentally different concepts of the Organization and its place in international politics, which could be seen also in the different attitudes towards the legal weight of decisions of the Organization.

It is in this context that the principle embodied in Article 100 of the Charter is of decisive significance. This principle, which has a long history, establishes the international and independent character of the Secretariat. Thus, it is said that the Secretary-General and the staff of the Secretariat 'shall not seek or receive instructions from any Government or from any other authority external to the Organization', and that they 'shall refrain from any action which might reflect on their position as international officials responsible only to the Organization'. In the same Article, the Members of the United Nations undertake to respect 'the exclusively international character of the responsibilities of the Secretary-General and the staff and not to seek to influence them in the discharge of their responsibilities'.

The significance of the principle stated in Article 100 is a dual one. It envisages a Secretariat so organized and developed as to be able to serve as a neutral instrument for the Organization, were its main organs to wish to use the Secretariat in the way which has been mentioned above and for which Article 98 has opened possibilities. But in doing so, the principle also indicates an intention to use the Secretariat for such functions as would require that it have an exclusively international character.

In the traditional conference pattern, participants in a meeting are mostly serviced by a secretariat drawn from the same countries as the participants themselves, and constituting a mixed group regarding which there is no need to demand or maintain an exclusively international character. It is therefore natural that those who favour the conference approach to the United Nations tend to give to Article 100 another interpretation than the one which the text calls for, especially in the light of its historical background and its background also in other clauses of the Charter.

There is no reason to go more deeply into this special problem here. Suffice it to say that, while the Organization, if regarded as a standing diplomatic conference, might well be serviced by a fully international Secretariat but does not need it, the other approach to the Organization and its role cannot be satisfied with anything less than a secretariat of an exclusively international character, and thus cannot be reconciled with a secretariat composed on party-lines and on the assumption that the interests represented in the main organs in this manner should be represented and advocated also within the Secretariat. Thus, again, the choice between conflicting views on the United Nations Secretariat is basically a choice between conflicting views on the Organization, its functions, and its future.

In order to avoid possible misunderstandings, it should be pointed out here that there is no contradiction at all between a demand for a truly international Secretariat and a demand, found in the Charter itself, for as wide a 'geographical' distribution of posts within the Secretariat as possible. It is, indeed, necessary precisely in order to maintain the exclusively international character of the Secretariat, that it be so composed as to achieve a balanced distribution of posts on all levels among all regions. This, however, is clearly something entirely different from a balanced representation of trends or ideologies. In fact if a realistic representation of such trends is considered desirable, it can and should be achieved without any assumption of political representation within the ranks of the Secretariat, by a satisfactory distribution of posts based on geographical criteria.

The exclusively international character of the Secretariat is not tied to its composition, but to the spirit in which it works and to its insulation from outside influences as stated in Article 100. While it may be said that no man is neutral in the sense that he is without opinions or ideals, it is just as true that, in spite of this, a neutral Secretariat is possible. Anyone of integrity, not subjected to undue pressures, can, regardless of his own views, readily act in an 'exclusively international' spirit and can be guided in his actions on behalf of the Organization solely by its interests and principles, and by the instructions of its organs.

V

After this brief review of the principles of the Organization, of the character of its decisions and of its structure, especially as regards arrangements for executive action, presented only as a background for the consideration of what basic concepts and approaches should guide the development of the

Organization, it may be appropriate, in conclusion, to give attention to the activities of the Organization and their relevance to the current international situation.

For years the Organization has been a focal point for efforts to achieve disarmament. This may still be considered as the main standing item on the agenda of the General Assembly. However, in recent years these efforts of the Organization have been running parallel to other efforts which are either outside of it or only loosely tied to the work of the United Nations. This may be justified on the basis that a very limited number of countries hold key positions in the field of armaments, so that any effort on a universal basis and by voting, to reach a decision having practical force, would be ineffective, unless founded on a basic agreement between those few parties mostly concerned. Therefore, direct negotiations between those countries are an essential first step to the solution, through the United Nations, of the disarmament problem, and do not in any way derogate from the responsibilities or rights of the Organization.

The situation may serve as an example of a problem which has become increasingly important in the life of the Organization: the right way in which to balance the weight of the Big Powers and their security interests against the rights of the majority of Member nations. Such a majority naturally cannot expect the Big Powers, in questions of vital concern to them, with their superior military and economic strength, automatically to accept a majority verdict. On the other hand, the Big Powers cannot, as Members of the world community, and with their dependence on all other nations, set themselves above, or disregard the views of, the majority of nations. An effort to balance the Big Power element and the majority element is found in the Charter rules regarding the respective competence of the General Assembly and the Security Council and regarding the special position of the Big Powers within the Council. Other efforts to solve the same problem are reflected in the way in which the disarmament problem has been attacked in recent years. No fully satisfactory or definitive formula has been found, but it must be sought, and it is to be hoped that when the time comes for a Charter revision, agreement may be reached on a satisfactory solution.

What is true of the disarmament problem is, of course, true also of those more specific questions in which security interests of Big Powers are or may be directly involved, as for example the Berlin problem. The community of nations, represented in the United Nations, has a vital interest in a peaceful solution, based on justice, of any question which – like this one – unless brought to a satisfactory solution, might come to represent a threat to peace and security. However, the problem of the balance to be struck between the rights and obligations of the Big Powers and the rights and obligations of all other nations applies, in a very direct way, also to this problem which is now so seriously preoccupying the minds of all peoples and their leaders. The United Nations, with its wide membership, is not, and can, perhaps, not aspire to be a focal point in the debate on an issue such as the Berlin question, or in the efforts to solve it, but the Organization cannot, for that reason, be considered as an outside party which has no right to make its voice heard should a situation develop which would threaten those very interests which the United Nations is to safeguard and for the defence of which it was intended to provide all Member nations with an instrument and a forum.

Reference has already been made in this Introduction to the work of the Organization devoted to furthering self-determination, self-government and independence for all peoples. In that context it was recalled that the General Assembly, at its last session, adopted a resolution regarding the colonial problem which elaborates the basic principles of the Charter in their application to this problem.

This is, likewise, a question which for years has been before the General Assembly and it is likely to remain a major item until a final result is achieved which reflects full implementation of the basic principles in the direction indicated by last year's resolution. Experience has shown that peaceful progress in that direction cannot be guaranteed solely by decisions of the General Assembly or the Security Council, within the framework of a conference pattern. Executive action is necessary, and neither the General Assembly nor the Security Council – which has had to deal with situations in which the liquidation of the colonial system has led to acute conflict – has abstained from such action in support of the lines upheld. As in the past, executive action by the Organization in the future will undoubtedly also be found necessary if it is to render the service expected from it under the terms of the Charter.

It is in conflicts relating to the development towards full self-government and independence that the Organization has faced its most complicated tasks in the executive field. It is also in the case of executive action in this context that different concepts of the Organization and of its decisions and structure have their most pointed expressions. As regards this specific aspect of the work of the United Nations, the front line has not been the usual one between different bloc interests, but more one between a great number of nations with aims natural especially for those which recently have been under colonial rule or under other forms of foreign domination, and a limited number of powers with other aims and predominant interests. This seems understandable if one takes into account that a majority of nations wishes to stand aside from the Big-Power conflicts, while power blocs or Big Powers tend to safeguard their positions and security by efforts to maintain or extend an influence over newly emerging areas. The United Nations easily becomes a focal point for such conflicting interests as the majority looks to the Organization for support in their policy of independence also in relation to such efforts, while power blocs or countries with other aims may see in the United Nations an obstacle in the way of their policies to the extent that the Organization provides the desired support. How this is reflected in the attitude towards the development of the executive functions of the United Nations can be illustrated by numerous examples. It may be appropriate in this context to say in passing a word about the problem of the Congo and the activities of the United Nations in that country.

Different interests and powers outside Africa have seen in the Congo situation a possibility of developments with strong impact on their international position. They have therefore, naturally, held strong views on the direction in which they would like to see developments in the Congo turn and – with the lack of political traditions in the country and without the stability which political institutions can get only by being tested through experience – the doors have been opened for efforts to influence developments by supporting this or that faction or this or that personality. True to its principles, the United Nations has had to be guided in its operation solely by the interest of the Congolese people and by their right to decide freely for themselves, without any outside influences and with full knowledge of facts. Therefore, the Organization, throughout the first year of its work in the Congo, up to the point when Parliament reassembled and invested a new national Government, has refused – what many may have wished – to permit the weight of its resources to be used in support of any faction so as thereby to prejudge in any way the outcome of a choice which belonged solely to the Congolese people. It has also had to pursue a line which, by safeguarding the free choice of the people, implied resistance against all efforts from outside to influence the outcome. In doing so, the Organization has been put in a position in which those within the country who felt disappointed in not getting the support of the Organization were led to suspect that others were in a more favoured position and, therefore, accused the Organization of partiality, and in which, further, such outside elements as tried to get or protect a foothold within the country, when meeting an obstacle in the United Nations, made similar accusations. If, as it is sincerely to be hoped, the recent national reconciliation, achieved by Parliament and its elected representatives of the people, provides a stable basis for a peaceful future in a fully independent and unified Congo, this would definitely confirm the correctness of the line pursued by the United Nations in the Congo. In fact, what was achieved by Parliament early in August may be said to have done so with sufficient clarity. It is a thankless and easily misunderstood role for the Organization to remain neutral in relation to a situation of domestic conflict and to provide active assistance only by protecting the rights and possibilities of the people to find their own way, but it remains the only manner in which the Organization can serve its proclaimed purpose of furthering the full independence of the people in the true and unqualified sense of the word.

The United Nations may be called upon again to assist in similar ways. Whatever mistakes in detail and on specific points critics may ascribe to the

Organization in the highly complicated situation in the Congo, it is to be hoped that they do not lead Members to revise the basic rules which guide the United Nations activities in such situations, as laid down in the first report of the Secretary-General to the Security Council on the Congo question, which the Council, a year ago, found reason, unanimously, to commend.

Closely related to a policy aiming at self-government and independence for all is the question of economic and technical assistance, especially during the first years of independence of a new Member State. The United Nations and its agencies and affiliated organs have at their disposal only very modest means for the purpose, but a rich experience has been gathered and the personnel resources are not inconsiderable.

Last year the Economic and Social Council and the General Assembly had to consider proposals designed to open up new possibilities for the Organization to respond to the demands of Member Governments facing all the problems of newly achieved independence. Naturally, the problems which are of special importance for such countries are basically the same as those which face all countries which have been left behind in economic development. Therefore, the urgent attention required by newly independent countries in this respect can in no way justify a discrimination in their favour against other countries with similar difficulties.

This year the General Assembly will have before it proposals initiated by the Scientific Advisory Committee and endorsed by the Economic and Social Council, for a conference under United Nations aegis, intended to provide possibilities for a break-through in the application of the technical achievements of present times to the problems of the economically less developed countries. It is sincerely to be hoped that, in the interest of international co-operation and the acceleration of the economic progress of those countries, this proposal will meet with the approval of the General Assembly.

So far, the economic and technical activities of the United Nations have been less influenced by the conflict between different concepts of the role of the Organization than its activities in other fields. However, it is impossible to isolate the economic and technical problems from the general question discussed in this Introduction. While receiving countries should have full freedom to take assistance from whatever source they find appropriate, they should not be barred, if they so wish, from getting all the assistance they need through United Nations channels or under United Nations aegis. The Organization is far from being able to meet all such demands, as donor nations continue to show a strong preference for bilateral approaches on a national or group basis. Again, the problem arises of the basic concept of the United Nations. With the conference approach to the work of the Organization a choice is made also in favour of bilateral assistance, while the alternative approach opens the door to a development under which international assistance, in implementation of the principle of equal economic opportunities for all, would be channelled through the Organization or its related agencies to all the extent that this is desired by the recipient countries and is within the capacity of the Organization.

Basic to the United Nations approach to economic and technical assistance is the principle, under all circumstances, that, although the Organization has to follow its own rules and maintain its own independence, its services are exclusively designed to meet the wishes of the recipient Government, without the possibility of any ulterior motives and free from the risk of any possible influence on the national or international policies of that Government. Whatever development the executive activities of the Organization may show in the field, there should never be any suspicion that the world community would wish or, indeed, could ever wish to maintain for itself, through the United Nations, a position of power or control in a Member country. Were political groups in a country really to believe in such a risk, the explanation would seem to be that, as had indeed happened in the case of Governments of Member countries with long established independence, they may find it difficult to accept the judgement of the majority of the nations of the world as to what in a specific situation is necessary in order to safeguard international peace and security, when such a judgement appears to be in conflict with the immediate aims of the group. With growing respect for the decisions of the Organization and growing understanding of its principles, the risks for such misinterpretations should be eliminated.

This Introduction has limited itself to general observations on questions of principle, leaving all problems of detail to the report itself. This has seemed appropriate in view of the fact that the Organization has now reached a stage in its development where Member nations may find it timely to clarify their views on the direction in which they would like to see the future work of the Organization develop.

DAG HAMMARSKJÖLD
Secretary-General

17 August 1961

Annex 2

Address given by the Secretary-General, Mr Dag Hammarskjöld, on the Occasion of Staff Day, General Assembly Hall, 8 September 1961

I am happy to have this opportunity to meet with you today. Both in the world at large, and by way of repercussion of world events on the Organization, much has happened during the two years which have elapsed since the last Staff Day.

During this period the General Assembly has met under most exacting circumstances and the Organization has had to undertake a major operation which in its magnitude and complexity has been quite unique in its history. As a result, the resources of the Secretariat have been heavily taxed, and I know that all of you have had to work under considerable pressure and that many of you have had to put in very long hours.

Those of you who have responded to the call to go out to the Congo, mostly at short notice, have displayed your readiness often despite considerable personal and family inconvenience. Quite a few of those who went out to the Congo are now back in New York and their place has been taken by others. I hope that all those of you who have had this opportunity of participating in the Congo operation feel as enriched by your experience as the Organization has been enriched by your contribution.

I have publicly paid tribute to all those who have participated directly in the Congo operation; but tribute is due equally to those who stayed behind and did the back-stopping from Headquarters. I therefore take this opportunity to record, and express, a deep gratitude to all of you for the way in which you have responded to the demands of the Organization.

The general world situation and its repercussions on the Organization have unavoidably left their mark on the Secretariat. In particular the discussions in the last session of the General Assembly have raised far-reaching questions on the nature of the Secretariat. What is at stake is a basic question of principle: Is the Secretariat to develop as an international secretariat, with the full independence contemplated in Article 100 of the Charter, or is it to be looked upon as an inter-governmental – not international – secretariat providing merely the necessary administrative services for a conference machinery? This is a basic question and the answer to it affects not only the working of the Secretariat but the whole of the future of international relations.

If the Secretariat is regarded as truly international, and its individual members as owing no allegiance to any national government, then the Secretariat may develop as an instrument for the preservation of peace and security of increasing significance and responsibilities. If a contrary view were to be taken, the Secretariat itself would not be available to Member Governments as an instrument, additional to the normal, diplomatic methods for active and growing service in the common interest.

I have dealt with this question at some length in various statements, most recently and fully in the Introduction to the Annual Report. It is a question which the Secretariat itself cannot answer as it is up to the Member Governments to decide what kind of Secretariat they want. But the quality and spirit of our work will necessarily greatly influence the reply.

In a situation like the one now facing all peoples of the world, as represented in this Organization, it is understandable that staff members should sometimes feel frustrated and even depressed. In that they are not different from their fellow beings in other positions influenced by the trend of world events. There is only one answer to the human problem involved, and that is for all to maintain their professional pride, their sense of purpose, and their confidence in the higher destiny of the Organization itself, by keeping to the highest standards of personal integrity in their conduct as international civil servants and in the quality of the work that they turn out on behalf of the Organization. This is the way to defend what they believe in and to strengthen this Organization as an instrument of peace for which they wish to work. Dejection and despair lead to defeatism – and defeat.

During this period of two years, one of the major changes affecting the Organization has been the introduction of many new Members, especially from Africa. The presence of these new Members is welcome, as it reflects the spread of independence and greater freedom, and as it greatly strengthens the Organization and its capacity for service. These new Members are entitled to get their fair share in the staff of the Organization. At the same time some of the older Members have shown greater interest than heretofore in the representation of their nationals in the Secretariat.

These two factors have lent added urgency to a problem which affects every one of you, namely the problem of adjusting geographical distribution. It has been obvious to me that adjustments should be made as quickly as possible to the new situation on the basis of the present formula, and without waiting for the consideration by the General Assembly of a new one. It has been our concern to ensure that these changes should be carried out with the least possible adverse effect on the promotion prospects and other service rights of the existing staff. I have the feeling that on the whole it has been possible to strike an equitable balance. Special hardship aspects are still under study.

I am advised that although the promotion registers have been issued only very recently, same 99 promotions have already been approved since the beginning of this year for staff subject to geographical distribution, including the G-5 level. In addition 25 promotions have also been authorized in the professional posts which are not subject to geographical distribution. In the general services category, excluding G-5, the number of promotions already approved for 1961 is 136, and 12 promotions have been authorized in the manual workers' category.

Consideration is being given to the possibility of requesting the General Assembly to authorize a certain number of personal promotions over and above those which may have taken place within the established Manning Table. This is one of the recommendations made by the Committee of Experts on the Activities and Organization of the Secretariat.

You are also aware that a number of important proposals dealing with salaries and allowances will be considered by the forthcoming session of the General Assembly. Some of these proposals have been based on the conclusions reached by the International Civil Service Advisory Board. Some others arise out of the recommendations submitted by the Expert Committee on Post Adjustments.

Elements like salaries and promotion naturally are very close to all of us and their significance for the feeling of security and quiet of staff members is obvious. But the spirit of a corps like the United Nations Secretariat, as it develops within the framework set by working conditions, is finally determined by other factors.

We all know that if we feel that what we do is purposeful, not to say essential for the progress of men and human society in a broader sense – yes, even if we believe that what we do is essential only for a small group of people and its future happiness – we are willing to accept hardships and serve gladly for the value of serving.

This common truth naturally applies to this Secretariat as to any other group in which people work together for a common aim. Of course, this does not justify those who decide on the conditions of service of the Secretariat to take advantage of the international spirit of service and of the idealism which may be found within its ranks by maintaining less than fair conditions of work. A good worker should be treated on a basis of equity whatever the motives which guide or inspire him. But it does mean that for the staff members themselves, given the proper conditions of work, the ultimate satisfaction they derive from the work will depend on their personal engagement in it and on their understanding of the collective aim which the work is intended to serve and its significance for the world in which we want to live and which we want to see built for future generations.

This leads me back to the international situation and to the role of the United Nations. It is true that we are passing through a period of unusual threats to human society and to peace. The dangers are too well known for me to add any comments here. If anything, you hear and see too much about them in the headlines of every paper. It is also true that the role of the Organization is necessarily a modest one, subordinated as it must be to Governments, and through Governments to the will of the peoples.

But, although the dangers may be great and although our role may be modest, we can feel that the work of the Organization is *the* means through which we all, jointly, can work so as to reduce the dangers. It would be too dramatic to talk about our task as one of waging a war for peace, but it is quite realistic to look at it as an essential and – within its limits – effective work for building dams against the floods of disintegration and violence.

Those who serve the Organization can take pride in what it has done already in many, many cases. I know what I am talking about if I say, for example, that short of the heavy work in which you, all of you, have had his or her part, the Congo would by now have been torn to pieces in a fight which in all likelihood would not have been limited to that territory, but spread far around, involving directly or indirectly many or all of the countries from which you come. I also know what the activities of the Organization in the economic and social fields have meant for the betterment of life of millions, and for the creation of a basis for a happier future.

This is not said in a spirit of boastful satisfaction with what this Organization has been able to do – which, alas, falls far short of the needs – but as a realistic evaluation of the contribution we all of us, individually, have been permitted to make through our work for this Organization. It is false pride to register and to boast to the world about the importance of one's work, but it is false humility, and finally just as destructive, not to recognize – and recognize with gratitude – that one's work has a sense. Let us avoid the second fallacy as carefully as the first, and let us work in the conviction that our work *has* a meaning beyond the narrow individual one and *has* meant something for man.

Those of us who have had the opportunity of working in a national civil service or the secretariat of a national government know, and understand fully, the added responsibilities and problems that one has to face when working in an international secretariat. These responsibilities cannot be discharged, and these problems cannot be solved, save by our own inner dedication to the cause which the world Organization is pledged to serve under the Charter. I am sure that all of you will continue to respond to any demand made on this Organization in the service of this common cause.

I would like very much to thank the Chairman of the Staff Committee for giving me this opportunity to share my thoughts with you on this occasion.

INDEX